A HANDBOOK OF
Living Religions
EDITED BY JOHN R. HINNELLS

VIKING

VIKING
Penguin Books Ltd, Harmondsworth, Middlesex, England
Viking Penguin Inc., 40 West 23rd Street, New York, New York 10010, U.S.A.
Penguin Books Australia Ltd, Ringwood, Victoria, Australia
Penguin Books Canada Ltd, 2801 John Street, Markham, Ontario, Canada, L3R 1B4
Penguin Books (N.Z.) Ltd, 182–190 Wairau Road, Auckland 10, New Zealand

First published 1984
Copyright © John R. Hinnells and Penguin Books Ltd, 1984
Illustrations, maps and diagrams by Raymond Turvey, except pages 203, 292, and 293

Filmset in Monophoto Sabon by Northumberland Press Ltd, Gateshead
Printed in Great Britain by
Richard Clay (The Chaucer Press) Ltd, Bungay, Suffolk

BRITISH LIBRARY CATALOGUING IN PUBLICATION DATA

Hinnells, John R.
  A handbook of living religions.
  1. Religions – Dictionaries
  I. Title
  291'.03'21   BL80.2

ISBN 0-7139-1626-5

This book is dedicated to the staff of Wrightington Hospital as a token of respect and gratitude for their work

Contents

Contributors

PROFESSOR MARY BOYCE, The School of Oriental and African Studies, London University

PROFESSOR JOSEPH EPES BROWN, Department of Religious Studies, University of Montana

DR W. OWEN COLE, Religious Studies Department, West Sussex Institute of Higher Education, Chichester, United Kingdom

DR B. COLLESS and DR P. DONOVAN, Religious Studies Department, Massey University, New Zealand

L. S. COUSINS, Department of Comparative Religion, Manchester University

PROFESSOR KENDALL W. FOLKERT, Department of Religion, Central Michigan University

JOHN R. HINNELLS, Department of Comparative Religion, Manchester University

DR DENIS MacEOIN, Department of Religious Studies, University of Newcastle upon Tyne

PROFESSOR J. GORDON MELTON, The Institute for the Study of American Religion, Evanston, Illinois

DR DAVID REID, Professor of Sociology of Religion, Tokyo Union Theological Seminary

PROFESSOR MICHAEL SASO, Department of Religion, The University of Hawaii at Manoa

DR AYLWARD SHORTER, Lecturer in African Theology, Kipalapala Seminary, Tanzania, and Downside Visiting Fellow in African Religions, Bristol University

DR HAROLD W. TURNER, Centre for the Study of New Religious Movements in Primal Societies, Selly Oak Colleges, Birmingham, United Kingdom

DR ALAN UNTERMAN, Rabbi of Gatley Synagogue, Lecturer in Comparative Religion, Manchester University

PROFESSOR ANDREW WALLS, Department of Religious Studies, Aberdeen University

SIMON WEIGHTMAN, The School of Oriental and African Studies, London University

PROFESSOR ALFORD T. WELCH, Religious Studies Department, Michigan State University

Introduction

This *Handbook* is the product of scholarly collaboration on an international scale. It presents the conclusions of some of the latest academic research in a readable manner for the general public as well as for the student of religions. The book has a clear focus, namely living religions in the twentieth century. It also has a carefully thought-out structure, so that the reader is entitled to an account of the presuppositions which lie behind it.

The most fundamental of these is the importance of religion in history. Whatever any individual's personal religious beliefs may be, or even if there is some antagonism towards religion, it is difficult for anyone to deny that religions have had considerable impact on societies in all continents. Religions have often been deeply involved in political matters, in cultural developments; they have been used to legitimate, suppress or inspire regimes, philosophies and artistic movements. Religious institutions have, for good or ill, dominated or undermined secular establishments of many kinds. Individuals have been inspired by religion to live up to the highest possible personal standards, or provoked to display the basest instincts. It is not possible to understand the history of most, if not all, countries without knowledge of the religions which have flourished there and influenced, moulded or corrupted both leaders and masses.

It is often said that this is a secular age; that religion is declining. A basic conviction behind this book is that such assertions are at most half-truths, if not wholly wrong. Perhaps formal membership of some established religious institutions is declining, but this represents only one part of the religious spectrum. In other parts religion can evidently be seen to flourish in the twentieth century: in new religious movements in primal societies in Africa or in the cities of Japan; on U.S. university campuses in the 1960s; in the powerful spirit of Islamic revivalism in the 1970s; and in the growth of 'alternative' religions or charismatic movements in various continents in the 1970s and 1980s. Religion is only seen to be declining if it is viewed from a limited and 'traditionalist' perspective. This *Handbook* is concerned with both established religions and the new movements.

With modern communications, religious institutions and people are in greater contact than ever before. Such contact produces an enormous impetus for change. This is true not only of international religions (for example Buddhism), as they have moved across political boundaries and been challenged by radical political change, but also of the traditions of 'small-scale' or primal societies, whether in Africa or the Pacific, as they have been confronted by the entry of such missionary religions as Islam and Christianity. The twentieth century can be characterized as a particularly dynamic period in the history of religions. Religious people of most generations in diverse cultures have considered 'the youth of today' as less religious than themselves. The truth is sometimes that the young are not so much less religious as religious in a different way. Living means changing; this *Handbook* is concerned with living religions as they have experienced change in the twentieth century.

However great, and valid, people's interest in modern movements may be, it would be rash, even wrong, to look at recent apart from earlier history. This is not only because religions, like people, are in some measure the products of their own history, but also because living religions commonly assert their identity with the past. Few movements, however new, stress their difference from their origins. Revival or reform movements often emphasize that they are returning to the purity of their tradition's original form. It is, therefore, necessary to understand both the history and the perceived history of the religions.

This *Handbook* is concerned with *living* religions in another sense also: how does each religion function as a vital force in the daily life of its adherents? Many books focus heavily on doctrines, making religion primarily a belief system or a cerebral activity. Right belief is an important factor for some traditions, but not in others. For a great many people in various countries religion is something which is part of the fabric of society and life. It is something 'done' and lived rather than something reasoned: however the scholars may theorize, whatever may be the 'official' teaching of a given 'establishment', the religion of the majority is often expressed mainly through custom and practice. So, whereas some books assume a 'pure' form of the 'original' religion which has been 'adulterated' by the 'superstitions' of the common people, writers in this *Handbook* give serious attention to both beliefs and practices, to the rites and customs as well as to the teachings of the religions. In recent years some scholars have used the distinction between the 'great' and the 'little' traditions to distinguish between the (inter)national or 'mainstream' formal expression of a religion and its local (e.g. village) expressions. Such a division may be inappropriate for some religions because it implies too great a gap between classical teachings and popular practices, or because there may be more than one 'great' tradition (as for example with the

Eastern Orthodox, Catholic and Protestant traditions of Christianity). Nevertheless, this distinction has served a useful function in that it has drawn to people's attention the variety of expressions of religion which conventional 'theological' approaches have neglected.

A real danger for a book on religions is that it can too easily assume, wrongly, that there are always definable, separate phenomena corresponding to the labels popularly used, such as Christianity or Hinduism. In practice the divisions between religions are sometimes artificial. It is not always the case that to believe one religion is 'right' necessarily involves believing that another is 'wrong'. Dual or multiple affiliation to religious organizations does occur, for example in contemporary Japan. The impact of missionary religions on primal societies has often produced new movements which do not naturally belong under any of the conventional labels. Religion must sometimes, therefore, be studied as a regional phenomenon rather than under the conventional headings of '-isms'.

Assumptions abound in the study of religion; they are at their most dangerous when they are unrecognized. This book seeks to challenge many commonly held assumptions: that india is changeless; that Christianity is a single, easily recognized phenomenon; that religions are monolithic wholes; that Jainism and Zoroastrianism are dead religions; that Islam is a 'Near Eastern' religion; or that Buddhism is an abstract philosophy. But it is not only popular assumptions which need to be questioned or clarified; it is just as important to spell out scholarly assumptions. There are few cold facts in the study of religions: all explanation involves interpretation. Rarely do general books on religions set out what scholarly methods and assumptions lie behind their accounts. Perhaps it is assumed that the general reader does not need such information. One conviction behind this book is that it is precisely the general reader, or the non-specialist, who *does* need such an account because she, or he, is the most vulnerable to an unbalanced or biased account. Authors in this *Handbook* have, therefore, given a brief account of the different scholarly methods and assumptions which have influenced the study of their subject. It is equally necessary for the reader to have some idea of the nature of the sources on which such studies have been based, because the questions which can be asked, if not always answered, vary according to the type of sources available. Contributors have added a brief survey of the range of materials available in order to aid a proper understanding of the tradition.

Because the various religions differ so much from each other it is not possible to devise a single appropriate structure for all the entries. A literary straitjacket is neither desirable nor possible. But in order to give some unity and coherence to this multi-author work, authors were asked to lay out their material under the following headings, in so far as they are appropriate:

1. Introduction covering: (a) a brief survey of the main primary sources; (b) an introduction to the history of the religion; (c) a survey of the main phases and assumptions of scholarly study of the religion.
2. A succinct account of the main *teachings* of the religion.
3. An outline of the main *practices* of the religion, including formal worship and 'rites of passage' (i.e. rituals thought to convey the individual from one stage of life to another, as at birth, initiation to maturity, marriage and death).
4. *Popular*, 'little' or 'local' traditions.
5. *Modern* or twentieth-century developments, not only in beliefs and practices but also with reference to major political and social changes.

In addition authors were asked to collect, where possible, appropriate data (e.g. statistics) which would make this a useful *Handbook* for the scholar as well as the lay person. Obviously this general structure and range of material had to be adapted to the nature of the respective traditions.

In addition to the study of modern developments in each of the religions or regions covered, it seemed important to include material which set these developments in a wider perspective. Thus chapters have been included on new religious movements in primal societies and on the 'alternative' religions in the West. The latter subject is one which few general books cover, yet it is one which is particularly important given the vitality of such groups and the ignorance with which they are so often reported. 'Alternative' religions have proliferated to such an extent that there is a real problem in providing full coverage in any one book. The solution adopted here is to give one general chapter on the main 'families' of such religions and a substantial entry on one case, namely Baha'ism, which may be considered something of a paradigm for possible future developments. Baha'ism can be seen in origin as an Islamic reform movement, but it has grown into an autonomous, self-aware religion with missions in many countries, in the U.S.A., for example, as well as in the Third World.

The sequence of chapters in a general book of this kind sometimes reflects a fundamental assumption regarding the priority of religions or a conviction relating to their supposed type. There is no such significance in the order of entries in this *Handbook*. It is intended to be a book to be enjoyed, but in practice it is unlikely that it will be read from one cover straight through to the other. Which tradition is at the front and which at the back is, therefore, not a significant issue. The important point is rather the groupings of traditions. Because of their historical interconnectedness it was thought helpful to group together the Semitic traditions of Judaism, Christianity and Islam. Similarly Hinduism, Sikhism and Jainism needed to be together. Zoroastrianism was placed between these two groups because it is a religion which has historically and geographically stood between them. Similarly the Buddhist material is placed between the entries on India and those on China and Japan because it spans these various Asian cultures. The primal traditions (so commonly neglected in books on living religions) are grouped together. The final three entries are on different aspects of the nature and development of new or 'alternative' religious movements.

Every reader will doubtless have his or her own ideas on what contents should go into a book and in what proportions. Obviously there are omissions. What single book could encompass a field that is so diverse, so changing and so complex? One topic which the editor regretfully omitted was a general discussion of methods, assumptions and definitions. But, given that such methodological issues are considered in relation to the individual topics, it was decided that a general chapter on such themes would have swung the overall balance of the book too far towards the theoretical. For the interested reader a list of challenging books on this topic is included in the General Bibliography.

As authors have taken as a priority the readability of their text and a broad view of the history and phenomena of their respective subjects, they have had to omit details which readers may find important and interesting. This is especially the case with regard to intercontinental movements such as Buddhism, Christianity and new religious movements. In such instances the reader is referred to *The Penguin Dictionary of Religions*. The two books can be used, for both pleasure and profit, independently. But they do complement each other. In various ways they are designed alike, not least in the presentation of bibliographical material. Each entry has a numbered bibliography. In the body of the text square brackets are used exclusively and consistently for bibliographical references. Arabic numerals before the colon refer to the number of a book in the bibliography. A roman numeral after the colon refers to a chapter in that book, whereas an arabic numeral after the colon refers to pages in that book. Thus [4: v] refers to chapter five of item four, whereas [4: 5] refers to page 5 of the same book. In this way references can be given to further reading on specific as well as on general points without interrupting the flow of the text. The guiding principle in the arrangement of the bibliographies is to provide the non-specialist reader with the information necessary to find the books in a library. Alternative editions (mainly, but not only, American and British) have also been listed. In addition to the bibliographies, some chapters carry a few end-notes, referred to by superior figures in the body of the chapter, or appendices of a specialist nature.

In contrast to the *Dictionary* it was decided, reluctantly, to omit the subjects of Marxism and Humanism. The *Dictionary* is intended to be more comprehensive than the *Handbook*. For the latter it was thought important to allow space for more extended consideration of the religions covered. The physical constraints of the size of the book made it necessary to concentrate on what are generally considered the major religious traditions, from which category Marxists and Humanists typically wish to distance themselves.

It should be noted that maps in the *Handbook* are intended to locate important places mentioned in the text. They do not distinguish chronological periods, so that ancient and modern sites appear on the same map.

Finally, it is the Editor's genuine pleasure to give thanks to the many people who have helped in the preparation of this book. First, naturally, are the authors who, without exception, have been cooperative and willing to adapt wherever possible to the requests of the Editor. Thanks also are due to Dr Valerie Roebuck for her specialist help on Hindu iconography. As ever, Miss Nora Firby, the bibliographer, worked efficiently and ably. She has also given very considerable help with the Index. It has been a real pleasure and privilege to work again with Michael Dover of Penguin Books. No editor could have asked for more effective, ready and kindly help. Special thanks are due to Peter Phillips for his considerable care and expertise in editing the text, and to Paul Bailey, Alasdair Hamilton and Raymond Turvey for their different roles at different stages in producing the artwork. My friend and colleague, Lance Cousins, as well as contributing to the book, has acted as a regular 'sounding board' for ideas, given encouragement at difficult times and advised over many problems. The responsibility for all errors of judgement and detail is, of course, mine alone. My family have, as always, been patient and supportive: no words can ever adequately express my thanks to them.

John R. Hinnells

A Handbook of
LIVING RELIGIONS

A Note on Terminology

Two common designations have been avoided in this book. The first is AD (= *anno Domini*, the year of 'Our Lord'), because this is taken by many to represent a Christian orientation. Instead, the more widely accepted CE (Christian Era) and BCE (Before (the) Christian Era) are used throughout. The second term which has been avoided is 'Old Testament', because this implies a belief in a 'New' Testament, reflecting a Christian assessment of texts which is offensive to Jews. Instead, the term 'Hebrew Bible' has been used, which by referring to the language of the texts is intended to be religiously neutral. In a book written for, and by, people of different religious positions, or of none at all, a neutral stance is considered essential.

Western publishing conventions generally treat Judaeo-Christian scriptures differently from those of other religions. Thus books from the Christian Bible, e.g. Matthew, are not printed in italics, whereas those of other religions are. In a technical, unbiased book such practice is questionable. In this *Handbook* the following practice has been adopted: the name of the main scriptural work (Bible, Qur'an, Avesta) appears in roman, because of the frequency with which such terms appear in the chapter. Sections or books within that scriptural collection and all other texts are italicized.

I

Judaism

Introduction

SOURCES OF JUDAISM

The primary source of Jewish religion is the Hebrew Bible, consisting of twenty-four books divided up into three sections: *Torah* (the *Pentateuch*), *Neviim* (the Prophets) and *Ketuvim* (the Writings or Hagiographa). Next in importance to the Bible is the *Babylonian Talmud*, a collection of rabbinical traditions edited in the fifth/sixth centuries CE, containing the main teachings of the oral Torah. Other early rabbinical writings such as the *Palestinian Talmud* (fourth/fifth centuries) and midrashic commentaries on the Bible are less authoritative than the *Babylonian Talmud*, which itself is an extended commentary to the Mishnah (a work redacted at the end of the second century). The most influential medieval works are the commentary of Rashi (1040–1105) to both the Bible and the *Babylonian Talmud*; the great law code, known as *Mishneh Torah*, of Maimonides (1135–1204), and the same author's philosophical *magnum opus, The Guide for the Perplexed*, which reinterprets Jewish theology in Aristotelian terms; and the collection of mystical traditions, known as the *Zohar*, which was written or edited by Moses de Leon (1240–1305). (See Figure 1.1.)

In the late Middle Ages the standard code of Jewish law and ritual (*halakhah*), the *Shulchan Arukh* or 'Prepared Table', was written by Rabbi Joseph Caro (1488–1575), who included the customs of Spanish and oriental Jewry, and was added to by Rabbi Moses Isserles (1525–72), who incorporated the customs of central and eastern European Jewry. This work has shaped the practice of Jewish communities throughout the world.

In the modern period rabbinical writings have mainly taken the form of commentaries on pre-modern texts, and Responsa. Responsa literature dates back to the early post-Talmudic period, and consists of published answers to questions about matters of law or ritual. In the changing environment of modernity many new situations have arisen calling for a reinterpretation of Jewish law and its application to differing circumstances. Rabbis have dealt with such issues in Responsa, which if their author is an acknowledged halakhic expert may be collected together and published. The last century and

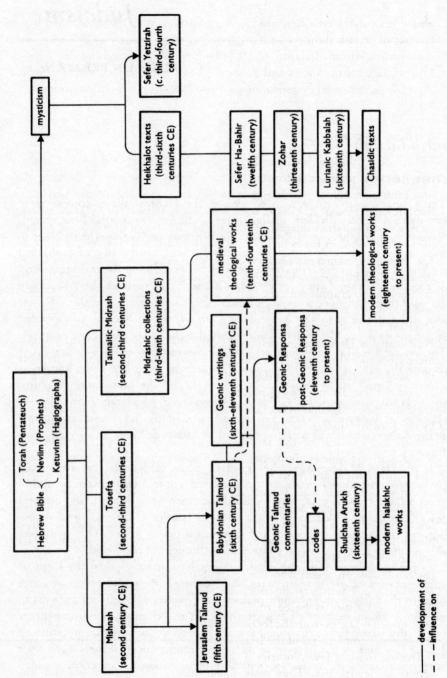

Figure 1.1   The religious literature of Judaism

——— development of
– – – influence on

Hebrew Bible { Torah (Pentateuch)
               Nevilim (Prophets)
               Ketuvim (Hagiographa)

mysticism

Sefer Yetzirah (c. third–fourth century)

Heikhalot texts (third–sixth centuries CE)

Sefer Ha-Bahir (twelfth century)

Zohar (thirteenth century)

Lurianic Kabbalah (sixteenth century)

Chasidic texts

Tannaitic Midrash (second–third centuries CE)

Midrashic collections (third–tenth centuries CE)

medieval theological works (tenth–fourteenth centuries CE)

modern theological works (eighteenth century to present)

Tosefta (second–third centuries CE)

Geonic writings (sixth–eleventh centuries CE)

Geonic Responsa
post-Geonic Responsa (eleventh century to present)

Babylonian Talmud (sixth century CE)

Geonic Talmud commentaries

codes

Shulchan Arukh (sixteenth century)

modern halakhic works

Mishnah (second century CE)

Jerusalem Talmud (fifth century CE)

a half have also seen a renewed interest in Jewish theology stimulated by the contact of Jewish thinkers with modern European thought. The various sub-movements within Judaism – Modern Orthodox, Conservative, Reform, Liberal, Reconstructionist and Zionist – have all produced works reflecting their own ideological understanding of Jewish existence and Jewish identity.

WORLD JEWRY

The modern religious Jew, whether he is affiliated to an Orthodox, Conservative, Reconstructionist, Reform or Liberal synagogue, sees himself as a member of a faith community which goes back some 4,000 years to its origins in the Patriarchal period of Abraham, Isaac and Jacob. For him or her the past is not merely of antiquarian interest, it lives in the rituals out of which his religious life is structured, in his beliefs, and it is constitutive of his very identity as a Jew. Since the eighteenth century, when Jews began to move *en masse* out of the medieval European ghetto (i.e. segregated area) into modern society, the Jew has had to grapple with the challenges to tradition presented by the norms and beliefs of a scientific understanding of man and the world (see Figure 1.2). Over the last half-century he has had to readjust his outlook in the face of the Nazi-inspired Holocaust, in which about 6 million Jews were brutally killed merely because they were Jews (see Figure 1.3), and in the light of the rebirth of a Jewish national home in the Land of Israel after 2,000 years of exile.

Today there are nearly 14½ million Jews in the world. The biggest demographic concentration is in the U.S.A., with just under 6 million Jews, followed by the State of Israel (over 3 million), and then by the Soviet Union (just under 3 million). The rest of the Jewish population is scattered throughout the world, with sizeable communities in France, Britain, Canada, South America and South Africa, and with much smaller concentrations in a host of other countries (see Figure 1.4). Because of the political situation in the Soviet Union Jews there make little contribution to the cultural, intellectual and religious life of world Jewry. The two main centres of Jewish life are therefore in the North American continent and in Israel. The majority of Jews in the former, and approximately half the Jews in the latter, are Ashkenazi Jews of central or eastern European origin who share a religious subculture with Yiddish as its lingua franca. The other main component of Jewry is the Sefardi-oriental grouping whose culture is based round the traditions brought by Spanish and Portuguese refugees from the Iberian peninsula, in the late fifteenth century, to the Jewish communities of the Islamic world with whom they merged. [1]

During the last few centuries it was the Ashkenazim who were the pace-setters in Jewish life. They were the founders and leaders of the Zionist

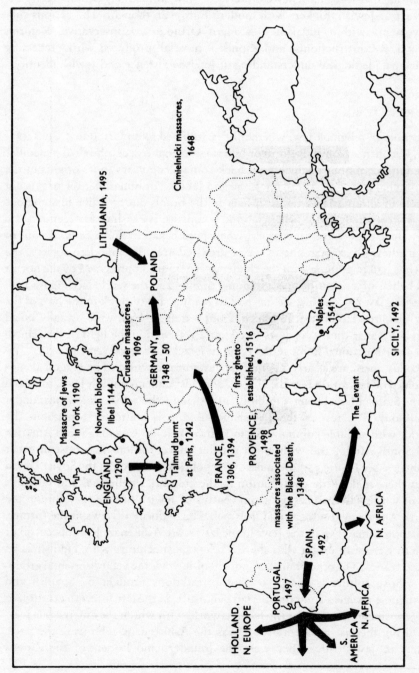

Figure 1.2 Dates of expulsions of Jews from Christian Europe and main sites of anti-Jewish persecution

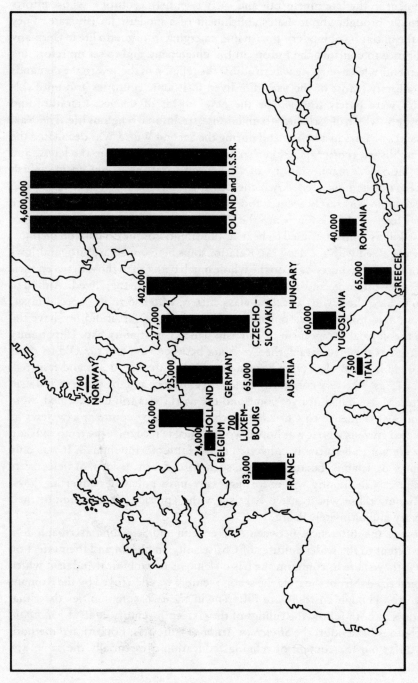

Figure 1.3 The destruction of European Jewry during the Nazi Holocaust (figures represent the minimum estimated casualties)

POLAND and U.S.S.R. 4,600,000

NORWAY 760

HOLLAND 125,000

BELGIUM 106,000

LUXEM-BOURG 700

GERMANY 277,000

CZECHO-SLOVAKIA 402,000

FRANCE 83,000

AUSTRIA 65,000

HUNGARY

YUGOSLAVIA 60,000

ITALY 7,500

ROMANIA 40,000

GREECE 65,000

movement in the late nineteenth and early twentieth centuries, whose efforts eventually brought about the establishment of a modern Jewish state. They were the initiators of modern Jewish life, emerging from ghetto life in Germany and France to confront the European Enlightenment, and to set up reforming movements whose purpose was to adjust the religion of the Jew to the demands of modernity. Most of the Sefardim lived in Islamic countries and until this century were barely touched by the new worlds of science, literature and philosophy which did so much to undermine traditional religious life. The Nazi massacres of Jews just before and during the Second World War decimated the old established centres of Ashkenazi Jewry [2:533]. They were the latest, and most horrific, manifestation of European anti-Semitism, from which Ashkenazim had suffered down the centuries [3: XVIII]. The life of Jews in Christendom was rarely secure, and pogroms (i.e. attacks against Jews) were always likely to break out, since the Christian Church taught that Jews were Christ-killers who continued to bear responsibility for the crucifixion of Jesus, and were allied with the devil [4]. Relationships between Sefardi-oriental Jews and their Muslim hosts were on the whole much better than those between their Ashkenazi brethren and the Christians among whom they lived. Although Islam treated the Jew as a second-class citizen, who had to pay special taxes, and imposed many restrictions on his life and behaviour, it did not have the same theological antagonism to Judaism which Christianity had. Christianity saw itself as the New Israel, the Covenant between God and the Old Israel as recounted in the Bible having been superseded by the life, death and resurrection of Jesus. The very continuity of Jewish existence and the claim of Judaism that the Messiah had not yet come and the world was still unredeemed, were a continual challenge to Christian teaching. Islam, by contrast, saw Jews as protected citizens who it was hoped would one day recognize the truth of Islam but were not to be forcibly converted to the faith of Muhammad. It was only at times of Islamic fanaticism that such forced conversions of Jews were attempted. Christianity was more aggressive in its policy of converting Jews, threatening those who resisted baptism with expulsion, confiscation of their property and ultimately death.

Despite the differences between Ashkenazim and Sefardim, ascribable to a large extent to the wider cultures of Christianity and Islam and their effect on Jewry, they share in common the basic elements of rabbinical Judaism which characterized it from the time the second temple was destroyed by the Romans in 70 CE. Though customs are different in the two communities the ritual practices of both follow the rulings of the sixteenth-century code of *halakhah*, or religious behaviour, the *Shulchan Arukh* (Figure 1.1). Educational methods also differ but the content of religious education is essentially the same: the

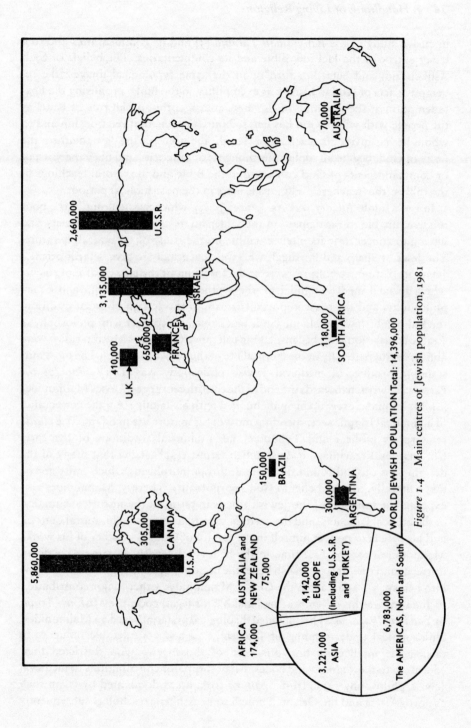

Figure 1.4 Main centres of Jewish population, 1981

U.S.S.R. 2,660,000

ISRAEL 3,135,000

FRANCE 650,000

U.K. 410,000

SOUTH AFRICA 118,000

AUSTRALIA 70,000

U.S.A. 5,860,000

CANADA 305,000

BRAZIL 150,000

ARGENTINA 300,000

WORLD JEWISH POPULATION Total: 14,396,000

AFRICA 174,000

AUSTRALIA and NEW ZEALAND 75,000

EUROPE (including U.S.S.R. and TURKEY) 4,142,000

ASIA 3,221,000

The AMERICAS, North and South 6,783,000

intensive study of the *Babylonian Talmud* [5] and its commentaries and to a lesser extent of the Hebrew Bible and its commentaries. The beliefs of both Ashkenazim and Sefardim turn upon the same typological images: the redemptive acts of God in history as exemplified in the Bible, promising the final redemption at the dawning of the messianic age; the special role of Israel as the people with whom God has entered into a covenantal relationship and to whom he has given his teaching or Torah; the need for the Jew to affirm the unity of God, negate all idolatrous thoughts or practices, and obey the *mitzvot* or commandments of God contained in the Bible and in the oral teachings of the rabbis (the 'teachers', religious leaders in the post-biblical period).

In the Middle Ages it was Ashkenazi Jewry which was culturally the poor relative, unable to participate in the wider interests of Christian society and having to concentrate its intellectual life on the study of rabbinical literature. The Jews of Spain and Portugal, who were eventually to give Sefardi-oriental Jewry its distinctive culture, were at the forefront of the two great movements which formed medieval Judaism: the synthesis between Judaism and Greek philosophy; and the most important stream of the Jewish mystical tradition, the Kabbalah. Jews in Islamic lands first came into contact with philosophy in Arabic translation, and because of the tolerance of various Muslim rulers were able to participate fully in the cultural life of their host countries. The most outstanding product of medieval Jewish philosophy was *The Guide for the Perplexed*, written towards the end of the twelfth century by Moses Maimonides [6]. Maimonides grew up in Spain but fled with his family from the persecution of a fanatical Islamic sect, spending most of his mature life in Egypt. The *Guide* reinterprets biblical and Talmudic (i.e. rabbinical traditions of the early Christian era) teachings in Aristotelian terms, emphasizing that many of the descriptions of God found there are anthropomorphisms which must not be taken literally, for any belief in God's corporeality is heresy. Maimonides also explains the function of the Jewish rituals in terms of the historical situation of the biblical Israelites, and the need for man to be refined in his moral outlook and his beliefs to perfect himself in the service of God. In another of his works Maimonides, for the first time in the history of Jewish doctrine, lays down thirteen fundamentals of Jewish belief the negation of which would lead the Jew into heresy [7]. Apart from the *Guide*, Maimonides' other major contribution to Judaism was his all-embracing halakhic (or legal) code, the *Mishneh Torah* or *Yad Ha-Chazakah*. This included theological material based on Maimonides' philosophical understanding of Judaism, and had considerable influence in raising the intellectual horizons even of those Jews who restricted their education to the *Talmud* and codes. All of the major contributions to medieval Jewish philosophy came from Spain or from areas dominated by Islam such as north Africa and the Orient. Though some Ashkenazi scholars subsequently read the philosophical works of their co-religionists, Ashkenazi culture as a whole did not absorb the ethos of free inquiry, and the consequent broad-based perspective on Judaism which was current in parts of the Islamic world. The Ashkenazim in northern France and Germany, and later on in Poland, Lithuania, Hungary and Russia, developed a very intricate system of study of Talmudic literature, and turned in on themselves away from interests which were more theological and general in nature. Ashkenazi religiosity was inclined to pietism, to an awareness of man's finiteness and sinfulness, and to a form of mysticism in which the adept underwent a severe regimen of spiritual training leading to a vision of the divine Glory seated on the heavenly throne [8: III]. Many elements of folk religion, with strong magical overtones, were absorbed by Ashkenazim and indeed came to be accepted as normative customs on a par with the *halakhah* itself.

The great flowering of medieval mysticism, however, took place precisely in those areas which had experienced the most intense development of philosophical religion, namely in Spain and Provence. In part the Kabbalah spread as a reaction to the changes that philosophically minded intellectuals had made in the traditional Jewish outlook. They had allegorized away much of the substance of Jewish theology, and reinterpreted the halakhic rituals as spiritual ideas. The great monument of kabbalistic religion was the *Zohar* [9], written in Spain but claimed by Moses de Leon, its promulgator, to be the teachings of the second-century sage R. Simeon bar Yochai [8: V, VI]. In this work we find a reversion to the modes of Talmudic Judaism, the rituals being interpreted as the mystical contact points between man and the divine. The *Zohar*, however, goes beyond the strengthening of halakhic norms by interpreting them as the primary means whereby the divine substratum underlying the world is kept in harmonious relationship with it. It also advocates a whole series of new rituals of its own, emphasizes the demonic forces at work in the creation, teaches that the difference between Jew and Gentile is not merely a question of degree but of kind, the Jew possessing a quality of soul absent from the non-Jew, and generally reinforces the sense of the magical which theologians influenced by Greek philosophy had argued was inimical to monotheistic belief.

Sefardi culture was deeply influenced by the Kabbalah of the *Zohar*, which began to circulate at the end of the thirteenth century, and by the kabbalistic teachings of Isaac Luria among a community of Spanish exiles in Safed, northern Palestine, in the late sixteenth century. While the philosophical religion of the Middle Ages left great works of literature to future generations, it was essentially an elitist perspective on Judaism. Kabbalah continued as a living movement within Judaism, eventually shaping exoteric religion through its special rituals and ideological assumptions about the emanations with which God created the world, the nature of the soul, the task of man in the world, and the means by which the messianic redemption could be brought about. At both its scholarly and popular levels Sefardi Jewry was transformed into an amalgam of rabbinical and kabbalistic Judaism, with its central images drawn from both the Bible and *Talmud* and the *Zohar* and Lurianic corpus. Although kabbalistic ideas spread among the Ashkenazim they never gained the almost complete dominance that they had among the Sefardim. Ashkenazi culture had never risen to the rarefied, and somewhat dangerous, heights of this synthesis with philosophy. It had its own traditions of pietism and mysticism, and its profound system of intellectual analysis of Talmudic and halakhic texts meant that it put as much store by scholastic knowledge as by religious or mystical intuition. The only major movement among the Ashkenazim almost entirely inspired by the Kabbalah was the Chasidic movement, which began in eastern Europe in the eighteenth century. This was originally a populist revolt against the scholarly elitism of the rabbinical leadership in the Ukraine and southern Poland, emphasizing the worth of the ordinary, unlettered Jew who could not engage in the very demanding life of Talmudic studies. Chasidism adapted kabbalistic teachings about the divine emanations within all creation, and singled out the inner state of the worshipper, rather than his understanding of the tradition, as the primary value in the service of God. Since the humble and simple Jew could attain to a state of *devekut*, or inner cleaving to God, he could play a central role in the spiritual scheme of things despite his ignorance [10: III; 11: 107]. In the course of time even the Chasidic movement gave way to the predominant Ashkenazi tradition of the meticulous following of halakhic norms and the study of the *Torah* as the main ideal of the religious life. Although it maintained its separate identity, and formed self-contained communities around the Chasidic rabbi or *tzaddik*, Chasidism ceased to be guided by the kabbalistic impetus and became part of Ashkenazi orthodoxy.

ATTITUDES TO JEWISH MYSTICISM AND JUDAISM

In the nineteenth century modernizing Jews associated with the early stages of Reform Judaism found the elements of kabbalistic Judaism among Ashkenazi culture to be the most recalcitrant to change, and to encapsulate the ethos of what they regarded as medieval superstition and magic. They had no sympathy for its symbolism and no understanding of its contribution to Jewish spirituality. To them it represented the worst form of the narrow-minded and obscurantist ghetto religion. It was only in the twentieth century that Jewish academic scholars shook off these prejudices and began to investigate the profound religious ideas which lay behind the magical and folkloristic elements of Kabbalah. This century too has seen a reassessment of Judaism by Christian scholars, whose picture was clouded by the negative attitude of the New Testament to the Pharisees, the spiritual ancestors of rabbinical Judaism. It was customary for Christians to think of ancient Judaism as the religion of the Bible and of modern Judaism as the religion of the Jewish people in the times of Jesus. Behind all this was the view that Judaism had somehow ceased all development and growth during the first century CE, and that at that period Pharisaic religion was as hidebound and hypocritical as the Gospel authors depict it. Although one still comes across this view in Christian writings about Judaism it has become less common as a result of the scholarly work of both Jewish and Christian academics [12]. The nature of rabbinical Judaism in the first few centuries has been extensively explored, and developments during the Middle Ages and up to modern times have been fully charted [13]. The great complexity of Judaism, made up as it is of a variety of different strands, makes overfacile comparisons between Christianity ('the religion of love, of compassion') and Judaism ('the religion of law, of divine judgement'), which were so common in a previous age, seem singularly unfounded. Within Judaism there are elements of both faith and works, both divine love and judgement, which have come to be recognized as constituting the very fabric of the religion.

The Basic Teachings of Judaism

At the centre of Jewish belief lies the faith in one God, who has made the heaven and the earth and all that they contain (*Genesis* 1; 2), and who took the Israelites out of their bondage in Egypt, revealed his divine teaching or *Torah* to them, and brought them into the Holy Land. This idea of God's redemptive acts in history has coloured the Jew's view of his situation since the biblical period, and proffers the hope that one day the Messiah, or anointed one of God, will come to usher in a messianic age when the Jews will be gathered once again to the Land of Israel. The idea that Israel is a people chosen by God is associated in Jewish consciousness with the revelation of the Pentateuchal teachings to Moses and the Israelites as they wandered in the wilderness after the Exodus from Egypt (*c.* fourteenth century BCE, the archetype for later Judaism of God's liberation of the Jews from bondage and suffering). An oft-repeated benediction of the liturgy runs: '. . . who has chosen us from all the nations and given us His Torah [i.e. teaching]. Blessed are you, O Lord, who gives the *Torah*' [14: 5, 71]. The Torah of God is not merely identical with the text of the *Pentateuch*, or even with the whole Hebrew Bible, which is also considered to be divinely inspired, but includes the oral teachings of Judaism, which are thought in essence to go back to the revelation to Moses. The fact that the religion has developed since the biblical period is not unrecognized, but the traditional Jewish view is that the developments all follow the principles of interpretation laid down in that period or are consequences of rabbinical enactments whose purpose was to make fences around biblical religion in order to strengthen it as circumstances changed.

Maimonides' analysis of the thirteen fundamentals of Jewish belief, although much criticized by subsequent scholars, has come to be accepted as something like the official creed of Judaism [7; 15: 3]. It has the following structure. The first five fundamental beliefs concern God: God is the creator of all that is; God is one; God is incorporeal; God is eternal; and God alone is to be worshipped. In the Middle Ages both popular piety and certain elements of the mystical tradition were less than happy about the belief in the corporeality of God being regarded as heretical. The popular imagination had always tended to take the biblical and rabbinical descriptions of God more or less literally, while the mystics developed a series of meditations on the gigantic dimensions of the 'body' of God, known as *Shiur Komah* [8: 63], which were not in line with Maimonides' more philosophical approach to the subject. Since then, however, the incorporeality of God has come to be accepted by all sections of Jewry as representing authentic Jewish doctrine, and the belief that God has physical dimensions or form as heretical [7: IV].

The next four fundamental beliefs concern revelation. They are: that God communicates to man through the medium of prophecy; that Moses was the greatest of the prophets to whom God communicated in the most direct manner; that the whole of the *Torah* (i.e. *Pentateuch*) was revealed to Moses by God; and that the *Torah* will not be changed or supplanted by another revelation from God. The idea of prophetic revelation was seen as a basic element of Judaism in the past, and has continued to play a central role among both Orthodox and modernizing trends in contemporary Jewry, with the exception of the Reconstructionist movement (see page 48). The other three doctrines have led to great controversy in the modern era, with Reform Judaism emphasizing the message of the purely prophetic books of the Bible more than the *Pentateuch* with its rituals; accepting the finding of biblical criticism that the Bible in general, and the *Pentateuch* in particular, are composite texts redacted over a long period of time by different editors; and firmly espousing the view that the biblical traditions have become outdated and must give way to modern religious sensitivities. All this is considered heretical by Orthodox thinkers and is regarded as undermining the very basis of Jewish religion as a response to the revelation of God. Against this, both Reform and Conservative Jews have argued that there is room for the idea of divine inspiration within the Jewish tradition, but that this inspiration is something less than the older idea of revelation by direct communication with the prophets. What is to be identified as divinely inspired and what as purely human within the Bible and Jewish tradition is very difficult to decide, and there has been no general agreement between the different modernizing movements within Judaism. [7: X, XI; 16: 223; 17: 290]

The tenth and eleventh fundamental beliefs are in God's knowledge of the deeds of mankind and his concern about them; and that he rewards and punishes people for their good or evil ways. This is meant to negate the idea that God has withdrawn from involvement in the day-to-day running of the world, and that there is no ultimate justice. The notion of a God who is interested in the doings of both nations and individuals, and who metes out the deserts of the righteous and the wicked, characterizes the salvation-history of the Bible and is the assumption behind the commandments and laws which presuppose that the Jew is free to choose how he behaves and is consequently responsible for his choices. Although some radical theologians have questioned these basic assumptions about God, particularly in the light of the killing of millions of Jews by the Nazis, which seems to make a mockery of the idea of a just world and caring God, they have remained part and parcel of mainstream Jewish thought in the modern world.

The last two of Maimonides' fundamental beliefs concern the coming of the Messiah (or anointed one), a descendant of the line of David, the famed ancient king of Israel, who will usher in the messianic age, and the resurrection of the dead. Both of these doctrines have been considered questionable by sections of Jewry since the beginning of Jewish emancipation in the late eighteenth century. The idea of a personal Messiah of the Davidic line was considered too particularistic and the Reform movement has preferred to talk instead about a universalistic messianic age which will dawn for all mankind. [7: 384; 17: 178] The resurrection was likewise considered a doctrine out of tune with modern ideas about the body and soul, and has been generally replaced among non-Orthodox Jews with a doctrine of the continuing existence of the soul after death. Such a doctrine is also part of traditional Judaism, where it coexists with the belief in the resurrection, and even Maimonides himself in his works devotes far more space to it than to the more formal doctrine of the resurrection. Nevertheless, in an essay about the resurrection, which Maimonides wrote to answer critics who accused him of neglecting this doctrine in favour of that of the immortality of the soul, he makes it clear that Judaism believes in the resurrection even if little can be said in philosophical support of it. The reason why he discusses the soul's immortality at greater length in his works is that more can be said about it in rational terms. It does seem clear, however, that Maimonides holds the disembodied bliss of the soul to be the ultimate state to which the righteous will attain and the resurrection to be merely a stage, albeit a doctrinally supported stage, prior to this spiritual bliss. The daily prayers offered by Jews contain references both to the Messiah and to the Resurrection, and the Reform prayer-book has changed these texts in line with its own interpretation of the doctrines.

Jewish Ritual

The Hebrew language is a very concrete mode of expression, preferring stories or images to express an idea rather than more abstract concepts. In a parallel way Judaism expresses its beliefs and attitudes more through its ritual nexus than through abstract doctrine. The earliest work of rabbinical Judaism, the *Mishnah* (end of second century CE), is concerned with agricultural laws, benedictions, festivals, the relationship between men and women, issues of civil and criminal law and damages, ritual purity, and the temple ritual and its sacrifices. In the discussion and formulation of such issues the rabbinical sages gave expression to the ethos of Judaism. The ordinary Jew today may know little about the sophisticated analysis of Jewish theology and doctrine which went on among philosophers in the Middle Ages, or about the speculations of the Kabbalists. In so far as he is a traditional Jew, however, his life will be structured around the halakhic rituals which shape his approach to God, to his fellows, and to the world about him. For him they are the prime repository of his faith. This is why there is such a large gap between the traditionalist and the modernist. It is not the differences in doctrine alone which divide them, but more important, the differences in life-style, liturgy, festival rituals, dietary laws, marriage and divorce procedures, etc. While variations in practice between one Jewish community and another do not substantially affect the overall religious orientation, the complete modernization of the *halakhah* by Reform Judaism and some sections of the Conservative movement present a ritual structure which on occasion is almost unrecognizable to the traditionalist, and seems to express a different set of beliefs and values. In what follows we shall describe some of the more important traditional rituals, it being understood that the extent of their observance varies from very strict to very light depending on the degree of modernization of the Jews concerned.

THE JEWISH YEAR

The Jewish ritual year is a lunar year of twelve months, approximately eleven days shorter than the solar year. Leap months are intercalated at regular intervals to prevent the lunar and solar years from diverging too far, since the festivals are tied to the agricultural seasons (see Figure 1.5). The year begins in late September/early October with the New Year festival (Rosh Ha-Shanah), which for Jews is a period of divine judgement in which the fate of the world in the coming year ahead is determined. Jews repent of their sins, the ram's

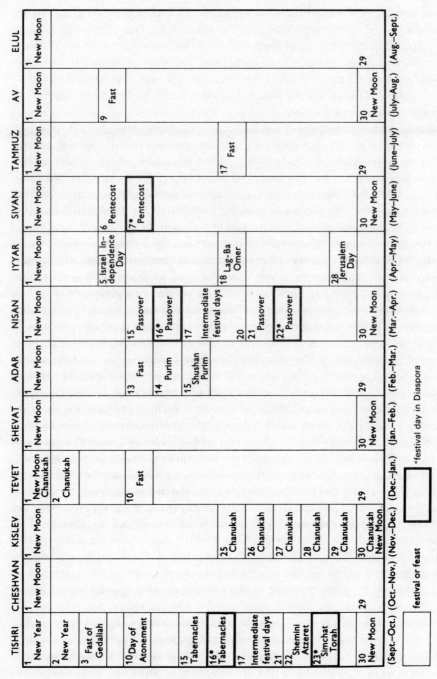

Figure 1.5 The Jewish calendar

horn (*shofar*) is blown in the synagogue (see page 38) summoning man to an awareness of his shortcomings, and the idea of God as the divine king is emphasized in the liturgy. For the two days of this festival Jews eat sweet foods as a symbol of the good year to come, and celebrate to show that they are confident of God's mercy [11: 173; 18: 145, 156]. The day after Rosh Ha-Shanah is a fast day (Tzom Gedaliah), lasting from dawn till nightfall, commemorating a tragic event in Israel's past.

Ten days after the New Year is the Day of Atonement (Yom Kippur), a twenty-five-hour fast day beginning at dusk and lasting till nightfall on the following day. All food and drink are forbidden, and no leather shoes, a sign of comfort, may be worn nor sexual relations take place between husband and wife. Most of the time is spent in the synagogue, seeking atonement from God for past sins, reciting the account of the entrance of the High Priest into the Holy of Holies, the most sacred area of the ancient temple, which took place on this day, and reading from the *Pentateuch* and the Book of *Jonah*. The day is the most solemn occasion of the Jewish year, and synagogues are usually crowded with worshippers, many of whom would not attend at other times. The message of Yom Kippur is that God forgives the truly penitent sinner, but for sins committed against one's fellow man one must first try to win his forgiveness before turning to God in prayer. [11: 178; 18: 151, 161]

Five days later comes the festival of Tabernacles (Sukkot), an eight-day festival in Israel and a nine-day one elsewhere because of uncertainty about when the lunar month began when this was fixed by the sighting of the new moon in the Land of Israel. The Jew lives for the duration of the festival in a little shack or booth (*sukkah*) covered with branches, remembering the time that his Israelite ancestors wandered through the wilderness after the Exodus from Egypt, protected only by the mercy of God. One of the most important rituals of Tabernacles is the taking of the four species, a palm branch, willows, myrtles and a special citrus fruit, the *etrog*, which are held together and shaken during the prayers. The first day (outside Israel the first two days) of the festival and the last day (or last two days) are festive days proper and no profane work may be done. During the intermediate days work is restricted but allowed. The last day (or last two days) are celebrated as the time of the Rejoicing of the Torah (Simchat Torah) when the Pentateuchal cycle of yearly readings is completed and begun again from the beginning of *Genesis*. This ceremony is accompanied by great rejoicing in the synagogue with singing, dancing and alcohol. [11: 180; 8: XIX, XX]

Some two months later Chanukah, an eight-day feast of lights commemorating the victory of the Hasmonean priests over the non-Jewish Seleucid rulers of Palestine in the second century BCE, is celebrated. On each night an extra candle is lit in the eight-branched candelabrum or *menorah*, until on the last night all eight candles are burning. The lighting is accompanied by benedictions and the singing of a hymn, 'Maoz Tzur', recounting God's saving acts during the course of Jewish history. Chanukah is not a true festival, and normal work is allowed. [11: 184; 18: XXIII, XXIV] A week after the end of Chanukah there is another daytime fast remembering a tragic event which took place in the biblical period. This is known as Asarah Be-Tevet (the tenth of the month Tevet). The month of Tevet is followed by the month of Shevat.

The next month of the Jewish year, Adar, is the most joyous month, on the fourteenth of which the carnival-like festival of Purim falls. This commemorates the events recounted in the biblical Book of *Esther* – how the Jews of the Persian empire were saved from the designs of the villainous Haman. The scroll of *Esther* is read publicly in the synagogue, once in the evening and once during the day (Jewish festivals always begin the evening before, at sunset). Whenever Haman's name is mentioned the congregation boo and stamp their feet. Jews often dress up in fancy dress on Purim; they send gifts of food to each other and give charity to the poor. The Purim feast is usually held in the afternoon, and Jews are encouraged to drink alcohol to the point when they cannot distinguish between 'blessed be Mordecai' (one of the heroes of the story) and 'cursed be Haman', signifying that divine help transcends the normal distinctions of human understanding. [11: 186; 18: XXVII, XXVIII]

A month after Purim is the seven-day (eight outside Israel) festival of Passover (Pesach). This festival must always fall in the spring, and commemorates the time of the Exodus of the Israelites from Egypt. No leavened bread may be eaten during the festival and the Jewish house is given a thorough spring-clean to remove all traces of leaven. The staple food eaten during Passover is flat wafers of unleavened bread (*matzah*). On the first night (outside Israel, on the first two nights) a ritual family meal, known as the Seder, is held. During the meal the story of the Exodus is read from a special Haggadah text, four cups of wine are drunk, bitter herbs symbolizing the suffering of the Israelite slaves in Egypt are eaten, as are other ritual foods including unleavened bread. The Seder is maintained even among Jews who do not keep up other Jewish traditions, for apart from its purely religious significance as a celebration of God's redemption it is intimately associated with family ties, which are extremely important for Jews [8: VII, IX].

Seven weeks after the second day of Passover the one-day (or two-day) festival of Pentecost (Shavuot) falls. The period between Passover and Pentecost is one of semi-mourning, and no weddings take place. Shavuot is celebrated as the time when the Ten Commandments were given to Moses on Mount Sinai, and the story of the theophany on Sinai is read in the synagogue. Jews customarily stay up all night on the first night of Pentecost studying the *Torah*, as if to show that they are ready to receive the word of God once more [11: 193;

18: x]. In the modern period a number of new festivals have been introduced in the period between Passover and Pentecost, associated with the modern state of Israel (Israel Independence Day and Jerusalem Day) and with the Nazi Holocaust (Holocaust Remembrance Day). As yet these have only gained partial acceptance as part of the Jewish ritual year.

Just over five weeks after Pentecost there is a three-week period of intense mourning remembering the events surrounding the destruction of the first and second Jerusalem temples in the sixth century BCE and the first century CE respectively. This period begins with a daytime fast (Shivah Asar Be-Tammuz) and ends with a twenty-five-hour fast (Tisha Be-Av), during which no leather shoes may be worn and Jews do not sit on normal chairs but on the ground or on low stools. Weddings are not allowed for these three weeks, and haircuts, the eating of meat and the drinking of wine are restricted – customs about these matters varying between different communities [11: 194; 18: x]. The mourning, though focused upon the destruction of the second temple, also symbolizes the sufferings experienced in the exile during the centuries that followed. The memory of what happened thousands of years ago is, therefore, at the same time a living memory of what has been happening since. The Jewish ritual year ends with the lunar month of Elul, falling around September time, which is a period of preparation and repentance leading up to the New Year festival.

Aside from the yearly cycle there is a minor festival falling at the beginning of each month (Rosh Chodesh) and, more important, there is the weekly Sabbath (Shabbat), which begins each Friday evening at sunset and lasts till nightfall on Saturday night. The Sabbath is a day of complete rest, and even those types of work which are allowed on festivals (associated with cooking) are forbidden. As with other festivals there is a special liturgy for the Sabbath, and the day is sanctified over a cup of wine (kiddush). Apart from attendance at the synagogue for prayers and the weekly reading from the Pentateuch much of the day is spent in the family circle. On Friday night the mother lights candles before the Sabbath begins, and on his return from synagogue the father blesses his children before reciting kiddush and making the blessing over two loaves of the special bread (challah). During the three Sabbath meals hymns are sung at the table, and the best food is served. At the conclusion of the Sabbath a prayer (havdalah) is recited over a cup of wine, over incense, and over a candle flame. [11: 169; 18: IV]

RITES OF PASSAGE

A child is considered a Jew if it is born of a Jewish mother; whether or not the father is Jewish is of no consequence for the religious status of the child, according to tradition. The male child is circumcised on the eighth day after its birth, if it is healthy, and is then given a Hebrew name. Circumcision, representing the entrance of the child into the covenant which God made with Abraham and his descendants, is accompanied by a celebratory meal. Till the age of twelve for a girl, and thirteen for a boy, a child is regarded as a minor. He or she will be gradually instructed in the keeping of Jewish rituals, will be taught Hebrew and learn to translate passages from the Bible and the prayer-book. At the age of twelve or thirteen the child is regarded as an adult who must keep the halakhic rules in their entirety. Its passage to maturity is marked by a Bar Mitzvah ceremony for a boy, and a Bat Mitzvah ceremony for a girl. The Bar Mitzvah consists of being called up in synagogue to read from the *Torah* scroll or the weekly portion from the *Prophets*. This is followed by an often elaborate party to which relatives and friends are invited. The Bat Mitzvah is a relative newcomer to the Jewish scene, having been introduced in modern times to give the girl more of a role in Jewish public life. It usually consists of a ceremony in which several girls participate together, and is more common in Reform communities than in Orthodox ones. [11: VIII]

Marriage is a high point in the life of a Jew, for it signifies the setting up of a new family – the family being the basic unit of Jewish ritual. Judaism does not allow marriage with a non-Jewish spouse, and the intermarriage between a Jew and a Gentile cannot be performed in a synagogue. Intermarriage is generally regarded as a tragedy for the parents and family of the Jewish partner, although it is an increasingly frequent occurrence in the modern Western world. The desire of a non-Jewish partner to be accepted by the family and community of the Jewish partner is one of the main reasons for the conversion of Gentiles to Judaism today, even though it is not considered to be a particularly good reason for conversion by the religious authorities.

Marriage usually takes place under a decorated canopy in the synagogue, with a minority of Ashkenazi Jews preferring the more traditional setting of marriage under a canopy in the open air. It is not necessary for a rabbi to perform the ceremony, any layman can do so in the presence of at least two witnesses. It has become customary for the rabbi, who is not a priest but an expert on *halakhah*, to officiate together with the synagogue cantor and to preach a short sermon containing words of encouragement to the young couple. The ceremony itself consists of various benedictions over glasses of wine, the giving of a ring by the groom to the bride, the reading of the wedding document, and the breaking of a glass indicating, at the time of greatest joy, a sense of sadness at the destruction of Jerusalem [11: 150]. Marriage is considered a desirable condition for every Jew, since there is a biblical commandment, or *mitzvah*, to have children. Jews are generally discouraged from remaining bachelors or spinsters by choice, and religious literature from the biblical story of the first human couple, Adam and Eve, onwards depicts the unmarried individual as an incomplete person. If there is a breakdown of the marriage relationship a religious divorce procedure is necessary before either party is allowed to remarry, civil divorce not being recognized as a means of dissolving the marital state.

Great store is set in Judaism by respect for the aged. Children have a duty to look after their parents, indeed the honouring of parents is one of the Ten Commandments. In established Jewish communities today old-age homes are often large and well endowed, providing a Jewish atmosphere for people to spend the twilight of their lives in. After death, which is defined in Judaism by the cessation of respiration, burial must take place immediately out of respect for the departed. Orthodox Jews do not practise cremation, and burial has to take place in consecrated ground, which means that Jews have their own cemeteries. It is customary to throw a small amount of earth from the Land of Israel on to the coffin, and some Jews who die in the Diaspora (i.e in the lands of the Jewish dispersion) are even taken to be buried in the Holy Land, particularly in Jerusalem. All this is an affirmation of the belief in the resurrection, which it is thought will take place essentially in the Land of Israel. According to a popular Jewish belief those who die outside of Israel will have to roll over in subterranean caverns till they reach the Holy Land to be resurrected there. Next of kin have to undergo an intense period of official mourning for the first week after burial. They sit at home on low stools, with their garments rent, and do not wear leather shoes. People come to conduct prayer services in the mourner's house and to comfort him. The mourning then gradually decreases in intensity, depending on the closeness to the dead relative, allowing the mourner eventually to resume his normal place in the community. The ritualized mourning procedure is intended to permit the mourner to express his grief, but at the same time to discourage him from taking his sense of loss to extremes. [11: 163]

THE SYNAGOGUE

The proto-synagogue began in the sixth century BCE, after the first temple was destroyed, when many Jews were deported in captivity to Babylonia. Its role then was as a house of assembly. It developed markedly after the destruction of the second temple in 70 CE, eventually becoming the centre for community prayers, for the reading of a section from the *Pentateuch* on Mondays, Thurs-

days, Saturdays, and on festivals, and for instruction in Jewish teachings. Both
the Christian church and the Islamic mosque were modelled after the synagogue prototype. Until the modern period the synagogue was overshadowed
by the Jewish home, which was the primary locus of ritual. In the last two
centuries, however, with the growing secularization of the home the synagogue
has become more important as the place where Jewish life finds its full
expression. [11: 197]

The influence of the non-Jewish environment is apparent in the architecture
of the synagogue building, and even in some cases in the internal layout. After
Jews emerged from the medieval ghetto they looked upon the European church
as a model for synagogue reform. The traditional platform at the centre of
the synagogue, from which the *Torah* scroll was read, was moved up to the
front, so that the congregation became more of an audience witnessing the
religious activities of the rabbi and cantor. The older style of synagogue, still
found in many Orthodox communities, was built on the assumption of the
equal participation of all worshippers. In the newer-style synagogues the
religious functionaries have adopted more of a priestly role.

When praying, Jews face towards Jerusalem, and the ark of the synagogue
(a type of cupboard often set behind a curtain) in which the *Torah* scrolls
are kept is set in the Jerusalem-facing wall, making it the focus of prayer.
The liturgy consists of three basic prayers, to be said in the morning, the
afternoon and the evening. On Sabbaths and festivals there are variations
in the liturgy reflecting the special character of the day, and the services are
generally much longer than on weekdays [19: VII, X]. A typical Saturday morning service including a sermon would last between two and a half and three
hours, while even the longest weekday morning service takes less than an
hour. Each service is built round an *amidah* (literally 'standing') prayer which
consists of blessings, requests and thanksgivings. On Sabbaths and festivals
the requests are replaced by special prayers for the occasion, and an additional
amidah is also recited modelled on the additional sacrifices brought in temple
times. The other main component of the morning and evening services is
the Shema (*Deuteronomy* 6: 4–9; 11: 13–21; *Numbers* 15: 37–41), which opens
with the affirmation of faith: 'Hear O Israel, the Lord is our God, the Lord
is One.' The rest of the liturgy consists of benedictions, psalms, hymns, and
selections from the Bible. Prayers are led by the cantor or any competent
layman, whose purpose is to keep the pace of prayer at a regular tempo and
to recite those portions of the liturgy said when there is a quorum (*minyan*)
of ten adult males. [11: 209]

The traditional synagogue is run entirely by men; the women do not play
a public role, lead the prayers, read from the *Torah* scroll, preach or indeed
sit with the men in the main body of the building (see Figure 1.6). They will

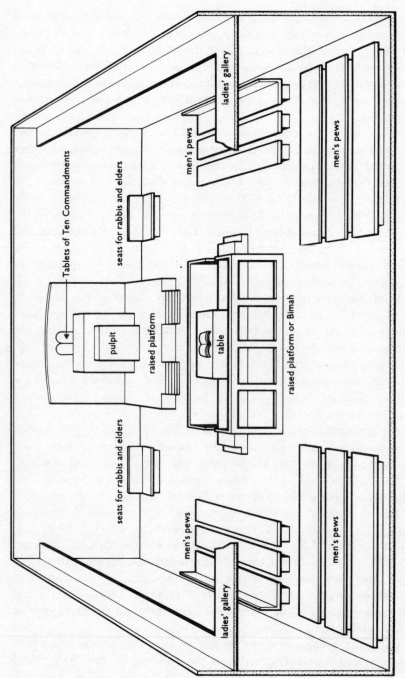

Figure 1.6 Plan of a typical synagogue

usually occupy a ladies' gallery, or sit downstairs behind a partition. Reform and Conservative synagogues (known as temples in the U.S.A.) have mixed seating and involve the female worshippers to a far greater extent than Orthodox ones. Women have even been ordained as rabbis in a number of Reform communities. Another difference between traditional and Reform synagogues relates to the covering of the head during prayer. In all Orthodox and Conservative synagogues the male congregants will either wear a hat or a skull-cap during the service, and many Orthodox Jews keep their heads covered even at home or at work as a sign of respect for God in whose presence man always is. Orthodox married women will also cover their hair in synagogue with a wig, hat or scarf, some even maintaining the covering at other times as well. In many Reform congregations, particularly in the U.S.A., the covering of the head in synagogue is not mandatory.

THE HOME

The home and family are very important for Jewish ritual. The doorpost of each door, with the exception of the toilet and bathroom, has a *mezuzah* scroll inside a metal, wooden or plastic case affixed to it. The *mezuzah* is a parchment on which the first two paragraphs of the Shema are written. It signifies to the Jew that his home is a place where God's presence dwells, and it reminds him of his religious duties. The food the Orthodox Jew eats is determined by the Jewish dietary laws. These forbid all animals which do not have a cloven hoof and chew the cud, all birds which are birds of prey, and all sea creatures which do not have fins and scales. *Kosher* (i.e. fit) animals have to be ritually slaughtered, certain forbidden parts removed, and the meat salted to remove the blood before it can be eaten. Meat and milk cannot be cooked or eaten together, and different kitchen utensils must be used for them. It is also necessary to wait for a period of time after eating meat before milk dishes can be eaten. The Jewish kitchen and the Jewish cuisine therefore have a distinctive character, and bring home to the Jew that even in this most basic mode of life he must serve God. [11: XII]

On Sabbaths and festivals the family eat their meals together, which are accompanied by hymns and grace before and after food. In general, no food may be eaten without a benediction acclaiming God as the creator and producer of the objects being consumed, and a prayer is to be said afterwards thanking God. Before bread is consumed the hands must be ritually washed, as they must be on arising in the morning from a night's sleep. Benedictions are said after going to the toilet, when the hands must be washed, before going to sleep at night, on smelling spices, on hearing thunder and seeing lightning, on seeing a rainbow, or even on hearing good or bad news. Life at home, for the Orthodox Jew, is structured round religious parameters which affect both the individual and the family.

The Jew's dress is also subject to halakhic rules. We have already mentioned the custom for males of wearing a head covering at all times and for married women to cover their hair. Clothes must not be woven from a mixture of wool and linen, and some Jews even continue to wear the style of garments which were common in Europe before Jewish emancipation. There is no halakhic requirement to wear the black hats and long black coats, or for the Sabbath the fur-rimmed caps, silk coats and white socks which Chasidic Jews dress in. Those who do insist upon them, however, feel that to abandon them would be too much of a concession to modern ways [10: XXIV]. The male Jew has to wear a four-cornered vest-like garment with strings attached to each corner. This is a miniature version of the fringed shawl (*tallit*) worn during morning prayers, which on weekday mornings accompanies the arm and head phylacteries (*tefillin*). Phylacteries consist of leather boxes, painted black, held in place by black leather straps. In the boxes are scrolls of parchment with various passages from the *Pentateuch* inscribed on them. These specifically ritual items of apparel are based on biblical commandments, but their effect on the Jew is to remind him that his life and activities must be oriented to God and to the fulfilment of the *mitzvot*.

Popular or Folk Religion

Most of our knowledge about Judaism in the past comes from religious literature which reflects the beliefs and attitudes of its authors, an intellectual elite. There is considerable evidence, however, about the beliefs and outlook of the ordinary, unlettered Jew in the pre-modern period. Some of this is contained in rabbinical literature itself, having been taken over and developed from oral motifs as a means of exemplifying religious truths and values. Many of the collections of *midrashim*, or homiletic commentaries on the Bible, edited during the first millennium of the Christian era, are replete with folkloristic themes [20]. To later readers the midrashic tales, originally meant to clothe an abstract idea or ethical principle, represented the literal truth about historical events. Angels, demons, magical powers, ascents to heaven, wise animals and birds, and all the other features of folklore were thus sanctioned as part of the Jewish tradition, and were used for oral transmission and embellishment. Jewish mystical texts also reflect this pattern. They use images from popular religion to symbolize mystical doctrine, and because of the awe in which kabbalistic teachings were held by ordinary Jews many of these images were accepted literally by popular belief [8: VI]. This is exemplified by the kabbalistic practice of making a *golem* or artificial man. For the mystics this was essentially a spiritual exercise, being a certain stage in the Kabbalist's inner development [21: v]. For the wider Jewish populace the making of a *golem* was a real act of magic power, and many legends circulated about wonder-working mystics and the doings of the *golems* they had created [22: 84]. The philosopher-theologians of the Middle Ages fought against the excesses of the popular imagination, their belief in semi-mythological beings, their literal approach both to the Bible and to rabbinical literature. They saw Jewish monotheism being qualified by the belief in angels and demons, by an interest in magic rather than in prayer and the service of God.

Over the centuries the attempts of the medieval philosophers bore fruit, and limited the extent to which folk religion developed. However, even the impact of the European Enlightenment, which has deeply affected Jews over the last 150 years, did not quite eradicate the belief in and practice of magic and superstition. These continued to exist side by side with the official religion in which the worship of the one, true God was taught. From early rabbinical literature onwards we find a divergence in attitude towards the *mitzvot*, some rabbis seeing the commandments as having only one purpose, i.e. enabling man to refine himself in the service of God, while other rabbis understood them as means for affecting the spiritual/physical condition of man, the environment, and even the state of higher levels of reality. The way halakhic rules were finalized often reflected the first interpretation of the *mitzvot*, and this is also the view of them that appears in medieval philosophical literature. Under kabbalistic influence the second interpretation gradually dominated the halakhic outlook, and acted as a conserving force, since any changes in ritual had to contend with the belief that the ritual was the means of maintaining harmony in the universe and therefore was sacrosanct [21: IV]. The popular approach to the *mitzvot* also invariably preferred the view of ritual in which it is operative as a quasi-magical force, and in folk religion halakhically prescribed ritual and purely magical practices coexist and are interwoven. Some newly introduced rituals were severely attacked by scholars, who believed them to be magical practices infiltrating the halakhic nexus. A case in point is the custom of slaughtering a chicken just before the Day of Atonement. The thirteenth-century Spanish talmudist, Rabbi Solomon ibn Adret, fought to eradicate this custom in his city on the grounds that it was a forbidden magical practice. A later scholar, the sixteenth-century author of the main halakhic code, the *Shulchan Arukh*, also sought to discourage this custom. Nevertheless it won widespread popular approval and the support of other rabbis, and eventually was taken up by standard works on Jewish ritual.

Magical practices were widely used by unlettered Jews for a variety of purposes. Many magical prescriptions, known as *segullot*, circulated to deal with ill health, barrenness, lack of love between a man and a woman, the evil eye, burglary, a bad memory, to discover whether a missing relative was still alive, witches' spells against people, children who cry continually, astrological forces, protection against bullets, difficult childbirth, unsuccessful business dealings, fire, storms at sea, imprisonment, drunkenness etc. [20: IX, X]. Some of these belong to the sphere of folk medicine, while others involve purely magical remedies [23: VIII]. The purveyors of this magic were known as *baalei shem* (singular *baal shem*), who were itinerant wonder-workers catering for a clientele of mostly poor, semi-literate Jews. The founder of the Chasidic movement, R. Israel ben Eliezer (1700–60), began his career as a wonder-working faith-healer, hence his title Israel Baal Shem Tov [10: III]. Another semi-magical practice, found both among Ashkenazi Jews in eastern Europe and Sefardi-oriental Jews in Islamic lands, was visiting the graves of dead holy men. A request might be written on a piece of paper and deposited inside the tomb on the site of the burial, or candles burnt. Sometimes the tomb was measured out in coloured string or candle wick. The idea behind these and similar practices was that the spirit of the deceased should intercede on behalf of the visitor, or that being in the mere presence of the mortal remains of such a saintly and powerful person would be of benefit. Criticism was directed against such practices by the rabbinical leadership, but ultimately they were unable to prevent Jews seeking out the help of the dead, even if there were ample warnings against such behaviour in early Jewish literature.

In the modern period people's exposure to scientific assumptions about the world and to secular education has meant that many of the magical procedures of the past are no longer practised. Ashkenazi Jews who still preserve the culture of the pre-modern ghetto, and who consciously reject some of the advances in man's outlook on the world, are likely to continue folk religion. This is even more true of the older generation of Sefardi-oriental Jews in Israel who have not received a modern education. For such Jews the evil eye, the machinations of demons, and the need for protective amulets against miscarriage and misfortune are part of the very reality of the world they inhabit. Magic fills the gap between their belief in God who has created heaven and earth and demands of the Jew that he fulfil the Commandments, and their immediate experience of life. There is no essential conflict between their monotheistic theology and their belief that the space between man and God is populated by a host of lesser powers at work.

Modern Movements

The last two centuries have seen some of the greatest changes in Judaism since it underwent its dramatic transformation after the destruction of the second temple in 70 CE. In the latter part of the eighteenth century Jews in

Germany and in France began to move outside the confines of their cultural ghetto and to participate in the intellectual life of Europe. Their emancipation and acceptance as citizens, rather than as aliens, was still to come, but some managed to surmount the obstacles in the path of the Jew and attained a measure of equality with their Christian fellow countrymen. One of these was Moses Mendelssohn (1729–86) who as a young boy moved on his own to Berlin, taught himself Latin, European languages and other secular subjects and attained considerable renown as a German writer and philosopher. Though he encountered anti-Semitism among some of his Christian contacts, and suspicion among his less modernizing co-religionists, he believed that a new age was dawning for the Jews. He encouraged them to learn German and cease using their Yiddish dialect. He urged them to study secular subjects, acquire a trade, and prepare themselves to become part of the wider community. At the same time, however, he wanted them to preserve their Jewish traditions and himself remained an Orthodox Jew. In succeeding generations many of those who followed Mendelssohn's lead went beyond their mentor's intentions. They found that the easiest method of acceptance into Christian society was to undergo baptism and shed their Jewish identity. The gap between Mendelssohn's view of Judaism and the somewhat liberal Christianity of their contemporaries did not seem large enough to warrant maintaining separate Jewish existence with all its inherent problems. [11: 71; 17: III; 24: 46; 25: 255]

Some Jews in the post-Mendelssohn era did not wish to lose their identity as Jews, but they could not identify with the ghetto-type Judaism of the majority of their co-religionists. They could not believe in all of the teachings of traditional Judaism, nor did they feel comfortable with aspects of synagogue ritual. They began, in their different ways, to introduce changes which were the forerunners of those associated with the later movement known as Reform Judaism. The areas of concern were the continued use of Hebrew in the services, rather than German; the references in the liturgy to return of the Jews to the Holy Land in the messianic age, which implied that Jews could not be regarded as loyal citizens of their country of residence; the use of an organ and choir in synagogue, which was not common practice in traditional communities; and a regular sermon in the vernacular. [17: 156]

During the first few decades of the nineteenth century new-style synagogues, known as temples, spread both in Germany and in other European countries. Their practices were opposed by the Orthodox rabbis, and both sides appealed for support to the government authorities. Gradually the reforming movement was taken over by intellectuals who began to formulate its ideological platform. The main assumption of this ideology was that Judaism was a historical religion developing through time, and that it had to change in line with the new conditions it was facing. A number of conferences of reforming rabbis were called in the 1840s at which there was some disagreement between those who favoured radical change, since Judaism was essentially a religion of ethical monotheism to which ritual was extraneous, and those who wished to preserve elements of the tradition. The conferences tried to dissociate themselves from those reforming movements which sought to abolish all ritual expression, but nevertheless took up a radical stance on some issues which alienated the moderates. In general the history of Reform Judaism in Germany was one a modified traditionalism, with only a small number of communities adopting a radical approach to the *mitzvot*. The same was true of Reform Judaism in Britain, which began in the 1840s. It was only with the beginning of Liberal Judaism in Britain, in the early twentieth century, that the more extreme reforming position was institutionalized. [26: 161] In the U.S.A., by contrast, the radical tendency has predominated in Reform Judaism from the 1880s.

Underlying Reform Judaism was the belief that a new age of tolerance was dawning for mankind, and that Jews would be accepted by the Christian world as equals. This optimism has gradually diminished, particularly in the light of Nazi atrocities and the support they had from European anti-Semitic movements. Today Reform Judaism is strongly Zionist in orientation, whereas it was once very hostile to nationalistic elements in Judaism. There is also a much more positive approach to Jewish ritual and to more traditional themes of Jewish theology among Reform Jews in the Western world. The antagonism between Orthodoxy and Reform, which characterized the early history of the latter movement, is still very much a feature of their relationship today. (See Figure 1.7.)

An offshoot of the more traditionalist branch of movements for reform in Judaism was the Conservative movement in the U.S.A. This was begun in the mid nineteenth century by European Jews who wanted to modify old-style Orthodoxy in the face of the realities of American life. They did not approve of Reform Judaism, and took as their model the attitudes of the European Historical school which affirmed both the validity of the Jewish past as well as the need for Jews to modernize. [17: VIII, XIII] After a slow start Conservativism began to expand at the end of the nineteenth century when the radicalness of the Reform platform made any attempt at compromise with official American Reform impossible. Conservative Judaism set up its own training college for rabbis, its own synagogue and rabbinical organizations. Today it is the biggest organized stream within North American Jewry, with branches throughout the U.S.A. and Canada [16: 254]. It claims to be the authentic continuation of the rabbinical Judaism of the pre-modern period, but the many changes it has introduced into Jewish ritual and the doctrinal position of some of its proponents have led Orthodox rabbis to outright condemnation of its institutions. During the 1920s Mordecai Kaplan, a member

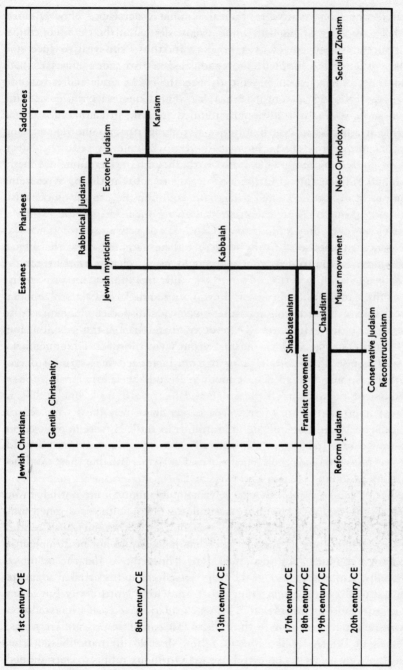

Figure 1.7 Jewish sects and movements

of staff of the Conservative rabbinical seminary, developed a new, more naturalistic theology of Judaism which eventually led to the founding of the Reconstructionist movement as a breakaway from Conservative Judaism. Reconstructionism has adopted a more radical stance towards changes in ritual and doctrine, but its appeal has mostly been to intellectuals and it has not won a large following [11: 219; 16: 241; 24: 535]. Conservativism has found its main support among traditionally minded reformers or modernist traditionalists. Its success in North America is due, in part, to the rejection of traditional mores by Reform Judaism there. In Britain, by contrast, it has had very limited success owing both to the greater moderation of British Reform and to the nature of Orthodoxy organized into the United Synagogue in London. Many of the United Synagogue communities are very modernist in outlook, and in an American context would be considered Conservative. In Britain, however, they affiliate to an Orthodox organization.

The general response of Orthodoxy to reforms was to affirm the divine basis of Judaism and to deny that man could simply change God's teaching at his convenience. In practice, however, two different approaches were taken. Many of the leading rabbis in eastern Europe closed ranks against any changes in Jewish life, even of a minor nature, since they suspected change to be a hallmark of Reform. Hungarian Orthodoxy took a lead in this position, but it was equally strong among Chasidic groups who forbade their members from studying secular subjects or even from changing their style of dress. The other response was to accept modernity and the culture of European Enlightenment, but to maintain the rituals and doctrines of traditional Judaism. The most important genre of this type of synthesis was the movement of German Neo-Orthodoxy founded in Frankfurt by S. R. Hirsch. In opposition to those who saw Judaism as a historically evolving religion Hirsch argued that it was a system of symbols, encapsulated in ritual, and that these symbols were equally valid in each age. [11: 221; 17: IX]

The varied religious responses to Jewish emancipation were not felt to be satisfactory by many of the more assimilated Jews in the late nineteenth century. The problem as they saw it was that anti-Semitism was endemic in the Christian culture of Europe, and that Jews would not be accepted as equals however much they shed their Jewish identity. Under the influence of nationalist movements in central Europe Jewish thinkers started to advocate Jewish national revival, seeing the Jews not as a religious entity but as an ethnic group whose members shared historical memory and a common culture. This contrasted markedly with the Reform view that Jews were Germans, Frenchmen or Britons of the Mosaic faith. Most of the nationalists, later known as Zionists, were completely secular in their outlook. They wished to see Jews established in their own homeland where they would at least be free from anti-Semitic prejudice. Jews would then be able to develop like any other nation. [17: 305; 24: XIII] The most important Zionist leader was Theodor Herzl (1860–1904), who is known as the founder of Zionism as a political movement. Herzl came to believe in Jewish nationalism after his experiences with French anti-Semitism during the notorious Dreyfus Affair in Paris in the 1890s, when a Jewish captain in the French army was falsely accused of spying. If France, which was the most highly cultured European country, could be the seat of such virulent anti-Jewish feeling then the idea that one day Jews would be accepted as equal members of Christian society was merely a pipe-dream. Herzl called together the various Zionist groups to attend the first Zionist congress in 1897, and spent the rest of his short life in seeking the backing of a major power for his goal of a Jewish homeland. [27: III] During the early twentieth century the Zionist movement grew, and groups of Jews went to resettle Palestine, the ancient homeland of the Jewish people, which was part of the Turkish empire and subsequently controlled by Britain under a mandate from the League of Nations. The Nazi-inspired massacres of 6 million Jewish civilians, during the Second World War, convinced many of the remaining Jews that a Jewish state was an absolute necessity. It also stimulated the United Nations to recognize the State of Israel, which was set up on 14 May 1948. The Arab countries of the Middle East were strongly opposed both to the existence of a non-Arab state in the centre of what they saw as essentially Arab territory, and to the mass immigration of Jews from all over the world to Israel [24: 559]. They fought a number of wars in order to eliminate Israel and to drive out the Jewish population (e.g. 1967, 1973). Although they had little purely military success the wars, and the political pressure backed up by the power of Arab oil, have meant that Israel has found itself constantly threatened since its inception. There has been considerable pressure on Israel to agree to the setting up of a Palestinian state in areas occupied by the Israelis since the Six-Day War (1967). Neither the Palestinians nor the Israeli government have as yet agreed to such a solution to the problems of the area.

The effect of all this on world Jewry has been profound. The shock of the Nazi Holocaust has made Jews much more aware of their insecurity and the depths of prejudice against them. Support for Zionism is strong, and for many Jews in the West Zionism has filled the gap in their sense of Jewish identity left by the diminishing of purely religious belief and rituals. Israel's isolation and the Arab-inspired resolution of the United Nations equating Zionism with racism have convinced many Jews that anti-Semitic prejudice did not end with the fall of the Hitler regime. It seems to be a permanent feature of the Gentile world's relationship to the Jew, with the State of Israel the only place where Jews can live without fear that their Jewishness may one day lead to a resurgence of the alienation and victimization that has characterized their existence down the ages. Israel also provides a spiritual focus for the Jews in the Diaspora. Its achievements have helped to enhance Jewish dignity, badly shaken by the Nazi atrocities. Its holy places serve as centres for visiting Jewish pilgrims (see Figure 1.8), and its religious leadership is looked to for guidance on issues which confront the traditional Jew in the modern world. The return of the Jews to Zion and Jerusalem, foretold by the biblical prophets as events associated with the onset of the messianic era, signifies that God has not forsaken his covenant or special relationship with the People of Israel. For many Jews this 'ingathering of the exiles' represents the beginning of a new epoch, perhaps the start of the messianic times themselves. [11: 90]

Judaism and Art

Over the centuries Judaism provided the framework, not merely for a set of religious beliefs and rituals, but also for a total cultural complex which Jews carried with them on their many migrations through different countries and host cultures. Even when they were relatively isolated from their surroundings, living in ghettos both for their own protection and because they were treated as social outcasts by their Gentile neighbours, they still borrowed from their general cultural habitat. These ongoing additions to Jewish culture can be shown simply by comparing the distinctive languages, dress, food, literature, music and art forms of Jewish communities with these features in their Gentile environment. The parallels between the two are marked, and the cultural differences between various Jewish subgroups are attributable in large measure to the influence of their different surroundings.

What was absorbed by Jews from the particular setting in which they lived, however, was rarely simply taken up wholesale. In every area of cultural life it was Judaism that determined both what was absorbable and the manner in which it came to be part of Jewish lore. Thus the cultural elements of Jewish life are an amalgam of early Hebraic forms and continually added new forms. The latter were Judaized, that is they were adapted to the existing cultural framework, so they could be readily integrated as part of an organic whole [28: 16, 18].

Basic to the expression of Jewish artistic creativity, in its most general sense, is the limited place of the visual in Judaism. The biblical and post-biblical antagonism to representative art, particularly three-dimensional forms, emerges from the need to avoid idolatry, i.e. the association of any objects or representations with God himself [7: IV]. Although in the synagogue art of the early Christian period biblical scenes feature on wall paintings and

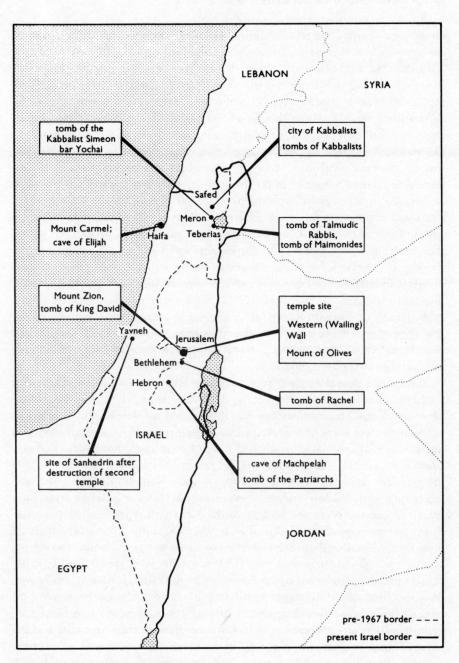

Figure 1.8   Jewish holy sites in Eretz Israel

on mosaics, with a large representational element of human and animal motifs, the opposition to such art was widespread both prior to and during this period. Josephus, the first-century CE Jewish historian, reports popular unrest at Roman attempts to set up figures or military insignia in Jerusalem. Early rabbinical works contain views prohibiting art even if used for purely decorative purposes, since this is an extension of the biblical injunction, contained in the Decalogue (*Exodus* 20: 4–5), not to make a graven image. In the Middle Ages these iconoclastic tendencies characterize much of rabbinical thought, and the revulsion at representational art was strengthened by the influence of Islamic antagonism on the subject. Jews also clearly felt the need to distance themselves from the icons, statues and paintings of the Christian churches, which were felt to be idolatrous. This is not to say that visual art had no form of expression among Jews of the pre-modern period, but rather that it was severely limited. An important outlet for visual art was in the shaping of artefacts for ritual purposes often in precious or semi-precious metals (candelabra, spice boxes, marriage rings, as well as synagogue furnishings and tapestries, scribal arts, the illumination of manuscripts etc.). The many rituals of Judaism in the home and the synagogue, the festivals of the Jewish year, and the central place played by religious texts of all types allowed Jewish craftsmen, and Jewish patrons employing non-Jewish craftsmen, to develop distinctive art forms.

The main cultural expression of Jewish creativity was, however, not in visual art but through musical, oral and literary forms. There was less danger of idolatry in the literary and story-telling imagination, and though the religious authorities were wary of heretical ideas finding their way into untrammelled flights of fancy, they had much less control over the dissemination of this cultural form than over visual art. The poetry, hymns, aggadic stories, and the great flowering of mystical speculation as well as the many legends and fables of Jewish folklore are all an expression of this emphasis on non-visual creativity [22: 11]. Were the images of the Kabbalah, with its interpretation of the ten aspects of the Godhead as mother and father, son and daughter, lover and beloved, and its understanding of all reality, both human and divine, as made up out of male and female elements, to have found iconographic expression they would have posed a major problem for Jewish monotheism. As it was they remained in oral forms and, after overcoming some opposition to their wider dissemination, also in literary forms. Jewish music has characteristically been expressed in liturgical form both in the synagogue and the home. Hymn singing, the chanting of prayers and the reading of Hebrew scripture to a fixed musical notation have long been a basic part of Jewish life. On more joyous occasions, such as family celebrations or festivals, dancing and instrumental music (e.g. for weddings) are quite common, although the different Jewish communities were influenced by the non-Jewish musical forms of their host cultures.

The cultural preference in Judaism for the primacy of the word (whether sung, spoken or written) over the visual object has had a more general effect on Jews, both in the pre-modern and modern periods. Jewish communities have frequently been uprooted from their areas of settlement and been forced to move across provincial or national boundaries to re-establish themselves once more in a new environment. Such moves were often accompanied by anti-Jewish turmoil, in which the refugees managed to salvage little of the material possessions which they owned in their old locale. Migrations and expulsions would normally completely disrupt the cultural life of the community because of the loss of the synagogues and of the works of art. The fact that Jews had mainly a musical, oral and literary culture enabled them to survive and to carry the main forms of their culture from place to place. In the modern world the cultural bias of Judaism, favouring verbal expression, has influenced Jews even far removed from their religious roots to find creative outlets in theatre, novels, films, poetry, singing and in music rather than in sculpture and the visual arts.

BIBLIOGRAPHY

1. ZIMMELS, H. J., *Ashkenazim and Sephardim*, London, Oxford University Press, 1958
2. REITLINGER, G., *The Final Solution: The Attempt to Exterminate the Jews of Europe, 1939–1945*, 2nd edn, New York, Yoseloff, 1961, repr. 1968; London, Vallentine, Mitchell, 1968
3. ROTH, C., *A Short History of the Jewish People*, rev. edn, London, East and West Library, 1969; Hartford, Conn., Hartmore, 1970; New York, Hebrew Publications, 1978
4. TRACHTENBERG, J., *The Devil and the Jews: The Medieval Conception of the Jew and Its Relation to Modern Antisemitism*, New York, Harper, 1966
5. THE BABYLONIAN TALMUD (tr. under the editorship of I. Epstein), 18-vol. edn, London, Soncino, 1961; in 35 vols., 1935–52
6. MAIMONIDES, i.e. MOSES BEN MAIMON, *The Guide of the Perplexed* (tr. S. Pines), 2 vols., Chicago, Ill., University of Chicago Press, 1974, prev. publ. 1963
7. JACOBS, L., *Principles of the Jewish Faith: An Analytic Study*, London, Vallentine, Mitchell/New York, Basic Books, 1964
8. SCHOLEM, G. G., *Major Trends in Jewish Mysticism*, 3rd edn repr., New York, Schocken, 1961; 3rd edn, New York, Schocken, 1954; London, Thames & Hudson, 1955

9. THE ZOHAR (tr. H. Sperling and M. Simon), 5 vols., London, Soncino, 1931–4

10. RABINOWICZ, H. M., *The World of Hasidism*, London, Vallentine, Mitchell/Hartford, Conn., Hartmore, 1970

11. UNTERMAN, A., *Jews: Their Religious Beliefs and Practices*, London, Boston, Mass., Routledge, 1981

12. MOORE, G. F., *Judaism in the First Centuries of the Christian Era*, 3 vols., Cambridge, Mass., Harvard University Press, repr. 1966; first publ. 1927–30

13. BARON, S. W., *A Social and Religious History of the Jews*, 2nd edn, 17 vols. and Index to vols. 1–8, Philadelphia, Pa, Jewish Publication Society of America/New York, London, Columbia University Press, 1952–76

14. THE AUTHORIZED DAILY PRAYER BOOK (with a tr. by S. Singer), new edn, London, Eyre & Spottiswoode, 1962, repr. 1968

15. SCHECHTER, S., *Studies in Judaism*, New York, Meridian, 1962, prev. publ. 1958

16. SKLARE, M., *Conservative Judaism: An American Religious Movement*, new edn, New York, Schocken, 1972

17. RUDAVSKY, D., *Modern Jewish Religious Movements: A History of Emancipation and Adjustment*, New York, Behrman, 1967, 3rd edn, 1979. Original title: *Emancipation and Adjustment: Contemporary Jewish Religious Movements*, New York, Diplomatic Press/London, Living Books, 1967

18. SCHAUSS, H., *Guide to Jewish Holy Days*, New York, Schocken, repr. 1970

19. IDELSOHN, A. Z., *Jewish Liturgy and Its Development*, New York, Schocken, 1967; prev. publ. New York, Holt, 1932

20. GINZBERG, L., *The Legends of the Jews*, 7 vols., Philadelphia, Pa, Jewish Publication Society of America, 1968; prev. publ. 1909–38

21. SCHOLEM, G. G., *On the Kabbalah and Its Symbolism* (tr. Ralph Manheim), New York, Schocken, 1965

22. TRACHTENBERG, J., *Jewish Magic and Superstition: A Study in Folk Religion*, New York, Atheneum, 1970; prev. publ. New York, Behrman, 1939

23. ZIMMELS, H. J., *Magicians, Theologians and Doctors: Studies in Folk-Medicine and Folk-Lore as Reflected in the Rabbinical Responsa, 12th–19th Centuries*, New York, Feldheim/London, Goldston, 1952

24. SACHAR, H. M., *The Course of Modern Jewish History*, New York, Dell, 1958, rev. edn 1977; prev. publ. Cleveland, World/London, Weidenfeld, 1958

25. KATZ, J., *Tradition and Crisis: Jewish Society at the End of the Middle Ages*, New York, Schocken, 1971

26. SHAROT, S., *Judaism: A Sociology*, Newton Abbot, Devon, David & Charles/New York, Holmes & Meier, 1976

27. HERTZBERG, A. (ed.), *The Zionist Idea: A Historical Analysis and Reader*, New York, Atheneum, repr. 1971; prev. publ. New York, Doubleday, 1959

28. UNTERMAN, A., *Judaism*, London, Ward Lock Educational, 1981 (The Arts and Practices of Living Religions)

2

Christianity

ANDREW WALLS

Introduction

NAME

The term 'Christian' was first used in *c.* 35–40 in Antioch in Syria, to describe a group of people who demonstrated attachment to 'Christos' [39: *Acts* 2: 26]. This was a Greek translation of the Hebrew term 'Messiah', used by Jews to designate their expected national saviour. The movement, which had reached Antioch from Jewish sources, identified the Messiah with the recent prophet-teacher, Jesus of Nazareth. The Antiochene sobriquet stuck. It is entirely appropriate. Over the centuries the Christian movement has produced a bewildering diversity of expressions, but allegiance to 'Christ', Jesus the prophet-teacher of first-century Palestine, is crucial to them all. [17: 28] The use of a Jewish technical term to designate this historical figure reminds us that the movement is rooted in the life and writings of ancient Israel. In all the transformations Christianity has undergone through its encounters with different cultures and civilizations the marks of its Israelite inheritance return again and again.

SOURCES

The Jewish scriptures. The earliest Christians were Jews, with the traditional threefold scriptures. Although Christianity became an overwhelmingly Gentile movement, the Christian communities continued to read the Jewish scriptures, using them as an authoritative source for teaching and debate, and seeing them as 'the Old Testament' (or 'Covenant'). [6: VII]

The New Testament writings. For the life and work of Jesus the Christ the collection of Christian writings known as the 'New Testament' is the only extensive early source. It contains the ideas and images of Jesus held in the early Christian communities, ideas and images powerful enough to bring those communities into being. The special status of the New Testament writings comes from their association in one way or another with the group of followers of Jesus known as the apostles. The members of this group, chosen by Jesus himself, were recognized as the founders and regulators of the Christian community, possessing the authoritative interpretation of Jesus and his teaching. When the living apostles passed from the scene their surviving writings, and those of their close associates, naturally had a special significance as preserving the interpretation of Jesus entrusted by him to his companions.

Taken together, the Old and New Testaments represented the 'prophets' and the 'apostles'. They were the record of a continuous and consistent series of revelations culminating in Christ as interpreted by those he appointed for that purpose, and formed a 'canon', or measuring rod, whereby the life of the Christian community might be tested. [23: XIX; 29: 56ff] It is not possible here to give any account of the literary discussions concerning the books which comprise the New Testament, nor is it necessary to our purpose [see summaries in 24 and 30]. All (or virtually all) come from the first century, some of them within the first half; all were, or were early believed to be, associated with people or communities within the apostolic circle and thereby as containing normative teaching. [8: XXIII; see XXIV and XXX for studies of particular writings]

The Christian community. From its origins, Christianity has had the idea of a shared life in a community of which Christ is the head. There is an almost universal conviction that God is active in the Church, guiding it into truth, though Christians differ widely among themselves as to the instruments by which that guidance is given. The widespread nature of this conviction requires us to see the Christian community, the Church, as one of the sources of Christianity. But while some Christians believe the Church to be entrusted by God with a tradition to transmit and develop through its accredited representatives and teachers, others deny the existence of any source of revelation independent of the scriptures. [11 vol. III: V, VI]

These differences relate to the interpretation of the role of the apostles. In much Christian thought, there is the idea that the apostolic office has been perpetuated in the Church over the centuries through a succession of bishops whose unanimity guarantees 'catholic', i.e. universal, truth. Other Christians hold that the office of apostle was a once-for-all institution for the establishment of the Church; the scriptures are now the sole reliable guide to what is 'apostolic' teaching, to which the institutional church should conform. To these we should perhaps add an idea characteristic of pentecostal and a good deal of African Christianity; that God still speaks through prophets and inspired people, particularly to apply the message of the scriptures to specific human situations. Christians differ in their identification of the Church, but virtually all groups recognize some form of consensus among believers as a test of authenticity, and virtually all accept that God in some way directs the life and deliberations of the Christian community.

HISTORY

Christianity has existed for two millennia. It has several times changed its geographical centre of gravity. It has adapted itself to diverse societies and been reshaped by them. It has been the most syncretistic of all the great faiths, while never losing the marks of its Jewish origins. There is no single 'Christian civilization' but an endless process of translation into various languages and cultures and into the various subcultures within them. Our periodization of Christian history will therefore be based on the dominant cultures with which it has been associated at various times.

The Jewish phase (c. 30 to c. 70). For a short but vital period Christianity was entirely Jewish. To a contemporary observer, the early Christian community described in the opening chapters of the *Acts of the Apostles* would have seemed but one among the infinite variations of Judaism. In most respects the Jerusalem Christians were indistinguishable from other observant Jews. They offered animal sacrifices, circumcised their male children and kept the seventh day punctiliously free from work. What distinguished them from other Jews was their identification of Jesus of Nazareth – known by all to have been crucified, and declared by them to have risen from the dead – with the scriptural figures of the Messiah, the Son of Man and the Suffering Servant. [23]

The companions of Jesus, the recognized leaders of his movement, shared this background. For many years they confined their preaching – as Jesus had done – to Jews, expounding the Jewish scriptures and explaining their fulfilment in Jesus. His resurrection proved him to be the divinely appointed Messiah. He had inaugurated the Age to Come described in the prophecies. His people were forgiven their past sins, and received an overflow of the divine presence and energy (the 'Holy Spirit'). [8: XIII–XVII; 23: I–IV; 39 *Acts* 2, 14–39]

One of the signs of the Age to Come, according to the same prophecies, was that non-Jews would seek and find the salvation which God had given to Israel. So the conversion of pagan Greeks in Antioch [39: *Acts* 11, 19f] could cause no difficulty in principle, even to the most devout upholders of the Jewish Law. Such things proved that the Gentiles were entering Israel, as Jews had always believed they would, when the Age to Come dawned. Many naturally expected that such would now be circumcised and keep the Law, as had always been expected of converts to Judaism. Had this expectation been fulfilled, Christianity would have remained a minor Jewish denomination, and its survival beyond the Roman period would have been questionable. But the Jerusalem Christians decided that Gentiles would be accepted on the ground of faith in Jesus Messiah, without being circumcised or required to keep the Jewish Law. In defiance of traditional practice, which enforced ritual separation from Gentiles in social intercourse, Jewish believers in Jesus met at the meal table with uncircumcised fellow believers. The bond with Jesus had precedence over the bond of national unity. It was possible to enter Israel without becoming a Jew. [8: XXII]

The full implications were probably not realized at the time. Many Christian Jews must have expected that Gentile followers of Jesus would gradually assimilate to their own Jewish model. In fact, Gentiles came flooding in and became the majority among Jesus' followers. The departure of the Christians from Jerusalem during the Jewish revolt against the Romans, and the destruction of the temple and the Jewish state in 70 CE, brought the end of the Jewish model of Christianity for ever. [6: XI; 8: XXVIII] A remnant of ethnic Jews then and since have recognized Jesus as Messiah; only a minority of these, however, have sought, like the earliest Christians, to express their faith in strictly Jewish terms. Most have assimilated to Gentile modes of worship and devotion. Some were compelled to do so.

The Hellenistic–Roman phase (c. 70 to c. 500). A major turning-point in Christian history occurred in Antioch when unnamed Jewish Christians began to talk about Jesus to 'Greeks', i.e. pagans.

Antioch was the centre of the first organized attempt to spread faith in Jesus in the Hellenistic world. The outstanding figure in this was a Dispersion-born rabbi, Saul. He had not been a companion of Jesus, but was convinced that he had seen him after his resurrection, and he was widely recognized as an apostle. Saul contended vigorously for accepting converts on the grounds of faith in Jesus without the requirement of the Jewish Law: they had very evidently received the divine life of the Holy Spirit, which showed that God had already accepted them. He took a Gentile name, Paul (by which he is usually known), lived equally readily within Jewish and Greek culture and, while himself thoroughly Hebraic in thought and instinct, encouraged Greek Christians to assert their freedom from the Jewish cultural tradition. For him the Christian community organically united ethnic and religious communities previously thought divided for ever. He travelled throughout Asia Minor and eastern Europe introducing Jesus to the synagogues of overseas Jewish communities like that in which he was born. These often had a fringe of sympathetic Gentiles influenced by Judaism, who seem to have been particularly open to Paul's message. Besides these 'God-fearers' many pagans without any significant background in Judaism were affected. [8: XVIII, XXI, XXIV]

The term 'Messiah' meant little to anyone not raised in Israel. For new Christians Jesus was 'Lord', a title regularly applied to the cult divinities of the eastern Mediterranean lands. They were influenced by various strands of Greek philosophy, Roman law, mystery cults, oriental magic and astral science. All this mental furniture had to stand in the same room with the essentially Hebraic faith in Jesus Messiah which the apostles had preached [cf. 15: 1–2; 29: 1]. And before long the typical Christian leader was no longer a son of Israel nourished in centuries of the Israelite inheritance. He was by birth or ancestry a Greek-speaking convert from paganism. This transformed the life-style of Christians and the expression of their beliefs [15: 43]. Observance of the Law, animal sacrifice, circumcision, Sabbath observance, all disappeared. Some Jewish features of the new faith were hard to assimilate. The doctrine of resurrection was a constant stumbling-block. Many Greek-speaking people had grown up to think matter the seat of evil, both in the world and in the personality, and wished to be free of the body. The conviction that Christ had risen was too central to Christian preaching to be abandoned, but many spoke of the resurrection of the body as though it meant the immortality of the soul, an idea well known to Greeks. (The Western form of Christianity has perhaps never ceased to confuse the two ideas.) 'Indigenizing' movements, seeking to make Christianity at home in the Hellenistic intellectual world, played down or rejected the most obviously Jewish features of the Christian inheritance.

The new Christians used the thought forms of Hellenistic culture. The formulation of 'orthodoxy', developing statements of correct belief, was brought about by using the categories and methods of Greek philosophical debate. The Christian pattern of organization owed something to Greek civic organization [23: 188]. The corporate leadership on the Jewish model of the earliest congregations gave way to a system of linked local hierarchies, each under a bishop. This system helped to maintain 'orthodox' or 'apostolic' tradition. Individuals or communities who insisted on teaching not approved by the local hierarchies found themselves excluded. This type of organization, strong, but not over-centralized, helped to cope with another peril. State persecution of Christians, at first spasmodic and local, increased by the middle of the third century, and in the early years of the fourth reached a desperate ferocity. [21] The Christians' insistence that their allegiance to Christ prevented their worshipping in the state cult, which involved veneration of the Emperor's 'genius' or spirit, and their frequent refusal to undertake military service, contributed to suspicions about their loyalty to the Empire. All this changed with Constantine's accession to power in 313. He first tolerated, then favoured, the Christian Church. Privilege replaced disability until Christianity effectively became the state religion of the Empire. Hitherto various attractions – the moral changes it offered, the majesty of its worship, the close, caring relationships it created – had drawn people towards Christianity from the declining popular religions, philosophical rationalism and the Eastern cults. From the fourth century on, however, Christian profession became the rule rather than the exception, and a period dawned in which Christianity and affairs of state were constantly entwined.

A guiding principle in the formulations of current belief was that of 'catholicity' or universality [29: 12]. This was a natural product of the doctrine that the apostles taught the same faith everywhere. Under the Christian Empire the practice developed of seeking a consensus on major matters of theology or practice which might otherwise be divisive. Bishops, who represented the teaching and ruling functions of the Church, met in council, implicitly agreeing to be bound by the outcome of that council's decisions. Constantine himself took a lead in promoting this activity, which lent colour to the idea of the Church as a corporate body with quasi-juridical powers. Outside that Church's organization, however, there boiled a cauldron of religious activity which Church writers simply denominate 'the heresies'. Some of these movements bore little relationship to the Christian faith with its Hebraic roots. Others were radical indigenization movements, striving to bridge the gap between Hellenistic culture and the Christian faith with its Jewish scriptures. Others again represent the penetration by Christianity of subcultures or minority cultures within the Hellenistic world. Some movements which the Church at large declared heretical may have been simply local forms of Christianity [21].

The Roman Empire was not, however, the first Christian state: the Kingdom of Armenia anticipated it by some years. Before 500, there were innumerable Christians in areas which had little or nothing to do with the Roman Empire. There were sizeable Christian communities in south India and south Arabia, in the Nile valley and the Sudan, in the Horn of Africa and the Caucasus. There were substantial Christian minorities in the Persian Empire, with their own scholars, saints and martyrs, but there the association of Christianity with the old enemy, Rome, worked against it.

The barbarian phase (c. *500–1100*). By 500 Christianity was solidly based on a considerable world empire, had clothed itself with the intellectual garments of a highly sophisticated literary civilization, and taken the tools of a high technology. With the Roman Empire as its principal base Christianity continued to expand among the tribal peoples north of the imperial frontiers, along the eastern trade routes, and into parts of eastern Africa. This expansion was made possible both by dedicated agents set apart to preach the faith and ordinary people carrying it in the course of their daily work and family life.

Christian Romans shared the attitude of their pagan predecessors and contemporaries to the 'barbarians', and trembled at the thought that Empire and

Christian civilization alike might be swept away in a barbarian flood. The flood eventually came, and the western half of the Roman Empire broke under a barrage of fierce and ugly little wars. But the effect on the Church was not what earlier writers had expected. Many of the barbarians were already Christians, if not always of a Roman kind. The Christianity some had imbibed was of the archaic 'Arian' type, banned in the Empire; gradually this gave place to the more developed Roman confessions. Indeed, despite the centuries of destruction and unsettlement, the northern and western peoples were surprisingly open to the religion and culture of the people whose Empire they had destroyed.

As the Empire broke down, Christianity spread among the states which arose from its ruins; and as new peoples achieved dominance in various parts of the West, Christianity spread among them also. [See 5 for the example of England.] It is a complex story. Rulers like the mighty Charlemagne (King of the Franks, 768–814, and Emperor) and the centralizing King of Norway Olav Trygvason (d. 1000), extending the numbers of Christians and their own power simultaneously, are one factor. Church-inspired missions, such as the one Pope Gregory the Great sent to southern England in 597, are another. Hundreds of monks and ascetics on their own missions, driven by the desire for holiness and obedience, are yet a third.

There were not many martyrs among the northern peoples. The progress of religious change was often rapid, whole communities moving behind their chief men. But there were periods of return to the old gods, and places which resisted long: much of Sweden and most of Finland was unpenetrated till the twelfth century. Nevertheless, the old gods died. Many people were weary and disillusioned with them. Christianity helped the adjustment from the obsolete warrior life to that of settled farming, albeit attitudes belonging to the old religion passed into the new. Saints and martyrs quietly replaced the local spirits. The symbols changed, the directions and motives of religious practice remained. Power and protection were still sought, but sought now from God. Of that power the Church was trustee, its saints and its ceremonies the channels.

Migration, war and settlement had already eroded local kinship-based identities; a universal Christian Church provided a greatly superior kinship. The use of Latin for scriptures, liturgy and learning forged another bond. The language and something of the sense of identity belonging to the old Roman Empire were preserved in the idea of an Empire of Christ, to whom all Christian princes and peoples owed allegiance.

In early Christianity churches associated with the apostles had special status. In all the West, there was only one such church, Rome, associated with Peter, chief of the apostles. It was easy, therefore, to see Rome as the crown of that system through which flowed the power of God, its bishop as successor of Peter and earthly representative of Christ. A multitude of factors, historical and cultural, political and theological, gave Rome and its bishop a unique place in the minds of Western Christians. Equally, Eastern Christians, with their Emperor still reigning in the New Rome, Constantinople, with another language, and other ancient and apostolic churches, saw things in a different light. However, the position of Christianity in the eastern Mediterranean was transformed when, by 642, the Arabs, united and inspired in their new-found faith of Islam, had overrun Egypt and Syria. Over the generations much of the population of these Christian heartlands embraced the faith of their new rulers. In North Africa, overset by both barbarian and Arab invasions, Christianity died out altogether. In the Middle East, it became the hereditary faith of a minority community. In Constantinople, a Christian Emperor ruling over eastern Europe and Asia Minor prolonged the Hellenistic–Roman phase of Christianity for several centuries more.

Greek Christianity also expanded northwards. In 988 Christianity was proclaimed the official religion in Kiev, and though it took several centuries to penetrate the countryside, the basis of Russian Christianity was laid. But while new Slavonic churches emerged to the north, the Empire's outlying provinces in the Mediterranean lands were gradually chipped away, their Christian populations following the same path as those of Egypt and Syria. As the political and cultural divide between East and West grew, Eastern and Western Christians entered different worlds.

Meanwhile, Oriental Christians of the Nestorian and Monophysite families, separated from both East and West, continued to spread their own forms of Christianity. Their merchants and their missionaries traversed Central Asia, and by 781 were practising their faith in T'ang China. [42 vol. 6: 74ff]

Another shift was taking place in the Christian centre of gravity, almost as remarkable in its effects as the transition from Jewish to Greek Christianity. No longer was the typical Christian consciously Roman, or literate, or Greek-speaking, or 'civilized' at all; he was now a peasant cultivator and what Greeks and Romans had long designated a 'barbarian'. Nevertheless Christianity, more than any other factor, connected these peoples with the inheritance of Greece and Rome. Literature, learning and literary habits were established by the Church among essentially pre-literate peoples. The Church maintained the creeds of the councils and asserted orthodoxy as it knew it; and its learning was inevitably shaped by the Hellenistic–Roman phase of Christianity.

One institution which had been born in that phase was developed and variously adapted by each group of Christians, Greek, Latin and Oriental. This was the monastery, the close-knit band of men or women, celibate, dedicated to religion, living together under rule. Monasteries served many functions, sometimes providing the task forces for religious operations, sometimes maintaining learning, sometimes acting as centres of religion, education or charity. Varied motives, not all of the highest, filled them, but above all they were the focus for those who wished to be radically Christian, to imitate the life-style of Christ and his apostles. And in the West they provided an alternative community for those who could see no possibility of leading a consistent Christian life amid the pressures of a violent society.

The Western phase (c. 1100 to c. 1600). In 1453 the Turks occupied Constantinople, and the Christians of the East passed under Muslim rule. The Nestorian adventure in China faded, the Mongols swamped Central Asian Christianity. Russia was still painfully acquiring its Christian rudiments. Western Europe became incontestably the centre point of Christianity. When men there spoke of 'Christendom' they thought of the complex of Western countries which acknowledged Christianity as their profession, accepted the bishop of Rome as its arbiter and used Latin in their worship. Only after the explosion of the Western peoples into new lands in the sixteenth century did any significant widening of the religious horizons take place. Within this period the foundations of the modern world were laid. The intellectual and artistic developments of the period, the foundations of scientific practice and the related technological advance, all owe something to the discovery by Latin-speaking Westerners of the legacy of Greece. Politically, the period shows the first signs of the development of nation-states as the consciousness of common nationality gradually became more important than allegiance to a particular ruler. [6: 108–16]

All these developments both affected and were affected by the Christian faith. A return to Greek-language studies opened up access to the Christian Scriptures afresh. The Greek intellectual tradition underlies the widely different expositions of Christian belief by Thomas Aquinas (1225–74) and John Calvin (1509–64), the most considerable encyclopedic thinkers produced by Western Christianity. The most important technological development, printing, received an immense impetus from the religious conflicts of the time, and may have done much to determine their outcome. The development of nation-states, each with its own distinctive features, and each equally professing to be a Christian community, produced local forms of Christianity.

From the pre-Christian centuries of primal religion the European peasant retained his lively sense of benevolent and malevolent spiritual forces always at hand, liable to break into daily life. To the hope that these forces would bring protection or prosperity in this life was now added the need of shelter from terrors of the next. It was natural to seek these things through the Church, and to see that Church as a reservoir of supernatural power operated by a specialist priesthood. Such ideas were obviously open to manipulation and commercial exploitation. The sixteenth century brought the end of the worst of these abuses, and the beginning of the end of the conditions which produced them.

The nature and meaning of salvation came under intense discussion. For a significant sector of the Church three affirmations on this topic became central. Salvation is 'by grace only', and this is a matter of divine initiative, contrary to the mechanical and quantitative methods of achieving it which dominated so much of popular religion. It is also 'through faith only', so that human merit is excluded. And the source of knowledge about it is 'from scripture only'. Another sector insisted on the need to couple these 'onlys' with other factors, the merits of the saints, the necessity of good deeds as a condition, not the fruit, of salvation, the ongoing tradition of the Church.

This social, intellectual and religious ferment was too much for the unitary structure of Latin Christianity. From the sixteenth century on, Western Christianity appears in three distinguishable branches. The conservative formulation, thinking of itself as 'Catholic', universal, could claim institutional continuity with earlier Christianity, preserving as it did the concept of a supra-national Church under the bishop of Rome. The 'Protestant' formulation, with the three 'onlys' as its watchword, could claim that many 'Catholic' features were in fact innovations, and no part of the teaching of the apostles. For them continuity with the apostles was achieved by attention to the apostolic scriptures. A reformation of the Church on lines indicated in scripture should take place in each nation. This produced a series of 'reformed' churches similar in their main teachings, but reflecting the local conditions of those countries and differing in their forms of government. The third formulation was that of the radical reformers whom Catholics and Protestants called 'Anabaptists'. It challenged an assumption which had underlain Western Christianity since Constantine: that membership of the Christian Church and membership of the community of the state were conterminous. By taking the Protestant understanding of salvation to its logical conclusion and identifying the Church with those who had personal faith, they broke the link between Church and state, and re-created the persecuted Church of early Christianity. In the process they enabled the concept of freedom of conscience to emerge.

The conservative, Catholic formulation left the monasteries in very much their traditional form. The Protestant reformers abandoned them, arguing that family life in society could be just as holy, just as dedicated to God and just as beneficial in its effects. The radical reformers went further. For them the Church was the holy community of dedicated people, the congregation. The Anabaptist congregation is the fully Protestant version of the monastery, with husbands, wives and children all incorporated in a community wholly

committed to a Christian style of life. In their different ways each of these
three competing manifestations represented a radicalization of Christianity,
a rejection of compromise with the pre-Christian concepts which had underpinned Christian practice for centuries. Each provided a path of adjustment
to the modern world, to more complex forms of society and a wider universe
of ideas. (See Figure 2.1.)

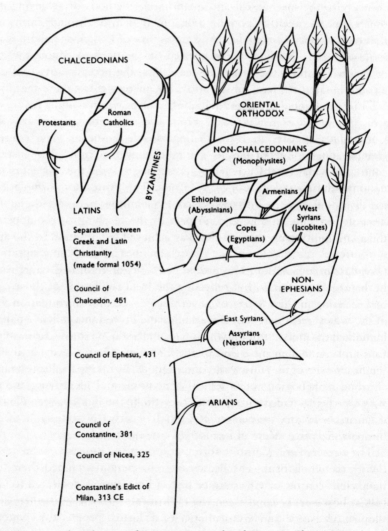

Figure 2.1   The relations of Eastern, Oriental and Western Christianity
(from the late J. M. Harness, by permission)

For a few years in the thirteenth century a few Western Christians glimpsed a possible understanding with the Mongol Empire. But Western vision was not yet able to cope with such horizons, and the contact, which might have been so potent for the religious history of the world, faded away.

The years that saw Western Europe become the Christian heartland saw also the balance of Eastern Christianity transformed. Bulgaria, Serbia and Russia successively became the seats of major new Christian populations. Their churches were organized on the model of that of the old Empire of Constantinople; but they were quite ready to challenge that Empire's power. In 1204 Crusaders from the West looted Constantinople and deliberately desecrated its churches. This event drove a wedge between East and West for centuries, and opened the way for the eventual Muslim triumph in the East. Before that triumph, however, the Greek Christianity of the old Empire had a late flowering. Its monasteries produced spiritual and mystical writers as disturbing as Gregory Palamas (d. 1359); its laity, theologians as profound as Nicholas Cabasilas (d. 1380). (The lay theologian has until lately been far more characteristic of Eastern than of Western Christianity.)

But the threat of eclipse was at hand for all the Eastern Christian communities. When the old Empire passed under Muslim rule, Russia had already known two centuries of Mongol domination. The difference was that under the Mongols the Russian Church was protected and quietly throve. Here was Constantinople's successor.

The phase of expanding Europe (c. 1500 to c. 1920). Between 1500 and 1900, the balance between Europe and the rest of the world was transformed. Europeans occupied whole continents as settlers and assumed control of vast areas. When the First World War broke out people of European origin dominated the globe, claiming many non-European territories as their possessions and controlling the economies of the rest, Japan being almost the only significant exception. During the same period Christianity moved from being a European phenomenon to a world faith, the signs of its approaching decline in Europe being evident just as it was expanding everywhere else. (This phase of Christian history overlaps with the last, since the expansion of part of Europe took place while elsewhere the reformulations described in the last section were still going on.)

With the whole of the eastern Mediterranean under Turkish rule by 1500, the ancient centres of Christianity became concerned mainly with survival. Russia, however, became a centre of Christian thought and spirituality, developing an ascetic and mystical style of its own. Throne and Church were closely linked, as they had been in Constantinople. If Constantinople was the Second Rome, Moscow was the Third, its Tsar (or 'Caesar') the defender of the Church and its orthodoxy like that of the Christian Roman emperors. As the Russian Empire extended eastwards, Russian Christianity followed it across all North Asia, and, in Alaska, even into North America. Russia assumed the role of protector of the Eastern Christians. Christian identity had much to do with the emergence of independent Balkan states, a movement pioneered by Greece in the early decades of the nineteenth century.

Western expansion was even more dramatic and the expansion of Western Christianity yet more significant. By 1550 Spain had set up a vast empire in Central and South America. By 1650 Portugal was established in Brazil, many African coastlands, India and South-East Asia, with footholds in China and Japan; and the northern European powers, England especially, were settling large tracts of North America and exploiting the commercial advantages of the Caribbean islands, as well as looking eastward to India and beyond.

There had been little previous contact between Western Christians and non-Christian peoples, other than European Jewish minorities. Relations with Islamic peoples were soured by centuries of warfare, crusades and folk-memories of escape from conquest. By 1650 adherents of all three branches of Western Christianity, Catholic, Protestant and radical, were living on close terms with native American peoples. Western treatment of these peoples was usually misguided and often beastly, but Christianity provides the main mitigating influences of its story. A genuine desire for their conversion led to some tragic consequences, but it forced Westerners to recognize their potential equality in faith. Christianity moderated the worst abuses of Western tyranny; it was almost the only source of self-criticism for the Western peoples, the principal source of challenge to Western rapacity. In Central and South America, conversion (by inducement, force and conviction), together with settlement from southern Europe and intermarriage, laid the foundations of a new Christian continent. North Europeans took their Christian profession to Australia, New Zealand, parts of Africa and, above all, to North America. By the end of this phase North America had replaced Europe as the main theatre of Christian activity. The United States provided new hope and new life for settlers from every country in Europe and every variety of Christianity. New expressions of Christianity and new institutions (such as the organized evangelistic campaign) developed to cope with its expanding frontier and rapid urban growth and then, in turn, acted upon Europe.

The missionary movement is also in some respects an aspect of the expansion of Europe – even if European economic and political interests have not always favoured, and have sometimes actively opposed, it. Indeed, the Church authorities of Europe, absorbed in their own problems, were not often concerned or equipped for the propagation of Christianity across cultural frontiers. The missionary movement, which undertook this task, was the work less of authorities than of enthusiasts. It developed characteristic forms of organization. Among Catholics, whose activities predominated before the late eighteenth century, the instrument lay in the religious orders. These were bodies of priests and laymen, or of women, vowed to live together under discipline, and able to work outside the normal Church structures to accomplish particular tasks. For Protestants, the leading influence in the early nineteenth century, the voluntary society offered a similar independence and flexibility for work overseas.

Between them, often in competition, the Catholic orders and the Protestant societies planted the Christian faith across Africa, Asia and the Pacific. Inevitably they brought with them the learning, technology and something of the outlook of the West. Side by side with this expansion of Christianity from Europe, came signs of a recession from Christianity within Europe. In intellectual circles, non-religious interpretations of the world became increasingly common. In the social sphere, resentment at the frequent alignment of the Church with power, wealth and privilege alienated others from Christianity. Above all, in the industrial countries, urban development and a huge increase in population left multitudes without any regular contact with the churches. The original organization of Western Christianity was designed for a primarily agricultural society, and found it impossible to cope with an industrial one.

Two features of this phase appear to be opposite in tendency, though they often coexisted. On the one hand, the intensive activism characteristic of the European of this period was reflected in his religion. The theatre of faith is the whole world of human activity, not the heavenly training ground of the monastery or alternative community of the elect. On the other hand, in this phase Western Christianity becomes increasingly a matter of private choice. Early Western Christianity inherited from the pre-Christian past an idea of religion as transmitted custom, binding on the whole community. The more open, plural societies of later times could not accommodate this. Newer countries like the United States acknowledged no link between Church and state. Meanwhile, movements like Pietism (originating in seventeenth-century Germany), and the Evangelical Revival (which deeply affected Protestants on both sides of the Atlantic in the eighteenth and nineteenth centuries), distinguished between the 'formal' or 'nominal' Christianity typical of their countries as a whole and the 'real' Christianity of inward experience of renewal and active faith known by a smaller number.

The southern phase (since 1920). The present phase of Christianity has seen another dramatic shift in its centre of gravity. Not long ago Christianity was the religion of nearly all the peoples of Europe and their New World descendants, and of few others. Today it is a faith distributed throughout the world, is specially characteristic of the southern continents and appears to be receding only among the peoples of European origin (see Figures 2.2 and 2.3).

The recession from Christianity observable in Europe in the last phase has accelerated. At the beginning of the present phase, Russia, once the Third Rome and the centre of Eastern Christianity, officially adopted an atheist ideology, and after the Second World War other Eastern European countries followed suit. Yet paradoxically, Christian expression is often more evident in Eastern than in Western Europe. Though accurate comparisons are hard to come by, the proportion of the population regularly attending worship in Russia may bear comparison with that in Britain, while Poland is the most strikingly Catholic country in Europe. Only in Albania, previously a predominantly Muslim country, has evidence of Christian activity completely disappeared.

In North America, technological development has been greater than in Europe, but the pace of recession from Christianity has been slower. North America has been the main source of the missionary movement for many years. In the United States the proportion of Catholics to Protestants has increased, but the influence of the radical tradition of Christianity (see page 65f), reinforced by the evangical distinction between nominal and real Christianity, is immense. It is held to underpin the traditional values of a libertarian and individualistic society; and a claim to the evangelical experience of faith-renewal has helped candidates for public office.

But Christian expansion outside Europe and the lands occupied by European peoples has continued unabated. The expansion has outlasted the European empires and the missionary movement. Whereas missionary effort gave prominence to the old civilizations of India and China, it is Africa and the Pacific, along with Latin America, which have become notable for their Christian populations. [4: 778] On one estimate Christian profession in sub-Saharan Africa has increased in geometrical progression since the mid nineteenth century, doubling every twelve years or so. Everything suggests that, by the end of the present century, Africa will have by far the largest Christian profession of any of the continents [4: IV]. This movement has gone along with the social revolutions brought to Africa through contact with the West and the effect of the forces of modernization; but the main agents and initiators in the spread of Christianity have always been Africans. Undoubtedly Christianity has assisted in the adjustment to change, as it did in earlier centuries for the peoples of Europe in a parallel situation. Since virtually all African societies have espoused some version of the development model, further substantial change can be expected.

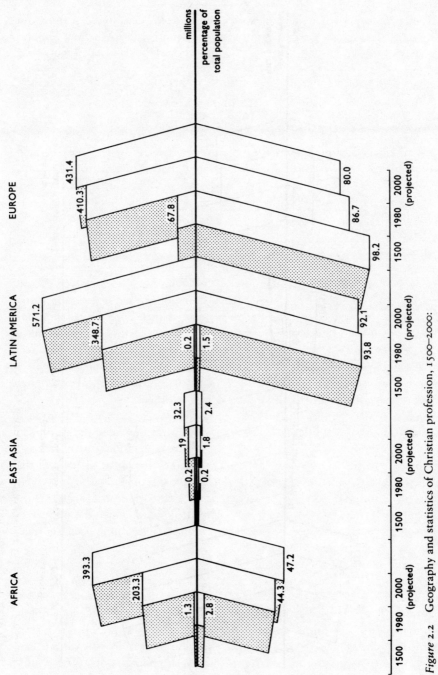

Figure 2.2　Geography and statistics of Christian profession, 1500–2000:
Africa, East Asia, Latin America and Europe

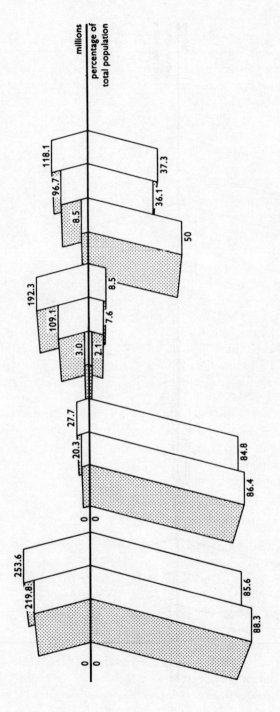

Figure 2.3 Geography and statistics of Christian profession, 1500–2000:
North America, Oceania, South Asia and U.S.S.R.

Latin America, where, as in early Western Europe, Christianity was imposed on top of peasant primal religions, has seen in the twentieth century movements of radicalization of Christianity which recall those which Europe saw in the sixteenth. There has been a reformulation of Catholicism [22], a notable increase of Protestantism [43], abundant manifestations of charismatic and 'enthusiastic' religion, and a new consciousness of the social implications of Christ's teaching. If Africa has been notable in the twentieth century for spectacular Christian growth, Latin America has been notable for revising and reshaping the inherited forms of Christianity. [46: 77ff; cf. 22: 1ff]

The same century has seen the old religions of Asia revive, reformulate and come to terms with the modernizing forces which in an earlier period of interaction with the West seemed to threaten their dissolution. Christianity there has, for the most part, remained the faith of small minorities. Only one Asian country, the Philippines, has a population substantially Christian in profession. There are important Christian minorities in South Korea and Indonesia, among others, and that of India, though a tiny percentage of that country's vast population, is remarkable both for its antiquity and for its members' capacity for fresh and constructive Christian thought [45]. China saw a sizeable movement towards Christianity in the course of its 'modernizing' revolution in the early part of this century. This was eclipsed in the Communist triumph a generation later. The strength of the Christian presence in China seems more significant than could have been guessed even a decade ago.

Christianity is now much more diverse in its forms and manifestations, its geographical spread and its cultural variety than at any previous time in its history. The only safe prediction appears to be that its southern populations in Africa, Latin America, Asia and the Pacific, which provide its present centres of significance, hold the key to its future. [9]

THE STUDY OF CHRISTIANITY

Eusebius of Caesarea (*c.* 265–339) is deservedly called the 'father of church history'. He relates the history and chronology of the world to the biblical history from Abraham to Christ, and traces the trials and triumphs of the Church from apostolic times to his own. Later Church historians, when writing of Christian history as a whole, tend to follow one or other of these models. Some write in terms of the history of God's salvation of the world, with Israel and the Christian Church marking successive stages in that cosmic history. Others write to explain the background and antecedents of the faith of the Christian readers of the author's time and place. Church-history writing has thus been a theological exercise; it is history written from the standpoint of faith.

Few writers, in fact, have been concerned with the history of Christianity as such, with all its plethora of local forms. Most have been concerned with the somewhat different exercise of the history of the Church. 'Church' is itself a theological term, standing in the writers' minds for 'People of God' or 'Body of Christ'; and Church historians have accordingly written either in terms of a particular institution or body of Christians ('a church' or 'churches') or accepted standards of 'authentic' belief and practice. Local factors have dominated in the selection of materials, for in effect the Church historian is linking the people of God as he recognizes them in past ages with the believers he knows and represents in his own day. The American K. S. Latourette (1884–1968) pioneered the genuinely global writing of Christian history; but his greatest work is concerned with one phenomenon only, advance and recession in the profession of Christianity. A comprehensive treatment from the stand-point of the discipline of the history of religions is still awaited.

The sense of the historical continuity of the people of God in all ages is characteristic of Christianity and will continue to generate study and writing. Its future form will be affected by the loss of Western dominance within Christianity, the increased understanding now manifest between different Christian traditions, and new perspectives on history and Christianity developing in the southern continents. Theological study of Christianity arises from the application of rational thought to the normative sources: the attempt to elucidate Christian belief as part of a total Christian world-view. But new developments in theology rarely arise as a result of abstract intellectual activity conducted for its own sake. It is the pressure of particular situations which forces the reflective process, and dictates its priorities. Not all theological topics are equally absorbing to all Christians. What is of high concern to one group in one age may be taken for granted or ignored completely in another. Theology is local and occasional in character. Thus situations unprecedented before the twentieth century have given a new prominence to questions about the responsibility of Christians in society at large, Christian attitudes to various manifestations of violence and the scope of Christianity in relation to other faiths. 'Liberation theology' could only have arisen in Latin America; 'Black theology' belongs to the experience of Blacks in the United States and in South Africa.

Western theology has been prone to systematize and synthesize theological thought. The Roman Catholic and Protestant Reformed traditions have been the most hospitable to systematic theology. The chart shown in Figure 2.4 was drawn (in 1590) to illustrate a work called A Golden Chaine, or The Description of Theology. It is meant to show the coherence (as of a 'golden chain') of all the biblical teaching. And it is for practical application: a map for the serious soul seeking salvation. It belongs to the Reformed tradition, but Catholic theology can equally lend itself to maps and diagrams. Later theologians went further, extending theology to a complete system covering art and culture, politics and economics. Eastern theology has never lent itself to maps and diagrams and there has always been a current in Western theology which has resisted schematization. Its representatives tend to work with a number of theological key concepts, or to use recurrent biblical themes as guiding principles. What is striking is that so many of the most influential Christian writers since early times have expanded their thought by means of biblical commentaries.

Teachings

Christians of a certain time and place sometimes stress things which would seem irrelevant or repellent to Christians of another. If a Martian observer were to visit, say, a meeting in the Jerusalem temple in about 37 CE, a session of one of the early councils, for example that of Nicea in 325, a convention of Irish monks in about 600 CE, a London meeting to promote civilization and missions in Africa in 1840 and a white-robed congregation singing through Lagos streets on its way to a healing service in Nigeria in the 1980s, he would in each case be meeting representative Christianity from the heartlands of their respective times. He would also be meeting Christian groups with a historical interconnection. But he might have difficulty at first establishing what they had in common; and each of the five groups would severely disapprove of some of the others' priorities and practices. What follows does not seek to supply a systematic account of Christian teaching. Instead, it asks what the communities which profess Christianity have in common. What links observant messianic Jews in the Jerusalem temple, Greek intellectuals at Nicea, ascetic monks on Iona, earnest early Victorian Protestants in Exeter Hall and the Eternal Sacred Order of the Cherubim and Seraphim in Nigeria? This means omitting from consideration of Christian teaching matters which any one of the Martian's chosen groups, and any large group of Christians today, would consider vitally important.

CHRISTIANS WORSHIP THE GOD OF THE JEWS

Christian worship of the God of the Jews indicates the historical particularity of the Christian faith. In every phase of Christian history it has been taken for granted that the revelation of God took place by a particular process, involving a particular people, the Jews. In each phase, too, Christians have seen themselves as in some way continuous with Israel, and the biblical history of Israel as part of their own, even in the periods of Christian hostility towards

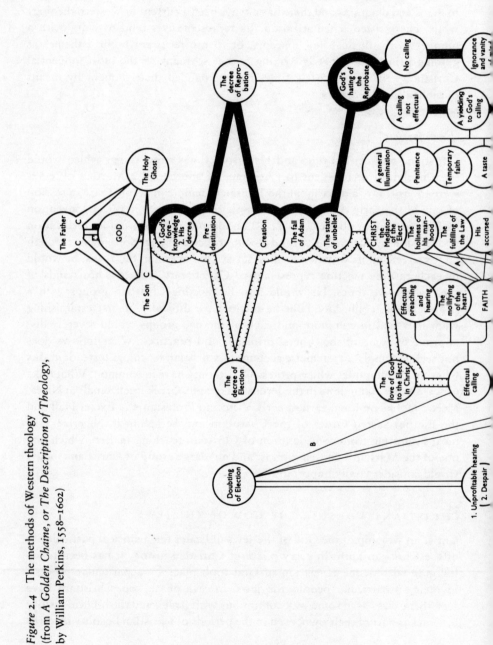

Figure 2.4 The methods of Western theology (from *A Golden Chaine, or The Description of Theology*, by William Perkins, 1558–1602)

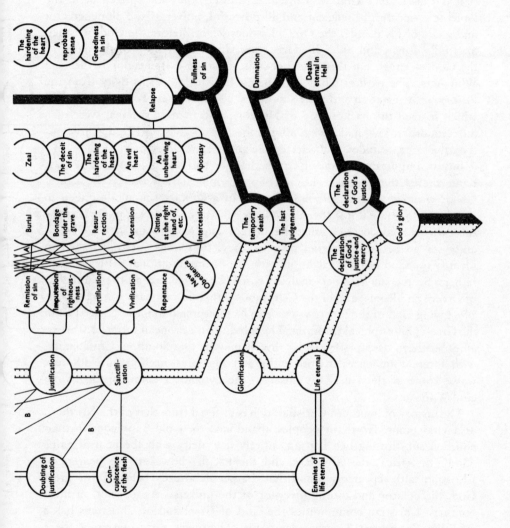

the Jewish community or amid harsh theological judgements on Jewish destiny. This 'scandal of particularity', the coupling of the divine purpose for the whole world to certain events, places and people, runs right through Christianity.

It is thus Israel's God who discloses himself, the God spoken of in the Israelite scriptures: beneficient and all-powerful, universal and alone, creator and guide of his people, the One who does Right. Before the God of Israel, man falls down, and hides his face. *I am* is one translation of the name of the God of Israel, but this does not indicate static existence; he is the God Who Acts. The earliest Christians, being Jewish, knew this deity from the history of their nation and their scriptures. The divinities of popular religion, which formed the background of Hellenistic–Roman Christians, were of a different order. Jews had always abused these as no-gods, anti-God. Christians took the same attitudes, and rejected the gods of the Greek past.

But an important stream of Greek thought had also rejected, or at least reinterpreted, these beings. The God of philosophical tradition was the highest Good: without a name, often spoken of in abstract terms or described in negatives. It was natural for early Greek Christians to fuse the God of the Bible with this concept of a somewhat distant, impersonal being. When Christianity spread to the barbarian peoples, they, too, were not encouraged to identify the God of their salvation with any of the traditional deities of their fathers. So the single impersonalized word 'God' replaced all the pantheons of Greece and Rome, and of the Celtic and Germanic and many other peoples. The Living God of the Hebrews came to be interpreted in terms derived from the Greek philosophical tradition. The mind of all European forms of Christianity has been deeply affected by this. It may be that Southern Christianity, with different influences at work within it, will express itself in quite different ways. Some of them may be closer to the dynamic Hebraic vision of the God Who Acts.

The history of Southern Christianity has differed from that of the Northern at a vital point. Northern peoples abandoned their old pantheons in their entirety, substituting belief in an entirely new deity with the neutral name 'God'. In Africa, the Americas and the Pacific, however, the bearers of Christian faith repeatedly found that the people already believed in a great God, the creator and moral governor of the universe. As a result, in most Southern Christian communities the God of Israel and of Christians has a traditionally venerated vernacular name. This gives a starting-point for a theology quite different from that of the earlier phases of Christian history.

JESUS CHRIST OF NAZARETH HAS ULTIMATE SIGNIFICANCE

The inescapable connection of Christianity with history ties it to a place, a time and a person. In Christian movements, Jesus is not considered simply to be a particular representative of a universal: he *is* the universal. Historically, Christian groups accord him ultimate significance, and for them life involves a commitment to following him.

There is an enormous range of interpretations of that significance, depending on what constitutes the ultimate for people of the particular time and place concerned. There is an equally wide range of understandings of the implications of following Christ, affected by the priorities of the situation in which the followers find themselves. Let us take, purely as examples, the Martian's five groups. The Jerusalem Christians saw ultimate significance in the Messiahship of Jesus. For them he was the long-expected saviour of Israel. He would rule it rightly, end its sufferings and make it in actuality what it already is in principle: the people of the holy and right-doing God. ('You shall call his name Jesus, for he shall save *his people* from their sins', the angel says to the devout family to which Jesus is born [39: *Matthew* 1:21].) This Messiah figure was fused with two other figures from the Jewish scriptures: the Son of Man, the divine agent who would bring the whole historical process to a climax, vindicate right and show the defeat of evil, and the Suffering Servant, who voluntarily underwent a sacrificial death on behalf of his people.

The Martian's second group, the fourth-century theologians assembled at Nicea, would have fully accepted all these statements, but for them the statements about Messiah, Son of Man and Suffering Servant were not the ultimate. The Greek intellectual habit forced them to make distinctions. If Jesus was the divine Son (and language like this was plain enough in the scriptures), what does that mean? For God must by definition be unchangeable, beyond pain, beyond pressures from his own creation, and Jesus was a human, historic figure who suffered and died. After agonizing debate – by no means ended by this assembly – the Nicenes decided on a formula, conditioned by the Greek intellectual vocabulary, with which to express their conviction about the ultimate significance of Jesus. He is 'of the same substance with the Father'; and they expressly renounced language which might suggest he was some sort of demigod or mixed being, higher than man but lower than God. [29: IX]

The Martian's remaining groups of Christians would all have been prepared to accept the Nicene conclusion. But in some cases they would do so rather formally, as a decision of the Church, a chapter in a book now concluded. The Irish monks, though supporting it strenuously, were perhaps more immediately concerned with Christ as the conqueror of evil, a 'strong name' with which they confronted the evil powers abroad in the universe, and the curses, incantations and sorceries of pagan opponents. The crucified and glorified Son of God also gave inspiration and hope of victory in the relentless austerity of their own lives.

For the early Victorian group in London, all these ideas – the exact definition of the person of Christ, the inspiration of his sufferings, the invocatory power of his name – were questions either taken for granted or rarely thought of. The principal affirmation about Christ was his completed work of atonement for human sin, appropriated by each true believer personally by faith. Otherworldly asceticism had passed away; they were seeking to bring their affirmations about Christ to bear upon a busy, complex life, Church and state, home and overseas.

Most of these questions are very secondary for the Nigerian charismatic group the Martian visits in the 1980s. For them Christ is power, ultimate power available now, triumphing over disease and all the multitudinous frustrations and privations of urban life in modern Africa. He is also exclusive power, not to be shared, as half-Christians try to share him, with the old powers of traditional Africa. [47: 192ff]

There are certain features common to the various Christian perceptions of the significance of Jesus:

1. The 'ultimate' has to be interpreted in the light of the earlier statement that Christians worship the God of Israel. If God is one and Jesus ultimate, then language used of one will penetrate that used of the other. Jewish Christians like Paul used the language of divine sonship about Jesus without feeling that they were compromising the centuries of fierce monotheism in their blood. There is no hint in the transition from Jewish to Greek Christianity of any crisis over the status of Jesus or the proper titles to describe him.

2. Jesus provides the moral yardstick for the believer. It is clear that ethical instruction had a substantial place in the early Christian communities. Some of this was in a form already well known to Jewish converts: avoid theft, lies, idolatry, sexual misbehaviour. Some dealt with family and society relationships. Some expounded the fundamental of Christian ethics, the principle of love. Jesus summed up the whole of the manward side of the voluminous Jewish law as 'You must love your fellow man as yourself', while Paul described love as 'patient and kind; not jealous or conceited or proud; not ill-mannered, or selfish or irritable. Love doesn't keep a record of wrongs; love is not happy with evil, but is happy with the truth. Love never gives up.' [39: 1 Corinthians 13: 4–7]

But this ethical instruction is not free-standing; it is tied to the person of

Jesus. Jesus himself associated his moral teaching with the idea of the Kingdom of God, the divine rule established on earth, inaugurated or brought near by his own coming. Paul and other early Christian writers linked the ethical dynamic of love to the figure of Jesus, who abrogated his privileges as divine son and voluntarily accepted unjust suffering on behalf of others [e.g. 39: *Philippians* 2: 2–11; 1 *Peter* 2: 18–25]. Jesus is the moral absolute for all forms of Christianity.

3. The ultimate significance of Jesus attaches especially to his death and its outcome. In each of the gospels, an amount of space which would be disproportionate in any normal biography is devoted to the last week of Jesus's life. The interpretations, doctrines and theories developed by Christians to explain the significance of the events of that week are beyond number. Their very multitude indicates how fundamental these events are in all Christian perceptions. Not for nothing has the cross become the most widespread of all symbols of Christian faith.

Three ideas occur time and again in all the doctrines and theories. The first is that Jesus' death was on behalf of others. The second is its association with forgiveness, and especially with God's forgiveness of men. The language of atoning sacrifice has dominated; but even those Christians who have depicted Jesus principally as the perfect teacher, and his death as the supreme example of self-sacrifice or patient submission and non-retaliation, link these ideas with the forgiveness of past human wrongs and the possibility of a new start. The third idea is that of resurrection. This characteristically Irano-Jewish belief (see pages 178–9), resisted even by some in Judaism, was a feature of Christianity from the start. The earliest preaching insisted that Jesus was actually alive after being actually dead. No feature of the Christian message caused more intellectual problems, or more rejection in the Greek world, and some recent trends in Western thought have found it equally hard to accommodate. But in the Christian movement as a whole, belief in the resurrection of Christ has obstinately remained a fixed point. It is fundamental to the conviction of the triumph of God and of good in the face of the crucifixion of Jesus [15: 177–242]. There has followed from it the conviction of the eventual resurrection of the rest of the race.

While the Christian belief in the resurrection of Jesus has usually stressed its historical nature, it has never been viewed solely as a past event. Most expressions of Christianity depend on the conviction that Christ is not only alive, but accessible, and this is as true of much popular religion as it is of Christian saints and mystics. While some stress the presence of the Lord when the Christian company gathers for worship, others concentrate on an ongoing relationship in daily life. Many of the simplest, and some of the sublimest, expressions of Christian experience amount to the conviction of a relationship that can only be expressed in personal terms.

4. The ultimacy of Jesus is associated with the end of history and the summing-up of the universe. Sometimes this has been expressed in the idea of a judgement of the righteous and the wicked; sometimes in the reversal of the fortunes of a proud oppressor and wretched oppressed; sometimes in the renewal of the earth and the establishment there of a righteous order directed by Christ; sometimes in an amalgam of all these things. Whatever the form, the underlying conviction is that Jesus – as Judge, Saviour, Ruler, Renewer – will bring world history to its climax, triumph over its evils, and inaugurate a new age. Christian beliefs about Jesus show the inescapable commitment of Christian faith to history. Nevertheless, the significance of Jesus for Christianity is not only past-historic, but present and future as well.

GOD IS ACTIVE WHERE BELIEVERS ARE

Some faiths which share with Christianity the idea of a Supreme God envisage him as distanced from the world. The believer approaches him, if at all, only in emergency. It has been a common thread of Christian belief that God is both active in the world and accessible from within it. That accessibility is in some expressions of Christianity commonly mediated through the saints, but there is never doubt as to its true source.

In the traditional theology of all the main confessions, this divine activity and the accessibility of the divine presence to the believer is associated with a doctrine of the Holy Spirit. The Jerusalem Christians spoke of 'Holy Spirit' in relation to the remarkable and spectacular capacity for ecstatic utterance which marked out their community. The fact that Gentile converts received the same capacity was one of the decisive factors in persuading Jerusalem believers to recognize their authenticity. [8: 206–9, 228–33]

By Nicene times these phenomena had disappeared; when anything similar appeared, it usually met with disfavour. Christians of the fourth century, however, spoke of the Holy Spirit as the special presence of God in the Church, leading it to right corporate decisions. The Irish monks thought of the power which gave a holy man boldness to speak the word of God even before mighty chiefs or rulers. The Victorians stressed the refining influence working in the individual Christian's character and personality, overcoming his natural self-centredness. The Lagos believers, perhaps rather vague about distinctions between the living divine Son and the divine Spirit (and indeed, the two are closely connected in much early Christian language), stress the manifest power of healing revealed in the community and its charismatic leader.

These examples – and others could be given – show that the precise formulation of the doctrine of the Holy Spirit is affected by the world-view of the
particular Christian group. Those groups whose world-view is oriented
towards personal effort and piety will stress a different type of divine activity
from those who stress corporate life. Similarly, those who think of the Church
primarily in universal terms will have different priorities from those who think
primarily in local terms. But, in some form or other, most groups of Christian
believers, even the least sophisticated, will insist on the ongoing divine activity
in the world. They will identify that activity with the Holy Spirit, even if
they use language in which the Spirit alternates with Christ. And, almost
certainly, that activity of the Spirit will be held to operate in a special way
in the sphere of the Church (however that body may be conceived by that
particular group) and among believers.

In traditional Christian theology the combination of the three constantly
recurring factors, the worship of the God of Israel, the ultimate significance
of Jesus and the immediacy of the divine presence to believers, has given rise
to the doctrine of the Trinity. Statements of this doctrine developed in the
first four centuries and (usually represented in English as 'one God in three
persons') have been commonly adopted by most Christian groups [29: IV, V, X].
Eastern and Western Christians have differed on the precise formula indicating
the relationship of the Holy Spirit to the other 'persons', but this difference
has not involved any question of the unity of God or the status of the three
'persons'. The formulations (which have indeed been explicitly rejected by
a small minority of Christian groups) owe much to the traditions and termi-
nology of Greek philosophy and Roman law, but the idea which underlies
them does not derive from these sources. The doctrine has been a way of
stating three basic convictions which go back to the earliest period of the
Christian traditions and reappear throughout its history: the One God of
Israel; the Ultimate Christ; the divine activity where believers are.

CHRISTIANS USE THE SAME SACRED WRITINGS

Christians with no ethnic relationship to Judaism adopted the Jewish scriptures
as their own. The resistance to this and other Jewish features during the
Hellenistic phase of Christianity has been followed by other controversies
about the 'Old Testament', notably among Western Christians of the last
two centuries. Some of these were disturbed over conflicts with scientific or
historical studies, or embarrassed at the possible moral implications of some
'Old Testament' passages [11 vol. III]. In one form or another, however, most
Christian communities have been able to accommodate their changing views
and emphases to the age-old Christian appropriation of the Jewish scriptures,

and with them the conviction that they relate to Christ, and reflect a process of divine revelation of which he was the climax. This way of reading the scriptures is reflected in the earliest Christian writings, and derives ultimately from Jesus himself.

The double corpus of sacred writings formed by the 'Old' and 'New' Testaments (see pages 56–7) has always been regarded as regulating Church life, and as the ultimate source of Christian doctrine. It has also been the regular court of appeal for prophets and reformers. Though sometimes Church authorities have restricted or discouraged lay access to the scriptures, public reading has always been a feature of Christian worship. Private reading has been deeply influential, especially in Western Protestantism, in recent Western Catholicism and in the churches of Africa and Latin America.

Not until the sixteenth century did the West follow the precedent of earlier Christianity, and the example of Eastern churches, in presenting the Bible in the languages commonly spoken. Since then no feature of Christian expansion has been more noticeable than the translation of the Bible. By 1980 the whole Bible had been translated into at least 275 languages, and substantial parts into more than 1,700. Many of the newer churches and movements in Africa and the Pacific have remodelled the Christian inheritance they originally received through Western missionaries on the basis of their reading of the Bible. This accessibility to translation has much to do with the immense cultural adaptations which have been such a feature of Christian history. Christians frequently draw the analogy between scripture, a divine message in human speech, and Christ, the divine in human form. Both are called 'The Word of God'.

CHRISTIANS BELONG TO A PEOPLE OF GOD

In view of the relationship already noted, it is not surprising that Christians feel a degree of continuity with Israel, and carry over Israel's sense of being a people of God. This idea of a people of God commonly transcends time, space and race, and comprehends all believers in Christ. If we look again at the Martian's five groups of Christians, we see that each recognizes a continuity with old Israel to which only the first belongs by birth. Each also recognizes that it is part of a Christian body which stretches back in time. The later groups, although apparently so different in their preoccupations from the earlier groups, still see them as part of their own history.

This sense of a people of God in and beyond history, analogous to and continuous with Israel, results in a doctrine of the Church. The consciousness of a universal, time-transcending, corporate body to which Christians belong is common to virtually all Christian communities. How that body is identified and expressed in time and locality, however, is another matter. Some Christians have sought to identify the universal body with a particular Christian community, with a single focus of authority, and an identifiable membership. Such an 'exclusive' type of doctrine of the Church has been a feature of both very large and very small Christian communities. Others have linked the concept of the universal Church with that of various autonomous 'churches', distinguished from each other by nationality, differences on secondary matters of doctrine, or even matters of convenience. Others stress the idea of a spiritual fellowship of Christians, drawing its reality from the experience of relationship with Christ, in which external and organizational matters are comparatively unimportant. Others again combine several of these ideas. (One common combination distinguishes between a visible organization of professing Christians and an invisible fellowship of authentic Christians.) Such different understandings inevitably issue in diverse forms of organization. They are also particularly prone to influence from the cultural setting and the nature of local society.

Practices

The range of Christian practice is even more immense than the range of doctrine, and equally impossible to summarize. The syncretistic nature of historical Christianity means that Christian elements appear in many different aspects of social life. Almost any of the practices found in other religions of the world may be found in Christianity – but only in certain forms of it. Pilgrimage or possession, meditation or monasticism are prominent and valued features in some types of Christian tradition, but regarded as alien to the essence of the faith in others. A mere catalogue of affirmations and denials would be tedious and unhelpful. A selection of Christian practices follows, some all but universal, some used by many, but not all, Christians, some used only by small minorities. The selected practices have in common only that they are explicitly referred to in the scriptures which are accepted as foundational by all Christians.

PRAYER

Prayer is generally held to be both an obligation upon Christians and a privilege arising from the accessibility of the transcendent world. The elements of public and private prayer do not greatly differ, save for what the solemnity of liturgical language may bring to the former, and the spontaneity which personal situations may impart to the latter. Both have been moulded by three influences in particular:

1. *The Jewish inheritance of Christianity.* In prayer Israel's high transcendent God is addressed by dependent, contingent and sinful men. Adoration, thanksgiving and confession are thus among the elements of prayer. The biblical *Book of Psalms*, originally designed for worship in the Jewish temple, has deeply affected the language of adoration. Its highly personal exultations and laments, its fierce aspirations and desperate cries for help, have also provided a fountain of expression and example for Christian private prayer.

2. *The short prayer taught by Jesus to his disciples and commonly known as the Lord's Prayer.* Occurring in the New Testament in two slightly differing forms, this has from early centuries been regularly used in public worship, and even by communities which use no other fixed form of words for prayer. Throughout the period it has also been taught to children and to new Christians. Its few clauses form an index of basic teaching on Christian life and practice: a daring address to God as Father; an acknowledgement of God's kingly rule and of desire for conformity to his will on earth; a quiet request for the immediate necessities of life; and a plea for forgiveness coupled with readiness to forgive. [17: 72ff]

3. *Other words of Jesus, backed by their exemplification in letters of Paul, which relate to the element of asking.* This element, whether on the petitioner's own behalf or on behalf of others, is thoroughly characteristic of Christian prayer. Indeed intercession, the act of representing the needs of others to God, is encouraged by the sense of community which underlies the various forms of the doctrine of the Church.

The meditative, contemplative tradition of personal prayer is also found, but not in all forms of Christianity. Christian mysticism has left a long record of spiritual experience and a rich deposit of literature [48]. It is most prominent in the Orthodox churches of Eastern Christianity, where deification is the recognized goal of the Christian life. Eastern spiritual writers speak constantly of a vision of boundless divine Light by which, in the words of the seventh-century Maximus Confessor, 'the mind is ravished, and loses all sensation of itself or of any other creature, and is aware of Him alone, who through love has produced this illumination'. A Syrian writer of unknown name and date, usually called Pseudo-Dionysius, was deeply influential. God, he says, is beyond affirmation, being or knowing; the divine is dark through very excess of light. It is therefore by *unknowing* that the divine is approached: inner stillness, requiring unceasing and absolute renunciation, bringing to bear the deeper powers of the soul. Pseudo-Dionysius was read in the West through a ninth-century Latin translation by the Irish monk John Scotus Erigena. The official attitude of the Western churches, while favourable to meditation and contemplation informed by the teaching of Church or scripture, has been cautious about mystical experience. Some mystics are among those recognized by the Latin Church as its saints, people of pre-eminent holiness; but others who used Dionysius' 'way of unknowing' remained suspect. Western Christianity has always feared any blurring of the distinction between transcendent God and contingent man; it has also been reluctant to admit what cannot be tested by scripture or Church.

The question is moving into a new phase in Asia, where some Christians are exploring the goals and modes of their own mystical and contemplative traditions in the light of other faiths.

A good deal of Western and African Christianity is essentially activistic in orientation, and hence the great intercessor is as likely as the great contemplative to be seen as a hero of spirituality.

Christian prayer is typically addressed to the Father in the name of Christ, and its motivation and effect are associated with the divine action of the Spirit. The use or absence of fixed forms or specific postures are secondary questions, and the variety of answers to them is beyond our scope here.

DAYS OF OBSERVANCE

In the overwhelming majority of Christian communities, Sunday, the first day of the week, is accepted as a time when the community meets for worship. The custom is of great antiquity and owes something to the Jewish sabbath [23:203f]. The Ten Commandments (frequently accepted by Christians as representing the permanent as distinct from the provisional aspect of the Jewish Law) require the seventh day to be kept holy, that is, separate. Early Christian practice was to use the first day of the week, the day associated with the resurrection of Jesus, as the special day of worship. As Christianity came to dominate society, Sunday was recognized as a 'holy-day', permitting or requiring worship, and remitting some of the duties attached to other days of the week. In subsequent Christian history, the association with the Jewish sabbath sometimes brought an emphasis on prohibition of unnecessary activity. By reaction, others stressed the recreational opportunities of Sunday.

In nineteenth- and twentieth-century Africa, the granting of a special status to Sunday (e.g. by prohibition of public markets) has often been a milestone in the acceptance of Christianity by a particular community. A minority of Christian groups, including the Seventh-day Adventists and some other bodies of American origin, the Church of Ethiopia and many African churches, insist on a literal observance of the Ten Commandments and the special status of Saturday.

About other 'holy-days' there has been less unanimity. In the Hellenistic phase of Christianity, Easter, which commemorates the resurrection of Jesus and occurred near the Jewish Passover festival, was a landmark in the year. It was a pre-eminent time for baptism and reception of new converts. As Christianity spread among the primal peoples of Europe, the indigenous festivals were often replaced by or altered into Church festivals. In particular, the great midwinter ceremony was linked with a commemoration of the birth of Christ, Christmas.

The sixteenth-century Reformation challenged the structure of festivals, and especially the saint cult with which it was associated. In some Protestant countries, such as Scotland, seasonal festivals were abolished altogether. For practical purposes today the more conservative traditions, Orthodox, Roman Catholic and Anglican, adhere to a structured Church year with numerous festivals commemorating events associated with Christ and the work of salvation, some other biblical themes, events or particular saints. Other Western-originated Christian traditions take particular note of only a few major festivals, usually Christmas, Easter and perhaps Pentecost, the festival of the Holy Spirit. The official tradition of most Western churches exalts Easter, as in early Christian times, as the main Christian festival. In popular esteem, however, this place is usually held by Christmas, which in the post-Christian West continues to bear special significance as a season of 'peace and goodwill'.

Some newer forms of Southern Christianity appear to be developing a new pattern of festivals, strongly influenced by ancient Jewish models. Many African Independent churches, for instance, have great open-air assemblies which draw inspiration from Jewish feasts like Passover or Tabernacles, but give them Christian significance, rooting them in the history and experience of the local community. [44: 168]

GIVING

In all Christian communities liberality is a requirement. Three particular obligations can be identified. The first is support for the Church itself; the upkeep of places of worship, provision for their services, and usually the maintenance of men (and now sometimes women) with special duties of ministry. The second (not invariable, but still very common) is the extension of the work of the Church. To combine intense attachment to the local building or worshipping community with recognition of kinship or obligation outside the locality has been a recurrent feature of Christianity.

The third is an obligation to give to 'the poor'. Paul devotes a surprising amount of attention to famine relief [39: *Romans* 15:25–8; 1 *Corinthians*

16: 1–4]. In modern societies this is expressed in a range of charitable objects and organizations for the relief of suffering. Most Christian bodies with anything more than a local organization sponsor or share in some such activity. Concern for 'the poor' is by no means unique to Christianity but it has been especially characteristic of Christianity to *organize* the consequent liberality. Institutions for education or healing, for relief of famine or for assisting those on the margins of society have been prominent in one form or another in every phase of Christian history.

Some Christian bodies, both in the West and in the southern continents, practise tithing of income, based on the Jewish model described in the Hebrew scriptures, as a minimum standard of giving. Quite small Christian communities can by this means produce a remarkably high level of activity.

BREAD AND WINE

It is recorded that immediately before the Crucifixion Jesus arranged a last meal with his disciples at which (as befitted the host or president at any Jewish meal) he took bread and wine and gave thanks to God. He then spoke words linking the bread and the wine with his approaching death, and urged his disciples to repeat this meal in memory of him. In every phase of Christian history, Christians have solemnly taken bread and wine, read or recited the words of Jesus at the Last Supper, offered prayer, and eaten and drunk. There are a few Christian communities which do not follow this custom. The best known is the Society of Friends (Quakers), who in stressing the internal action of the Spirit of God have abandoned many external and traditional forms of worship and the rites thought of as sacraments (i.e. channels of divine action) by most other Christians. A few communities have substituted articles of local fare for the bread or the wine (which were, of course, the local fare of first-century Palestine); for instance, the 3-million-strong Kimbanguist Church in Zaire uses sweet potatoes and honey.

There are immense differences in the external action of the various Christian communities. Some have sumptuous language, dress and music meant to indicate the very presence of the King of Heaven, and ritual to mark the high drama of his appearance among men. Others recall the domestic simplicity of the original meal which the rite repeats, and the humble human circumstances in which the historical Jesus displayed God. There are communities, notably in the Eastern churches, where the people stand throughout as though in the heavenly courts with the risen Jesus among them. There are some Western traditions, notably Roman and Anglican, wherein they receive the consecrated bread and wine kneeling, as in solemn adoration of the Lord present at the feast; and others where they sit, as though his guests, as the disciples did at the first supper and as all his people will at the ultimate heavenly feast. There have been chapters in the life of the Latin Church when in view of the significance of the bread and wine as the body and blood of Christ, only priests took them, the people watching; and in the Greek, when only priests have taken them regularly, the people infrequently. The frequency of the rite also varies: weekly or even daily in some Christian circles, annually in others.

In their different ways, all these things underline the importance which this practice has for Christians. But the significance attributed to the practice is as varied as its forms. Some interpretations use the language and ideas of expiatory sacrifice to take away sin, while insisting that the sacrifice represented is the death of Christ. Some associate it with a special and particular presence of Christ. Others stress the nature of the broken bread and poured-out wine as 'visible words', a representation of the work of Christ in material form. Others eschew any language which might suggest that the rite has effect in and of itself, or requires the presence of a consecrated priest, or that the self-offering of Christ needs to be repeated in some way. These insist that the practice is essentially a solemn commemoration of that self-offering.

The names given to the practice reflect these differing ideas: Mass, Eucharist, Lord's Supper, Communion. The idea of communion, in fact, underlies them all. All, probably, think of the act as affording opportunity for heightened sharing in the accessibility of Christ to his people. And its original significance as a shared meal, taken together by the friends of Jesus, has never quite been lost. Centuries of separation were broken down when Jewish Christians first sat at the table with Gentile believers. From earliest times the ultimate discipline has always been excommunication – exclusion from the table set for the Christian family. Conversely a welcome to the same table is the ultimate sign of acceptance.

THE SPECIAL USE OF WATER

Prophecy was revived in Israel in the first century CE in the person of John the Dipper (i.e. the Baptist) whose appearance and impact reminded people of a prophecy that the first great prophet, Elijah, would reappear one day to herald the Messiah. John's preaching had an ethical urgency, demanding a change of heart and style of life. Those who responded were symbolically immersed in water. It seems that this rite had previously been used to symbolize the cleansing of a Gentile convert to Judaism. John insisted that true-born Israelites needed the same transformation, and the same cleansing, as any pagan outsider. [8: XII]

Jesus continued John's movement and his followers continued to administer baptism. With them, however, baptism symbolized not only a change of heart but the coming of the Holy Spirit which was to mark the messianic age. The early Christian preaching sometimes speaks of 'repentance and baptism' and sometimes of 'repentance and faith', as though these were interchangeable. Baptism was an act of open identification with, i.e. faith in, Jesus. Paul saw an added symbolism: passing down into, then up out of the water recalled the death, burial and resurrection of Jesus. The believer identified with him, died to the old life, rose to a new life 'in the Spirit'. Baptism was a great symbolic entrance to the Christian community.

We cannot tell when the question of baptizing children first arose, but the practice of baptizing whole families is very understandable. As Christianity became a state religion virtually all children in 'Christian' countries were baptized, and few people other than children. The original link between baptism and active faith was lost, and immersion was largely abandoned. The sixteenth-century radical reformers in the West sought to restore it by abandoning infant baptism, restoring immersion and requiring profession of faith from those of responsible age. Their successors in this 'Baptist' approach today represent a substantial minority of Western Christians, particularly strong in the United States, and with a fair minority in Russia. Some sections of African Christianity have also restricted baptism to actively participating adults, often administering it in a river or the sea, and applying it both to mark entrance to the Church and to mark acknowledgement of divine power there.

The association of baptism with entrance to the Christian community makes it a 'rite of passage'. In 'Baptist' communities, active profession of faith tends to be most frequent at adolescence. Churches which practise infant baptism have often developed other rites of confirmation or church membership to mark the passage to full responsibilities within the Christian community. Two complexes of ideas have been associated with Christian baptism from earliest times, that of repentance–faith–commitment (inherited from John) and that of bestowal of the Holy Spirit. Sometimes one and sometimes the other is most in the mind of Christians. Where the first is uppermost, baptism is the sign of the committed Christian who has taken up his place in the community over against 'the world'. Where the latter prevails, baptism is principally a sign of divine activity, of God's initiative for man's salvation.

Some African groups see a further significance in water, consecrated by prayer, as a medium or sign of healing.

THE SPECIAL USE OF OIL

Earliest Christianity inherited the Jewish traditional language of anointing with oil to mark the divine appointment of prophets, priest and kings. The very word 'Christ' reflected the idea. They also used oil, accompanied by prayer, in healing their sick. The former use led to the anointing of newly baptized Christians, as a sign of their entrance to a community prophetic, priestly and royal in character. This rite of 'chrismation', using consecrated ointment, remains important among Eastern ('Orthodox') Christians, who link it with the gift of the Holy Spirit.

In Latin Christianity the prayerful use of oil for healing gradually gave place to anointing as a solemn preparation for death. The healing use has periodically been revived in various traditions.

Cultural changes have diminished the special use of oil; for many Christian communities the symbolism has been too remote. Westerners have linked the sign of the endowment of the Holy Spirit rather with the imposition of hands, and Africans have more often seen water than oil to be the appropriate accompaniment of divine healing. Eastern Christianity, however, consistently uses oil in both connections, and the biblical allusions to these associations have led to the recurrence of its use, in diverse forms, throughout Christian history elsewhere.

LAYING ON OF HANDS

The laying on of hands is now no longer universal among Christians, and where it occurs it has a range of significance. The origins lie in Jewish practice, where the range was equally wide. The commonest examples in modern Christianity are as follows:

For appointment to office. According to the earliest Christian writings, the apostles set aside leaders for the Church after prayer and laying on of hands, and most branches of Christianity employ this practice at the ordination or appointment of ministers (called 'priests' in some traditions, though others reject the word because of its sacrificial and mediatorial connotations) and sometimes of other leaders. It signals both continuity and corporate solidarity.

For some major branches of Christianity it means much more, in that it is held that the authentic Church is continued through a visible line of succession of bishops reaching back to the apostles and continuing their office. This belief is strenuously resisted by many other Christians, who maintain that it undermines the fundamental principle of faith in Christ as the entrance to the Church. This difference has probably been in recent years the greatest stumbling-block to the union of different branches of Christianity.

For confirmation. We have already seen that the development of infant baptism as the norm led to a need for another ceremony marking the transition to full participation in the Christian community. Such rites of confirmation in many communities use imposition of hands on this occasion. Since most Christians think of the Church as in a special way the sphere of the Holy Spirit, it is natural that the practice should be associated, at least symbolically, with the gift of the same Holy Spirit.

For healing. Jesus commonly laid his hands on the sufferer when healing, and the early accounts of healings in his name by his followers indicate that they did so, at least on occasion. The practice is still widespread in African Christianity, where Christian healing is a common feature.

THE USE OF TONGUES

The early Christian communities knew a heightened consciousness which they attributed to the gift of the Holy Spirit. One aspect of it was the capacity to utter fluently a range of sounds outside normal speech. Paul seems to have thought this capacity overvalued, and insisted that it should be controlled and the utterances interpreted for the benefit of those without it [39:1 *Corinthians* 12–14]. The phenomenon (known as 'glossolalia') died out. It was thus thought of as special to the apostolic age and its occasional appearance thereafter was ascribed to hysterical or even diabolical sources. Since the nineteenth century, however, it has reappeared on an increasing scale. The London congregation of Edward Irving (1792–1834) experienced it, and its presence in revival movements in America and Europe early in this century led to the separate growth of Pentecostal churches [28]. In the past few decades it has established itself as a dominant feature in a burgeoning Latin American Protestantism, and become part of the regular experience of a significant number of Protestant and Roman Catholic members (frequently called 'charismatics') elsewhere.

Among some churches and groups which practise it, it is regarded as a *sine qua non* of authentic spirituality, by others as a valuable, intense and liberating, but not essential, experience of divine love. Many outside those churches and groups regard it with reserve or dislike, as a source of disorder or division.

CHRISTIAN ART

The needs of Christian worship have obviously brought about special forms of architecture. In any society where Christians are secure enough to build, they usually produce distinctive buildings, instantly recognizable as churches. At the same time there is no single, universal 'shape' for a church (Figure 2.5). Some of the reasons for this are simply cultural, but different strains within Christianity have affected the nature and the scale of Christian architecture. The great cathedrals rising massively above the cold and wretched hovels of medieval European towns expressed grandeur and permanence amid hard struggle and brief, uncertain life. The imposing structure of the Medak church in a hunger-ridden area of south India was a joint possession in which the desperately poor people who made up its first congregation could take pride. A different strain of Christianity rejects the symbols of grandeur and permanence. Here the people of Christ (himself often homeless) are pilgrims seeking a better land. Their true symbol is the traveller's tent. The church they need is a modest – but still distinctive – building which reflects this.

Throughout Christian history attitudes to art have reflected two strains of Christianity. Neither can be identified simply with any one Christian tradition, or any particular Christian community. One strain insists that God has a right to the best, the highest and the costliest offerings of human riches, skill and labour. This instinct has been fruitful in grand conceptions, superb achievements and rank bad taste. With it has often gone another conviction: that the world belongs to God, that Christ redeemed the whole of human life and every human activity. One fruit of this may be the artist's belief in his freedom to follow his art to God's glory. Another may be the legislator's belief that there is a certain pattern of law and learning, art and music, appropriate to a Christian society.

A different strain emphasizes the poverty of even the most magnificent human offering to God, and the central Christian belief that God himself came to earth in the humble circumstances of a Palestinian peasant family. Rich adornment and complex art may discourage the poor, while the wealthy bask in the false security of the outlay which provided it. The finest human creations all too readily call attention not to God, but to themselves, and thus lead not to adoration, but to idolatry.

With this strain there also often goes a sharp mental division between this present world, the world of nature, perverted in all its courses, but transitional and temporary, and the next world, the world of spirit, God-ordered and permanent. The effect of this division is sometimes that certain activities – in this case, art – are associated with the world of nature, the 'secular' world. There is therefore little or no place for art in worship or in the religious life; it is at best a luxury, at worst a distraction. Alternatively, the activities may be regarded as legitimate only in so far as they directly serve the interests of the 'sacred' world of the spirit. Either way, the result is to create quite separate styles for the religious and the secular life.

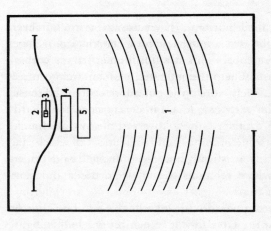

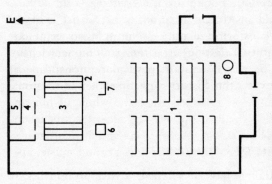

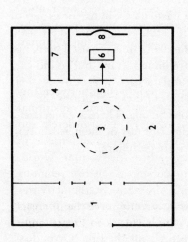

E ←

A EASTERN

1. Narthex – porch for preparation
2. Nave – no seating; congregation stands, walks
3. Dome above, painted with Christ as ruler
4. Iconostasis – screen covered with icons
5. Central door – opened during service
6. Altar
7. Chapel for preparation of bread and wine
8. Bishop's seat in semi-circular 'apse'

B WESTERN: 'Parish' type

1. Nave – seated congregation
2. Screen (in older churches) – open door
3. Choir (where service is led)
4. Sanctuary (railed)
5. Altar table
6. Pulpit (for preaching)
7. Lectern (for reading Scriptures)
8. Font (for baptism)

C NORTHERN: 'Meeting-house' type

1. Congregation seated
2. Pulpit (where service is led)
3. Bible (open for service)
4. Communion table (no rails)
5. Baptistery (covered when not in use)

Figure 2.5 Types of church building: some different uses of religious space

The second strain is often called 'puritan'. (If we use this term, however, we must not confuse it with the much more complex historical movement of that name in England and America.) This strain is found in every century and in every Christian tradition. Where it dominates, worship rarely makes an immediate aesthetic appeal. Such worship is not addressed to the senses and does not court easy popular response; it is, rather, considered to be the worship of the elect. Such an attitude is not, however, always destructive of Christian art; the strain has sometimes purified religious art of excess and gaudy display. Nor is it necessarily artistically uncreative. Indeed, by declaring a separate, 'secular' sphere, where religious themes were not a necessary feature, it helped to create secular art.

Christian art has always faced a paradox. It inherits the Semitic revulsion at the idea of depicting God. At the same time it recognizes one human figure as the image of God, with a definite bodily form, identifying with all men. And if with all men, why should an African artist not depict Christ as black? Yet Christians insist on Christ's historical identity – so must he not be always depicted as a Jew of first-century Palestine? It is the paradox which runs throughout the Christian faith, because it insists on particular times and places and persons and events, yet invests this history with timeless and universal meaning.

The Principal Traditions of Christianity

Differing traditions of Christianity have developed, giving prominence to different elements of doctrine and practice. These differences have often been sharpened by geographical or communal isolation. In the modern world five such 'great traditions', each associated with a particular Church or group of churches, may be identified: Eastern, Oriental, Latin, Northern and African. Cultural rather than doctrinal or ecclesiastical appellations are used here, not because the questions of doctrine or practice are unimportant, but to indicate the significance of certain historical and cultural factors in producing their present shape and characteristics. To one or other of these traditions the vast majority of Christian churches and congregations belong. There are inevitably some mixed forms. It would be misleading to describe any of them as 'central' in a way which suggested that any of the others are peripheral.

THE EASTERN TRADITION

Nomenclature. Two Christian traditions share a common origin in the early Christianity of the eastern Mediterranean. Each claims to be the authentic continuation of that early Christianity, and each claims the title 'Orthodox'.

'Eastern' here identifies those Christians who think of themselves as constituting the Holy Orthodox Church, or the Orthodox Church of the East, and are called by others 'Greek Orthodox' or 'Russian Orthodox'. It is the descendant of Byzantine Christianity.

Geographical distribution. Eastern Christianity has survived as the faith of a small minority in some of its old heartlands (Turkey, Syria). In parts of these heartlands (Egypt, Lebanon) the majority of Christians today belong to other traditions. In Greece it has retained its ancient hold, and in all the Balkan countries except Albania it is the main religious force. But by far the largest number of Eastern Christians are Russians. The considerable Russian diaspora has today spread the faith of Holy Russia to Western Europe, North America and Australia, and Greeks and others have increased this Eastern presence amid Western societies. A spontaneous and indigenous development in East Africa has linked numbers of Kenyan and Ugandan Christians to the Eastern Church (Figure 2.6).

Conditioning factors. Eastern Christianity is marked by a sense of continuity, of embodying the ancient in the modern world, of being 'living antiquity'. The East had no Middle Ages, and the patristic period of the Early Fathers, complete in the West by 600 at the latest, lasted until the fifteenth century. Among Greeks, for whom the very language of the faithful is the language of the apostles and their scriptures, the sense of timelessness can be overwhelming.

Eastern Christianity has a long history of persecution and disability. Pre-Constantinian Christians in the eastern Mediterranean bore the fiercest attacks of the pagan Roman state, a memory kept alive by the assiduous veneration of the martyrs. Over the long centuries of Muslim rule every inducement was given to conversion from the faith, and conversion to it was wellnigh impossible. So attrition became the norm, survival the goal, fierce attachment to a glorious past the means. Russian Christians, spared Turkish overrule, generally thought of themselves as the defenders of their persecuted brethren; but under the Soviets they too were to know persecution, of varying degrees of ferocity. To its adherents, therefore, Eastern Christianity is, simply, Christianity; their Church not a denomination, but *the* universal and orthodox Church. It is in this light that one must view both the 1,500-year-old dispute with the Oriental churches, and the gulf, enlarged by history and geography, that has until recently divided Eastern Christians from the churches of the West. From an Eastern point of view, the divisions within Western Christianity are insignificant. As the Russian thinker Alexei Khomiakov (1804–60) put it, 'The Pope was the first Protestant' [49: 10].

Characteristic features. Two twentieth-century developments break a long cultural and theological isolation and may bring about profound changes. One is the emigration of Eastern Christians to Western lands, where they are a minority among Christians. There are particularly large communities in the United States. The other is the new preparedness of Eastern Christians to engage in discussion and shared activity with other Christians, exemplified in their lively participation in the World Council of Churches.

Tradition is the guide of Eastern Christianity. The elements of the tradition, in their approximate order of importance, are: the scriptures; the Ecumenical Councils (the meetings of bishops in the early centuries which furnished the great creeds); the Fathers of the Church (the early Christian writers in Greek); the Liturgy (which expresses in words and action the presence of God with his people); the canons or codified Church law; and the icons (literally 'images'), or holy pictures which transmit sacred doctrine and history. [49: 10; 53: VIII]

Eastern Christians are less given than Western to the exact formulation of doctrine. Tradition is an organic fusion of all the elements expressed in thought, word, action, line and colour. The painstaking critical studies of the Fathers characteristic of Western scholarship find little favour, for what matters is not the actual words of the Fathers but the cultivation of their temper of mind. The Eucharist is the theatre of God's action but the controversies over it and attempts at definition which have divided Western Christians have had little place. Icons are 'tradition' since they express, not the mind of the artist, like other forms of painting, but the mind of the Church. The icon, a characteristic external mark of Eastern Christianity, is also a key to Eastern Christian thought. Jesus the Divine Son was himself an icon; not only the image of God, but an image of what man redeemed can be. Eastern Christianity speaks of redeemed humanity. The aim of the Christian life is to be taken up into God. A saying of the fourth-century Greek Father Athanasius is much quoted, that Christ 'became what we are in order that we might become what he is'. The path to deification is through the Church with its rites, especially baptism and the Eucharist, with prayer, the study of scripture, and by following the commands of Christ. In the end, man is not absorbed into God, but transfigured by the divine indwelling. This transfiguration of the body explains the care taken with the relics of the saints, who have known that indwelling.

Eastern Christianity has no central authority; it is a family of self-governing churches. The four ancient patriarchates remain, though a shadow of their former selves, alongside the 'autocephalous' churches of Russia, Eastern Europe and the Balkans, and 'autonomous' churches elsewhere. (See Figure 2.6.)

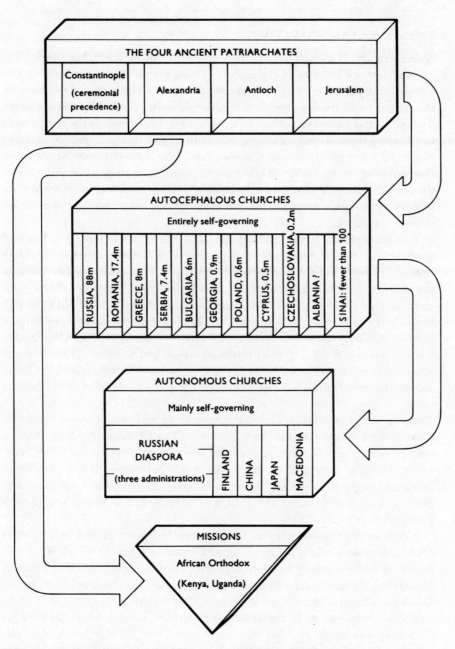

Figure 2.6 Eastern Christianity today: the Orthodox Church

THE ORIENTAL TRADITION

Nomenclature. 'Oriental' identifies a group of ancient churches originating within Eastern Christianity, and also describing themselves as 'Orthodox'. The Council of Chalcedon of 451 was meant to secure a consensus of teaching on the person of Christ [29: XII], but its decrees were opposed by some Eastern Christians and passed unnoticed by others. This was especially the case among the Empire's non-Greek-speaking minorities, and in those provinces most aggrieved at the extortion and misrule of the central government. Attempts by that government to coerce submission to Chalcedon only produced greater dissidence. Political, ethnic and theological factors all therefore assisted division; the theological were probably matters of emphasis and approach rather than of substance.

Two main groups refused to conform to the norms of Chalcedon and central government: the Nestorian (from a patriarch of Antioch degraded through imperial power) and the Monophysite (meaning 'one nature', a key word in their formulation of the doctrine of Christ), also called Jacobite (after a great sixth-century leader) [3: IX]. Both were rooted in the peoples of old Christian lands, Syria and Egypt; both spread the Christian faith far outside the Roman Empire. A few Oriental churches have entered into association with the Roman Church while maintaining their traditional rites and liturgies. These 'Uniate' churches represent a mixed form of the Oriental and Latin traditions. (There are also Eastern European Uniate churches, notably the Ukrainian Catholics.)

Geographical distribution. Oriental Christianity was once a more significant part of the Christian world than it is now. The Christianity of the Persian Empire was largely Nestorian. It spread across Central Asia and into China. Most of it was destroyed by the Mongols in the thirteenth and fourteenth centuries. Its principal remnant, the so-called 'Church of the Assyrians', was decimated in Iraq between the First and Second World Wars. The present patriarch lives in the U.S.A.

Monophysite Christianity has fared better. In Egypt, its first centre, most Christians today belong to the Coptic Orthodox Church, which is of this family. So is the ancient Church of Ethiopia. The still older Church of Armenia ignored Chalcedon, and belongs today, with its important offshoot in the U.S.A., to Oriental rather than to Eastern Christianity.

The Maronite Church, the principal Christian community of Lebanon, is Uniate. [3: 404–23]

Indian Christians claim that Thomas, the apostle of Jesus, founded a church in India. It is beyond doubt that Christianity has been there from early centuries. The oldest Christian community is rooted in a high-caste Malayalam-speaking sector of Kerala. Its history is so complex as to defy summary here. Nestorian, Jacobite and Western forces have played a part. There are Uniate sections and one displaying Protestant influence. [3: 359–88]

Conditioning factors. The Oriental churches (if we except those of India and Ethiopia) have known persecution and restriction perhaps beyond any other. Persecution has all but destroyed the Nestorians. They have not only maintained a Christian presence in a hostile environment; they have helped whole communities to survive and keep an identity. But they now represent – Ethiopia again excepted – the faith of self-conscious cultural minorities. Over the centuries, the intense conservatism which the need to maintain an identity often produces has meant that abandoned vernaculars have become 'sacred' languages for Church purposes. The Egyptian Church uses Coptic in its services; its members speak Arabic outside. The Ethiopian Church maintains the obsolete language Ge'ez (though signs of its increasing supercession by Amharic are now clear). Even in India, liturgies are performed in Syriac. The transmission of the faith in Oriental churches has accordingly been by common worship and prayer rather than through Scripture and doctrine.

The Oriental churches, so firm in rejecting the domination of the Easterns, have sometimes been a little more open to overtures from Western sources. Some of the Uniate churches, which acknowledge Rome, originated in this way, while other Oriental churches have been prepared to accept Protestant help in medical care or education, or even in the training of the ministry. But they have always been jealous of their separate identity. In Ethiopia different conditions prevailed. No persecuted minority here, the Church became interlocked with the imperial state apparatus. Ethiopia's geographical isolation, the interaction of Christian with ancient African traditions, and the presence of Judaic features of rather mysterious origin have also contributed to a unique development. [3: VIII]

Characteristic features. The Oriental churches have retained their old confessions, reflecting differences from the old churches of East and West in the statement of the doctrine of the person of Christ. But their distinctive theological formulations have rarely lain at the heart of their life. While relations with Western churches have often been sensitive they have rarely foundered on the Chalcedonian issue. These communities have generally been the local representatives of Christianity, rather than of some particular branch of it. Transmission of their faith has been possible only within families in distinctive communities. Expansion into another culture group has long been denied them (Ethiopia being a rare exception). Their survival is itself a marvel, their conservatism an inevitable accompaniment. The idea of timeless tradition dominates them. Their claim to present the apostolic tradition is not a formal statement or a theological judgement; it is a historical affirmation, soaked in the sense of direct historical connection.

The churches, however, have not all been immobile. Ethiopia and India provided plenty of evidence of creative response to new situations. They have also kept up a notable network of communication. Until recently the Coptic patriarch appointed the head of the Ethiopian Church, and Indian churches traditionally took their bishops from Mesopotamia.

Monasticism first developed in the Egyptian desert and the Syrian hinterland, and remains a potent force in the Oriental churches to this day.

The Ethiopian Church has some special features, such as observance of the Sabbath, circumcision, and a vast clergy and monastic community. Emperor Haile Selassie II promoted a cautious modernization, with increasing use of the widely spoken Amharic, instead of the archaic Ge'ez, for Scripture reading, and better training of the clergy. These measures were overtaken by the revolution of 1976, but at the time of writing, despite an obscure situation, the ancient Church appears to remain a significant force at local level.

THE LATIN TRADITION

Nomenclature. The Latin tradition of Christianity today is represented above all by the vast body of Christians presided over by the Pope (= *Papa*, Father) in his capacity as Bishop of Rome, and known to its members as the Catholic (i.e. universal) Church, or, simply, the Church. To avoid any confusion arising from these terms it is known in many settings as the Roman Catholic Church.

The term 'Latin', however, draws attention to some of the factors which have determined the shape of this tradition. It arose and was shaped by the conditions of the West, and its use of the language of the Western Roman Empire had a decisive effect. From one point of view the disruption of Western Christianity in the sixteenth century is the result of a vernacular movement, reflecting the triumph for Northern Christians of the local over the universal principle in that tension between local and universal which has always marked Christianity. Accelerated change has taken place within the Catholic Church in the second half of the twentieth century along with the diminished status of Latin and the rise in the importance of the vernaculars.

Geographical distribution. A specifically Latin tradition, guided more by legal precedent than by speculative theology, is discernible by the fourth century. Latin Christianity developed apace thereafter, in the wake of the destruction of the Western Empire. The peoples of Western Europe who wrought that destruction, and their successors, slowly became Christians, and were Latinized as they were Christianized. They became late Romans. They also recognized the special position of the church of Rome, the only one they knew to be founded by the apostles. All Europe west of a line from Scandinavia through the Carpathians to the Danube became a single Christian entity, linked by the special use of Latin and the active recognition of the Roman see, factors which distinguished it from the other Christian lands to the east and south. Small wonder if it began to think of itself as 'Christendom'.

In the fifteenth and sixteenth centuries 'Christendom' expanded with the beginnings of European domination in the Americas. At the same time, however, the disruption within European Christianity meant that vernacular-speaking 'Protestant' churches came to predominate throughout northern Europe; still influenced by Latin models, but no longer determined by them. The Latin tradition was henceforth centred on the southern lands of Western Europe: Portugal, Spain, France, Italy and Austria. Germany, Switzerland and the Low Countries were divided. The rise of the maritime power of Portugal, accompanied by a new zeal to spread the faith in the wake of colonization, established Latin Christianity not only in Central and South America, but on many parts of the African coastline and in parts of Asia. Missionary operations in the nineteenth and twentieth centuries spread this further; immigration from Ireland, Italy and other countries produced substantial Latin Christian enclaves in North America, Australia and other areas previously dominated by Northern or Protestant Christianity. In the same period anti-clerical secularist or Marxist influences have shaken the hold of Latin Christianity on France, and on sectors of the population in other southern European countries also. Today, Latin Christian influence is virtually world-wide, and the Catholic Church has more adherents, on any method of computation, than any other single Christian body.

Conditioning factors. By the use of Latin the Christianity of the Western, rather than the Greek Eastern, Roman Empire was transmitted to the majority of the new Christians of the 'barbarian' phase of Christianity, and Latin rather than the European vernaculars continued to be the language of the Church. It became the language of learning also, because it was the Church which preserved learning; and remained so long after Latin had ceased to be an ordinary spoken language. The Western peoples came to a common faith and a common cultural inheritance at the same time. Over the years that faith was transmitted to peoples outside Europe – but still with that language, and within a culture necessarily shaped by it. Even vernacular translations of the scriptures were for centuries often treated with great suspicion. All this helped to give cohesiveness, the consciousness of belonging to a supranational entity. At the same time the connection of so much that belongs to the heart of religion with a 'special' language has helped to concentrate power in the hands of the priesthood.

In the last few decades the central feature of Latin Christianity has changed dramatically. The liturgy is given in the language of the worshippers and reading of the scriptures in the worshippers' language is encouraged. The eventual effect of this change on Latin Christianity is incalculable.

The Western peoples converted to Christianity *en masse*. Latin Christianity thus developed from an early stage as the religion of whole communities, with the Church accorded a jurisdiction over the whole of society and all its members. For a long time this was the norm; it was many centuries before it was accepted that a community might be diverse in faith. This assumption of uniformity, and the persecution of 'deviants' which it engendered, was inherited by most Protestant states after the sixteenth-century Reformation. Today there are still Catholic states in which the Church holds a position of privilege, but most Catholics now live in plural or secular societies.

The special position accorded to Rome and its bishop has enabled the development of a degree of centralization not achieved by any religious body of remotely comparable size. It has also modified the ancient Christian custom of reaching major decisions after consideration by the bishops of different churches meeting in council. In Latin Christianity councils have not been frequent, at least in recent centuries. Since the Council of Trent, which fixed a standardized pattern after the great disruption in the Western Church in the sixteenth century, only two have met: the first Vatican Council of 1869–70, which considered some of the major new movements of the nineteenth century; and the crucial second Vatican Council almost a century later. Since then, however, a conference of bishops has met regularly – another sign of the transformation of Latin Christianity in the late twentieth century. [35: 106–10]

Latin Christianity has been deeply affected by the major disruption which it suffered in the sixteenth century, usually called the Protestant Reformation. This led to the withdrawal of many Christians from the acknowledgement of Roman headship, and the development of another tradition of Christianity characteristic of the Northern peoples. Much of the standardization of doctrine and practice which was arrived at in the wake of the disruption was expressly formulated with the positions or assertions of the Protestant leaders in mind. One result has been that definitions or practices which had their origin in purely local or temporary circumstances have been given permanence or significance. The conditions of European history meant that from the sixteenth century some powers were 'Catholic' and others 'Protestant'. To profess the faith of the nation's enemy was to render one's own loyalty suspect; and emotional loyalties and deep-set repugnances that had little to do with religion became associated with the name of 'Catholic', which became a badge of national or communal identification to friend and foe alike. Some of this legacy remains today.

Characteristic features. In practice Latin Christianity has been able to combine a supranational structure and a strong sense of community identification with fair success, maintaining a firmly centralized decision-making power in major matters, but allowing scope for local peculiarities. The latter has enabled local cults to flourish, with devotion to local saints, images or appearances; it has also enabled newly Christianized societies to adapt their own institutions or reconcile old and new beliefs. In addition, the apparently rigid hierarchical structure admits of exceptions and modifications. Latin Christianity is marked by a strong emphasis on the institutional Church as the possessor, the guarantor and the interpreter of the tradition of Christ, including the scriptures. The Church is the sphere of the Spirit's activity on earth, within which the truth is taught and the divine life made actual among men.

No Christian tradition has sought to define doctrine, law and practice as closely as the Latin with the exception, perhaps, of some forms of Northern Christianity themselves influenced by Latin models. [35: 223f] Hence the centuries-old insistence that the sacraments are seven in number: the rites of baptism, marriage, confirmation, Eucharist, penance, anointing of the sick before death, and ordination. Thence also the pronouncement by the first Vatican Council of the infallibility of the Pope when speaking in the name of the Church; or the succession of pronouncements over many centuries about the Virgin Mary, culminating in the declaration of 1950 that at the end of her earthly life she was taken up, body and soul, into heaven. The two last indicate also the cumulative process of definition; a widely held belief often takes centuries before it is formally defined. [35: 212]

The tradition stresses the objective presence of the life of Christ in the Church, made available in the sacraments. The sacraments carry out what they signify; and, assuming they are carried out within the Church, they are independent of the agent who carries them out. The characteristic sign of the Church's presence, and of Christ's presence, has therefore been the celebration of the Eucharist, the Mass.

THE NORTHERN TRADITION

Nomenclature. In the sixteenth-century disruption of Western Christianity known as the Reformation, a section of it abandoned Latin and the acknowledgement of Roman leadership, and produced a vernacular reformulation of Christianity. The name usually applied to it, 'Protestant', is not a particularly descriptive term, and names used by the Reformers themselves, such as Evangelical or Reformed, have the disadvantage that they are now used in different senses, or to describe particular forms of Protestantism. 'Northern' is used here since, while this tradition of Christianity has spread throughout the world, it has been especially characteristic of Northern Europe and its peoples.

In the sixteenth century, the earliest period of its separate existence, the Northern tradition developed two forms. The first, the type properly called Protestant, sought a reformed version of that Latin Church which had held the allegiance of the Western European peoples since their conversion. The supremacy of the Roman see would be ended. National churches, no longer dominated from outside, and using the languages of the people, would be purged of doctrines and practices out of tune with the scriptures. But these churches would still be the churches of the whole community, as that of Rome had been. Some Reformers of this type, essentially conservative, made only the changes which seemed to them to be absolutely demanded by scripture. Others sought to remodel the Church completely in the light of the scriptures, to make it more like what they saw there of the New Testament church. Generally speaking, the Lutheran churches result from the former, and the Calvinist or Reformed from the latter. (The English development was unique in combining rather advanced doctrine with a fairly conservative form of Church government. In later times Anglican doctrine has been developed in a conservative direction to the extent that many Anglicans now prefer not to be called Protestant.) All the Protestant Reformers, however, sought to reform the whole of the Church within their particular state, and looked to the rulers of that state to assist in the work of reformation.

But another group sought a more radical reformation. If, as all Protestants held, faith was personal trust in Christ, then, argued the radicals, the Church could not consist of the whole population of a state; it consisted of those who had faith. So they developed 'believers' churches' – close-knit fellowships of families with personal commitment: a form of organization quite different from the Christian state with its priests or pastors instructing their parishes. The radical reformers were thus disturbing to the state as well as to the Church, and Protestant reformers feared these 'Anabaptists' as much as conservative Catholics did. [51] Baptists, Congregationalists, Mennonites and Quakers are among the modern descendants of the radical reformers.

The Protestant and radical streams within Northern Christianity have mingled with each other increasingly since the eighteenth century. On the one hand, the significance of any link between Church and state in Western Europe has waned since the Enlightenment, and when Northern Christianity spread to the Americas, Africa and Asia, the question of the Christian state did not arise. On the other hand, especially since the Evangelical Revival of the eighteenth century, an important section of Northern Christianity, usually designated 'evangelical', has emphasized the distinction made by the radical reformers between 'nominal' Christians, baptized simply because they were born in a Christian community, and 'real' Christians, defined by personal faith-commitment (Figure 2.7).

Geographical distribution. Southern Europe produced outstanding Protestant Reformers, but they made little headway in their own lands. It was Northern Europe that responded. A Lutheran, conservative Reformation was adopted in many German princedoms and the Scandinavian kingdoms within the sixteenth century, more advanced forms in the German and Swiss city-states and in Holland and Scotland. The radicals were persecuted. Holland proved more hospitable than many places, and in seventeenth-century England radicals enjoyed a brief period of ascendancy. But it was America that brought the radicals into their own. Much of the huge complex of American Protestantism is of radical origin. [25]

Since the eighteenth century both emigration and vigorous missionary activity have taken all branches of Northern, like Latin, Christianity, to all six continents.

Conditioning factors. The factors which have conditioned Latin Christianity have affected the Northern tradition also.

Characteristic features. Northern Christianity is essentially *vernacular*. The break with Latin, brought about by the desire that the faith should be widely apprehended by the people, meant the growth of local and national expressions of the faith. The *diversity* of Northern Christianity is a natural result. Freed from external constraint, the Church government of a Tudor monarchy was unlikely to resemble that of a Swiss democracy. The waves of immigrants to America naturally brought their own diverse expressions of Christianity with them; the totally new urban conditions of the nineteenth century produced new forms, attracting different social groups. The characteristic form of the Church in Northern Christianity is the denomination. It is infinitely adaptable, at the price of being infinitely diffuse.

The Northern tradition has produced a *laicization* within Western Christianity. The preaching of God's initiative for man's salvation and of faith as the instrument by which salvation was received reduced the place of the sacramental system of the Church, to which popular religion had earlier looked for salvation. This in turn undermined the power of the priesthood, which dispensed the sacraments. The stress on Scripture as the sole norm of guidance, and the popularization of the Scriptures, meant that the same sources were open

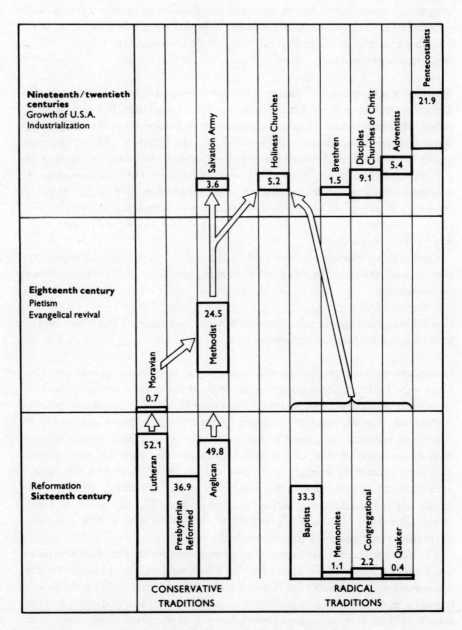

Figure 2.7 Northern (non-Latin Western) Christianity, 1980:
world figures (after Barrett, 1982 [4])

to laity and to ministers. Ministers openly married and had families, just like laymen. Luther insisted that a married cobbler could live as holy a life as a celibate monk; so a separate monastic class was no longer needed. Virginity, so long exalted, lost its special status of holiness.

Laicization originally meant a consecration of the 'ordinary' life of work and family. *All* Christians were called to holiness and to prepare for heaven. It has often been argued that the values this fostered favoured the accumulation and investment of capital and helped to shape the economic and industrial pattern of the West. Laicization has helped to produce *secularization* when the motives for the consecration of ordinary life have waned. In the post-Christian West, anti-religious and anti-clerical movements are strongest in the Catholic countries; the pace of secularization, and the disappearance of the overt signs of Christian attachment, are faster in Protestant ones.

THE AFRICAN TRADITION

Nomenclature. At the beginning of the century there were perhaps 10 million professing Christians in Africa. Today there are 203 million, and by the year 2000 there could be 393 million. Besides representatives of Oriental Christianity in Egypt and Ethiopia [4: 4], some late adherents to Eastern Christianity in Kenya and Uganda, and the fruit of the missionary efforts of Latin and of Northern Christianity, the figure includes churches which cannot be called Catholic or Protestant or Orthodox. The so-called African Independent churches draw from springs deep in the heart of African culture [47: 35–118 and see Chapter 11 below]. They are found, to different degrees, in every part of the continent, and no one set of causes or conditions explains them. They are another example of the way the Christian faith clothes itself in different cultural garments. Many of these characteristics also appear in members of the churches which derive directly from Catholic and Protestant missions. In other words, a profound modification of Latin and Northern Christianity may well take place in Africa, with the Independents giving some indication of the direction the modification may take.

Conditioning factors. African Christianity is shaped by the fact that it arrived in conjunction with the impact of modern, Western forces upon the primal societies of Africa. The colonial period was short, the missionary period not much longer, but the effect of Western trade, technology, education and ideas, and the fundamental shift of activities and values brought about by the period of Western domination, shows every sign of being permanent. Primal societies are holistic. Sacred and secular duties are not distinguished; both are submerged in all-embracing custom, sanctioned by the ancestors. The religious effect of the new developments therefore, even the apparently 'secular' ones, has been shattering. The Christian faith has been embraced as a substitute world-view for the primal one, or in less sharp transition has supplemented a partly rejected, partly retained world-view. In either case, the primal world-view, even in its broken form, poses religious questions which have no meaning in European society, and cannot be answered in terms of the Latin or Northern forms through which the Christian faith originally came to Africa.

The encounter of modern and primal societies has produced a disturbance of values causing ambiguity and moral uncertainty by overlapping codes of practice. It has also linked people who previously had no common bond of kinship. Christianity itself has made people consciously part of a universal community. It has also frequently provided a means of knitting together the torn fabric of moral choice in African society. The extent to which churches of missionary origin have not been able to reintegrate old and new is the extent of the significance of the Independent churches.

Characteristic features. The experience of African Christianity and that of other newer Christians of the southern hemisphere has been different from that of Europe at two vital points.

In both, the acceptance of Christianity brought pre-literate peoples into the sphere of literary culture; but whereas for the Northern peoples literary culture meant an alien language in which only religious specialists could be expected to be competent, for the Southern peoples the change has favoured the growth of vernacular literature. This process has theological effects: the explanation and elucidation of the Christian faith in one's own vernacular, in dialogue with other vernacular speakers, is a wholly different matter from its recapitulation in a fixed form in an alien language, however carefully learned, by a specialist. What is even more important, in the conversion of the Northern countries, is that new Christians turned from many gods to 'the One'. The Christian faith found no shadow of itself in the faiths which it displaced. But in Africa, Christian missionaries frequently found knowledge of a Being, often associated with the sky, with no altars, no priests, perhaps no regular worship, but present and behind the constitution of reality. The coming of Christianity was less bringing God to the people than bringing God near. Thus, however severe the Christian judgement may have been about a society's religion and life (and it was often uncomprehendingly harsh), a traditional name for God remained as the name of the Christian God. This makes a link between old and new which leads to important questions about the relation of the old religion of Africa to the new.

In Africa salvation has a solid, material context: the power of God, Christ and the Holy Spirit is revealed in healing, in protection from evil powers, in combating frustration and fear. These themes are particularly prominent among the Independents, and constitute part of their appeal; but the immediacy of salvation is a regular theme of African preaching.

African Christianity puts strong emphasis on the word. Christianity came with the book and the literary revolution, and in Africa is generally biblicist; but the inspired preacher, the charismatic leader who has 'utterance', is held in high honour. Among the Independents the special words of revelation received through prophecy and the use of sacred 'revealed' words are also common. By contrast the sacraments as defined in the West are probably less significant, though shared meals have an important place in Church life as in community life.

The fear of witchcraft is a desolating fact of African life; attempts to remove it by means of rationalistic assurance that there is no such thing as witchcraft are doomed to failure [26: 60–76]. African Christianity has to cope with this, and to argue both in the light of scripture and of experience about questions of duty to ancestors (for death does not divide the African family) and to the land. It is already showing more attention to sacred places than has been common in Northern Christianity, and in a different way from that of Latin Christianity; and an interest in uses of water as a symbol and medium of divine action beyond those uses seen in Christianity elsewhere. [47: 228f]

In general, African churchmen have been happy enough to retain the denominational structures inherited from the missions, and sometimes to diversify them. The Independents have added thousands of new denominations. The plethora of religious bodies does not, however, mean a harsh exclusive sectarianism. It is associated with the tendency to produce cohesive units where the leader is known and can be active among his people. [26: 17–20] African Church order has combined complex hierarchical structures with scope for spontaneity and congregational expression.

In relation to the state, there have been cases of individual heroism, some leading to martyrdom, in Uganda and elsewhere; but the attitude of the Church under indigenous leadership in independent Africa has been continuous with that under missionary leadership in colonial Africa. In one respect, the experience of European and Latin American Christianity is unlikely to be repeated; almost all African states (outside the Islamic states of the north and east) are plural in religious allegiance. There are few where any one Church can ever expect to be exclusive.

OTHER SOUTHERN TRADITIONS

The largest single Christian culture will probably soon be the Spanish- and Portuguese-speaking mestizo complex of Latin America [4: 9], and it might be proper to devote a section to Latin American Christianity. However, most of its features either are to be found within the Latin tradition, which is the dominant strand, or (like the 'liberation theology', characteristic of many of its principal theologians [22]) are local extensions of that tradition. Latin American Protestantism, which has seen phenomenal growth within the present century, is distinguished by a marked Pentecostal strain – evangelical, enthusiastic, stressing the immediacy of the Holy Spirit's activity – and is marked by the gift of tongues (see page 93 above). It may be, however, that the Hispano–Portuguese movement in theology and life will influence the Latin and Northern traditions of Christianity which originally produced it, rather than becoming identifiable as a separate Christian tradition.

The Pacific islands, to a greater extent even than Africa, have produced new Christian nations, where Christian profession is almost universal; but their total population is small in relation to the world population. There are movements in some respects parallel to the African Independent churches. Some of the most spectacular, however, are properly seen as movements of adjustment of traditional society to Christian and modern influences rather than as part of the Christian tradition itself. (See Chapter 11, B and D, below.)

Other modern traditions might be identified but for the present small size of their Christian communities relative to the total number of Christians in the world. India and China may yet produce important versions of Christianity. The former in particular operates in a world of thought quite different from that in which Christianity has hitherto thrived, differing in all its assumptions about time, nature and the being of God. It also operates in a land with age-old traditions of renunciation, asceticism and the mystical quest, as well as one in the throes of rapid social change. An expression of Christianity which takes account of all these is likely to display striking differences from any that have gone before.

MARGINAL TRADITIONS

There are movements which are only intelligible in relation to Christian faith, but which do not clearly have the marks of historic Christianity. In some cases, however, a degree of movement or fluidity is discernible, so it is best to take these movements as belonging to the margins of Christianity.

Three groups may be distinguished:

1. *Folk religions.* A synthesis of Christian and pre-Christian elements is common in many rural communities. Latin America and parts of southern Europe have, for example, processions which are in all essentials re-enactments of traditional events of pre-Christian religion associated with fertility and renewal. These include some reference to the Virgin or saints and some re-

interpretation of old rituals. Such ceremonies vary in the degree of adaptation used; some are frankly plural, while in others, notably the influential spirit movements of African origin in Brazil or the Caribbean, the Christian element is imported and relatively superficial.

2. *Hebraist movements*. In many primal societies religious reformers arise, influenced by Christian models, who induce in whole communities a clear break with the traditional world-view, perhaps recognizing the Christian God; but who make no clear confession of the ultimate significance of Christ. There are also cases, such as the Ratana movement in New Zealand, which began as Christian movements but in which the personality of the founder has tended to replace the figure of Christ. Such movements gather round the margins of historic Christianity, and may flow backwards and forwards across these margins.

3. *Post-Christian Western denominations*. Here we should perhaps distinguish between Unitarianism and a succession of nineteenth- and twentieth-century new Western movements. In Unitarianism two separate strands are noticeable: one, which is biblicist, resisting dogmatic statements which seem to go beyond biblical warrant, has modified confessions about Christ, but kept contact with the main Christian tradition; the other is rationalist, endeavouring to construct a universal 'rational' religion in which the miraculous plays no part.

Some movements have produced new 'revelations' to supplement the Christian scriptures, such as *Science and Health with a Key to the Scriptures*, the textbook of Christian Science by Mary Baker Eddy (1821–1910); or *The Book of Mormon*, associated with Joseph Smith (1805–44), the founder of the Mormons; or mandatory interpretations of the scriptures, like those characteristic of the Jehovah's Witnesses since the days of their founder C. T. Russell (1852–1916). These three originate in American Christianity but have greatly modified the significance of Christ, compared with that characteristic of historic Christianity.

Modern Developments

If its previous history is anything to go by, Christianity is on the verge of a transformation. In the present century its centre of gravity has moved from the north to the south; its centres of present growth make it likely that this will continue (Figure 2.8). It is too early to predict the precise nature of the changes, but in the past such changes of centre of gravity have altered priorities, preoccupations and the way in which Christianity has been expressed. Christian thought has hitherto developed in relation to the pressing

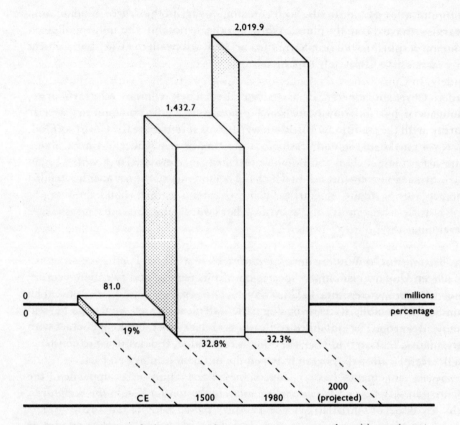

Figure 2.8 Statistics of Christian profession as a percentage of world population (after Barrett, 1982 [4])

needs of particular situations. It is likely that new developments will be increasingly dictated by the situations of Africa, Latin America and Asia [4: 1–20]. A sign of this is that, for the past two decades at least, issues arising from race, poverty, institutionalized oppression and the use of the world's resources have figured on the agenda of Christian theology in a way not conceivable at an earlier time. South Africa, where these issues appear in a peculiarly painful form, and which has a large Christian population, has figured prominently in the debate. There is, perhaps, no country where theological activity is more noticeable.

Such concerns arise from a widespread belief that the relief of distress – always recognized as a Christian duty – is in itself not a sufficient response to human suffering. To fulfil God's will for mankind, changes in society are necessary. The spread of this belief has made Christians more aware than before of questions posed by Marxist thought. Historically Christianity and Marxism have been hostile to each other, and the first Marxist political triumph resulted in the transformation of Holy Russia into an atheistic state. In practice, the condition of Christianity in Marxist countries has differed widely. In Cuba, where the Church was traditionally allied with the old social order, Christian adherence has halved since the Revolution [4: 252–5]; in Hungary it has fallen only by some 10 per cent [4: 363–7] and in Poland hardly at all [4: 569–74]. While Western Marxist intellectuals show a readiness to enter into dialogue with Christians on such topics as the nature of man, Marxist economic analysis has powerfully affected Christian theologians in Latin America. A feature of the 'theology of liberation' which has developed there is the insistence that theology involves action on behalf of the poor [22: 1–34, 163–83]. Many Latin American clergy, therefore, increasingly see developing the political awareness of the poor as part of their calling, and a Church which was long associated with the maintenance of the old regimes has become linked with revolutionary sentiment.

The missionary era, which helped to transform Christianity, has practically ended. There are still thousands of Western missionaries (as well as a growing number of missionaries from Africa and Asia) serving 'overseas', and, while many are engaged in philanthropic work or specialized services, an increasing recognition of large numbers of 'unreached peoples' in all continents may well result in an expansion in the numbers of missionaries in evangelistic enterprise. But if every missionary were withdrawn from Africa overnight, congregational life in the vast majority of cases would continue unaffected [27: 35]. Western domination of the Church is as dead as the old empires. In the 'high days' of the missionary movement, Christians looked for the collapse of all other religions. Despite the phenomenal response to Christianity since then, no one would now predict the imminent collapse of any of the major world faiths. Christians are pondering anew the significance of a plural universe of faiths [6: III–IV], and one result has been the development at various levels of a dialogue with members of other faiths. This is an activity which demands seriousness about truth; if one begins with the assumption that all religions are the same in essence, dialogue is hardly a priority. The increased Christian awareness of issues of peace and justice has also led to a desire to discuss with representatives of other faiths the shared human responsibility for the peace and health of the world.

Among internal developments within Christianity in the past generation is a re-emergence of the council as a means of consultation and consensus among Christians of different areas. Early Hellenistic–Roman Christianity developed this, before the separate development of Eastern, Oriental and Latin traditions. We have already seen that since the second Vatican Council the

Roman Catholic Church, the largest of the Christian bodies (Figure 2.9), has built regular conferences of bishops into its system. A wider conciliar system is seen in the World Council of Churches. The origins of this body lie in a series of conferences, beginning in 1910, to consider the missionary movement; it results, that is, from the world-wide spread of Christianity. The initiative came from Protestant churches of the Northern tradition, but Eastern and Oriental Orthodox and some African Independent churches later joined, and the development of self-governing churches in the southern continents has completely altered its balance since its formation in 1948.

So far the Roman Catholic Church has not joined the council; and a sector of Northern Christianity, associated with part of the evangelical stream of Protestantism, has also viewed it with suspicion or hostility. These evangelicals distrust the wide range of theological viewpoint represented in the council and believe that its social, political and humanitarian concerns have displaced the proper priority of proclaiming the Christian gospel. This belief has been strongest in North America, where evangelicals have tended to form distinct churches, rather than (as in Europe) remaining as a wing of the older Protestant churches. Since the Lausanne Consultation on World Evangelization of 1974, however, a conciliar movement has been developing among evangelicals. One fruit has been a deepening manifestation of evangelical concern about social issues and behaviour and their relation to the gospel.

One of the original hopes of the new conciliarism, the union of churches, arose in Northern Christianity, the most diffuse of the Christian traditions. Despite the emergence of large united churches such as the Church of South India (1947) and the later Church of North India, there has been less enthusiasm for union schemes in the southern continents. Some unions have taken place in North America, Australia and Europe; but far more significant is the much greater degree of understanding and mutual acceptance visible between the Christian traditions than at earlier times.

The so-called 'basic Christian communities', which developed most noticeably in Latin America, are communities in which, to quote a recent joint statement, 'the poor celebrate their faith in the Liberating Christ and discover the political dimension of love' [46:234]. By contrast, the house churches of Western Europe, in which Christians, mostly young, enjoy together the enthusiastic expression of their faith, are not often touched by political concerns; but they are a rare example of community in Western urban life. Related changes seem to be in progress in worship. Until recently, however, almost all forms of Christianity, apart from some fringe groups, avoided the dance in worship, retaining it as a purely 'secular' activity or rejecting it altogether as irreligious in its tendency. There are now signs of a break in these attitudes in some parts of Western and Latin American Christianity. In areas exposed

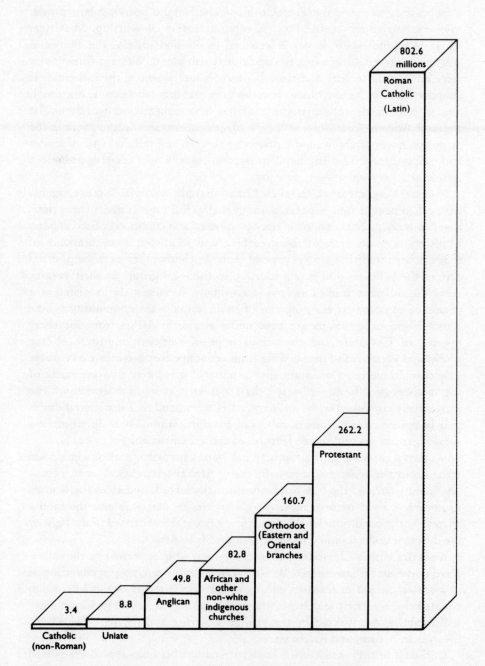

Figure 2.9   Christianity, 1980: world figures (after Barrett, 1982 [4])

to popular culture or to the 'Pentecostal' or 'charismatic' movements, a strong, rhythmic movement of the body is often a feature of worship. In Africa, where the dance is so deeply entrenched in life and society, the change is still more marked. Originally, the traditional attitudes of Western Christianity were introduced to Africa. Gradually, most notably among the Independent churches but among the older churches also, dancing has become a normal, almost unnoticed, accompaniment of much congregational worship. The characteristically African combination of spontaneity and order appear in the gripping power of traditional patterns of rhythm and the dialogue of leader and respondents. The rhythmic movement of a whole congregation is a powerful expression of corporate joy.

In Church organization, the older Christian traditions, with few exceptions, have relied heavily on a separated and (usually) full-time ministry (or 'priest-hood', but see page 92) which in the case of the Latin tradition is also celibate. Ministers perform most of the preaching and in all but some branches of the Northern tradition always preside at the Eucharist; they exercise pastoral care of the believers and give leadership to the local group. In their various ways the different traditions have accordingly envisaged the minister as a person of comparative learning and of some status in the community. These centuries-old expectations are now under strain: in Africa from the sheer number of Christians, which forbids hope of sufficient ministers on the traditional pattern; and in the West from economic forces which make it less easy than formerly to maintain such a pattern. It is likely that the ranks of the ministry will be more varied than formerly, that such service will be increasingly combined with 'ordinary' daily work, and that ministerial duties may be spread over various members of a congregation. These developments would seem to resemble some features of earliest Christianity.

Women's entrance to the ministry has been canvassed, and in some cases effected, in the older traditions. In many African churches women play a dominant part, and the Independents especially have found roles for women of notable insight or utterance. Also, attitudes to marriage and the family shaped by the conditions of Western life are being reformulated in the light of the different understanding of these institutions in Africa.

Attitudes within Christianity to sexuality may also be revised by the south-ward move. Both Eastern and Western Christianity were powerfully affected at a critical period of their growth by indigenous currents of thought which equated the material, and hence the body, with evil. Southern Christianity will doubtless be affected by the exaltation of life and the reproduction of life dear to African and Pacific societies.

Christian history has seen a constant tension between the forces which localize and indigenize it, and those which universalize it. Both forces belong to its earliest sources and message. Its present situation in the world shows both to the full. The universalizing forces are the same as ever: the worship of Israel's God, the according of ultimate significance to Christ, the use of the scriptures and the consciousness of a time-and-space-transcending community. It will be surprising if the localizing forces do not lead it into new paths.

BIBLIOGRAPHY

1. ABBOTT, W. M. (ed.), *The Documents of Vatican II*, New York, Association Press & Herder/London, Dublin, G. Chapman, 1966
2. ARBERRY, A. J. (ed.), *Religion in the Middle East: Three Religions in Concord and Conflict*, Cambridge, Cambridge University Press, 1969
3. ATIYA, A. S., *A History of Eastern Christianity*, London, Methuen/Notre Dame, Ind., University of Notre Dame Press, 1968
4. BARRETT, D. B. (ed.), *World Christian Encyclopedia: A Comparative Study of Churches and Religions in the Modern World, A.D. 1900–2000*, Nairobi, Oxford University Press, 1982. Contains a mass of statistics, analysis and information on 223 countries, plus an atlas
5. BEDE, *A History of the English Church and People* (tr. Leo Sherley-Price), rev. edn (by R. E. Latham), Harmondsworth, Penguin Books, 1968
6. BOSCH, D. J., *Witness to the World: The Christian Mission in Theological Perspective*, London, Marshall, Morgan & Scott/Atlanta, Ga, John Knox, 1980
7. BROWN, P. R. L., *Augustine of Hippo: A Biography*, London, Faber/Berkeley, Calif., University of California Press, 1967
8. BRUCE, F. F., *New Testament History* (1st U.S. edn), Garden City, NY, Doubleday, 1971 (copyr. 1969); rev. edn, London, Oliphants, 1971
9. BÜHLMANN, W., *The Coming of the Third Church: An Analysis of the Present and Future of the Church* (tr. R. Woodhall and A. N. Other), Slough, St Paul Publications, 1976
10. BUTLER, J. F., *Christianity in Asia and America after A.D. 1500*, Leiden, Brill, 1979 (Iconography of Religions)
11. CAMBRIDGE HISTORY OF THE BIBLE: I. ACKROYD, P. R. and EVANS, C. F. (eds.), *From the Beginnings to Jerome*; II. LAMPE, G. W. H. (ed.), *The West from the Fathers to the Reformation*; III. GREENSLADE, S. L. (ed.), *The West from the Reformation to the Present Day*, Cambridge, Cambridge University Press, 1963–70
12. CHADWICK, O., *The Popes and European Revolution*, Oxford, Clarendon Press/New York, Oxford University Press, 1981

13. CONE, J. H., *God of the Oppressed*, New York, Seabury, 1975; London, SPCK, 1977. An example of American 'black theology', a phenomenon also important in South Africa.

14. CROSS, F. L., and LIVINGSTONE, E. A. (eds.), *The Oxford Dictionary of the Christian Church*, 2nd edn, London, New York, Oxford University Press, 1974

15. CULLMANN, O., *Christ and Time: The Primitive Christian Conception of Time and History* (tr. F. V. Filson), rev. edn, London, SCM, 1962; Philadelphia, Pa, Westminster, 1964

16. DICKENS, A. G., *Reformation and Society in Sixteenth Century Europe*, London, Thames & Hudson/New York, Harcourt, Brace, 1966

17. DODD, C. H., *The Founder of Christianity*, London, Collins, 1971; New York, Macmillan, 1970

18. DOUGLAS, J. D. (ed.), *The New International Dictionary of the Christian Church*, Grand Rapids, Mich., Zondervan/Exeter, Paternoster, 1974

19. DOWLEY, T. (ed.), *The History of Christianity*, Tring, Lion, 1977; as *Eerdmans Handbook to the History of Christianity*, Grand Rapids, Mich., Eerdmans, 1977

20. FASHOLÉ-LUKE, E. W., GRAY, R., HASTINGS, A., and TASIE, G. (eds.), *Christianity in Independent Africa*, London, R. Collings/Bloomington, Ind., Indiana University Press, 1978

21. FREND, W. H. C., *The Early Church*, London, Hodder, 1965; Philadelphia, Pa, Lippincott, 1966

22. GIBELLINI, R. (ed.), *Frontiers of Theology in Latin America* (tr. John Drury), Maryknoll, NY, Orbis, 1979

23. GOPPELT, L., *Apostolic and Post Apostolic Times* (tr. R. A. Guelich), London, Black/New York, Harper & Row, 1970

24. GUTHRIE, D., *New Testament Introduction*, 3rd edn, London, Tyndale/Downers Grove, Ill., Inter-Varsity, 1970

25. HANDY, R. T., *A History of the Churches in the United States and Canada*, Oxford, Clarendon Press, 1981; prev. publ. Oxford, New York, Oxford University Press, 1976

26. HASTINGS, A., *African Christianity: An Essay in Interpretation*, London, G. Chapman, 1976

27. HASTINGS, A., *A History of African Christianity, 1950–1975*, Cambridge, Cambridge University Press, 1979

28. HOLLENWEGER, W. J., *The Pentecostals: The Charismatic Movement in the Churches* (tr. R. A. Wilson), Minneapolis, Minn., Augsburg Publishing, 1972; London, SCM, (1972)

29. KELLY, J. N. D., *Early Christian Doctrines*, London, Black, 2nd edn, 1960, 5th rev. edn, 1977; rev. edn, New York, Harper & Row, 1978

30. KÜMMEL, W. G., *Introduction to the New Testament* (tr. H. C. Kee), London, SCM, 1975, 2nd edn, 1977

31. LANTERNARI, V., *The Religions of the Oppressed: A Study of Modern*

Messianic Cults (tr. Lisa Sergio), London, MacGibbon & Kee/New York, Knopf, 1963

32. LATOURETTE, K. S., *A History of the Expansion of Christianity*, 7 vols., London, Eyre & Spottiswoode, 1938–45; New York, Harper, 1939–47; Grand Rapids, Mich., Zondervan, n.d.; London, Paternoster, 1971

33. LEHMANN, A., *Christian Art in Africa and Asia* (tr. E. Hopka, J. E. Napola, O. E. Sohn), St Louis, Mo, Concordia, 1969

34. LEWIS, C. S., *Mere Christianity*, rev. edn, London, Bles/New York, Macmillan, 1952

35. MCKENZIE, J. L., *The Roman Catholic Church*, London, Weidenfeld/New York, Holt, Rinehart, 1969

36. MARSDEN, G. M., *Fundamentalism and American Culture: The Shaping of Twentieth Century Evangelicalism, 1870–1925*, New York, Oxford University Press, 1980 (1981)

37. MARTIN, M.-L., *Kimbangu: An African Prophet and His Church* (tr. D. M. Moore), Oxford, Blackwell, 1975; Grand Rapids, Mich., Eerdmans, 1976

38. MOORE, P., *Christianity*, London, Ward Lock Educational, 1982 (The Arts and Practices of Living Religions)

39. NEW TESTAMENT. There are many available versions in English. Good and convenient is *Today's English Version*, London, The Bible Societies, Collins, 1976 (The Good News Bible); New York, American Bible Society, 1974

40. NIEBUHR, R., *Christ and Culture*, London, Faber, 1952; New York, Harper, 1951

41. PARKER, T. H. L., *John Calvin: A Biography*, London, Dent, 1975; Philadelphia, Pa, Westminster, 1976; Tring, Lion, 1977

42. PELICAN HISTORY OF THE CHURCH (ed. W. O. Chadwick), 6 vols., Harmondsworth, Baltimore, Md, Penguin Books, 1960–71; repr. London, Hodder, 1962–72: 1. CHADWICK, H., *The Early Church*; 2. SOUTHERN, R. W., *Western Society and the Church in the Middle Ages*; 3. CHADWICK, O., *The Reformation*; 4. CRAGG, G. R., *The Church and the Age of Reason, 1648–1789*; 5. VIDLER, A. R., *The Church in an Age of Revolution, 1789 to the Present Day*; 6. NEILL, S., *A History of Christian Missions*

43. READ, W. R., MONTERROSO, V. M., and JOHNSON, H. A., *Latin American Church Growth*, Grand Rapids, Mich., Eerdmans, 1969

44. SUNDKLER, B. G. M., *Zulu Zion and Some Swazi Zionists*, London, New York, Oxford University Press, 1976

45. THOMAS, M. M., *The Acknowledged Christ of the Indian Renaissance*, London, SCM, 1969; Indian edn, Madras, CLS, 1970

46. TORRES, S., and EAGLESON, J. (eds.), *The Challenge of Basic Christian Communities* (tr. John Drury), Maryknoll, NY, Orbis, 1981

47. TURNER, H. W., *Religious Innovation in Africa: Collected Essays on New Religious Movements*, Boston, G. K. Hall, 1979

48. UNDERHILL, E., *Mysticism*, 6th edn, London, Methuen, 1916; many edns issued London, Methuen/New York, Dutton
49. WARE, T. (Kallistos), *The Orthodox Church*, Harmondsworth, Baltimore, Md, Penguin Books, 1963
50. WILLIAMS, C. W. S., *The Descent of the Dove: A Short History of the Holy Spirit in the Church*, London, SCM & Longman, 1939; New York, Meridian, 1956
51. WILLIAMS, G. H., *The Radical Reformation*, Philadelphia, Pa, Westminster/London, Weidenfeld, 1962
52. WRIGHT, A. D., *The Counter-Reformation: Catholic Europe and the Non-Christian World*, London, Weidenfeld, 1982; New York, St Martin's Press, 1982
53. ZERNOV, N., *Eastern Christendom: A Study of the Origin and Development of the Eastern Orthodox Church*, London, Weidenfeld/New York, Putnam, 1961

3

Islam

ALFORD T. WELCH

Introduction

For Muslims Islam has been from the beginning much more than what is usually meant by the Western concept 'religion'. Islam, meaning in Arabic 'submission (to God)', is at the same time a religious tradition, a civilization and, as Muslims are fond of saying, a 'total way of life'. Islam proclaims a religious faith and sets forth certain rituals, but it also prescribes patterns of order for society in such matters as family life, civil and criminal law, business, etiquette, food, dress and even personal hygiene. The Western distinction between the sacred and the secular is thus foreign to traditional Islam. In the Muslim view there are few if any aspects of individual and social life that are not considered to be expressions of Islam, which is seen as a complete, complex civilization in which individuals, societies and governments should all reflect the will of God.

SOURCES

The primary sources for the study of Islam are vast in number and scope. For convenience they can be divided into two fairly distinct, although not exclusive, categories: works in classical Arabic, of which very few have been translated into English or other European languages; and works in modern languages – modern Arabic, Persian, Turkish, Urdu, Swahili and many others, including the European languages. Among the innumerable works on Islam in classical Arabic the one that all consider to be the 'first source' for Islam is the Islamic scripture, the Qur'an (Arabic, *al-qurʾan*, 'the recitation'). The Qur'an is divided into 114 independent liturgical units of widely varying length called suras (from the Arabic, *sura*, 'unit'). Each sura begins with the formula, 'In the name of God, the Merciful, the Compassionate', usually followed by a longer liturgical introduction, and often ending with a formulaic conclusion. Except for the first sura, a seven-verse prayer that serves as an introduction to the Qur'an (see page 138 below), the suras are arranged roughly in order of descending length. Islamic orthodoxy and modern critical scholarship agree that the contents but not the final arrangement of the Qur'an go back to Muhammad. It is also virtually certain that Muhammad began but did not complete the task of compiling a written text of the Qur'an. About twenty years after his death an official recension of the consonantal text was issued by the third caliph, 'Uthman. A system of seven canonical readings of 'Uthman's text was established in the tenth century, and gradually one of these came to be used in nearly all parts of the Islamic world. In 1924 a standard edition of the printed text, complete with signs for recitation (indicating pauses, elision, etc.), was issued in Cairo. This edition has gained widespread acceptance by Muslims and Islamicists alike, although other texts are still used. There is no critical edition of the Qur'an, nor are there standard translations of the Arabic text into European languages. Among the many English translations, those by Yusuf Ali (1934) and M. M. Pickthall (1930, 1976) are preferred by most English-speaking Muslims. The most popular English translation by a non-Muslim is that of the Cambridge Arabist, A. J. Arberry (1955). A two-volume translation by Richard Bell (1937, 1939) is the most useful for critical purposes.

Next to the Qur'an stand the Hadith works, multi-volume collections of accounts called hadiths (from the Arabic, *hadith*, 'story, tradition') that report or allege to report the sayings and deeds of the Prophet Muhammad. These hadiths provide an official guide for all aspects of Muslim daily life, for which Muhammad stands as exemplar *par excellence*. Six canonical collections were compiled in the ninth century, and others such as Ahmad b. Hanbal's *Musnad* have also gained widespread respect. Among these the most highly regarded are the two called *al-Sahih*, 'the sound (hadiths)', compiled by al-Bukhari (d. 870) and Muslim (d. 875) [10 and 31; and also 35, a later compilation]. The traditional Muslim view is that at least the 'sound' hadiths compiled by al-Bukhari and Muslim are valid statements going back to Muhammad's contemporaries, and that orthodox Islamic life and thought must be based on the Qur'an and these hadiths. Modern critical scholarship is divided on the question of the authenticity of the Hadith accounts. It is clear that many of them, including some in the collections by al-Bukhari and Muslim, grew out of the legal and theological debates of later generations. In any case, the Hadith accounts can be taken as primary sources for orthodox Islam today and for the classical Islam of the first three centuries of the Islamic era. The debate is on the extent to which these accounts represent the Islam of the third rather than the first century of the Islamic era. Some Muslim modernists have rejected the Hadith altogether as representing a stage in the history of Islam long after the time of Muhammad.

In addition to the Qur'an and the Hadith, the primary sources for the study of Islam include biographical studies of Muhammad and other Muslim leaders, historical works on the development of Islam in various parts of the world, legal and theological writings, commentaries on the Qur'an (which often reflect stages in the later development of Islamic thought and practice), Islamic poetry and other literature, and a wide variety of devotional and pilgrimage manuals, as well as mystical, philosophical and sectarian works. Very few of these works have been translated into English or other European languages.

THE SCHOLARLY STUDY OF ISLAM

The task of understanding Islam is immense, and a variety of methods or approaches are necessary for gathering and analysing information and then reaching valid conclusions. Approaches that have been used successfully to increase our understanding of Islam range from descriptive to normative and ideally should proceed in the following order.

Historical and philological. The first task is to seek factual information about the Islamic tradition from the time of its origins to the present. This calls for, among others, the use of historical and philological methods, which involve primarily the interpretation of literary texts. This textual approach to the study of Islam has been very productive since about the middle of the nineteenth century, when a succession of extremely competent scholars – working primarily from Arabic, Persian and Turkish texts – began producing critical editions, translations and analytical studies of the primary sources of the Islamic 'Great Tradition'. Students at the beginning of their studies of Islam now have the benefit of translations of some of the most essential primary sources mentioned above. Historians and other interpreters of classical and modern Islamic texts are now going beyond the initial stages of research accomplished by the great scholars of earlier generations and are providing a deeper understanding of Islamic history and culture by applying new methods of historiography and literary-critical analysis.

Social-scientific. Also involved in the task of gathering and analysing factual information about the Islamic world are the newer approaches of the social sciences, notably sociology, anthropology and political science. Most of the research in these fields, however, has been devoted to the study of modern politics, economics, etc. in countries where Islam is dominant, particularly in the Middle East, rather than the study of how these developments have affected Islam, e.g. the continuing effects of the abolition of the caliphate in 1924 and the cessation of the traditional Zakat system (see below) in most countries of the Islamic world. Reuben Levy's *The Social Structure of Islam* [29] provided an excellent foundation for a sociology of Islam, and other studies have offered keen insights into the contemporary situation of Islam in certain countries, for instance Clifford Geertz's *Islam Observed* [17], on Morocco and Indonesia, and Nikki Keddie's *Roots of Revolution* [27], on Iran, but much more needs to be done in terms of social-scientific analysis of contemporary Islam in the various regions of the world.

Comparative and phenomenological. After a sufficient amount of factual information and analysis has been gathered, the next step is to compare Islamic beliefs, practices and institutions with those of other religious and philosophical traditions, including Marxism. Until about the end of the nineteenth century most European comparative analysis of Islam was done from Jewish, Christian or other non-Islamic perspectives, with the apparent purpose of showing up the inferiority of Islam. During the twentieth century the comparative study of Islam and other traditions has proceeded in a more positive manner, although at a very slow pace. The rise of the phenomenological approach to comparative religion (see especially G. van der Leeuw, *Religion in Essence and Manifestation*, London, 1938) has had considerable impact on the Western study of Islam, mainly in promoting attempts to understand Islamic faith and practice from Muslim points of view. Major comparative analyses involving Islam and one or more other traditions following the methods of phenomenology have yet to appear and, with the exception of a few writers such as Kenneth Cragg, Islam has seldom been taken into consideration in comparative theological studies.

Normative. The ultimate stage in one's appraisal of Islam involves the normative disciplines of philosophy and theology, which yield value judgements. The question of the relative truth and value of Islamic beliefs and practices as compared with those of other traditions should be treated only in the light of a solid foundation of historical and comparative analysis. Normative approaches to Islam have historically been pursued from several perspectives ranging from the older Christian missionary – and more recent Marxist – attacks against Islam to contemporary irenic and apologetic approaches. In recent years the older Christian missionary spirit has given way to an irenic attitude, which strives to appreciate Islamic religiousness and foster a new Western attitude towards Muslims. One immediate goal of this new approach is to seek ways of 'dialogue' with Muslims in the hope of building bridges of mutual sympathy and understanding. The writings of Kenneth Cragg and W. Cantwell Smith are typical of these concerns. At the same time, the apologetic approach offered by many Muslims who write today for a Western and Muslim audience, such as Khurshid Ahmad [3], provides valuable source material for the attitudes and beliefs of contemporary Muslims. [On these approaches, see 2: 34–54]

THE HISTORY OF ISLAM

Islam dates from the last ten years of the life of the Prophet Muhammad (d. 632). Born probably around 570, Muhammad was orphaned at a young age and was reared by his grandfather and then an uncle, Abu Talib. At about the age of twenty-five Muhammad gained financial security when he married Khadija, a wealthy widow. Then when about forty he began seeing visions and receiving revelations, which he proclaimed publicly in the streets of Mecca, his native city and also the centre for commerce and religious pilgrimage for western Arabia (Figure 3.1). Fearing the economic repercussions of Muhammad's preaching against the deities worshipped by the pilgrims at Mecca's central shrine, the Ka'ba, the leading families of the city persecuted Muhammad and his followers and imposed an economic boycott against his clan. This boycott gave rise to opposition within Muhammad's clan, and on the death of Abu Talib in about 620 Muhammad lost his clan protection and had to seek refuge elsewhere. After failing to find a new home for his followers in nearby al-Taif, Muhammad reached an agreement with representatives of Yathrib, an agricultural settlement some 445 kilometres north of Mecca, and in 622 he and his followers made the *hijra* ('migration') to this settlement, which came to be called Medina, from *madinat al-nabi*, 'the city of the Prophet'. There within the short period of ten years Muhammad, the religious leader of a small band of emigrants, rose to become political leader of virtually all of central and western Arabia. A military victory over a much larger force of Meccans at Badr in 624 was a turning-point, followed by what turned out to be a diplomatic victory over the Meccans in the signing of the Treaty of al-Hudaybiya in 628 and the peaceful surrender of Mecca to Muhammad in 630.

After Muhammad's death the political and spiritual leadership of the majority of Muslims was assumed by a succession of caliphs or 'deputies' of the Prophet, who ruled Islam in his place in all aspects except as prophet. Within a decade of Muhammad's death the Arabs, under the leadership of the second caliph, 'Umar (d. 644), took control of Egypt, Palestine, Syria, Mesopotamia and the heart of ancient Iran, capturing Damascus in 635, Jerusalem in 640, Cairo in 641, Alexandria in 642, and Isfahan in 643. During the reign of the third caliph, 'Uthman (d. 656), the Arab empire expanded westwards to Tripoli, north to the Taurus and Caucasus mountains, and eastwards to what is now Pakistan and Afghanistan. After the death of the fourth caliph, 'Ali (d. 661), Muhammad's cousin and son-in-law, the Muslim community split, with the majority, who later came to be called Sunnis, following the Umayyad dynasty of caliphs (661–750) and then the 'Abbasid dynasty (750–1258). In 711, one century after the advent of Islam in Mecca and midway

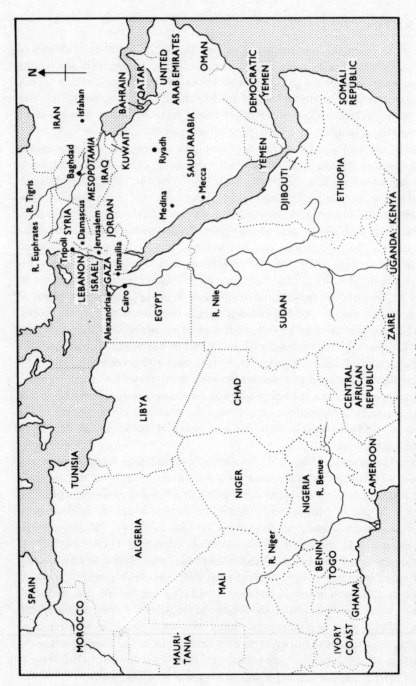

Figure 3.1 The Islamic homelands in North Africa and the Middle East

through the Umayyad period, the Arabs entered Spain from North Africa and also crossed the Indus river into the subcontinent of India. The farthest expansion into western Europe is marked by the Arab defeat at the hands of Charles Martel near Tours in 732, exactly a solar century after the Prophet's death and ten years before the birth of Charlemagne. The Arabs were forced to withdraw from France, but they remained in Spain for seven and a half more centuries. In the east the Arab, Umayyad empire spread north to the Aral Sea and across the Oxus river (now called the Amu-Dar'ya) to Tashkent, and eastwards to include almost the whole of what is now Pakistan and Afghanistan. During the caliphate of the 'Abbasids with their capital in Baghdad, the extent of the 'Islamic territories' in the west remained the same as under the Umayyads, while in the east Muslims gained control of northern India and the area down to the bay of Bengal. But this vast region, from the Pyrenees to what is now Bangladesh, was soon divided into a number of independent territories, ruled for centuries by successions of Islamic dynasties, and 'Abbasid rule was eventually reduced to just part of what is now Iraq [8].

While most areas that came under Muslim control remained so, this was not the case in Europe and the subcontinent of India. In Muslim Spain the Spanish Umayyads ruled from 756 to 1031, and then several Islamic dynasties, including the Almoravids and Almohads from North Africa, ruled an ever decreasing Muslim Spain during the period of the Christian Reconquista that culminated in the fall of Granada in 1492, when many Muslims (and the Jews) were forced to leave Spain. The Ottoman Turks, whose leaders, called sultans, assumed the title of caliph, crossed into eastern Europe from Anatolia in the fourteenth century and rapidly took over most of the Balkans. Then during the next two centuries their empire gradually encircled the Black Sea and spread north-west almost to Vienna and north-east almost to Kiev, while to the south the Ottomans gained control of Egypt, North Africa and the Fertile Crescent. During the nineteenth century the Ottomans lost most of their holdings in Europe and across northern Africa, and by the beginning of the First World War Turkey in Europe was reduced to the small area called Eastern Thrace that surrounds Istanbul. When the last Ottoman sultan, Muhammad VI, was deposed by Atatürk, the title of caliph went briefly to a cousin and then in 1924 the caliphate was abolished altogether. The Muslim Mughals by the end of the seventeenth century controlled virtually all of the subcontinent of India, in addition to what is now Pakistan, Afghanistan, Kashmir and Bangladesh. In the eighteenth and nineteenth centuries, however, they gradually lost control of the outlying areas and eventually northern India. The last Mughal emperor was deposed by the British in 1858. So the Arabs were forced out of western Europe, the Turks out of virtually all of eastern Europe, and the Mughals out of India, but not until these groups left their permanent Islamic imprint.

A distinction must be made between the rapid political and military expansion of empires ruled by Arabs and other Muslims and the spread of Islam or religious conversion, which proceeded at a much slower pace. Those areas where the rulers and the majority of the people became Muslims came to be called Dar al-Islam, the House of Islam. Eventually the overwhelming majority of the people across northern Africa, the Fertile Crescent and Anatolia converted to Islam from the various forms of Christianity, and an even higher percentage of the people of Iran converted from the Zoroastrian faith; a very small percentage of the Jewish people, on the other hand, converted to Islam. Since the time of the 'Abbasids, Islam has continued to spread, mostly by peaceful, missionary means, eastwards through Asia to parts of China and South-East Asia, notably Malaysia and Indonesia where a large majority are now Muslim, and also across a wide band of northern sub-Saharan Africa, where Islam continues to gain new converts.

Perhaps the most persuasive evidence of the vitality of Islam today is that it continues to be a missionary force in various parts of Asia and Africa, with remarkable successes especially in sub-Saharan West and East Africa, where Islam has the advantage of not being identified with white, European colonialism. Today, Muslims are represented in all the major races and cultures, but the vast majority live in a nearly contiguous band around the globe from the Atlantic shores of North and West Africa eastwards to Indonesia in the Pacific. The largest community of Muslims is that of the Indian subcontinent (most in Pakistan, India and Bangladesh) numbering about 225 million. Over 135 million are in South-East Asia and Indonesia, about 120 million in the Arab countries of the Near East and northern Africa, and about 90 million in the non-Arab countries of the Middle East (Turkey, Iran and Afghanistan). In other areas it is estimated that 95 million Muslims live in sub-Saharan Africa, 70 million in Russia and China, and about 7 million in Europe (not counting European Turkey), mostly in the Balkans. Altogether there are well over 700 million Muslims, or about one-sixth of the world population. Shi'a Muslims, mostly in Iran and Iraq, make up about one-tenth of the total Muslim population of the world. For more exact statistics, see Appendix B (pages 164–5)

Basic Doctrines

The basic Islamic beliefs are given in the Qur'an, where several creedal statements occur. One example is Sura 4.136/135:

O believers, believe in God and His Messenger and the Book He has sent down on His Messenger and the Book He sent down before. Whoever disbelieves in God, His angels, His Books, His Messengers, and the Last Day has surely gone astray, far into error.

The Qur'an has much to say about these beliefs, but no systematic treatment of any one doctrine is given. Also, the Qur'an appears to contain a number of contradictions on the essential beliefs; but the apparent inconsistencies are best understood as reflecting different stages in the gradual development of several complex, interrelated teachings.

GOD AND THE SPIRIT WORLD

Early parts of the Qur'an are striking for their lack of statements about God, other deities, and the various members of the world of spirits. The earliest passages – several short, rhythmic suras that are in the style of the pre-Islamic Arabian soothsayers – contain no references to God, nor any indication that they are messages from a deity. The earliest revelations that mention Muhammad's God refer to him only as 'Lord' (*rabb*), as in the expressions 'your Lord', 'his Lord', etc. (see the beginning of Suras 74, 87 and 96). Sometime later, Muhammad's Lord began to be called 'the Merciful' (*al-rahman*). This name seems to have been preferred for a while (see, for instance, Suras 19 and 43, and the important statements in 13.30/29, 25.60/61 and 55.1ff). At about the same time, the name 'Allah', known to the Meccan polytheists before Muhammad's time, was introduced into the revelation. The well-known verse, Sura 17.110, which begins, 'Say: Call upon Allah or call upon the Merciful; whichever you call upon, to Him belong the most beautiful names', had the effect of replacing the dominant usage of 'the Merciful' with that of 'Allah'.

Later parts of the Qur'an provide the ingredients of a rich theology in their frequent use of a wide variety of divine epithets, as for instance in the following liturgical passage at the end of Sura 59:

> He is God – there is no god but He.
> He is the Knower of the unseen and the visible.
> He is the Merciful, the Compassionate.
> He is God – there is no God but He.
> He is the King, the Holy, the Peaceable, the Faithful,
>   the Preserver, the Mighty, the Compeller, the Sublime.
> Glory be to God, above what they associate (with Him).
> He is God – the Creator, the Maker, the Shaper.

> To Him belong the most beautiful names.
> All that is in the heavens and the earth magnifies Him.
> He is the Mighty, the Wise.

From such lists of divine epithets later Muslims made lists of Ninety-nine Names of God. Those who were concerned to state Islamic beliefs about God in creeds developed other themes, as seen in Article 2 of the document that has come to be called Fiqh Akbar II:

> God the exalted is one, not in the sense of number, but in the sense that He has no partner; He begetteth not and He is not begotten and there is none like unto Him. He resembles none of the created things, nor do any created things resemble Him. He has been from eternity and will be to eternity with His names and qualities, those which belong to His essence as well as those which belong to His action. Those which belong to His essence are: life, power, knowledge, speech, hearing, sight and will. Those which belong to His action are: creating, sustaining, producing, renewing, making, and so on. [49: 188]

The doctrine that 'God is One' is so prominent in later parts of the Qur'an that it is easy to overlook the fact that earlier parts of the Islamic scripture do not reject the existence of other deities. The three goddesses whose worship flourished in and around Mecca in Muhammad's time, al-Lat, al-'Uzza and Manat, are mentioned by name in Sura 53.19–20. In a series of revisions of this sura these goddesses at first seem to have been accepted as intercessors with God, then are said to have been angels, and finally are said to be merely names invented by the Meccans' forefathers. In other Meccan parts of the Qur'an, that is, passages dating from before the Hijra in 622, deities other than Allah are demoted to the level of jinn before they are said not to exist at all (see Sura 6.100, 34.40–42/39–41, 37.158–66).

The existence of the jinn, those shadowy, invisible spirits of pre-Islamic Arabia that, like man, can be either good or evil, is also assumed in Meccan parts of the Qur'an, especially in the expression 'jinn and men', which occurs a number of times. The jinn also appear in the Qur'an in mythic and legendary accounts, for instance as listeners at the gate of heaven seeking knowledge of the future (Sura 72.8–9, one of the Qur'anic versions of an ancient Near Eastern myth explaining shooting stars), as slaves of Solomon working on the Temple (27.39, 34.12–14/11–13), and as the host or army of Iblis, the fallen archangel (18.50/48) (for Muhammad's attitude to Jewish Scripture see page 135 below). Iblis is the Qur'anic and Islamic name for the archangel Lucifer, who was cast from heaven for revolting against God and became Satan, the Tempter. In other contexts, the jinn are presented as 'satans', a term that is synonymous with 'jinn' whenever the latter are presented as evil or mischievous. It is significant that the jinn, demons and Iblis are not mentioned in parts of the Qur'an dating from after the establishment of distinctively Islamic beliefs and practices at about the time of the battle of Badr in 624. In place of these 'lower' spirits, the Qur'an presents an exalted view of angels, who appear as invisible, abstract symbols of God's power, and of Satan as an abstract symbol for evil and disbelief. This polarization and exaltation of spiritual powers for good and evil parallels the gradual exaltation of God as the One Creator, Sustainer of life, and Judge at the end of time. The Islamic creeds do not expand on the Qur'anic statements about angels, the jinn, Satan, and other members of the spirit world, but popular Islam has maintained belief in these spirits and has elaborated a vast spirit world that touches all aspects of life in this world and the hereafter.

THE NATURE AND DESTINY OF MAN

A second complex of ideas central to Islamic faith as it arose in the Qur'an and developed in later creeds and theological treatises involves the origin, nature and destiny of man. In the Qur'an man's creation and judgement are frequently mentioned together, often with references to the resurrection. In the earliest contexts the idea of creation is closely related to the conception and birth of each individual, as in Sura 80.17–22/16–22:

> Woe to man! How ungrateful he is.
> From what did He create him?
> From a sperm-drop has He formed him.
> Then He makes his path easy for him.
> Then He causes him to die and buries him.
> Then, when He will, He raises him.

In later passages the biblical idea of the creation of the First Man from dust or clay occurs a number of times, as in the following version of the Iblis story in 15.28ff, which begins: 'And when your Lord said to the angels: "See, I am about to create a human being from clay, formed from moulded mud. When I have shaped him and breathed My spirit into him, fall down all of you and bow before him."' This idea of creation is then incorporated into statements on man's life-cycle, as in 71.17f/16f: 'God caused you to grow out of the earth, then He will return you into it, and bring you forth [from it again].' Finally both views of creation are combined into several elaborate accounts, such as in 23.12–16:

> We created man from an extract of clay;
> Then We placed him as a sperm-drop into a safe receptacle;
> Then We fashioned the clot into a lump; then We fashioned the

lump into bones; then We clothed the bones with flesh; then
We made him into a new creation. So blessed be God the
fairest of creators!
After this you will surely die,
And on the Day of Resurrection you will surely be raised up.

As for the basic nature of man, whether man is 'born in sin' as a result of the Original Sin of Adam and Eve or is intrinsically good, the glory and crown of God's creation, Islam adopted what appears to be a compromise view, seen in Sura 91.7–10:

By the soul and [Him who] formed it,
And implanted into it its wickedness and its piety!
Blessed is he who purifies it.
Ruined is he who corrupts it.

Thus the potential for both good and evil are breathed into each person by God at birth. Then throughout life each person is tested by his Maker, as the Qur'an says in 21.35/36: 'And We try you with evil and good as a test; then unto Us you will be returned.' The clear Qur'anic teaching is that some people will choose good and will be rewarded, while others will choose evil and will be punished. Eternal reward and punishment are to be meted out by God at the Last Judgement, around which a central doctrine of the Qur'an and later Islamic theology developed. In the early stages of the development of Qur'anic credal statements, the most frequently occurring requirement for being a believer was that one 'believe in God and the Last Day'. This great eschatological event, also called the Day of Judgement, the Day of Resurrection, and sometimes simply 'the Day', is vividly described in the Qur'an, as are the pleasures of the Garden of Paradise and the torments of the hell-fire, called Jahannam (cf. the Hebrew Gehenna), the Fire etc. (see 22.19–23/20–24, 56.11–56, 69.13–37, 76.11–22 etc.).

The Islamic doctrine of the hereafter, with its stress on reward and punishment, seems to require the corollary belief in individual responsibility for one's faith and actions. But the ancient Arabian belief in Fate found its way into the Qur'an and developed later into the Islamic doctrine of predestination. According to the ancient view, four things are decided for each individual before birth: the sex of the child; whether it will have a happy or miserable life; what food it will have; and its term of life. This idea of a predetermined term of life occurs in the Qur'an, as in 6.2: 'It is He who created you from clay, then determined a term, and a term is stated with Him' (cf. 3.145/139). Man's predestination is said to involve everything in life, as in 9.51: 'Nothing will befall us but what God has written down for us ...' It was left for later theologians to correlate this teaching with other Qur'anic statements saying that each person is responsible for his or her own actions.

REVELATION — GOD'S MESSENGERS AND BOOKS

The earliest parts of the Qur'an do not mention revelation or God's prophets and their scriptures. When prophets are mentioned in later Meccan passages they are referred to as 'messengers' (*rusul*, singular *rasul*) or 'ambassadors' (*mursalun*). The most common context for the activities of these messengers from God is the punishment-story, where a messenger such as Noah or Lot brings God's message to his tribe, is ridiculed and rejected by most of his people, and then is rescued by God along with his family and followers, while most of his tribe perishes in a flood, fire or some other natural calamity. Details of Muhammad's experience in Mecca are frequently included in the stories of the earlier prophets, and there is only an inference that Muhammad is also such a 'messenger' and that his city, Mecca, is being threatened with the same type of terrestrial destruction. The Qur'an does not, during this period, explicitly describe Muhammad as a 'messenger of God' (*rasul Allah*) to be classed with the great messengers of the past.

It is only after the Hijra in 622, and after the Muslims' victory at the battle of Badr in 624, that the role of 'prophet' (*nabi*) became prominent in the Qur'an, and Muhammad came to be included explicitly among the prophets. Prophets are said to descend from Abraham, the first monotheist and thus the first 'Muslim' (one fully surrendered to God alone), and each is said to have been given a Book or scripture (*kitab*). The Torah of Moses and the Gospel of Jesus receive special attention in the Qur'an and in later Islamic belief, but the Psalms of David, the 'scrolls of Abraham' and others are mentioned briefly in the Qur'an and are assumed for each prophet. In Medinan parts of the Qur'an, that is, passages dating from after the Hijra in 622, or to be more precise, in post-Badr parts of the Qur'an, Muhammad is frequently called 'the Prophet' or 'the Messenger of God', two expressions that came to be used synonymously in later revelations (see for instance their usage in Sura 33). The precise meaning of the expression 'Seal of the Prophets', applied to Muhammad in 33.40, is uncertain. It seems to have meant that Muhammad put a seal of divine approval on the true teachings that have come down from earlier prophets. That is, he confirmed the true teachings that came down in the Jewish community from Moses and in the Christian community from Jesus, while showing other Jewish and Christian beliefs to be false notions invented by later Jews and Christians, for instance the Jewish food laws and the Christian belief that Jesus was the Son of God. This expression, Seal of the Prophets, later came to be interpreted to mean that

Muhammad was the 'last and greatest of the prophets'. [For the development of these ideas in later Islamic thought, see 49.]

Basic Practices

There are five essential Islamic practices, known as the Pillars of Islam. These are Shahada (profession of faith), Salat (worship), Zakat (alms-giving), *saum* (fasting) and Hajj (pilgrimage). Each is prescribed in the Qur'an, but none is described there in detail. During the first three Islamic centuries these practices came to be strictly regulated by Islamic law. The exact manner of observance of these Pillars varies between Sunni and Shi'ite practice, and among the four Sunni legal schools or rites, the Shafi'ites, the Hanafites, the Malikites and the Hanbalites [see 34: IV]. The times for observance of the annual practices, notably the fast during the month of Ramadan and the pilgrimage during the month of Dhu-l-Hijja, are determined by the Islamic lunar year established by Muhammad during the last year of his life. A lunar year of twelve revolutions of the moon around the earth lasts about 354 days, or eleven days less than a solar year. Thus the beginning of the Islamic year, and each of the annual festivals, moves back through the solar calendar one season every eight years or through the entire solar year once in about thirty-two and a half years. Some time after Muhammad's death, the year of the Hijra, 622 (see page 127 above), was chosen as the beginning of the Islamic era, often designated AH from the Latin *anno Hegirae*. (See Appendices C and D, pages 166–7, on the Islamic calendar and its relation to the Julian and Gregorian calendars.)

THE SHAHADA

The beginning and essence of being a Muslim is to recite with sincere 'intention' (*niyya*) the simple Islamic creed called the Shahada (confession), consisting of two statements: 'There is no god but God' and 'Muhammad is the Messenger of God'. Both occur in the Qur'an, but not together. This formula is pronounced by new converts as part of the ceremony of becoming a Muslim, and it is recited in each performance of the Salat (see below). The term in the Shahada translated above as 'God' is *Allah*, the Arabic proper name for God used by Christians as well as Muslims. This name probably comes from *al-ilah*, 'the god', the common Arabic noun for a deity, with the definite article. Since Christians, Jews and others agree with Muslims on the first statement of the Shahada, it is the second that distinguishes Muslims. Implying much more than casual assent that Muhammad is 'a prophet', it carries with it the conviction that Muhammad is the last and greatest of the prophets, and also the exemplar of all proper religious faith and practice. As mentioned above, the expression 'messenger of God' is used synonymously with 'prophet' in later parts of the Qur'an. In later Islamic thought a distinction was made between these two expressions.

THE SALAT AND FRIDAY WORSHIP

The earliest Islamic practice to arise was the daily prayer ritual called the Salat. Until some time after the Hijra in 622 it seems to have been required only of Muhammad and it was performed only twice each day, at sunrise and sunset (see Suras 11.114/116, 17.78/80, 20.130, 40.55/57, 50.39/38, 52.48f etc.). Then in Medina performance of the Salat was required of all Muslims, and a third Salat, called 'the middle Salat' in Sura 2.238/239, was added, possibly influenced by the fact that the Jews performed their prayer three times a day. The Friday noon worship service was also instituted by Muhammad in Medina. For the first year or so after the Hijra the Muslims faced towards Jerusalem during the performance of their prayer, as was the Jewish practice. Then at the time of the so-called 'break with the Jews' the direction of prayer (*qibla*) was changed from Jerusalem to Mecca, and the Meccan *qibla* has been an obligatory aspect of the Salat ever since. To what extent the present complex ritual had developed during Muhammad's lifetime is difficult to determine. Some essential parts of the later Salat are mentioned in the Qur'an, for instance, the bowing (*ruku'*) in 2.125/119, 22.26/27, 48.29 etc., and the prostration (*sujud*) in 2.125/119, 4.102/103, 25.64/65 etc. The three daily Salats required of all Muslims during Muhammad's lifetime are mentioned by name in the Qur'an (in 24.58/57 and 2.238/239). Within a century of the Prophet's death the number of required daily Salats was firmly set at five, and a number of hadiths arose supporting this number [see 10: VIII and 31: IV].

The beginning of the period for performing each of the prescribed daily Salats and the time to go to the mosque on Fridays (see page 143 below) are announced by a public call to prayer called the *adhan*, given by an official of the mosque called the muezzin (Arabic *mu'adhdhin*, 'caller'). The call to prayer consists of seven short statements: 'God is most great./I testify that there is no god but God./I testify that Muhammad is the Messenger of God./Come to prayer./Come to salvation./God is most great./There is no god but God.' The first statement is repeated four times, the last only once, and all the others twice. In the call to the morning prayer the statement, 'Prayer is better than sleep', is inserted after the fifth statement, or, in one of the legal rites, at the end. The Shi'ites (see page 154 below) insert 'Come to the best work' after the fifth statement, and they recite the final statement twice. The worshipper must be in a state of ritual purity, accomplished by performing either the minor ablution called *wudu'*, for minor impurities, or the major one called *ghusl*, for major impurities. Some of the legal rites have ruled that one ablution ceremony in the morning serves for all five prayers of that day unless it has been invalidated by some impurity.

Proper observance of the Salat is a required duty of all Muslims, and its essential elements are prescribed by Islamic law and customary practice. The exact performance of the Salat varies among the various legal schools or rites (see above), but there is a general uniformity of practice regarding thirteen essentials (*arkan*) – six utterances or recitations, six actions or positions, and the requirement that these twelve must proceed in the prescribed order. The description given below is based largely on that of the great theologian al-Ghazali (d. 1111) in explaining the practice of the Shafi'ites, the legal rite that predominates today in Egypt, Syria, India and Indonesia. The system of numbering the utterances and giving letters for the positions makes the description of the essentials valid for all the major legal rites. In addition to the thirteen essentials, there are also a large number of 'customary' (*sunna*) elements that are recommended but not required. There is considerable variation among the major rites on the *sunna* elements.

The Salat begins (Figure 3.2) with the worshipper in (a) the 'standing position' (*qiyam*), facing the Ka'ba in Mecca. In a congregational Salat, whether performed in a mosque or elsewhere, a second call to prayer, called the *iqama*, is recited, followed by the statement, 'Worship has begun.' Then comes (1) the statement of 'intention' (*niyya*) indicating which prayer is about to be performed, followed by (2) a *takbira*, the statement, 'God is most great.' Remaining standing, the worshipper then begins the first *rak'a* or liturgical cycle with (3) recitation of the *Fatiha* ('Opener'), the first sura of the Qur'an:

> In the name of God, the Merciful, the Compassionate. Praise belongs to God, the Lord of the worlds, the Merciful, the Compassionate, the Master of the Day of Judgement. Thee only do we serve; to Thee only do we pray for succour. Guide us in the straight path, the path of those whom Thou hast blessed, not of those against whom Thou art wrathful, nor of those who go astray.

This is followed by a second recitation from the Qur'an, either individually or in silence as the leader recites aloud. Next comes (b) the 'bowing' (*ruku'*), with the worshipper bending the upper part of the body to a horizontal position with his hands on his knees. In this position he says 'Glory be to God' or a longer statement of praise, varying in different rites. The worshipper then (c) resumes the standing position (*i'tidal*) and, with the hands raised to the sides of the face, says 'May God hear him who praises Him', or a longer formula. Then follows (d) the first 'prostration' (*sujud*), with the toes, knees, palms and forehead all touching the floor or ground. In this position the worshipper says, 'Praise be to Thee, my Lord, the Most High.' This is followed by (e) the sitting position (*julus*), usually a half-sitting, half-kneeling position, sitting on the left foot but kneeling with the right, in which another *takbira* is recited. Then there is a second 'prostration', which is required but not counted separately in the lists of essentials. During this prostration the worshipper says, 'My Lord, forgive me, have mercy on me, grant my portion to me, and guide me.' This completes the first rak'a or cycle of the Salat. The second follows immediately as the worshipper stands and recites the *Fatiha* again and then proceeds through the same sequence of essentials. The morning Salat has two rak'as, the sunset one has three, and the noon, afternoon and evening ones each have four. After the second prostration of the last rak'a the Salat then concludes with the final four essential elements. The worshipper assumes (f) the 'sitting position' (*qu'ud*) and recites (4) the Shahada (see above), (5) a blessing on the Prophet and his family, and (6) the 'salutation of peace' called the *salam* or *taslim*, simply 'Peace be upon you', pronounced once with the head turned to the right and once to the left. Originally this greeting seems to have been intended for one's guardian or recording angels, but al-Ghazali said it should also be for one's fellow worshippers, and this later interpretation has become widely accepted. In the Salat, which culminates in the prostration before God, the faithful Muslim performs a daily ritual that symbolizes the essence of Islam, submission (*islam*) before God, the Almighty, and public participation in the rituals instituted by Muhammad [see 11: 63–84 and 26: 463–80].

At noon on Fridays Muslims throughout the world congregate in their local mosques for a special worship service called 'the assembly' (*al-jum'a*). The mosque is a unique, Islamic institution that is essentially different from the Jewish and Christian counterparts, the synagogue and the church (see Figure 3.3). Its most characteristic architectural features are (1) the minaret or tower, from which the call to prayer is given, (2) the 'niche' (*mihrab*) indicating the direction of Mecca, which the worshippers face while praying, (3) the 'pulpit' (*minbar*), a usually ornate staircase with an enclosure at the top from which the Friday sermon is delivered, and (4) some type of fountain or source of water for ablutions. The most important mosque officials are the 'leader' (*imam*) of the Salat, the 'preacher' (*khatib*), who delivers the Friday sermon, and the muezzin, who issues the call to prayer. In smaller mosques these offices are often combined in one or two persons, while in larger ones there are sometimes several imams and muezzins. The 'essentials' (*arkan*) of the Friday worship service are (1) a sermon, usually presented in two parts,

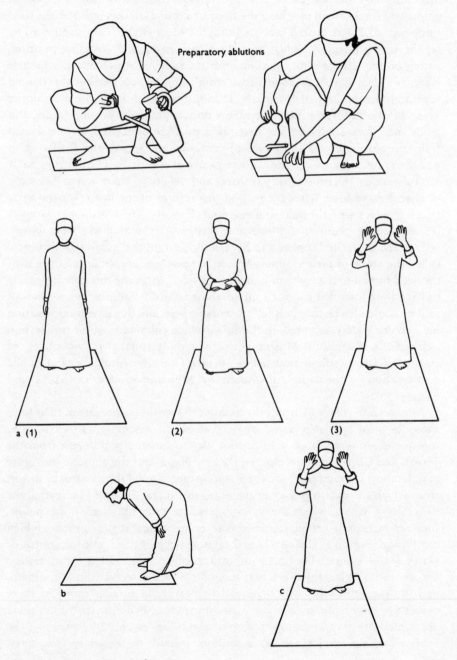

Preparatory ablutions

a (1)

(2)

(3)

b

c

Figure 3.2   The positions of prayer

(second prostration)

f (4)

(5)

(6)

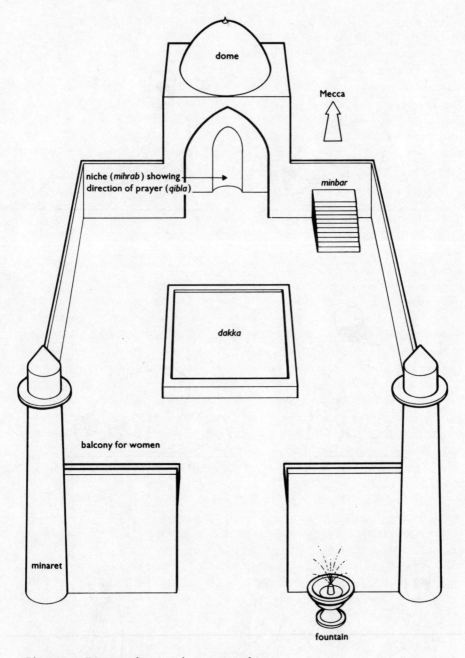

dome

Mecca

niche (*mihrab*) showing
direction of prayer (*qibla*)

minbar

dakka

balcony for women

minaret

fountain

Figure 3.3   Diagram showing characteristic features
of mosque architecture

followed by (2) a special Salat of two rak'as called the *salat al-jum'a*, led by the imam. It is recommended that a *sunna* or 'customary' Salat of two rak'as be performed by the worshippers individually before the service begins. Performing ablutions before the service, wearing perfume, arriving early, and reciting suras from the Qur'an and blessings on the Prophet are also considered *sunna* and meritorious. [For a more detailed description of the mosque and Friday worship, see 47: 289–99; for hadiths on this service, see 10: XI, 31: VII, and 26: 537–49; for specific regulations according to the Shafi'ite rite, see 11: 144–72 and 26: 480f.]

ALMS-GIVING

The broad lines of the origin and early development of the Islamic institution of alms-giving are fairly clear. Before the Hijra the sharing of wealth with the poor was stressed in the Qur'an as a pious act, but the technical term Zakat and even the common noun *sadaqa* were not used. After the Hijra, when the small Muslim community of emigrants found themselves in need of support from new converts in Medina, alms-giving acquired new significance as an Islamic welfare system in which those who had extra income shared with those who did not have enough. But no set amount was stipulated. In response to the question posed by a group of believers, 'How much do we pay?', the Qur'an says simply (in 2.219/216f), 'The surplus!', meaning 'whatever you do not need'. In the course of time this 'surplus' came to be interpreted differently, and a minimum assessable amount called the *nisab* was set for each type of property. The Zakat then became a tax of a certain percentage of one's wealth or produce, or a specified ration of livestock. The Zakat was to be paid on food crops and fruit at the time of harvest, on livestock after a full year of grazing, and on precious metals and merchandise on hand at the end of the year. The Zakat system, which varied in different geographical areas and among different legal rites, came to be carefully regulated by the Muslim religious and political leaders. With the establishment of modern secular states throughout the 'Islamic world', the traditional Zakat was in most cases replaced by national taxation and welfare systems. Only a few countries such as Saudi Arabia and Libya have maintained official Zakat systems along traditional lines. In most parts of the Islamic world today alms-giving has become a voluntary practice carried out at the local level. Egypt and a few other countries have large national agencies that collect and distribute Zakat, but still on a completely voluntary basis [26: 486–91].

FASTING

During the first year after the Hijra Muhammad instituted a one-day, twenty-four-hour fast called the Ashura ('tenth'). This was apparently the name used by the Jews of the Hijaz for the fast on the Day of Atonement, which falls on the tenth day of Tishri. The Qur'an does not mention the Ashura fast, but Hadith accounts have much to say about it, acknowledging that it was borrowed from the Jews and that it was kept for a while as an Islamic fast before the Ramadan fast was instituted. The establishment of the thirty-day daytime only fast of Ramadan seems to have been related to the Muslim victory at the battle of Badr in Ramadan, 624. From the beginning recitation of the Qur'an has had a special place in the Ramadan activities, when it is customary for Muslims to recite or read one-thirtieth of the Qur'an each night of the month. For this reason the text has been divided into thirty equal parts, marked in the margins of all oriental editions.

The basic requirements of the fast are given in two verses of the Qur'an 2.185/181, the verse that instituted this fast, and 2.187/183, which replaced and relaxed the fasting regulations given earlier and recorded now in 2.184/180. The first verse states that the fast is to be kept throughout Ramadan, and that anyone who is sick or on a journey may break his fast for these days, but must make them up later. The second verse states: 'You are permitted during the night of the fast to go in to your wives ... and eat and drink until so much of the dawn appears that a white thread can be distinguished from a black one. Then keep the fast completely until night and do not lie with them when you should remain in the mosques.' According to later Islamic law the essentials of the fast are that it is to be kept from just before sunrise until just after sunset during the thirty days of Ramadan by all adult Muslims who are in the full possession of their senses and, for women, it is to be kept only on those days when they are free from menstruation and the bleeding of childbirth. The fast is regarded as having been broken on any day on which certain violations occur, the exact lists of which vary among the different legal rites. Violations are usually listed in four categories: (1) allowing food, beverages or anything else, to be swallowed intentionally, and in modern times inhaling tobacco smoke has also been prohibited; (2) intentional vomiting, even when this is done under a doctor's orders; (3) sexual intercourse; and (4) the emission of semen when caused by any type of sexual contact. Muslims are encouraged to break their fast as soon as possible after the sun has set and to eat in the morning as late as possible before sunrise. Indecent talk, gossip, slander and anything else that would cause anger or grief to anyone should also be avoided, along with any actions that might arouse passion in oneself or someone else. Any days during Ramadan on which the fast is broken should be made up as soon as possible during the following month. Although carefully regulated by Islamic law and custom, fasting by its very nature becomes a voluntary act of piety on the part of the observant Muslim [see 26: 491–6, and for a translation of the section on fasting in al-Bukhari's *Sahih*, ibid., 88–123].

THE GREAT PILGRIMAGE

The fifth Pillar of Islam is the Great Pilgrimage or Hajj to the sacred monuments in and near Mecca, required of all Muslims at least once in a lifetime if they are physically able to make the trip and can afford it (see Figure 3.4). From before the time of Muhammad these rituals have been divided into two groups, the *'umra* (visitation), sometimes called 'the Lesser Pilgrimage', which takes place in and near the Sacred Mosque in Mecca and can be performed at any time of the year, and the *hajj* (pilgrimage), which begins in Mecca and proceeds out to 'Arafat and back and is performed only on certain days of the month of Dhu-l-Hijja (see Figure 3.5). Islamic law and custom stipulate three methods of performing these two groups of ceremonies: (1) 'one by one' (*ifrad*), the preferred method, completing the *hajj* ceremonies first and then the *'umra* ones; (2) 'enjoyment' (*tamattu'*), performing the *'umra* first and then breaking the state of ritual purity or sanctification (*ihram*) to enjoy the pleasures of Mecca for a few days before resuming the *ihram* for the *hajj*; and (3) 'conjunction' (*qiran*), beginning the *'umra* and then the *hajj*, and then completing both at the same time.

For several days and even weeks before the Hajj begins, a steady stream of pilgrims, numbering over 1 million in recent years, flows into Mecca. Before crossing into the *haram*, the sacred territory that surrounds Mecca, the pilgrims enter a state of ritual purity (*ihram*) by performing a major ablution (*ghusl*) and a special Salat of two *rak'as*, expressing their 'intention' (*niyya*) to perform one of the three types of pilgrimage mentioned above, and then donning a white, seamless garment called also an *ihram*. On entering Mecca all pilgrims visit the Sacred Mosque as soon as possible and perform a sevenfold 'circumambulation' (*tawaf*) of the Ka'ba. Then they perform a Salat of two *rak'as* and drink from the nearby sacred well called Zamzam. Those who intend to fulfil an *'umra* either as a ceremony separate from the Hajj proper – essentially a mark of respect paid to the city on entering it for the first time – or as part of a *tamattu'* performance of the Hajj then leave the courtyard of the Sacred Mosque and climb the stairs to the ancient 'high place' called al-Safa. Here begins the second major ceremony of the *'umra*, the 'running' (*sa'y*) between al-Safa and al-Marwa, another hill about 385 metres away. First, the 'intention' to perform the 'running' ceremony is

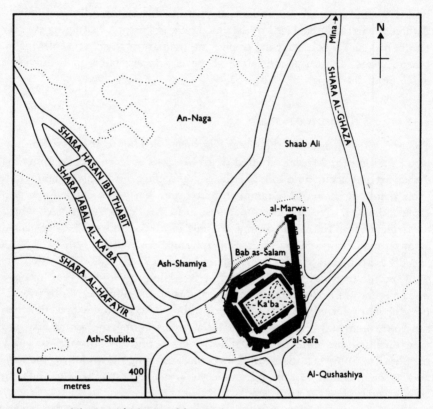

Figure 3.4   The Sacred Mosque, Mecca

expressed and verses from the Qur'an and other pious sayings are recited.
Then the pilgrims traverse 'the running course' (*al-mas'a*), walking part way
and running part way. On al-Marwa they face the Ka'ba and recite more
pious sayings, and then retrace their steps back to al-Safa. They go back and
forth until they have traversed the 'running course' seven times, thus ending
up at al-Marwa, where a ritual desacralization is performed by having the
hair trimmed or a single lock of hair cut off. Those pilgrims who follow the
other two methods (*ifrad* and *qiran*) are not required to perform the 'running'
ceremony before the rituals of the *hajj*.

On the 7th of Dhu-l-Hijja the pilgrimage ceremonies are officially opened
with a service at the Sacred Mosque in Mecca which includes a ritual purification of the inside of the Ka'ba and a sermon or *khutba* delivered from the
pulpit (*minbar*) that stands near by. According to the pilgrimage manuals
the *hajj* then begins on the 8th of Dhu-l-Hijja in Mina (a small uninhabited

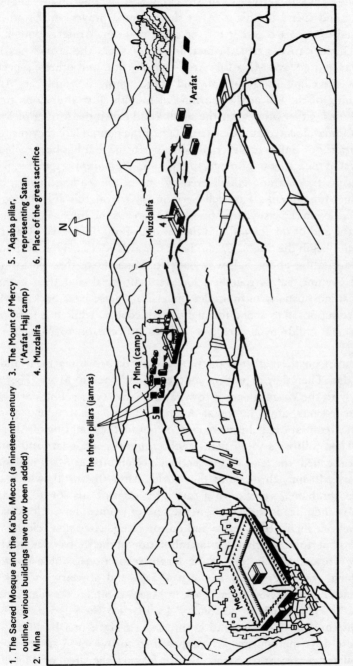

1. The Sacred Mosque and the Ka'ba, Mecca (a nineteenth-century outline, various buildings have now been added)
2. Mina
3. The Mount of Mercy ('Arafat Hajj camp)
4. Muzdalifa
5. 'Aqaba pillar, representing Satan
6. Place of the great sacrifice

Figure 3.5 The *hajj*: the route followed by the Hajji around Mecca (the distance from Mecca to 'Arafat is about twenty-four kilometres)

village about eight kilometres east of Mecca), where the pilgrims are supposed to assemble and spend the night. After the morning prayer on the 9th they are supposed to depart together for the great plain of 'Arafat, about fifteen kilometres farther to the east. In fact, in recent years the crowd has been so large that many leave Mina for 'Arafat on the 8th, and others, especially the Shi'ites travelling in from Iran and Iraq, simply assemble at 'Arafat on the evening of the 8th or the morning of the 9th. Just after noon on the 9th the pilgrims gather on or near the small knoll called the Mount of Mercy (Jabal al-Rahma), located at the eastern edge of the plain. Here they recite the noon and afternoon Salats together and then perform what has been called the central ritual of the entire pilgrimage, the 'standing' (*wuquf*) ceremony, which lasts until sunset. A sermon is delivered by one of the leading imams, commemorating Muhammad's Farewell Sermon, given on this hill during the pilgrimage he led in the last year of his life. As soon as the sun has set, cannon-fire marks the end of the *wuquf*, and the throng of pilgrims leave 'Arafat immediately and begin the 'flight' (*ifada*) back towards Mecca. They stop in the valley of Muzdalifa, about half-way back to Mina. Here they perform the sunset and evening Salats together, have a light meal and then gather a number of stones, usually in multiples of seven, for use later back in Mina. The men are supposed to spend the night in Muzdalifa, while it is customary for the women, children, and elderly men to proceed on to Mina for the night.

Before dawn on the 10th the pilgrims are awakened for a meal and the morning Salat. Then they depart on another 'flight' back to Mina. They proceed directly to the western end of town and throw seven pebbles at a stone pillar that represents Satan (Jamrat al-'Aqaba). This is a ritual cursing of Satan, driving away temptation, believed to commemorate the tempting of Abraham by Satan. Then follows a vast ritual slaughtering of sheep, goats and camels, and the meal called 'the feast of the sacrifice', celebrated at Mina and simultaneously by Muslims throughout the world. After this meal, which commemorates Abraham's sacrifice of a ram after offering his son to God, the pilgrims have their heads shaved, or, in the case of women, have a lock of hair cut off. They are then free to bathe and put on clean, often new, clothes. But they must still perform another circumambulation of the Ka'ba back in Mecca before they are completely free of the *ihram* restrictions. There must also be a 'running' (*sa'y*) ceremony between al-Safa and al-Marwa if this was not performed earlier. These rituals back in Mecca complete the requirements (*arkan*) of the Hajj, but it is 'customary' (*sunna*) for the pilgrims to return to Mina for three days of celebration on the 11th–13th of Dhu-l-Hijja. On each of these days the pilgrims are supposed to throw seven stones at each of three pillars representing Satan. Before leaving the area of Mecca the pilgrims must perform a final circumambulation of the Ka'ba, called 'the farewell *tawaf*', and then many visit Islam's second holy city, Medina, before returning to their home countries [see 26: 496–509].

OTHER PRACTICES AND CUSTOMS

In addition to the five Pillars of Islam other practices and customs are commonly observed throughout the Islamic world. The Qur'an is explicit in its regulations on such matters as marriage, divorce, inheritance and food laws (2.228–32, 4.3, 11/12–14/18, 22/26, 5.1, 96/97 etc.), and in prohibitions against usury, gambling, drinking wine, eating pork etc. (2.173/169, 3.130/124, 5.3, 90/92 etc.). There are distinctively Islamic customs involving weddings, circumcision and funerals, which vary in details in different countries. There are supererogatory fasts, such as the Ashura Day fast on the 10th of Muharram and the 'Arafat Day fast on the 9th of Dhu-l-Hijja. And there are supererogatory prayers such as the 'Salat of the Pauses', a long prayer service interrupted by pauses that is performed in the mosques during the evenings of the month of Ramadan. (On Sufi practice, see page 152 below.)

Religiously men and women are equal in Islam. Muslim women are required to keep the Pillars of Islam and other religious and moral duties, and basic education, especially in religious matters, is a right and duty for women as well as for men. In other respects, however, the Qur'an and Islamic law and custom place men above women, for instance in the man's responsibility to provide for his wife and children. For this reason a higher percentage of inheritance goes to male heirs. The extent to which the lives of men and women are kept separate, and women's lives are restricted, varies from country to country. The custom of keeping women in partial seclusion in some Muslim societies seems just as oppressive to modernist Muslims as it does to most Westerners, but it is seen by other Muslims as a way of being respectful and protective of women. The Qur'an enjoins modesty in dress and behaviour for men and women (e.g. 24.30f); it does not explicitly require the veiling of women. Today the customs of dress among Muslim women vary in different parts of the Islamic world. Some women, especially those from the villages and smaller towns, cover themselves completely from head to toe; others dress in the usual Western manner or cover their heads discreetly with scarves [14; 29: 11].

Unity and Diversity

Since the time of Muhammad the Muslim community has tended to split up into various groups. Often political and cultural factors were as significant as theological and philosophical ones in this process. The formative period in the development of Islamic thought, culminating in the work of al-Ash'ari (d. 935), was an exciting battleground of ideas that in retrospect can be seen as a complex dialectical process that culminated in what became Sunni orthodoxy, the established doctrines of the vast majority of Muslims. The main issues involved faith and works, predestination and free will, revelation and reason, the implications of the unity of God, the eternity of the Qur'an, and whether or not the Qur'an must be taken literally.

This dialectical process can be seen as beginning with the group that came to be called the Kharijites, the 'seceders', since they withdrew from the 'party of 'Ali' (see page 154 below) and later from the Umayyads, claiming that the Muslim leaders at that time did not follow the Qur'an strictly and leave major decisions to God. The Kharijites, who have continued as a small sect in North Africa, also conclude that Islam should be a community of saints and that those who commit grave sins forfeit their identity as Muslims. Those who differed on this point, emphasizing the importance of proper faith over works and arguing that the decision on grave sinners should be deferred to God at the Judgement Day, came to be called Murji'ites, 'postponers' or 'those who hope' [43: V]. Those who emphasized human responsibility over predestination or predeterminism came to be called Qadarites, 'determiners', meaning in their case that people determine their own fate [43: IV].

The Traditionists, that is, those who based their faith and practice strictly on the 'traditions' (*ahadith*, singular *hadith*) of the Prophet and were suspicious of the use of reason in ascertaining religious truth, rallied round Ahmad b. Hanbal (d. 855), who defended the concept of the eternity of the Qur'an as the Speech of God (*kalam Allah*), and argued for a literal interpretation of the Qur'an, including its vivid descriptions of creation and the afterlife and its anthropomorphic statements about God. This latter point involved the doctrine of God's attributes, that is, the belief that God literally sees, hears, speaks etc., because these human attributes are ascribed to him in the Qur'an. His followers, the Hanbalites, came to reject all use of critical reason in determining doctrinal issues. Their opponents, known as Mu'tazilites, 'separatists', attempted to give equal weight to revelation and reason as sources of religious knowledge and truth, but their methods and conclusions tended to come down on the side of reason. The system of the Mu'tazilites was built around the twin emphases, 'the unity and justice of God'. The first point led them to deny the doctrines of the attributes of God, the eternity of the Qur'an, and literal interpretation of the Qur'an; the second led to a denial of the doctrine of predestination. The views of the Mu'tazilites were adopted as official doctrine by the caliph al-Ma'mun (d. 833) and were imposed on the leading judges and religious teachers through an Inquisition that lasted from 833 to about 849. Most of those questioned yielded to the pressure of the government and publicly affirmed the doctrine of the createdness of the Qur'an. Among the few who firmly refused was Ahmad b. Hanbal, who was imprisoned for two years for his insistence on the doctrine of the uncreatedness, and hence eternity, of the Qur'an [43: VIII; and on the Inquisition, ibid., 178f].

A synthesis between the Traditionist-literalist position of the Hanbalites and the rationalist approach of the Mu'tazilites was achieved by al-Ash'ari (d. 935), who studied under the leading Mu'tazilites of his day and accepted their methods and their conclusions until he was about forty. He then 'converted' to Hanbalite views and spent the remainder of his career defending them, but using the methods of the Mu'tazilites. Al-Ash'ari's thought can be summarized in four main points: (1) The Qur'an is uncreated and is the very speech of God, and like his other attributes it is eternal and is in some sense distinct from his essence. (2) The anthropomorphic statements about God in the Qur'an must be accepted, but 'without asking how', that is, without asking how God sees, hears, speaks etc. (3) Eschatological descriptions in the Qur'an must also be accepted as they stand, but 'without asking how'. One of the key issues here involved the Qur'anic phrase 'looking to their Lord' and whether in the afterlife people will be able to 'see' God in the normal sense. (4) The Qur'anic teaching on predestination must be accepted on the basis of the formula, 'God creates the acts of a person, and the person acquires the acts', that is, the omnipotence of God is to be taken seriously, while people 'acquire' responsibility for their deeds by willing at the moment of acting to do them [44: IX]. The Hanbalites continued to distrust al-Ash'ari's use of reason, but his system of theology came to be accepted as Sunni orthodoxy.

The extreme representatives of the Greek, rationalist outlook were the group that came to be called the 'philosophers' (*falasifa*). They differed from the 'theologians' (*mutakallimun*) not only in their view that observation and reason are the primary sources of knowledge and truth, but also in their preference for discussing traditional philosophical questions rather than theological ones. Al-Kindi (d. *c.* 870) is usually regarded as the first major philosopher to write in Arabic, and the only great one of Arab lineage. His main accomplishment was that he adapted Greek thought and science to fit the Arab and Islamic world. His theological views were close to those of the Mu'tazilites, and, in contrast to later Islamic philosophers, he accepted the doctrine of *creatio ex nihilo*. The Turkish-born al-Farabi (d. 950) was the founder of Arabic Neoplatonism. Especially favoured by the Shi'ites (see page 154 below) because of his political philosophy, which is consistent with their religious beliefs, al-Farabi has received much attention and acclaim in recent times in the West, where he is sometimes hailed as the most original thinker among the Islamic philosophers. The Andalusian philosopher-physician-scientist, Ibn-Rushd (d. 1198), known in the West as Averroës, seems to have made the greatest impact on European thought, especially among the Scholastics, such as Thomas Aquinas (d. 1274) and Albertus Magnus (d. 1280). Ibn-Rushd's main contribution lay in his meticulous commentaries on the writings of Aristotle and his conscientious grappling with the perennial question of the relation of revelation to reason [15: 82–112, 125–47, 302–25].

But the person most often deemed the greatest philosopher to write in Arabic is the Persian-born Ibn-Sina (d. 1037), known in the West by his Latin name, Avicenna. His major philosophical work, the *Kitab al-Shifa'* (Book of Healing), is an encyclopedia of eleventh-century Greek and Islamic learning, ranging from logic and metaphysics to mathematics and science. The philosophical parts he later abridged into a more popular work, the *Kitab al-Najat* (Book of Salvation). Ibn-Sina, also a Neoplatonist, made a major contribution to Oriental and Western philosophy, not so much for his original ideas as for his synthesis and systematic elaboration of the ideas of his predecessors, including especially al-Farabi [15: 147–83].

Mystical ideas began to flow into the stream of Islamic thought as early as the first century AH, when an ascetic pietism arose in the Muslim community. The growing emphasis on the need for obedience to divine law within official Islam was another factor leading Muslim mystics and ascetics, who came to be called Sufis, to turn inward. Calling for a life of love and pure devotion to God, the Sufis developed a spiritual path to God, consisting of a series of 'stages' of piety (*maqamat*) and gnostic-psychological 'states' (*ahwal*), through which each Sufi was to pass. The 'stages' are similar to the *scala perfectionis* of the medieval Christian monks, while the 'states' resemble Hindu and Buddhist concepts, as may be partly seen in the simplified version shown in Table 3.1. The Sufi emphasis on this twofold spiritual path led to a doctrine of 'annihilation' (*fana'*) of the individual in God, exemplified in the famous statement by al-Hallaj (d. 922), 'I am the Truth', Truth being one of the names or attributes of God and a cognate of the term translated in the table as 'The Reality'. The idea that there are various levels of Islamic piety, and that only a few of the elite can reach the highest goal, led to a concept of sainthood in Islam, along with the related belief that saints could perform miracles.

The Sufi tradition within Islam also stands out for its distinctive practices. While orthodox Islam frowns upon any use of music in religious rituals, Sufi orders throughout the Islamic world, particularly in Turkey, Iran and the Indo-Pakistani region, have developed a wide variety of ritual observances involving singing, drums and other musical instruments, and dance. Music is used in ritual processions, often commemorating the birthday (*mawlid*)

Table 3.1. The Sufi mystical path and the Christian *scala perfectionis*

The Sufi mystical path according to al-Sarraj's *Book of the Radiances of Sufism*:	The *scala perfectionis* according to the fourteenth-century *Theologia Germanica*:
I *The Law*	I *Purification*
1. Repentance	1. Remorse for sin
2. Abstinence	2. Confession of sin
II *The Way*	3. Reconciliation of life
3. Renunciation	II *Enlightenment*
4. Poverty	4. Avoidance of sin
III *The Gnosis*	5. Living life of virtue and good works
5. Patience	
6. Trust in God	6. Bearing trial and temptation
IV *The Reality*	III *Union*
7. Satisfaction	7. Pureness and integrity of heart
	8. Love
	9. Meditation on God

of the founder of the order. Each order also developed its own distinctive ritual observance called a *dhikr*, a Qur'anic term meaning 'remembrance (of God)'. These rituals often include some form of dance, the best known in the West being that of the Turkish Mevlevi order, often called the 'whirling dervishes', whose cosmic dance around their master (*shaykh*) simulates the rotation of the planets around the sun. Sufi belief and practice often degenerated into saint cults and superstition that were clearly outside the realm of Islamic orthodoxy.

During the two centuries from the time of the famous al-Junayd of Baghdad (d. 911), said to be the greatest orthodox exponent of the 'sober' type of Sufism, to the even more celebrated al-Ghazali (d. 1111), said to be the most original thinker that Islam produced and its greatest theologian, there was a steadily growing reform movement within Sufism. Al-Ghazali, an Ash'arite theologian (i.e. a follower of al-Ash'ari) and a master of the Sufi way, effected a reform of both paths, rejecting the radical Sufi idea of 'annihilation' and such popular practices as the veneration of saints, while bringing about a major reorientation and revival of orthodox Islam. Al-Ghazali's synthesis between Sufi and Sunni Islam provided a permanent bond between these two traditions [44: XIII].

Al-Ghazali also brought about a synthesis between theology and philosophy, deeply affecting the course of subsequent Islamic thought. In his famous work, *The Inconsistency of the Philosophers*, he attacked the Neoplatonism of earlier Islamic philosophers such as al-Farabi and Ibn-Sina, while accepting some aspects of Aristotelian thought, especially syllogistic logic. Just as al-Ash'ari overcame the first wave of Greek influence by combining Mu'tazilite methods and Hanbalite views, so al-Ghazali overcame the second wave, that is, the philosophical movement that culminated in Ibn-Sina, by combining Aristotelian methods and Ash'arite views. Al-Ghazali's accomplishment in bringing together Ash'arite theology and elements of Aristotelian philosophy and Sufi mysticism brought about the last great synthesis in the dialectical process that established the Sunni orthodoxy of the great majority of Muslims [15: 244–61].

Some Muslims, however, chose to remain outside the fold of Sunni orthodoxy. The largest minority group, the Shi'ites, take their name from their identification as the 'party of 'Ali' (*shi'at 'Ali*), the cousin and son-in-law of Muhammad. The Shi'a began as a political movement among those who supported 'Ali and his descendants (who were also descendants of Muhammad through his daughter, Fatima) as the only legitimate successors of Muhammad as heads of the Muslim community. With the success of the Umayyads and the 'Abbasids and the rise of Sunni Islam, the Shi'a became a separate religious community, eventually centring their activities in Iran. They rejected the Sunni view that orthodoxy should be determined by a 'consensus' (*ijma'*) of the religious authorities, and developed in its place the doctrine that there was an infallible *imam* ('leader' or 'guide') for each generation. These Imams, 'Ali and a direct line of his descendants, were the only source of religious instruction and guidance. According to the majority of Shi'ites, called Imamites or Twelvers, the line of succession of Imams proceeded as shown in Figure 3.6. When the twelfth Imam mysteriously disappeared in 878 the Imamate came to an end and the collective body of Shi'ite 'religious scholars' or ulema assumed his office awaiting his return as the 'rightly guided one' (*al-Mahdi*). The present ayatullahs (meaning 'signs of God') see themselves as joint caretakers of the office of the Imam, who is to return at the end of time. The Shi'ites also developed their own theology, Qur'an commentaries, legal system and distinctive manner of performing the various Islamic rituals. They are thus by intention clearly set apart from the majority Sunnis [40].

The second largest group of Shi'ites are called Ismaelis or Seveners, because of their contention that the rightful seventh and last Imam was not Musa al-Kazim, but his elder brother Isma'il (Ismael) who died as a child. This sect arose sometime in the ninth century, possibly as late as the time of the

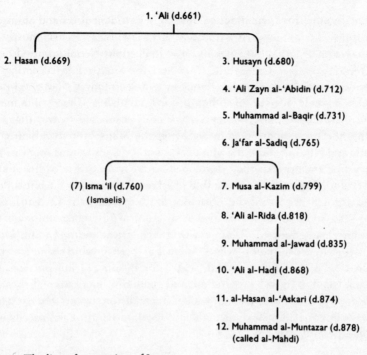

Figure 3.6 The line of succession of Imams

death or disappearance of the twelfth Imam, al-Mahdi. The Ismaelis developed their own distinctive ideas, based on Neoplatonism and the concept of gnosis or hidden knowledge passed down to man through emanations from God. The Ismaelis flourished in the tenth century and were influential in the establishment of the Fatimid dynasty in Egypt, Palestine and Syria. They have also been active missionaries for Islam and have spread especially to southern Arabia and East Africa. The main body of Ismaelis is divided into two branches, the Musta'lis, whose headquarters are in Bombay, and the Nizaris, led by the Aga Khan. Other offshoots of the Ismaelis include the Nusayris and the Druzes, the latter stemming from belief in the deification of the Fatimid leader al-Hakim (d. 1020), whose return they seek. The Druzes are an esoteric sect, meeting on Thursdays instead of the usual Friday Muslim assembly, holding firmly to monogamous marriage, having their own strict ethical code and distinctive beliefs such as that 'Ali was an incarnation of God. The Hashshashin (Assassins) should also be mentioned briefly. They, too, broke off from the Ismaelis in Syria during the period of the early Crusades in the eleventh century. They received their name from their use of hashish, and became famous for their practice of seizing Crusader forts and assassinating Christians. Today, known as Khojas or Mawlas, they live mostly in the Bombay area of India, but some live also in northern Syria, Iran and Zanzibar [40: 78–83].

Besides these clearly defined Islamic sects and a number of others like them, there is a wide variety of other groups involving Islam. In some cases Islamic and non-Islamic elements have been combined to form syncretistic groups, the most notable example being the Sikhs of India, who combine Islamic and Hindu beliefs and practices. In other cases groups began as Islamic reform movements, but then developed so far from orthodoxy that they are now excluded by most from the fold of Islam, for example the Babis, founded in the 1840s in Iran, and the Ahmadiyyans, especially the Qadians, founded in the 1880s in India. There are also many cultural differences among orthodox Muslims throughout the Islamic world. In Africa, India, China, Indonesia and virtually every region where Islam has been established, local cultural features have been incorporated. Thus, for instance, Islam in Africa looks African, Islam in India looks Indian, and Islam in China looks Chinese. These cultural differences are seen not only in their distinctive art and architecture, but also in variations in the rituals and local varieties of popular beliefs [21 vol. II, especially 329–68; 532–74].

Modern Developments

In modern times traditional Islam has been challenged by a bewildering array of forces, from outside and inside the Muslim community. The strongest outside forces have been political, economic and social, and have come from the West. A large part of the Islamic world, from North Africa to Indonesia, came under European, colonial rule. With the rise of nationalism among Islamic peoples and the establishment of independent states, there has been a continuing struggle for control among the various factions, some wanting secular states with Western-style law, education etc., while others demand some form of Islamic state where traditional Muslim life can continue unhampered. The most vigorous outside force challenging Islam during the twentieth century has been socialist ideology, both Marxist and non-Marxist. Muslim response to these outside forces has taken a variety of forms, and the struggle within the Islamic community has given rise to a number of competing movements and trends.

EARLY REVIVALIST REFORM

The first throbs of new life in Islam after a period of several centuries came in the form of revivalist reform movements in Arabia, India and parts of

Africa during the late eighteenth and early nineteenth centuries. One of the first and most influential of these movements was established in central Arabia through the tireless efforts of Muhammad b. 'Abd-al-Wahhab (d. 1792), who set out to purify Islam from foreign accretions. He argued that Muslims should return to the simple beliefs and practices that prevailed during Muhammad's lifetime. In their militancy and puritanism the Wahhabis were not unlike the Kharijites of early Islam with their call for a pure Islam regulated by a literal interpretation of the Qur'an. The Wahhabis revived the conservative legal school of Ahmad b. Hanbal and elevated it to a position of influence it had never enjoyed before. They joined forces with the family of Su'ud who, from their capital at Riyadh in central Arabia, captured and 'purified' Mecca in 1806 and continued to flourish until 1818 when their power was broken by the famous governor of Egypt, Muhammad 'Ali. At the beginning of the twentieth century Su'udi power began to be restored in central Arabia, and in 1932 'Abd-al-'Aziz b. Su'ud established the Kingdom of Su'udi (or Saudi) Arabia. Since then Wahhabi beliefs and practices have enjoyed official sanction throughout Arabia, including the holy cities of Mecca and Medina, from which they have influenced Muslims throughout the world, especially in the developing areas. The Wahhabis teach that it is polytheism to visit the graves of saints or to seek intercession through a prophet or saint. They are against observance of the Mawlid al-Nabi (Birthday of the Prophet), which is widely celebrated throughout the Islamic world. They hold that it is unbelief to employ allegorical interpretation of the Qur'an or to accept as knowledge anything not confirmed by the Qur'an, the canonical hadith accounts, or strict reasoning. They also discourage such Western innovations as cinemas, tobacco and dancing, and are justly called the Puritans of Islam.

Modern Islamic reform in India began as early as the seventeenth century. After a period of widespread popularity and influence of Sufism, which was responsible for large-scale conversions of Hindus to Islam, the orthodox Muslims found a champion in Ahmad Sirhindi (d. 1625), who attacked the philosophical monism of Sufi extremists such as Ibn-al-'Arabi, but retained certain Sufi views and techniques in a system that stressed the traditional Islamic values and Islamic law. Sirhindi's reforms were later espoused and enforced by the Muslim ruler and strong defender of Sunni orthodoxy in India, Aurangzeb (d. 1707). A half century later Indian Islam found a new intellectual leader in Shah Wali-Allah of Delhi (d. 1762), who, like Ibn-'Abd-al-Wahhab in Arabia, was concerned with 'purifying' Islam from un-Islamic beliefs and practices and returning to the simple teachings of early Islam. His system stressed social and economic justice with a broad humanistic base, but he also retained a Sufi interpretation of the universe. A later disciple, Sayyid Ahmad of Bareli, transformed this intellectual reform school into an active *jihad* (holy war) movement, which has sometimes been called the Wahhabi movement of India. After returning from a pilgrimage to Mecca, Sayyid Ahmad recruited an army and captured a large part of north-west India from the Sikhs. Muslim rule in India continued until 1858 when the great Mughal empire was brought to an end by the British.

The nineteenth century witnessed the birth of several reform movements in Africa. As in India, these movements combined the call to return to the simple teachings of early Islam with the use of Sufi methods of organization and propagation of ideas. The Idrisi order, founded by Ahmad b. Idris (d. 1837), rejected the Sufi idea of union with God, and instead proposed a union with the spirit of Muhammad as the only legitimate goal of Islamic mysticism. Ibn-Idris was not only a practising Sufi but also a specialist in Islamic law. Like Ibn-'Abd-al-Wahhab, he rejected the classical Islamic concept of 'consensus' (*ijma'*) and insisted on the right of 'individual opinion' (*ijtihad*) for himself. From the Idrisi order sprang other independent orders, the most important being the Sanusiyya, founded in 1837 by the Algerian disciple of Ibn-Idris, Muhammad b. 'Ali al-Sanusi (d. 1859), who established his own Sufi-type ritual and organized over twenty centres or cells (zawiyas), mainly in North Africa. Like Ibn-Idris, al-Sanusi claimed the right of *ijtihad* and thus made legal rulings on economic and social matters for his followers. His teaching emphasized the goal of living the good life in this world, as contrasted with the other-worldly stress that often characterized orthodox Islam. The Sanusi order provided an activist social-reform programme involving political action. It was active in pan-Islamic and anti-colonial causes including the liberation of Libya from Italian rule. When the Kingdom of Libya was founded in 1951 (it lasted until 1969, see page 161 below) the leader of the Sanusi order at that time became Idris I, the first king of the new nation.

These revivalist reform movements shared several characteristics, including a deep concern with the social and moral degeneration of Muslim society, a call to return to 'original Islam' and shed the later accretions especially of popular Sufism, a rejection of the idea that true Islam reached its final form in medieval times, an acceptance of *ijtihad* and new ideas, and a willingness to carry out revivalist reform through armed force (*jihad*) if necessary [34: XII].

MODERNIST REFORM

In the mid nineteenth century, reform of a definitely modernist mode began to make significant inroads into Muslim life and thought, especially in India and Egypt. In India Muslims were boycotting the government schools and consequently shutting themselves out of government service and other employment, mainly because they considered British-ruled India as a non-Muslim society, literally an 'abode of war' (*dar al-harb*). Sayyid Ahmad Khan (d. 1898) saw that Muslims were only hurting themselves, so he encouraged loyalty to the British, arguing that Muslims in India lived in a society in which they were free to practise their religion as they pleased. He urged Muslims to pursue modern education as a means of bringing themselves into the modern world, and in 1875 he founded a college, now the University of Aligarh, where all that was best in Western thought could be taught, to women as well as to men, in an Islamic atmosphere. He insisted that modern Muslims should be free to interpret and adapt traditional Islamic beliefs and practices in the light of reason and modern science, and he further argued that Islam and science could not be contradictory. For instance, he encouraged Muslims to rethink traditional Islamic practice regarding polygamy and slavery, which he saw as social evils. His influence continues to be strong among Indian and Pakistani Muslims.

Another prominent Indian reformer was the Shi'ite jurist, Amir 'Ali (d. 1928), who was also British-trained and educated. His book, *The Spirit of Islam*, still widely read by Muslims and non-Muslims alike, has had widespread influence on contemporary Muslim life and thought. Many of his views are now generally accepted, at least by Western-oriented Muslims, even though he, like Sayyid Ahmad Khan, was severely criticized as a modernist by the ulema of his day. Amir 'Ali remained orthodox in most aspects, but he devised modern, rational explanations for the meaning of the Salat, fasting and other religious duties, and he called for sweeping changes in certain social institutions that had long characterized traditional Muslim life, for instance, the abolition of slavery and polygamy. His justification for these changes lay in his central thesis that Islam, properly understood, embodies certain moral and social values that tend towards modernization. He argued that, while the spiritual teachings of the Qur'an are eternal and changeless, the specific Qur'anic regulations of Muslim life were not intended to be permanent. They represented great steps forward in Muhammad's time, establishing a pattern of progress that God intended to continue through the centuries. Thus, when society as a whole had made sufficient progress, it was God's intention that such institutions as slavery and polygamy should be abolished. He also went further than any of his followers were prepared to go in regarding Muhammad as the author of the Qur'an, arguing that this was the view of the early generations of Muslims. And he urged Muslims to read the Qur'an on its own and interpret it for themselves, without the unnecessary burden of official interpretations that were placed upon it in medieval times [13: IV].

Meanwhile, in the Middle East similar concerns were being expressed by the leading Egyptian modernist of the period, Muhammad 'Abduh (d. 1905), who argued that Islam and modern science were completely compatible.

Influenced on this point by Jamal al-Din al-Afghani (d. 1897), 'Abduh urged Muslims to cultivate modern philosophical and scientific academic disciplines and expand the curricula of Islamic educational institutions. He was especially well situated to effect such reforms after being appointed head of the thousand-year-old mosque school, and now university, al-Azhar in Cairo. Trained as a theologian along traditional lines, 'Abduh became convinced that faith and reason were not only compatible, but that both must be utilized in order to understand the world and man. He sought to reform Islamic thought and modernize Islamic practice so Islam could survive in the modern world and meet the needs of the younger generations of Muslims who were being introduced to Western ideas. 'Abduh saw his main task to be a restatement of the basic tenets of Islam in terms that were acceptable to the modern mind. One of the best-known examples of his method and concerns involves the Qur'anic teaching on polygamy. 'Abduh argued that the well-known verse that seems to allow a man to have up to four wives (4.4/3) must be interpreted in light of another verse (4.129/128). Since the first says a man may have more than one wife only if he can treat them equally, and the second says that it is impossible to treat two or more wives equally, the real teaching of the Qur'an is that a man should have only one wife [34: XIII].

CURRENT DEVELOPMENTS

The twentieth century has seen the formation of a variety of Islamic groups and movements, which have either continued or reacted against the concerns and programmes of the nineteenth- and early twentieth-century Muslim modernists. Several of these new movements have been active in social and political matters, as well as being very vocal in expressing their views through a variety of journals, pamphlets and books. In Egypt the legacy of Muhammad 'Abduh continued for a while in a movement called the Salafiyya (the Founding Fathers), led by Muhammad Rashid Rida (d. 1935), who completed 'Abduh's Qur'an commentary and published it in an influential journal he founded, called al-Manar (The Lighthouse). The Salafiyya, a group of conservative reform leaders who saw themselves as Neo-Hanbalites, called for some social and legal reforms, while distrusting the freedom for radical change espoused by the 'modernists'. The movement drifted towards a fundamentalist and anti-intellectualist position and gradually died out. The direct heir of its legacy was the Muslim Brotherhood, founded in Ismailia, Egypt, by Hasan al-Banna' (d. 1949), who in his student days in Cairo was a follower of Rashid Rida. Al-Banna' continued the journal al-Manar for a while after the death of its founder, but he came to sense that the task of revitalizing Muslim society demanded an active campaign among the masses, rather than literary, intellectual ventures. He thus organized some fifty centres throughout Egypt for classes and discussion groups, and eventually the movement spread to Syria, Palestine, the Sudan and other parts of the Arab world. In Egypt it became more and more political in its activities until 1954, when it was banned along with other political parties after the revolution. In recent years sentiment towards the concerns and aims of the Brotherhood has been revived in Egypt and other countries, often coupled with anti-Western views, but the movement remains frustrated and virtually powerless to effect changes of policy within the various governments [13: 31–47, 110–20].

The Indo-Pakistani equivalent of the Muslim Brotherhood is the Islamic Party (*Jama'at-i Islami*), founded in 1941 by the energetic and prolific Abu-l-A'la al-Mawdudi (d. 1979). Pakistan, meaning the 'nation of the pure (*pak*)', was established in 1947 as a new experiment in modern Muslim statehood. The idea of Pakistan, proposed by the philosopher-poet Muhammad Iqbal (d. 1938) and later put into effect by Muhammad Ali Jinnah, Pakistan's first President, was to carve out the Muslim majority areas from British India and form an independent state for Muslims. Jinnah, who was not a particularly religious man and did not have in mind a theocratic state ruled by mullahs, died in 1948 before a constitution could be adopted. The absence of strong, positive leadership since then and the lack of a consensus among the politicians have prevented the realization of any of the various dreams of Pakistan as an ideal Muslim state. Al-Mawdudi's conservative Islamic Party at first opposed the idea of establishing Pakistan, arguing that Islam was a universal force that should maintain its presence and strength in India. Since 1947 the Islamic Party in Pakistan, like the Muslim Brotherhood in Egypt, has been politically ineffective. But, unlike the Brotherhood, the Islamic Party has not been purely activist. Al-Mawdudi developed a theoretical basis for its social and political programmes and led in a vigorous educational campaign. Islamic Party publications, many by al-Mawdudi himself, have had widespread influence outside Pakistan, for instance among Muslims living in Europe and North America [13: 120–24].

The twentieth century has also seen the disestablishment of the Ottoman Empire and the caliphate, along with the establishment of a secular state in Turkey (led by Kemal Atatürk in 1923), while Islamic revolutionary regimes have been established in the Sudan (led by Jaafar al-Numeiry in 1969), Libya (led by Muammar al-Qadhafi in 1969) and Iran (led by Ayatullah Khumaini in 1979). Each country and geographical region has its own unique problems and opportunities for Islam. It is clear that Islam is today a vibrant, living force that will continue to hold its own against the onslaught of Marxist and other socialist pressures. At the present time we are witnessing dramatic changes in the political and social structures that constitute the Islamic world, from

Morocco and Senegal to Indonesia and the Philippines, so that the Islam of future decades will appear just as different from the Islam of today as today's Islam appears from that of past centuries.

APPENDIX A   *Key Dates in the History of Islam*

(d. = 'death of')

c. 570	Birth of Muhammad
622	The Hijra or Emigration to Medina (622 CE = 1 AH)
624	Battle of Badr, first Muslim major victory in battle
630	Battle of Hunayn, last battle led by Muhammad
632	d. the Prophet Muhammad
632–4	Caliphate of Abu Bakr, Muhammad's first 'successor' (caliph)
634–44	Caliphate of 'Umar
639	Muslim conquest of Egypt
644–56	Caliphate of 'Uthman
c. 651	'Uthman issued official recension of the Qur'an
656–61	Caliphate of 'Ali, cousin and son-in-law of Muhammad
661–750	Umayyad dynasty ruled from Damascus
680	Battle of Karbala and death of Husayn b. 'Ali
728	d. the theologian Hasan al-Basri
748	d. the early rationalist Mu'tazilite, Wasil b. 'Ata'
750–1258	'Abbasid dynasty ruled from Baghdad
756–1037	Umayyad dynasty in Spain
767	d. Abu Hanifa, founder of the Hanafite legal rite
785	The great mosque at Cordova built
786–809	Caliphate of the great Harun al-Rashid
795	d. Malik b. Anas, founder of the Malikite legal rite
813–33	Caliphate of al-Ma'mun and controversies with the Mu'tazilites
820	d. al-Shafi'i, founder of the Shafi'ite legal rite
834	d. Ibn-Hisham, author of the biography of Muhammad
845	d. Ibn-Sa'd, author of the *Tabaqat*
855	d. Ahmad b. Hanbal, founder of the Hanbalite legal rite
861	d. the caliph al-Mutawakkil, with whom orthodoxy triumphed
870	d. the Traditionist al-Bukhari
875	d. the Traditionist Muslim
878	Twelfth Shi'ite Imam died or disappeared

886	d. the Traditionist Ibn-Maja
888	d. the Traditionist Abu-Dawud
892	d. the Traditionist al-Tirmidhi
909–1171	Fatimid dynasty in northern Africa
915	d. the Traditionist al-Nasa'i
923	d. the historian and Qur'an commentator, al-Tabari
935	d. the theologian al-Ash'ari
944	d. the theologian al-Maturidi
951	d. the philosopher al-Farabi
969	Fatimid conquest of Egypt
1013	d. the theologian al-Baqillani
1037	d. Ibn-Sina (Avicenna)
1037–1492	Moorish dynasties rule in Spain
1055	The Seljuq Tughril Beg takes over rule in Baghdad
1099	Capture of Jerusalem by the Crusaders
1111	d. the theologian al-Ghazali
1138	d. the philosopher Ibn-Bajja (Avempace)
1193	d. Saladin, the Muslim victor over the Crusaders
1198	d. the philosopher Ibn-Rushd (Averroës)
1209	d. the theologian and Qur'an commentator, Fakhr al-Din al-Razi
1240	d. the Sufi master Ibn-al-'Arabi
1254–1517	Mamluk rule in Egypt
1258	Hulagu the Mongol takes Baghdad
1273	d. the Sufi master Jalal al-Din al-Rumi
1277	d. the Traditionist al-Nawawi
1316	d. the Qur'an commentator al-Baydawi
1326	d. the theologian Ibn Taymiyya
1336	Compilation of the *Mishkat al-Masabih*
1406	d. the historian Ibn-Khaldun
1453	Fall of Constantinople to the Turks
1492	Fall of Granada and end of Moorish dominion in Spain
1505	d. the historian and Qur'an scholar, Jalal al-Din al-Suyuti
1517	Ottoman sultan, Selim I, assumed title of Caliph
1625	d. Ahmad Sirhindi of India
1762	d. Shah Wali-Allah of Delhi
1792	d. Ibn-'Abd-al-Wahhab, founder of Wahhabis
1837	d. Ahmad b. Idris, founder of the Idrisi order
1858	End of Muslim Mughal rule in India
1859	d. al-Sanusi, founder of the Sanusi order
1875	Islamic university founded in Aligarh, India
1881	Muhammad Ahmad declared himself Mahdi in the Sudan

1897   d. Jamal al-Din al-Afghani
1898   d. Sayyid Ahmad Khan
1902   Ibn-Su'ud begins conquest of Arabia
1905   d. Muhammad 'Abduh
1922   Last Ottoman sultan deposed by Atatürk
1923   Standard edition of the Qur'an published in Cairo
1924   Caliphate abolished
1928   d. Sayyid Amir 'Ali, author of *The Spirit of Islam*
1929   Muslim Brotherhood founded by Hasan al-Banna'
1932   Islamic, Wahhabi kingdom of Saudi Arabia established
1935   d. Muhammad Rashid Rida, founder of *al-Manar*
1941   Jama'at-i Islami founded in India by al-Mawdudi
1947   Pakistan founded as an Islamic state
1969   Islamic socialist regime established in Libya by al-Qadhafi
1979   Islamic revolutionary regime established in Iran by Khumaini
1979   d. Abu-l-A'la al-Mawdudi

APPENDIX B   *The Islamic World*

Approximate Muslim populations and percentages of total populations in countries where Islam is dominant or is a significant minority are as follows (source: [47a]):

THE MIDDLE EAST

	millions	%		millions	%
Turkey	41·1	98	Lebanon	1·4	51
Iran	34·1	98	Kuwait	1·0	93
Afghanistan	14·4	99	Oman	0·8	100
Iraq	11·2	95	West Bank	0·6	80
Saudi Arabia	7·2	95	Gaza	0·4	98
Syria	6·8	87	Israel	0·4	8
Yemen Arab Republic	5·5	99	Bahrain	0·3	91
Jordan	2·7	93	United Arab Emirates	0·2	92
Democratic Yemen	1·6	90	Qatar	0·1	100

THE REST OF ASIA

	millions	%		millions	%
Indonesia	123·2	90	Philippines	2·3	5
India	80·0	13	Thailand	2·0	4
Pakistan	72·3	97	Burma	1·3	4
Bangladesh	70·8	85	Sri Lanka	1·0	7
U.S.S.R.	50·0	19	Singapore	0·4	15
China	17·9	2	Brunei	0·1	60
Malaysia	6·5	50	Mongolia	0·1	10

NORTH AND SAHARAN AFRICA

	millions	%		millions	%
Egypt	35·4	91	Niger	4·2	85
Morocco	18·3	99	Mali	3·5	60
Algeria	17·3	97	Libya	2·6	98
Sudan	11·7	72	Chad	2·1	50
Tunisia	6·1	99	Mauritania	1·4	96

EAST AND SUB-SAHARAN AFRICA

	millions	%		millions	%
Nigeria	31·3	47	Sierre Leone	1·0	30
Ethiopia	11·8	40	Malawi	0·8	15
Senegal	4·3	82	Uganda	0·7	6
Tanzania	3·8	24	Madagascar	0·6	7
Somalia	3·4	99	Gambia	0·5	90
Guinea	3·1	65	Zaire	0·5	2
Ghana	2·0	19	Comoro Islands	0·3	80
Ivory Coast	1·8	25	Liberia	0·3	15
Upper Volta	1·4	22	Guinea-Bissau	0·2	30
Kenya	1·3	9	Mauritius	0·2	17
Cameroon	1·0	15	Togo	0·2	7
Mozambique	1·0	10	Central African Republic	0·1	5

BALKANS (EXCLUDING EUROPEAN TURKEY)

	millions	%
Yugoslavia	4·1	19
Albania	1·8	70
Bulgaria	0·9	11

APPENDIX C   *Islamic Calendar*

THE MONTHS

1. Muharram (formerly, Safar I)
2. Safar (formerly, Safar II)
3. Rabi' I
4. Rabi' II
5. Jumada I
6. Jumada II

7. Rajab
8. Sha'ban
9. Ramadan
10. Shawwal
11. Dhu-l-Qa'da
12. Dhu-l-Hijja

PRINCIPAL EVENTS OF THE ISLAMIC YEAR

1 Muharram	New Year's Day
10 Muharram	Ashura Day, voluntary fast day for Sunnis; commemoration of battle of Karbala for Shi'ites
16 Muharram	Imamat Day (for Ismaili Khojas only)
12 Rabi' I	Mawlid al-Nabi (Birthday of the Prophet)
23 Jumada II	Birthday of Aga Khan IV (Ismaelis only)
27 Rajab	Laylat al-Mi'raj ('Night of the Ascent' of Muhammad to heaven)
1 Ramadan	Beginning of the month of fasting
27 Ramadan	Laylat al Qadr ('Night of Power', commemorating the sending down of the Qur'an to Muhammad)
1 Shawwal	'Id al-Fitr (Feast of the Breaking of the Fast)
8–13 Dhu-l-Hijja	Annual Pilgrimage ceremonies in and near Mecca
10 Dhu-l-Hijja	'Id al-Adha (Feast of the Sacrifice) – also called 'Id al-Hajj (Feast of the Pilgrimage)

APPENDIX D   *Islamic and Christian Calendars*

Prevailing Christian calendar dates for the first day of given Islamic years are as follows:

1 AH	16 July 622	800	24 September 1397
100	3 August 718	900	2 October 1494
200	11 August 815	1000	19 October 1591
300	18 August 912	1100	26 October 1688
400	25 August 1009	1200	4 November 1785
500	2 September 1106	1300	12 November 1882
600	10 September 1203	1400	21 November 1979
700	16 September 1300		

The Gregorian calendar dates equivalent to the first day of the Islamic year and the first day of Ramadan, the month of fasting, are as follows:

	1st Muharram	1st Ramadan
1400 AH	21 November 1979	14 July 1980
1401	9 November 1980	3 July 1981
1402	30 October 1981	23 June 1982
1403	19 October 1982	12 June 1983
1404	8 October 1983	31 May 1984
1405	27 September 1984	21 May 1985
1406	16 September 1985	10 May 1986
1407	6 September 1986	30 April 1987
1408	26 August 1987	18 April 1988
1409	14 August 1988	7 April 1989
1410	4 August 1989	28 March 1990
1411	24 July 1990	17 March 1991
1412	13 July 1991	5 March 1992
1413	2 July 1992	23 February 1993
1414	21 June 1993	12 February 1994
1415	10 June 1994	1 February 1995
1416	31 May 1995	22 January 1996
1417	19 May 1996	10 January 1997
1418	9 May 1997	31 December 1997
1419	28 April 1998	20 December 1998
1420	17 April 1999	9 December 1999
1421	6 April 2000	29 November 2000

BIBLIOGRAPHY

1. 'ABDUH, MUHAMMAD, *The Theology of Unity* (tr. I. Musa'ad and K. Cragg), London, Allen & Unwin, 1966

2. ADAMS, C J., 'Islamic religious tradition', *The Study of the Middle East* (ed. L. Binder), New York, London, Wiley, 1976, pp. 29–87

3. AHMAD, K. (ed.), *Islam: Its Meaning and Message*, London, Islamic Council of Europe, 1975

4. ANDRAE, T., *Mohammed: The Man and His Faith* (tr. T. Menzel), London, Allen & Unwin/New York, Scribner, 1936

5. ARBERRY, A. J. (tr.), *Muslim Saints and Mystics: Episodes from the Tadhkirat al-Auliya' by Farid al-Din Attar*, London, Routledge/Chicago, Ill., University of Chicago Press, 1966

6. AZAD, A. K., *The Tarjumān al-Qur'ān* (tr. S. A. Latif), 2 vols., Bombay, London, New York, Asia Publishing House, 1962–7

7. BALJON, J. M. S., *Modern Muslim Koran Interpretation, 1880–1960*, Leiden, Brill, 1961

8. BOSWORTH, C. E., *The Islamic Dynasties*, 2nd edn, Edinburgh, Edinburgh University Press, 1980

9. BROCKELMANN, C., *History of the Islamic Peoples* (tr. J. Carmichael and M. Perlmann), New York, Capricorn, 1960; tr. prev. publ. New York, Putnam, 1947/London, Routledge, 1949

10. AL-BUKHARI, *Ṣaḥīḥ al-Bukharī* (tr. M. A. Khan), 9 vols., Medina, Islamic Bookstore, 1976–9

11. CALVERLEY, E. E., *Worship in Islam, Being a Translation, with Commentary and Introduction, of al-Ghazzali's Book of the Iḥyā' on the Worship*, London, Luzac, 1925, 1957; Madras, Christian Literature Society for India, 1925

12. COULSON, N. J., *A History of Islamic Law*, Edinburgh, Edinburgh University Press, 1964

13. CRAGG, K., *Counsels in Contemporary Islam*, Edinburgh, Edinburgh University Press, 1965

14. ESPOSITO, J. L., *Women in Muslim Family Law*, Syracuse, NY, Syracuse University Press, 1982

15. FAKHRY, M., *A History of Islamic Philosophy*, New York, Columbia University Press, 1970

16. GÄTJE, H., *The Qur'ān and Its Exegesis: Selected Texts with Classical and Modern Muslim Interpretations* (tr. and ed. A. T. Welch), London, Routledge/Berkeley, Calif., University of California Press, 1976

17. GEERTZ, C., *Islam Observed: Religious Development in Morocco and Indonesia*, New Haven, Conn., Yale University Press, 1968

18. GOLDZIHER, I., *Introduction to Islamic Theology and Law* (tr. A. and R. Hamori), Princeton, NJ, Princeton University Press, 1981

19. GUILLAUME, A. (tr.), *The Life of Muhammad: A Translation of Ibn Isḥāq's Sīrat Rasūl Allāh*, London, Oxford University Press, 1955

20. HAYKAL, M. H., *The Life of Muhammad* (tr. I. R. al-Faruqi), n.p., North American Trust Publications, 1976

21. HODGSON, M. G. S., *The Venture of Islam: Conscience and History in a World Civilization*, 3 vols., Chicago, Ill., University of Chicago Press, 1974

22. HOLT, P. M., LAMBTON, A. K. S., and LEWIS, B. (eds.), *The Cambridge History of Islam*, 2 vols., Cambridge, Cambridge University Press, 1970

23. IQBAL, SIR MUHAMMAD, *The Reconstruction of Religious Thought in Islam*, Lahore, Muhammad Ashraf, 1968; Delhi, Kitab, n.d.; prev. publ. London, Oxford University Press, 1934

24. JANSEN, J. J. G., *The Interpretation of the Koran in Modern Egypt*, Leiden, Brill, 1974

25. JEFFERY, A. (tr. and ed.), *Islam: Muhammad and His Religion*, New York, Library of Liberal Arts, 1958

26. JEFFERY, A. (tr. and ed.), *A Reader on Islam: Passages from Standard Arabic Writings Illustrative of the Beliefs and Practices of Muslims*, The Hague, Mouton, 1962; repr. New York, Arno, 1980

27. KEDDIE, N. R., *Roots of Revolution: An Interpretative History of Modern Iran*, New Haven, Conn., Yale University Press, 1981

28. KRITZECK, J., and LEWIS, W. H. (eds.), *Islam in Africa*, New York. Van Nostrand-Reinhold, 1969

29. LEVY, R., *The Social Structure of Islam*, Cambridge, Cambridge University Press, 1969; prev. publ. 1957; the 2nd edn of *The Sociology of Islam*

30. MAUDUDI, A. A., *The Meaning of the Qurān*, 4 vols., Lahore, Islamic Publications, 1970–73

31. MUSLIM, ABU AL-ḤUSAYN, *Ṣaḥīḥ Muslim* (tr. A. H. Siddīqī), 4 vols., Lahore, Muhammad Ashraf, 1976, prev. publ. 1972–5

32. NASR, S. H., *Islam and the Plight of Modern Man*, London, New York, Longman, 1975

33. PADWICK, C. E., *Muslim Devotions: A Study of Prayer-Manuals in Common Use*, London, SPCK, 1961

34. RAHMAN, F., *Islam*, 2nd edn Chicago, Ill., University of Chicago Press, 1979

35. ROBSON, J. (tr.), *Mishkat al-Masabih: English Translation with Explanatory Notes*, 4 vols., Lahore, Muhammad Ashraf, 1965–6, prev. publ. 1960–65

36. SCHACHT, J., *An Introduction to Islamic Law*, Oxford, Clarendon Press, 1964

37. SCHACHT, J., *The Origins of Muhammadan Jurisprudence*, Oxford, Clarendon Press, 1950

38. SMITH, WILFRED CANTWELL, *Islam in Modern History*, Princeton, NJ, Princeton University Press, 1957

39. STODDARD, P. H., CUTHELL, D. C., and SULLIVAN, M. W. (eds.), *Change and the Muslim World*, Syracuse, NY, Syracuse University Press, 1981

40. ṬABĀṬABĀ'Ī, M. H., *Shi'ite Islam*, 2nd edn, Albany, NY, State University of New York Press, 1977

41. TRIMINGHAM, J. S., *A History of Islam in West Africa*, London, New York, Oxford University Press, 1962

42. TRIMINGHAM, J. S., *Islam in East Africa*, Oxford, Clarendon Press, 1964; prev. publ. London, Edinburgh House Press, 1962

43. WATT, W. M., *The Formative Period of Islamic Thought*, Edinburgh, Edinburgh University Press, 1973

44. WATT, W. M., *Islamic Philosophy and Theology*, Edinburgh, Edinburgh University Press, 1962, 1979

45. WATT, W. M., *Islamic Political Thought*, Edinburgh, Edinburgh University Press, 1968

46. WATT, W. M., *Muhammad: Prophet and Statesman*, London, Oxford University Press, 1961, 1974

47. WATT, W. M., and WELCH, A. T., *Der Islam*. I: *Mohammed und die Frühzeit – Islamisches Recht – Religiöses Leben*, Stuttgart, Kohlhammer, 1980 (Die Religionen der Menschheit series, vol. 25, 1, ed. C. M. Schröder)

47a. WEEKES, R. (ed.), *Muslim Peoples: A World Ethnographic Survey*, Westport, Conn., Greenwood, 1978

48. WELCH, A. T., 'al-Ḳur'ān', *The Encyclopaedia of Islam*, new edn, V, fasc. 85–6, Leiden, Brill, 1981, pp. 400–429

49. WENSINCK, A. J., *The Muslim Creed: Its Genesis and Historical Development*, Cambridge, Cambridge University Press, 1932; London, Cass, 1965

4   *Zoroastrianism*

MARY BOYCE

Introduction

SOURCES

Zoroastrianism has a long oral tradition. Its prophet Zarathushtra (known in the West as Zoroaster) lived before the Iranians knew of writing, and for many centuries his followers refused to use this alien art for sacred purposes. The Avesta, their collection of holy texts, was finally set down in a specially invented alphabet in the fifth/sixth century CE. Except for the *Gathas*, seventeen hymns composed by Zoroaster, all parts of it are anonymous, the composite works of generations of priestly poets and scholars. Its language, known simply as Avestan, is otherwise unrecorded. It was written down in Persia, under the Sasanian dynasty; and the Sasanian Avesta was a massive compilation in twenty-one books. Only a few copies were made, and in the destruction which later attended the Arab, Turkish and Mongol conquests of Iran all were destroyed. The surviving Avesta consists of liturgies, hymns and prayers. The manuscript tradition goes back to Sasanian times, but the oldest existing manuscript was written in 1323 CE. The Avesta has been printed [1], and translations exist in German, French and English.[1] None can be regarded as authoritative, since research is still constantly producing new insights.

Some Avestan manuscripts have an interlinear translation in Pahlavi, known as the Zand or 'Interpretation'. Pahlavi, the language of Sasanian Persia, was written in a difficult script. There exist in Pahlavi translations and summaries of lost books of the Sasanian Avesta, and also a considerable secondary religious literature. [6] This too is mostly anonymous. Almost all Pahlavi works have been edited and translated, but some of the translations badly need revision.[2] The later religious literature is in Persian, Gujarati and English.

SHORT INTRODUCTION
TO THE HISTORY OF THE FAITH

The internal evidence of the *Gathas* shows that Zoroaster lived before the Iranians conquered the land now named after them, probably, that is, between 1400 and 1200 BCE. [8: 189ff; 9: 1–3; 10: 18ff] The Iranians then, as pastoral nomads, inhabited the south Russian steppes east of the Volga. The prophet succeeded in converting one of the tribal princes, Vishtaspa, and saw his faith take root. It spread among the eastern Iranians, and eventually reached western Iran, which had been settled by the Medes and Persians (see Figure 4.1). It became the state religion of the first Persian Empire (550–531 BCE), founded by Cyrus the Great, its western priests being the famed magi. [9] Its doctrines had great influence then on some of the Persians' subjects, notably the Jews. Direct evidence for Zoroastrian beliefs and practices at this time comes from Persian monuments and inscriptions and from Greek writings. The conquest of the empire by Alexander seems to have done much harm to the oral tradition, with sacred texts being lost through the deaths of priests.

In due course the Parthians, a people of north-eastern Iran, founded another Iranian empire (c. 141 BCE to 224 CE), which again had Zoroastrianism for its state religion [10: 78–100]; and this was succeeded by the second Persian Empire, that of the Sasanians. They created for the faith a strong ecclesiastical organiza-tion, with a numerous priesthood and many temples and colleges. [10: 101–44] With the Arab conquest in the seventh century Islam supplanted Zoroastrian-ism as the state religion of Iran, but it was some 300 years before the Semitic faith became dominant throughout the land.

Towards the end of the ninth century a group of Zoroastrians sailed east in search of religious freedom, settling eventually, in 936, at Sanjan in Gujarat [10: 156f]. Others joined them there, forming the nucleus of the 'Parsi' (Persian) community of India. At first the Parsis prospered only modestly, as farmers and petty traders, spreading northward along the coast as far as Broach and Cambay. But from the seventeenth century, with the coming of European merchants, they advanced rapidly, and by the nineteenth century individuals had amassed huge fortunes. By contrast, the mother-community in Iran (then concentrated around the desert cities of Yazd and Kerman) was enduring ever greater poverty and oppression. The Parsis played a notable part in the develop-ment of Bombay, and by the twentieth century had become a predominantly urban community, with a well-educated middle class. Partly through their help the Iranis were freed from persecution and were able to follow suit, with a thriving community developing in Tehran; but the majority still remain in farming villages. With the end of British rule in India a number of Parsis settled abroad, notably in cities in England, Canada, Australia and the U.S.A. Although prosperous the community is numerically very small (see Figure 4.2).

SCHOLARLY STUDIES OF ZOROASTRIANISM

The Zoroastrians, enclosed as tiny minorities within Muslim and Hindu societies, were unknown to Western scholars until the seventeenth century,

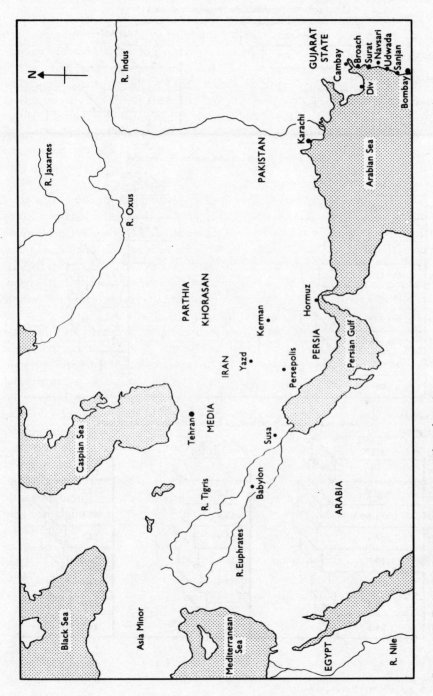

Figure 4.1 Zoroastrianism: some ancient and modern sites

Rural and urban distribution of population of India (1961)

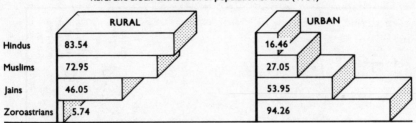

	RURAL	URBAN
Hindus	83.54	16.46
Muslims	72.95	27.05
Jains	46.05	53.95
Zoroastrians	5.74	94.26

Comparison of Parsi population growth in decades

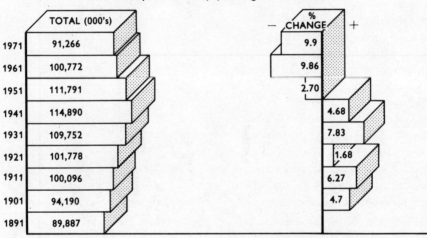

	TOTAL (000's)	% CHANGE
1971	91,266	9.9
1961	100,772	9.86
1951	111,791	2.70
1941	114,890	4.68
1931	109,752	7.83
1921	101,778	1.68
1911	100,096	6.27
1901	94,190	4.7
1891	89,887	

Parsis in Bombay city, percentage compared with that for all India

	INDIA (000's)	BOMBAY (000's)	%
1971	91.3	70.1	69.5
1961	100.8	71.8	69.1
1951	111.8	68.6	61.4
1941	114.9	59.9	52.1
1931	109.8	57.7	52.6
1921	101.8	52.1	51.3
1911	100.1	50.1	50.8
1901	94.2	46.1	49.1

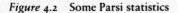

Figure 4.2 Some Parsi statistics

when merchants and other travellers brought back accounts of them. In 1700 an English divine, Thomas Hyde, published a study in Latin of the religion, drawing on these accounts and on meagre literary sources. He respected Zoroaster as a great seer and tried to prove that he had been a strict monotheist, and that Greek evidence about his dualism was misleading. In the eighteenth century a French scholar, Anquetil du Perron, travelled to India and persuaded a Parsi priest to part with Avestan and Pahlavi manuscripts, and to teach him how to read them. His published translations startled Europeans, since they gave evidence not only of dualism, but of the worship of many divine beings through intricate rituals [10]. Most were unwilling to abandon Hyde's interpretation, and so they concluded that Zoroaster's followers must have distorted their prophet's teachings. This theory was strengthened when it was discovered through linguistic studies of the Avesta that the Parsi priests no longer fully understood their holy texts. This was especially true of the *Gathas*, which present enormous difficulties. In the mid nineteenth century a German philologist, M. Haug, realized that these hymns alone represent the words of Zoroaster, although most other Avestan texts are piously attributed to him. Because of their many obscurities it was possible at that stage to interpret the *Gathas* fairly freely, so owing to his preconceptions Haug translated them in a way that supported the idea of Zoroaster's own monotheism and rejection of rites. [12] Thenceforth the theory that all the remaining Avestan and Pahlavi texts represented a corruption of the prophet's teachings became academic dogma in the West.

In the twentieth century a Swedish scholar, H. S. Nyberg, influenced by ethnographic studies, suggested that Zoroaster had been a 'shaman', who composed his hymns in inspired trances [13]; and a Frenchman, G. Dumézil, sought to apply to Zoroastrianism his idea that Indo-European peoples grouped their gods according to three 'functions', corresponding to the social roles of priest-king, warrior and farmer. Much scholarly energy was spent on working out this theory, without generally convincing results. [For an application of his theories to Zoroastrianism see 14: 38ff.]

Meantime some scholars who visited the Parsis were impressed by their high ethical standards and philosophy of life, which seemed to accord with Gathic teachings; and they began to question whether there could really have been a serious break in the tradition. Then philologists discovered allusions to existing beliefs and practices in the *Gathas* themselves, as their vocabulary and style became better understood. The case was thus slowly built up for regarding the Zoroastrians as having been, in fact, strikingly steadfast – as having maintained over three millennia an unbroken tradition, handed down by precept and practice as much as by holy texts. Earlier interpretations of the history of the faith had prevailed too long, however, to be easily discarded, and they still claim their adherents.

Another problem dividing scholars was the date of Zoroaster. Probably during the Parthian period the magi sought to establish when exactly their prophet had lived; and they produced a date equivalent to 558 BCE. This seemed so precise that some scholars accepted it as genuine. Others maintained that it was far too late to fit the facts of the Avesta and early Persian history; and their view now prevails. The date appears in fact to have been calculated some time after the establishment of the Seleucid era in 312/311 BCE [15].

Basic Doctrines

Inhabitants of vast empty steppes, the Iranian priests evolved a severely simple creation myth [8:130ff, 192ff; 10:19ff]. They saw the world as having been made by the gods, from formless matter, in seven stages: first the 'sky' of stone, a firm enclosing shell; then water, filling the bottom of this shell; then earth, lying on the water like a great flat dish; then at its centre the original Plant, and then by it the uniquely created Bull, and the First Man, Gayo-maretan ('Mortal life'); and finally the sun, representing the seventh creation, fire, which stood still above them. Fire was thought to be present too in the other creations, as a hidden life-force. Then the gods made sacrifice. They plucked and pounded the Plant and scattered its essence over the earth, and other plants grew from it. They slew the Bull and Gayo-maretan, and from their seed sprang other animal and human life. Then a line of mountains grew up along the rim of the earth, and at the centre rose the Peak of Hara, around which the sun began to circle, creating night and day. Rain fell, so heavily that the earth was broken into seven regions (*karshvars*). Man lives in the central region, cut off by seas and forests from the other six. One great sea, called Vourukasha ('Having many bays'), is fed by a huge river which pours down ceaselessly from the Peak of Hara (see Figure 4.3). These final details the priestly thinkers evidently took from still more ancient myths, while the threefold sacrifice reflected the three offerings they themselves once made, of a pounded plant (*haoma*), cattle and human victims. Their belief, it seems, was that as long as men continued pious sacrifices and worshipped the gods the world would endure, governed by the principle of *asha*. This represents order in the cosmos and justice and truth among men. As well as venerating 'nature' gods, the Iranians worshipped three great ethical beings whom they called the Ahuras ('Lords'): Ahura Mazda, Lord of Wisdom, and beneath him Mithra and Varuna, Lords of the covenant and oath which, duly kept, bound men together according to *asha*.

Zoroaster was himself a priest, born into this hereditary calling; but in his lifetime, it appears from the *Gathas*, the long-established pastoral society of the Iranians was being shattered. The Bronze Age was then developing among them, and warrior-princes and their followers, equipped with new weapons

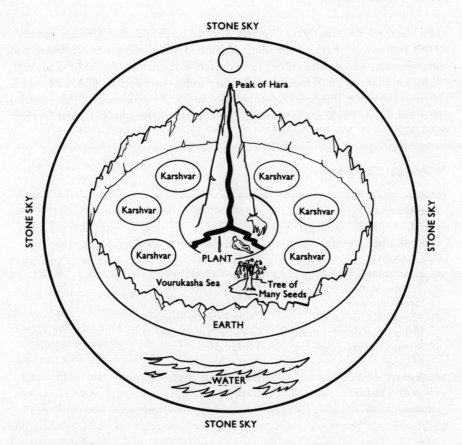

Figure 4.3 The Iranian world picture

and the war-chariot, were indulging in continual warfare and raiding. The prophet's own people seem to have been victims of more advanced and predatory neighbours; and the violence and injustice which he thus saw led Zoroaster to meditate deeply on good and evil, and their origins. In due course he came to experience what he perceived as a series of divine revelations, which led him to preach a new faith. He taught that there was only one eternal God, whom he recognized as Ahura Mazda, a being wholly wise, good and just, but not all-powerful, for in his own words: 'Truly there are two primal Spirits, twins renowned to be in conflict. In thought and word, in act they are two: the good and the bad' (*Yasna* 30.3). God, that is, had an Adversary, Angra Mainyu (the Evil Spirit), likewise uncreated; and it was to overcome him and destroy evil that Ahura Mazda made this world, as a battleground where their forces could meet. He accomplished this through his Holy Spirit, Spenta

Mainyu, and six other great beings whom he evoked, the Amesha Spentas, 'Holy Immortals'. Each of the seven fashioned one of the seven creations, and now protects and dwells within it; and each is at once an aspect of God, and, as his emanation, an independent divinity to be worshipped. Ahura Mazda is transcendent; but through the Holy Spirit he can be immanent in his especial creation, man. Table 4.1 gives the great heptad's names, in the order of their creations.

Table 4.1. The Amesha Spentas

Avestan (Pahlavi)	Approximate English renderings	Creation
1. Khshathra Vairya (Shahrevar)	Desirable Dominion/Power	Sky
2. Haurvatat (Hordad)	Wholeness/Health	Water
3. Spenta Armaiti (Spendarmad)	Holy Devotion/Piety	Earth
4. Ameretat (Amurdad)	Long Life/Immortality	Plants
5. Vohu Manah (Vahman)	Good Purpose/Intent	Cattle
6. Spenta Mainyu (Spenag Menog)	Holy Spirit	Man
7. Asha Vahishta (Ardvahisht)	Best Truth/Righteousness, Order	Fire

The heptad evoked the other lesser Immortals, the *yazatas*, beings 'worthy of worship'. They were the beneficent old gods, including the two lesser Ahuras. Angra Mainyu countered by bringing into being evil spirits, including the *daevas*, ancient amoral gods of war; and with them he attacked the good creations. By Zoroastrian doctrine it was he who destroyed the first Plant, Bull and Man, bringing death into the world, while the Amesha Spentas turned evil to good by creating more life from death. This is their function, to combat evil and strengthen good. Their creations strive instinctively to this same end, all except man, who should do so by deliberate choice, in the light of Zoroaster's revelation. At death each individual will be judged. If his good thoughts, words and deeds outweigh his bad, his soul crosses a broad bridge and ascends to heaven. If not, the bridge contracts and he falls into hell, with its punishments.

The ultimate aim of all virtuous striving is to bring about the salvation of this world. The last days will be marked by increasing wretchedness and cosmic calamities. Then the World Saviour, the Saoshyant, will come in glory. He is to be born of the seed of the prophet, miraculously preserved within a lake, and a virgin mother. There will be a great battle between *yazatas* and *daevas*, good men and bad, ending in victory for the good. The bodies of those who have died earlier will be resurrected and united with their souls, and the Last Judgement will take place. Metals in the mountains will melt and cover the earth in a fiery flood, which will destroy the wicked and purge hell. (By a later softening of this doctrine, first attested in the ninth century CE, the wicked, purified by the ordeal, will survive to join the blessed.) The saved will be given ambrosia to eat, and their bodies will become as immortal as their souls. The kingdom of Ahura Mazda will come on an earth made perfect again, and the blessed will rejoice everlastingly in his presence.

One small modification was early made in the original doctrine: to keep Khshathra Vairya, who was patron of warriors, linked with the substance of their weapons, the substance of the sky was reinterpreted as rock-crystal, which was classified as a metal. This Amesha Spenta thus became lord of metals. In his honour these should be kept burnished, and coins dispensed wisely and generously in charity.

Only one major Zoroastrian heresy is known, Zurvanism, which probably arose in Babylon (then a Persian possession) in the fifth century BCE [9:231– 42]. It was a monism, and its central doctrine was that there was only one uncreated being, Zurvan ('Time'), father of both Ahura Mazda and Angra Mainyu. This was grievous heresy, since a common origin was thus postulated for good and evil. But the Zurvanites held that Zurvan, a remote god, bestowed his powers on his good son, who then created this world. Hence Zurvanites and the orthodox were able to worship together in common veneration of the Creator, Ahura Mazda, despite their doctrinal differences.

Basic Observances

A Zoroastrian has the duty to pray five times daily (at sunrise, noon, sunset, midnight and dawn) in the presence of fire, the symbol of righteousness. [For further on this section see 16, 17 and 18.] He prays standing, and while uttering the appointed prayers (which include verses from the *Gathas*) unties and reties the *kusti*. This is the sacred cord, which should be worn constantly. It goes three times round the waist and is knotted over the sacred shirt (*sedra*). Before praying, the Zoroastrian performs ritual ablutions, for the faith makes cleanliness a part of godliness, seeing all uncleanness as evil. The Zoroastrian purity laws are comprehensive but are now largely neglected by urban dwellers. Nevertheless even they abhor pollution of earth or water, and maintain the strictest cleanliness in their persons and homes. The conviction that unbelievers are necessarily unclean still operates among Parsis and prevents non-Zoroastrians entering fire-temples or being present at Zoroastrian acts of worship.

The ancient veneration of fire among the Iranian peoples evidently centred on the ever-burning hearth fire. The temple cult of fire was, it seems, instituted as late as the fourth century BCE [9: 221–5]. It, too, centres on an ever-burning wood fire, set either in the top of an altar-like pillar or in a metal vessel. There are three grades of sacred fire: the Atash Bahram ('Victorious fire'), which is consecrated with many rites and kept blazing brightly; the Atash-i Aduran ('Fire of fires'), more simply installed and allowed at times to lie dormant beneath its hot ashes; and the Dadgah ('(Fire) in an appointed place'), which is virtually a hearth fire placed in a consecrated building. This may be tended, if necessary, by lay people. There is no obligation on a Zoroastrian to visit a fire-temple, since he may pray before any 'clean' fire; but the sacred fires are much beloved, and in devout families children are taken to them from an early age. Some believers pray regularly at a temple, others attend only on special occasions. Some offering is always made, usually of wood or incense for the fire, with often a money gift for the priests (see Figure 4.4).

Men and women have equal access to the temples, and boys and girls undergo the same initiation into the faith. This usually takes place between the ages of seven and nine among Parsis, twelve and fifteen among Iranis. The occasion, called by Iranis *sedra-pushun* ('putting on the sacred shirt'), by Parsis *naojote* (probably 'being born again'), is an important family one. The child has already learnt the *kusti* prayers. On the day he bathes, drinks a consecrated liquid for inward cleansing and puts on the sacred shirt. The priest then performs the simple ceremony of investing him with the *kusti*, after which relatives dress him in new clothes and give him presents amid general rejoicing. This ceremony takes place at home or in some public hall or gardens, as do weddings. Again before marriage bride and groom undergo a ritual purification and put on new garments. Iranis and Parsis share a common ceremony of marriage, in which Avestan and Pahlavi words are spoken by the officiating priest in the presence of assenting witnesses from the two families. Both communities have in addition a wealth of popular customs, and the festivities last several days.

A birth is also naturally rejoiced at, but there is then concern for purity, and in a few strictly orthodox families the mother is still segregated for forty days. Formerly the infant was given a few drops of consecrated *haoma*-juice soon after birth; but its naming is a simple matter of declaration by parent or priest.

Ceremonies at death are far more important and have a double aim: to isolate the impurity of the dead body and give help to the soul. The body is given into the charge of professionals, who live to some extent segregated lives, as unclean persons. Wrapped in a cotton shroud it is carried on an iron bier, after due prayers by priests, to a stone tower (*dakhma*), where the polluting flesh is quickly devoured by vultures and the bones are bleached by sun and

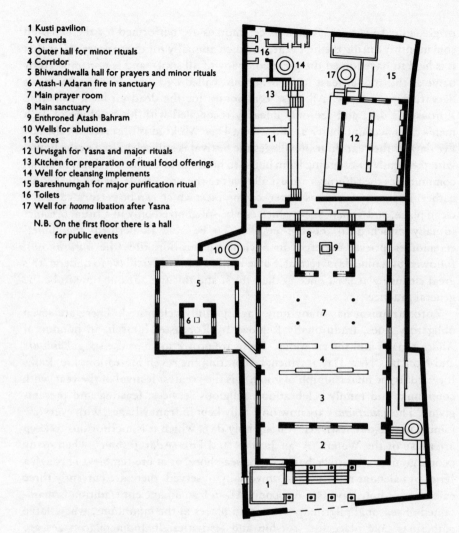

1 Kusti pavilion
2 Veranda
3 Outer hall for minor rituals
4 Corridor
5 Bhiwandiwalla hall for prayers and minor rituals
6 Atash-i Adaran fire in sanctuary
7 Main prayer room
8 Main sanctuary
9 Enthroned Atash Bahram
10 Wells for ablutions
11 Stores
12 Urvisgah for Yasna and major rituals
13 Kitchen for preparation of ritual food offerings
14 Well for cleansing implements
15 Bareshnumgah for major purification ritual
16 Toilets
17 Well for *haoma* libation after Yasna

N.B. On the first floor there is a hall
for public events

Figure 4.4 Ground plan of Anjuman Atash Bahram, Bombay

wind. Mourners follow the bier at a distance, two by two, and afterwards make
ablutions. Some families now prefer cremation (by electrical means), or burial,
with the coffin set in cement to protect the good earth. The funeral should take
place within twenty-four hours; but the soul is held to linger on earth for three
days, during which time priests say prayers and perform ceremonies to help it.
Before dawn on the fourth day family and friends gather to bid it farewell. They
pray and undertake meritorious acts for its sake, for example say extra prayers

or give gifts to charity. Religious ceremonies are performed for the departed soul monthly during the first year, and then annually for thirty years. After that it is held to have joined the great company of all souls, and is remembered by name at the annual feast in their honour, called by Parsis Muktad, by Iranis Farvardigan or Panje. All these ceremonies for the dead go back to before Zoroaster's day, and are only uneasily reconciled with his teaching of each man's own accountability at Judgement Day. Muktad is observed on the last five days of the year. In Irani villages the festival is still celebrated in the home, with the family priest going from house to house to bless the offerings. In urban communities the offerings are usually sent to the fire-temple, where the people gather. Zoroastrianism has 'outer' ceremonies, which can be performed in any clean place, and 'inner' ones, which can be solemnized only in a ritual precinct (usually attached to the fire-temple). To be able to perform the 'inner' ceremonies priests undergo an ancient purification rite (the *barashnom*), followed by a nine days' retreat. Some Irani villages also still try to undergo this great cleansing at least once in their lives, and this used at one time to be the general practice.

Zoroastrianism has many holy days, joyfully celebrated. There are seven obligatory ones, traditionally founded by Zoroaster himself, in honour of Ahura Mazda and the creations. These are now known as the six *gahambars* and No Ruz ('New Day'), which, celebrating the seventh creation, fire, looks forward to the final triumph of good. It is the greatest festival of the year, with communal and family celebrations, religious services, feasting and present-giving. The *gahambars* are now only fully kept in Irani villages, with everyone joining in five-day festivals. Among holy days which it is meritorious to keep are those of the Waters (Aban Jashan) and Fire (Adar Jashan), when many people go to pray at river-banks or the sea-shore, or at fire-temples. Through a series of calendar reforms, not universally observed, there are currently three calendars of holy days (see Appendix A). In Iran an ancient tradition is maintained of seasonal pilgrimages to sacred places in the mountains, where large gatherings take place for worship and festivities. In India pilgrimages are regularly made to the oldest Parsi sacred fire at Udwada, a village on the coast.

Priests and laity remain two distinct groups, though they intermarry. Priests wear white, the colour of purity, and some Parsi laymen also do so on religious occasions. Parsi women wear the sari. In Iran Zoroastrian village women keep a distinctive traditional dress, but in towns all Zoroastrians have now adopted standard clothing. No Zoroastrian women have ever worn the veil. In dietary matters their religion gives Zoroastrians great freedom, in that they are required only to refrain from anything that might belong to the evil countercreation (e.g. a hideous fish). Under Muslim and Hindu pressures many now refrain, however, from pork and beef, and some Parsis are vegetarians by choice.

Popular Customs

Underlying some popular customs is the belief that light is good, darkness evil. [For this section see 18: 219–20 and 17.] A blessing is generally murmured when a light is lit. In village homes the housewife will sprinkle incense on a pan of embers and carry this through all the rooms at dawn or before sunset, in purification. No cock is killed after it has begun to crow, since it is then a holy creature, announcing daybreak. Water is not drawn in villages after dark, nor money exchanged.

Other popular customs arise from respect for the creations and their immanent divinities. A flame is not blown out, but allowed to die. Care is taken not to spill anything on a fire, and if this happens, a penance is performed. Offerings are regularly made and prayers said at sources of pure water (there is one very holy well in Bombay), and in Iran noble trees are venerated. It is held a sin to cut a sapling or kill a young animal (since neither has yet fulfilled its part in the scheme of things). Animals are treated well, especially dogs. By custom, still locally observed, bread is given regularly to a dog before the family eats; and in Vahman month Hindus drive cows into Parsi quarters and the Parsis acquire merit by feeding them.

The devout feel the presence of the *yazatas* everywhere. In Iran at *sedra-pushun* a child takes one of them as its especial guardian, and individual Parsis do the same, praying often to him and lighting lamps at the fire-temple on his feast day. The Iranis have many small shrines dedicated to individual *yazatas*, and on great holy days will visit all the local ones, kindling fire and lamps, and offering incense and prayers. They also regularly dance and sing at the shrines, believing that gladness pleases the divine beings. There are special rites to heal the sick, to restore lost purity, or to help a woman conceive a child. When performed by priests these always include Avestan prayers, in the presence of fire; but village women sometimes perform their own rites, verging on magic, without these elements. Such practices are strongly discouraged by the community elders.

Modern Developments

From about the ninth century Zoroastrians were cut off from contact with general advances in learning, and could do no more than practise and preserve their own faith. Increasing wealth among the Parsis did not bring any real change in this position until the early nineteenth century, when the laity were able to send their sons to Western-type schools in Bombay. [19] A Parsi priest then set up the first printing-press in that city, and Parsi newspapers were published. Soon afterwards a Scottish missionary, J. Wilson, made a determined effort to convert the Bombay Parsis, whom he admired, to Christianity. [For this section see 10: 196ff; 20.] He had studied Avestan and Pahlavi texts in translation, and now made use of the new newspapers for scornful attacks on their contents, especially their dualism. The Parsi laity had had no knowledge of these ancient texts, for they themselves used their Avestan prayers as holy *manthras*, potent but not literally understood. So, much startled, they turned to their priests to rebut Wilson's criticisms. But the priests, who were still trained in wholly traditional fashion, were ill-equipped to meet his challenge. One high priest simply published a restatement of orthodox beliefs, without making any attempt to reinterpret the ancient myths which they incorporated, and at which Wilson had mocked; and the laity felt accordingly that he had failed them. Two other priests took refuge in occultism, interpreting the Avesta allegorically in the light of Sufi and Hindu concepts. Its 'inner' teachings, they declared, concerned a remote, almighty God, while 'Ohrmazd and Ahriman' were no more than allegories for man's own better and worse selves. The *yazatas* they held to be a series of intermediate intelligences; and they found that Zoroaster had implied the doctrine of reincarnation, with salvation to be achieved by self-denial and fasting. Although all this was in fact alien to Zoroastrianism, a number of Parsis accepted it as offering an escape from the perplexities suddenly thrust upon them.

Others tried to modernize their faith more rationally; and in 1851 the Zoroastrian Reform Society was founded, 'to break through the thousand and one religious prejudices that tend to retard the progress ... of the community'. Some of its members adopted the extreme Western theory (publicized by Wilson) that Zoroaster had preached a simple monotheism, rejecting virtually all rituals; and their position was strengthened when Haug, lecturing in Bombay in the 1860s, expounded his own interpretation of the *Gathas*. Those who held to traditional observances received their share of Western support later, when Theosophy, with its occultism and regard for the esoteric value of rituals, was brought to Bombay from the U.S.A. in 1885. A number of Parsis joined the Theosophical Society, and came into danger of adulterating their own beliefs and practices with alien (largely Hindu) ones. For this they were censured by adherents of Ilm-i Khshnoom ('Science of (Spiritual) Satisfaction'). This is an exclusively Zoroastrian occultist movement which was founded in 1902 by an uneducated Parsi, Behramshah Shroff. He interpreted the Avesta in the light of his own visions and again taught of one impersonal God, and of planes of being and reincarnation, with much planetary lore intermixed. He showed a total disregard for textual or historical accuracy, but stressed the importance of exactly performed rituals and adherence to the purity laws. There are some Ilm-i Khshnoom fire-temples, but the movement, though it has grown, is now subdivided into contending factions.

Reformists had earlier published, in Gujarati script, cheap printed copies of the Khorda (Little) Avesta, the Zoroastrian prayer-book, so that every Parsi now had direct access to the sacred texts. This further diminished the role of the priests, who had fallen rapidly from being respected for their learning to being despised as ignorant, not only of the new secular knowledge but also of the true meaning of the holy books. The need for better understanding of the latter led a layman, K. R. Cama, to introduce their study on Western philological principles. His pupils, all young priests, worked admirably at editing and translating Pahlavi and Avestan texts, but attempted no fundamental theological studies. The Parsis, who lack any one recognized ecclesiastical authority, remained perplexed and divided into contending religious groups. Among these the old dualistic orthodoxy was largely lost, overlaid by declared monotheisms of either the Western or the occultist type. In the 1970s, however, a new Western respect for Zoroastrian dualism began to exert an influence, and yet another movement was launched among the laity to revive more traditional beliefs, and to reconcile ancient myths with current scientific knowledge.

From the late nineteenth century the Parsi reform movement influenced the urban community in Iran, but an unquestioning orthodoxy still survives in country regions there. In cities abroad Parsis and Iranis mingle and every shade of religious opinion is represented, together with widespread secularism. Survival of the faith is often seen as part of the preservation of communal identity, and both for this and for truly devout reasons vigorous efforts are often made locally to maintain the religious life. These usually centre on a meeting-house, or even (in London and New York) on a sacred fire. Special efforts are now made to publish attractive books of instruction for children, and to ensure that they are initiated into the faith. Whether those with a non-Zoroastrian mother or father may properly be admitted, or converts made, are controversial matters, discussed all the more urgently because of the community's dwindling numbers (due both to a falling birth-rate (see Figure 4.2) and to absorption into surrounding societies).

Despite doctrinal confusions, the traditional moral theology can be seen still shaping the lives of Zoroastrians. Their prophet taught the need for each of his followers to be constantly active in furthering the good creation; and from the time the Zoroastrians first re-emerge into general history individuals can be seen exerting themselves to benefit others, through charitable gifts, public works, medical care and the like. Latterly they have entered local and national politics, caring thus not only for their own communities but for society at large. Three Parsis have sat in the British House of Commons [21: 69ff], and others have been active in Indian politics, while an Irani was a founding member of the first Iranian parliament, established in 1906. The strikingly parallel achievements of the two Zoroastrian communities, separated since the ninth century, and both for a long time impoverished and oppressed, appear to result from the two factors which they have in common: valiant ancestors, prepared to sacrifice almost everything for their faith; and that faith itself, demanding of them courage and integrity, love of God and their fellow creatures, and an undaunted active opposition to evil in every form.

NOTES

1. Darmesteter and Mills [2] is still the only complete English translation, but is badly in need of revision. For the *Gathas* it is best to look at more than one translation, e.g. Moulton [3], Duchesne-Guillemin [4] and Insler [5].
2. This includes the pioneer translations of West [7], which are still valuable for their introductions and notes.

APPENDIX A   THE SEVEN HOLY DAYS OF OBLIGATION

Gahambar is the Middle Persian term for six of the seven obligatory Zoroastrian festivals, neglect of which was formerly held to be a sin. The *gahambars* appear to have been ancient seasonal festivals, refounded (tradition says by Zarathushtra himself) to honour Ahura Mazda and the six great Amesha Spentas, together with the seven creations. Each festival lasted originally one day, but after a calendar reform in the third century BCE they were extended to six days, later reduced to five. The seventh festival is called in Middle Persian No Roz ('New Day'), and celebrates the beginning of the year. The dates of the celebration of the festivals according to the three existing Zoroastrian calendars are shown in the table opposite.

Festival/Ancient name		Dates celebrated	
		In 1980–83	In 1984–7
1 Midspring/Maidhyoizaremaya	S	5–9 October	4–8 October
Associated 'Holy Immortal':	K	5–9 September	4–8 September
Dominion	F	30 April	30 April
Associated creation: Sky		to 4 May	to 4 May
2 Midsummer/Maidhyoishema	S	4–8 December	3–7 December
Associated 'Holy Immortal':	K	4–8 November	3–7 November
Wholeness	F	29 June	29 June
Associated creation: Water		to 3 July	to 3 July
3 Bringing in corn/Paitishahya	S	18–22 February	17–21 February
Associated 'Holy Immortal':	K	19–23 January	18–22 January
Devotion	F	12–16 September	12–16 September
Associated creation: Earth			
4 Homecoming (of the herds)/	S	19–22 March	18–21 March
Ayathrima	K	19–22 February	17–21 February
Associated 'Holy Immortal':	F	12–16 October	12–16 October
Immortality			
Associated creation: Plants			
5 Midwinter/Maidhyairya	S	7–11 June	6–10 June
Associated 'Holy Immortal':	K	8–12 May	7–11 May
Good Intent	F	31 December	31 December
Associated creation: Cattle		to 4 January	to 4 January
6 All Souls (Parsi Muktad,	S	21–25 August	20–24 August
Irani Farvadigan)/	K	22–26 July	21–25 July
Hamaspathmaedaya	F	16–20 March	16–20 March
Associated 'Holy Immortal':			
Holy Spirit/Ahura Mazda			
Associated creation: Man			
7 New Day/No Ruz	S	26 August	25 August
Associated 'Holy Immortal':	K	27 July	26 July
Righteousness	F	21 March	21 March
Associated creation: Fire			
'Old' No Ruz (Hordad Sal,	S	31 August	30 August
celebrated on day Hordad,	K	1 August	31 July
see Appendix B)	F	26 March	26 March

APPENDIX B   THE ZOROASTRIAN CALENDAR

From ancient times the Iranians had a year of twelve months with thirty days each. The Zoroastrian calendar, created probably early in the fourth century BCE, was distinctive simply through the pious dedication of each day and month to a divine being. Four days were devoted to 'Ahura Mazda the Creator (Dadvah)', probably as an esoteric acknowledgement of Zurvan, who was worshipped as a quaternity. In later usage the first of these days is named 'Ohrmazd', the other three 'Dai' (for Dadvah); the three 'Dai' days are distinguished by adding to each the name of the following day, e.g. 'Dai-pa-Adar', 'Dai-by (the day)-Adar'. The names are given here in their Persian forms.

THE THIRTY DAYS

1. Ohrmazd
2. Bahman
3. Ardibehisht
4. Shahrevar
5. Spendarmad
6. Khordad
7. Amurdad

8. Dai-pa-Adar
9. Adar
10. Aban
11. Khorshed
12. Mah
13. Tir
14. Gosh

15. Dai-pa-Mihr
16. Mihr
17. Srosh
18. Rashn
19. Farvardin
20. Bahram
21. Ram
22. Bad

23. Dai-pa-Din
24. Din
25. Ard
26. Ashtad
27. Asman
28. Zamyad
29. Mahraspand
30. Aneran

THE TWELVE MONTHS

1. Farvardin (March/April)
2. Ardibehisht (April/May)
3. Khordad (May/June)
4. Tir (June/July)
5. Amurdad (July/August)
6. Shahrevar (August/September)

7. Mihr (September/October)
8. Aban (October/November)
9. Adar (November/December)
10. Dai (December/January)
11. Bahman (January/February)
12. Spendarmad (February/March)

Every coincidence of a month and day name was celebrated as a name-day feast. There was thus one such feast in every month but the tenth, when four feasts were celebrated in honour of the Creator, Ohrmazd. The chief name-day feasts still celebrated by the Parsis are Aban and Adar. The Iranis also celebrate the festivals of Spendarmad, Tir and Mihr with special observances.

THE FIVE GATHA DAYS

By the reform of the third century CE five extra days were added at the end of the 360-day year. These were named after the five groups of Zoroaster's hymns. (All but the first of these are known by the opening word of the first hymn in the group. *Gatha Ahunavaiti* is called after the 'Yatha ahu vairyo' prayer, which precedes it in the liturgy.)

1. Ahunavad
2. Ushtavad
3. Spentomad
4. Vohukhshathra
5. Vahishtoisht

The *gahambar* of Hamaspathmaedaya is now celebrated throughout these five days.

Various subsequent calendar reforms were directed at trying to stabilize the 365-day calendar in relation to the seasons. (The old 360-day calendar had been adjusted from time to time by the intercalation of a whole extra month.) It is these attempts which have led to the existence of three Zoroastrian calendars today.

BIBLIOGRAPHY

1. GELDNER, K., *Avesta: The Sacred Books of the Parsis*, 3 vols., Stuttgart, Kohlhammer, 1896 (text with introduction)
2. DARMESTETER, J., and MILLS, L. H., *The Zend-Avesta*, Oxford, Clarendon Press, 1883–95 (Sacred Books of the East, IV, XXIII, XXXI), prev. publ. 1880–87; repr. Delhi, Motilal Banarsidass, 1965/New York, Krishna, 1974
3. MOULTON, J. H., *Early Zoroastrianism*, London, Williams & Norgate, 1913; repr. Amsterdam, Philo Press, 1972/New York, AMS, 1980
4. DUCHESNE-GUILLEMIN, J., *The Hymns of Zarathustra* (tr. M. Henning), London, John Murray, 1952 (Wisdom of the East Series)
5. INSLER, S., *The Gāthās of Zarathustra*, Leiden, Brill, 1975 (Acta Iranica 8)

6. BOYCE, M., 'Middle Persian literature', *Iranistik*, Leiden, Brill, 1968, pp. 31–66 (Handbuch der Orientalistik, ed. B. Spuler, 1.iv.2.1)

7. WEST, E. W., *Pahlavi Texts*, Oxford, Clarendon Press, 1882–1901, first publ. 1880–97 (Sacred Books of the East, V, XVIII, XXIV, XXXVII, XLVII); repr. Delhi, Motilal Banarsidass, 1965, New York, Krishna, 1974

8. BOYCE, M., *A History of Zoroastrianism*, vol. I, *The Early Period*, Leiden, Brill, 1975 (Handbuch der Orientalistik, ed. B. Spuler, 1.viii.1.2A)

9. ibid., vol. II, *Under the Achaemenians*, 1982

10. BOYCE, M., *Zoroastrians, Their Religious Beliefs and Practices*, London, Boston, Mass., Routledge, 1979 (paperback, 1984)

11. ANQUETIL DU PERRON, A. H., *Zend-Avesta, Ouvrage de Zoroastre*, 2 vols. in 3, Paris, Tilliard, 1771

12. HAUG, M., *Essays on the Sacred Language, Writings and Religion of the Parsis*, 3rd edn, London, Trübner, 1884, 4th edn, 1907, repr. Amsterdam, Philo Press, 1971

13. NYBERG, H. S., *Die Religionen des Alten Iran* (tr. into German by H. H. Schaeder), Leipzig, Hinrichs, 1938, repr. Osnabrück, Zeller, 1966

14. DUCHESNE-GUILLEMIN, J., *The Western Response to Zoroaster*, Oxford, Clarendon Press, 1958

15. SHAHBAZI, A. SH., 'The "Traditional date of Zoroaster" explained', *Bulletin of the School of Oriental and African Studies*, XL, i, 1977, pp. 25–35

16. MODI, J. J., *The Religious Ceremonies and Customs of the Parsees*, 2nd edn, Bombay, J. B. Karani's Sons, 1937; first publ. Bombay, British India Press, 1922, repr. New York, Garland, 1980

17. BOYCE, M., *A Persian Stronghold of Zoroastrianism*, Oxford, Clarendon Press, 1977

18. SEERVAI, K. N., and PATEL, B. B., 'Gujarāt Pārsīs', *Gazetteer of the Bombay Presidency*, IX. 2, Bombay, Government Central Press, 1899

19. HINNELLS, J. R., 'Parsis and British education, 1820–1880', *Journal of the K. R. Cama Oriental Institute*, 46, 1978, pp. 42–59

20. WILSON, J., *The Pārsī Religion: As Contained in the Zand-Avasta and Propounded and Defended by the Zoroastrians of India and Persia*, Bombay, American Mission Press, 1843

21. HINNELLS, J. R., 'Parsis in Britain', *Journal of the K. R. Cama Oriental Institute*, 46, 1978, pp. 65–84

22. BOYCE, M., *Sources for the Study of Zoroastrianism*, Manchester, Manchester University Press, 1984.

5

Hinduism

SIMON WEIGHTMAN

Introduction

WHAT IS HINDUISM?

The word Hinduism is used to refer to the complex religious tradition which has evolved organically in the Indian subcontinent over several thousand years and is today represented by the highly diverse beliefs and practices of more than 500 million Hindus. Apart from communities in neighbouring states, and those communities in such places as Bali, South-West Africa and the Caribbean that have been created by migration (together forming less than 10 per cent of the totality) the majority of Hindus live in India, where they constitute over four-fifths of the entire population. Hinduism is so diverse internally that the only way of defining it acceptably is externally, in terms of people and places, and 'Hindu' is, in origin, simply the Persian word for Indian. The land of India is crucial to Hinduism; its sacred geography is honoured by pilgrimages and other ritual acts and has become deeply embedded in Hindu mythology and scriptures.

There are two principal reasons why it is preferable to regard Hinduism as an evolving religious tradition rather than as a single, separate 'religion' in the sense that the term is usually understood. The first reason is that Hinduism displays few of the characteristics that are generally expected of a religion. It has no founder, nor is it prophetic. It is not creedal, nor is any particular doctrine, dogma or practice held to be essential to it. It is not a system of theology, nor a single moral code, and the concept of god is not central to it. There is no specific scripture or work regarded as being uniquely authoritative and, finally, it is not sustained by an ecclesiastical organization. Thus it is difficult to categorize Hinduism as a 'religion' using normally accepted criteria.

The second reason for this preference is the extraordinary diversity of Hinduism, both historically, and in the contemporary situation. Such diversity is scarcely surprising when it is remembered that Hinduism refers to the mainstream of religious development of a huge subcontinent over a period of several thousand years, during which time it has been subject to numerous incursions from alien races and cultures. The subcontinent is not only vast, but it is also marked by considerable regional variation. Regions differ from one another geographically, in terms of terrain, climate, natural resources, communications etc., and also ethnographically, in terms of the many and varied ethnic, cultural and linguistic groupings that inhabit them. Diversity is, therefore, to be expected in almost every domain.

Hinduism evolved organically, with new initiatives and developments taking place within the tradition, as well as by interaction with and adjustment to other traditions and cults which were then assimilated into the Hindu fold. These two processes of evolution and assimilation have produced an enormous variety of religious systems, beliefs and practices. At one end of the scale are innumerable small unsophisticated local cults known only to perhaps two or three villages. At the other end of the scale are major religious movements with millions of adherents across the entire subcontinent. Such movements have their own theologies, mythologies and codes of ritual and could, with justice, be regarded as religions in their own right.

It is then possible to find groups of Hindus whose respective faiths have almost nothing in common one with another, and it is also impossible to identify any universal belief or practice that is common to all Hindus. Confronted with such diversity, what is it that makes Hinduism a single religious tradition and not a loose confederation of many different traditions? The common Indian origin, the historical continuity, the sense of a shared heritage and a family relationship between the various parts, all these are certainly important factors. But these all equally apply to Buddhism, Jainism and Sikhism, each of which arose within the Hindu tradition but separated from it to become an independent religion. Crucial, however, is the fact that Hindus affirm it is one single religion. Every time a Hindu accepts someone as a fellow Hindu, in spite of what may be radical differences of faith and practice, he is making this affirmation. Whatever its seeds, Hindu self-awareness certainly developed in early confrontations with Buddhists and Jains, acquired greater potency as Hinduism was confronted by Islam and then Christianity, finally being considerably strengthened in recent times by the growth of nationalism and political identity. It is Hindu self-awareness and self-identity that affirms Hinduism to be one single religious universe, no matter how richly varied its contents, and which makes it a significant and potent force alongside the other religions of the world.

APPROACHES TO HINDUISM

The first attested usage of the word 'Hinduism' in English was as late as 1829. This is not to say that the beliefs and practices of the Hindus, or 'Gentoos' as they were referred to in the eighteenth century, had not been previously studied.

Indeed serious work had already begun, spurred on by the exciting 'discovery' of Sanskrit and the realization that it was related to Latin and Greek. [1:1] Philological work, the editing and translation of texts, has been a continuing and major scholarly concern. Because the corpus of religious and philosophical works is so vast, however, there still remains much that awaits thorough investigation. Nevertheless the huge body of religious writings, sometimes referred to as Hindu scriptures, has helped to form a mistaken view of Hinduism. Certainly these works are of primary importance. But it must be remembered that they were written by a priestly elite, the Brahmans, and are, of necessity, unrepresentative of the beliefs and practices of the great majority of Hindus at any given time. They are, moreover, not a coherent corpus, but as diverse as the history of Hinduism itself. Some authors, through excessive reliance on texts, and through failing to place these texts in their overall contexts, have perpetuated an image of Hinduism as being concerned solely with the higher realms of metaphysical and theological teachings when, in fact, a very great deal more is entailed.

The writings, beliefs and practices of the Brahmans were understood by early observers in contact with the everyday realities of Hinduism to represent the true 'orthodoxy' and they were thus obliged to relegate much of what they found to the status of folklore and superstition. More recently, ethnographic and anthropological research has gone a long way towards removing this misleading polarization and has partly succeeded in integrating both aspects into a single totality. This process has itself generated further dualities, however, such as 'The Great' and 'The Little Tradition' which may prove in the long run to be equally unhelpful.

The Christian missionaries were highly critical of most of what they encountered in India, although they welcomed monotheism wherever they found it as providing further evidence of the universality of this phenomenon. Subjected to the scorn of the missionaries, the more Westernized and educated Hindus took the opportunity that the new word 'Hinduism' offered to reinterpret and project Hinduism almost as they wished, since it was never clear precisely what the term referred to. As will be seen later, Hinduism came to be projected as 'the most ancient and mother of all religions', and through being, by implication, the best of all religions, it was naturally the most tolerant. This new mythology was coupled with the notion of the spiritual East and the materialistic West, as if there were no spirituality in the West and no materialism in the East. Such dubious popular images were supported by the equally false notion of the changelessness of India. In fact Hinduism and India are characterized by both continuity and change, and no single image can be appropriate either to so complex an agglomeration as Hinduism or to so vast a continent as India.

There is still a relativism in the use of the word Hinduism. To someone reading the literature it becomes clear that there are almost as many 'Hinduisms' as there are authors who write about it. Recently one scholar has commented trenchantly on the term Hinduism, describing it as 'a particularly false conceptualization, one that is conspicuously incompatible with any adequate understanding of the religious outlook of Hindus'. While the arguments cannot be rehearsed here, there is much validity in them, although it is improbable that his wish to have the word dropped will ever be fulfilled. The word is here to stay. In this article it will be used as many now use it to embrace the totality of beliefs and practices of all Hindus, both as they are now, and as they have evolved over the centuries. [1; 2; 3; 5; 6]

HISTORY AND SOURCES OF HINDUISM

All that is known of the earliest stage of religious life in India – designated by some as protohistoric Hinduism – is derived from excavated seals and statuettes belonging to the Indus valley civilization (? 4000–2200 BCE) [1: 1] (see Figure 5.1). These are usually interpreted as indicating that veneration was shown to a male god, seated in a yogic posture and displaying characteristics of the god known in later Hinduism as Shiva (see Figures 5.4–5.6 below); also to female goddesses, phallic symbols and certain animals and trees. Ritual purification with water seems also to have been an important element. Fragmentary as these details are, however, all of these features reappear in classical Hinduism and are widespread in current belief and practice – testimony to the persistence of religious forms in India. [1: 11]

The second historical phase, that of Vedism or Vedic religion, is usually taken to extend from about the middle of the second millennium BCE until about 500 BCE. It was ushered in by the arrival of the semi-nomadic Aryan tribes who, by conquest and by settlement and assimilation, spread during these centuries across north India. The Aryans were that branch of the Indo-European peoples who moved down into Iran and Afghanistan and then into India. What is known of their religion when they were in India derives mainly from the Veda, a remarkable corpus of religious literature which displays a considerable evolution of religious attitudes throughout the period. [1: 11]

The oldest of these works is the *Rig-veda*, a collection of hymns addressed to various gods or divine powers (*devas*) and used during the main official religious rites. These rites centred round fire sacrifices and the use of a sacred plant, Soma, from which a drink was made which was believed to heighten spiritual awareness [8]. The ceremonies were complex and required specialist priests for whose use two further works, the *Sama-veda* and the *Yajur-veda*, were added to the corpus. Alongside the official religion there was a domestic cult requiring rites to be performed by the householder. The fourth and latest

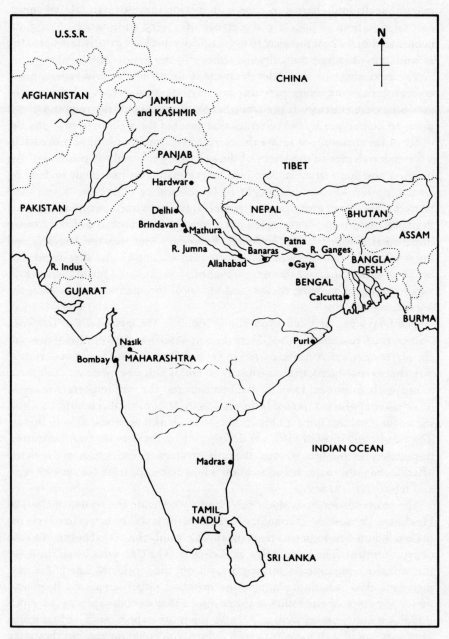

Figure 5.1   General map of India

work, the *Atharva-veda*, presumably also intended for domestic use, contains magical spells and charms to cope with a wide range of natural and supernatural situations. This early acceptance of a very wide range of religious concern, from the cosmological to the magical, must have greatly facilitated the assimilation of indigenous cults and tribes into the Aryan fold. [7; 9]

The next stage in Vedic development is found in the *Brahmanas*, prose commentaries containing practical and mythological details relating to the sacrifice. Here ritualism is pre-eminent. No longer was it the response of the *devas* to human praise and offerings that ensured the welfare of man and the order of the cosmos, but rather the correct performance of the sacrifice itself. This major change in the status of the sacrifice weakened the position of the *devas*, a position further undermined by the search for one single underlying cosmic power which was thought to be the source of the *devas* and their powers. This one great cosmic power was sometimes personalized – as Prajapati or Purusha for example – but eventually was conceived of as the single impersonal absolute called *brahman*. *Brahman*'s seat was the sacrifice, and knowledge of *brahman* was the key to cosmic control. Another trend that becomes apparent about this time is that of asceticism and meditation, which was represented as being the internalization of the sacrifice within man, the microcosm. [2; 7; 9]

The final stage of Vedic evolution is found in the last works of the Veda proper, the *Upanishads* [7; 10]. Here the emphasis is away from ritual towards the personal and mystical experiencing of the One. When the various worldly influences are reduced, the human self (*atman*) is able to experience itself as, or at one with, *brahman*. Here for the first time too the very important doctrine of *samsara* appears. *Samsara* is the endless cycle of birth and rebirth to which each soul is subject until it obtains liberation (*mukti* or *moksha*) in *brahman*. The conditions of each birth are determined by the acts (*karma*) performed during the previous life. Whereas the early hymns were little concerned with the afterlife, now the major preoccupation is how to escape from the cycle of birth and rebirth. [1: VII; 2; 7; 9]

The ten centuries from about 500 BCE to 500 CE are the period of classical Hinduism. Because the chronology is problematic it will be better to review the main religious developments thematically. Certainly the period began in a time of great ferment. The Vedic cult was in decline. The *Upanishads* and the quest for *moksha* represented a turning away from the world. Meanwhile a new merchant class was flourishing whose members either supported their own non-Vedic cults, or else followed the new sects that were then arising, of which Buddhism and Jainism were to become the most important. The Brahmans, as priests, could well have lost much influence in consequence, but they were also the educated elite, sole guardians of Sanskrit and the textual traditions. It is they who were the principal agents in creating a sufficiently flexible religious and social framework within which they were able to assimilate the new classes, peoples and cults. One of the main powers and functions of the Brahmans at this time was of legitimation. Perhaps the first really significant exercise of that power, as well as the first affirmation of Hindu self-awareness, was to establish allegiance to the Veda, however contrived, as the criterion of orthodoxy. In consequence, some of the newly arisen sects, notably Buddhism and Jainism, were treated as heterodox and separated to go their own way, although cross-fertilization continued for many centuries. [1: II, VII]

The change of emphasis to living-in-the-world was firmly established in the religious law books, *dharma sutras* and *dharma shastras*, which codified how Hindu society should be and how Hindus should live, at least according to Brahmanical prescription. The essential concept was *varnashrama dharma*, that is, the duties or right way of living of each of the four classes of society (*varnas*) in each of the four stages of life (*ashramas*). Although there is also a general *dharma*, righteousness or moral code, incumbent on all, this relativist code of behaviour was founded on the belief that people are not the same and that their duties or ethics vary according to who they are and where they are in life. The four *varnas* – Brahmans (priests and teachers), Kshatriyas (rulers and warriors), Vaishyas (merchants and cultivators) and Shudras (menials) – were ordered hierarchically on Vedic authority and the first three, the 'twice-born', had full religious rights, while those of the menials were much restricted. Unsubjugated tribes or groups with unacceptable practices were considered 'untouchables' and outside the Hindu pale. These prescriptive works, the *dharma shastras*, deal with domestic rituals, life-cycle rites, sin, expiation, ritual pollution, purification and many other matters fundamental to the Hindu way of life. [12] The three aims of life were *dharma*, the acquisition of religious merit through right living, *artha*, the lawful making of wealth, and *kama*, the satisfaction of desires: thus embracing the major aspects of human life. Only later was *moksha*, the quest for liberation, added as the fourth. Right living in this world, *dharma*, had displaced *moksha*, liberation from this world, at the very centre of Hinduism. [1; 12; 28; 29; 31] But *moksha* was never ignored. It was explored by schools of speculative philosophy, often with very sophisticated metaphysical systems, all purporting to be valid means of salvation. Six of these *darshanas* (doctrines) were accepted as orthodox, but only one of them, Vedanta, was to evolve and play an important part in the later development of Hinduism. [2; 32]

There is ample evidence that non-Vedic theistic cults were widespread throughout the Vedic period. The process whereby these cults and divinities were brought within Hinduism and somehow connected to the Veda is both complex and little known. Suffice it to say that, for Hinduism, the rise, or re-emergence, of theism was one of the most profound developments of the period. Two gods, Vishnu and Shiva, both relatively unimportant in the Veda, became pre-eminent, although many other gods were also worshipped. [4; 14; 15]

Vishnu (see Figures 5.2 and 5.3) became identified with various existing deities, and this syncretism has given him the character of a benevolent god, concerned for the welfare of the world, who periodically, in times of moral

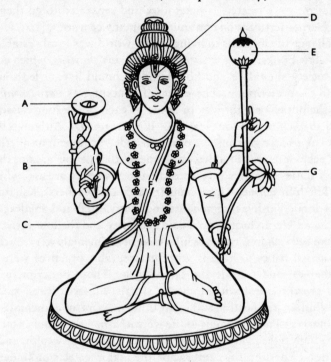

A *Cakra* (discus), a weapon and a symbol of kingly power

B *Shankha* (conch), used as a trumpet in both war and ritual

C *Vana-mala* – a garland of forest flowers. Often worn by Vishnu and Krishna.

D Sectarian mark, as worn by Vishnu's devotees

E *Gada* (mace)

F *Yajnopavita*, the sacred thread

G *Padma* (lotus), representing beauty and purity, often associated with Vishnu's wife
Lakshmi and other goddesses

A, B, E and G are the four most usual attributes
by which Vishnu is identified

Figure 5.2   Vishnu and his attributes

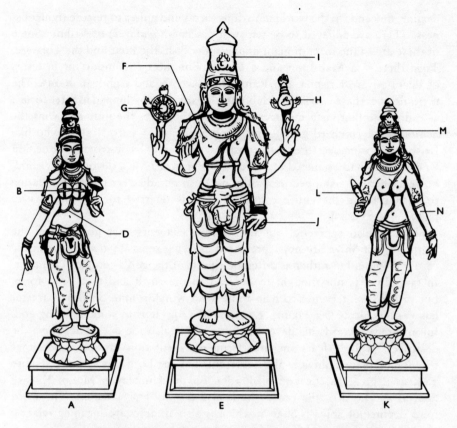

A Shridevi (Lakshmi), goddess of good fortune, standing as the first wife on the right
B Breast band, sign of the senior wife
C Hand in pose of relaxation
D The elaborate arrangement of threads on the chest is characteristic of Lakshmi. Vishnu
   and Bhudevi both wear the simpler form of sacred thread (*yajnopavita*). Although mortal
   women do not wear the thread, goddesses can be so shown
E Vishnu as 'Abode of Shri' (splendour, good fortune)
F *Shrivatsa* ('beloved of Shri') mark on Vishnu's chest
G *Cakra* (discus or quoit), decorated with flames
H Conch, decorated with flames
I Kingly crown (*kirita mukuta*) and ornaments
J Hand on thigh, symbolizing that for his worshippers the ocean of *samsara* is only thigh deep
K Bhudevi (Prithvi), the Earth Goddess, the second wife
L Water-lily bud (the Earth Goddess flower)
M Queen's crown (*karanda-mukuta*)
N Pose of relaxation

Figure 5.3 Vishnu as Shrinivasa with consorts (South Indian bronzes from
Srinivasanallur, Tiruchirapalli district, fifteenth/sixteenth century CE)

decline, descends to the world in various forms and guises to restore righteous-ness. There are believed to be ten such descents (*avataras*) of Vishnu. Some of these are in the form of giant animals: the Fish, the Boar and the Tortoise. Then there is a Man-Lion and a Dwarf. But the most important in terms of devotion are Krishna and Rama, the seventh and eighth *avataras*. The mythology of these two is very elaborate. Krishna is worshipped in three forms: as a divine infant; as a mischievous youth who plays the flute and wins the hearts of the cowherd girls (*gopis*); and as a mighty hero. Rama, who like Krishna is a prince, restored righteousness to the earth by destroying the demon Ravana who had abducted his wife Sita. The word for a devotee of Vishnu, however he is worshipped, is Vaishnava (also an adjective meaning 'relating to Vishnu') and the entire cult of Vishnu is referred to as Vaishnavism. [1: VII; 4; 14; 15; 30]

Shiva is also syncretic, but the various elements that go to form the mythology of Shiva are not represented as being separate *avataras* as in the case of Vishnu, but rather as different aspects of the god's complex character. In fact Shiva is not thought to descend to the earth and take on a form, but rather he intervenes to help those who worship him. Shiva's character has various facets (see Figures 5.4, 5.5 and 5.6). He is to some a loving god, full of grace towards his devotees. But there is also the dark side, Shiva the destroyer, who is fearsome and frequents cremation grounds and other frightening places. Shiva is also represented as the Lord of the dance (Figure 5.6), as a great ascetic god meditating on the Himalayan Mount Kailash and, as the Lord of the beasts, he is also a god of procreation. The word for a devotee of Shiva is Shaiva, which is also an adjective meaning relating to Shiva, and the cult of Shiva is referred to as Shaivism.

Vishnu's wife is Lakshmi, goddess of prosperity (see Figure 5.7). The wife of Shiva is Durga (Figure 5.8) in her fierce aspect, and Parvati in her benevolent form (Figure 5.5). It was around Durga–Parvati that, at the end of this period, the Mother Goddess cult re-emerged. Its followers were called Shaktas because they believed the goddess to be the immanent active energy (*shakti*) of the transcendent and remote Shiva who was otherwise inaccessible. [1: VII; 2; 4; 14–16; 30]

The two great epics, the *Ramayana* and, particularly, the *Mahabharata*, are rich encyclopedic sources for the religion of this period [13]. Included in the *Mahabharata* is the *Bhagavadgita*, a poem which has become one of the most influential Hindu scriptures [11]. In it Lord Krishna speaks of three ways to salvation: that of enlightenment; that of action, including religious rites; and, the most highly recommended, that of loving devotion to the Lord (*bhakti*). It is *bhakti* that has inspired and informed the greater part of Hinduism to the present day. [2; 11] Other consequent developments also

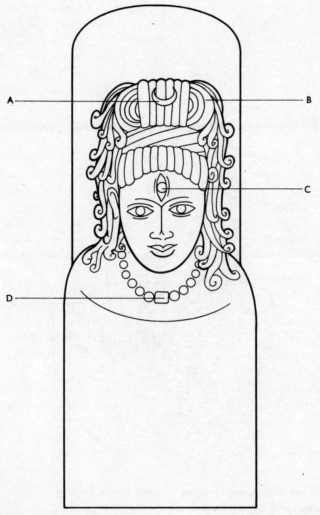

A Crescent moon

B *Jata*, the ascetic's unkempt locks of hair

C Third eye, representing Shiva's wisdom but also his power of destruction – he can blast enemies with fire from it. It is a sign of yogic power

D *Rudraksha-mala*, a rosary of Rudraksha (eye of Shiva) seeds, sacred to Shiva.

Only the upper part of the sculpture would have been visible: it was made to fit into a pedestal (possibly representing the *yoni*)

Figure 5.4 Eka-mukha-linga (*lingam* with one face of Shiva)

A Shiva, with third eye, snake necklace, the typical ear-rings and long
  unkempt hair of an ascetic. He wears only a *kaupina* (G-string)

B Parvati serves him with bhang (cannabis in yoghurt). She is shown in the costume of a
  lady of the time and place when the drawing was made (note the nose ornament and
  ear-ring)

C The Goddess's lion

D Ganesha, here shown as a four-armed child eating *laddus* with Shiva's animal mount

E Nandi, Shiva's bull

F Karttikeya, the six-headed, six-armed war god shown here as a child, feeding his
  peacock mount

Figure 5.5   The domestic life of Shiva and Parvati (from a late eighteenth- or early
nineteenth-century Kangra drawing for a miniature in the British Museum)

A Goddess of River Ganga, which flows from Shiva's hair. She is here shown as a snake-tailed woman in the gesture of *namaskara* (to honour Shiva)

B Drum, giving the rhythm of the dance of creation

C Cobra

D *Abhaya-mudra*, the gesture granting freedom from fear

E Hand pointing to the raised foot signifies salvation

F The upraised foot, coming forward from the circle, represents salvation

G Ascetic's skull

H Moon

I Third eye

J Long swirling locks full of flowers and snakes

K One male, one female ear-ring because Shiva combines both attributes

L Sacred head

M Short dhoti of the ascetic

N The dance steps are the creation and destruction of universes. Shiva dances on one spot, at the centre of the universe/the human mind-heart

O Fire, the periodic destruction and re-creation of the universe

P Ornamental *prabha-mandala*, the circle of glory, representing the universe/human heart

Q Demon of Ignorance, who is glad to be trodden on by the God

Figure 5.6   Shiva as Nataraja, king of dancers

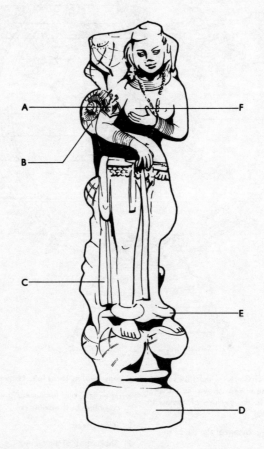

A Armband in the shape of a peacock

B The back of the image is carved with peacocks and lotuses. Peacocks are associated with the rainy season, hence fertility

C Diaphanous skirt, characteristic of the style from Mathura

D Pedestal, taking the form of the *purnaghata* ('full vase') of lotuses, which is still associated with Lakshmi

E Heavy anklets – the goddess is shown richly adorned

F She offers her breast and unfastens her garment, suggesting her power of fertility

Figure 5.7   Lakshmi, as goddess of prosperity (Kushana, second/fourth centuries CE). This early image represents Lakshmi (who is Kamala, the lotus goddess) in association with symbols of water, fertility and female beauty

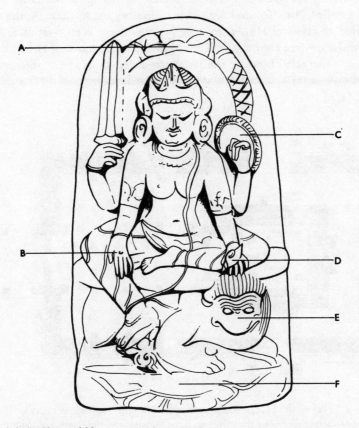

A halo (*prabha-mandala*)

B *Varada-mudra*, the gesture of granting favours (the small round object in the palm is perhaps a wishing gem). This suggests her benevolence to her worshippers

C The sword and the buckler (seen from the inner side) represent the goddess in her fierce aspect, in which she fights demons. The image combines fierce and gentle aspects

D Conch shell, showing that Durga is a *shakti* of Vishnu as well as of Shiva (in mythology she is Vishnu's sister, and Shiva's wife)

E Lion, the mount (vahana) of Durga

F Lotus footstool and pedestal

Figure 5.8 Durga and her attributes (from a *c.* tenth-century relief from eastern India)

took place. The Vedic sacrificial rites had to give ground to new forms of worship (*puja*) often performed in front of an image or a statue symbolizing or representing the deity in question. A rich mythological literature evolved in works called Puranas, and temple-building began, so that, by the end of this period of classical Hinduism, temples must have been a familiar feature of the landscape (see Figure 5.9). The characteristic features of Hindu temples are: (1) a 'sanctuary' housing the image, referred to as the *garbhagriha* (or 'womb-house'); (2) a spire (*shikhara*) over the sanctuary; and (3) a porch or canopy. [4; 6]

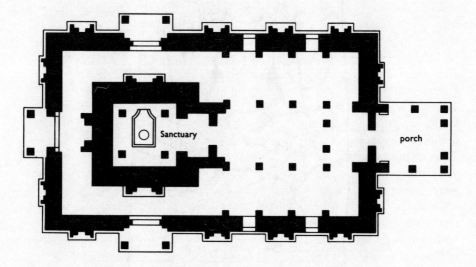

Figure 5.9 Plan of the Svarga Brahma temple, Alampur (seventh century CE). In the appropriate niches of the outer walls are positioned the Dikpalas, the guardians of the eight directions of space

The next period, that of middle or medieval Hinduism, from the sixth century to the nineteenth century of our era, is characterized by proliferation in almost every domain. It is also interesting that many of the major initiatives, especially in the earlier centuries, took place in the south of India where Buddhism and Jainism were in decline and new Hindu kingdoms arose fostering Hindu self-awareness. [1: III, VII] At a social level this period saw the proliferation of castes (*jatis*), but no theory as to their origin is, as yet, conclusive. It is not thought that they arose through the mixing of the four classes (*varnas*), from which they differ substantially, but clearly the *varna* model of hierarchy, specialization of functions and social separation provided an ideological backing. Whatever the defects of the system, and various sects attacked it vehemently, it served to provide social stability in times of political turbulence, to ensure the continuity of a richly diversified culture, and, above all, to give Hindus a social identity, even if it was not the identity that they themselves wished. [1; 38]

The major developments in religious philosophy, the *darshanas*, or schools of salvation, took place within Vedanta. Shankara (?788–850 CE), who advocated the way of knowledge (*jnana*), formulated his system of Advaita, non-duality, as an exposition of Upanishadic thought, and also founded a monastic order which was to be the forerunner of many others. [17; 18] The Advaita position is held by many Hindus to this day. Briefly, Shankara asserted that only *brahman* was real, all else, including the phenomenal world, the sense of individuality, even the *devas*, was unreal. It only appeared to be real because of *maya*, *brahman*'s power of illusion. When the human spirit, through meditation and enlightenment, realizes that it is itself of the substance of *brahman* and has no separate identity, then it merges with *brahman*, as the drop is absorbed in the ocean. This non-dualistic position, that the soul and God are of the same substance, is unsatisfactory for theists, because it does not allow for there to be a relationship between the individual soul and God. Thus in the twelfth century Ramanuja produced a system called Vishishtad-vaita, differentiated non-duality, which, while accepting that the soul and God were of the same essence, also taught that the individual soul retained its self-consciousness, and hence was able to exist in an eternal relationship with God. [17; 18; 19] This new system of Ramanuja opened the way for theism, especially Vaishnavism, within Vedanta, and provided the initial theological impetus for later schools such as those founded by Madhva (thirteenth century), Nimbarka (fourteenth century), Vallabha (sixteenth century) and Caitanya (sixteenth century), all of whom followed and advocated the way of *bhakti*, devotion. [32]

As the three principal currents of theism evolved, so each diversified and produced its own literature. The main genres, the Vaishnava *Samhitas*, the Shaiva *Agamas* and the Shakta *Tantras*, are primarily handbooks dealing with doctrine, yoga and meditation, temple-building and the consecration of the image of the deity in the temple, worship and festivals and the conduct expected of the adherent. At a less institutional level, *bhakti* was transformed from a restrained respect into a passionate and ecstatic experience by the Tamil devotional poets, the Vaishnava Alvars and the Shaiva Nayanars. These saint-poets in the south of India expressed their impassioned spirituality in hymns to Vishnu and Shiva respectively not in Sanskrit but in Tamil from the eighth to the tenth century. It has been said that, with them, *bhakti* ceased to be a way to salvation, but became salvation itself. [22]

Within Vaishnavism this new attitude was reflected in the Sanskrit *Bhaga-vata Purana* (*c*. ninth century), which became a powerful source of inspiration for Krishna *bhakti* (devotion to Krishna) in the north [24]. Numerous new sects arose and many fine devotional poets used the vernacular languages such as Hindi, Marathi, Gujarati and Bengali for their verses thus enabling millions to come into direct contact with the scriptural traditions for the first time. [26] Devotion to the other important *avatara* of Vishnu, Rama, found powerful expression in the *Ramacaritamanasa* of Tulsidas (sixteenth century), which is one of the most loved works in north India. [25]

Shaivism too developed strongly. A distinctive school of Shaivism arose in Kashmir, certainly before the ninth century, which was much influenced by Advaita [21]. The devotional outpourings of the Nayanars of the south were incorporated into a theological system called Shaiva-siddhanta which was formulated in the twelfth century. [20] Also in the twelfth century, a movement came into being called Vira-Shaivism whose followers were called Lingayats. Vira-Shaivism, which rejected both the caste system and temple worship, exists to this day in a somewhat modified form. [20; 23]

Shaktism too developed and proliferated. One aspect of Shaktism that had a strong influence on both Shaivism and Buddhism was called Tantrism. The movement was of a highly esoteric nature and had its own form of yoga, a secret language, a psychophysiological theory and characteristic modes of worship and practice designed to lead to self-realization and liberation. Although some of its practices have been much criticized, Tantrism, whose boundaries are difficult to define, is now generally thought to have added a new vitality to much of medieval Hinduism. [16]

There remains one movement of major significance, the Sant tradition. The Sants, themselves mainly from the lower castes, rejected the caste system and all forms of external religion, both Muslim and Hindu. They preached a form of interior religion based on constant awareness of and love for a personal God who was without attributes. Kabir, Raidas and Dadu, all in the fifteenth and sixteenth centuries, were three of a long line of preacher-poets in whose name sects were later formed. One such sect, whose 'founder' was Guru Nanak, later developed into Sikhism [17; 27; and see Chapter 6 below].

Thus during the Muslim period in India, and especially from the fifteenth century, Hinduism was vital and alive. *Bhakti* sects flourished, the vernacular languages were used, most of the population was involved at some level, and caste, however much loathed by certain groups, provided social stability and identity. In the face of this, Islam made surprisingly little headway, except perhaps to strengthen Hindu self-awareness. But it is in the modern period, in the nineteenth and twentieth centuries, which will be considered in the final section, that Hinduism faced its greatest self-examination as it confronted Western culture and Christianity.

Hindu Presuppositions and Belief

It will be apparent from the above examination of the inherently diverse nature
of Hinduism that any attempt to produce a concise exposition of 'basic teachings' or 'fundamental beliefs' could only be misleading and partial. Beliefs
and teachings there are in abundance, but few command universal acceptance.
Well-articulated systems of belief, theology and philosophy are found in
specific sectarian traditions or philosophical schools, most of which have their
own recommended *sadhana* (method of practical realization) for their
adherents. But these are the particulars, not the universals, of Hinduism. At
the most general level there are, however, certain underlying presuppositions
which together constitute a kind of received understanding, although this
understanding is modified for each individual by personal, family, caste,
regional and, maybe, sectarian viewpoints. The most important of these presuppositions will now be examined, together with certain other areas of
Hindu concern and belief.

One of the most important and potent concepts for all Hindus is that of
dharma. *Dharma* has various levels of meaning, but no single English equivalent. The word 'Hinduism', though, is often rendered in Indian languages
by the term *Hindu dharma*, the *dharma* of the Hindus. Here it signifies the
religion or the right way of living for Hindus. At the cosmic level *dharma*
is *sanatana dharma*, the eternal *dharma*, which is the unchanging universal
law of order which decrees that every entity in the universe should behave
in accordance with the laws that apply to its own particular nature. Coming
to the world of man, *dharma* is the source of moral law. There is, on the
one hand, *sadharana dharma*, the general code of ethics that applies to everyone. This includes injunctions to perform meritorious acts such as going on
pilgrimages, honouring Brahmans and making charitable endowments, as well
as prohibitions against causing injury, lying etc. On the other hand there is
the relativist *varnashrama dharma*, which has already been discussed above.
In fact, today, *varnashrama dharma* is understood as accepting and following the customs and rules of one's caste (*jati*). Thus *dharma* means, among
other things, eternal order, righteousness, religion, law and duty. The central
importance of *dharma* has led some to state that Hinduism is a way of life,
a proposition that has much, but not total, validity. [28; 29; 31]

A person is a Hindu because he is born to Hindu parents, and thereby
into their caste. Caste is the principal factor that determines an individual's
social and religious status. Caste is too complex a subject to discuss in any
detail here, but it is underpinned by, or expresses itself by means of, the
religious notion of purity and pollution which is one of the most fundamental
Hindu ritual concerns. [38] Nobody can escape from pollution, since the
natural functioning of the body produces sources of pollution. All human

emissions, for example, are polluting: saliva, urine, perspiration, faeces, semen, menstrual flow and the afterbirth. Menstruating women, and women for a period around childbirth, are considered impure and are subject to restrictions, which vary from caste to caste, to prevent them from polluting others, especially by means of food. But perhaps the most powerful source of pollution is death. Not only are those who handle corpses heavily polluted, but a dead person's household and certain of his relatives are also polluted by the death and have to observe various types of prohibition for varying periods. There are many ways of coping with the different types of pollution, but a particularly common one is the use of running water. A pious Hindu's morning bathing is not simply a wash, but a ritual purification to bring him to the state of purity considered necessary in Hinduism before approaching a deity. [30]

A caste is a separate, hereditary group which is normally endogamous, that is, marriage takes place usually only within the caste. A caste protects its corporate purity by restricting various types of contact with other castes it considers to be polluting, and hence impure. Thus the attribution of 'pure' or 'impure' to castes is, to some extent, relative to the status of those making the judgement. The Brahman castes, though, are always at the top of the hierarchy, being the most pure, and hence the most vulnerable to pollution. At the bottom are those castes who, for example, handle dead animals, skins or function as menials at funerals. The middle-ranging castes in any locality rank themselves hierarchically between these two extremes. Food is a major area subject to restrictions, because it readily carries pollution. The inter-caste hierarchy in any locality is clearly demonstrated in food transactions, since it quickly becomes apparent which castes or group of castes will accept or reject water, cooked food and raw food from which other castes. Physical contact used to be another sensitive area, hence the 'untouchable' castes, now called Harijans, but this is much less of an issue nowadays, perhaps because of legislation making untouchability illegal. The Harijan castes, however, still remain at the very bottom of the hierarchy. In a close-knit community, for example in a multi-caste village, the system results in the most minute discriminations being made in the sphere of interpersonal relations, but in the looser society of a town there is much greater relaxation. If a member breaks his caste's purity rules, the pollution he incurs can affect the whole caste group, so the social sanctions against the offender can be severe, and he can be required to perform various ritual acts of purification before he is entitled to resume full caste rights. An individual's ritual status is determined by the status of the caste group into which he is born. [31; 38]

But caste-linked *dharma* is not solely concerned with whom a person may marry and with purity rules that affect interpersonal behaviour. It can also determine, for example, what work a person may do, whether meat may be eaten or alcohol drunk, or whether widows may remarry. What one caste finds acceptable another does not, so that, at this level, *dharma* produces a relative morality, based on conformity to custom backed by social sanctions and scriptural authority. This by no means exhausts *dharma*. The most intimate group to which a Hindu belongs is the family. It is within the family mainly that *dharma* is transmitted from one generation to another, by custom and example in the normal process of growing up, by stories and myths which are usually highly moral and contain idealized relationships and situations, and finally by scripture and precept, although this is probably the least significant in practice. The handing down of *dharma* to the next generation is made easier by the extended nature of the Hindu family, which results in a greater exposure to adult moral and religious influences than is usually found in Western families. The Hindu family ethic is very strong so the structure of authority and the roles and responsibilities of different relationships are usually strictly adhered to. The Hindu life-cycle rites as well as various lineage and caste cult observances take place within the family and form an important part of its religious life. Thus the Hindu is initiated into both the specific and the generalized *dharma* as a natural thing from his earliest years. [38]

Dharma is more than an ethical system, but, in so far as it is viewed as such, it contrasts with the moral systems of those theistic religions which posit an ethical god. *Dharma* is ideologically supported by other important presuppositions, the already mentioned doctrine of *samsara* (the endless cycle of birth and rebirth to which the soul is subject), the allied doctrine of *karma*, that every action produces its inevitable result so that one's status in this life is determined by one's conduct in a former birth, and the notions of *papa* (sin) and *punya* (merit). Actions that deviate from *dharma*, whether by omission or commission, are *papa*, sin, and increase an individual's store of demerit. To follow *dharma* is meritorious, and especially meritorious are such acts as pilgrimage, making gifts to Brahmans or sponsoring a religious recitation. The merit, *punya*, so attained adds to one's own store, or can be transferred to, say, a departed ancestor. Certain expiatory rites, such as bathing in the Ganges, reduce *papa* and hence increase the merit balance. It is the balance between sin and merit that will eventually determine, through the law of *karma*, how a person is born in a future life, as an insect, animal or man, and, if human, with what status. The law of *karma* is used by most Hindus to explain people's present status and situation, but thoughts of future lives do not, on the whole, act as a factor in determining immediate behaviour, since the acquisition of merit through following *dharma* is an end in itself, being one of the four Hindu aims of life. [28; 29; 31]

If there are many restrictions for a Hindu in the domain of conduct, in belief there is almost total freedom. Provided that a Hindu observes the rites and cults inherent in his *dharma*, he may believe what he likes. There are, however, certain metaphysical presuppositions, like *samsara* and *karma*, to which Hindus are heir, reject them or modify them as they may. [For a broad study of Indian beliefs see 3; 28; 32.] Primary among these is the concept of *brahman*, the impersonal Absolute or World Soul that underlies the phenomenal diversity of the universe and is, at once, both immanent and transcendent. Questions about God can produce the answer *brahman*. Other answers represent *brahman* in a more personal form as *bhagvan* or *ishvara*, the Lord. Those who worship Vishnu or Shiva may replace *bhagvan* with their chosen deity. Broadly speaking, the Hindu position, in so far as there is a single position, can be described as a mixture of pantheism and monotheism, the blend being determined by the emphasis given to the concept of *brahman* as World Soul or to that of *bhagvan* as High God.

There are certain other aspects of the Hindu approach to the divine that need to be considered. One is the principle of the *ishtadeva*, the chosen deity, which accepts that individuals worship their preferred deity exclusively as the Supreme God. Connected with this is the inclusiveness of the Hindu approach. Other deities and beliefs are not denied or opposed, but are accepted as valid for others, although not regarded as of the same order of excellence as one's own. Thus a devotee of Vishnu, for example, will subordinate all the other major gods, seeing them as servants or manifestations of the one supreme Vishnu. A devotee of Shiva will do likewise. While, therefore, to enumerate all the various deities worshipped in India would produce a formidable list, and perhaps be suggestive of polytheism, to do so would be misleading without taking into account the position of the individual worshipper. For the individual there is one supreme God, however conceived or named, and various other *devas*, gods or spiritual powers. These merit respect and perhaps worship, but are conceived of as subordinate manifestations, often with specialized functions. One author has rightly pointed out that one could spend a lifetime in India and never find a 'polytheist' in Western terms, because even an unlettered peasant who has just made offerings at several shrines will affirm that 'Bhagvan ek hai', God is one. Finally the divine is also seen in men of great sanctity, in animals such as the cow, in certain trees, rivers, mountains and in countless sacred sites across the subcontinent (Figure 5.10).

Another concept central and essential to Hinduism is *moksha* (liberation), which is also one of the four Hindu aims of life. That from which liberation is sought is *samsara*, the cycle of birth and rebirth. The part of man which is immortal – variously described and designated by different schools of

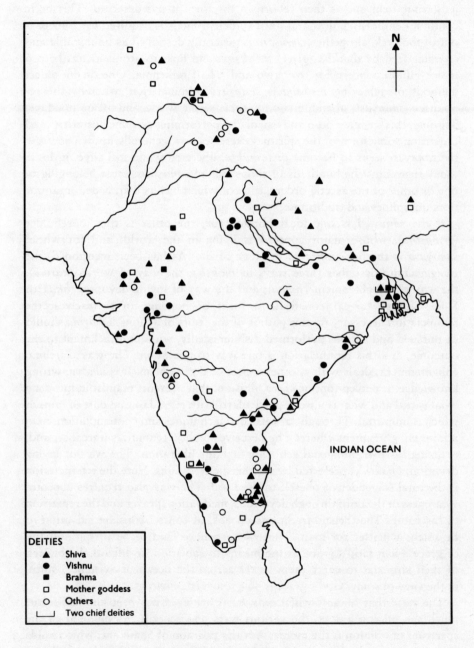

Figure 5.10   Chief deities at sacred places in India

DEITIES
- ▲ Shiva
- ● Vishnu
- ■ Brahma
- □ Mother goddess
- ○ Others
- ⨆ Two chief deities

INDIAN OCEAN

thought – passes at death to diverse heavens and hells where it works out its karmic debt and is then reborn in the form it has deserved. This cycle continues endlessly unless and until sufficient merit is acquired for it to pass out of the cycle altogether. *Samsara* is generally described as unbearable and characterized by *dukkha* (grief). *Moksha*, and how to attain it, has been a major Hindu concern for over two and a half millennia. One of the oldest methods of achieving *moksha* is *sannyasa*, renunciation, whereby the renouncer (*sannyasi*) abandons home, society, the world and all its bondage. Through this renunciation, and usually by performing extreme austerities and practising some form of the spiritual exercises now generally known as *yoga*, the *sannyasi* seeks to become *jivanmukta*, liberated while still alive. In India today there must be hundreds of thousands of *sannyasis*, most belonging to one or other of the ascetic orders, each of which has its own code, organization, disciplines and traditions.

If the *sannyasi* is one ideal Hindu type, the other is the householder (*grihastha*), whose major concern is living in the world, and for whom *sannyasa* is the final *ashrama* or stage of life. As has been mentioned, the *Bhagavadgita* describes three ways to *moksha*: the way of works (*karma*); the way of enlightenment (*jnana*); and the way of loving devotion (*bhakti*). Since works (*karma*) constitute a form of bondage in themselves, the renunciation necessary on this path is of the fruits of actions. *Dharma* should be pursued and actions performed disinterestedly, without attachment to the outcome, and this renunciation is one way to liberation. The way of *jnana*, enlightenment, deals with another aspect of the problem. It is *avidya*, wrong knowledge or perception, or *maya*, illusion, that prevents man from knowing what is real and what is unreal, particularly with regard to that part of himself which is immortal. Through various *yoga* techniques and contemplation, man attains enlightenment whereby he perceives reality, renounces unreality, and, realizing his own immortal self, thus obtains liberation. The way of loving devotion, *bhakti*, is preferred by the theistic traditions. Here the renunciation is the total surrender of oneself to the Lord. The way also requires constant awareness of the Lord through devotions, meditation, prayer and the repetition of his name. The theistic traditions do not, of course, consider salvation to be solely a matter for man. Those who believe God to be loving and full of grace await God's grace as the means to salvation, to lift off the burden of their sins and to carry them safely across the ocean of existence, since, in the view of some, God's grace is able to override *karma*.

The state that obtains when *moksha* is achieved has been the subject of much speculation among the various sects and schools. At one end of the spectrum of opinion is the monist Advaita position of Shankara, which holds that the immortal self of man is identical with *brahman* and is absorbed into *brahman* as the drop of water into the ocean. At the other end of the spectrum are the theists, who hold that the immortal soul of man lives in an eternal relationship with God. Thus Vishnu, Shiva and Krishna each have their own abodes, heavens, in which selves retain their identity in various states of nearness to God. Between these two extremes there are a range of intermediate positions. For sinners, though, there is the certainty of hell, whose horrific tortures, matching the seriousness of different sins, are graphically described.

Just as man is subject to cycles of birth and rebirth, so the universe itself is thought to go through cycles of dissolution and re-creation within immense time spans. The gods responsible for this cyclicity vary with the sectarian sources in which the myth is recorded. Within these cycles are lesser periods – *yugas*, or ages. The present age, the Kali-yuga, is thought to last 432,000 years and to have begun in the year 3102 BCE. The characteristics of this age are a decline in righteousness, piety and human prosperity. At the end of the age the world will be destroyed again by flood and fire, although there are alternative versions of what might happen. [1; 28]

The presuppositions and concerns that have just been discussed form the central elements of the received Hindu religious understanding, at least at the most general level. There are, of course, other elements, of which astrology is one important example, but the essentials have been covered. At the level of the particular, one would need to examine the nature and the mythology of the various gods, and the theology and philosophy of the different schools and sects. It is, however, within the general conceptual framework just presented that the particular systems and beliefs are articulated, and the individual Hindu derives his personal faith.

Hindu Practice

The concept of *dharma*, and how it can affect almost every aspect of a Hindu's life, has already been discussed. One author refers to this as the 'ritualization of daily life', while others consider Hinduism itself to be primarily a way of life. There is another view that sees Hinduism essentially as a *sadhana*, a way, or ways, to self-realization and the attainment of *moksha*. In considering Hindu practice, therefore, one should remember that it has a far more total application than simply the performance of rites and rituals, being concerned with the practical realization of religious values at every level. That said, however, few religions have devoted so much attention to ritual as has Hinduism. From the earliest times, the ritual manuals contain details of the most astonishing complexity and elaboration. [33] Many of these works were, of course, produced for officiating Brahman priests, and absolute accuracy in performance is considered essential, since the smallest mistake invalidates the entire rite and brings retribution. It is, however, clear that the domestic rituals that the twice-born householder, in particular the Brahman, is expected to perform daily are no less complex and demanding. [3]

A Brahman should perform a sequence of devotional rituals called *sandhya* three times a day, at dawn, at midday and in the evening. He should also worship his *ishtadeva*; make offerings to the *devas*, the seers of old and his ancestors; perform an act of charity, pay reverence to his teacher and read from the scriptures. Some of these rituals are very elaborate. The morning *sandhya* includes rituals on rising, answering the calls of nature and on brushing the teeth. The sequence continues with the Brahman purifying himself by bathing, purifying his place of worship, practising breath control, invoking the deity by the ritual touching of his limbs, meditating on the sun, making offerings of water and constantly uttering various prayers that he may be pure, free from his sins and strong enough to remain holy. One of the most important prayers, which may be repeated as many as 108 times, sometimes with the aid of a rosary, is called the 'Gayatri', a Vedic verse addressed to the sun as the Inspirer and Vivifier, and now understood as referring to the Supreme God. It has been estimated that, if the enjoined rituals were performed in full, they would take at least five hours a day. Certainly there are some pious Brahmans who do in fact perform such rituals every day, but for most daily rituals are very much abbreviated, and observance decreases proportionately as one descends the socio-ritual scale. [34]

Of great importance among domestic rituals are the *samskaras*, or sacraments, which are the life-cycle rites that mark the major transitions of a Hindu's life. In the early texts there were as many as forty such rites, but now fewer than ten are generally performed. Their purpose is to sanctify each transition of an individual's life, to protect such individuals from harmful influences and to ensure for them blessings. The pre-natal rites have nowadays fallen from use and the first observances are those attending birth. These are designed primarily to contain the pollution generated by the birth and to protect the mother and child, who are considered to be particularly vulnerable to harmful influences. The exact time of birth is noted so that a horoscope may be drawn up. On the sixth day, or sometimes on the twelfth, there is the *namakarana*, or name-giving ceremony; the house is purified and a number of the restrictions on the mother are lifted. Some castes and families observe rites on the child's first sight of the sun, and the first taking of solid food. More widely observed is the rite of ritual tonsure, when the child's head is shaved. This can take place in the child's first year or later and is often done at a temple or religious fair, sometimes as the fulfilment of a vow made by the mother to a *deva* in return for the *deva* having kept the child healthy. Another rite, that of ear-piercing, is also fairly common, although there is wide variation as to when it is performed.

The next rite, the *upanayana*, initiation, has great traditional importance, because it is the rite by which the three highest *varnas*, or classes, become 'twice-born' through receiving initiation into the Hindu fold. Nowadays, however, the rite is not regarded with the same importance as previously, and it appears to have become mainly the concern of the Brahman castes. At this ceremony the young man is invested with the sacred thread, *janeu*, which must be worn at all times and kept free from impurity. He is also initiated into the 'Gayatri' prayer by the presiding Brahman priest, who thereby often becomes his *guru*, or spiritual preceptor. In some castes a different kind of initiation takes place when, for example, a Vaishnava ascetic acts as the *guru* and whispers a *mantra*, sacred formula, to those being initiated.

The rite that signals the ritual climax of the life-cycle is *vivaha*, marriage. Standing midway between the impurity produced at birth and death, it represents the point of maximum ritual purity, in token of which the couple are treated as gods. It is a Hindu's religious duty to marry. Through marriage the religious debt to the ancestors is paid off by the production of progeny. Marriage is, therefore, a sacrament of the utmost social and religious significance in Hinduism, and usually the greatest expense a Hindu incurs is that arising from having his children married. The elaborate complex of marriage rituals can take a week or more. Because of this there is great variation in practice. The actual marriage is sealed by a rite called *phera* during which the couple walk seven times round the sacred fire, although this is only one small part of the extremely elaborate series of social and religious rituals that constitute Hindu marriage.

The *antyeshti samskara*, the funeral sacrament, is the last of the rites performed. Again there is variation in practice, but the observances have a twofold purpose. The first is to enable the departing spirit (*preta*) to leave this world and attain the status of an ancestor (*pitri*) so that it does not remain as a ghost (*bhuta*) to trouble the living but can pass to its next destination. The second is to deal with the massive pollution that is released at death, which automatically affects certain of the deceased's relatives. The body is cremated on a pyre lit preferably by the eldest son of the departed. Then begins a period of ten or eleven days of ritual restrictions on the relatives, at the end of which offerings of milk and balls of rice or barley (*pindas*) are made. These offerings, which are made at ceremonies called *shraddha*, usually take place between the tenth and twelfth days and thereafter annually. Their purpose is to enable the departing spirit, the *preta*, to acquire a new spiritual body with which it can pass on. The funeral rites should properly by performed by a son so that the deceased may best be assured of a good rebirth. It is for this reason that Hindus long above all to have a son. [3; 34]

One of the major differences in the style of domestic ceremonies is whether or not they are conducted by a Brahman priest. Not all Brahmans are priests; in fact, few are: nor are all religious practitioners Brahmans. The Brahman is a priest first because of his ritual purity, a necessary condition for acting as an intermediary between man and God, and second because of his specialized knowledge of ritual and sacred prayers and utterances. When a priest presides the rite will be more elaborate and in accord with scriptural prescription than when a head of household officiates. Rites without a priest are not invalid, but are less prestigious. An experienced priest can perform highly complex rituals and deliver a stream of sacred utterances and instructions at great speed, but many have to resort to handbooks to guide them through the ceremonies. A Brahman priest who serves a family is called a *purohita*. He will serve a number of families, usually by hereditary right, in return for an annual fee. After each ritual he will be paid a sum called *dakshina*, but this is not thought of as a fee, rather as a meritorious gift made to a Brahman. Brahmans will normally only serve as priests to twice-born castes.

Hindu worship (*puja*) falls into three categories: temple worship; domestic worship; and a form of congregational worship. This last type, *kirtana*, mainly consists of hymn-singing, and is the characteristic mode of *bhakti* devotion. It has to be said that the majority of temples in India are small, although there are a significant number of large ones, especially in the various sacred centres. A temple is the home of the enshrined deity, who will have been installed by a rite of consecration in the inner sanctuary. The god's consort may also be present, and other associated deities are often represented in different parts of the temple. Vishnu and his *avataras*, mainly Rama and Krishna, are usually represented by images – statues, often of considerable complexity – portraying many of the god's mythological attributes. This is also the case with the Goddess in her various forms. Shiva, however, is usually represented by the *lingam*, an object (usually a black stone) shaped like the male organ, and often set in the *yoni*, the shaped form of a female organ; these are the universal symbols of Shaivism. [36]

Temple priests called *pujaris* serve the deity, treating him (or her) either as royalty or as an honoured guest, or both. They carry out, at set times of the day, a schedule of worship and attendance which begins before dawn. The deity is awakened, bathed, fed, holds court, rests, is anointed, decorated, and finally is retired for the night. This schedule is accompanied by various ceremonies such as *arati* (the waving of lamps), the sounding of bells, the performance of music, hymns, prayers, the offering of flowers, fruit, grain, food and incense, together with other forms of worship and supplication. On festival days connected with the deity there are often spectacular ceremonies and processions which draw people from far around. There is no requirement for any Hindu to go to a temple, although many do, and worship is private. A Hindu goes to a temple in the hope of obtaining a *darshana*, sight or experience, of the deity, to make offerings, to pray to or petition the deity, or perhaps to make or fulfil a vow. Often food which has first been offered to the deity and hence has become consecrated (*prasada*), is available for worshippers for whom it is a much desired blessing. [36]

Domestic worship takes place in most households, but rarely with the elaboration of the temple routine. In most houses there is an area set aside for worship and maintained in a state of ritual purity. Here the *ishtadeva* of the household is represented by an image, by some symbol of the deity concerned, even by a poster. It is usually the women of the household who attend the deity and carry out the various rituals. These can comprise *arati*, offerings, prayers and acts of supplication. Geometrical designs called *yantras* and *mandalas* are sometimes used as symbols for worship. These range from fairly complex mystical symbols, used mainly in Tantric rites, to simpler designs made on the ground with different-coloured powders which can be used in the worship of any deity. [3]

The devotees who gather together to worship by chanting *bhajanas* or hymns are usually, but not necessarily, affiliated to a sect. The chanting, the music, the rhythm and the atmosphere of fervent devotion can produce a deep effect and some enter a state of trance. At these gatherings there is also sometimes an *arati* ceremony and the distribution of *prasada*. Groups who gather together in this way to worship through hymn-singing occur all over India and at most levels of society. In those parts of Assam where *bhakti* has become institutionalized, *bhajanas* are the principal mode of worship.

A different kind of communal worship is the *katha*, or the recitation of a work of scripture. It is meritorious to sponsor such a recitation and priests are commissioned and an audience invited. Each text normally relates in specific terms exactly what benefits will accrue to those who hear the text and to those who sponsor its performance.

Another highly meritorious and widely practised religious act in Hinduism is pilgrimage [35] All over India pilgrimages are taking place daily, on every scale and in every region (see Figure 5.11). There are local and regional pilgrimage sites as well as all-India pilgrimage sites like Banaras and Conjeeveram. Each site has its own characteristics, its own benefits to offer the pilgrims. There are regional sites, for example, which offer help to the blind, to the childless or to those suffering from skin complaints. Banaras and Gaya are particularly concerned with salvation, the absolution of sin and the making

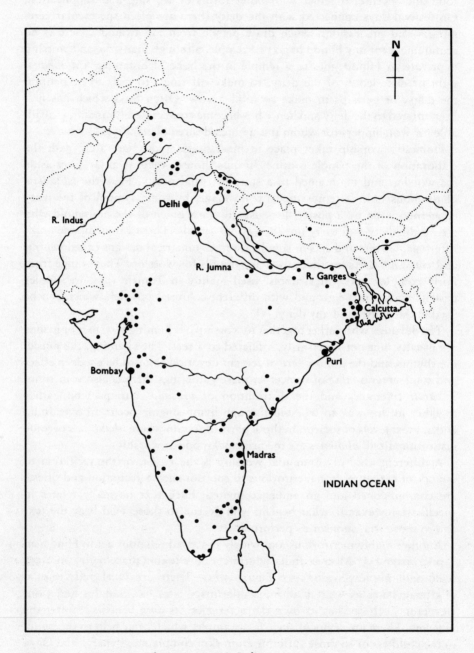

Figure 5.11   Important pilgrimage sites in India

of offerings for ancestors. Mathura and Brindavan are associated with Krishna, and hundreds of thousands of pilgrims go every year in the hope of obtaining *darshana*, an experience, of their Lord Krishna of whom they are devotees. Thus people undertake pilgrimages for a mixture of motives: for merit and salvation, for absolution of sins, to worship or experience the divine, to propitiate ancestors or to appease an angry deity, to obtain relief from illness or misfortune, or to ensure prosperity or some more specific blessing. The consequence of hundreds of thousands of Hindus mingling together away from their own localities is to reinforce the sanctity of the sacred geography of India to which Hinduism is so closely tied, and to continue to foster the sense of Hindu unity and self-awareness.

Pilgrimage sites are usually very well organized, with guides and priests who receive the pilgrims and then take them through the round of locations and ceremonies. There are booklets describing the various features and temples of each site, detailing their respective mythological associations, praising their merits and enumerating the benefits that accrue from each. Sometimes pilgrimages take place on particular days of the year when there is some great festival or religious ceremony at a certain site, such as the Jagannatha festival at Puri. By far the largest gatherings, which run into several million people, take place at the *melas*, religious fairs, which occur every twelve years at Allahabad, Hardwar, Ujjain and Nasik.

Perhaps, however, the most colourful aspect of Hindu practice is the annual cycle of festivals [39]. Indeed, Hinduism has been described as a religion of fasts, feasts and festivals, since fasting, vigils and feasting are usually integral parts of the celebration of Hindu festivals. [37] As with pilgrimage, festivals are local, regional and all-Indian. When festival lists from villages in the same region are compared, often there are very few common to all. The number of festivals celebrated throughout India must run into thousands, but the number actually celebrated in any given locality will rarely exceed twenty, and is usually much less. It is not only, of course, a matter of location. Certain castes and sects have their own festivals, and devotees of a particular deity will be concerned in the main with the festivals associated with that deity. No attempt can be made here to describe even the most notable all-India festivals. There are festivals connected with the seasons – new year, spring and autumn festivals – as well as many festivals connected with the major gods of Hinduism, Shiva, Rama, Krishna, Lakshmi, Durga, Ganesha and Hanuman. But even with these major all-India festivals there is considerable regional variation in the manner of their celebration, in the mythology and sometimes in the deity connected with each date. Although therefore this treatment of Hindu festivals has been short, their significance in the life of Hindus is great. They bring life and vitality to Hinduism. They provide an annual

•

reminder of religious values as well as occasions for great joy and celebration.

Many sweeping generalizations have been made about the position of women in Hinduism, but the diversity of sources and the contradictory nature of their pronouncements cannot sustain a single view. Apart from the omission of certain Sanskrit *mantras* from some of the life-cycle rites, and the fact that marriage is regarded as such a significant event in a woman's life that initiation (*upanayana*) is not performed, there are almost no major areas of Hindu practice from which women are excluded. A woman is held to be an equal partner in *dharma* with her husband, and thought to share his destiny, which is why many Hindu women fast regularly for the welfare of their husbands. As the mistress of the household, ritual purity is in her charge, as are many of the household rituals. Women go on pilgrimages, sponsor *kathas*, visit temples, fast, and make vows and offerings. In fact, much of the living practice of Hinduism is dependent on the participation of women.

One of the ideals of Hindu womanhood is Sita, the wife of Rama, who is portrayed as ever obedient and subservient to her Lord's wishes [4]. But although the Hindu woman is expected to show public deference to her husband, this in no way indicates the nature of their private relationship. As manager of the household, and as mother, the Hindu woman wields considerable authority. Child marriage is now illegal and the remarriage of widows lawful. The practice whereby a widow immolated herself on her husband's funeral pyre (*sati*) – which was always the exception rather than the rule – has been forbidden in law for over a century. The battle to overcome prejudice against the education of girls was won in the nineteenth century. In short, there is little reason to think that the Hindu woman is at any greater disadvantage than women elsewhere in the world, as the presence of women in many leading positions in India conclusively demonstrates.

Hinduism in the Villages

Of the total Hindu population of India, over 80 per cent, that is over 400 million Hindus, live in villages. The number of villages is over 500,000. Thus the Hinduism of the villages must certainly be regarded as the religion's most prevalent if not its most characteristic form. It is in the villages that one meets the full diversity of Hinduism. Some have regarded the religion of the villages as a 'level' of Hinduism, as folk or popular religion, but this is a mistake. There is no separate 'village Hinduism' any more than there is a separate 'village Christianity'. The entire spectrum of Hinduism, from its most sophisticated to its most unsophisticated manifestations, can be found in the villages. There is certainly a specific emphasis. The majority of villagers are simple, unlettered folk who struggle for their livelihood in the face of poverty, disease, climatic uncertainty and many other kinds of threats and difficulties. As is to be expected such people are concerned not so much with the higher realms of metaphysical speculation, nor with elaborate ritualism, but rather with the practical, pragmatic side of religion. This latter aspect of religion, which seeks to attain ends in this world – a son, a good crop, recovery from illness etc. – is as much a part of Hinduism as any other aspect, and has been since at least the time of the *Atharva-veda*. This is, however, only a matter of emphasis. Dispersed and localized in the villages of India, the continuing tradition of Hinduism flourishes and is still evolving in all its multiplicity and diversity. [40–42]

There is no such thing as a typical Indian village. Almost every village is different. This is not surprising given the great regional variations of the subcontinent, especially with regard to terrain, climate, ethnic and linguistic groupings and cultural traditions. The population of India, moreover, is not wholly Hindu. There are Muslims, Christians, Sikhs, Jains, Buddhists, Parsis and some Jews. Thus in religious terms, too, the population of the villages is not homogeneous. This lack of homogeneity is further increased by the segmentation of the Hindus into castes. There are single-caste and multi-caste villages. The nature and number of castes, and the strength of their representation, crucially affects the types of religious beliefs and practices found in a village, as well as determining its social structure. It is often the case in a multi-caste village that the pattern of residence reflects the caste composition, with, perhaps, each caste having its own quarter, and sometimes the Harijans occupying a separate hamlet.

The effect of having a number of different caste groups and also maybe households, sometimes hamlets, of adherents of other religions, is to produce considerable religious diversity within a single village. It may be that some of the castes are high, aspiring to Brahmanical norms in their behaviour and practices. Other castes, like the Harijans, who are denied the service of Brahman priests, have had to develop their own forms of religious expression. Not only are their customs quite different from those of the higher castes, but the deities they venerate are usually more local and tend to be more specific in their functions (like, for example, a smallpox goddess). Some castes have a traditional association with a particular deity, who functions rather like a patron saint, and in large castes which have a complex internal organization there are also clan and lineage deities. These caste cults add further diversity to the religious life of any particular village. It is because of this range and diversity that one must reject the notion of there being a special 'village Hinduism'. [41]

The hierarchy into which the castes arrange themselves is determined at the village level. But, usually, unless there are some special factors, there will not be a marked difference between the ranking of a caste in one village and the way the same caste is ranked in the villages around, provided that the caste composition of the villages is more or less the same. The hierarchy is not, however, fixed, except that the Brahman is always at the top and the Harijan at the bottom. If a caste group does well economically and seeks to have its newly won material position ritually recognized in an enhanced position in the hierarchy, it will abandon those of its customs and religious practices which are considered 'low', adopting instead those of the castes above it in the hierarchy. In a generation or two it will have established itself higher up and become accepted in its new ritual status. Likewise a caste group might, for some reason, lose prestige or standing and slowly slip down in the hierarchy. Although at any one time the hierarchy seems fixed, in fact there is perceptible and constant movement when measured over decades. Low castes do not humbly accept their lowly status. There is generally much bitterness, and continual effort to improve their position. [38; 41]

It used to be thought that villages were somehow self-contained units; but this is not the case and probably never has been. In the religious sphere, as well as in every other, villages are integrated into the locality and the region of which they form a part. There are considerable differences between the varieties of Hinduism found in the major regions of India: between, for example, Bengal, Gujarat and Tamil Nadu. Not only do these regional forms determine the religious outlook of the villagers, but the location of a village within a region can also be influential. It could be situated near a major temple, the centre of a sect or an ascetic order, a place of regional pilgrimage, or some other sacred site with a long mythological pedigree. These can create sub-regional influences that again colour the beliefs and practices of the villagers in that locality. Some of the villagers might be drawn to join a sect whose centre was near by, or become disciples of a *guru* who had taken up residence in the vicinity. Local cults can develop around the tomb of a man who was considered to be of great holiness. Those elements of Hinduism that are considered to have an all-India spread, like certain festivals, in fact are mediated through regional and sub-regional traditions to the individual villagers. Although the names and dates may correspond, there are major differences in the rationale and significance of such festivals in different regions, and even greater differences in the significance they might hold within the total structure of each village's sacred year. [39]

It is often the case that there are several small temples in a village, perhaps Rama, Shiva or Hanuman temples, but by far the most numerous structures are the small shrines that house the *grama devatas*, the village deities. If the various divine beings of Hinduism were to be ranked in terms of importance or power, first would come *brahman* or *bhagvan*, the Godhead or God, secondly would come the *devas*, the major gods of Hinduism, and lastly would come the *grama devatas*, the village deities. If the ranking is in terms of immediacy and the amount of attention received from the villagers, then the order is reversed. The reason for this is that, in the unsophisticated understanding of a substantial proportion of the village population, *bhagvan*, God, is too transcendent, too remote, too concerned with the cosmos to be interested in a villager's problems. The *devas* too, who do *bhagvan*'s work at a universal level, are also thought to be too busy or too grand to be concerned with humble peasants. But the various *devatas* or local deities are believed to be the supernatural powers which not only affect a villager's life and welfare, but which also demand his attention and can be extremely angry if they are not given it, with dire results for the villager.

The term *grama devata* is generic, and refers to all the deities of this category associated with a village. In a sense they all have a general function as guardian or tutelary deities of the village and they are all considered powerful and liable to bring disaster if not suitably propitiated. In fact, though, they are very varied. Some have specialized functions, like the goddesses of hydrophobia or smallpox. Others are associated with a specific part of the village for which they are the guardians. Many come into being as deifications of natural forces or the spirits of both the benevolent and the malevolent dead. One type of *grama devata* which is common to almost all parts of India is called *mata*, mother. In reality this is a euphemism, because *matas* are far from being maternal. Some are positively bloodthirsty, demanding animal sacrifices and offerings. They are among the most feared and most propitiated spirits in the villager's experience.

Not all *devatas* have shrines. Those that do, such as the special deity of a caste group, are usually represented by a statue or a brightly decorated figure of some kind. Sometimes, however, it is only possible to know that a *devata* lives in a thorn-bush or a clump of bamboos because rags are tied to them as votive offerings by the villagers. Sometimes bricks placed in a particular way or stones painted with lead oxide are the only indications of a *devata*. [41] It should not be thought that all villagers are entirely convinced about the power, even the existence, of many of the *devatas*. The higher castes in particular usually have little to do with them, regarding them as just the sort of thing that low castes would believe in. But the higher castes and the sceptical apart, this still leaves a substantial proportion of the village population who do accept that they live in an environment peopled with supernatural powers and spirits who can help them or harm them, and who require attention, propitiation and worship, as a matter of prudence if nothing else. No villager, however, will confuse this type of supernatural with *bhagvan*, although sometimes an identification is made between a particular *devata* and one of the *devas*.

When a villager is in some kind of difficulty, facing a crisis or an illness, he will first exhaust natural causes and remedies. If the problem persists, he may decide that supernatural causes are at work and turn to one of the village specialists in the supernatural. All villages have some such specialists, maybe one of the informal priests who tend the *grama devatas*, or perhaps an exorcist or a diviner. A quite different idiom operates here from that of the *devas*, who are approached by Brahman priests and in purity. The informal priests are nearly always from the lower castes and they have a special relationship with the village *devatas* of whom they are the instruments through which the deities speak to the villagers. In many parts they are ecstatics and become possessed by their tutelary deity or some other deity who is then able to speak directly to the villager. These informal priests or ecstatics attain the trance state, in which they become possessed, often by means of drumming, flagellation or the use of intoxicants. Sometimes the worshippers and petitioners standing around also enter a trance and nod or collapse or howl. [39; 41] The kind of answer that a villager with a problem will be given by these priests is that such and such a deity is angry with them for some reason, usually neglect, and demands an offering, or that they are troubled by a hostile spirit or a ghost, or that their problem is caused by the effects of the evil eye on their crops or on a child. Whatever the diagnosis, the priest will prescribe a remedy which is usually the performance of rituals of various kinds that the villager must carry out. If the ecstatic is possessed by the deity that is causing the problem, then it speaks directly to the person concerned explaining what is required and why.

Exorcists are another kind of supernatural specialist commonly resorted to in the villages. They deal with people possessed by a spirit or more usually a ghost. A ghost is the spirit of someone who has died an unnatural or untimely death and for whom the funeral rites were not effective (in which case ghosts remain on earth haunting people and places). The most powerful male ghosts are the ghosts of Brahmans and the most feared female ghosts are those of women who died childless or in childbirth. When a possessed person comes to an exorcist, the exorcist, having enlisted the aid of his own tutelary deity, will perform a few rituals and then ask the ghost to leave. A long conversation might then ensue with negotiations about the offering the ghost will require before it consents to leave the victim. Whatever the technique of the exorcist, he will usually try to coax the ghost out and confine it in a clove or small object. Later he will 'seat' the ghost elsewhere. The patient will have to provide offerings for the ghost, the tutelary deity, and some form of payment for the exorcist. [39; 41]

But a villager's contact with the *devatas* is not always through these kinds of intermediaries. The most common religious act in villages is a simple act of worship, like the making of an offering, by a single person in private. Sometimes it is made out of piety, sometimes in thanksgiving, sometimes as propitiation. One of the most common practices is the making of vows. This is very much like a contract between a villager and a *devata* made in the villager's head. It will specify that if a desired event comes about, then the villager will worship the *devata* by making a special offering, keeping a vigil or some such act. The desired event might be that the villager finds a spouse for an offspring, has a good harvest or locates a lost animal. If the event does not take place, then there is no obligation on the villager. If it does then the vow must be fulfilled otherwise there could be serious consequences. Many of the troubles of villagers are attributed by the *devatas'* priests to the non-performance of vows and the resulting anger on the part of the deity concerned.

These local deities and their cults have been treated at length because they constitute an important part of many villagers' religious life. But they are by no means all of it. Those selfsame villagers might also venerate one or more of the *devas*, the major gods of Hinduism. That this should not be thought of as polytheism has already been explained. The major events in the religious life of a village are the festivals that punctuate the year and are observed usually with great enthusiasm according to the manner of the place. Life-cycle rites too, a birth, a wedding or a funeral, provide important ceremonial occasions which are remembered for years and often bring relatives from far and near. Sometimes a wandering holy man or singer comes to the village and attracts much interest with *bhajanas*, recitations or preaching. Then there are the occasions when the villagers go out on small-scale pilgrimages or to visit a temple or some other sacred spot. All of this, both what is seen and what is unseen, forms part of the living Hinduism of the villages. [40; 42]

Finally it should again be stressed that the entire range of Hinduism is to be found in the villages, from the most orthodox Brahmanical observance to the purely local lower-caste cult. Also it must be remembered that it is the entirety that constitutes Hinduism, not just those elements that are Brahmanical or which have an all-India spread.

Modern Developments

It is now generally accepted that, when the British arrived on the scene in India in the eighteenth century, Hinduism was static if not stagnant. When the British left India in the middle of the twentieth century, Hinduism had become self-aware, self-confident and even self-assertive. It now sees itself, and is seen by others, as a world religion. There are Hindus spread over most parts of the globe, and there are Hindu movements or teachers with many thousands of followers in Europe, Britain and America. The processes whereby this came about are complex. The fact of British rule, the development of communications within India, the introduction of the printing-press, the development of prose in the Indian languages, Western education, the use of English, the challenge of Christianity and its missionaries, all these were significant factors. Equally important was the growth of political awareness, nationalism, the pressure of national and international events and the final development into independent nationhood. These and many other factors have all been profoundly influential in their own ways, but above all else it has been the revival and response from within Hinduism that has brought about this truly remarkable transformation. [See in general 43–4.]

At the beginning of this process stands Ram Mohan Roy (1772–1833) [2; 45]. He was born into a well-to-do Bengali Brahman family and was educated first in Patna, a centre of Muslim learning, where he formed an intense dislike for image-worship. In 1814 he joined the East India Company in Calcutta. There he embarked on a study of the *Upanishads*, from which he concluded that they contained a pure theism and certainly provided no justification for idol-worship. He learnt English and was deeply influenced by Western culture and scientific thought. He also had much contact with Christian missionaries. While thoroughly approving of the ethical teachings of Christianity, he could not, however, accept the divinity of Christ. He brought a rationalist approach to Hinduism and rejected not only image-worship but the doctrine of reincarnation as well. Appalled by certain Hindu practices he became an active social campaigner. So effective was his campaigning against *sati*, the practice where widows immolated themselves on their husband's funeral pyre, that in 1829 it was made illegal. A strong advocate of Western education, for women and girls as well as men and boys, he founded the Hindu College in Calcutta which opened in 1819. In 1828 he founded the Brahmo Samaj, a society that met once a week to hear readings from the *Upanishads*, sermons and to sing theistic hymns. Prayer, or any attempt to approach the divine, formed no part of this rather cold, austere approach, which appealed mainly to the educated intellectual elite. Reminiscent of eighteenth-century deism, and also peculiarly un-Indian, Roy felt this to be a return to the former purity of Hindu worship.

The next effective leader of the Brahmo Samaj after the death of Roy was Debendranath Tagore, father of the famous poet, who joined the society in 1842. He was an intensely religious man who added prayer to the Samaj service. He initiated a study of the Veda and concluded that its claim to inerrancy and to be the unique scriptural authority could not be accepted. From then on reason and conscience became the primary sources of authority for the Samaj, and Debendranath himself compiled an anthology of passages taken from various scriptures, mainly the *Upanishads*, which accorded with the position of the Samaj. A book, the *Brahma Dharma*, became the principal sacred work for the Samaj. [45]

In 1857 a young radical reformer called Keshab Chandra Sen joined the Samaj and quickly became part of the leadership, greatly impressing Tagore. At his instigation the Samaj rejected the Hindu sacraments, the *samskaras*, and produced rites of its own. It was the question of caste, however, that led Tagore and Sen to separate, and the Samaj to split. Sen wished to repudiate caste and for the twice-born to abandon the sacred thread. This was too much for the more conservative members of the Samaj. They remained with Tagore while Sen and his followers left to found the Brahmo Samaj of India. Sen thereafter became increasingly influenced by Christianity, and he compiled a scriptural work for the new Samaj drawing on sources some of which were not Hindu but were taken from other religions, particularly Christianity. He also made various changes in the service, incorporating elements of Bengali *bhakti*. But his greatest achievements were in the field of social reform. He campaigned strongly to improve the position of Hindu women and girls, and against child marriage. Under his leadership the Samaj celebrated inter-caste marriages and also the remarriage of widows, both revolutionary moves to the orthodoxy of the day.

The Brahmo Samaj was to split yet again, and Sen to found another movement called the Church of the New Dispensation. This was even more eclectic, and included a great deal from Christianity, but it did not survive his death in 1884. Meanwhile the Samaj itself continued and had a certain amount of influence in Bengal and in missionary centres elsewhere. Its real importance, however, is that it began the process of Hindu self-examination and heralded the awakening of the Hindu social conscience. The campaigning eventually proved to be successful. Not only were Brahmo marriages recognized in law, but so were inter-caste marriages and the remarriage of widows, while child marriage was made illegal. [2; 45]

Mention should also be made of the Prarthana Samaj in Maharashtra, which was not dissimilar to the Brahmo Samaj with which it had links. Its members too were theists, opposed image-worship, rejected the authority of the Veda and the doctrine of reincarnation, but they saw their theism to be a continuation of medieval Maharashtrian *bhakti*. Under the leadership of Mahadev Govind Ranade (1842–1901) their main effort was in the field of social reform and social welfare, particularly with regard to the depressed castes. In this their achievement was not inconsiderable.

Quite different from both the Brahmo and the Prarthana Samaj was the

Arya Samaj which was founded in 1875 by Dayananda Sarasvati (1824–83) [46]. Dayananda, after a childhood experience, had become disillusioned with image-worship. Eventually he found a *guru* under whom he studied and to whom he gave a pledge to remove from Hinduism all the corruptions and accretions that had entered it after the Veda. Whereas the trend of previous reform movements had been towards Westernization, here was a movement that was Hindu through and through, intent on returning Hinduism to its Vedic purity. Dayananda's view, however, of what constituted the message of the Veda was highly idiosyncratic and is beyond the scope of this account. What is really significant about the Arya Samaj is that Hinduism had gone on to the offensive. Dayananda fiercely attacked both Islam and Christianity since he saw them as threats to Hinduism in that they were attracting converts, especially from the lower castes. The Samaj instituted a ceremony for reconversion to Hinduism, and began to invest untouchable castes with the sacred thread, a procedure not recognized by the orthodox. The Samaj had some success, particularly in the Panjab and the North. Colleges were established and the use of Hindi encouraged. Seeking to establish itself as a universal church, the Arya Samaj was militant, dogmatic and aggressive. It still exists in various parts of the world. Most Hindus did not like either its message or its methods, but it gave Hinduism a boost of self-confidence when it was needed.

A further boost came from an unlikely quarter. In 1877 Mme Blavatsky and her helper Colonel Olcott arrived in India. They had opened the Theosophical Society two years earlier in New York, but with little success. However, there is no doubt that both Mme Blavatsky and her successor Mrs Annie Besant (1847–1933) greatly raised the self-confidence of Hindus. Hailing Hinduism as a repository of ancient wisdom and the source of all religions, these two formidable ladies travelled round India lavish in their extravagant and uncritical praise of all things Hindu, awakening pride in the religious heritage of Hinduism and removing any feelings of inferiority that had developed following the activities of Christian missionaries, about whom they were scathing.

The next really significant influence came from deep within Hinduism. In 1852 Gadhadhar Chatterji, the son of poor Brahman parents, became a priest at the Kali temple near Calcutta. Here, in his longing for the Mother, he went through endless trances and mystical states until finally he was granted a vision of the Goddess. He turned to Tantric disciplines to control the stream of spiritual experience he was passing through and eventually was initiated by a monk of the Advaita school into the Vedantic teaching of pure monism. The name he received on initiation and by which he is generally known is Ramakrishna Paramahansa. Ramakrishna's deep spirituality made a powerful impact on all who came in contact with him, often producing in them some form of spiritual experience. Many came to see him, including Keshab Chandra Sen and other reformers, and they found that what they could only speak of from their minds, he spoke of from the depth of his own spiritual experience. Much that he said was not new, but his own consciousness enabled him to see God in every man and in every religion. He affirmed that all religions were true and that everyone should follow their own as their way to God realization. He was also insistent on the need to serve one's fellow men. [2; 47]

Among Ramakrishna's disciples was a young Bengali called Narendranath Datta who had received a Western education in Calcutta and had been hovering on the edge of the Brahmo Samaj until he had met Ramakrishna. This meeting transformed his life. After Ramakrishna's death he became a *sannyasi* with the name of Vivekananda and travelled throughout India. [48] In 1893 he went as the representative of Hinduism to the first session of the World Parliament of Religions in Chicago. Here he made a very great impact, presenting Hinduism for the first time to the world as a universal faith. His message, although questionable in part, was that all religions were true, that Hinduism is the most ancient, the noblest and the mother of all religions, that India was spiritual and the West materialistic, though he believed that India should use Western science and methods to improve her lot. His philosophical position was that of Advaita. He spent four years lecturing in America and England and as a result Vedanta centres were set up in several cities. His return to India was greeted with great enthusiasm, for Hinduism had found an outstanding exponent and it was even thought that he had converted most of America. He immediately set up the Ramakrishna Mission, which devoted itself to social work and the relief of suffering as well as to promoting its religious message. [48] The Ramakrishna Mission has not had a great impact, although it still exists. But Vivekananda had made an unprecedented contribution. He had raised Hinduism to the status of a world religion in the outside world, and he had affirmed to Hindus that all parts of Hinduism were good, though some had been misunderstood and distorted. It was on these foundations that Mahatma Gandhi was to build.

Mohandas Karamchand Gandhi (1869–1948) was born to a family of Gujarati Kshatriyas and, after a somewhat unsettled education, he was sent to London to study law, being called to the Bar in 1891 [49; 50]. After two years in India he went to South Africa where he remained for twenty years. He worked with the Indian community there and led them with some success in their struggle for justice, and against oppressive measures. By the time he returned to India in 1915, Gandhi was forty-six. Most of the values, convictions and techniques for which he later became famous in India had already been formed and tested. He had already formulated his concept of *satyagraha*, adherence to the truth, which he combined with *ahimsa*, non-violence, and *sarvodaya*, universal uplift or the welfare of all, as the three main essentials of his approach. His passionate belief in human equality and justice he had demonstrated in his work, and by personally taking an untouchable to live in his house in South Africa. His favourite religious reading was the *Bhagavad-gita*, the *Ramacaritamanasa* of Tulsidas and the Sermon on the Mount. He was greatly influenced by the writings of Tolstoy, Ruskin, Thoreau and William Morris. He had established a community in a farm near Durban which sought to achieve simplicity of life, and it could be that it is to these authors that he owed his belief in the virtue of manual labour and his aversion to large-scale industry. Also deeply rooted in him was the belief that *brahmacarya*, total self-control, was essential to the pursuit of truth.

On his return to India, Gandhi established an ashram, or spiritual community, and set about both his political activities and also his campaign to improve the position of the untouchables, initially fasting until temples were opened to them for the first time ever. The history of the national movement, the winning of Independence and Gandhi's central part in this cannot be chronicled here, but what must be realized is that Gandhi was a religious leader first, and a political leader second. He came to the masses of India as an ascetic, a *sannyasi*, and they regarded him as a *mahatma*, a saint or great soul, and even as an incarnation of Vishnu. He called himself a follower of *sanatana dharma*, the eternal *dharma* or righteousness, and he believed that the soul of India must first become liberated from its vices before there could be freedom from the British. [50] That is why he campaigned so strongly against untouchability, calling the untouchables Harijans, the people of God; that is why he fasted and prayed endlessly that there should be neither violence nor intercommunal hatred between Hindus and Muslims; and that was why partition and the blood-bath that followed were for Gandhi failure, even though the British had gone and India had achieved nationhood.

But if Gandhi felt this to be a failure, and if his efforts to remove untouchability have not succeeded, still his achievement is immense. Gandhi was truly a *mahatma*, a great soul, for he embraced within himself the entire people of India, imbuing them with his own deep spirituality, and led them to independent nationhood. Certainly this was a major political triumph, but, more important, it was the realization of religious values in the hearts and minds of men on a prodigious scale. In the process he, perhaps more than any other before, brought Hindu self-awareness and self-identity to a new maturity.

After the death of Gandhi, and since the Republic of India has become an independent secular state, Hinduism has paused for breath, as has India herself. Some have claimed to see major changes, especially detecting the collapse of the caste system, but this is premature and the evidence unconvincing. History should indicate that deep processes of change in so conservative a religion as Hinduism are inevitably slow and usually undetectable at any given time. But India now has its place in the world, and Hinduism stands alongside other world religions as an equal. It would seem probable that the next developments, perhaps in all religions, will come in response to the pressures of world events. Whatever the future holds, however, there can be no doubt that the contribution of Hinduism will be rich and valuable, and will mark yet another stage in its continuing evolution.

BIBLIOGRAPHY

General

1. BASHAM, A. L., *The Wonder That was India*, London, Sidgwick & Jackson, 1954, 3rd rev. edn 1967; New York, Taplinger, 1968; London, Fontana, 1971
2. ZAEHNER, R. C., *Hinduism*, London, New York, Oxford University Press, 1962, new edn 1966
3. MORGAN, K. W. (ed.), *The Religion of the Hindus*, New York, Ronald Press, 1953
4. O'FLAHERTY, W. D. (ed.), *Hindu Myths: A Sourcebook, Translated from the Sanskrit*, Harmondsworth, Penguin Books, 1975
5. DE BARY, W. T., *et al.* (eds.), *Sources of Indian Tradition*, New York, Columbia University Press, 1958, repr. 1969

Introduction to Hinduism

6. FARQUHAR, J. N., *An Outline of the Religious Literature of India*, London, New York, Oxford University Press, 1920
7. KEITH, A. B., *The Religion and Philosophy of the Veda and Upanishads*, Cambridge, Mass., Harvard University Press/London, Oxford University Press, 1925
8. O'FLAHERTY, W. D., *The Rig Veda: An Anthology*, Harmondsworth, Penguin Books, 1981
9. MACDONELL, A. A., *Vedic Mythology*, Strassburg, Trübner, 1897
10. HUME, R. E., *The Thirteen Principal Upanishads*, London, Oxford University Press, 1921, 2nd edn 1931, repr. 1934; Madras, Oxford University Press (India), (1949), repr. 1958
11. EDGERTON, F., *The Bhagavad-Gita, Translated and Interpreted*, Cambridge, Mass., Harvard University Press/London, Oxford University Press, 1944, 1952; prev. publ. Chicago, Ill., Open Court Publishing, 1925

12. BÜHLER, G., *The Laws of Manu, Translated with Extracts from Seven Commentaries*, Oxford, Clarendon Press, 1886 (Sacred Books of the East, XXV); 2nd edn, Delhi, Motilal Banarsidass, 1967

13. HOPKINS, E. W., *Epic Mythology*, Strassburg, Trübner, 1915; Ann Arbor, Mich., University Microfilms, 1961

14. BHATTACHARJI, S., *The Indian Theogony: A Comparative Study of Mythology from the Vedas to the Purāṇas*, Cambridge, Cambridge University Press, 1970; repr. Columbia, Mo, South Asia Books, 1978

15. GONDA, J., *Viṣṇuism and Śivaism: A Comparison*, London, Athlone Press, 1970; New Delhi, Oriental Books, 1976

16. GUPTA, S., HOENS, D. J., and GOUDRIAAN, T., *Hindu Tantrism*, Leiden, Brill, 1979

17. CARPENTER, J. E., *Theism in Medieval India*, London, Constable, 1926, first publ. London, Williams & Norgate, 1921 (Hibbert Lectures, 2nd ser., 1919)

18. LOTT, E. J., *Vedantic Approaches to God*, London, Macmillan/Totowa, N J, Barnes & Noble, 1980

19. CARMAN, J. B., *The Theology of Rāmānuja*, New Haven, Conn., Yale University Press, 1974

20. DHAVAMONY, M., *The Love of God According to Śaiva Siddhānta: A Study in the Mysticism and Theology of Śaivism*, Oxford, Clarendon Press, 1971

21. CHATTERJII, J. C., *Kashmir Śaivism*, Srinagar, Research Department, Kashmir State/London, Luzac, 1914

22. RAMANUJAN, A. K., *Speaking of Śiva*, Harmondsworth, Penguin Books, 1973 (Kannada poetry, tr. with introduction)

23. DESAI, P. B., *Basaveśvara and His Times*, Dharwar, Kannada Research Institute, Karnatak University, 1968

24. ARCHER, W. G., *The Loves of Krishna in Indian Painting and Poetry*, London, Allen & Unwin/New York, Macmillan, 1957

25. HILL, W. P. D. (tr.), TULASĪDĀSA, *The Holy Lake of the Acts of Rāma: An English Translation of Tulasī Dās's Rāmacaritamānasa*, Bombay, Oxford University Press (India), 1952, 1971

26. RANADE, R. D., *Indian Mysticism: Mysticism in Maharashtra*, Poona, Aryabhushan, 1933 (S. K. Belvalkar and R. D. Ranade, *History of Indian Philosophy*, vol. 7)

27. VAUDEVILLE, C. (tr.), *Kabir*, vol. 1, Oxford, Clarendon Press, 1974

Hindu Presuppositions and Belief

28. BOWES, P. *The Hindu Religious Tradition*, London, Boston, Mass., Routledge, 1978

29. KANE, P. V., *The History of Dharmaśāstra*, 5 vols. in 7, Poona, Bhandarkar Oriental Research Institute, 1930–62

30. MONIER-WILLIAMS, SIR M. B. H., *Brahmanism and Hinduism*, 4th edn, London, John Murray/New York, Macmillan, 1891

31. PRABHU, P. N., *Hindu Social Organisation*, new edn, Bombay, Popular Book Depot, 1954, repr. 1972; first publ. as *Hindu Social Institutions*, London, New York, Longmans, 1939
32. DASGUPTA, S. N., *A History of Indian Philosophy*, 5 vols., Cambridge, Cambridge University Press, 1922–55, and repr.; Atlantic Highlands, NJ, Humanities, 1975; Delhi, Motilal Banarsidass, 1976

Hindu Practice
33. DIEHL, C. G., *Instrument and Purpose: Studies on Rites and Rituals in South India*, Lund, Gleerup, 1956
34. STEVENSON, M. S., *The Rites of the Twice-Born*, London, New York, Oxford University Press, 1920; repr. New York, International Publications Service, 1971; New Delhi, Oriental Books, 1971
35. BHARDWAJ, S. M., *Hindu Places of Pilgrimage in India*, Berkeley, Calif., University of California Press, 1973
36. MICHELL, G., *The Hindu Temple: An Introduction to Its Meaning and Forms*, London, Elek/New York, Harper & Row, 1977
37. UNDERHILL, M. M., *The Hindu Religious Year*, London, New York, Oxford University Press/Calcutta, Association Press, 1921

Hinduism in the Villages
38. HUTTON, J. H., *Caste in India: Its Nature, Function and Origins*, Cambridge, Cambridge University Press, 1946; 4th edn, Bombay, Oxford University Press (India), 1963
39. BABB, L. A., *The Divine Hierarchy: Popular Hinduism in Central India*, New York, Columbia University Press, 1975
40. O'MALLEY, L. S. S., *Popular Hinduism: The Religion of the Masses*, Cambridge, Cambridge University Press/New York, Macmillan, 1935
41. POCOCK, D., *Mind, Body and Wealth: A Study of Belief and Practice in an Indian Village*, Oxford, Blackwell/Totowa, NJ, Rowman & Littlefield, 1973
42. CROOKE, W., *The Religion and Folklore of Northern India*, London, Oxford University Press, 1926; first publ. as *The Popular Religion and Folklore of Northern India*, 2 vols., Westminster, Constable, 1896; republ. Delhi, Munshiram Manoharlal, 1968, and (as *The Religion ...*) New Delhi, Chand, 1972

Modern Developments
43. FARQUHAR, J. N., *Modern Religious Movements of India*, New York, Macmillan, 1915, repr. 1919; New Delhi, Munshiram Manoharlal, 1967
44. SHARMA, D. S., *The Renaissance of Hinduism*, Benares, 1944
45. KOPF, D., *The Brahmo Samaj and the Shaping of the Modern Indian Mind*, Princeton, NJ, Princeton University Press, 1978
46. RAI, L. L. (LAJPAT RAI, L.), *History of the Arya Samaj*, New Delhi,

Bombay, Orient Longman, 1967; first edn publ. as *The Arya Samaj*, London, Longman, 1915

47. NIKHILANANDA, *The Gospel of Sri Ramakrishna*, Madras, Sri Rama-krishna Math., 1947, 1957
48. DEVDAS, N., *Swāmī Vivekānanda*, Bangalore, Christian Institute for the Study of Religion and Society, 1968
49. FISCHER, L., *The Life of Mahatma Gandhi*, London, Cape, 1951
50. GANDHI, M. K., *Autobiography: The Story of My Experiments with Truth* (tr. from the original Gujarati by M. Desai), Ahmedabad, Navajivan, 1962; first publ. in English as *The Story of My Experiments with Truth*, 1927–9. Other edns include Washington DC, Public Affairs Press, 1948, 1954; London, Phoenix, 1949

6

Sikhism

W. OWEN COLE

Introduction

SOURCES FOR THE STUDY OF SIKHISM

The Punjabi movement which came to be known as Sikhism attracted no more literary attention from its contemporaries than did the beginnings of other groups which developed into Christianity and Islam. Consequently the principal primary sources for the study of Sikhism in its formative period, considered to date from 1469 to 1708, are Sikh. These must be checked against Indian writings of the time, especially Muslim, to place the emergence of the faith in its socio-historical context. The documents fall into two categories. First, there are the scriptures which are contained in the Guru Granth Sahib, also known as the Adi Granth. This consists of religious teachings expressed in metrical form composed by six of the Gurus, the first five and the ninth (see page 242), as well as the verses of some Hindu and Muslim teachers who had a similar religious outlook [1: III]. Though anthologies of these hymns were made during the period of the second Guru and possibly in the lifetime of the founder, Guru Nanak, the first definitive collection, known as the Adi Granth, or first book, was compiled in 1603–4 under the supervision of the fifth Guru. The last recension of the Adi Granth was made by the tenth Guru, Gobind Singh, in 1706. He included verses composed by his father, but none of his own. Two years later, on the eve of his death, he installed the collection as his successor, since which time the names Guru Granth Sahib and Adi Granth have been used synonymously and the book has been the authoritative guide and scripture of the Sikhs.

The Adi Granth contains no historical narratives and little explicit biographical material about the Gurus who established the Sikh faith. For such information it is necessary to turn to a number of hagiographic biographies of Guru Nanak known as *janam-sakhis* [4; 5; II; 21], and to similar traditional accounts of the lives and achievements of the later Gurus [2]. To these must be added the *Vars* of the bard Bhai Gurdas, ballads or heroic poems composed in the time of the fifth or sixth Gurus, epitomizing the work of the early Gurus and providing a commentary on the Sikh way of life. An important source for the life and teachings of the tenth Guru is the *Dasam Granth*, or book of the tenth Guru, compiled some years after his death by Bhai Mani Singh, one of his disciples [2: III]. However, it is by no means certain that all its contents are authentic compositions of the Guru and it still awaits thorough analytical study. Knowledge of the concerns of the Sikh community during the eighteenth and nineteenth centuries can be obtained from various codes of discipline issued during that period.

SHORT INTRODUCTION TO THE HISTORY OF THE RELIGION

Sikhism owes its origins and early impetus to the sense of mission and dynamism of a man known reverentially as Guru Nanak. He was born in April 1469 at Talwandi, now called Nankana Sahib in his honour, a village not far from Lahore (see Figure 6.1). The *janam-sakhis* portray him as a precocious child who outstripped his teachers in knowledge while questioning the traditional standards and practices of piety which he encountered, both Hindu and Muslim [21: 4–9]. When he was thirty years old Nanak underwent an experience which resulted in him becoming a religious teacher. This is described in the *janam-sakhis* [e.g. 21: 18–21], but the earliest account is given in one of his hymns which is preserved in the Adi Granth (p. 150):

I was a minstrel out of work,
The Lord gave me employment.
The mighty one instructed me,
'Sing my praise night and day.'
The Lord summoned the minstrel to his high court.
On me he bestowed the robe of honouring him and singing his praise.

On me he bestowed nectar in a cup,
The nectar of his true and holy name.
Those who at the bidding of the Guru
Feast and take their fill of the Lord's holiness
Attain peace and joy.
Your minstrel spreads your glory
By singing your word.
Nanak, through adoring the truth,
We attain to the all-highest.

The form this experience took is not known. One morning Nanak took his customary bath in the river near his home at Sultanpur where he was in the employment of a local Muslim governor, Daulat Khan; and disappeared for three days, during which the river was dragged and the banks searched.

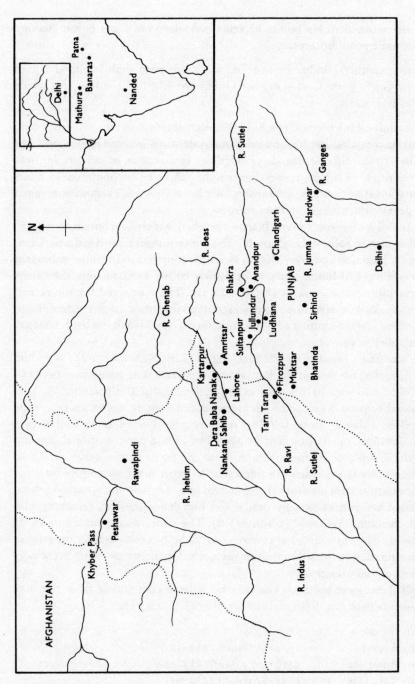

Figure 6.1 Sites in India relating to the Sikh religion

When he returned to his family he remained silent for a day before making the enigmatic pronouncement,

> There is neither Hindu nor Muslim, so whose path shall I follow? I shall follow God's path. God is neither Hindu nor Muslim and the path which I follow is God's.

From a study of his life and teaching the interpretation of these words would seem to be that God lies beyond religious systems. Whether Guru Nanak felt that God could also be found within them is a matter of debate. He was severely critical of the expressions of religion which he encountered, so much so that it must sometimes seem ironic that his own work eventually resulted in the development of yet another religion.

For over twenty years Guru Nanak travelled widely, encouraging women as well as men to follow 'God's path'. The *janam-sakhis* record visits to Tibet, Sri Lanka, Baghdad and even Mecca, as well as journeys to the most important religious centres of India. Then, in or shortly before 1520, he built the village of Kartarpur on the bank of the River Ravi. There he lived for the rest of his life, making a few brief journeys but giving most of his attention to establishing and developing a Sikh community. Guru Nanak died at Kartarpur in September 1539.

The attractive personality and teaching of Guru Nanak naturally won him many disciples, for whom the Punjabi term is *sikh*. The immediate needs of these Sikhs was met by his own example, leadership and teaching. A daily devotional routine developed with morning and evening devotions beginning and ending a day given to fulfilling one's responsibilities as a member of a family. Personal meditation had its place but so had congregational worship using the Guru's own compositions. At some point in the development of the community Guru Nanak decided that he must make some provision for its continuation after his death. He groomed one of his disciples, named Lehna, for leadership and eventually designated him his successor, renaming him Angad, meaning 'my limb' [2 vol. II: 1–11]. The name was intended to assert continuity. The choice of a successor was to be of considerable importance in ensuring that a pietistic movement gained permanence and eventually became a distinct religion.

In all there were ten Sikh Gurus, who led the community from the time that Guru Nanak began his teaching until 1708. They were:

Guru Nanak	1469–1539
Guru Angad	1504–52 (Guru 1539–52)
Guru Amar Das	1479–1574 (Guru 1552–74)
Guru Ram Das	1534–81 (Guru 1574–81)

Guru Arjan	1563–1606 (Guru 1581–1606)
Guru Hargobind	1595–1644 (Guru 1606–44)
Guru Har Rai	1630–61 (Guru 1644–61)
Guru Har Krishan	1656–64 (Guru 1661–4)
Guru Tegh Bahadur	1621–75 (Guru 1664–75)
Guru Gobind Singh	1666–1708 (Guru 1675–1708). (See also Figure 6.2.)

All the Gurus came from the Khatri jati, a mercantile caste regarded by Sikhs as belonging to the Kshatriya varna (see page 197). With the fourth Guru the office became hereditary in the line of his male descendants, all of whom, like him, were Sodhis [5: v]. Sikhism regards each of the Gurus as of equal standing. Two of the Sikh bards whose compositions are included in the Guru Granth Sahib expressed their spiritual relationship thus (AG 966):

> The divine light is the same, the life form is the same. The king has merely changed his body.

The same concept is also expressed by the use of the word Mahala followed by the appropriate number, instead of a personal name, when assigning a composition of the Adi Granth to its author. The formula Mahala I denotes Guru Nanak, Mahala V Guru Arjan. Sometimes this is abbreviated to MI, MV or even I, V. Occasionally Sikh writers will convey the same idea by referring to Guru Nanak's successors as 'the third Nanak' or 'the fifth Nanak' [21: 3].

In the development of the Sikh Panth, as the community is called, some Gurus played a more important part than others [1: II; 5: III]. Guru Angad's task was to consolidate the Panth. This he did by writing down Guru Nanak's hymns in a script developed either by himself or his predecessor. Now called Gurmukhi, it has become the script of written Punjabi. He may also have encouraged the compilation of the first *janam-sakhi*. These would provide scattered communities, known as *sangats*, with an example to follow, instruction to study, and a collection of material for use in worship.

Guru Amar Das felt the need to ensure that the growing and widespread Panth should remain under his direction. He established himself at the village of Goindwal on the River Beas. He summoned the Sikhs to assemble in his presence three times a year at Magha-shivatri, a Shaivite festival (see pages 200–203), Diwali (associated with Ram Chandra), and Baisakhi, the beginning of the New Year and spring harvest in the Punjab. He also divided the Sikhs into twenty-two districts, called *manjis*, each supervised by a *masand*.

The fourth Guru, Ram Das, began the building of the city of Amritsar. Though it now lies on the famous Grand Trunk road from Kabul to Calcutta it was then some miles north of it. Guru Ram Das may have moved from

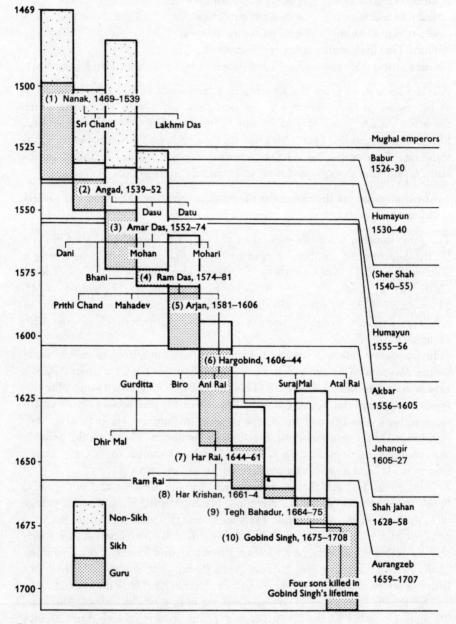

Figure 6.2 The place of the ten Gurus in the Sikh religion

Goindwal to Amritsar because the site had associations with Guru Nanak, but he encouraged merchants and business men to establish themselves there, so it may be assumed that his motives were commercial and perhaps political as well as pious. However, the brevity of his leadership prevents the scholar from adducing his purpose with certainty.

With Guru Arjan intentions became clear. He established other towns at Taran Taran, Sri Hargobindpur (named after his only son) and Kartarpur (not to be confused with the village created by Guru Nanak). These gave him a political and economic base in a region of the Punjab populated to a large extent by Jats, an agrarian social group noted for its military traditions and democratic spirit. Guru Arjan also set about building a place of worship in Amritsar and authorizing the compilation of the Adi Granth, which he installed in the new building called the Harimandir or Darbar Sahib. Its site is now occupied by the Golden Temple.

During the late sixteenth century the Sikhs enjoyed good relations with the tolerant Mughal Emperor Akbar the Great (reigned 1556–1605) (see page 242). Indeed it may be that it was the interest he showed in the movement (as well as in other expressions of religion) which encouraged the Sikhs to hope that they might be the reconciling agent between Hinduism and Islam for which the Emperor seemed to be seeking. On the birth of his son, whom he named Hargobind, Guru Arjan wrote (A G 396):

> The Sat Guru (God) has sent the child,
> The long-lived child has been born by destiny.
> When he came and made his
> abode in the womb his mother's heart became very glad. The son, the
> saint of the Lord, is born. The primal
> writ has become manifest amongst all. In the
> tenth month, by the Lord's command the baby has
> been born.

However, within two years of the installation of the Adi Granth in the Harimandir, Akbar had been succeeded by Jehangir who had the Guru imprisoned on suspicion of being implicated in a move to support his defeated rival. Guru Arjan died in captivity, providing Sikhism with its first martyr.

Guru Hargobind, it is said, armed himself in obedience to his dying father's advice. He lived and ruled as a temporal as well as spiritual leader, keeping court, enjoying hunting yet remaining the Guru of the Sikhs, though unlike his predecessors he did not compose religious verses. Doubtless this prompted some shift of emphasis from the living Guru to the Adi Granth as spiritual guide. Though relations with Jehangir, the Mughal emperor, were sometimes strained, nevertheless he occasionally accompanied the ruler on hunting expeditions.

The seventh and eighth Gurus did not make outstanding contributions to the religion's development. With the ninth Guru, Tegh Bahadur, leadership seems to have reverted to a more traditional form. This surviving son of Guru Hargobind was a devout poet, though also a man of strong character. He succeeded to the *gaddi*, or seat of authority, at a time when Emperor Aurangzeb's policy of Islamization was beginning. (In 1669 orders were given to close Hindu schools and demolish temples. Ten years later the poll tax (*jizya*) imposed on non-Muslims was reintroduced.) Guru Tegh Bahadur was among those who opposed the emperor. In 1675 he was executed in Delhi and is revered by Sikhs as a martyr who died not only for the Sikh faith but also for the principles of religious liberty.

His son, the tenth Guru, was also a man whose relationships with the Mughal emperor were variable. With regard to the development of Sikhism his importance lies in two decisive acts. In 1699 at the Baisakhi gathering in Anandpur he founded the Khalsa brotherhood [1: VI; 5: 1]. The word 'Khalsa' may be translated as 'pure', but the land which is the personal property of a sovereign is also called *khalsa*. The term, therefore, denotes the Guru's own people. Those who responded to the Guru's call for loyalty at Anandpur received initiation through a ceremony known as Khande ka Amrit, or Amrit Pahul, using a mixture of sugar and water stirred by a two-edged sword (a *khanda*) while a number of Sikh hymns were recited. Those initiated took certain vows, and adopted five 'K's'. These are five symbols which, in Punjabi, each begin with the letter K. They are *kesh* (unshorn hair), *kangha* (comb), *kirpan* (sword), *kara* (steel wristlet) and *kachch* (short trousers). To these, male members of the Khalsa added the turban worn traditionally by the Sikh Gurus. The result was a distinctiveness of appearance which has marked the Sikh ever since. Male members of the Khalsa replaced their *gotra* or caste name by Singh and females used Kaur. The theoretical significance of using these names, meaning 'lion' and 'princess', is the elimination of caste identity in that everyone is raised to the status of a Kshatriya (warrior class) – if in practice the *gotra* name is often retained to assist identification.

As Guru Gobind Singh lay dying from wounds inflicted by an assassin, he installed the Adi Granth as his successor. Since then it has been called the Guru Granth Sahib, though Sikhs still use the name Adi Granth. The reason for conferring guru-ship upon the collection of sacred writings was to prevent succession disputes, because the Guru's four sons had all pre-deceased him [16: v]. However, the move is also seen in the context of Guru Gobind Singh's doctrine that the Khalsa was his other self. While the spiritual guide was to be the scripture, political or temporal authority was to reside in the Khalsa Panth (community).

The creation of the Khalsa was a device for sanctioning the use of force and disciplining it by bringing it under the control of the Guru. Certainly

from the time of Guru Hargobind, who kept a small standing army, Sikh fight-
ing units had existed [3 vol. I: IV]. Often these were irregular war bands
responsible to local commanders. Now they owed allegiance to the Guru,
who would only call upon them to fight in a *dharm yudh*, a struggle on behalf
of justice, in defence of religious freedom [3 vol. I: V]. The sanctioning of armed
resistance is not regarded by Sikhs as contrary to the spirit of Guru Nanak.
There is no evidence that he was a pacifist or that the purpose of his mission
was the reconciliation of Hindu and Muslim. At the same time there are many
examples that can be given of his speaking out against falsehood and exploitation [e.g. 4: III]. The use of force when all other methods had failed was
regarded as necessary in the unstable political climate of the late seventeenth
century.

So far the development of Sikhism has been attributed to the policies of
the Gurus. It is now necessary to mention another factor, the nature and
composition of the Sikh community itself. Sikhism is, and always has been,
a fiercely democratic movement. The Gurus attracted to themselves men and
women from many groups but by the time of Guru Arjan, a strong influx
of Jats had taken place [5: I, V]. The Jats, a militant, egalitarian, north
Indian agrarian group, traditionally opposed to Brahmanism (see pages 206ff),
began to influence the lay movement, which Sikhism is, as soon as they joined
it. The work of Guru Hargobind and of Guru Gobind Singh, as well as the
policies of Guru Arjan in building his three towns, might be seen as attempts
to bring the Jats under their control.

The year 1708 marks the end of what might be described as the canonical
period of Sikhism. The eighteenth century saw long and bitter struggles between Sikhs and Mughals until, at the end of the century, one of the Sikh
resistance leaders succeeded in creating, maintaining and expanding an independent state in the Punjab. The man was Maharaja Ranjit Singh [3 vol.
I: X, XI]. The kingdom which he founded with the capture of Lahore in 1799 survived until 1849 when his son Maharaja Dalip Singh handed his kingdom
and the Koh-i-noor diamond over to the British after the second Punjab war.

Four other events in the history of Sikhism need to be mentioned if
present-day Sikhism is to be understood fully. First, in the late nineteenth
century, the influential Singh Sabha movement emerged [3 vol. II: IX; 5: V].
This was a response to the successful Christian evangelism in the Punjab but
even more to the activities of the Arya Samaj (see page 230). In 1877
Dayananda Saraswati came to the Punjab and opened a branch of the Arya
Samaj in Lahore. Though at first his movement was well received by Sikhs
it soon became clear that he held their Gurus in low esteem. The Sikhs
responded by increasing their support of a Singh Sabha (Singh Society) which
had been founded in Amritsar in 1873 and quickly extended its work to
Lahore and other cities. Its main function was the revival of Sikhism through

literary and educational activities, especially the founding of such institutions as the Khalsa College, Amritsar (1892). This recovery also took the form of political agitation, leading to the Anand Marriage Act (1909), which gave legal recognition to the Sikh form of wedding service, and the Gurdwara Act (1925). This ended a protracted and bitter struggle to regain control of *gurdwaras*, Sikh places of worship, which had often passed into the ownership or custody of Hindus.

Sikhs, who took part with other Indians in the Independence struggle, were to find their homeland divided between India and Pakistan in 1947 [3 vol. II: XVII]. The civil unrest that ensued was particularly marked in the Punjab, with perhaps as many as 2 million Sikhs leaving the eastern part and a similar number of Muslims emigrating from the west. Enmity between Sikh and Muslim remains strong, a generation later. This second significant event in Sikh history led to the third. The demand for a separate Sikh state was ignored in 1947 but in 1966 the Punjabi Suba was established, a Punjab state with redrawn boundaries, containing 85 per cent of the Sikh population of India and having Punjabi as its official language [3 vol. II: XIX]. This might not be Independence, but it gave the Sikhs some measure of autonomy.

Fourthly, mention must be made of the migrant Sikh community. From about 1870 until 1947 Sikhs served in the British army outside India. On discharge some of them settled in such places as Hong Kong and Singapore. In common with many Punjabis other Sikhs who had not been in the armed forces joined the migration, though maintaining their roots in the Punjab. Now Sikhs are to be found in many English-speaking parts of the world, usually Commonwealth countries, but also the U.S.A. It is too soon to say what influence this group of migrants, some 1 million or about 8 per cent of the total Sikh population, will have upon the Panth, but it could be considerable. Already Sikhism regards itself as a world religion. As yet, however, the phrase relates more to its distribution and self-awareness than to the universality of its appeal. In reality all Sikh communities are still Punjabis and the religion might be categorized as ethnic, but as roots put down in Britain, Canada and elsewhere strengthen, the link with the Sikhs of the Punjab may become less one of a single culture, yet remain that of a common faith.

INTERPRETATIONS OF SIKHISM

The Sikh religion has been viewed in a variety of ways by the comparatively few Western scholars and observers who have given it their attention since the British first made contact with Sikhs at the beginning of the nineteenth century. Sometimes the conclusion has been drawn that Sikhism was an Indian reform movement critical of the influence and power of the Brahmans, of caste oppression, and of *sati*, the burning of widows on the husband's funeral pyre (see page 228). It has also been regarded as a form of *bhakti* (see pages 200f), owing its teachings to two north Indians: Kabir (d. ?1448), from whom it is asserted Guru Nanak derived his message, and Ramanand (b. ?1299). Their *sampradaya* (teaching) will be discussed later. Another interpretation sees the movement as an attempt to reconcile Hinduism and Islam by creating a syncretism which would be acceptable to both. Lt-Col. Sir John Malcolm's *Sketch of the Sikhs* (London, 1812), in what might be called the first serious account of the religion by a European, wrote (p. 113):

> Born in a province on the extreme verge of India, at the very point where the religion of Muhammad and the idolatrous worship of the Hindus appeared to touch, and at a moment when both those tribes cherished the most violent rancour and animosity towards each other, his [Nanak's] great aim was to blend those jarring elements in peaceful union, and he only endeavoured to effect this purpose through the means of mild persuasion. His wish was to recall both Muhammadans and Hindus to an exclusive attention to that sublimest of all principles, which inculcates devotion to God, and peace towards man. He had to combat the furious bigotry of the one and the deep-rooted superstition of the other; but he attempted to overcome all obstacles by the force of reason and humanity.

Here is the beginning of the scholarly interpretation of Sikhism as a movement for reconciliation.

A few years earlier Q. Crauford (*Sketches of the Hindoos*, London, 1790) had defined the essense of Guru Nanak's teaching in one sentence: 'It appears that he soon became an admirer of Nirganey worship, and used to declaim against the folly of idols, and the impiety of offering adoration to any but the Supreme Being.' 'Nirganey' is the way Crauford recorded the word *niranjani*, worship of the one formless God. *Niranjan* means the Supreme Lord. This view may be nearer the mark than many expressed subsequently, though at a time when human rights and sexual equality are being stressed throughout the world, and inter-faith dialogue is a matter of importance to the religious, Sikhs eagerly and quite rightly point to the spirit of egalitarianism, democracy and social awareness which characterizes the movement, and depict Guru Nanak as a reconciler, a sixteenth-century Gandhi.

The Teachings of Sikhism

The most distinctive concept of Sikhism is its doctrine of guru-ship. The *Srimat Bhagavata* (11.3.21) advises the spiritual seeker who wishes to achieve liberation to 'find proper instruction at the feet of a guru who is well versed in the Vedas that lead to a knowledge of God'. The first known gurus, or spiritual preceptors, in the Indian tradition were imparters of Vedic knowledge and many of them were Brahmans. However, there is another parallel tradition in India, that of spiritual teachers whose authority lay not in their membership of the Brahman *varna* or in the Vedas but in a personal sense of enlightenment and a belief that they had been commissioned directly by God. Often they saw their responsibilities as being to guide to liberation anyone, man or woman, regardless of caste, who approached them. Such a teacher was Guru Nanak. However, the Sikh concept of guru-ship is far richer than that of merely believing in an enlightened human teacher. The Adi Guru, or Primal Guru, is God himself, often named in Sikh writings as the 'Sat Guru' (True Preceptor). The essence of God is beyond human knowledge or understanding but he graciously communicates himself to mankind. This he does through his word, his message of enlightenment. In doing so he manifests himself as divine teacher, the Sat Guru.

The ten human Gurus of Sikhism, listed earlier, were emphatic that God was the Guru, and that any importance they had was as faithful messengers through whom his word was revealed. Here Guru Nanak and his successors were taking hold of an ancient Indian idea of the *shabda* as sound, the sound associated with *brahman*. What they believed was that this sound was the manifestation of *brahman* which became articulate and coherent in the words which they uttered. Thus the terms used for the verses in which the teaching is enshrined, *shabad* or *bani*, are often prefixed by the syllable 'gur' to give expression to this view (*gurbani, gurshabad*). When the tenth Guru installed the Adi Granth as Guru (whence its alternative name Guru Granth Sahib, he was in one respect doing no more than reaffirming the original doctrine that guru-ship belonged to the divine author and that the message was received from him rather than from the person conveying it.

This is not the end of the story of guru-ship. When Guru Gobind Singh created the Khalsa in 1699 he was himself initiated as its sixth member. He described it as his other self and recognized the guru-ship of the Khalsa. During the eighteenth century guru-ship seems to have been shared between the community and the Scripture, being complete when the Khalsa gathered in the Guru Granth Sahib's presence. Such assemblies were eventually terminated; awareness of the guru-ship of the Khalsa became a memory rather than a present reality. In the late twentieth century, at a popular level, guru-ship is sited in the ten Gurus and the scripture: though that of God is acknowledged and explored by the theologians, that of the community has been neglected, albeit some scholars are now once more turning their attention to it.

The antecedents of Sikh thought are to be found in the Sant tradition of north India [4:151–8; 22:IV, sect. 3]. Sant is a convenient way of referring to a group of teachers and mystics united by a similarity of ideas, though not by any historical connection. Those who are assigned to the Sant group, such as Namdev (1270–1350), Ravidas (?fifteenth century) and Kabir are often described as disciples of Ramanand, but this must be seen as no more than an attempt to provide them all with a Brahman guru, to offset Smarta criticism of unorthodoxy, probably in the seventeenth century. (The Smartas were, above all, believers in the Hindu revealed scriptures of secondary order (*smrti*), the epics, lawbooks and Puranas.) The relationship of Guru Nanak to Kabir, as of Kabir to other Sants, is to be explained by an affinity of ideas. Guru Nanak was not Kabir's disciple [1:41]; both belonged to the Sant tradition whose ideas they would receive through the religious songs (*bhajans*) which the teachers composed and which were transmitted orally from one generation to another.

The unifying core of Sant belief was, first, that God is *nirguna* (unconditioned, without qualities) rather than *saguna* (manifested, possessing qualities and form, usually as a divine 'incarnation' *avatara*, see page 200). He is, therefore, not to be worshipped in the form of statues or other physical manifestations. Second, Sant belief stressed that God is the only ultimate reality, all that is, the one without a second. The Sant tradition was uncompromisingly monotheistic. From these ideas, realized through personal spiritual experience, other teachings were derived. *Avataras* were rejected; so was the efficacy of ritual acts, pilgrimages and asceticism, as well as the concept of pollution. The ministrations of Brahmans were considered unnecessary and the authority of the Vedas was implicitly denied. *Varna* and *jati* were thought to be illusory distinctions resulting from ignorance, as, ultimately, were sexual differentiations. Sant teachings were open to Brahmans and untouchables, women as well as men, so spiritual liberation was open to everyone.

Although God, it was believed, had no need to become incarnate and did not take any animal or human form, nevertheless one quality is assumed for the purpose of revelation, that of speech. In this respect, in Sikhism God is *saguna* as well as *nirguna* [1:75], a personal God, the divine Guru and inner teacher. Whoever becomes aware of the inner activity of God as Guru, and responds to that voice by obedient living, attains spiritual liberation while in this present body. The effects of *karma* have still to be worked out but no more *karma* will be accumulated (see page 211). At death the spirit will live in the divine presence, never to be reincarnated. Effort cannot induce this immanent revelation, it is a sovereign act of God's will, an act of divine grace. The inner spiritual experience is developed by meditation until a person's whole being is God-permeated. In Sikhism the name given to this activity is *nam simran* [1:89], calling to mind God's name and thereby becoming so immersed in the divine unity that the illusion of duality is overcome.

Corporate worship as well as individual meditation is a means of achieving God-realization. The bard Bhai Gurdas (d. 1629) was nephew of Guru Amar Das and amanuensis of the fifth Guru during the compilation of the Adi Granth. His poems are regarded by Sikhs almost as commentaries upon the sacred writings and guides to the Sikh way of life. He wrote, 'One is a Sikh, two is a *sangat* [community or congregation], where there are five [Sikhs] God is present' (*Var* 13, 19). This line accurately reflects the teaching of Sikhism about the importance of the congregation. Guru Nanak himself said (*AG* 228):

> The company of those who cherish within them
> the true Lord, turns mortals into godly beings.

The emphasis which Sikhism places upon becoming God-oriented (*gurmukh*), rather than self-centred and self-reliant (*manmukh*) which is man's natural state, does not require the Sikh to turn to the forest or follow an ascetic life; on the contrary, domestic life, engagement in commerce, farming and industry are to be pursued. In serving one's fellow man one obeys God, living uncontaminated by the five evil impulses of lust, covetousness, attachment, wrath and pride, like a lotus in a pond. The duties of a Sikh have been summed up in three phrases: *nam japna, kirt karni* and *vand chakna* – keeping God's name continually in mind, earning a living by honest means and giving to charity. *Seva*, service on behalf of the community, is also a highly praised virtue.

The ideals and teachings of Sikhism are present in the north Indian Sant traditions, but in Guru Nanak they achieve a coherence and completeness not found hitherto. In fact it may be said that he takes them to a point where the *varnashrama dharma* of Hinduism (page 209), with its four classes of society, four stages of life and four goals, is reduced to one in an ethical monotheism open to men and women alike, living as householders (*grihastha*). [17] While such Sant teachers as Namdev or Kabir may be regarded as composing hymns to express, explain or testify to their experience of God, Guru Nanak is to be seen as having a greater ambition, that of providing the villagers of north India and beyond with an alternative to Islam. The egalitarian monotheism of Islam must have been attractive, especially to those classes of Hindu society whose members, according to brahmanical teaching, could not hope to attain *moksha* (see page 212) in this present round of existence. In a Punjab under Muslim rule Islam may also have offered possibilities of social improvement. If the development of *bhakti* may be seen as a response of Hinduism to this threat, so the work of Guru Nanak should be regarded as a carefully conceived, broadly based movement providing an indigenous alternative to Islam.

The Sikh scriptures include the compositions of Hindus and Muslims who may be listed among the members of the Sant tradition or whose teaching had a close affinity to its ideas. The purpose of this unique catholicity may have been to invite the disparate groups, whose adherents might be called disciples of Kabir, Farid (1173–1265), Ravidas and others, to unite within the Sikh fold.

Religious Practices

The focal point of Sikh life and worship is the Guru Granth Sahib. Sikh worship takes place in its presence and consists of the congregational singing of hymns from the scripture, led by musicians, and the reading and exposition of the scriptures by members of the congregation. The place where acts of worship are held is called a *gurdwara* (literally the door (*dwara*) of the guru – see Figure 6.3), the abode of the guru [1: IV]. In fact this name may be applied to the room of a private house as well as to a place of public worship owned by the community, provided it contains a copy of the scripture. A family possessing a Guru Granth Sahib should consult it, that is read from it, daily and will probably do so in the evening. Public worship (*diwan*) may take place on any day. No weekly holy day is observed by Sikhs, but as *ekadashi*, the eleventh day of a lunar month, is important to Vaishnavite Hindus (see pages 200ff), and *sangrand* too is a day of customary significance in north India, these are often the occasion for special *gurdwara* services. However, individuals and families may visit the *gurdwara* at any time on any day, make an offering and listen to the Guru Granth Sahib being read. At the Golden Temple in Amritsar, the principal Sikh shrine on the site of a building originally constructed by Guru Arjan, the daily reading of the scripture begins before dawn and continues beyond sunset.

There are times when the Adi Granth is read from beginning to end without a break. As public acts of the Sikh community the occasions are the *gurpurbs* [1: 132], anniversaries of the birth or death of one of the Gurus. These are Sikhism's only distinctive festivals: its others – Magha, Diwali and Hola Mohalla – are Hindu in origin [1: 129]. Sometimes as an act of piety before a wedding, after a funeral or when new business premises are opened, families will also organize such continuous readings. These are carefully timed to take about forty-eight hours and are called *akhand paths*. The Guru Granth Sahib is 1,430 pages long in the printed form now universally used. It is not always possible for families to organize *akhand paths* so a normal reading (*sidharan path*) in such circumstances might be arranged to take place over a period of one or two weeks, family and friends assembling daily to participate in the spiritual exercise.

The scripture is also used when a child is named and at a wedding

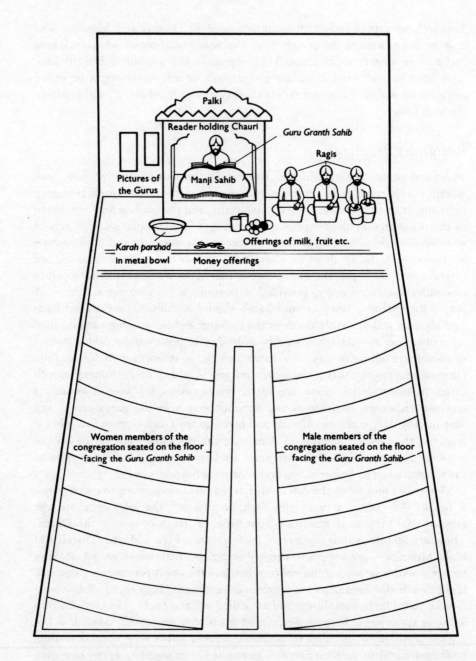

Figure 6.3   **Plan of a typical *gurdwara***

[1: 112–14]. At the naming of a child someone should open the Adi Granth at random and read out the first word of the first hymn on the left-hand page. The first letter of the word should provide the initial letter of the name. When a couple have agreed to marry one another they will circumambulate the scripture four times in a clockwise direction while the four verses from the wedding hymn (*lavan*) of Guru Ram Das are sung. Consent and marriage in the presence of the Guru Granth Sahib are all that is required in Sikh eyes to legitimize a marriage. Funerals consist of readings from the scripture but the body will not be taken in to the presence of the holy book [1: 119]. At some point in most of these rites will occur two features which conclude the act of worship. The first is the saying of a formal prayer (*ardas*) [1: 180–83] spoken by a member of the standing congregation facing the Guru Granth Sahib; the second is the sharing of *karah prasad*. This is a warm pudding of flour, semolina, water, sugar and ghee which is distributed among all members of the congregation. The simple meal symbolized equality and the rejection of caste distinctions, which have often been a bar to commensality in Hindu society.

The distinctive Sikh rite of initiation [12], Amrit Pahul or Khande ka Amrit [1: 122–9], is also centred on the Guru Granth Sahib in the presence of which it must take place, and the re-enactment of the ceremony which took place when the Khalsa was founded in 1699. Five male Khalsa members, wearing the five K's and turban, dissolve sugar crystals in water with a *khanda* while they chant prescribed hymns from the Adi Granth and some verses composed by Guru Gobind Singh. The nectar (*amrit*) is then administered to the eyes and hair of the male or female initiate, who is also given some of it to drink. They then take certain vows and repeat the words of the *Mool Mantra*, a terse statement of belief composed by Guru Nanak. It reads:

> There is one God, his name is truth eternal.
> He is creator of all things, the all-pervading spirit.
> Fearless and without hatred, timeless and formless.
> Beyond birth and death, he is self-enlightened.
> He is known by the Guru's grace.

In the *Mool Mantra* the Guru is God-manifest.

Sikhism has never succeeded in separating itself completely from its Hindu parent. In fact Hindus would regard Sikhs as heterodox Hindus. As a minority tradition existing in the midst of such a Great Tradition, not to mention the strong presence of Islam, it may seem remarkable that Sikhism has survived at all. That it has done so must be in no small part due to the centrality of the Guru Granth Sahib as a basis of belief and focus of practice and to the development of a strong pride in the Sikh heritage. However, in practice Sikhs have never entirely freed themselves from the influence of caste [5: V], especially, for example, in marriages. The theoretical equality of women is no more a complete reality than in other societies boasting the same ideology. The Hindu concept of pollution has not been fully eradicated from Sikh life despite the teachings of the Gurus. This can be seen from such things as the use of *akhand paths* to purify a building, and the insistence of some Sikhs upon vegetarianism. The experience of the eighteenth century, the martyrdom of two Gurus, and the recent memory of Muslim–Sikh tensions before and during the partition of India at the end of the Raj still affect relations between the two religions, although the emphasis of Sikhism is upon tolerance and coexistence based on mutual respect.

BIBLIOGRAPHY

1. COLE, W. O., and SAMBHI, P. S., *The Sikhs: Their Religious Beliefs and Practices*, London, Boston, Mass., Routledge, 1978
2. MACAULIFFE, M. A., *The Sikh Religion*, 6 vols., repr. Delhi, Chand, 1963, 1970; first publ. Oxford, Clarendon Press, 1909. A faithful and comprehensive account of the Sikh tradition covering the period 1469–1708
3. SINGH, KHUSHWANT, *A History of the Sikhs*, 2 vols., 2nd edn, Delhi, Oxford University Press (India), 1977; prev. publ. London, Oxford University Press/Princeton, NJ, Princeton University Press, 1963–6; Bombay, Oxford University Press, 1967
4. MCLEOD, W. H., *Guru Nanak and the Sikh Religion*, Oxford, Clarendon Press, 1968; Indian edn, Delhi, Oxford University Press, 1976
5. MCLEOD, W. H., *The Evolution of the Sikh Community*, Oxford, Clarendon Press, 1976; Delhi, Oxford University Press, 1975
6. ĀDI-GRANTH, *Selections from the Sacred Writings of the Sikhs* (tr. Trilochan Singh *et al.*), London, Allen & Unwin/New York, Macmillan, 1960
7. *Guru Nanak and Indian Religious Thought . . . Commemorative Lectures*, 1966–9 (ed. Taran Singh), 2 vols., Patiala, Punjabi University, 1970
8. SINGH, SHER, *Philosophy of Sikhism*, Lahore, Sikh University Press, 1944
9. FAUJA SINGH *et al.*, *Sikhism*, Patiala, Punjabi University, 1969
10. SINGH, TEJA, *Essays in Sikhism*, Lahore, Sikh University Press, 1944
11. SINGH, TEJA, *Sikhism: Its Ideals and Institutions* (new edn, Bombay, 1951), repr. Calcutta, Bombay, Orient Longman, 1964/Amritsar, Khalsa, 1970; first publ. London, New York, Longman, 1938
12. SINGH, SIR JOGINDRA, *Sikh Ceremonies*, Chandigarh, Religious Book Society, 1968; Bombay, International Book House, 1941

13. GREWAL, J. S., *Guru Nanak in History*, Chandigarh, Panjab University, 1969
14. GREWAL, J. S., *From Guru Nanak to Maharaja Ranjit Singh: Essays in Sikh History*, Amritsar, Guru Nanak University, 1972
15. GREWAL, J. S., and BAL, S. S., *Guru Gobind Singh: A Biographical Study*, Chandigarh, Panjab University, 1967
16. COLE, W. O., *The Guru in Sikhism*, London, Darton, 1982
17. COLE, W. O., *Sikhism and Its Indian Context, 1469–1708*, London, Darton, 1982
18. *Perspectives on Guru Nanak: Seminar Papers* (ed. Harbans Singh), Patiala, Punjabi University, 1975
19. *Essays in Honour of Dr Ganda Singh* (ed. Harbans Singh and N. G. Barrier), Patiala, Punjabi University, 1976
20. JAMES, A. G., *Sikh Children in Britain*, London, New York, Oxford University Press, 1974
21. MCLEOD, W. H., *The B40 Janam-sākhī*, Amritsar, Guru Nanak Dev University, 1980
22. VAUDEVILLE, C. (tr.), *Kabir*, vol. 1, Oxford, Clarendon Press, 1974. Sheds light upon many of the areas which Guru Nanak and Kabir shared as common, while recognizing the differences

It should be noted that there is no completely satisfactory version of the *Guru Granth Sahib* in English. Many Sikh writers use the translations in [2]. Two complete translations are:

Sri Guru-Granth Sahib, Gopal Singh, Delhi, Gur Das Kapur, 1962
Sri Guru-Granth Sahib, Mannohan Singh, Shiromani Gurdwara Parbandhak Committee, Amritsar, 1969

A compendium of new translations of important and diverse Sikh texts is MCLEOD, W. H., *Sources for the Study of Sikhism*, Manchester, Manchester University Press, 1984.

7

Jainism

KENDALL W. FOLKERT

Introduction

Jains have been present in India's religious life for at least 2,500 years, and continue to be a visible and active community, holding tenaciously to a rigorous discipline whose roots pre-date the Buddha. The community at present includes only some 3 million persons (roughly one-half of 1 per cent of India's population); and its relative size has been small throughout its history. Yet the influence of the Jains on Indian culture and the continuity of their history have been such that Jainism is commonly regarded as one of India's major indigenous religious traditions.

At Jainism's core lies an ascetic ideal. Jains take their name from the term 'Jina', which means 'conqueror'. 'Jina' is an honorific term, not a proper name (cf. 'Buddha'); it is given by Jains to twenty-four great teachers. The message and example of these teacher-conquerors was that the human being, without supernatural aid, is capable of conquering the bondage of physical existence and achieving freedom from rebirth; and that this conquest is to be achieved only by the most rigorous renunciation of all physical comforts and social constraints. These teachers are also called Tirthankaras, a title meaning 'crossing-maker', which points to their role as teachers and exemplars for others who seek the same goal.

Though relatively small in numbers, Jainism is not monolithic. Regional and linguistic divisions, and differences in religious practice, have been present in Jainism since at least the beginning of the Christian Era. Jains are, by and large, divided into Shvetambaras (so named because their monks and nuns are 'white-clad'), Digambaras (so named because their male ascetics are 'sky-clad', i.e. nude), and several reform movements which have arisen in recent centuries. It is also important to note that, while Jainism has an ascetic basis, the majority of those who call themselves Jains are lay persons whose religious life is not monastic.

PRIMARY SOURCES FOR THE STUDY OF JAINISM

Sources for study are best treated as three categories of literature: (1) early scriptures; (2) later Sanskrit writings; and (3) more recent literatures. The first category comprises the oldest texts of Jainism, which were composed in various Prakrits (early Indian vernacular languages). By the fifth century CE, the Shvetambara Jains had assembled a collection of forty-five extant texts into a canon [1: 47ff; a complete list is found in the Appendix (A) below], commonly called the Siddhanta. This canon's oldest and most venerated texts are the *angas*, which present early accounts of Jain monastic discipline and contain sermons and dialogues of Vardhamana Mahavira (sixth century BCE), the last of the twenty-four Tirthankaras.

Not all Jains, however, regard these forty-five texts as normative. In the sixteenth century CE a reform movement called the Sthanakavasis produced a canon of texts that contains only thirty-two of the forty-five texts in the Siddhanta; and the Digambara Jains, while not repudiating most of the dog-matic content of the Siddhanta, hold that the language and form of this canon are not authentic. The Digambaras preserve two very old Prakrit texts that pre-date the compilation of the Shvetambara canon. These earliest Digambara texts, the *Shatkhandagama* ('Scripture in Six Parts') and the *Kashayaprabhrta* ('Treatise on the Stain of Passion'), were supplemented by commentaries and writings which, together with the older texts, give the Digambaras their own body of normative literature, called the *Anuyoga* ('Expositions').

The second category of primary-source literature, written in Sanskrit largely from 700 CE onward, signals a major change in Jainism. Alongside commen-taries on older texts, this large body of literature contains new didactic texts, philosophical writings, and narrative and technical works. An important feature of this literature is that much of it deals with the lay community, and includes writings (resembling the Hindu Puranas) that give a Jain view of world prehistory and of the origins of basic human institutions and everyday religious activity.

These Sanskrit sources thus point beyond themselves to a major develop-ment in Jainism: the systematization of lay life, including religious discipline and temple, home and life-cycle rituals. These sources are, therefore, important for understanding the full range of Jain religious life. [For the reader's guidance, a list of major works in several categories is provided in the Appendix (B) below.]

The third area of primary-source material, of more recent origin, consists of works in modern Indian languages (including early forms of such languages as Gujarati and Marathi) and, over the last century, in English. The vernacular works cover a range of popular religious material, including recastings of

Sanskrit narratives. There are also works written in the last few decades that are directed towards Jain renewal and contemporary problems [2: 301–2].

Jain writings in English were often directed towards European and American audiences, and include efforts at presenting ancient Jain texts and ideas to the Western world. Notable in this connection, though many more examples could be cited, is the work of J. L. Jaini, a Digambara layman, whose *Outlines of Jainism* and many other works present something of a modern apologetic for Jainism.

JAIN HISTORY

It is common to refer to Vardhamana Mahavira, who lived from 599 to 527 BCE (the traditional dating), as the 'founder' of Jainism, and to regard Jain history as beginning with him. However, Jains hold that the universe is eternal and uncreated and, as do Hindus, conceive of time in vast, cyclic terms. A full cycle of time consists of two main periods of some 600 million years, each subdivided into six parts. One of these main periods is a period of ascent, in which all conditions improve; the other is a time of descent, in which knowledge, behaviour, human stature etc. all decline. In each main half-cycle there appear twenty-four great teachers, the Jinas or Tirthankaras referred to above.

In the current cycle of cosmic time (which is a period of decline), twenty-four such teachers are thus held to have lived. The last of these was Vardhamana Mahavira. His predecessor in the series was a man named Parshva, whom the Jains place in the ninth century BCE, and for whose life there is some (but very little) historical evidence. Modern accounts of Jain history thus begin with Mahavira, but Jain literature and religious life include all twenty-four Tirthankaras.

Mahavira was born Vardhamana Jnatrputra in north-east India, near modern Patna. (Jnatrputra is his clan-name; 'Mahavira' is an honorific title meaning 'great hero'.) At thirty years of age, he abandoned his life as a member of the warrior (Kshatriya) class, and took up the life of a possessionless mendicant. For more than twelve years Mahavira devoted himself to renunciation and detachment from all physical needs and comforts. At the end of this time, having reached complete understanding of the nature of the universe and absolute detachment from worldly desires, he began teaching others. By Jain accounts, he had assembled a following of several hundred thousand by the time of his death at the age of seventy-two.

Leadership of the Jains thereafter passed to Mahavira's senior disciples, and under these men and their successors the movement began to spread from north-eastern India into eastern and north-western population centres. The

Jains, like the Buddhists, benefited from the support for monastic ideals of the Mauryan dynasty (third century BCE), and the growth and geographical spread of Jainism accelerated, carrying it into central and southern India.

In the period after Mahavira's death, divisions emerged within Jainism, in particular the Shvetambara–Digambara schism mentioned above. The two groups disagreed largely over monastic practice. The Digambaras maintained that an ascetic who had truly renounced the world would also renounce clothing, and go naked, as Mahavira apparently had done. The Shvetambaras maintained, however, that Mahavira's life and teachings did not make nudity an absolute requirement, and that the wearing of simple white garments would be a sufficient act of renunciation. From this particular disagreement have come the names (see above) that characterize this lasting division within Jainism.

Other areas of disagreement also arose, no less significant than the matter of clothing, but often more technical and less subject to popular debate. These included the question of scriptures, as detailed earlier; there were also disagreements over other particulars of monastic life, and differing versions of the life story of Mahavira, plus a significant and lasting disagreement concerning the status of women. Shvetambaras admit women to full monastic vows, but Digambaras do not, arguing that women are not capable of attaining liberation and must await rebirth as males in order to pursue full ascetic careers.

All these differences were accentuated (and may well have been partly caused) by the fact that the two groups were concentrated in different regions and subcultures of India during Jainism's period of growth. The Digambaras were the principal Jains in south and central India, while the Shvetambaras concentrated in the north and west. Thus it is appropriate to think of the Shvetambara–Digambara division as being in many ways like the difference between Orthodox and Roman Catholic Christians.

Internal divisions notwithstanding, the Jains entered a period of growth and influence by the fifth century CE. In central and southern India, the Digambaras won royal patronage and were a notable cultural force, especially in such matters as the development of vernacular literatures. A few centuries later the Shvetambaras played much the same role in the north, and even more so in western India.

This was the period, as noted above, that gave a coherent and lasting pattern to the Jain lay community. As Jainism had moved into diverse regions and had grown in numbers, the absorption of lay persons into the movement required that the lay Jain be given a distinctive identity. Thus narrative texts and models of lay discipline are prominent in this period's literature.

By the eleventh and twelfth centuries CE Jainism was beginning to retreat geographically into its present area of concentration (see Figure 7.1). A rising tide of Hindu theistic religion in south and central India, with accompanying royal patronage, led to the Jains falling into disfavour in those regions. The Digambaras gradually retreated to the north and west, leaving behind only a shadow of their earlier presence in the central and southern regions. In the Shvetambara-dominated areas less contraction occurred, although the Shvetambaras also declined in influence as new Hindu movements gained a following. The Shvetambaras also experienced the increasing presence of Islam in India from the twelfth century onwards. Thus the growth of Jainism was deflected in the north-west as well as in the Digambara regions.

By 1500 CE, Jainism had largely reached its current geographic status, and from this time onwards began to see various movements of reform and renewal. Prominent among these was a fifteenth- and sixteenth-century Shvetambara movement called the Sthanakavasis. Still active today, its members are recognizable by their practice of wearing a cloth or mask over the mouth and nose (see page 226). This group produced, as noted, its own canon of scripture; and it objected to the veneration of images as practised by Jains, and to the entire complex of temple-cultus and activity that had developed in Jainism by that time. Other movements followed, notably a similar Digambara group, known as the Taranapanthas, which originated in the sixteenth century; and the eighteenth-century Shvetambara Terapantha movement.

Jainism has thus passed through periods of formative, largely monastic life (from Mahavira to the early Christian Era); of spread, growth and engagement with laity (early Christian Era to twelfth century); and of contraction, reform and redevelopment.

SCHOLARLY STUDY OF THE JAINS

The Jains came to the notice of Western scholarship largely through the efforts of Albrecht Weber, Georg Bühler and Hermann Jacobi. Weber and Bühler combined efforts in the 1880s to present to scholars a comprehensive account of the Jain scriptures; and Jacobi pioneered the translation of Jain Prakrit texts into European languages. A number of other scholars, too numerous to catalogue here [cf. 3: 1ff], contributed to early Jain studies, but the work of the three just mentioned was formative. This is so for two reasons. First, it was not uncommon for nineteenth-century scholars of India to portray Jainism as subordinate to Buddhism. The Jains were often treated merely as predecessors of Buddhism or as a schismatic offshoot. Some scholarly attempts were made to show that Vardhamana Mahavira and Siddhartha Gautama, the Buddha, were one and the same, the Jain schismatics having altered the founder's portrait just enough to make it appear that they had their own

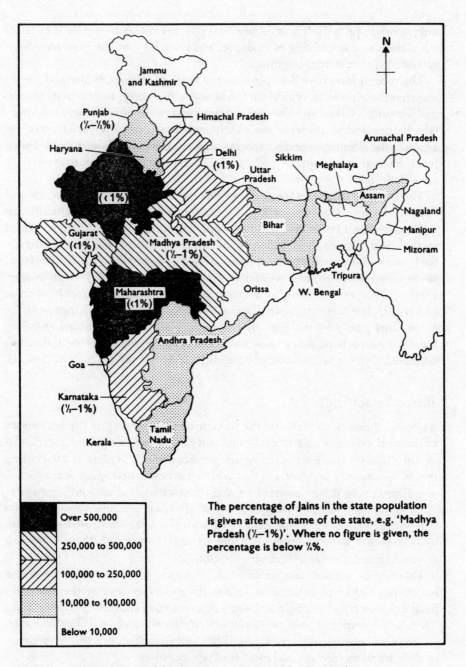

Figure 7.1 Distribution of the Jain population (in India) by number and as percentage of state population

unique origin [4: ixff]. It was Jacobi who put this notion to rest by his tireless translation and assembling of evidence, and since his time the Jains have been accorded appropriate recognition.

The second formative dimension of the work of Weber, Bühler and Jacobi was that their interests, typical for the nineteenth century, were heavily textual and historical. Given this, they were drawn first to the Shvetambara tradition, which appeared to preserve the oldest and most complete set of texts. As a result, the Western world's earliest complete picture of Jainism was drawn from Shvetambara sources, while the Digambaras were portrayed in a secondary light.

The effect of this early focus on the Shvetambaras and on Jain texts is still felt. Subsequent Jain scholarship, by such eminent figures as Helmuth von Glasenapp, Ernst Leumann, Walther Schubring and Ludwig Alsdorf, remained textual and historical in focus, with an emphasis on the Shvetambaras. Such work still represents the dominant approach to the study of the Jains. More comprehensive, topical and social-structural study of Jainism is rare. Efforts to portray the Jains as a living, practising community, such as those of Mrs Sinclair Stevenson early in this century, and of V. A. Sangave in the 1950s, only partly fill this gap. By and large it must simply be said that Jain scholarship, perhaps more than any other part of the study of India, has remained where it began: in an almost exclusively textual and historical mode.

Basic Teachings

As noted, Jainism teaches that the human being can conquer the limitations of physical existence and attain immortality by means of rigorous ascetic discipline. Jainism bases its teaching on a fundamental division of all existing things into two classes: *jiva*, i.e. that which is sentient; and *ajiva*, that which is not. Every living thing consists of a *jiva* (often translated as 'soul', but better understood as a 'sentient essence') and of *ajiva*, i.e. a non-sentient, material component that has become associated with the *jiva*. This association with *ajiva* prevents the *jiva* from realizing its true nature, which is immortal, omniscient and absolutely complete in itself.

There is an infinite number of *jivas*, and each is an eternal and discrete entity, not linked to other *jivas* in any fashion. The *jivas* neither emanate from a common source nor in any way merge with one another upon liberation. There is no 'supreme *jiva*' or supreme deity/creator, and the Tirthankaras, or Jinas, are not regarded as divine. They are venerated; but this is in virtue of their status as teachers and models of renunciation.

Jains also hold that each *jiva* has eternally been associated with *ajiva*, i.e. that there was no 'fall' of the *jiva* into an impure state. The *jiva*'s association with *ajiva* is beginningless, like the universe; yet the condition is not unchangeable. The association of the two is understood to be the work of *karma*, a concept that the Jains share with the larger Hindu tradition (see pages 196, 211–12), but which they understand in a unique fashion. In the Jain view, *karma* is a subtle form of matter that clings to the *jiva*, obscuring (but not actually altering) the *jiva*'s innate capacities. This obscuring of its faculties causes the *jiva* to be reborn into an infinite series of physical existences, another basic premise that Jainism shares with Hinduism as a whole.

There is only one way in which the *jiva* can be set free of this karmic bondage and resultant physical rebirth, and that way involves the ascetic life. The goal of ascetic discipline is to stop any further association of the *jiva* with *karma*, and to hasten the decay of such *karma* as has previously obscured the *jiva*. When the *jiva* is at last rid of all karmic association, it is held to be freed of rebirth, and to rise to the uppermost reaches of the universe, the *siddha-loka* (see Figure 7.2), to abide there eternally in its innate perfection: total knowledge and self-containment.

An interesting dimension of the Jain consideration of *jiva* and *ajiva* is the system of philosophical analysis known as *anekantavada*, the teaching of 'non-one-sidedness', which Jain philosophers developed as a way of dealing with the multiple dimensions of reality. Jain metaphysics considers the soul to be both essentially unchanging and yet capable of various qualitative alterations, and seeks to synthesize conflicting analyses of reality (e.g. either as permanent or as constantly changing). In the Jain view, any philosophical system that holds reality to be ultimately reducible to one ontological dimension (e.g. to permanence, or to constant change) is an *ekantavada*, a 'one-sided view', and is condemned to error by its very failure to take account of the several equally important dimensions of being. Thus the Jains insist on 'non-one-sidedness'.

These core teachings contain certain key elements related to basic Jain values. The first such matter is the nature of the *jiva*. Jains infer the existence of the *jiva* from its function as 'knower' and agent of activity in living things, and argue that the *jiva*'s innate nature must be whole and complete, or else there would be an inconsistency in its existence, even though it has been eternally associated with *karma*. Thus it is that the *jiva* is held to be innately omniscient and eternal. It is this capacity for omniscience that gives authority to Jain teachings, for the Tirthankaras are held to have attained omniscience in virtue of their ascetic detachment from all physical things. There being no supernatural agency, there can be no divine revelation; the truth of a Tirthankara's teaching thus ultimately rests on the Jain conviction that all *jivas* are capable of total knowledge [5: 61–4]. The work of a Tirthankara is to show the way, to 'make a crossing', based upon his attainment, which is, properly speaking, the recovery of his own *jiva*'s true nature, not the discovery of something new.

A second key element in Jain teachings is the nature of *ajiva* and the working of *karma* [see 5:IV]. All insentient existents are included in the category of *ajiva*, particularly space, time and matter, the latter conceived of as atoms. It is important to note that the actual existence of *ajiva* is not denied by Jains, and that matter is therefore real and eternal. *Karma*, then, as a subtle form of matter, is not an illusion or result of perceptual error. It is real, and must be dealt with in a physical way, as must be all components of worldly existence.

Dissolution of the *jiva*'s association with *karma* thus requires the cultivation of actual and extreme detachment from all that is not-*jiva*. No purely 'spiritual' or 'mental' exercise will suffice. Thus Jain monastic life has always had, and has today, a quality of concreteness and actual physical rigour to it.

A third key element is the practice of *ahimsa*, 'non-injury'. As Jainism evolved, *ahimsa* came more and more to the fore as a key component of detachment from *ajiva*, from the material world of *karma*. For Jains, *ahimsa* has come to embody one's willingness to separate oneself altogether not merely from acts of injury or killing, but also from the entire mechanism of aggression, possession and consumption that characterizes life in this world. Thus *ahimsa* has come to be a hallmark of the Jain commitment to detachment. It is not only an ethical goal, but also a metaphysical truth for Jains that non-injury is part of the path to liberation.

The central place given to this teaching has resulted in a number of characteristic Jain practices, including the monastic practice of carrying a small broom or whisk with which to brush away gently any living creatures before one sits or lies down; the Sthanakavasi practice of wearing a mask stems from a desire to prevent even the accidental ingestion of invisible creatures. The concern for *ahimsa* has also involved the entire community, monastic and lay, in a characteristic insistence upon vegetarian diet, and opposition to animal slaughter in general, as important dimensions of non-injury; and Jain lay persons are enjoined to engage only in occupations that minimize the destruction of living beings. Thus most Jains are members of mercantile or professional classes.

The achievement of such detachment, in total reliance upon one's innate capacities, is an arduous task. The Jain lay person has no expectation of final liberation. Living outside of monastic orders means that release from physical existence can come only in some future life. Moreover, even the ascetic is understood to live many lifetimes of renunciation before achieving total conquest. The casting of this rigorous teaching into day-to-day practice dominates the history of Jainism and its concrete everyday life.

Characteristic Jain Practices

INTRODUCTION

In matters of religious practice Jainism presents an interesting case. Since Jain teachings give absolute centrality to the ascetic ideal, monastic practice is the most direct outcome of the teachings. At the same time, one cannot quickly and sharply draw a line between monastic and lay religious practice in Jainism, and treat the former as orthopraxis and the latter as the 'little' tradition in Jainism. Such a bifurcation fails because there is a body of lay Jain practice that is modelled on the monastic life, and because Jainism has regularly sought to link together monk and lay person, ascetic and lay life.

Therefore, Jain religious practices are best seen as being of two basic types: first, those practices – monastic and lay – that are most informed by the ascetic ideal; and second, those practices – largely of lay persons – that are less directly linked to asceticism and which are thus more representative of popular religious practice.

The more ascetic model is framed by a vision of the complete path to liberation as consisting of fourteen stages, called *gunasthanas* [1: 272–3; 5: 268–80]. These stages trace the progression of the *jiva* from a state of total karmic bondage to its final release and the regaining of its full capacities. Only at the fourth *gunasthana* is the *jiva* sufficiently free of bondage to enable one to live as a pious lay person, and the monastic path proper begins at the sixth *gunasthana*. Thus the formal orthopraxis of Jainism assumes a continuity between the lay and monastic careers.

MONASTIC ASCETICISM

Entry to the sixth *gunasthana* is marked by the taking of monastic vows. Jains have always taken the specifics of monastic practice with great seriousness; as noted above, differences over monastic practice have led to divisions within Jainism. Despite these differences, however, there is a basic set of monastic practices that is widely shared [6: 139ff]. The aspirant to monastic orders must be physically and morally fit, and will have prepared for entry into orders by studying under a chosen preceptor who is already in orders. When the aspirant is ready, a formal ceremony of initiation is conducted.

In this ceremony, the new ascetic takes five great vows (*mahavratas*): vows to observe *ahimsa*, and to avoid lying, stealing, sexual intercourse, and ownership of any possessions. He or she will be given a new name, usually the name of the preceptor's monastic lineage. (Beginning early in the movement's history, Jain ascetics formed themselves into monastic lineages, called *gacchas*, whose members follow the monastic example of a series of leaders; major *gacchas* to be found today are the Kharatara, Tapa and Ancala *gacchas*. [For details of monastic organization, see 6: 337ff and 7: 76–7.])

If the aspirant is entering a Digambara order, he gives up all his possessions and clothing, and is given a small whisk of peacock feathers as his only possession. A Shvetambara initiate is given three pieces of cloth to wear, a whisk made of wool, and a begging-bowl and staff. The Sthanakavasis add a face-mask to this set of items. Thereafter, the new monk or nun is expected to join with at least two or three others and to live a life of increasingly rigorous discipline. Such a small group of ascetics generally remains relatively mobile eight months of the year, spending periods of time in various temples, study centres, places of pilgrimage, or simply in wandering. They beg for all their food and accept no possessions beyond those given them at their initiation. During the four remaining months, specifically in the rainy season (late June to early October), monks and nuns congregate in various towns and villages, to be with their preceptors and the leaders of their larger monastic groups. Here the monks and nuns are instructed, formally confess their transgressions of monastic discipline to their superiors, and in turn instruct and assist the lay community that hosts them for this period of time.

In the course of this day-to-day life, the monk or nun engages in study, meditation and physical discipline designed to further the *jiva*'s continuing dissociation from the bonds of *karma* and to advance it along the subsequent *gunasthanas*. As noted above, many lifetimes of monastic discipline are required to traverse these stages; and as the Jain ascetic reaches old age, he or she may choose to die voluntarily, undertaking a ritual death by fasting, which is called *sallekhana*. Performed under the close supervision of one's preceptor, this ideally passionless death ensures that one will not void one's spiritual progress by clinging to material existence at the end of one lifetime. It is a powerful sign of Jainism's dedication to the conquest of material existence by renunciation.

LAY ASCETICISM

As noted in the introduction Jainism passed through a period of change from *c*. 500 to 1300 CE, particularly in respect of its lay community. While there is evidence for the presence of lay persons in Jainism from early on, their role *vis-à-vis* the monastic orders probably remained somewhat fluid until the early centuries of the Christian Era. Growth in Hindu popular piety and Jainism's growing presence among new populations in the Deccan and western India led to the accomplishments of this period, namely, the development of a distinctive lay Jain religious identity.

One of the foci of this development was the ordering of lay discipline modelled on the monastic orders. To further this, some forty texts and manuals of lay discipline (called *shravakacaras*) were produced [8: xxvii–xxx]. A basic pattern of lay requirements emerged from these texts, consisting of a set of prescribed disciplines that leads the Jain lay person through eleven stages of heightened renunciation.

These eleven stages, known as *pratimas*, are essentially a lay version of the monastic career,[1] and all Jain lay persons are expected to reach at least some point of progression through these stages. Linked to the *pratimas* is a collection of some twenty vows. These are also modelled on monastic requirements, and involve restraint in diet, travel, clothing and the like. These vows are taken at the second *pratima*, and full practice of them is attained as one moves through the stages. There is even a final vow, recommended but not obligatory, that is a lay version of the ascetic death by starvation.

The *pratimas* clearly carry the lay person along a path of increasing ascetic rigour, leading at the eleventh stage to virtual ascetic renunciation. There is nothing here of the Hindu or Buddhist notion that the lay person can find salvation through alternative disciplines or devotional religion. The lay discipline of the Jains can have only one of two results: (1) rebirth in circumstances that permit an ascetic life, brought about by partial progression through the stages; or (2) full ascetic renunciation in one's present life. In neither case will the lay vows and stages themselves lead to liberation.

There is, thus, remarkable consistency between Jainism's basic ascetic teaching and this view of lay life. Arising as it did in Jainism's period of greatest growth and change, it represents a major effort to bind together the lay and monastic community.

Daily Religious Life

Notwithstanding the significance of formal lay discipline, a great many Jains do not practise the ascetic model of lay piety, but rather participate in the Jain tradition by means of other religious activities that are often the more visible features of Jainism. These include temple worship, pilgrimage, observance of holidays, and participation in Jain 'rites of passage'. Many of these would appear to have only a tenuous connection with Jainism's ascetic core; yet the ascetic model has at least penetrated these to some extent, and long historical association has woven them into a whole that is largely consonant with Jainism's basic teachings.

TEMPLE WORSHIP

The most visible non-ascetic practice is the temple cult. Although Jainism teaches no supreme deity or creator, there is an extraordinary profusion of Jain temples to be found in India, so that few Jain communities, however small, are likely to be without one or more. The cult itself centres on veneration of images of the Tirthankaras. Evidence of such a cult of images is as old as Mauryan times (third century BCE), and votive slabs from the early Christian Era, found at Mathura, show images of Tirthankaras in standardized forms identical to those in later temples: seated in deep meditation or standing erect, arms and hands held at the side, in an attitude of immobile bodily discipline (cf. the great statue of Bahubali (Gommateshvara) at Shravana-Belgola in Karnataka, Mysore).

The seated image came to dominate Jain iconography, and at least one such image is the focal point of each Jain temple. This image is offered *puja* ('worship', i.e. homage shown by acts of symbolic hospitality) by lay persons according to their private patterns of temple attendance. Jains are enjoined to perform *puja* especially in the early morning, after bathing and before breakfasting. The ceremony itself has at least four parts (though it may be more elaborate):

1. The worshipper approaches the image, reciting a litany of homage, named the *Panca-namaskara-mantra*, then forms a diagram with rice grains. The form of the diagram is as shown in the centre drawing (dotted-rectangle area) of Figure 7.2.[2] The text of the litany (translated into English) is as follows:

> Homage to the Jinas!
> Homage to the souls that have
>   attained release!
> Homage to the leaders of the
>   Jain orders!
> Homage to the preceptors!
> Homage to all the Jain
>   mendicants in the world!
> This fivefold salutation,
>   destroyer of sin, is of all
>   auspicious things the most
>   auspicious!

Thereafter the worshipper offers the image a symbolic bath, or actually shower-baths a small adjacent image.

2. The name of the Tirthankara whose image is present is invoked, and an offering of eight substances, each representing a religious virtue, is made.

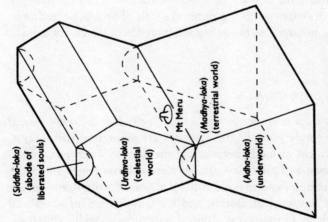

The portion shown inside the dotted rectangle is a sign commonly made during *puja*.
The palm of the hand carries a stylized version of the word *ahimsa* :

(*Jain pratika*, symbol of Jain faith, officially adopted in 1975 at celebration of the 2,500th anniversary of Mahavira's nirvana.)

The symbol clearly reflects the archaic view of the universe (see left).

(*The archaic view of the universe, representing in rough outline the human form, and its four levels of abode.*)

Humans dwell in the *Madhya-loka*. The celestial world and underworld comprise many internal levels corresponding to the type of celestial or infernal being.

(*Siddha-loka* (abode of liberated souls)

(*Urdhva-loka* (celestial world)

Mt Meru

(*Madhya-loka* (terrestrial world)

(*Adha-loka* (underworld)

Figure 7.2   Loka-akasha: the Jain conception of the universe

3. The names of all twenty-four Tirthankaras are recited.
4. Lighted lamps are waved before the image.

Many Jains do not perform temple *puja* daily, often choosing to perform much the same act in a home shrine. The temples more commonly draw the entire community to them on festival occasions, particularly those that celebrate events in the lives of the Tirthankaras. On such occasions elaborate *puja* ceremonies are staged, often including decorations and renewal of a temple's images.

This act of worship is related to ascetic Jainism in that its stated purpose is to focus the lay person's desires on detachment from material existence as represented by the Tirthankara's image, and thus to reduce karmic bondage. But it is doubtful that its significance ends there. It is also fruitful to see *puja* in Jainism as a particularly lay institution, one that gives the lay community a sense of identity that it cannot easily obtain from the ascetic ideals of Jainism. The temple cult is largely the province of lay persons. Monks and nuns are not to serve as temple officiants, nor is their presence during *puja* even welcomed. Temple officiants, who may assist with *puja* and who care for the images and the temple itself, are most often chosen from the lay community. This remains true despite the fact that ascetics have often attached themselves to temples for purposes of study and teaching, and in some regions have become almost a class of temple specialists. (As noted in the introduction, the Sthanakavasis object to the temple-complex and the veneration of images; in place of the temple, they focus on the *upasraya*, a building constructed and maintained by lay persons for monks and nuns to use as a centre for instruction, confession and study [2:245].)

Briefly put, the temple-cultus in Jainism, while penetrated by the ascetic ideal and orthodox Jain teachings, is also kept apart from asceticism by being – at least ideally – outside the domain of monastic control. Thus the Jain lay person, while being drawn towards the rigorous ideals of an ascetic tradition, also has an institutional arena in his or her religious life in which lay control is dominant.

PILGRIMAGE AND HOLIDAYS

Pilgrimage to holy places is an important act for Jains, and is closely related to the purposes of temple *puja*. Pilgrimage sites are associated with events, especially the attainment of final liberation, in the lives of Tirthankaras and other great Jain saints, and pious lay persons have endowed such sites with great complexes of temples and shrines. Among major sites of pilgrimage are Sameta Sikhara and Pavapuri (in Bihar), and Mt Girnar (in Saurashtra), all of which are sites where Tirthankaras attained liberation; as well as Shatrunjaya (in Gujarat), Mt Abu (in Rajasthan) and Shravana-Belgola (Karnataka), which are sites of major temples and monuments celebrating the asceticism of Tirthankaras and other Jain saints.

Jains also celebrate a complex calendar of holidays whose principal festivals are, like pilgrimage rites, linked to major events in the lives of the Tirthankaras, especially Rshabha (the first Tirthankara), Mahavira and his predecessor Parshva. (The events are: (1) descent into the mother's womb; (2) birth; (3) ascetic renunciation; (4) attainment of omniscience; (5) physical death and final liberation.) Many of these events are particularly celebrated by pilgrimage to sites associated with the Tirthankaras; and the birth date and death/liberation date of Mahavira (in Caitra (March/April) and Karttika (October/ November), respectively) are widely celebrated by all Jain communities. A wide range of other celebrations and monthly fast-days are also observed [see 2:245–54]. Notable among these is Akshayatrtiya ('the immortal third', celebrated on the third day of the waxing moon in Vaishakh (April/May)), commemorating the first giving of alms to the first Tirthankara, Rshabha, and emphasizing the virtue of alms-giving to ascetics in general.

But perhaps the most significant holiday period is Paryushana, held for eight days (by Shvetambaras) or ten days (by Digambaras) in the month of Bhadrapada (August/September), while the monks and nuns are in their rainy-season retreat [2:246–8]. In this period, lay persons particularly seek to perform fasting and austerities on the ascetic model, and to spend time with monastic leaders. The holiday thus takes advantage of the rain-retreat, which brings ascetics and lay persons together for a protracted period; and it also serves the lay community itself, for on the final day of Paryushana, known as Samvatsari, lay persons make a general confession for the transgressions of the past year, not only to their monastic confessors, but also to each other. Letters are written and visits paid for the purpose of asking and extending forgiveness. Persons will often return to home villages and towns for these holidays and the accompanying activities. Thus Paryushana, while it emphasizes the lay person's efforts to participate in ascetic activities, also serves to bind together the lay community and strengthen its identity.

RITES OF PASSAGE

As one would expect in a tradition whose fundamental basis is ascetic and which counsels absolute detachment from social values and material existence, the oldest Jain teachings do not establish norms in the area of religious life to do with life-cycle rites, an area of great importance for communal identity in a social setting. In the period after 500 CE, when Jainism was growing vigorously, the problem became critical. Various efforts at defining the Jain relationship to Hindu day-to-day religious culture came to full fruition in the eighth century CE in Jinasena's *Adipurana*, a Jain *purana*, or 'account of ancient things'. In it, Jinasena sought to establish a Jain version of the Hindu *samskaras*, or life-cycle rites (see pages 216–17).

In this case, however, the ideal has not fully penetrated day-to-day practice. Jinasena's vision of the life-cycle rites extends to fifty-three 'sacraments', of which the first twenty-two cover the life-cycle of the lay householder, while the remaining thirty-one 'sacramental' stages trace one's life through post-householder ascetic renunciation, rebirths on the ascetic path and, finally, absolute liberation. But Jains, by and large, use a series of life-cycle rites only somewhat different from its Hindu counterpart. Sixteen sacraments, from pre-natal observances up to funeral rites, are usually observed, with some variation between Shvetambara and Digambara communities [2: 259–63].

Yet one significant difference remains between the Jain and Hindu rites, in that most Jains do not observe the rites of *shraddha*, the post-funeral rites that Hindus observe in order to effect the transition of the deceased's soul from one existence to the next. These rites have been sharply decried by Jain teachers as being contrary to Jain views concerning the *jiva* and the workings of *karma* [1: 302ff]. Jains thus cremate their dead ceremonially, but there the formal life-cycle rites end.

Hence, even where Hindu practice appears to have been adopted by Jains, at least one characteristic sign of Jain orthodoxy remains, enough perhaps to mark a distinctive identity even in this area where the Jain lay community most resembles its larger Hindu context.

Twentieth-Century Trends in Jainism

In the first half of the twentieth century, the Jain community appeared to be shrinking as a percentage of India's population. In the 1881 census, Jains had represented 0.48 per cent of India's total population; by 1941 this figure stood at 0.37 per cent. By the 1970s, however, this trend had reversed itself, so that the population percentage represented by Jains now has nearly returned to its level of a century ago; and the equivalent percentage represents a growth in actual numbers of nearly 1.5 million (from *c.* 1.22 million in 1881 to *c.* 2.6 million in the 1971 census).

Notwithstanding this growth, the Jain community remains a very small part of India's total population, and continues to face the problem of main-taining its distinctive identity in the midst of the rapid change and vast popula-tion of modern-day India. This is not to say that the problem is insoluble. The community has shown considerable strength in recent times, particularly in the recovery of its classical ideals, and the monastic orders contained more than 5,500 monks and nuns as of 1977 [1: 247].

Nineteenth-century Western Indology exerted on the Jains much the same force as it did on the Hindu tradition, creating a strong interest in ancient sources, history and, especially, in sacred literature. In addition to the efforts of those European scholars who took a particular interest in Jainism, the Jains themselves undertook to collect and publish their own ancient literature, a task that is still under way today. Underwritten by donations from lay persons, Jain publishing-houses in Calcutta and Bombay produced printed editions of the *Shvetambara Siddhanta*; and Digambaras set out to publish the normative texts of their tradition as well. In this connection, it is noteworthy that this undertaking, once launched, has been carried forward almost exclusively at Jain initiative and effort, despite some early reluctance in parts of the community to see sacred texts printed. European scholars have edited and translated scattered texts, but no comprehensive publication of Jain texts has been done by anyone but the Jains themselves.

In addition to publishing-houses, Jains established numerous centres for research and study, and such centres became the focal points for the unearthing of a great treasure of manuscripts contained in Jain temple libraries. Since medieval times it has been held to be meritorious for a Jain to commission the copying of a text; and Jain libraries, carefully preserved and catalogued, were discovered to contain great literary reserves, including non-Jain texts.

The renewed availability of this classical heritage also stimulated efforts to place Jain teachings into modern vernacular languages, and led to attempts to relate contemporary religious and social issues to the norms established in older models. While modern Jain thinkers have often struggled with such relatively archaic teachings as those concerning *karma* or Jain cosmology (see Figure 7.2), Jainism's ethics, especially its emphasis on *ahimsa*, have proved to be a continuing source of inspiration able to bring classical norms into modern-day contexts.

Twentieth-century Jains have been moved by their ethical heritage, and by the fundamentally egalitarian concept of the *jiva*, to engage in a wide range of charitable undertakings and social concerns; and it may well be that these classical Jain perspectives are significantly responsible for the community's disproportionate effect on Indian life in recent times. Perhaps nowhere is this more the case than in the life of Mohandas K. Gandhi who, though a Hindu, was significantly influenced by a Jain layman, Raychandbhai Mehta, and whose early efforts in labour reform in Ahmadabad brought him into a curious and apparently formative relationship with Jain mill-owners in that city.

At the same time, Jainism faces critical pressures in maintaining its distinctive day-to-day religious life. Jains have tended to live in cities and big towns in large numbers, so much so that the urban population of Jains already approached 50 per cent early in this century [2:31]. This is in large measure due to their traditional occupational role in India, as merchants and professionals in law, education and related fields. In the twentieth century, however, the relatively urban character of the Jain community poses particular challenges, for it is in India's urban centres that the impact of rapid change and non-Indian cultural and social forces is greatest.

The Jains do bring strengths to this situation. Though their community has, over the centuries, adapted itself to a caste-like social structure (see pages 209–10), the Jain 'castes' tend to be agents more of familial and social stability than of hierarchical distinction; and considerable occupational flexibility obtains within them. Jains have, therefore, been relatively able to engage in the newer occupations brought by technology without the accompanying religious and social strains that affect Hindu society. The Jains are a comparatively wealthy subculture, and are thus able to underwrite the educational and institutional costs involved in preserving and transmitting their tradition.

But the homogeneous culture of the late-twentieth-century world stands in stark contrast to the archaic asceticism of Jainism's core. Thus, just as Jainism faced the problem of forming and maintaining a distinctive community over a millennium ago, it now appears to face the same problem again, in a new context, which threatens to undercut the extraordinary goal of Jainism: to look far beyond one's present life, and seize upon the absolutely human endeavour to recover one's original being.

NOTES

1. The stages are: (1) right views; (2) taking vows; (3) practising equanimity through meditation; (4) fasting on certain holy days; (5) purity of nourishment; (6) sexual continence by day; (7) absolute continence; (8) abandoning household activity; (9) abandoning possessions; (10) renouncing all concern for the householder's life; (11) renouncing all connections with one's family [1: 186].
2. Jains interpret the *svastika* as representing the four possible levels of rebirth: divine, human, nether world and animal/vegetable; the three dots are the religious virtues of insight, knowledge and conduct; and the crescent represents the abode of liberated *jivas* [1: 108, 200].

APPENDIX

A. THE 'ŚVETĀMBARA SIDDHĀNTA'

The texts listed below were all written in Prākrit, but, following the common practice, the Sanskritized forms for their titles are given here. (Prākrit titles are given, within parentheses, in the Index.) An asterisk indicates that the work is available in translation into European languages (see Bibliography).

Aṅgas:
*1. *Ācārāṅga*
*2. *Sūtrakṛtāṅga*
3. *Sthānāṅga*
4. *Samavāya*
5. *Vyākhyāprajñapti (Bhagavatī)*
6. *Jñātṛdharmakathāḥ*
*7. *Upāsakadaśāḥ*
*8. *Antakṛddaśāḥ*
*9. *Anuttaraupapātikadaśāḥ*
10. *Praśnavyākaraṇa*
11. *Vipākaśruta*
12. *Dṛṣṭivāda* (extinct)

Upāṅgas:
1. *Aupapātika*
2. *Rājapraśnīya*
3. *Jīvājīvābhigama*
4. *Prajñāpanā*
5. *Jambūdvīpaprajñapti*
6. *Sūryaprajñapti*
7. *Candraprajñapti*
8. *Nirayāvalī*
9. *Kalpāvataṃsikāḥ*
10. *Puṣpikāḥ*
11. *Puṣpacūlikāḥ*
12. *Vṛṣṇidaśāḥ*

Prakīrṇakasūtras:
1. *Catuḥśaraṇa*
2. *Āturapratyākhyāna*
3. *Bhaktaparijñā*
4. *Saṃstāraka*
5. *Taṇḍulavaicārika*
6. *Candravedhyaka*
7. *Devendrastava*
8. *Gaṇividyā*
9. *Mahāpratyākhyāna*
10. *Vīrastava*

Chedasūtras:
*1. *Ācāradaśāḥ*
2. *Bṛhatkalpa*
3. *Vyavahāra*
4. *Niśītha*
5. *Mahāniśītha*
6. *Pañcakalpa* (extinct)
7. *Jītakalpa*

Mūlasūtras:
*1. *Daśavaikālika*
*2. *Uttarādhyana*
3. *Āvaśyaka*
4. *Piṇḍaniryukti*

Cūlikāsūtras:
1. *Nandīsūtra*
2. *Anuyogadvārasūtra*

B. MAJOR SANSKRIT WORKS

What follows is a highly limited selection of works by major authors, divided according to subject-matter. An asterisk indicates that the work is available in translation into European languages (see Bibliography). The most comprehensive account of this literature in general is contained in Maurice Winternitz, *A History of Indian Literature*, vol. 2, *Buddhist Literature and Jaina Literature*. The literature concerning lay disciplines is best surveyed in R. H. B. Williams, *Jaina Yoga*.

1. Narrative literature, including Jain 'Puranas':
   Ādipurāṇa, Jinasena (Digambara), eighth century CE
   Uttarapurāṇa, Guṇabhadra (Digambara), ninth century CE
   *Triṣaṣṭiśalākāpuruṣacaritra, Hemacandra (Śvetāmbara), twelfth century CE

2. Writings on lay discipline:
   Ratnakaraṇḍa, Samantabhadra (Digambara), fifth century CE
   Śrāvakācāra, Amitagati (Digambara), eleventh century CE
   *Dharmabindu, Haribhadra (Śvetāmbara), eighth century CE
   Yogaśāstra, Hemacandra (Śvetāmbara), twelfth century CE

3. Didactic and philosophical writings:
   *Tattvārthādhigamasūtra, Umāsvāti (claimed by both Digambaras and Śvetāmbaras), second century CE(?)
   Āptamīmāṃsā, Samantabhadra (Digambara), fifth century CE
   *Pramāṇamīmāṃsā, Hemacandra (Śvetāmbara), twelfth century CE
   *Anyayogavyavacchedikā, id.
   *Syādvādamañjarī (a commentary on the foregoing), by Malliṣeṇa (Śvetāmbara), thirteenth century CE

BIBLIOGRAPHY

WORKS CITED IN THE TEXT

1. JAINI, P. S., *The Jaina Path of Purification*, Berkeley, Calif., University of California Press, 1979; first Indian edn, Delhi, Motilal Banarsidass, 1979
2. SANGAVE, V. A., *Jaina Community: A Social Survey*, Bombay, Popular Book Depot, 1959
3. SCHUBRING, W., *Die Lehre der Jainas, nach den alten Quellen dargestellt*, Berlin, De Gruyter, 1935; English tr. W. Beurlen, *The Doctrine of the Jainas*, Delhi, Motilal Banarsidass, 1962
4. JACOBI, H., *Jaina Sūtras*, vol. 1, Oxford, Clarendon Press, 1884 (Sacred Books of the East, vol. 22); repr. Delhi, Motilal Banarsidass, 1968, New York, Dover Publications, 1968

5. TATIA, N., *Studies in Jaina Philosophy*, Banaras, Jain Cultural Research Society, 1951
6. DEO, S. B., *History of Jaina Monachism*, Poona, Deccan College, 1956
7. MEHTA, M. L., 'Jaina monastic discipline', in: Gurbachan Singh Talib (ed.), *Jainism*, Patiala, Punjabi University, 1975, pp. 68–77
8. WILLIAMS, R. H. B., *Jaina Yoga: A Survey of the Mediaeval Śrāvakācāras*, London, New York, Oxford University Press, 1963

TRANSLATIONS OF JAINA TEXTS LISTED IN THE APPENDIX

9. *Ācārāṅga*: JACOBI, H., *Jaina Sūtras*, vol. 1 (see entry 4 above)
10. *Sūtrakṛtāṅga*: JACOBI, H., *Jaina Sūtras*, vol. 2, Oxford, Clarendon Press, 1895 (Sacred Books of the East, vol. 45)
11. *Upāsakadaśāḥ*: HOERNLE, A. F. R., *The Uvāsagadasāo, or The Religious Profession of an Uvasaga*, 2 vols., Calcutta, Bibliotheca Indica, 1888–90
12. *Antakṛddaśāḥ (Antagaḍadasāo)*: see entry 13
13. *Anuttaraupapātikadaśāḥ*: BARNETT, L. D., *The Antagaḍadasāo and Aṇuttarovavāiyadasāo*, London, Royal Asiatic Society, 1907
14. *Ācāradaśāḥ*: JACOBI, H., *Jaina Sūtras*, vol. 2 (see entry 10 above)
15. *Daśavaikālika*: LALWANI, K. C., *Daśavaikālika-sutra*, Delhi, Motilal Banarsidass, 1973
16. *Uttarādhyana*: JACOBI, H., *Jaina Sūtras*, vol. 1 (see entry 4 above)
17. *Triṣaṣṭiśalākāpuruṣacaritra*: JOHNSON, H. M., *The Lives of Sixty-Three Illustrious Persons*, Baroda, The Oriental Institute, 1962
18. *Tattvārthādhigamasūtra*: JAINI, J. L., *Tattvārtha-sūtra of Umāsvāti*, Arrah, Central Jaina Publishing House, 1920
19. *Pramāṇamīmāṃsā*: MOOKERJEE, S., and TATIA, N., *Pramāṇamīmāṃsā of Hemacandra*, Varanasi, Tara Publications, 1970
20. *Anyayogavyavacchedikā*: THOMAS, F. W., *The Flower-Spray of the Quodammodo Doctrine*, Berlin, Akademie-Verlag, 1960
21. *Syādvādamañjarī*: THOMAS op cit. (see entry 20)

L. S. COUSINS

Introduction

A VAST EXPANSE

The history of Buddhism extends over two and a half millennia. It has spread into a number of originally unrelated cultures and exercised great influence over much of Asia. No other religion has existed in such disparate cultures as a major influence for so long. Over 50 per cent of the population of the world live in areas where Buddhism has at some time been the dominant religious force. Inevitably it has responded to differing circumstances, and local customs and ideas have influenced it in many ways. Adaptability has historically been a marked feature, arising no doubt from some of Buddhism's most distinctive and central notions. Yet there is also continuity.

All forms of Buddhism today derive from the same roots. So the approach adopted here is to begin with this common source in ancient Indian Buddhism and then go on to describe separately the Buddhism of the three main twentieth-century geographical areas. This treatment of the subject should not blind us to the fact that most kinds of Buddhism are motivated by similar concerns. The aim is nearly always to create conditions favourable to personal medita-tional or spiritual development. The general understanding is that insights of the right kind can transform the individual in ways usually expressed in terms of 'liberation', 'freedom' or 'spontaneity'. This is generally seen as re-quiring a long period of training. Underlying this practice is an elaborate classification of states of mind as they relate to the path leading to liberation and a rather exact methodology of spiritual training – a kind of 'spiritual technology'. No two schools of Buddhism describe these matters in precisely the same way, but there is a constant similarity of concern and parallelism of method. An underlying common purpose has been adapted to different situations with great flexibility.

THREE GREAT TRADITIONS

The three great traditions of Buddhism are distinct historically and geographically (Figure 8.1). (Older names for these areas that reflect particular prejudices are best avoided and have not been used here.)

1. Southern Buddhism, often known as Theravada Buddhism, has about 100 million adherents, most of whom live in the five countries of Sri Lanka (Ceylon), Burma, Cambodia, Laos and Thailand (Siam). Smaller numbers are found in parts of Vietnam, Bangladesh and India, and as emigrants to the U.S.A.

2. Eastern Buddhism, practised in China, Japan, Korea, Vietnam and among various emigrant populations. A meaningful estimate of numbers cannot be given. The close relationship between Buddhism and various indigenous religions (Confucianism, Shinto, Taoism, folk religion) is such that a family or individual may adhere simultaneously to various practices. Moreover, Communist rule in much of the area has made reliable information unobtainable. Some estimates give numbers of actively committed Buddhists, but this is misleading when set beside figures for nominal adherence. It may be said that Buddhism is one of the most widely influential religious traditions within a population of the order of 1,200 million.

3. Northern Buddhism, current in Tibet, Mongolia, the Himalayas, in parts of China and the Soviet Union and among a scattered emigrant population, with perhaps 10 million adherents. Its influence has been somewhat greater than numbers might suggest. It has preserved a rich and independent cultural, spiritual and philosophical tradition derived directly from classical Indian Buddhist teachings.

INCOMPLETENESS

One common feature of the three great traditions should be noted. Everywhere it has penetrated, Buddhism coexists with indigenous religious traditions in complex ways. This is true both of elaborate and varied systems such as Hinduism, Confucianism or Taoism and equally of simpler forms of local folk religion and cultus. This is no accident. It is a consequence of the founder's concentration upon the most essential. Nor has it proved a weakness. It has enabled Buddhism to adjust successfully and sensitively to varied environments, seeking to adapt and transform rather than to destroy. It is an error to think of a pure Buddhism, which has become syncretistically mixed with other

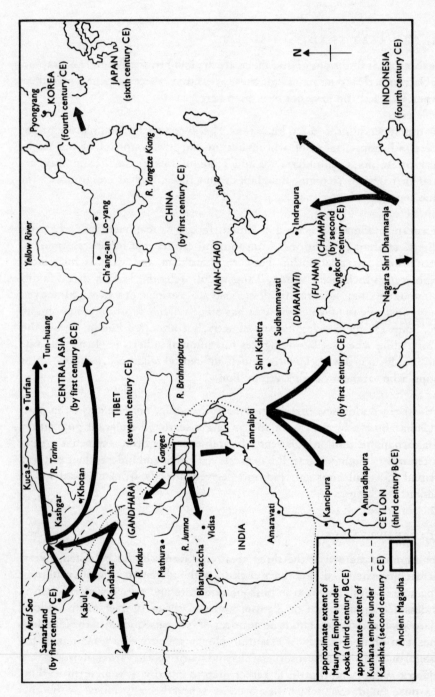

Figure 8.1 The expansion of Buddhism

religions, even corrupted and degenerate in later forms. Such a pure Buddhism has never existed. Buddhism has always coexisted with other religious beliefs and practices. It did not usually seek to involve itself in every sphere of human ritual activity. Many such things are 'not conducive to' the path, i.e. not relevant to the spiritual endeavour. Its strength perhaps lies in this very incompleteness.

So the superstition and 'animism' of the villager, the widespread Asian interest in magic, numerology and astrology, the rituals of the Brahman or Taoist priest are not part of the fundamental orientation. They may be practised if desired so long as the main aim is not lost. Buddhism as such has no more to say about them than the natural scientist about the laws of tennis. They are irrelevant. This very fact entitles the Buddhist modernist to reject such things however much they have historically been entwined with the life of ordinary Buddhists. If he goes on to claim that Buddhism is opposed to such things, this is perhaps a natural exaggeration or sometimes an excessive wish to accord with alien values.

Ancient Buddhism

THE BACKGROUND TO EARLY BUDDHISM

Origins. The early history of India is less well known than that of the other great civilizations of the ancient world. Much of what is known cannot be placed in a secure chronological framework. Most scholars believe that the founder of Buddhism was born in the second quarter of the sixth century BCE and remained active well into the first quarter of the fifth century. He was certainly a contemporary of the founder of Jainism. We know also the names of most of the important kings ruling in northern India during his lifetime.

The context in which the Buddha lived and taught is clear. Most of northern India seems to have been inhabited by people speaking early forms of the Middle Indian languages, still rather close to Sanskrit. These dialects were probably mutually comprehensible; so communications across India would have been easier at this time. Outside India important developments were taking place. While the Buddha was striving for his goal, Cyrus the Great was completing the extension of the Persian Empire into Central Asia and perhaps what is now known as Afghanistan (see page 172). Within two decades Darius had made the Indus valley into the richest province of the empire. Henceforth the Middle Indian world was in a situation similar to that of the Greek world to the west. Overshadowed by the enormous territories of the Great King, both experienced great cultural and economic impact. Skills, techniques and ideas from the ancient civilizations of the area could spread more rapidly than ever before. The similarity with Greece is striking in other respects also. In both these frontier areas we find a proliferation of ideas and systems of belief, offering different prescriptions for life. Just as the Greek philosophical tradition emerges to influence the subsequent intellectual history of Western civilization, so too Buddhism emerges to influence the intellectual and religious history of Asian civilization.

The Buddha appears to have made a conscious attempt to avoid the dogmatism of competing religious systems. He aimed to teach only what was essential for spiritual development and carefully excluded from his system everything not directly relevant to that purpose. The result is radically unusual. The Buddha set out a middle way, based mainly upon pragmatic considerations. One-sided viewpoints and aims were rejected. Materialistic views of life and spiritually oriented beliefs in personal immortality were considered equally misleading. Mistaken too were extreme goals, seeking either self-satisfaction through indulgence in pleasure or self-purification through ascetic discipline. Traditional religious beliefs, rites and customs were re-evaluated, not so much on the basis of 'reason' as of what might be called 'spiritual common sense'. Extreme forms of superstition and ritualism were opposed, but so was a naïve materialism which sought to deny the real experiences of the spiritual path.

Buddhism and Hinduism. It is sometimes suggested that the Buddha was a Hindu. If by Hindu is meant 'anyone adhering to a religion of Indian origin', then he obviously was. If Hinduism is understood as that synthesis of various traditions oriented towards the Brahmanical Vedic tradition which has been the religion of most educated Indians since at least the fifth century CE, then the Buddha was certainly not a Hindu. Indeed Buddhism was one of the influences which led to the formation of the Hindu synthesis. If Hinduism is taken as synonymous with 'Brahmanism', then it is uncertain what exactly was the Buddha's relation to that. During the period of the formation of Buddhism there were at least three major sources of religious authority in India:

1. The hereditary priestly class of the Brahmans, preserving the scriptures of the Vedic tradition and much ancillary learning.

2. The naked ascetics, emphasizing ascetic practices.

3. The clothed wanderers (*parivrajakas*) with a less extreme discipline. While some in groups two and three may have adhered to the Vedic tradition, it is clear that many did not. From the naked ascetics developed the religions of the Jains and Ajivakas. Buddhism may have been more closely related to the third group.

Some scholars believe that the non-Brahmanical traditions derive from indigenous Indian beliefs stemming from the Indus valley civilization (*c.* 2000 BCE), before the entry of the speakers of Indo-European languages who brought the beginnings of the Vedic tradition to India. More probably native and immigrant elements had become inextricably mixed long before the sixth century BCE.

Buddhism is clearly influenced by and aware of all three contemporary tendencies. The Vedic tradition was certainly important, but not yet fully formed. The classical spiritual literature of that tradition contained in the *Upanishads* is not easily datable. The very earliest *Upanishads* are probably pre-Buddhist, others may be contemporary with early Buddhism, but probably the majority of the fourteen or so major *Upanishads* are post-Buddhist and perhaps influenced by Buddhism. [1: 28–42]

THE THREE JEWELS

The Buddha. The reliability of the accounts we have of the life of the Buddha is a matter of much scholarly debate. Our sources cannot be shown with certainty to be sufficiently close in time for absolute reliability. It is not that we know nothing. The traditional life story handed down largely in common among all Buddhists is quite full. We may be fairly sure that it contains much accurate information of a historical kind. We are quite sure that it contains later elaboration and additions. What we often do not know is which is which.

The future Buddha was born as a princeling named Siddhattha (Sanskrit: Siddhartha)[1] in the Gotama clan among a people dwelling near the present-day border with Nepal, known as the Sakkas (see Figure 8.2). After a royal up-bringing he renounced family life, studied under various spiritual teachers, went his own way, practised self-mortification for a while, rejected this in favour of moderation and finally achieved a spiritual realization after a night of striving beneath a tree at the place now known as Bodh-gaya. He pro-claimed his teaching to a small group of disciples in an animal park at Isipatana (Sarnath) near Banaras and spent the remainder of his life giving spiritual instruction both to the public at large and to an ever-growing body of disciples. By his death in his eighty-first year his following had become a large and well-organized community. More than this we cannot say with certainty. Nevertheless we should remember that the Buddha legend which has inspired and motivated so many for so long is enormously important in its own right. [2]

Buddhas and the dhamma. The word *buddha* means 'one who has woken up' – i.e. from the mental sleep of the untrained mind – but Buddhists have often preferred a traditional explanation. A buddha is 'one who knows' the *dhamma* or basic truth of things. So anyone is a buddha who has achieved

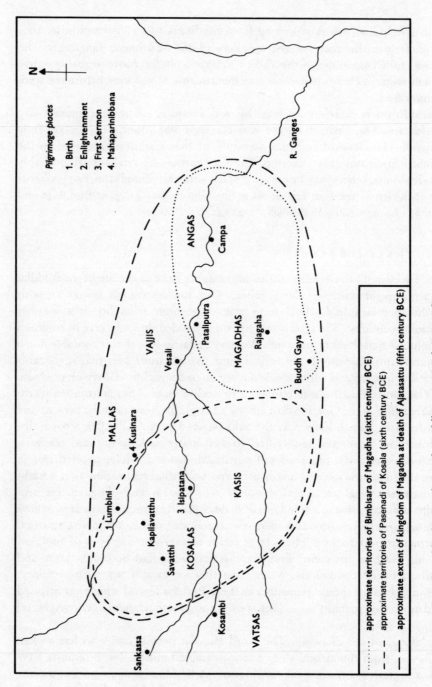

Figure 8.2   The political background to early Buddhism in North-East India

the goal of the Buddhist path. More usually the word is used only of an individual of much greater cosmic significance: the Samma-sambuddha, 'one who has fully awakened in the right way' or 'one who has fully known in the right way'. Such a Buddha is extremely rare in the universe. Whole aeons may pass before one is born.

Buddhist modernists often lay stress on the human nature of the Buddha, partly as an understandable response to pressure from theistic missionaries. This can be misleading. Buddhahood is achieved in human circumstances as the culmination of many lives, but the penultimate life is always divine. It is in fact the result of striving for perfection for countless lives, reborn in many different forms and conditions of being. Traditional Buddhism understands by the word Buddha neither man nor god, but one who has far transcended the nature of both – the Teacher of gods and men.

From an early date accounts of the life of the Buddha contained both human and cosmic elements. Modern historical scholarship attempted at first to construct a biography by eliminating all miraculous and marvellous elements as later additions, but there are serious methodological objections to this. Moreover by removing the more poetic and mythic elements of the Buddhist tradition, it creates a false impression of a rather dry intellectual philosophy. This obscures the devotional aspect of early Buddhism.

The lives of all Buddhas conform to a pattern, which is not envisaged as mere historical accident but rather exemplifies the spiritual law or truth taught by all the Buddhas. It is this truth which early Buddhists called *dhamma* (Sanskrit: *dharma*). In practice the word was used in a number of slightly differing ways. *Dhamma* is the law of the cosmos – the true nature of things, their intrinsic lawfulness as it were. It is also the law of the mind, of the good life and of the spiritual path. The understanding gained by the Buddhas enables them to be the embodiment of this. To realize *dhamma* is at once to comprehend the law of the spiritual life and to achieve its goal. So the Buddha declared: 'Who sees *dhamma* sees me. Who sees me sees *dhamma*.' The teachings and texts of Buddhism are the outward embodiment of *dhamma*. They are *dhamma* to be learnt as opposed to *dhamma* to be practised or *dhamma* to be penetrated in the moment of liberation. [3: 131–5]

The Sangha. Many Buddhist ceremonies begin with the act of going for refuge to the 'three jewels'. Added to the Buddha and the *dhamma* is the community, or Sangha. In its more universal aspect this refers to those who have realized the transcendental *dhamma* – the holy community of the noble ones or *ariya-sangha*. It is this which is taken as refuge. In its more historical sense it is the community of *bhikkhus* or religious mendicants. It is not known how much of the organization of that community evolved during the Buddha's long life, how much was already current in earlier Indian mendicant groups and how much developed during the following century. However it happened, it was a remarkable achievement. No other religious or non-religious community combines so long a history with so wide an influence and spread. As late as the mid twentieth century members of the Buddhist Sangha numbered well over 1 million and although the hostility of Communist governments has reduced that number considerably, it certainly exceeds a quarter of a million.

The secret of the success of the Buddhist Sangha lies in the set of training rules known as the *Patimokkha*. This is now current in three distinct recensions among Southern, Eastern and Northern Buddhists respectively (others are preserved but no longer in use). It is enlarged from a common core of 150 major rules, but differing social conditions have led to a fairly wide variation in the way in which the rules are now applied.

In ancient India the most distinctive feature of the Buddhist Sangha was probably its adoption of a compromise between the settled life-style of many orthodox Brahmans and the wandering characteristic of other traditions. By establishing fixed residences for three months in the rainy season, the Buddha ensured that the life of the *bhikkhu* would provide both for the establishing of local centres of operation and for the retention of at least something of the simplicity necessitated by the life of the wandering religious beggar. Larger settled institutions tended to develop later, but great individual mobility usually remained possible. This kind of inherent compromise is natural to the Buddhist 'middle way' and quite characteristic of the training rules of the *Patimokkha*. A similar balance is clearly expected between the demands of discipline and a relaxed approach as well as between respect for seniority and individual autonomy. Authority was collective rather than hierarchical, but a certain minimum observation was enforced. Only the breach of four specific rules led to expulsion (*parajika*, i.e. 'defeat'): the act of sexual intercourse; taking human life; theft; or dishonest claim to some spiritual attainment. The majority of the lesser rules are concerned either with ensuring simplicity of life-style or with maintaining a disciplined deportment.

The *Patimokkha* can be approached fairly laxly and each *bhikkhu* is in principle free to leave the Sangha if he wishes. Yet taken with a full commitment it represents a most demanding training, requiring great attention and awareness in every action – especially for the inexperienced. Such of course is its purpose. It is part of the spiritual training directed towards the Buddhist goal.

[4: 86–110]

THE DEVELOPMENT OF ANCIENT BUDDHISM

Asoka. The Buddhist scriptures were not committed to writing until the first century BCE. So the earliest independent evidence for Buddhist ideas is found in the inscriptions of the Emperor Asoka (Sanskrit: Ashoka) of the Mauryan dynasty in the third century BCE. Asoka states that he turned to a serious commitment to Buddhist practice as a result of revulsion at the horrors of war. His authority extended over the greater part of South Asia and his prestige must have greatly aided the wider extension of Buddhism. In subsequent Buddhist tradition Asoka is portrayed as the ideal Buddhist ruler, heavily committed to the spread of the teaching.

Asoka's personal position is clear. He worshipped at Buddhist shrines, enlarged Buddhist monuments, went on Buddhist pilgrimages and formally expressed adherence to the Sangha. Nevertheless he spoke always of *dhamma* in his edicts and avoided the more abstract forms of Buddhist teaching. While *dhamma* can be interpreted in terms of the general background of Indian religion as good or right behaviour, this should not be taken too far. Asoka was following the Buddha's own example in seeking to find common ground and to conciliate without conceding essentials. His edicts are similar in content to Buddhist texts addressed to the ordinary layman. If they also differ little from comparable Jain and Brahmanical works, this is quite natural in a philosophy which aims at consensus, at a 'middle way'. Asoka's attitude to other religions is set out clearly in his Twelfth Rock Edict:

> His Majesty ... gives praise to all religious teachers whether monks or householders ... both by giving (*dana*) and by various kinds of worship (*puja*). But his Majesty does not think giving or worship to be as valuable ... as strengthening the real essence ... the foundation of this is control of speech so that praising one's own religious teachers or criticism of other people's should not occur without reason or, if there is reason, it should be mild. Other people's teachers should be given praise in every way. By doing so one profits one's own religion and benefits the other's religion. By doing otherwise one damages one's own religion and does harm to the other person's.

Asoka's edicts evince a concern for animal and human welfare both on a practical and on a moral level: 'This will profit in this life and also in the next life.' He tried to set an example of diligent endeavour and non-violence to his successors, apparently adopted vegetarianism but was clearly not an outright pacifist. He was hostile to animal sacrifice even though this could not have been welcome to traditional Brahmans. He was, above all, concerned with moral purification and self-awareness. He gave his own definition of *dhamma*: 'Few faults, many good deeds, pity, generosity, truthfulness, purity.' So *dhamma* is what you are and do, rather than what you believe. This emerges directly from his Buddhism. If he conceived it as strengthening the 'real essence' of all religion, perhaps this was because he conceived of Buddhism in the same way, as the Buddha before him certainly did. [1: 242ff]

Early Buddhist literature. During the early period a considerable body of oral literature had developed in vernacular Middle Indian. Eventually this was organized into three sections or 'baskets': the Tipitaka. When later it was set into writing, slightly different dialects were used in different localities. The general tendency was to use a more 'learned' style closer to classical Sanskrit. In North India a highly Sanskritized form of Middle Indian, sometimes referred to as Buddhist Hybrid Sanskrit, was widely used. In the south Sanskrit was not so important until a later date. So in Ceylon a much less Sanskritized but stylish form became current, known traditionally as Magadhi but now usually referred to as Pali. In fact the Pali Canon or Tipitaka in Pali appears to have been written down rather earlier than elsewhere (first century BCE) by a conservative group which relegated later material to commentaries. Some other branches incorporated directly into their recension of the canon.

The three sections are distinct in subject-matter and method. The *Vinaya-pitaka* or 'Basket of Discipline' is concerned with the order and discipline of the Sangha. It contains an elaborate case-law, based upon the convention that each rule was established by the Buddha as a result of a specific incident. The *Vinaya-pitaka* must be rather early in date as, apart from various appendices, it is almost identical in the different recensions. Still earlier is the Patimokkha code, which is likely to have been laid down by the Buddha himself, at least in its main portion.

The second section – the *Sutta-pitaka* – mostly consists of discourses attributed to the Buddha and given at specific places to specific people. It is organized in four or five *nikayas* ('parts'), later known as *agamas* ('traditions'). The fifth *nikaya* is probably a later addition. It varies considerably in different recensions, but usually contains some quite early works as well as some much later compositions. A number of recensions of the discourses survive – complete in Pali, partial in Sanskrit and in Chinese and Tibetan translations. Although there are differences as to details and many variations of arrangement, the four *nikayas* contain more or less the same fundamental ideas in all recensions. Such variation as exists is probably due to chance rather than sectarian differences. Indeed this is wholly to be expected in an oral literature. The texts contain much repetition of stock passages and formulaic patterns. This is a technique to ensure accurate preservation of oral traditions, but it is one which allows considerable variation of the exact form. Such oral works, we know from studies elsewhere, are rarely recited identically. Their content, however, is very traditional and conservative. [64; 65: 1–10]

The abhidhamma *movement.* The third section of the Ancient Buddhist canon is the *Abhidhamma-pitaka.* Here the case is rather different. Each of the main recensions of the canon seems to have included different works in this section. So it is probable that the *abhidhamma* works are later than the four *nikayas.* However, it is important to distinguish the *abhidhamma* movement from the *abhidhamma* literature. For although particular works differ, the *abhidhamma* method differs much less. The movement of thought and practice which brought the *abhidhamma* approach into prominence probably occurred during the Mauryan period (third century BCE), if not earlier. Indeed the *nikayas* already show signs of influence from such a movement.

Abhidhamma classifies experience in terms of fleeting groups of events. These events are called *dhammas* because in aggregate they constitute the *dhamma* or truth realized by the Buddha and because they are, as it were, the constituent parts of his teaching. In later *abhidhamma* each *dhamma* is something unique and indivisible in its nature. *Dhammas* always occur in groupings and cannot be subdivided. Strictly speaking they are changing events not static realities. Philosophically this leads to a process-oriented view of experience in which only properties are recognized. There is no substantial core which owns the properties. Above all, there is no permanent and unchanging soul or ground of being in man or the universe. In fact, however, the earlier *abhidhamma* is not so much concerned with ultimate events as to show the fluidity and subtle structuring of experience. The aim is to produce a changed perception of reality. So an elaborate map of psychological states and spiritual levels was constructed on the basis of earlier traditions. The whole subsequent history of Buddhism is coloured by the *abhidhamma* endeavour. All the later systems of Buddhist thought are constructed upon an *abhidhamma* edifice. [1: 218ff]

Other developments. Ancient Buddhism was not static. We can identify a number of developing tendencies. Naturally these had roots in the earliest form of Buddhism known to us, equally naturally they are related to the general evolution of Indian thought. Brahmanical religion was slowly moving from its earlier sacrificial and intellectual emphases towards an approach based on devotion (*bhakti* – see pages 207–8). So too was Buddhism. Devotional elements had probably always been present in both. Emphasis on such elements was not a sectarian move. Rather a climate of opinion led gradually to new practices. The natural tendency to use more and more exalted language in praise of the Buddha led inevitably to a more and more exalted conception of his status. No doubt the founder had never been conceived of as an 'ordinary' human being any more than many living Indian holy men are today. Devotional practices, based upon the worship of various kinds of relic, gradually increased in importance. Initially a matter purely for the laity, they later came to involve the Sangha too.

If the Buddha was radically superior to his enlightened disciples, then the path to buddhahood must necessarily also be superior. Gradually this began to be explained in detail as the path of the *bodhisatta* (Sanskrit *bodhisattva*) – 'one bound for awakening'. The explanation was based upon older conceptions of the path. The same terms were used but viewed as 'perfections', i.e. exalted to the highest possible degree. The Buddha had always been seen as motivated by concern for the welfare of all beings. The path to buddhahood is naturally viewed as based upon compassion. Just as the Prince Siddhattha was depicted as striving heroically over many lives, so every *bodhisatta* must strive similarly. The same general tendency led eventually to the introduction of the Buddha image in the early centuries of the Christian Era. In early Buddhism Buddhas were represented not in human form but by symbols (see Figure 8.3). This is perhaps because prior to Greek influence such representation was characteristic of the cult of the inferior deities. Later a rich artistic heritage of iconographic forms was to develop, expressing some of the central spiritual ideals in visual form (see Figure 8.4). [5: 1–82]

The early Mahayana. The developments outlined so far are the heritage of all later forms of Buddhism. It was from this milieu that a new kind of Buddhism was to emerge. At first it was simply a convergence of these existing tendencies. Some scholars have seen the new direction, usually referred to as the Mahayana, as a highly radical departure. This is clearly wrong. It is only true, if at all, of later fully developed Mahayana Buddhism. The early Mahayana literature developed over a period of centuries and did not at first differ greatly. It was simply another step in the same general line of development. Existing institutional forms were not altered by the early Mahayanists. The Sangha continued to function in much the same way as before. Such change as occurred came mostly much later and as part of general trends affecting the whole of Indian Buddhism. Down to the twelfth century at least the great centres of Mahayana Buddhism tended also to be centres for schools adhering to the earlier traditions. Many monks seem to have studied or practised both.

THE PLACE OF THE MAHAYANA

The essence of the Mahayana. What then did the new departure involve? Three main tendencies can be identified: the full adoption of a heroic ideal, a new cosmology closely related to visualization practices and a new philosophical expression based upon the experience of 'emptiness' in insight

Bodhi tree, throne
and royal umbrella

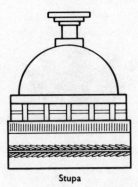

Stupa

Wheel and throne

Footprint

Fertile vase

Shrivatsa and svastikas

Standard

Lustration

Figure 8.3   The symbols of Ancient Buddhism

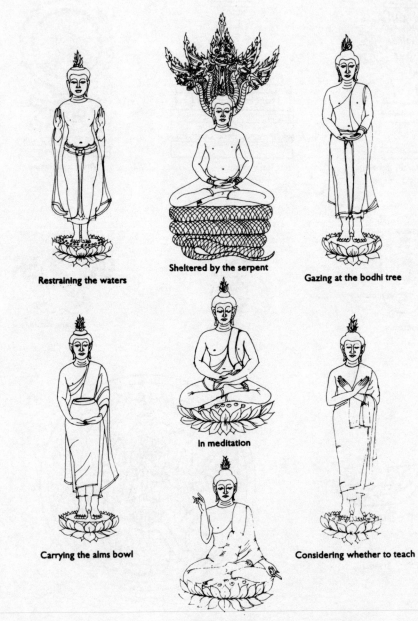

Restraining the waters

Sheltered by the serpent

Gazing at the bodhi tree

Carrying the alms bowl

In meditation

Considering whether to teach

Summoning rain

Figure 8.4   The Buddha figure in Thai tradition

Contemplating the corpse

Practising austerities

Revealing the worlds

Conferring ordination

Defeating *Mara*

Releasing the life faculty

Mastering his illness

meditation. The heroic ideal of the *bodhisattva* path was not new. What was new was the claim, explicit or implicit, that this should be adopted by all. Immediate personal enlightenment (arahatship) was now to be seen as an inferior goal. Greater stress was laid on altruistic action based upon 'skill in means' and compassion. This too was not new, but was now emphasized more than ever before.

The background world picture of early Buddhism was that of Indian religion in general but modified to fit the Buddhist meditational 'map' (see page 304). Meditation practices included recollection of the qualities of the Buddha and various kinds of visualization exercise. The Mahayana took these earlier cosmological and meditational elements and combined them in a new way. The final result was much more specifically Buddhist in form. Such earlier Indian deities (see page 197) as Brahma and Indra were overshadowed by new figures – Buddhas and spiritually advanced *bodhisattvas*. Their names and much of their nature derive from earlier devotional responses to the Buddha. They could and did become much more closely associated with the most spiritual and uniquely Buddhist teachings.

The philosophy of emptiness develops from earlier insight meditation and the related *abhidhamma* thought. The aim of both is to dissolve rigid views (*ditthi*) and bring about a fresher perception of the world. Apparent entities such as the mind are merely changing collections of evanescent events – a direct intuition of this is the experiencing of emptiness. *Abhidhamma* developed detailed analyses of this ever-changing world. The aim was to break down the apparent unity of things and so free the mind from rigidity.

The Mahayanists felt that these analyses had themselves created a prison similar to the old. The constituent parts were being taken as fixed entities and this was just as entrapping as older notions of soul or spirit. They emphasized the complete emptiness of all phenomena including all parts. Nothing has real existence in that nothing exists independently and nothing which has come into being has any permanence. This is from their standpoint not nihilism or pessimism; it is this very non-fixity which makes liberation possible. Indeed liberation is precisely the recognition of this emptiness. It is not an escape to somewhere else. Rather it is a transformed understanding of this world itself.

A dynamic balance. These three tendencies arise from different aspects of the earlier tradition. They were there part of a dynamic whole. In the Mahayana too they are skilfully interconnected. The heroic ideal of the *bodhisattva* path begins with the undertaking of a resolve to attain buddhahood. The commitment required in such a resolve is seen as an act of great spiritual and kammic potency (see page 302) productive of enormous results. Hence the realm of wondrous paradises and awe-inspiring spiritual beings to be visualized. Conversely such wondrous results can only reinforce the desirability of the *bodhisattva* path. To follow that path it is necessary to develop the perfections, last and greatest of which is the perfection of wisdom. That perfection of wisdom is nothing other than the realization of emptiness.

Between the emotionally attractive realm of vision and the inspiring but detached knowledge of emptiness is a necessary complementarity. Each is needed to balance the other. Without devotion and visionary experience emptiness is cold and dry. Without perfect wisdom such marvellous visions can only entrap. In this way the Mahayana sought to preserve the balanced synthesis so characteristic of the Buddhist spiritual path from its beginning. [6: 121–40]

Mahayana and Hinayana. The new movement gradually became systematized. There was gain in precision but perhaps some loss of the initial freshness and insight. Gradually it diverged more and more from the earlier tradition. The two were distinguished in terms of the goal at which they aimed. So they became known as the *bodhisattva-yana*, 'vehicle of the *bodhisattvas*', and the *shravaka-yana*, 'vehicle of the disciples'. As the superiority of the former became more emphasized (by its adherents), the terms Mahayana, 'Great vehicle', and Hinayana, 'Inferior vehicle' or 'Incomplete vehicle', became increasingly common. There is great confusion over the different senses in which these terms are used. In later Eastern and Northern Buddhist usage it is mainly a distinction of spiritual level. The Mahayana is superior in three ways: in its motivation (greater compassion); its goal (buddhahood); and its level of understanding (supreme wisdom). Teachings on these subjects represent a deeper level of exposition of the Buddha's message. The Hinayana is correspondingly seen as selfish in motivation, inferior in goal (arahatship), and lacking depth of understanding.

Too often these distinctions have been uncritically applied to early Buddhism or to Southern Buddhism. In both cases there are problems. Early Buddhism places a high value on the motivation of concern (*anukampa*) for others and never views the *arahat* as selfish. Rather he 'goes forth for the welfare and benefit of the world'. So too in later Southern Buddhism. Both recognize the legitimacy of the *bodhisatta* path and its goal of buddhahood. Some Southern Buddhists aspire to practise the perfections of the *bodhisatta*. They do not, however, consider this suitable for all and they do not accept the authority of the Mahayana literature. Many Southern Buddhists have great faith in the depth of understanding of their teachers.

The later Southern tradition is not monolithic. It contains various traditions from both the earliest and subsequent periods as well as important elements reflecting both influence from and reaction against the Mahayana. All forms of modern Buddhism have been influenced in their assessments of the past (and of their more distant co-religionists) by Western historical scholarship. Unfortunately this has introduced inappropriate issues and value judgements derived from European Protestant–Catholic controversy.

Southern Buddhism

INTRODUCTION

Sources. The Pali Text Society (founded by T. W. Rhys Davids in 1881) has published most of the Pali Canon in the Roman alphabet, as well as many translations and a great deal of commentarial material. Much remains to be done. Especially valuable are the translations of I. B. Horner [7] and T. W. Rhys Davids [8]. The most influential later work is the *Visuddhimagga* of Buddhaghosa (fifth century CE) [9]. The traditional manual of *abhidhamma* is the *Abhidhammatthasangaha* of Anuruddha (*c.* eleventh century) [10]. The main historical sources are the *Ceylon Chronicles*, admirably studied by Wilhelm Geiger. They can be compared with archaeological and epigraphic evidence.

The recent history of Southern Buddhism is essentially the history of Ceylon and South-East Asia. This is based partly upon local traditions and chronicles and partly upon outside sources, notably travellers' accounts and missionary writings. Much information on the modern practice of rural Buddhism is to be found in social anthropological studies. [11] Important are the works of M. E. Spiro [12] for Burma, S. J. Tambiah for Thailand, F. Bizot for Cambodia and R. F. Gombrich for Ceylon [13]. The last of these integrates the present-day picture with that given in the ancient Ceylon commentaries. [64]

History. The *Ceylon Chronicles* inform us that Buddhism was introduced into the island by a mission sent by the Emperor Asoka and led by his son Mahinda. The dominant school was the Vibhajjavada 'Separative Teaching' or 'Teaching which distinguishes', one of four main divisions of the Sangha in Ancient Buddhism. In the first century BCE its canon of scriptures was written down in Pali in Ceylon. The early history of Vibhajjavada outside the island is little known, but it is quite possible that it remained widespread in India and had already missionized parts of South-East Asia.

Certainly by the fifth century CE various forms of Vibhajjavada using Pali were widespread in southern India and among the Pyu and Mon peoples of present-day Burma and Thailand. The capital city of Ceylon at Anuradhapura was a centre of Vibhajjavada learning to which monks came from far afield.

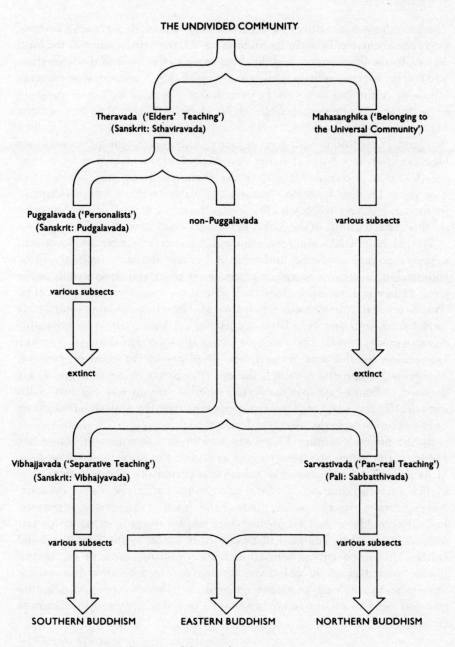

THE UNDIVIDED COMMUNITY

Theravada ('Elders' Teaching')
(Sanskrit: Sthaviravada)

Mahasanghika ('Belonging to
the Universal Community')

Puggalavada ('Personalists')
(Sanskrit: Pudgalavada)

non-Puggalavada

various subsects

various subsects

extinct

extinct

Vibhajjavada ('Separative Teaching')
(Sanskrit: Vibhajyavada)

Sarvastivada ('Pan-real Teaching')
(Pali: Sabbatthivada)

various subsects

various subsects

SOUTHERN BUDDHISM

EASTERN BUDDHISM

NORTHERN BUDDHISM

Figure 8.5 The main divisions of the Sangha

The prestigious Mahavihara ('great monastery') claimed to preserve authoritative commentaries brought by Mahinda and later written down in the local dialect. In the fifth century Buddhaghosa came to Ceylon and rendered these into Pali in order to make them more widely available. A considerable literature followed, continuing down to the present day. Provided with a strong sense of historical continuity through their chronicles, the followers of the Mahavihara proved very resistant to Mahayana ideas and preserved their own independent traditions with great tenacity. Although North Indian Buddhist ideas are known to some Pali writers, especially Dhammapala, they are utilized only so far as is compatible with Mahavihara traditions. [14] The name of Theravada ('Elders' teaching'), strictly applicable to many schools, came to be used exclusively by this tradition as a result of their claim to represent the unaltered teaching of the Elders in the undivided Sangha of old.

The first half of the second millennium saw a series of attempts by monarchs to unify the Sangha under the leadership of the orthodox Mahavihara tradition. Ultimately this became accepted, especially at court and government, as the most authentic form of Buddhism. There remained much local variation. Traditions deriving from other branches of Theravada, from ancient North Indian Buddhism and even from the Mahayana continued to be influential down to modern times. Theravada was strikingly successful during this period. One reason for this was probably the simplicity of the relatively uniform Mahavihara tradition. Although the ancient centres in South India slowly declined, in South-East Asia the decline of other schools was matched by the growth of Theravada. Large areas formerly dominated by Mahayana Buddhism or Hinduism became the preserve of Theravada.

By the fifteenth century Theravada Buddhism was dominant among the Burmese, the Mons, the Thai peoples and even the Khmers, covering most of its present-day territory. The subsequent period saw various attempts at unification, centralization or reform and various hazards of war or invasion. Nevertheless the overall picture altered little down to the nineteenth century. In Ceylon Buddhism had a more difficult time. Invasions from mainland Asia and, more seriously, conquest of much of the island by the Portuguese and Dutch with consequent missionization, persecution and destruction weakened the economic base of the island and severely damaged Buddhist institutions. Despite such problems Buddhism retained the allegiance of most Sinhalese and was able to recover much ground in a revival during the eighteenth century. [15]

Academic study of the Theravada. We do not know how much the Hellenistic Greeks and Romans knew of Buddhism. The name is mentioned a few times. The occasional travelling monk may have reached the Mediterranean.

Buddhism was certainly well known to the later Asiatic Greeks and in the Iranian world. At any rate almost no knowledge of Buddhism survived the decline of classical learning. Thereafter Europe was dependent upon travellers' reports: a few missionary monks travelling in Asia, occasional envoys and traders – the most famous is Marco Polo. In the sixteenth and seventeenth centuries more became known of the Asian countries through trade and conquest. A number of travellers' accounts of various Buddhist countries appeared. Such writings however treat of religion only incidentally. The first accurate knowledge of the Indian cultural background came only with the gradual development of Sanskrit studies. In the early nineteenth century this led to the first studies of Sanskrit Buddhist literature, mostly Mahayana, as preserved especially in Nepal.

The study of Ancient Buddhism had to await the creation of the linguistic tools necessary for the study of the Pali texts. To the traditional scholarship of Ceylon was applied the method of classical philology. English colonial officers and missionaries played some part in this pioneer work. So too did Danish travellers and scholars. Valuable though this was, it went hand in hand with a missionary-based account of Buddhism. Despite making available much important information both on the texts and on contemporary practice, this account was unsatisfactory. It focused attention upon areas where European opinion would consider Buddhism defective and propagated far-reaching negative evaluations which remain influential in certain circles. Buddhism was portrayed as 'pessimistic', 'life-denying' and so on. Yet this was partly based upon selective attention to particular statements out of context and a tendency to disregard the great variety of practice and attitude in Buddhism.

A reaction followed. The Pali Text Society made the Pali Canon fully accessible. The work of its founder, Rhys Davids, and a number of other scholars, mainly from England, Germany and Scandinavia, established a new school of Buddhist studies. It was believed that in the Pali texts an authentic early version of the Buddhist canon was preserved, more reliable than any other and providing accurate and detailed information as to the life and teachings of the Buddha. A rather favourable picture of Ancient Buddhism emerged, strongly influenced by rationalist and Protestant ideas. Miraculous, ritual and devotional elements in the literature were viewed as later innovations. Influences from Ceylon played an important part in the formation of this school, but ultimately it was itself to exercise a strong influence on Buddhist modernism. [16; 17: 15–26, 69ff]

THE STRUCTURE OF THE TEACHING

Many observers have found difficulty in reconciling Buddhist theory with the actual practice of the ordinary villager in the countryside. Much of the apparent discrepancy is due to an unbalanced presentation of Buddhist thought. Elements connected with popular practice tend to be minimized. They may be thought of as less interesting or not significant for the Western reader, or sometimes as later introductions of peripheral importance. Often too there is a bias towards the intellectual as opposed to the emotional. The result is a very misleading picture. This is quite clear if the traditional structure of Buddhist teaching is examined.

A passage which occurs about twenty times in the Pali Canon sets this out explicitly:

> Then the Lord gave a step-by-step discourse ... as follows: discourse on giving, discourse on precepts, discourse on the heaven worlds; he made known the danger, the inferior nature and the tendency to defilement of sense desires and sense objects and the advantage in being without them. When the Lord knew that the heart of the listener was fit, open, free from hindrances, happy and at ease, then he revealed the *dhamma* teaching particular to the Buddhas: suffering, arising, ceasing, path.

Usually the listener gains direct perception of *dhamma* 'just as a clean and dirtless cloth would easily take a dye'.

There are distinct levels to the teaching given here:

1. Step-by-step discourse: (a) first part: giving (*dana*), precepts (*sila*) and the heavens: (b) second part: the defects of sensuality and positive gain in freedom from it.
2. The particular teaching, i.e. the Four Noble Truths: suffering; its arising; its cessation; and the path to its cessation.

The step-by-step discourse does not contain anything specifically Buddhist. It was common ground in ancient Indian religion. The first part is mainly concerned with outward behaviour and way of life. The second is more to do with inner purity of heart. For those interested in spiritual practice it would be highly inspiring and lead to a transformed state of mind. Only in such a state is the hearer ready for the more profound particular teaching, usually known as the Four Noble Truths.

The Four Noble Truths are well known (see page 305 below). Too often they are approached out of context. They are intended for the spiritually advanced hearer who has both ordered his outer life in accordance with the harmony of things and cleansed his heart from fear and the grosser forms of attachment. He is now ready for a life which unifies compassion and experiential knowledge of *dhamma*. To expound the Four Noble Truths as a purely rational philosophy is to miss much of their purpose. The exposition here follows the sections of the traditional teaching, beginning with the first part of the step-by-step discourse.

Step-by-step discourse: first part

Giving. Dana, or giving, is the foundation of Buddhist practice. Charity and hospitality, although valued, are not what is meant here. Buddhist *dana* is a religious act, performed with great care and a sense of purpose. It is usually directed towards a person of religious commitment, especially a member of the Buddhist Sangha. Giving to such an individual is felt as a special and awesome act of great potency. It explicitly replaces the Brahmanical sacrifice with its strong magical and religious quality. Indeed *dana* retains something of this magical element. No doubt the Buddha aimed to retain the religious power of the sacrifice while rejecting its superstitious and life-destroying elements. The power of *dana* as a sacrifice of one's own possessions is attributed not to the intervention of divine beings or divine power, but to the workings of mental law. It is held that *dana* can transform the mind. The inner intention of the giver is reflected in the care, attention and joy with which the giving is performed. The higher the state of mind the more powerful the action (*kamma*). Important too is the state of mind of the recipient, made infectious as it were by the special nature of the act of giving. Either of these is sufficient to make the act effective. The two together are even more powerful.

Dana is usually explained in terms of its future effects, especially those in subsequent lives. Careful questioning soon discovers more immediate rewards also. The giver (*dayaka*) often has an enjoyable or moving experience, made stronger by the slightly formalized or ritual context in which *dana* usually occurs. In Buddhist theory this is a short-lived experiencing of a higher state – a foretaste of later stages of the path. Buddhist texts and sermons are fulsome in praise of *dana* precisely because it leads simply and naturally to the more advanced stages. Above all it reduces possessiveness and selfishness, leading naturally to sensitivity for the needs of others. This makes possible a correctly motivated commitment to control of one's external actions – the next stage.

Precepts. So the step-by-step discourse now turns to *sila*, or 'precept'. In this context what is meant is the act of undertaking precepts or training rules, especially the set of the five precepts. The formal undertaking of these normally follows the act of 'going for refuge' to the 'three jewels' (see page 283 above). The two together amount to declaring acceptance of Buddhist teaching as one's guide and undertaking to put it into practice in one's daily life. In some ways they represent the act of becoming a Buddhist. In Southern Buddhism they are not given on a single occasion in life, but tend to accompany every Buddhist activity, especially at the beginning to set the right atmosphere. The repetition of the formula 'I undertake the training rule of refraining from ...' is a purposive act (kamma), effective in its own right. The intention involved is an action which helps to condition one's future. Its frequent repetition accumulates merit. Mere lip-service would be of limited value, but an impressive ritual context is normal. This is intended to improve the state of mind at the time of undertaking sila. The better the state of mind the better will be the future effect.

The precepts are explained by the principle of 'doing to others as you would be done by'. In Southern Buddhism the emphasis is on avoiding harm either to oneself or to others. This is considered superior to a one-sided concern for either, perhaps because of a sense of the ultimate unity of life. The five precepts represent the fundamental discipline of external behaviour to which the Buddhist aspires. They entail refraining from: (1) destroying life; (2) taking what is not given; (3) wrong behaviour in regard to sense pleasures; (4) untrue speech; (5) causes of intoxication such as wines, beers and spirits. Additional precepts are taken with varying frequency in different areas. So eight precepts are often taken on special days connected with the lunar cycle: full-, new- and quarter-moon days. They involve temporary restriction of adornment, entertainment and physical comfort. They are specifically intended as an opportunity for the ordinary person to partake of the life-style of the Sangha. Again the aim is to create conditions which favour a better state of mind. [18: 87ff]

Kamma. A great part of popular Buddhism is based upon the performance of dana and sila. Each of these is only fully effective when accompanied by the appropriate understanding. The operation of the law of kamma (Sanskrit karma – see page 211) or action must be understood. It is this which determines the future condition of the individual both in this life and in future lives. Every act of will is considered a seed which will one day bear fruit in results of like kind to the original act. Our own actions in the past have created much of our present life and environment. This includes the material and social conditions in which we are born, the physical condition of our body and even much of our mental capacity. In modern terms both environment and genetic inheritance are the result of past actions. They are the wages of our deeds. This week's wages are based upon last week's work. Next week's depend upon what we do now. Comprehension of this law is known as 'knowledge of the ownership of deeds'. Such knowledge reinforces dana and sila;

for awareness of personal responsibility affects the whole calibre of an action.

Such understanding liberates the mind from fatalistic or superstitious views. Past actions, environment, genetics, history – none of these totally determines the individual's fate. He himself creates his own future. When the laws of gravity and motion are understood, it is no longer necessary to explain the movements of the heavenly bodies by means of angels or divine intervention. So, too, for the spiritual life. If the laws of the mind are comprehended, it is not necessary to imagine constant supernatural intervention. Of course in practice the sun 'rises' and 'sets'. There is nothing wrong with this as figurative or conventional language. The case is similar in spiritual matters. We assume that the law of gravity operates throughout the universe. Similarly the law of *kamma* applies to all conscious experience, past, present and future. Human, subhuman or above-human – all are subject to it. Since actions produce states and states produce conditions of being, all are subject to change of state and change of being. Conscious existence necessarily leads to birth and death. [7 vol. 3: 248–62]

The cosmos. The Buddhist conception of the universe is large-scale: worlds are organized into a spatial hierarchy – grouped in 'clusters' which are grouped in 'galaxies' which are grouped in 'super-galaxies' each containing billions of worlds. Each of these comes into being and passes away again and again over a very long period of time. None of this corresponds exactly with modern scientific cosmology, although Buddhist modernists find it quite possible to reconcile the two. For the more traditional, however, such a cosmos is only a part of the whole. The universe also has many levels.

The inferior levels are the four descents (*apaya*): (1) *asuras* or fallen *devas*; (2) *petas*, literally, the dead; (3) animals; (4) *niraya* or hell-dwellers. The last of these inhabit numerous states of torment located on eight major levels. The others are intended to accommodate the vast variety of the spirit world and the animal kingdom, considered as existing at or near the same level as human beings. Superior levels are more numerous. They are best set out in a simplified form (see Table 8.1). Higher in some respects are the Formless Brahmas, who have transcended the limitations of bounded existence.

A detailed correspondence between heaven worlds and states of consciousness is traditional: parallelism of psychology and cosmology is a fundamental feature of Buddhist thought. Indeed most Buddhist statements about the cosmos can be converted into statements about individual spiritual experience. Some Buddhist modernists argue that the traditional cosmology is merely symbolic. Hell realms, for example, are states of guilt and self-torment. This has some support even in ancient literature, but most Buddhists still accept a more literal interpretation based upon the law of *kamma*.

Table 8.1. The twenty-one heavenly realms

Number of heavens	Name and nature	Corresponding states of consciousness	Method of attainment
Five	*Pure abodes:* inhabited by Brahmas of great spiritual attainments	Transcendent states	*Samatha* and *vipassana* meditation
Ten	*Brahmas:* each over-lord of a universe	*Jhana*	*Samatha* meditation
Six	*Devas:* enjoyment of paradisaical pleasures	Skilful states	*Dana* and *sila*

The heavens. The first stage of the step-by-step discourse culminates in description of the realms of the *devas* who enjoy heavenly pleasures. For the more subtle and refined are the acts of *dana* and *sila*, the more subtle will be the resultant level of consciousness and the ensuing state of rebirth. The lower heavens may be depicted quite concretely – filled with palaces and gardens, places of beauty and wonder with marvellous wishing-trees to fulfil every desire. Many ordinary Buddhists are quite happy to aim at such a goal. It is often wrongly supposed that this is somehow improper. It should rather be seen as the necessary basis for the commencement of the spiritual path proper. The renunciation and quest of the Buddha-to-be began from the luxuries of the royal palace. So too the good life with full experience of wholesome pleasures is the ideal starting-place for dissatisfaction with them. [19]

Step-by-step discourse: second part. This part comprises the world of sense and the higher heavens.

The world of sense. The step-by-step discourse now turns to sensory experience (cf. page 300 above). The aim is to show how the attractions of colour, sound, smell, taste and touch take possession of the mind and distort it. So too in dream and imagination. On the most concrete level the search for wealth and possessions leads either to envy (if unsuccessful) or to possessiveness and fear of loss (if successful). This search is the ultimate cause of much violence, dishonesty and theft. Too easily it undermines generosity and *sila*. This is the danger in sensory experience. Compared with the higher achievements to come, the sensual is inferior even as a source of pleasure and happiness. The mind preoccupied with it loses contact with its own central nature.

Freedom from too much concern with sensory experience brings real advantage. The functioning of the mind is no longer obstructed by partialities and graspings which interfere with spontaneity of action. Free from cares and concerns it returns to a simpler and cleaner kind of functioning. The natural result is greater openness towards other living creatures and a more universal type of conduct. This is summed up as the four Brahma abidings: loving-kindness to all beings; compassion for their sorrow; joy in their joy; and balanced observation of their faults and virtues.

The higher heavens. Such states open the way to the Brahma heavens. These are reached by some form of calm meditation (*bhavana*). Their inhabitants dwell in power, radiance and beauty. The senses play a much smaller role there, but the inhabitants are still subject to the law of action. They may eventually fall to some lower level. The danger of their state is that it may be too satisfying. Yet it has one advantage. The mind has the kind of sensitivity, receptivity and stability necessary for the full comprehension of the profoundest teaching. [19]

The particular teaching. The particular teaching comprises the Four Noble Truths and Buddhist meditation.

The Four Noble Truths. The four truths are often referred to as the *ariya* or noble truths, because they bring one to true nobility – attained not by birth but by inner purification. They are traditionally explained by the simile of the physician. A doctor recognizes illness, diagnoses its cause, removes the cause and prescribes treatment to bring about health. The four truths apply the same method to the general human condition. But the matter is not quite as simple as that. In a famous passage the Buddha reproves his attendant Ananda for suggesting that the Four Noble Truths are clear and easy to understand. Knowledge of the idea is not enough. Only a full and existential comprehension can bring about the hoped-for transformation. Hence the need for the right prior state. The four truths are not so much *descriptive* as *prescriptive* truth. The important thing is not that the universe is this way. Rather when the mind is suitably at peace, one should see things in this way in order permanently to change the mind for the better. [20; 21]

1. The first truth is usually given as *dukkha*, or suffering, but other terms are sometimes substituted. For example, the first truth can be given as 'the world', the second as 'the arising of the world' and so on. In fact the first truth is meant to include most of ordinary human life. So the word 'suffering' must be interpreted with care. Even the most pleasurable experiences are *dukkha*. When life is described as suffering, it does not mean that pleasurable experiences are not pleasurable. It is simply that they remain subject to change

and loss. By comparison with spiritual pleasures they are not satisfying. Indeed the human condition is unsatisfactory so long as it lacks the lasting harmony and balance of the mind which contacts the transcendent.

Suffering is taught to arouse *samvega*. This is a kind of inner stirring and stimulation which motivates the individual to spiritual effort and, if prevented by cheerfulness from turning to depression, leads to mental awakening. So the first truth is usually explained by the great shocks of life: birth, sickness, old age and death. In normal life it is these which arouse *samvega*, but it can be the result of a vision of the unending process of birth and death or of the transitoriness of things.

2. The second truth is the arising of suffering. The cause of suffering is *tanha* ('thirst'), explained as craving for sense pleasure, for being and for non-being. *Dukkha* arises because we desire to have or control things, to experience in one way rather than another. We are dissatisfied with the way things are because we seek something different. This is a rather simplified explanation, albeit far-reaching. The full account of the second truth is given by the formula known as *paticca-samuppada*, 'conditioned origination'.

The history and interpretation of conditioned origination is a matter of much debate, but as far as later Buddhism is concerned, the basic principles are quite clear. Our present life and circumstances are largely due to past acts (*kamma*). These acts arose from ignorance (*avijja*) of *dhamma*. They must then be distorted in some way and create distorted results. Even now we continue to try to force experience into a false mould, by our craving. So our likes and dislikes generate attachment and rejection, forming a more or less fixed pattern made rigid by habitual desires and prejudices. These form the prison of our future. Yet understanding the nature of the process makes possible an escape from that prison.

3. The escape is *nibbana* (Sanskrit: *nirvana*), for the Buddhist the supreme bliss and the final liberation. This is the ceasing of suffering: the third truth. Craving and ignorance are ended. Just as when the cause of disease is removed, the state of health returns, so when the cause of suffering is removed *nibbana* ensues. The individual who reaches this final goal experiences great joy and happiness. All doubts and burdens are gone. His mind is free from prejudice and complication. He has a firm knowledge of freedom and liberation.

Many Western observers have seen something negative in *nibbana* as a goal. This seems perverse to the Buddhist, for whom *nibbana* is above all supreme happiness. The main schools of Indian Buddhism agree that *nibbana* is not a mere negation. Rather it is the unconditioned *dhamma*, not expressible in spatial or temporal terms; knowledge of it dissolves ignorance and ends craving. The question of the subsequent fate of the individual who achieves the goal is often raised. This is an unanswered question. Such matters as the temporal and spatial extent of the universe and the precise relationship between living being and body are placed in the same category. The reason given for the Buddha's silence is practical: such matters are time-wasting and distracting; they do not conduce to the aim.

It might seem that this could not apply to the spiritual goal itself, but in fact it is even more important here. Buddhism is a middle way between eternalism (belief in personal immortality) and annihilationism (belief that death is the final end). If eternalism is a rigid view (*ditthi*), motivated by craving and obstructing the path to liberation, it is counter-productive to describe the goal as if it were some permanent state of being. If annihilationism is another such view brought about by a different form of craving, then the opposite description is equally unhelpful. Buddhist teaching is primarily prescriptive. There is no point in including in the prescription anything which will diminish the chances of health.

4. The fourth truth is the truth of the path leading to the ceasing of suffering: the eightfold *ariya* path (see Table 8.2). It is easy to see that the fourth truth includes a much wider range of Buddhist teachings about the spiritual path than just the eight factors. All these teachings should be seen as forming an intricate and harmonious whole which naturally tends and inclines towards the goal – 'just as whatever great rivers there be, all tend and incline towards the ocean'.

The way can be divided into an ordinary (*lokiya*) and a transcendent (*lokuttara*) path. The Buddhist path is not so much a series of stages or steps as a particular grouping of states of mind with the property of flowing naturally towards the goal. In the ordinary path they have not yet reached a full and harmonious balance. When they do, the mind transcends ordinary understanding and acquires direct knowledge of the unconditioned truth. It is this knowledge which brings permanent change and leads to freedom of heart and understanding.

Buddhist meditation. Each of the four truths requires some activity. The first truth is to be *fully comprehended*. The second is to be *abandoned*. The third is to be *made visible*, while the fourth is to be *brought into being*. The four are symbolized (in three aspects) by a twelve-spoked wheel: the wheel of *dhamma*. No doubt this is intended to emphasize the interrelatedness of the truths. The activity of the fourth truth is then *bhavana*, 'bringing into being', often rendered as 'meditation'. What is meant is the bringing into being of the path and the training necessary for this. Two types of *bhavana* exist, based upon calm and insight respectively.

The normative method is to take calm or *samatha* as one's vehicle (*yana*) and seek first to develop the higher states of consciousness which lead to the Brahma realms (page 304). The *samatha* meditator tries to purify his

Table 8.2. The fourth truth: the way

	Faculties	Factors of the path	Factors of awakening	
3. Wisdom	5. Wisdom	1. Perfect view 2. Perfect thought	2. Investigation of dhamma	Insight (vipassana)
1. Sila	1. Faith	3. Perfect speech 4. Perfect action 5. Perfect livelihood		
2. Concentration	2. Strength 3. Mindfulness 4. Concentration	6. Perfect effort 7. Perfect mindfulness 8. Perfect concentration	3. Strength 4. Joy 5. Tranquillity 6. Concentration 7. Equipoise 1. Mindfulness	Calm (samatha)

mind from distractions and hindrances in order to reach mental absorption of a very subtle kind in one of the four meditations or *jhanas*. This could then be developed to the fourth *jhana* which is the basis for even subtler states or for various psychic abilities. Eventually he must turn to the development of insight in order to achieve the balance necessary for the transcendent path.

The alternative is to take insight or *vipassana* as one's vehicle. This was at one time unusual, but recent years have seen a strong revival of insight meditation, especially in Burma. This needs a special type of self-observation which remains slightly detached in order to avoid interfering with the natural flow of mental and physical phenomena. With clarity and alertness, greater awareness of mental and physical events and processes will arise. This leads to experiential knowledge of the four truths. Ultimately a poised and equable state of great understanding will be constantly present. Now the mind will naturally tend towards stillness and great inner peace, bringing about the necessary balance of *samatha* and *vipassana*.

Such a balance completes the ordinary path and the transcendent path will arise when conditions are appropriate. At the moment of its arising there is contact with the truth which is not a product of causes or conditions: the *ariya dhamma*. The meditator attains the stage known as 'stream-entry'. He is freed from doubt and superstitious religious practice, as well as from identification with the body. He has joined the family of the Buddha and won through to the *ariya* lineage. He cannot be reborn in the four descents nor break his observance of the precepts. A permanent change has occurred and henceforth he will always tend towards the final goal. The stream-enterer may train his mind to experience at will the transcendent attainment and can seek to unite it with his every action. He is now an *ariya*, noble by purification and within seven lives will attain the final and highest state of the *arahat*. In Southern Buddhism the *arahat* is a rare and lofty ideal man, who has attained the goal of ending every kind of mental defilement. He has done all that is to be done. He is the full embodiment of the *ariya* path – his actions accord fully with the needs of the situation. [21: 61–87; 22; 23]

BUDDHISM IN ORDINARY LIFE

Merit-making. Traditional Buddhism plays an important part in village life. Custom is important, but in principle it is a question of making merit by giving, taking precepts (*sila*) and sometimes a little meditation. Giving here includes transferring merit in order to benefit others and above all 'rejoicing' (*anumodana*). Taking pleasure in the good deeds of others is a mental act, productive of beneficial future results. So giving, undertaking precepts and so on potentially benefit the onlooker almost as much as the doer. In other words these are inherently participatory activities by way of joyful approval.

A wider sense can be given to the notion of keeping the precepts by including conscious acts of service to others and the act of deliberately honouring or paying respect to others. Similarly meditation practice can also include teaching *dhamma* and hearing *dhamma*. Hence listening to the chanting of Pali texts is a meritorious activity. This is partly independent of comprehension. Provided the listening produces a positive response or recalls previous meritorious acts it will still be effective. Of course understanding is even better. [12: 92ff; 13]

Paritta. Such chanting is especially common in the form of 'protection' (*paritta*) discourses. The practice is mentioned only rarely in the Pali Canon and always in contexts of healing and protection. There is a recognized manual of such discourses, selected from the more awe-inspiring and potent contexts. At some point (we do not know when) many new Pali verses and formulae were added in order to create a complex set of recognized forms for ritual purposes. Indeed its strong ritual component has been a major factor in the growth and success of Southern Buddhism.

Together with other merit-making activities the chanting of Pali discourses accompanies ceremonial occasions of many kinds, including some of the major events of the individual life-cycle. There are also many traditional ceremonies in which specifically Buddhist ritual plays little part. Chanting *paritta* comes into its own, however, with events which are in some way dangerous or potentially so: death, illness, possession, danger, embarking upon some new activity or entering a new house. It may take place on quite a small scale, but often there is an impressive and colourful ceremonial context, involving a great deal of careful preparation, all of which is, of course, also meritorious activity. [24: 109ff; 13: 201ff]

Worship. Worship is often supposed to be unimportant in Southern Buddhism. This is not true for the step-by-step discourse though it may be for the particular teaching. Focusing on the latter allows Buddhist modernists to minimize ritual and worship. But in fact there have probably always been elements of this kind in Buddhist teaching. The usual result is in practice a relaxed attitude to traditional devotion. Nevertheless it is probably more usual to view worship as a necessary preliminary.

Southern Buddhism recognizes three kinds of object of worship: corporeal relics of a Buddha or *arahat*; relics of use (i.e. those made use of in some way by such an individual); and symbolic relics which remind one of the Buddha or *dhamma*. The cult of relics has canonical sanction and certainly considerably pre-dates the reign of Asoka. Offerings to a relic and any act honouring or paying respect to a relic are forms of giving and of *sila* respectively.

Relic shrines may be very large buildings, often of historical significance, or smaller buildings – and they may even be portable. These are most frequently referred to by the Sanskrit term, *stupa* (Pali *thupa*), but other names are current in different localities. The best known are probably the Sinhalese *dagaba* and its derivative, 'pagoda'. Pagodas themselves often acquire great sanctity and become cult centres. Important also, especially in Ceylon, is the bodhi tree (a relic of use) usually planted in the monastic precincts. In principle this should be a descendant either of one of the trees planted by Mahinda, especially the one at Anuradhapura, or of the original tree at Bodh-gaya. The Buddha image is also very important, especially if it contains relics. Such images may be enshrined in large halls, for worship, in the environs of pagodas or in small shrines at home or work-place. Archaeology shows that the Buddha image is a later introduction to Buddhism, but Buddhist tradition hardly recalls its earlier aniconic phase (see page 291). It is meritorious to worship any relic. Offering of appropriate substances (incense, oil lamps, candles, even water, food or clothing are all common); paying respect by act or gesture, especially prostration; service by cleaning, adorning or embellishing; chanting appropriate verses – all these things give merit and so simultaneously give hope of advantageous future results and lead towards readiness for the path. [13; 24: 79ff]

Festivals. Southern Buddhism has its own traditional lunar calendar, varying only slightly from country to country. The full-moon days mostly have some special association in the life of the Buddha or in the history of Buddhism (see Table 8.3). Together with three other special days in the lunar month they are known in Pali as *uposatha* days and are important in the life of the Buddhist monastery. Lay people may visit the monastery. Special clothes, usually white, may be worn, particularly in Ceylon, and additional precepts may be undertaken (see page 301 above). Although considered highly meritorious such observances are not in any way compulsory. Most village Buddhists probably do attend at least a few times a year, especially on the more important full-moon days.

Annual festivals vary considerably, both locally and nationally. Festivals connected with the agricultural year (ploughing, sowing), with particular deities or spirits and with particular localities are widespread. The Buddhist element in these varies greatly. All of the Southern Buddhist countries have a New Year festival in the spring, fixed by a solar calendar. In Ceylon the two most important full-moon days are those of Vesak and Poson. The latter

Table 8.3. Annual festivals of Southern Buddhism*

Season	Pali name of month	Significance of full-moon day	Other festivals in this month
Summer	1. Citta		Solar New Year festivals
	2. Vesakha	Birth, enlightenment and final enlightenment of the Buddha	Rocket festival (Laos)
	3. Jettha	Arrival of Mahinda in Ceylon	
	4. Asalha	Conception, renunciation, first sermon and ascent to second heaven of the Buddha	Local festivals (Ceylon)
	An intercalary month sometimes added to reconcile the lunar and solar calendars		
Rains {Period of partial retreat}	5. Savana†		
	6. Potthapada†		
	7. Assayuja†	Descent from second heaven after preaching *abhidhamma*	Ancestor festival (Thailand) Sowing festival (Ceylon)
	8. Kattika†	Sending forth of the first Buddhist missionaries	Robe-offering ceremonies (*Kathina*)
Winter	9. Maggasira	Establishment of the community of nuns	
	10. Phussa		Harvest festival
	11. Magha	Assembly of disciples and Buddha's renunciation of his life-span	
	12. Phagguna	Origin of world in each world cycle	Festival of sand pagodas (Burma) Vessantara festival (Thailand)

* Each month ends on the full-moon day. The length is alternately thirty and twenty-nine days. The year begins near the spring equinox.
† Three of the four months of the rains season are kept as a period of partial retreat and intensified activity by the Sangha.

commemorates the arrival of Mahinda in Ceylon. Of more general importance is Vesak, which is associated with the birth, enlightenment and death of the Buddha. More important in South-East Asia are three full moons connected with the *vassa* (rains) when Buddhist monks remain domiciled in the same monastery for three months. Asalha begins the *vassa* and commemorates the first sermon of the Buddha. Assayuja commemorates the Buddha's return from preaching the *abhidhamma* to his mother in the second heaven and is the usual end of the *vassa*. Kattika recalls the sending forth of the first Buddhist missionaries and the permissible end of a late *vassa*. Both are festivals of lights. The ending of the *vassa* is associated with elaborate presentations of robes to the Sangha.

Most Buddhist festivals may be taken in more serious or less serious ways. There is usually much festivity and merry-making, an air of enjoyment and gaiety. There may be a great deal of colourful and careful decoration. Different festivals may involve the use of lights or fireworks, dramatic representations, entertainments, fairs, processions, making models or water sports. A few more committed individuals will use the occasion as an opportunity for more serious religious practice. Typically it is very much a matter of individual preference. [12: 209ff; 24: 199ff]

Pilgrimage. The ancient tradition of pilgrimage to the Buddhist centres in India associated with the life of the Buddha fell largely into abeyance after the Muslim conquest of North India. It has revived considerably in the last century. More local pilgrimages are very widespread. In particular the many sites on the island of Ceylon connected with Buddhist history and monuments have long been centres of pilgrimage. Some have their own season and special activities. They are seen as enjoyable as well as virtuous activities. [13: 108ff; 25: 35ff]

Buddhism and the spirit world. Buddhism has had little difficulty in accommodating a large number of local beliefs concerning various gods, spirits and the like. Naturally the powers of such entities are circumscribed by the law of *kamma* and other laws. The Buddhist perceives the universe as vast enough to encompass many such entities. Numerous different cults coexist with Buddhism – some barely tolerated, some irrelevant and ignored, some incorporated to a greater or lesser degree into the larger scene. Such cultic activities may play a considerable part in the life of the villager.

There has been much discussion among scholars as to the precise relationship between Buddhism and such cults. Some see a supernatural hierarchy with the Buddha at the summit. Others contrast the 'great tradition' with the 'little tradition'. The profane or secular level of spirit cults can be set against the superior sacred level of the Buddhist teaching. Many early European observers, followed by some Buddhist modernists, saw the existence of such cults as due to a corruption of the original 'pure' Buddhism. [11] In actual fact Buddhism is not concerned with such matters. They are not rejected. They are simply a different sphere of human activity. Provided there is no direct opposition to Buddhist teaching they can be left to regulate themselves.

There is no inconsistency between believing in the law of *kamma* and at the same time making offerings to a deity to obtain some desired result. This is no different to asking aid of a king or doctor. Such aid is itself part of a complex set of relations and subject to various causes and conditions. The help given by a deity is a matter of fact or falsehood. So the striking contrast between the role of spirit cults in Buddhist villages and the tendency of Buddhist modernists to minimize or deny such elements is only superficially a problem. Contact with Western scientism often leads to the supposition that such spirits or deities do not exist. In that case they are not a fact and can be discarded. Buddhism is committed to the notion that various entities and levels of being exist, but not to most particular names. In practice Buddhist traditionalists tend to be committed to at least a part of the local spirit cult. [26; 27]

MODERN DEVELOPMENTS

The nineteenth and twentieth centuries have been a period of great economic, social and political change in the Southern Buddhist countries. Buddhist thought and institutions have responded to an influx of ideas and practices from elsewhere. The linguistic and cultural diversity of these countries makes the identification of general tendencies unusually difficult. Three important trends are best characterized as reformism, 'ultimatism' and modernism.

Reformism. A notable feature of the recent history of the Buddhist Sangha is the growth of reformist fraternities (*nikayas*): the Shwegyin, Dvara and Veluvan *nikayas* in Burma; the Thammayut *nikaya* in Thailand and Cambodia; the Ramanna *nikaya* in Ceylon. The aim is closer conformity to the ideals of the Sangha. This is not new. In Ceylon both the largest fraternity, the conservative Siam *nikaya*, and the second largest, the Amarapura *nikaya*, trace their origins to earlier reformist movements. In time such movements become less homogeneous and overall discipline may decline.

The great majority of monks in Burma have remained in the much larger and more diverse Sudhamma *nikaya*. The same is true for the Maha *nikaya* in Thailand, Cambodia and Laos. These two fraternities and to some extent the Siam *nikaya* in fact represent the mass of the Sangha, grouping monasteries and traditions of diverse origins and long-standing local roots. Their membership includes monks and groups of monks very similar in practices and views to those of the reformist fraternities as well as many who would be considered lax and even corrupt by the committed reformist.

In Ceylon and Burma the ending of the monarchy and its replacement by foreign non-Buddhist rulers tended to undermine the discipline of the Sangha. This did not occur in Thailand and Indo-China. Accusations of laxity are often based upon a rather exacting spiritual ideal, seeking to restore an idealized situation of poverty and simplicity of life-style. [28: 66ff; 29]

'Ultimatism'. It seems useful to adopt the term 'ultimatism' to identify the tendency to take what is true from the viewpoint of ultimate truth or at an advanced level of spiritual practice as if it were the whole of Buddhism. In effect 'ultimatism' discards, ignores or even rejects the step-by-step discourse in favour of the particular teaching (page 300). This is a perennial possibility, frequent also in the history of Mahayana Buddhism. In Southern Buddhism today it takes the form of a rejection of much traditional practice and ceremonial as well as many of the outward forms customarily associated with merit-making activities. It is often supported by reference to early Buddhism. In more extreme forms it may be associated with symbolic interpretation of rebirth and of supernatural elements in Buddhist tradition. The emphasis tends to be directed towards insight meditation and a more rigorous interpretation of the Four Noble Truths. [30]

Buddhist modernism. During the modern period a certain amount of institutional change has taken place. Particularly striking is the development of lay Buddhist organizations based upon European models. Some customs and values based upon Christian practices have been introduced. Non-Christian strands of thought (notably scientific rationalism, but also theosophy) exercised a marked influence. A tendency arose to see Buddhism as essentially scientific and not really a religion at all. If religion is defined in theistic terms as was usual in the nineteenth century, then this is quite clearly the case. Perhaps, however, it is better to widen the definition of religion. At all events the result was a movement, often associated with ultimatist ideas, to reject ritual and superstition as later accretions to the pure original teaching. [29: 191ff]

Present-day situation. Among the general population in the Southern Buddhist countries a rather traditional form of Buddhism is still the norm, but diluted influences stemming from reformist, ultimatist and modernist trends are widespread. In those groups that have been exposed to Western education and a middle-class life-style some form of Buddhist modernism is common, often combined with ultimatist notions and support for reformist groups within the Sangha. These tendencies do not usually become sectarian, perhaps because of a general dislike of extremism and a theoretical adherence to the 'middle way'.

Meditation revival. It is often suggested that the twentieth century has seen a considerable revival in the practice of Buddhist meditation. The situation is a little more complex. It is necessary to distinguish between the situation in the Sangha and among lay people as well as to examine the differences between countries and meditation schools. A large number of practices and methods are current among the Sangha and, at least in South-East Asia, this has probably always been the case. In Burma the modern period has seen widespread growth in the practice of *vipassana* meditation. More traditional schools, usually laying more emphasis on *samatha* meditation, remain strong in Thailand and Indo-China. In the Thammayut *nikaya* this is often combined with reformism and some degree of modernism.

There has been a considerable increase in numbers of centres for the practice of lay meditation in recent years. In Ceylon this is, perhaps, an innovation, but in South-East Asia, where almost all youths traditionally spend a period of weeks or months as members of the Sangha, lay meditation practice has probably always been present. Such centres have also been established in a number of other Asian and Western countries. [22: 116ff; 31: 303–13]

Eastern Buddhism

INTRODUCTION

The Buddhism of China, Vietnam, Korea and Japan was influenced by the cultural background, the existing religious beliefs and practices and the historical development of the area. Understanding of it has been influenced by the presuppositions of study in the area generally. These matters are discussed in the sections of this volume concerned with Chinese and Japanese religions (Chapters 9 and 10).

Sources. The Chinese Buddhist canon is very large. The first printed edition, made between 971 and 983 CE, used more than 130,000 wood-blocks. Many other editions have since been made in China, Korea and Japan. The nineteenth-century Japanese scholar Nanjio compiled a catalogue based upon the arrangement which had been usual in recent times, listing some 1,662 items (see Table 8.4). A more historical arrangement is used in the modern standard edition, published in Japan 1924–34. The vast majority of works included are

Table 8.4. Number of items in Nanjio's catalogue

1. *Discourses (sutra)*	
(a) Mahayana	541
(b) Hinayana	240
(c) Later additions	300
2. *Vinaya*	
(a) Mahayana	25
(b) Hinayana	60
3. *Abhidharma*	
(a) Mahayana	94
(b) Hinayana	37
(c) Later additions	23
4. *Miscellaneous*	
(a) Indian works	147
(b) Chinese (and Korean) works	195
Total	1,662

translations from Sanskrit, Middle Indian and possibly from Central Asian languages. The modern edition contains about 1,700 such translations. [17: 77–101]

The first three sections in the table are the three main divisions of the Ancient Buddhist canon. Works drawn from various recensions of this are the main content of the Hinayana sections. North Indian Buddhism distinguished between *sutra* – works attributed to an enlightened being – and *shastra* – a later work of exposition. Many *shastra* works were included in the first part of the third section. The beginning of the fourth section is very diverse but includes a number of Mantrayana works (see page 333 below), while the second part contains a number of works belonging to Chinese schools. [33]

Unlike South Asia, East Asia has a well-developed tradition of historical studies. Moreover, Eastern Buddhism itself has a considerable historical literature. [17: 101ff]

History. The history of Eastern Buddhism may be considered under the following headings: early history; developments in India; the second turning of the wheel of *dharma*; the third turning; consolidation in China; and later times.

Early history. Although South China was probably influenced by forms of Buddhism coming from Indo-China, Buddhism initially entered the Chinese heartland mainly from Central Asia and eastern Iran. This occurred during the Han dynasty (206 BCE to 220 CE) not later than the first century CE. Some form of Ancient Buddhism, probably still mainly an oral tradition, was introduced. A clear distinction between the nascent Mahayana and the earlier schools had probably not yet developed. Central Asian influence predominated until the end of the period of the three kingdoms (220–65 CE). The two main approaches were the Meditation school of the Iranian An Shih-kao (fl. 148–68), which was less interested in the Mahayana, and the more specifically Mahayanist Wisdom school of the Kushan Lokakshema (fl. 168–88) concerned with the early Mahayana *sutras*. Both of these trends continued for many centuries. At first Buddhism was mainly popular among immigrant communities and with ordinary people outside the governing class.

Early Chinese Buddhism tended to employ native Chinese terms, especially Taoist ones. Indeed the Chinese probably saw Buddhism as a strange foreign kind of Taoism. The development of new trends in Chinese thought, especially the 'Dark Learning' based upon the *Book of Changes* (*I Ching*), provided the opportunity for Buddhism to penetrate the ruling circles. By the end of the third century a Chinese 'gentry Buddhism' oriented towards the Mahayana had developed. At the same time contact had grown up with Buddhist centres in Kashmir, closer to the Indian mainstream. In the fourth century Buddhism achieved full official recognition both in China and Korea. [34; 35: 182ff]

Developments in India. The date, geographical location and sectarian affiliations of the early Mahayana have each been the subject of considerable discussion. Much depends on how the term 'Mahayana' is defined; for the trends from which Mahayana emerged may well be considerably older than the distinctive Mahayana. Probably its origin cannot be much before the first century BCE or later than the first century CE. As to its geographical source, plausible arguments have been advanced for East India, for South India or for the North-West. Similarly it can be related to three of the four major groups in the Sangha. The most likely explanation for so much evidence pointing in different directions is that the early Mahayana very quickly became a pan-Indian and non-sectarian movement.

New *sutras* proliferated. It was not claimed that these had been known previously, although most were expounded as the 'word of the Buddha'. They had been preserved in some realm other than the human because they dealt with matters of great profundity which earlier generations had not been able to comprehend or even remember. Only now had teachers of sufficient calibre arisen – men able to journey to such realms and understand the teachings found there. In other words the early Mahayana works were written down by spiritual teachers as a result of some kind of meditational or spiritual attainment – a type of 'inspired literature'. [1: 352ff]

The second turning of the wheel of dharma. Two distinct phases of the Mahayana can be identified. Later Indian Buddhism distinguishes these as the second and third 'turnings of the wheel of *dharma*'. (The first turning was the first sermon of the Buddha and the whole canon of Ancient Buddhism.) The most noticeable feature of the second 'turning' is its emphasis upon 'emptiness' (Sanskrit: *shunyata*). In the third 'turning' there is a more positive assertion of ultimate truth, reacting against the apparent nihilism of emptiness teachings when inadequately understood. Stress is placed upon such notions as *tathata* ('thusness'), *dharmata* ('*dharma*-ness') and *buddhata* ('Buddha-ness'). More importance is given to the role of mind. By and large the Mahayana *sutras* represent a creative outflow and not a rigid systematization. Consistency is not a strong feature. Inevitably more philosophically sophisticated expositions arose in the form of *shastra* literature.

The *sutras* of the second 'turning' provided the inspiration for the first great *shastra* system – the Shunyatavada ('emptiness teaching'), also known as the Madhyamika ('of the Middle'). Its chief exponent was Nagarjuna (second or third century CE), but there were many later authorities. The Shunyatavada used the systematic method of the *abhidharma* (page 289) to support the teachings of the Mahayana. The aim was to prove that all positions and supposed realities are purely arbitrary. If the earlier teaching is that the apparent world is a fragile house of cards, the Shunyatavada went further and suggested that there were not even any cards. Reality is like a shifting palace made out of soap bubbles! The aim is to create an attitude of flexible spontaneity – a more natural and flowing response to life. [1: 373–92; 36: 381–2; 37: 238–49]

The third turning. It is the last phase of the *sutra* literature which is connected with the formation of the second great *shastra* system – the doctrine of Vijnaptimatra ('information only'). This emphasized meditation practice and so acquired its second name: Yogacara ('practice of yoga'). The school was probably founded by Asanga and his younger brother Vasubandhu (*c.* fourth century). Some scholars believe that the true originator of the Yogacara was Maitreyanatha the teacher of Asanga, but it is more likely that this is a reference to the *bodhisattva* Maitreya as the inspirer of Asanga.

The Yogacara may be seen as uniting the teachings of the Mahayana with those of the earlier *abhidharma* schools. The result was a kind of Mahayanist *abhidharma*, giving an elaborate map of the Buddhist path and offering quite detailed descriptions of the stages of meditational experience. [38: 233ff] The diverse teachings of the Mahayana *sutras* were brought within a single all-embracing system. More extreme interpretations of the notion of emptiness were rejected. In this respect Asanga certainly considered that he was remaining faithful to Nagarjuna's intention of adopting a middle position. Not all later Madhyamikas agreed, but many still made use of Asanga's teachings. The most characteristic teaching was the idea of 'information only'. In a dream we have many apparent experiences, but on waking we realize that they are only valid as experiences. We truly received them as information but they do not correspond to any external reality. The Vijnaptimatra school extends this to waking life; only the information itself is 'real'. This is often described as idealism, although strictly speaking even mental events are purely 'information'. However, the school does speak of mind as more real than matter. [1: 392–447; 36: 382–3; 37: 250–60]

Both of the great *shastra* systems have had many exponents in Eastern and Northern Buddhism down to modern times. Each has influenced the later forms of the other. They are the two great orientations of the Mahayana. Indeed they continue the two great traditions of Ancient Buddhist meditational practice. The Shunyatavada represents the insight or wisdom-oriented approach, while the Yogacara returns rather to the calm or concentration-oriented approach (page 307).

Consolidation in China. Influences from Kashmir increased markedly in China during the fourth and fifth centuries. More systematic attempts to introduce Indian Buddhist ideas and literature began to take place. The pilgrimage of Fa-hsien to India (399–413 CE) increased contact still further, while the arrival of Kumarajiva (401 CE) led to the large-scale introduction of Shunyatavada literature. [17: 77–101] By the sixth century relations with India had grown greatly. For some centuries monks from all over India came to China and Chinese pilgrims visited Indian Buddhist centres, especially the large-scale monastic universities in the ancient heartland. The arrival of Paramartha (546 CE) signalled the introduction of many Yogacara works. Still more were brought back from India by the Chinese pilgrim Hsuan-tsang who returned in 645 CE.

A massive quantity of Buddhist texts and practices of varying provenance were brought to China. Not surprisingly the Chinese found this confusing. So they began to develop schools of thought which sought to make overall sense of the many different traditions. Indeed, similar processes were at work in India too. The result was the emergence of the two great theoretical traditions of Eastern Buddhism: the T'ien-t'ai and the Hua-yen (see below).

During the T'ang dynasty (618–907 CE) Buddhism reached a very high level of influence not only in China and Korea, but also in Japan where it had been introduced in the sixth century. The period saw the introduction to China of the last phase of Indian Buddhism: the Mantrayana (see page 333). Most important of all, the dynasty saw the formation of two new movements which gradually came to dominate the Chinese Buddhist scene: the Pure Land school emphasizing devotion to the Buddha Amitabha, and the Meditation school, laying stress on an individual breakthrough to illumination. [39]

Later times. Towards the end of the T'ang period in 845 CE Buddhism experienced a severe persecution from which many of the smaller and older groups never recovered. During the following centuries native Chinese religious traditions gradually regained much of the ground previously lost, partly because they had successfully incorporated elements learnt from Buddhism and renewed their own vitality. Under some emperors Buddhism continued to receive great favour. Increasingly it was disapproved of as a foreign and non-Chinese cult. Attempts to harmonize the different schools seem to have increased in the medieval period. Indeed, some efforts were made to provide a basis for unity between Buddhism, Confucianism and Taoism. Eventually many Chinese came to believe in the harmony of the three religions and even more tended to practise it. Although a slow decline in influence did take place, Chinese Buddhism retained considerable strength into the twentieth century. The period of maximum influence came rather later in Korea and Japan, but there too a reaction in favour of Confucian and Shinto notions ultimately occurred.

Academic study of the Mahayana. Early interest in the Mahayana, stimulated by the discovery of Sanskrit texts from Nepal and the work of Eugène Burnouf and other scholars, had rather weakened by the end of the nineteenth century. This was due to the natural enthusiasm at the discovery of the Pali literature (see page 299 above). A number of scholars active during the first half of the twentieth century sought to re-emphasize the value of works available in Chinese and Tibetan translation. Many of these represent North Indian traditions just as ancient as that from Ceylon. One group of scholars working in Russia is especially associated with the name of T. Shcherbatsky. Influenced by contact with the living tradition of Northern Buddhism, they sought to comprehend Buddhist thought in terms of European philosophical development.

A second group, composed mainly of Belgian and French scholars, was more interested in the Mahayana as a religion and in the history of Buddhism. The most influential writer of this group was probably Louis de La Vallée Poussin. Eastern Buddhist traditions and studies of Hinduism were more influential. The period since the Second World War has seen a strong continuance of this Franco-Belgian school, most notably with the work of E. Lamotte. Moreover the researches in Tibet of the Italian scholar, G. Tucci, have given a new impetus to studies of Northern Buddhism. Important contributions have been made by scholars from India, especially in the study of Buddhist philosophy and history, and by Japanese scholarship, notably in the field of Eastern Buddhism.

At the same time new discoveries from the sands of Central Asia, the caves of Tun-huang, Gilgit in Kashmir and from the libraries of Nepal and Tibet have recovered lost Buddhist literature and opened up new fields for research. Text-critical and historical critical studies using these new materials have developed, especially in Germany. The recent expansion of Buddhist studies in North America seems likely to develop new approaches. [17: 15ff; 39: 1–32]

THE SCHOOLS OF EASTERN BUDDHISM

Eastern Buddhism is much more diverse than the Northern and Southern traditions. It contains a number of distinct schools which have tended on occasion to form separate sects (see Table 8.5). Originally there were rather more such schools, including a number stemming directly from Ancient Buddhism. Indeed the schools listed in group A are really just two of these, one specializing in *vinaya*, the other in *abhidharma*. Only the former continues as a living tradition in some temples – few in number but influential. The second is now merely an object of study. The two schools of the Indian Mahayana are widely influential, although only the Yogacara survives, as a distinct but minor organized sect. [36: 381–6; 40: 14ff; 41: 148ff]

T'ien-t'ai. The T'ien-t'ai school is named after the mountain on which Chih-i, its most famous teacher, established himself. Chih-i (538–97 CE) may be accounted the founder of the school even if he derived much of his teaching from various predecessors. Indeed T'ien-t'ai gathered into itself a number of earlier lines of teaching based upon the *Lotus sutra* and the Mahayana *Nirvana sutra*. Although the school is usually considered as primarily intellectual, it is important to note that it emphasized very traditional forms of meditation practice. Important works concerned with calm and insight meditation derive directly from the teachings of Chih-i himself.

The most characteristic feature of T'ien-t'ai is the elaborate classification of the Buddha's preaching into the 'five periods and eight teachings'. Different levels of teaching and different methods of giving that teaching are related to distinct periods in the Buddha's life and to the various forms of Buddhist literature. In this way a hierarchy is defined, giving an appropriate place to every extant form of Buddhism. The result is a comprehensive and encyclopedic system. In Japan the T'ien-t'ai school had great success and remains an important sect there. From it emerged the specifically Japanese school of Nichiren (see Chapter 10 below). Eclectic by nature, Japanese Tendai was influenced by a number of other Chinese schools, notably the Mantrayana and the Pure Land. [39: 303–13; 42: 437–96; 43]

Hua-yen. Although traditionally founded by Tu-shun (557–640 CE), the Hua-yen or Garland school received its most complete form with Fa-tsang (643–712). Its inspiration came from a group of Indian *sutras* known in Eastern

Table 8.5. Eastern Buddhist schools

India	China	Korea	Japan	English
A. Ancient traditions				
1. *Vinaya*	Lu	Kyeyul	Ritsu	Discipline
2. *Abhidharma-kosha*	Chu-she	Kusa	Kusha	
B. Indian Mahayana theory				
3. Shunyatavada or Madhyamika	San-lun	Samnon	Sanron	'Nihilist' or 'Three Treatise school'
4. Yogacara or Vijnaptimatra	Fa-hsiang or Wei-shih	Popsong or Yusik	Hosso	'Idealist'
C. Chinese Mahayana theory				
5. Based on the *Nirvana sutra*	Nieh-p'an	Yolban or Sihung	–	
6. Based on the *Lotus sutra*	T'ien-t'ai	Ch'ont'ae	Tendai	Lotus
7. Based on the *Avatamsaka sutra*	Hua-yen	Hwaom	Kegon	Totalism
D. New modes of practice				
8. Mantrayana or Vajrayana	Chen-yen	Milgyo { Ch'ongji / Sin'in	Shingon or Mikkyo	Esoteric
9. Based on the Pure Land *sutras*	Ch'ing-t'u	Chongt'o	Jodo Shin Ji	Pure Land
10. Dhyana	Ch'an { Lin-chi / Ts'ao-tung	Son or Chogye	Zen { Rinzai / Soto	Meditation

Buddhism as the *Avatamsaka* or *Garland sutra*. Hua-yen gave systematic form to a group of Indian teachings which are not quite so systematized in any surviving Indian text. Traditional Chinese philosophy also influenced Hua-yen. Perhaps partly for this very reason it is widely regarded in Eastern Buddhism as philosophically the most advanced school and has had wide influence.

Hua-yen developed its own classifications of the different kinds of Buddhist teaching on similar lines to T'ien-t'ai, but it is best known for its 'philosophy of totality'. A rich and striking symbolism verging on extravagance is employed. Everything in the universe is connected and harmoniously related to everything else. Indeed the result may be described as a 'hologram universe' in which every part contains the whole. This is all set out in some detail and taken to great depth. [39: 313–20; 44; 45]

Pure Land teachings. One branch of early Indian Buddhist meditation seems to have concentrated upon the visualization of the figure of the Buddha. In the early Mahayana this took the form of visualizing the Buddha Amitabha ('boundless radiance') in his pure land of Sukhavati ('land of happiness'). The practice involved recitation of the name of this Buddha. The practitioner aspired to a vision of Amitabha and rebirth in his paradise. Reciting the name eventually became widely popular far outside the circle of meditation specialists. In East Asia the cult of Amitabha became the most widespread form of Buddhist devotion. A specific school came into being, known in China as the Ch'ing-t'u.

The Indian authority for this school lies in three texts: the two *Sukhavati-vyuha sutras* ('sutras on the vision of the land of happiness') and the *sutra of meditation on the Buddha of Boundless Life*. At first it was simply one popular form of meditation and devotion, but later it came to displace many of the earlier forms. Sometimes it is suggested that the emphasis on devotion as providing a special kind of salvation is unnatural in Buddhism and alien to the earlier tradition. Yet even the earliest form of Buddhism known to us taught that faith in the Buddha was able both to bring about a heavenly rebirth and to set one firmly on the path to liberation. The difference is in the Mahayana emphasis on the 'power of resolve' of a Buddha, which is capable of creating enormously favourable conditions. This gradually became a doctrine of grace, reaching its most extreme development in Japan.

Devotion to Amitabha as part of the general Mahayana is very ancient. Many Chinese teachers played an important role in furthering both meditation on Amitabha and recitation of his name. But the Ch'ing-t'u does not really become a distinctive school until later. This was mainly the work of Tao-ch'o (562–645) and his disciple Shan-tao (613–81). The emphasis was on the power of simply 'reciting the name' to ensure rebirth in Amitabha's paradise. This was considered to be a simple approach, easy for ordinary people to adopt and still effective even in a period in which the original teaching was in decline. As a result of the work of Honen (1133–1212) and his disciple Shinran, Pure Land had great success in Japan, eventually becoming the largest single school (see page 376). [39: 338–50; 46]

The Meditation school. The traditions of meditation practice begun by An Shih-kao continued for many centuries. They were constantly augmented by new lines of teaching from India and Central Asia. During the T'ang dynasty a new Ch'an 'Meditation' school arose (best known in its Japanese form as Zen). No doubt it derived much from earlier schools, but by the end of the dynasty it had developed a kind of genealogy tracing its lineage of teachers through a series of six patriarchs. The first patriarch was considered to have been Bodhidharma, an Indian monk supposed to have arrived in China *c.* 520 CE. Around the lives of the patriarchs a rich and colourful spiritual literature came into being. So vital was this tradition that it absorbed into itself numerous other traditions. Almost all later Chinese meditation schools claimed affiliation to a lineage deriving from the Ch'an patriarchs. Already by the end of the T'ang period five such lineages had arisen. The two most important were: the Lin-chi (Japanese: Rinzai) and the Ts'ao-tung (Japanese: Soto). Although both claimed to derive their tradition from the sixth and last patriarch – Hui-neng (638–713) – they differ somewhat in approach.

Ch'an Buddhism has become well known for its emphasis on spontaneity and for a certain tendency towards iconoclasm. The teachers of this school were wary of any kind of routine or habitual spiritual practice. Similarly they showed a measure of hostility to ritual and to scriptural or scholastic literature. None of this should be exaggerated. Ch'an taught – 'not clinging to written words and not separating from written words'. The aim was to undermine *attachment* to particular religious forms. There was no wish to abolish the forms themselves: indeed such a wish would be seen as itself a form of attachment. In fact Ch'an eventually developed a very large literature of its own, concentrating on stories of the sayings and deeds of the Ch'an masters.

The main aim is to re-emphasize the immediate accessibility of direct realization. Enlightenment is to be striven for and realized in this very life. The Ch'an teachers claimed 'a special transmission outside doctrines' – a direct and wordless communication between teacher and pupil. Later tradition lays great stress on this transmission. Practical action was preferred to study. Ch'an often stresses the suddenness of the realization of enlightenment but in fact different degrees of realization were usually recognized. It is sometimes suggested that Ch'an represents a radically new development, even one which is no longer Buddhist at all. This is an exaggeration. In fact there is almost nothing in Ch'an which cannot be paralleled in earlier Indian Buddhism. The difference is in *style* rather than *content*. Ch'an adopted unconventional and unusual forms of expression. Probably the example of Taoism is very important here, especially for its tradition of simplicity and naturalness. [47; 48; 49 (history); 50]

DIFFUSION AND ADAPTATION

Chinese Buddhism. Buddhism has been changed by the culture and customs of every country to which it has come. Equally it has brought change to those countries. Yet China is a special case. Here Buddhism was the medium of contact between two of the great civilizations of the ancient world. There was no question of replacing the existing culture; inevitably Buddhists had to adapt to Chinese forms and customs. Chinese people asked new questions and offered new problems. Native Chinese religion and philosophy influenced and mingled with the new teachings.

It is customary to speak of Buddhism becoming Chinese, but this should not be taken too far. Even before it arrived in China Buddhism was a rich and varied religious tradition. It is not so much that it adopted Taoist or other Chinese ideas wholesale, rather it selected from a rich repertoire those elements which appealed in the Chinese situation. Naturally this led to a measure of convergence – the more so as the native traditions also brought to the fore elements which resembled Buddhist ideas or methods.

Buddhism in Korea. Prior to the arrival of the Ch'an school in the eighth century, Korean Buddhism had become dominated by the O-kyo or 'five doctrines'. These were the Vinaya, Yogacara, Nirvana (a precursor of T'ien-t'ai), Hua-yen and Popsong schools. The two last were the most important. The Popsong is an eclectic school founded in Korea by Wonhyo (617–86). Ch'an eventually established nine branches, known as the nine mountains after the location of many of the leading temples.

In the eleventh century T'ien-t'ai was introduced and sought to reconcile the existing trends. Ch'an was then reorganized under the name of Chogye and stimulated by the introduction of Lin-chi traditions. Buddhism was very influential under the Koryo dynasty (918–1392), but less so under the Yi dynasty (1392–1910) when Neo-Confucianism gained in importance.

Sectarianism and syncretism. There is some doubt as to the precise nature of the schools of Chinese Buddhism in the T'ang period (618–907 CE). It may be guessed that the Sangha at large was more than merely the sum of the different schools. If the schools had a certain independence of organization and action, they yet remained very much part of the larger grouping. For this reason the gradual decline of most of the schools as separate entities did not necessarily mean the complete elimination of their influence. Teachings deriving from other schools remained widespread even when the vast majority of temples were committed to the two practical schools of Ch'an and Pure Land.

Korean Buddhism took a slightly different direction partly as a result of government intervention. A reform in the sixteenth century reduced the numbers of monks and grouped the existing schools into two administrative sects: the Son and the Kyo. The former, meditation-oriented grouping was dominated by Ch'an but included also T'ien-t'ai, Vinaya and the Mantrayana. The Kyo contained the remaining doctrinal schools. This division continued until the twentieth century when it was replaced by a single umbrella organization. In fact separate schools continued within this body – at present no fewer than nineteen are officially recognized and more are unofficial.

In Japan the ancient schools grew more and more into independent sects with their own organization and separate lay following. It is important not to read this Japanese development back into the classical Chinese situation. The ancient Chinese schools were much less institutionalized sectarian entities than their successors in Japan. In China there arose a movement towards syncretism which tended to unite the Buddhist sects and in some cases sought to harmonize the teachings of Buddhism with those of Taoism and Confucianism. This led to a much more integrated and united form of Buddhism. Japanese writers tend to view this as a degeneration, but it can also be viewed as a successful victory for ecumenism over sectarian intolerance. [51: 395–407]

The religion of ordinary people. Buddhism in East Asia is closely connected with the native religious traditions in many ways, as is only natural when religions have been in such close contact for so long. For treatment of the religious situation as a whole in two of those countries, China and Japan, see Chapters 9 and 10 below. Here we can mention only some specifically Buddhist elements.

Most of the Chinese population before Communist rule took part occasionally in Buddhist activities of one kind or another. This might include festivals, ceremonies, pilgrimages and various kinds of merit-making activity. In this they perhaps differed little from the population of most other Buddhist countries – except perhaps in greater willingness to take part similarly in activities associated with other religions. Things can have been no different in ancient India. Of course many of the above activities could equally be undertaken with serious intent by the more committed – a relatively small percentage of the population. [51: 357ff]

Buddhist festivals. Buddhist monasteries theoretically celebrate between thirty-five and forty events, but most are of minor importance. Apart from festivals common to all Chinese, especially the New Year festival, five are particularly significant for Buddhists:

Month	Day	Event
Second	19	Birth of the Bodhisattva Kuan-yin (Avalokiteshvara)
Fourth	8	Birth of the Buddha
Sixth	19	Enlightenment of Kuan-yin
Seventh	9–15	Ullambana ('Festival of Hungry Ghosts')
Ninth	19	Death of Kuan-yin

The rains retreat (see Table 8.3) runs from the fifteenth of the fourth month to the fifteenth of the seventh month, but this is now of less importance in Chinese Buddhism. Nevertheless it is the festival which terminates the rains retreat which is the most important specifically Buddhist festival. The same is the case quite widely in the Buddhist world, although calendar differences tend to obscure this. [51: 108–10]

RECENT DEVELOPMENTS

The Sangha in Eastern Buddhism. The monastic community in China probably came from various sources, but two sects were more important: the Sarvastivadins and the Dharmaguptakas. The Dharmaguptakas were either a branch of the Sarvastivadins or an early branch of the Vibhajjavadins (see Figure 8.5). In addition a branch of the Ceylonese order of nuns was transmitted to China. Ultimately it was the Dharmaguptaka recension of the *Vinaya* which was the most influential in China.

In modern times, before Communist rule, the Chinese Buddhist Sangha was quite large – of the order of half a million monks and a quarter of a million nuns. About 5 per cent of these lived in larger public monasteries, which were generally well ordered and disciplined. The remainder lived in a large number of very small temples. Some of these were also occupied by monks with a strong personal commitment to the life-style of the Sangha. Others, we are told, were very nominal, even lax in their observance of the monastic discipline. Of course, some criticism of this kind comes from sources hostile to any form of monasticism.

A set of rules created by the Ch'an monk Pai-chang (d. 814 CE) was generally accepted as authoritative (in addition to the fundamental rules of the *Vinaya* and the Mahayana *Brahmajala-sutra*). Some of the minor rules of the Indian *Vinaya* had fallen into abeyance, but by and large the basic principles of Ancient Buddhist monasticism were still acknowledged in China, Vietnam and Korea. Indeed the peripatetic nature of the ancient Sangha was perhaps better preserved in China than elsewhere. Many monks, especially in their youth, spent several years wandering from province to province studying and practising in different temples. [51]

In Japan the situation changed most noticeably after the Meiji restoration in

1868. The requirement for celibacy was abolished by law and eventually marriage became widespread. This should not be confused with the much older tradition of a married priesthood in some branches of the Japanese Pure Land school. The new practice was also introduced into Korea under Japanese rule but has met opposition there. The vast majority of non-Japanese Buddhists regard a married monk as a contradiction; so, too, did the Japanese founders of most of the sects which now practise it. Protestant Christian attitudes to celibacy have given some outside reinforcement to monastic marriage.

Chinese Buddhism in the nineteenth century. Compared with its cultural and intellectual importance during the T'ang period or the great numbers of the Sangha in Mongol times, Buddhism had diminished considerably by the Manchu dynasty (1644–1911). During the T'ai-p'ing rebellion (1850–64) Buddhist temples and monasteries suffered much destruction. In the latter part of the dynasty the government was not sympathetic and Buddhism was restricted in its activities. By and large the Neo-Confucian bureaucracy viewed Buddhism as non-Chinese, non-productive and anti-family. This attitude influenced early Western missionaries and scholars, who then produced somewhat exaggerated reports of the decay of Buddhism because their observations were not sufficiently based upon first-hand knowledge. In fact Buddhism still remained influential and widely practised, but more so in some regions and less in others.

The Buddhist revival. The fall of the Manchu dynasty in 1911 brought both problems and opportunities. On the one hand there was a movement to expropriate the lands of the monasteries and thereby destroy the basis of Buddhist religious life. Yet this was successfully resisted during the Republican period. On the other hand old restrictions disappeared. Forms of preaching activity and association which had been prohibited under the Manchus to non-Christian religions now became possible. A number of new movements sprang up: various traditions of study were revived; publishing activity increased; some social and educational work was undertaken. The nucleus emerged of an ecumenical movement directed towards Buddhists in Japan, Tibet and South-East Asia.

The work of a relatively small number of monks representing modernist tendencies is noteworthy, the most famous being Tai-hsu (1890–1947). We have here in a Mahayana form the same varying mixture of reformism, modernism and ultimatism that we found in Southern Buddhism. Here, too, it is important to adopt a balanced approach. Reform movements tend to be committed to presenting what preceded as in some way unsatisfactory or degenerate. More traditionalist Chinese Buddhists would not accept that there was a revival at all. Of course almost all Buddhists believe that the faith has declined – indeed such a belief is itself an act of faith in the teaching of impermanence and hence a sign of vitality. It is important to be aware of values alien to Buddhism. Social activities by monks can be seen as an admirably modern innovation. Many Buddhists would see this as a wholly inappropriate imitation of Christian missionaries and destructive of the proper role of the Sangha. Outsiders have tended to be unsympathetic towards the values of silence and contemplation, but these are as essential to Mahayana Buddhism as the giving of material help to others, which is the task of the lay Buddhist.

Buddhism in both the Manchu and Republican periods was still a lively and powerful force in Chinese religious affairs. What is referred to as a revival is best seen as a form of Buddhist modernism – part of the response of Buddhism to the arrival of European religious and secularist ideas and practices. [39: 455–460; 52; 53]

The Communist period. With Communist rule established in China, North Korea and Vietnam a very different situation emerged. In China during the 1950s a policy of moderate restriction, modelled on Soviet policies developed in a Christian context, was initially adopted. Russian practice was much more hostile to monasticism than to the clergy. The application of the Soviet model in Buddhist contexts with 'monks' and no married clergy was necessarily very destructive. Monastic lands were nationalized and monks required to support themselves by some kind of work. Such a policy was already severe and destructive of the spiritual training of the monks. Moreover, many activities were restricted. The government for its part claimed to be engaged in a programme of reform which, no doubt, was sometimes justified. Some Buddhist cultural activities received government support; so, for example, Buddhist temples and monuments considered to be of cultural importance were repaired. According to government figures there were 100 million Chinese Buddhists in the 1950s.

From about 1958 the situation worsened markedly. By the climax of the Cultural Revolution a decade later Buddhism was totally prohibited throughout China, at least in theory. Buddhist monasteries and temples were closed and in many cases suffered damage at the hands of Marxist fanatics. How far this was universal is uncertain. It seems likely that there was some variation in different areas. With the abatement of the more extreme tendencies came a move to return towards the pre-1958 situation. By about 1980 many of the leading centres were again functioning and there was some action to repair damage. The future is obviously uncertain. Yet after all Buddhism has survived persecutions in the past and doubtless it still has many centuries of activity to come.

Outside the Chinese mainland the period has seen an increase in Buddhist activities in Taiwan, Hong Kong and in the Chinese diaspora. This seems partly due to Buddhist refugees from Communist rule, but also to influences from other Asian countries and even from the West. [54]

Northern Buddhism

INTRODUCTION

Sources. Tibetan Buddhism possesses two great canonical collections: the *bKa"gyur*; and the *bsTan'gyur*. The former contains translations of Indian scriptures and is usually arranged under six headings: (1) *Vinaya*; (2) *Prajna-paramita* ('perfection of wisdom'); (3) *Avatamsaka* ('garland'); (4) *Ratna-kuta* ('jewel heap'); (5) *Sutra*; (6) *Tantra*. It consists of about 100 volumes and contains around 700 works. The *bsTan'gyur* has over 200 volumes and more than 3,600 works. These are mainly the works of Indian authorities – in effect *shastra* literature of various kinds. The three main sections are: (1) a short collection of hymns; (2) commentaries on *tantras*; and (3) commentaries on *sutras*. Tibetan also has an enormous literature of its own, much of which is known only to Tibetan scholars.

History. The history of Northern Buddhism may be divided into four periods: early history; developments in India; the spread of Mantrayana; and the second diffusion of Buddhism in Tibet.

Early history. According to Tibetan tradition Buddhism was introduced to Tibet in the reign of Srong btsan sgam po (d. 649 CE) by two of the king's wives, one from Nepal and one from China. This can only have been on a small scale. It was in the reign of Khri srong lde brtsan (756–97?) that Buddhism made significant progress, culminating in the foundation of the monastery of bSam yas. The inspiration for this came from the Indian scholar Shantarakshita. Later tradition gives a major role to the yogi and sage Padmasambhava, said to have been invited by Shantarakshita to overcome supernatural opposition to the spread of Buddhism. In fact Buddhism came from various sources. We hear of a contest between followers of the Chinese Ch'an tradition and supporters of Indian schools, to some extent a contest between gradualist and sudden approaches to enlightenment. There were also influences from Central Asian Buddhism (Figure 8.6).

In due course resistance arose from followers of the native Tibetan religious tradition known as Bon. This led to persecution in the reign of gLang dar ma. After the death of this king in 842 CE the Tibetan kingdom broke up and Tibet lost control of Central Asia. Buddhism was affected by the general chaos

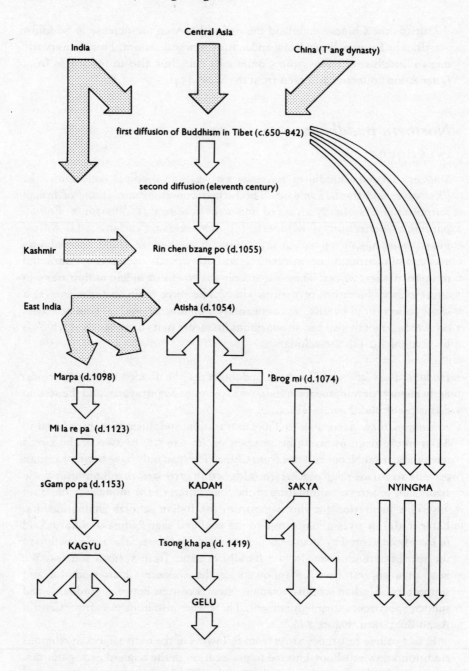

Figure 8.6   The evolution of Northern Buddhism

and largely disappeared from historical view. Yet it continued to develop, especially in outlying areas, and gradually penetrated Tibetan culture, both influencing and being influenced by the Bon religion. [55: 66–110; 56: 1–15]

Developments in India. The religious creativity of Indian Buddhism had produced another great flowering of sacred literature: the *tantras*. Like the earlier Mahayana *sutras* these claimed to be the teaching of a Buddha or equivalent figure. They represent the third and last major phase in Buddhist thought and practice. Just as the Mahayana did not replace the teachings of Ancient Buddhism, so too the new school did not displace the Mahayana. The new school developed within the old and was superimposed upon it.

The movement based upon the *tantras* is known as the Mantrayana, 'Vehicle of the *mantra*'. A *mantra* is a word or phrase used for meditation and devotion. According to an explicatory 'etymology' it 'protects the mind'. An alternative name is Vajrayana ('Vehicle of the diamond'), i.e. the indestructible vehicle. The origin of the tantric literature is still obscure; there were certainly parallel developments in both Hinduism and Buddhism. Much folk tradition and magical technique was incorporated in the new movement, including materials of very ancient origins. Two features are perhaps the most important. First, it involved the elaborate use of magical methods – esoteric teachings, ritual and ceremonial, initiations, incantations, sacred circles etc. – in effect the skilful and joyful use of sense experience and imagination to bring about individual transformation. Secondly, it emphasized the possibility of enlightenment in this very life, claiming that its methods could provide a direct path to the goal in contrast with the more gradual approach of the later Indian Mahayana. Great importance was given to the role of the teacher. A rich and vivid symbolism was employed. At first this probably emerged from and formed part of visualization exercises, but it soon began to take artistic form. Especially noticeable is the use of imagery connected with sexuality or with death. A new pantheon of specifically Mantrayana deities comes into existence, including many goddesses and female consorts or aspects of Buddhas and *bodhisattvas*.

Mantrayana developed into an articulated and sophisticated system. Elaborate correspondences were established between the pantheon, the body, meditational experiences and the world at large. In some schools the ritual performance of sexual acts seems to have taken place, but (at least in Buddhism) this should not be exaggerated. It can only have played a minor part in the Mantrayana movement as a whole. Tantra has a marked tendency to make use of activities which are psychologically 'loaded', especially in its visualization methods. The aim is partly to free the mind from ambivalent attractions and partly to startle the mind from rigid habits. In this there is some similarity with the methods of Ch'an Buddhism. [1: 482–502; 36: 386–7; 41: 116–23]

The spread of Mantrayana. In the last part of the first millennium CE the Mantrayana spread widely over most of the Buddhist world. It was present in Ceylon and South-East Asia as well as influential in Indonesia. In none of these places did it endure into modern times, although it left many traces of its influence. It was primarily in the area influenced by the Buddhism of Tibet that the Mantrayana remained important.

Yet there is one major exception; for the Chinese Mantrayana school was introduced into Japan by Kukai (774–835), best known as Kobo Daishi. The school which he founded, the Shingon, remains one of the larger Japanese sects. Shingon may be seen as a synthesis of an earlier phase of Mantrayana with the Chinese theoretical schools. Its practice, however, is essentially tantric in nature, although not deviating from conventional morality. [36: 389–90; 39; 57]

The second diffusion of Buddhism in Tibet. The end of the tenth century and the course of the eleventh saw renewed contacts between Tibet and Indian Buddhism. Relations were established with Kashmir and the centres of Buddhism in eastern India. New translations were made from the large body of Buddhist literature still available in the Indian monastic universities, soon to be destroyed by the invading Muslims. A number of Tibetan translators who had studied in India or Kashmir were at work in this period, notably Rin chen bzang po (d. 1055), 'Brog mi (d. 1074) and Marpa (d. 1098). Just as important were Indian teachers who came to Tibet. Particularly notable was Atisha (982–1054), one of the leading figures of contemporary Indian Buddhism.

The following century saw the rapid growth of Tibetan monasticism and the formation of the principal schools. This culminated in the thirteenth century when the Mongols established the head of the Sakya[2] school as ruler of Tibet. Later a new school was formed by the reformer Tsong kha pa (1357–1419), known as the Gelu. The heads of the Gelu school eventually acquired the title of Dalai Lama and gradually became rulers of Tibet. In the eighteenth century the Manchu rulers of China established effective suzerainty. Tibetan Buddhism showed great vitality, spreading not only throughout the Tibetan cultural area but also winning over the Mongols and establishing itself on a small scale quite widely in northern Asia. Indeed it was showing definite signs of expansion in the period just before the arrival of Communism. [56: 16–28; 55: 160ff]

Changing assumptions. Tibetan religion was very little known before the influx of Tibetan refugees into Western countries during the 1960s and later. Many very distorted accounts had become current. On the one hand Tibet was seen as a country in the grip of medieval religious superstition, dominated by demonolatry and a completely decadent and corrupt form of Buddhism. On the other hand it was portrayed as the home of the mystical, the spiritual and the magical – a land of great Masters filled with occult lore and profound knowledge. No doubt there is a measure of truth in each of these pictures, but they have made a fair understanding more difficult.

It is now quite clear that Tibet was the direct heir of later Indian Buddhism. It had both preserved the learning of the great monastic universities of India and added to that learning in a creative and constructive, if rather conservative, way. As such the monasteries of Tibet were the repositories of a very considerable and unique heritage – not only in religion, philosophy, logic and so on, but also in artistic and cultural products. The growth of Tibetan studies in the twentieth century has begun to bring real knowledge of that heritage and has replaced more extreme notions with realistic and balanced assessment of Tibetan religion.

THE NATURE OF NORTHERN BUDDHISM

The structure of the teaching. Tibetans sometimes argue that their teaching includes all three vehicles: the Hinayana, the Mahayana and the Vajrayana. There is some truth in this. Ancient Buddhism is represented in the Vinaya discipline and the practice of moral restraint. Moreover the Tibetan monastic curriculum sometimes included quite detailed study of the *abhidharma* and there are in any case many elements surviving from an early period. Yet it is clearly with the second and third vehicles that most Northern Buddhist teaching is concerned. Tibetan Buddhism contains large elements both of Mahayana and of Mantrayana. The former, often referred to as the 'Vehicle of the perfections', Tibetans see as the *bodhisattva* path developing perfections over many lives as set out in the Mahayana *sutras* and the two great *shastra* systems of the Shunyatavada and the Yogacara. The *shastra* systems were widely known and studied in the Tibetan schools.

The vehicle of the *mantras* is seen as the direct route, utilizing specific practices as a skilful means enabling buddhahood to be reached in years rather than lives. On one level this is reserved for the experienced practitioner at a relatively advanced stage. On another level it can be said to pervade the whole of Tibetan religion. Tibetan art and devotion are filled with the figures of deities, *bodhisattvas* and Buddhas whose origins lie in the *tantras* or who are presented in a guise based upon the *tantra*.

Perhaps the most striking feature of Tibetan Buddhism to the observer is the part played by ceremony and ritual, especially the public conferment of various kinds of blessing and initiation. This aspect of Northern Buddhism is in fact immensely successful and popular, even quite outside the normal limits of the religion. Recently such ceremonies have been performed fairly widely in both Europe and North America with visible effectiveness and impact. Their form and arrangement, however, is based upon Mantrayana theory of a quite detailed and sophisticated kind. [60]

The role of the Lama. Mantrayana Buddhism emphasizes the role of the teacher (Sanskrit: *guru*, Tibetan: *blama*), as any religious tradition which stresses initiations and esoteric teachings is likely to do. So much is this the case that the Lama is often added as a fourth refuge to the refuge in the three jewels usual in Eastern or Southern Buddhism. It is incorrect to apply the term to any Northern Buddhist monk, as is sometimes done. Tibetans understandably tend to object to the name 'Lamaism' for their religion because it implies that it is not authentic Buddhism.

One significant innovation that certainly has been made in Tibet is the introduction of the institution of so-called 'incarnate lamas' or *tulkus* (Sanskrit: *nirmanakaya*). Originally the idea was simply that a past teacher might return to new life as a child or might be especially connected to a child. The first Karmapa Lama (Dus gsum mkhyen pa: 1110–93) introduced a new notion by predicting his own immediate rebirth after death. Eventually the custom of finding a child to succeed a dead teacher became widespread. In some cases such 'lines' of succession were considered to act as the vehicle for the manifestation of the power of a *bodhisattva* or Buddha. The most famous example is of course the Dalai Lama, considered to be a focus for Avalokiteshvara, the *bodhisattva* of compassion. [56: 134–5]

Meditation methods. The same combination of Mahayana and Mantrayana applies in the realm of meditation practice. There is basic training in calm and insight meditation (see page 307), modelled especially on the accounts of the Yogacara school. This is widely practised but is often, though not always, regarded as only a preliminary stage. More typical is some kind of meditative ritual. This is essentially some combination of an appropriate *mantra* with a corresponding visualization exercise. So for example one may visualize oneself as taking the form of a Buddha while picturing that Buddha before one in an appropriate context (e.g. surrounded by circles of attendant Buddhas, *bodhisattvas* and deities). Such a practice will usually be initiated by ceremonial authorizations from a teacher, preferably one who has himself mastered that particular method. The practitioner must thereafter repeat a series of chants and visualizations, make offerings, repeat the relevant *mantra*, make appropriate gestures (*mudra*) at intervals and so on. Eventually the visualization should come joyfully alive, only to be dissolved again in emptiness.

Such methods occur in many different forms using a multiplicity of different techniques. Successful ritual service of a given deity is seen as bringing both inner and outer rewards, as well as advancing one on the path to liberation. It is almost impossible to separate this kind of meditation from more general popular devotion and cult. Each can lead into the other. Rituals performed by Tibetan monks are based upon the patterns and theoretical structure of tantric meditation and are at the same time intended to create conditions in the participant favourable for meditation. [56: 47–109; 61: 148–58; 62; 63: 25ff]

The schools of Northern Buddhism. Tibetan Buddhist schools differ as to precisely which texts they hold to be authoritative and in the deities to which they pay most attention; in some cases they possess particular teachings or practices in which they specialize. They remain quite similar in general features and perhaps do not amount to distinct sects. Three general groups can be distinguished: (1) the tradition deriving from the first diffusion of Buddhism in Tibet – the Nyingma ('old ones'); (2) the schools stemming from the second diffusion – especially the Kadam, Sakya and the Kagyu; and (3) the reform which gave rise to the Gelu or New Kadam school, often known as the 'Yellow Sect'. The earlier Kadam was absorbed by the Gelu school. This left four main schools as well as a number of less well-known ones.

The Sakya and Kagyu may perhaps be seen as the intellectual and yogic wings of the same many-branched tradition. The latter in particular is well known for its cotton-clad yogis, going back to the teachings of the poet-saint Milarepa (1040–1123). Especially important for this school are the Six Doctrines attributed to the Indian yogi Naropa (the teacher of Marpa), leading to the spiritual achievement known as *mahamudra*.

The Nyingma is partly a response to the success of the schools belonging to the second diffusion. On the one hand it retains many ancient traditions and practices of varying origin. On the other hand it has been one of the most creative schools. It gives authority to texts supposedly hidden during the period of persecution and later found by clairvoyant masters, even to some which are openly the product of contemplation. In this, of course, it simply continues the practice of the ancient Mahayana. The Nyingma school underwent a considerable renaissance in the fourteenth century, creating its own collection of *tantras* and developing a cult based upon the legendary figure of Padmasambhava, seen as its founder.

The Gelu school represents an attempt to return to the tradition of Atisha, re-emphasizing monastic discipline, which its founder Tsong kha pa (1357–1419) felt had become lax. Tsong kha pa had studied in all three of the schools of the second diffusion and stressed the importance of following authentic Indian tradition. The school had great success and founded large monastic universities in Lhasa and elsewhere, requiring a long and impressive period of study. Shunyatavada teaching played an important role. Unusual emphasis was placed on the study of logic and on public debate. [36: 388–9; 56: 33–9, 47–109]

The Sangha. Only one Vinaya tradition was established in Tibet – that of the Mulasarvastivada. In principle it is adhered to by all schools, but in practice it is overlaid to some extent by various Mahayana and Mantrayana traditions. A fairly complex organization had naturally developed in the larger monasteries. Before 1959 Tibet had a rather large Sangha, according to some accounts as much as 25 per cent or more of the population, though this is probably an exaggeration. There were certainly a few very large monasteries, especially in Lhasa and at the principal centres of various sects. [55: 237ff; 56: 110ff]

Festivals. The Tibetan calendar is related to the Chinese, with some differences. It is a lunar calendar, each month beginning at the new moon with the full moon on the fifteenth day. New Year and harvest festivals play an important part everywhere, as do festivals of sect founders and tutelary deities in particular monasteries. The following were generally recognized:

Month	Day	Event
One	10–15	Great miracle at Shravasti
Four	7	Birth of the Buddha
Four	15	Enlightenment and entry into *nirvana* of the Buddha
Six	4	First sermon
Nine	22	Descent of the Buddha from heaven (end of the rains retreat) [56: 146ff]

RECENT HISTORY

The Manchu rulers of China had established suzerainty over Tibet and their representatives exercised a measure of authority in Lhasa throughout the nineteenth century. The fall of the Manchu dynasty in 1911 ended that suzerainty as far as Tibet was concerned. Tibetan culture and religion continued still to be largely out of contact with the rest of the world. The Chinese Communist invasion in 1950 established Chinese overlordship under an agreement providing for Tibetan self-government. This collapsed in 1959, the Dalai Lama fled to India and direct Chinese colonial rule was forcibly imposed. Eventually the Cultural Revolution led to an attempt to destroy totally Tibetan religion. This appears to have involved the large-scale destruction of Tibet's artistic, sculptural and architectural heritage – probably the worst cultural crime of one people against another in recent centuries. At present there are signs of a return to more moderate policies.

Tibetan religion is still active in the Himalayan territories of India and Nepal as well as in the small kingdom of Bhutan and among refugee communities in India and elsewhere. Moreover, it has had some success in the field of missionary endeavour.

Afterword: The Three Traditions in the World Today

The twentieth century has brought mixed fortunes for Buddhism. Communist rule has meant wholesale destruction, especially to the Sangha, first in the Asian territories of the Soviet Union and in Mongolia, then successively in North Korea, China, Tibet, Vietnam, Laos and Cambodia. Each of the three traditions has suffered. The same period has seen a revival of activity and a return to lands long lost. Notably in Indonesia and in India Buddhism has re-established its presence and won new support.

More remarkably, new fields for expansion have emerged. In Europe, Southern Buddhism began to establish itself on a small scale as early as the beginning of the century. Eastern Buddhism in its Zen form started to attract a significant following outside the Asian immigrant communities in the 1950s, especially in North America. The work of Tibetan refugee teachers in the 1960s and 1970s won support for Northern Buddhism. By the early 1980s some hundreds of Buddhist groups and centres were widely scattered across the Western world. Much of this activity is on a fairly small scale, but in many cases quite well established. [41: 198ff; 61 248–58]

NOTES

1. Where Buddhist names and terms are current both in a Sanskrit and a Pali form (see page 288), only one form is generally given in the text: Sanskrit where dealing with Northern or Eastern Buddhism or with specifically Mahayana notions, Pali in the case of Southern Buddhism or the remainder of Ancient Buddhism. The alternate form may in most instances be found in the Index to this volume.
2. The written form of the Tibetan language is unusually different from the present-day spoken forms. Simplified forms have been used here for words which already have some current usage in English, e.g. names of sects. The full form may be found in the Index to this volume.

BIBLIOGRAPHY

1. WARDER, A. K., *Indian Buddhism*, Delhi, Motilal Banarsidass, 1970
2. PYE, M., *The Buddha*, London, Duckworth, 1979
3. CARTER, J. R., *Dhamma: Western Academic and Sinhalese Buddhist Interpretations: A Study of a Religious Concept*, Tokyo, Hokuseido Press, 1978
4. CH'ÊN, K. K. S., *Buddhism: The Light of Asia*, Woodbury, NY, Barron's Educational Series, 1968
5. SNELLGROVE, D. L. (ed.), *The Image of the Buddha*, London, Serindia/Paris, Unesco, 1978
6. CONZE, E., *Buddhism: Its Essence and Development*, Oxford, Cassirer, 1951, new edn, 1974; New York, Philosophical Library, 1951, Harper, 1959
7. HORNER, I. B. (tr.), *Middle Length Sayings*, 3 vols., London, Pali Text Society, 1954–9, repr. 1975–7
8. RHYS DAVIDS, T. W. and C. A. F., *Dialogues of the Buddha*, 3 vols., London, Pali Text Society, 1899–1921, repr. 1977
9. BUDDHAGHOSA, *The Path of Purification* (tr. Nāṇamoli), 2nd edn, Colombo, Semage, 1964; Berkeley, Calif., Shambhala, 1976
10. ANURUDDHA, *Compendium of Philosophy* (tr. S. Z. Aung), London, Pali Text Society, 1910, repr. 1979
11. LING, T. O., 'Sinhalese Buddhism in recent anthropological writing: some implications', *Religion*, vol. 1, pt 1, Spring 1971, pp. 49–59
12. SPIRO, M. E., *Buddhism and Society*, London, Allen & Unwin, 1971; New York, Harper & Row, copyr. 1970
13. GOMBRICH, R. F., *Precept and Practice: Traditional Buddhism in the Rural Highlands of Ceylon*, Oxford, Clarendon Press, 1971
14. ADIKARAM, E. W., *Early History of Buddhism in Ceylon*, Colombo, Gunasena, (1953); Migoda, Puswella, 1946
15. MALALGODA, K., *Buddhism in Sinhalese Society, 1750–1900: A Study of Religious Revival and Change*, Berkeley, Calif., University of California Press, 1976
16. WELBON, G. R., *The Buddhist Nirvāṇa and Its Western Interpreters*, Chicago, Ill., University of Chicago Press, 1968
17. JONG, J. W. DE, *Buddhist Studies*, Berkeley, Calif., Asian Humanities Press, 1979
18. SADDHATISSA, H., *Buddhist Ethics*, London, Allen & Unwin, 1970; New York, Braziller, 1971
19. MARASINGHE, M. M. J., *Gods in Early Buddhism*, Vidyalankara, University of Sri Lanka, 1974
20. RAHULA, W., *What the Buddha Taught*, Bedford, Gordon Fraser, 1959, 2nd edn, 1967; New York, Grove Press, 1962
21. SADDHATISSA, H., *The Buddha's Way*, London, Allen & Unwin, 1971; New York, Braziller, 1972

22. KING, W. L., *Theravāda Meditation*, University Park, Pa, Pennsylvania State University Press, 1980
23. NARASABHA, S., *Buddhism: A Guide to a Happy Life*, Bangkok, Mahachulalongkorn Buddhist University, 1971
24. DE SILVA, L., *Buddhism: Beliefs and Practices in Sri Lanka*, 2nd edn, Colombo, n.p., 1980
25. CARTER, J. R. (ed.), *Religiousness in Sri Lanka*, Colombo, Marga Institute, 1979
26. SLATER, R. H. L., *Paradox and Nirvana*, Chicago, Ill., University of Chicago Press, 1951
27. TAMBIAH, S. J., *Buddhism and the Spirit Cults in North-East Thailand*, Cambridge, Cambridge University Press, 1970
28. MENDELSON, E. M., *Sangha and State in Burma: A Study of Monastic Sectarianism and Leadership*, Ithaca, NY, Cornell University Press, 1975
29. BUDDHADĀSA, *Toward the Truth* (ed. D. K. Swearer), Philadelphia, Pa, Westminster, 1971
30. TAMBIAH, S. J., *World Conqueror and World Renouncer: A Study of Buddhism and Polity in Thailand Against a Historical Background*, Cambridge, New York, Cambridge University Press, 1976
31. KORNFIELD, J., *Living Buddhist Masters*, Santa Cruz, Calif., Unity Press, 1977
32. NANJIO, B., *A Catalogue of the Buddhist Tripitaka*, Oxford, Clarendon Press, 1883; Tokyo, 1930
33. ZÜRCHER, E., *The Buddhist Conquest of China*, 2 vols., Leiden, Brill, 1959
34. MORGAN, K. W. (ed.), *The Path of the Buddha: Buddhism Interpreted by Buddhists*, New York, Ronald Press, 1956
35. ENCYCLOPAEDIA BRITANNICA, 15th edn, *Macropaedia*, vol. III, Chicago, Ill., EB, copyr. 1982, 1974
36. CONZE, E., *Buddhist Thought in India*, London, Allen & Unwin, 1962; Ann Arbor, Mich., University of Michigan Press, 1967
37. GUENTHER, H. V., *Philosophy and Psychology in the Abhidharma*, rev. edn, Delhi, Motilal Banarsidass, 1974; Berkeley, Calif., Shambhala, 1976
38. CH'EN, K. K. S., *Buddhism in China: A Historical Survey*, Princeton, NJ, Princeton University Press, 1964, repr. 1972
39. CONZE, E., 'Recent Progress in Buddhist studies', in (his) *Thirty Years of Buddhist Studies*, Oxford, Cassirer, 1967; Columbia, SC, University of South Carolina Press, 1968
40. TAKAKUSU, J., *The Essentials of Buddhist Philosophy*, 3rd edn, Honolulu, Office Appliance Co., 1956; (1st Indian edn) Bombay, Asia Publishing House, 1956
41. ROBINSON, R., and JOHNSON, W. L., *The Buddhist Religion: A Historical Introduction*, 2nd edn, Encino, Calif., Dickenson, 1977
42. GODDARD, D., *A Buddhist Bible*, 2nd edn, Thetford, Vt, Author, 1938, repr. Boston, Beacon Press, 1970

43. HURVITZ, L., 'Chih-i', *Mélanges chinoises et bouddhiques*, 12 (1962)
44. CHANG, C. C., *The Buddhist Teaching of Totality: the Philosophy of Hwa Yen Buddhism*, London, Allen & Unwin, 1972; University Park, Pa, Pennsylvania State University Press, copyr. 1971
45. COOK, F. H., *Hua-yen Buddhism: The Jewel Net of Indra*, University Park, Pa, Pennsylvania State University Press, 1977
46. SUZUKI, D. T., *Shin Buddhism*, London, Allen & Unwin/New York, Harper & Row, 1970
47. CHANG, C. C. (CHANG CHEN-CHI), *The Practice of Zen*, London, Rider, 1960; New York, Harper, 1959
48. SUZUKI, D. T., *An Introduction to Zen Buddhism*, London, Rider, 1949, 1969; New York, Philosophical Library, 1949, Grove, 1964; prev. publ. Kyoto, Eastern Buddhist Society, 1934
49. DUMOULIN, H., *History of Zen Buddhism* (tr. Paul Peachey), London, Faber, 1963; New York, Pantheon, 1963, McGraw-Hill, 1965
50. YAMPOLSKY, P. B., *The Platform Sutra of the Sixth Patriarch*, New York, Columbia University Press, 1967
51. WELCH, H., *The Practice of Chinese Buddhism*, Cambridge, Mass., Harvard University Press, 1967
52. WELCH, H., *The Buddhist Revival in China*, Cambridge, Mass., Harvard University Press, 1968
53. CHAN, WING-TSIT, *Religious Trends in Modern China*, New York, Columbia University Press, 1953
54. WELCH, H., *Buddhism under Mao*, Cambridge, Mass., Harvard University Press, 1972
55. SNELLGROVE, D., and RICHARDSON, H., *A Cultural History of Tibet*, London, Weidenfeld/New York, Praeger, 1968
56. TUCCI, G., *The Religions of Tibet* (tr. G. Samuel), London, Routledge/ Berkeley, Calif., University of California Press, 1980
57. KIYOTA, M., *Shingon Buddhism: Theory and Practice*, Los Angeles, Calif., Tokyo, Buddhist Books International, 1978
58. XIVth DALAI LAMA (Ngawang Lobsang Yishey Tenzing Gyatso, Dalai Lama, 1935–), *The Opening of the Wisdom-Eye and the History of the Advancement of Buddhadharma in Tibet*, Bangkok, Social Science Association Press of Thailand, 1968
59. SGAM. PO. PA, *Jewel Ornament of Liberation* (tr. H. V. Guenther), London, Rider, 1959, 1970; Berkeley, Calif., Shambhala, 1971
60. LESSING, F. D., and WAYMAN, A., *Introduction to the Buddhist Tantric Systems*, The Hague, Mouton, 1968
61. PREBISH, C. S., *Buddhism: A Modern Perspective*, University Park, Pa, Pennsylvania State University Press, 1975
62. BLOFELD, J. J., *The Way of Power: A Practical Guide to the Tantric Mysticism of Tibet*, London, Allen & Unwin, 1970
63. BEYER, S., *The Cult of Tārā: Magic and Ritual in Tibet*, Berkeley, Calif., University of California Press, 1973

64. NORMAN, K. R., *Pāli Literature*, i.e. J. Gonda, *A History of Indian Literature*, vol. VII, fasc. 2, Wiesbaden, Harrassowitz, 1983
65. DENWOOD, P., and PIATIGORSKY, A., *Buddhist Studies – Ancient and Modern*, London Curzon Press/Totowa, NJ, Barnes & Noble, 1983

Chinese Religions

MICHAEL SASO

Introduction

Religion, in the modern Chinese context, is festive, celebrating the passage of men and women in the Chinese community through the cycle of life and death. Chinese religion is traditionally defined by the rites of passage, i.e. birth, maturation, marriage and burial, and the annual cycle of calendrical festivals. Membership of the Chinese social community is demonstrated by participation in the rites of passage and the annual festivals, rather than by intellectual assent to a body of revealed scripture. Chinese religion is therefore a cultural rather than a theological entity. All of the religious systems coming from abroad into the Chinese cultural complex found it necessary to accommodate to the religious and cultural values of China in order to survive and function. The success of Western religions especially has depended upon acceptance of the strong Chinese values of family and social relationships, and adaptation in some way to the customs of the Chinese people. The seasonal festivals as well as the rites of passage have equally survived the iconoclastic rigours of the socialist state of mainland China and the even more devastating secularized education and industrial revolution of maritime China. ('Maritime China' and 'diaspora China' are almost synonymous: maritime China refers to all Chinese living outside of mainland China on the Pacific basin or the islands of South-East Asia, while China of the diaspora refers to all Chinese living abroad owing to the political and economic situation on the mainland.)

The term for religion in China, *tsung-chiao*, refers literally to a *tsung* or lineage of *chiao* or teachings, of which the common men and women of China have traditionally admitted three: the Confucian system of ethics for public life; the Taoist system of rituals and attitudes towards nature; and the Buddhist salvational concepts concerning the afterlife. The three teachings, Buddhist, Taoist and Confucian, act as three servants to the faith and needs of the masses, complementing the social system. Confucius regulates the rites of passage and moral behaviour in public life. Taoism regulates the festivals celebrated in village and urban society, and heals the sick. Buddhism brings a sense of compassion to the present life and salvation in the afterlife, providing funeral rituals for the deceased and refuge from the cares of the world for the weary. But the Chinese commonly say that 'the Three Religions all revert to a common source' (*San-chiao kuei-i*), meaning in modern times that in fact the functionaries or priests of the three religions are dependent on the beliefs and needs of the common people of China, and attain meaning and livelihood as servants of the people. Religion is therefore a celebration by and for the people.

THE MAIN PRIMARY SOURCES

The main primary sources for the study of Chinese religion are: (1) the Confucian ritual classics, histories and local gazetteers; (2) Taoist canonical writings, popular manuals and fiction; and (3) Buddhist canonical texts and popular devotional *Shan-shu* books. The Confucian sources for religious custom and the rites of passage include later dynastic summaries in the form of sumptuary or ritual laws governing provincial and local variations in the rituals used at birth, maturation, marriage and burial [1]. Local and provincial officials frequently summarized the state-approved ritual laws in popular manuals commonly known as *Complete Home Rituals*, still available in temple and village bookshops in maritime China [2]. Though the variations found by anthropologists throughout mainland and maritime China often seem too disparate for systematic comparison, in fact at the deep structural level the Chinese rites of passage always follow the Confucian model.

The primary source for public ritual where a Taoist priest or liturgical expert is required is the Taoist Canon, now available in inexpensive photo-offprint for scholarly and ritual use [3]. The Canon contains hundreds of *chiao* rituals of renewal and *chai* funeral liturgies used today for festival and for burial. The Canon also preserves philosophical treatises, exorcisms and healing rituals, internal 'alchemy' or meditative tracts, alchemical formulae, medicine and herbal texts, and other rich sources of myth and popular Chinese religious practices. Field research in East and South-East Asia has uncovered a vast quantity of primary materials concerning the modern practice of Chinese religion in mainland and maritime China of the diaspora (South-East Asia). These modern sources are now in the process of publication [4].

Popular Buddhist sources of Chinese religious practice are found in the *shan-shu* publications, privately funded treatises on meritorious lives, legends and myths for public distribution [5]. For other sources of Buddhist practices, see the chapter on Buddhism in this volume (Chapter 8 above). Popular fiction dating from the Ming and the Ch'ing dynasties onwards, available in corner bookstores and penny lending libraries throughout maritime China, has been used as a first-hand source for popular beliefs and practices. The pioneering work in these vernacular publications has been done by the noted sociologist and sinologist Wolfram Eberhard [5].

AN INTRODUCTION TO THE HISTORY OF CHINESE RELIGION

Chinese religious history is divided into four major periods, listed traditionally as the spring, summer, autumn and winter of cultural development [6]. The birth of Chinese religion is traceable to the oracle bones, prognostications made by inscribing queries to the spirits on the carapace of a tortoise or the leg bone of an ox, and then applying heat to the bone to obtain an oracle reading. The cracks appearing in the bones gave the negative or positive response of the spirit to the problems posed by the Kings of Shang, c. 1760–1100 BCE, China's first historically documented period [7]. The religious cosmology depicted in the oracle readings is not unlike the cosmology of later summer and autumn Chinese history.

The later spring of China's religious history extends from the beginning of the Chou kingdom, c. 1100 BCE, through the Warring States era to the beginning of the Han dynasty in 206 CE. During this extended period six ways of thought are generally recognized to have formed the core of the Chinese cultural/religious system. Three of these, the moral/ethical directives of Confucius, the penal codes of the Legalists, and the secular agnosticism of the logicians, form what came to be called the Confucian way (Ru-chiao). The teachings of the Confucian school are traditionally considered to be collected in the Four Books and the Five Classics [8]. The legalist writings and the works of the logicians, along with the writings of the Confucian classics, are well summarized in the History of Chinese Philosophy of Fcng Yu-lan, translated and annotated by Derk Bodde [9].

The second set of three teachings from ancient China, the Taoist, Muoist and yin–yang Five-Element schools, form what came to be called spiritual Taoism (Tao-chiao) in the summer of Chinese religious history. The works of Lao-tzu (sixth/fifth century BCE), and Chuang-tzu (fourth century BCE) are the fundamental mystical and theoretical sources for religious Taoism [10]. The treatise on the brotherhood of man and universal love of Muo-tzu is now included as a part of the Taoist canon, providing inspiration for the sworn brotherhood and fraternal societies of modern China [11]. The yin–yang Five-Element (or Five-Mover–Five-Phase) cosmology which derives from the Tsou Yen school of ancient China formed the theoretical system of the so-called 'New Text' Confucian liturgists of the Han dynasty and inspired the first converts to religious Taoism [12].

In a more holistic sense such generalizations, which create a false dichotomy between the philosophical and the religious, the Confucian and the Taoist, are purely academic, i.e. simple heuristic devices to explain the richness of the Chinese religious/cultural heritage. In practice the Confucian statesman, Taoist poet and master of ceremonies for popular household ritual were often the same person. Like two sides of the same precious coin, Confucian social ethics and Taoist communion with nature formed the core of the Chinese religious spirit [13].

The second period of Chinese religious history, extending from 206 BCE to 900 CE, the summer or maturity of the three religions of China, witnessed the introduction of Buddhism into China from India; the formation of liturgical or spiritual Taoism as the priesthood of the popular religion; and the supremacy of Confucianism as custodian of the moral/ethical system of Chinese social culture. The rites of passage summarized by the New Text Confucianists of the early Han period, and the grand Taoist liturgies of renewal, became standardized for all of China [16].

The third period of Chinese religious history, the autumn or religious reformation, extended roughly from the beginning of the Sung dynasty c. 960 CE to the end of the Ch'ing dynasty and the imperial system, 1912 CE. During this period a true reformation of the religious spirit of China occurred, some 500 years before the reformation of European religious systems. The Chinese religious reformation was typified by lay movements in both Buddhism and Taoism, a syncretism, even ecumenism, between Buddhist and Taoist spiritual elements, and the growth of local popular cultures [16]. Secret societies, religious cults, clan and temple associations, merchant groups or *huikuan* flourished throughout China. Christianity was brought to China by Jesuits in the sixteenth century, and by increasing waves of missionaries in the nineteenth and twentieth centuries, but owing to the inability of Christian missionaries to adapt to the religious cultural system of China, it never equalled the popularity of Buddhism in the Chinese context [16].

The modern period of Chinese religious history is compared to winter in the four seasons of nature's constant cycle. Like a phoenix rising from the ashes of a burnt-out fire, or the drop of *yang* in the sea of *yin* which brings about cosmic rebirth in the depths of winter, the spirit of Chinese religion is at present experiencing a new vitality and rebirth both in the People's Republic and the maritime diaspora of China. To study Chinese religion in the modern era is indeed illuminating, since the structure of the religious system, which was often hidden by the proliferation of local customs and rituals in the recent past, is now laid bare by the necessities of secular society, and the exigencies of cultural continuity in a world filled with political as well as technological upheaval. Chinese religion continues to be a vehicle of self-expression and identity for the people who comprise China's masses, whether in continental, maritime or emigrant China overseas.

THE MAIN PHASES AND ASSUMPTIONS
OF SCHOLARLY STUDY OF CHINESE RELIGION

The modern study of Chinese religion can be broken down into three main phases, namely: (1) the nineteenth-century scholars who approached the study of China from the superior colonialist attitude or as missionaries who saw Chinese practices as gross superstition; (2) the early and mid-twentieth-century scholars who as historians of religion or anthropologists approached the Chinese experience from the 'objective' or 'scientific' approach; and (3) the structural phenomenologists who by participatory observation attempt to see Chinese religion from its own experiential 'eidetic' vision.

The major works of the first group of sinologists who studied Chinese religions were published between the late nineteenth and early twentieth centuries. De Groot's massive *The Religions of China* and Henri Doré's *Superstitions chinoises* are classics of this period [17]. The second group – historians of Chinese religion and anthropologists, with extensive field-work published during the past thirty years – are typified by the British social anthropologist Maurice Freedman and the American positive school of anthropology, represented by Arthur Wolf [18]. Where Freedman holds for the structured systematic view of Chinese religious practice, Wolf emphasizes the local, non-systematized and eclectic nature of field evidence. The excellent bibliography of Chinese religion prepared by Lawrence Thompson and the textbook of Chinese religion by the same author summarize modern studies in the field [19].

The third and most modern form of Chinese religious studies is typified by the intensive participation of the scholar in the religious life of the Chinese environment, an approach to Chinese religion based on laying aside one's own cultural assumptions and adopting the eidetic vision of the subject. This approach, which is basically structural in nature, owes much to the insights of Claude Lévi-Strauss, who in the study of South American myths first proposed a deep-structure theory underlying the seemingly contradictory nature of field evidence. The works of Kristofer Schipper, Emily Ahern, David Jordan and Liu Chih-wan are typical of scholars who have gone deeply into field experience to explain their insights into Chinese religion [20]. To the above names and titles must be added the impressive work of Professor Kubo Noritada, whose field experiences in China (both maritime and mainland), and publications, are significant [21].

The Basic Assumptions of the Chinese Religious System

Chinese religion as practised in the twentieth century is based solidly on the *yin–yang* Five-Element theory of nature. This is a composite of the Taoist, the Tsou-yen and the Fang-shih schools of the late-spring period of Chinese religious history [22].

COSMIC GESTATION

From the Taoist tradition, specifically the forty-second chapter of the *Lao-tzu*, is taken the definitive statement of cosmic gestation:

> The Tao gave birth to the One.　(*T'ai-chi*)
> The One gave birth to the Two.　(*yin* and *yang*)
> The Two gave birth to the Three.
> The Three gave birth to the myriad creatures.

The meaning of the text (see Figure 9.1) is dramatically expressed in Taoist ritual, seen throughout maritime China, South-East Asia, Taiwan, Hong Kong and modern Honolulu. The ritual is called Fen-teng ('Dividing the new fire') and is an essential part of the Taoist Chiao rites of cosmic renewal [23].

YIN AND YANG

From a new fire struck from a flint is lit a first candle, representing the immanent, visible Tao, *T'ai-chi* or primordial breath within the (head) microcosm of man. From the *T'ai-chi* is lit a second candle, representing primordial spirit, or soul within man, the chest or heart of the microcosm. A third candle is lit symbolic of vital essence, the gut or intuitive level within man. These three candles represent *T'ai-chi*, the immanent, moving Tao of nature, *yang* and *yin*. They also represent the Three Spirits of the Transcendent Tao's working in nature: *San-ch'ing*, Primordial Heavenly Worthy who governs heaven; *Ling-pao*, Heavenly Worthy who governs earths; and *Tao-te*, Heavenly Worthy who rules water and rebirth. Thus on the macrocosmic level the Tao gestates heaven, earth and water; on the microcosmic level, head, chest and belly (intellect, love, and intuition). On the spiritual level the Tao is seen to be ever gestating, mediating and indwelling within man [24].

THE FIVE ELEMENTS

Just as the cosmic-gestation chapter of the *Lao-tzu* is dramatically expressed in modern ritual, so the *yin–yang* Five-Element theory is still enacted during the

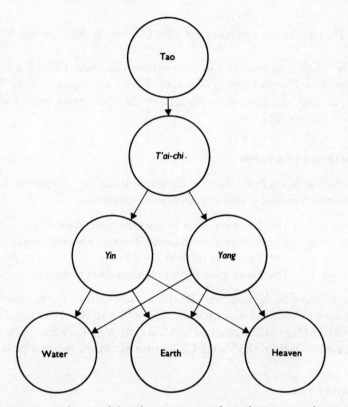

Figure 9.1   A structural view of the Chinese cosmos (from the *Lao-tzu*, chapter XLII).
The Tao gives birth to the One: *T'ai-chi* or primordial breath.
The One gives birth to the Two: *yin* and *yang*. The Two give birth to the Three:
watery underworld, earth and heaven. The Three give birth to the myriad creatures

annual celebration of cosmic renewal, in modern maritime China. The ritual is
called Su-ch'i and occurs on or about the winter solstice, or whenever a Chiao
festival of renewal is being celebrated. During the rite, a Taoist ritual expert,
called 'Master of Exalted Merit', plants the five elements, i.e. wood, fire, metal,
water and earth, into five bushels of rice, which represent east, south, west,
north and centre, i.e. the entire cosmos [25]. The elements are symbolically
represented by five talismans, drawn on five pieces of silk, green, red, white,
black and yellow respectively. Once the talismans have been planted in the
bushels of rice, the Taoist draws a series of 'true writs' in the air, striking a
sacred feudal contract with the spiritual powers of the cosmos, asking for the
blessings of new life in spring, maturity and full crops in summer, rich harvest in
autumn, and rest and security in the old age of winter [26].

UNION WITH THE TAO

After the five elements have been ritually renewed in nature, the Taoist always completes the ritual cycle of rebirth by a special meditative prayer for bringing about union with the transcendent Tao. This ritual, the highlight of most temple liturgies practised in maritime China or wherever Chinese religion flourishes, is called the Tao-ch'ang (making the Tao present in the centre of the microcosm) or the Cheng-chiao (attaining true mystical union with the Tao). The ritual is the converse of the Su-ch'i described above. Having planted the five talismans in the five bushels of rice on the first day of the Chiao festival of renewal, on the last day the Taoist dances the sacred steps of Yü (playing the role of China's Noah who stopped the floods of antiquity) and 'harvests' the talismans, one by one, ingesting them meditatively into the five organs within his body. The five organs (liver for east and wood, heart for south and fire, lungs for west and metal, kidneys for north and water, spleen/stomach for centre and union) act as a sort of divine mandala making the presence of the gestating Tao felt within the centre of the microcosm. The mystic experience of union with the Tao is thus taught by ritual performed in the village temple for the men and women of the village to see. What could not be taught by the theologian verbally is understood by the peasant through the visible expression of liturgical drama. [27]

The theory of Chinese religion is, therefore, seen as an eternally cycling progress outward from the Tao to the myriad creatures, and returning to the Tao for renewal by the very process of the seasons in nature. By following the path of nature, man attains eternal union. Ritual acts as a dramatic, non-verbal source of instruction for the laity in the Chinese religious system.

CONFUCIAN VIRTUE

Ritual is to Taoist cosmology as behavioural norms are to the Confucian ethic; just as the theory of Chinese religion is demonstrated in the liturgies of the Taoist Chiao festival, so the definitions of the Confucian ethic are drawn directly from the experience of the human encounter at the practical level of everyday experience. The Confucian norms for behaviour, written down in the spring of the ancient Chinese cultural system, are very much alive in the winter of the modern present. *Li* or respect, *hsiao* or family love, *yi* or mutual reciprocity among friends, *jen*, benevolence towards the stranger, and *chung*, loyalty to the state, are values deeply embedded in the hearts of the men and women of China, equally valid for mainland and maritime communities. [28]

Li is, like many Chinese characters, a symbol not limited by a single linear definition. The word means religious ritual as well as heartfelt respect, an attitude which is basic to the ego in approaching human relationships. The word reflects the virtue of the *chun-tzu*, the man or woman of outgoing, giving nature, who imitates heaven in generous liberality, and like the great ocean conquers by 'being low', letting all things flow into its embrace [29]. *Hsiao* is the virtue governing family relationships. Its definition embraces the love of children for parents and parents for children, making the family the very centre of Chinese social life. *Yi* represents the sense of deep commitment that friend must give to friend, and reciprocity governing the transactions of honest business. *Jen*, literally all the good things which happen when two humans meet, is best translated by the word 'benevolence' (Latin root, *bene-volens*), meaning 'wishing good things' for others. The comment of tourists coming back from mainland China, 'how kind everyone is', reflects the modern sense of *jen*, welcoming the stranger (*hao-k'o*), for which the great cities of China were traditionally famous. Finally *chung*, the sense of loyalty to the reigning power of state, coupled with an immense sense of democratic vote or common decision at the village and community level, makes China one of the most stable cultural systems in human history [30].

THE COSMOS

The *yin–yang* Five-Element theory governs not only the rituals of religious Taoism, but also the concepts of the present and the afterlife of the ordinary men and women of China. The principles of *yang* and *yin* when joined together in harmonious union – often represented as a dragon and a tiger in a sort of cosmic struggle of gestation – form the visible earth. Separated, *yang* floats upwards to form the heavens, and *yin* sinks downwards to form the watery and fiery underworld. [30] The three stages of the cosmos, heaven, earth and under-world, are reflected in the head, chest and belly of the microcosm (see Figure 9.2). Upon death the soul, which has completed its life-cycle, is thought to sink downwards into the realms of *yin*, where it is purged of its darkness and sins for a period before release to the heavens. [31] During this period the soul can cause sickness in the family or other calamity if unattended by the prayers and food offerings of the living. The function of the medium, or shaman, throughout Asia, as in China, Japan, Korea and South-East Asia, is to descend to the underworld (shaman) or act as a channel for the voice of the deceased (medium) to inquire about the needs of the unattended or sickness-causing soul. Buddhist ritual, especially, is thought to be efficacious in freeing the soul from the tortures of hell to ascend to the western heavens and paradise [32].

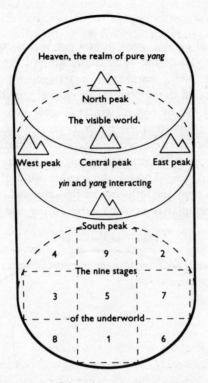

Figure 9.2   The spatial structure of the Chinese cosmos. Heaven is pure,
separated *yang*; earth is the visible world, *yin* and *yang* interacting. The watery or fiery
underworld is the realm of pure *yin*, divided into the nine sections of the magic square

HELL

Hell is seen in the drawings of modern temple frescoes and devotional books to
have nine cells or stages of punishment, each governed by a demon king [33].
The role of Buddhist and Taoist ritual is to lead the soul through these stages,
paying off the evil politicians whose role in the afterlife, as in the present, is
to tax and punish the common man and woman. In the Chinese system, only
politicians stay eternally in hell, in charge of the tortures of the damned. The
paper money burned at funeral and other rituals in China is symbolic of the
merits of the living whose acts of love and giving are like bank notes in hell,
drawing interest to free the souls of the deceased into eternal life [34].

LIFE-CYCLES

Finally, the theory of cyclical growth and renewal is equally reflected in the annual cycle of festivals of the lunar almanac, and the cycle of life of mankind in the cosmos. Birth, maturation, marriage, old age and death in the cycle of life are reflected in the planting of spring, growth of summer, harvest of autumn, and old age or rest of winter (Figure 9.3). The annual cycle of festivals liturgically celebrates these natural events of life, as explained below. Chinese religion is therefore eminently practical, integrating the individual into family and community, celebrating the passage of men and women through the cycle of life and of nature. Though the secular mind of the modern Chinese intellectual tends to deny the influence of the religious cultural system on the individual, the contemplative mystic of the Taoist and Buddhist community

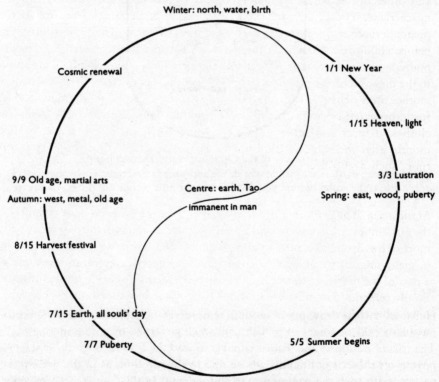

Figure 9.3 The temporal structure of the Chinese cosmos. *Yang* is born at the winter solstice, *yin* at the summer solstice. The life-cycle of man and the annual cycle of festivals follow the same pattern

and the banquets of the common people of the Chinese community draw the politician and the academician into the joys of festive celebration.

Characteristic Practices of Chinese Religion

THE RITES OF PASSAGE

Birth, maturation, marriage and burial have been regulated from the Han period onwards by the sumptuary and ritual law of the Confucian tradition.

Birth. Birth is the least regulated of the life rituals. Tradition allows the pregnant mother a respite from unwanted labour before birth by placing taboos on excessive needlework, tying of bundles or bales, lifting, moving furniture, and other duties which by psychological or physical pressure may cause a miscarriage. The *T'ai-shen* or 'foetus spirit' is made ritual protector of the pregnant mother, a jealous deity who punishes any person harassing the parent before childbirth. Directions for the birth process itself prescribe a woman midwife or doctor to care for the mother in labour, and pay special attention to the disposal of the placenta. Strict custom decrees one month of rest for the mother after delivery, with special foods rich in protein and vitamins, and so forth, prepared by family members. The wife's family must provide complete clothes, diapers and other necessary items on the first, fourth and twelfth months after the baby's birth. Presents given to the child or the mother at this time, such as fresh eggs, specially prepared chicken, health wines, or rice, symbolize good health and prosperity for both [35].

Maturation. The elaborate ritual of 'capping' for the boy and 'hair-styling' for the girl, important events in traditional educated families in the past, have been more or less dropped in modern times. Some communities still celebrate the boy or girl going off to college, or commemorate the *kuan* maturation rituals as a part of the marriage festivities. Otherwise the rite of puberty, or maturation, is only celebrated in the more traditional families, and often only by a banquet in which a chicken is served to the young adult to commemorate approaching maturity [34].

Marriage. Marriage in modern China of the diaspora is still a most elaborate affair, with the six stages observed in a fashion adapted from the traditional past. The stages or steps of Chinese marriage are as follows: [36]
  Proposal, consisting in the exchange of the 'eight characters' – the year, month, day and hour of birth for both parties. The eight characters of the boy are placed by the family altar of the girl's household, and any untoward event in

the family during a three-day waiting period signals that the girl rejects the marriage.

Engagement is announced by the bride's side sending out invitations for the auspiciously chosen wedding day, with a box of moon-shaped biscuits.

The bride's dowry is sent to the groom's home in a solemn procession through the streets. The entire community sees the gifts *en route*, and notes whether the bride's vanity box is prominently displayed. The groom-to-be opens the vanity box with a special key, symbolizing that the love of the young couple is sincere. The bride price is usually sent by the groom's family, counted, and sent back at this time. The groom's gifts to the bride, in the form of jewellery, clothes and other items, match the value of the dowry.

The bridal procession, formerly carried out by means of a bridal palanquin, now makes use of a limousine or taxi. The groom must go to meet the bride at her home, and accompany her back to his residence to the accompaniment of music, fireworks and streamers. On arrival at the groom's home, the bride pretends to be weak as crossing the threshold she steps over a smoking *hibachi* or cooking-pot, a saddle and an apple at the gate, symbolizing (by homonyms) a pure and peaceful crossing into the new household.

The exchange of marriage vows frequently takes place in a Christian church in the modern setting. The bride and groom toast each other with a small cup of rice wine, and then proceed to an extensive banquet. During the banquet the bride and groom must toast each table of guests. Tea coloured to look like whisky is taken by the young couple, while each guest must swallow a complete glass of spirits. The traditional custom of reciting poetry and giving long speeches is frequently but not always shortened.

The morning after is celebrated by the young bride serving breakfast to her new parents-in-law, and in turn being served breakfast by them. A basket of dried dates and seeds is given to the new parents-in-law, a homonym for 'many children' (many seeds) from the bride. The bride returns home to her own parents 'for the first time as a guest' on the third day after marriage.

Funeral ritual. Funeral rites in modern China of the diaspora may be extensive and costly, using Taoist and Buddhist forms as in the past, or completely Westernized in mortuary and church-burial form. Even when performed in a mortuary or church, certain aspects of the traditional rites of burial are observed, however, as noted in the following traditional account, taken from Chinese manuals [37]:

The moment of death. When death occurs at home, or sometimes in a modern hospital, the dying person often asks to be put on the floor, as near as possible to the ancestor shrine in the main hall of the room. Death is signalled to the neighbours by wailing. The family immediately goes into mourning, by removing all jewellery and fine clothes, and dressing in coarse cloth, hemp or muslin, as custom decrees. The burial day is chosen, and invitations are sent out to all paternal relatives to the sixth degree, and all maternal relatives to the third degree, to attend the funeral.

Preparing the corpse and coffining. The corpse is washed ritually and put in a coffin. Layers of white paper money or talismans are put over the corpse, symbolizing purification and protection from harmful germs or baleful influences after death. Even when done in a mortuary with an open coffin, the custom of laying white paper talismans across the body of the deceased is observed. Mourning visitors put incense in the incense pot, offer condolences to the bereaved family, and money gifts to help meet the expense of a funeral. The family altar and all decorations in the front room are covered with white cloth during the entire funeral. Food and precious belongings are put into the coffin before the closing and sealing.

Mourning at home or in the funeral parlour. A Taoist or Buddhist priest, or a Christian minister (sometimes all three), is asked to perform the funeral ritual at home or in the funeral parlour. Paper houses containing complete furnishings, symbolic clothes and paper money for the bank of merits in hell are burned. The burning of paper signifies the merits of the living, and the prayers of the community for the eternal salvation of the deceased. Flowers, incense and paper items, funeral wreaths and a special ancestor shrine for the deceased are presented during the funeral rite.

The funeral procession. Chinese and Western bands, playing traditional and modern dirges, children portraying the twenty-four scenes of filial piety as burial drama, a willow branch symbolizing the soul of the deceased, and the entire mourning family accompany the coffin to the grave. All of the invited mourners pause before the cemetery, with only the immediate family and the officiating ministers or priests going to the grave-side. After burial the willow branch is carried back to the family altar and used ritually to 'install' the soul of the deceased in the memorial tablet. The ancestor shrine, less and less frequently seen in the families of maritime China, acts as a reminder to the living of the central place of family and its virtues of love and mutual care in the present life.

Post-funerary liturgies are performed for the deceased by Buddhist, Taoist or Christian ministers on the seventh, ninth and forty-ninth days after burial, and on the first and third anniversaries of death in a special manner. The Taoist rituals are especially colourful, depicting a journey of the Taoist high priest into the underworld where the demonic politicians of hell are tricked and cajoled into releasing the soul into paradise. A huge funerary banquet is provided for all guests, relatives and coffin-bearers who attended the funeral when the burial is completed.

Through much of the diaspora of maritime China ancestor worship within the family has been supplanted by ancestor tablets which are kept for a fee at a Buddhist shrine, pagoda or temple. The altar in the main room of the traditional Chinese household, with the patron spirits of the family in the centre and the ancestor shrine on the left or 'west' side, is less and less frequently seen in Honolulu and South-East Asia. Education in Chinese religion at the college level, however, and the influx of Chinese from mainland China (who are, as a rule, more religious than those from secularized Taiwan or Hong Kong) tend to restore the practice of such traditional religious customs.

THE ANNUAL CYCLE OF FESTIVALS

The festive cycle of Chinese religious life follows the farmer's almanac, reflecting the busy time of the planting, weeding and harvesting process when religious festivals are relatively infrequent, and the rest periods when festivals predominate. Cyclical festivals fall in the odd-numbered or *yang* months, and farming activity in the even-numbered or *yin* (earth) months. The festivals are doubly symbolic, representing the progress of men and women through life as well as the ripening, harvesting and storing of crops. The calendar is followed enthusiastically by Chinese communities of the diaspora, and recognized cognately by mainland communities. [38]

First (lunar) month, first day. The lunar New Year, or festival of spring, is a family banquet in honour of the ancestors and the living members of the family who assemble from distant places to affirm identity. The New Year festival is the most important and widely celebrated of Chinese festivals today. Five or seven sets of chopsticks, wine, tea and bowls of cooked rice are laid out in memory of the ancestors on the family altar or table. Then a sixteen- or twenty-four-course banquet is served. Flowers, freshly baked cake, sweets, sweet dried fruit, three or five kinds of cooked meat, fish, noodles, bean curd, and various kinds of vegetable dishes, all with homophonic meaning for blessing and prosperity in the New Year, are served at the banquet. Women wear flowers in their hair, children receive presents and cash in a red envelope, new clothes are donned and fireworks signal the beginning of the first lunar month of spring. Good-luck characters are pasted by the door and the lintels, and visits made to friends, shrines and churches on New Year's Day.

First month, fifteenth day. This is the festival of light. The first full moon of the New Year is celebrated by a lantern procession and a dragon dance. Children carry fancy lanterns in the streets, and contests are held for the best lantern, best poems and best floats in the lantern parade.

Third month, third day. The lustration festival is celebrated from the beginning of the third lunar month until 105 days after the winter solstice, in the fourth lunar month, as a sacrificial cleaning of the graves and the celebration of the bright and clear days of spring. The graves are cleaned and symbolically 'roofed' or covered with talismanic tiles, begging for blessing in spring. The family holds a picnic in the hills after offering food at the grave.

Fifth month, fifth day. The beginning of summer is celebrated by the eating of *tseng-tzu* (rice cakes), by dragon boat races on the river and by rituals to keep children healthy and safe from the colds of summer. The colourful Taoist ritual exorcising the spirits of pestilence is seen throughout the coastal areas of south-east China and the diaspora.

Seventh month, seventh day. The festival of puberty, or the seven sisters day, is celebrated throughout maritime China, Japan and the diaspora with the charming tale of the spinning-girl and the cowherd boy, whose eternal tryst is commemorated on this evening.

Seventh month, fifteenth day. 'All souls' day' or the Buddhist Ullambhana is celebrated throughout Asia as a pre-harvest festival. The souls are freed from hell in a ritual of general amnesty before the rice and other crops are harvested from the soil. As on new year's day, the entire family celebrates with a banquet.

Eighth month, eighth day. The full moon of autumn marks the harvest festival, celebrated with a banquet of fresh fruits and round mooncakes eaten under the rising harvest moon. Poetry reading and family evenings after the harvest express thanks for nature's bounteous plenty.

The winter festivals. From the ninth month, ninth day until the eleventh month, eleventh day, various festivals celebrate the autumn and the winter period of rest and recycling. The Taoist rite of cosmic renewal or *Chiao* is most frequently celebrated at this time, up until the winter solstice [39]. Besides the cyclical festivals, various birthdays celebrating the heroes or saints of the folk religion occur at even and odd month intervals throughout the year, according to local custom. These patron saints festivals include the festivals of the local patron saints of the soil, on the first and fifteenth day of each month; the Heavenly Empress Ma-tsu, who protects fishermen, sailors and immigrants, on the fourth month, twenty-third day; Kuan-kung, patron of merchants and martial arts, on the sixth month, fifteenth day, and Tz'u-wei the patron of the pole-star, on the ninth month, ninth day. Taoist, Buddhist and popular temples usually offer rituals on all festive occasions. The spirit of Chinese religion, ecumenic or irenic rather than syncretistic,[1] moulds all religious systems to the needs of the people for ritual to celebrate the rites of passage.

RELIGIOUS FUNCTIONARIES

Three functionaries assist the people of the village in the practice of the rites of passage and the festivals. These are the Buddhist monk, the Taoist priest and the possessed medium or shaman. The Buddhist monk provides Pure Land-motivated chants, Ch'an (Zen) meditation and tantric, that is, mantric chant, *mudra* (hand gesture) and eidetic visualization[2] as regular services in the local Buddhist monasteries. The majority of the temples (*miao*) of popular Chinese religion are ministered by Taoist priests under the direction of a lay temple board of directors. Taoists provide various rituals for healing and blessing, including the universally popular ritual asking blessing from Ursa Major, the constellation of the pole-star. Both Buddhist and Taoist temples offer a modernized version of the method of prognostication of the yarrow stalk and *I Ching* book (that is, numbered wooden sticks are drawn from a wooden container by chance, and the corresponding hexagram is read by a monk or nun in the temple) for reading one's fortune or common-sense advice in practical home and business matters. The temple or religious centre in the Chinese village is truly a cosmic as well as a cultural axis, providing fairs, opera, puppet shows, story-tellers, and meeting-places as well as religious services. As with the medieval cathedrals of Europe, the villagers build their own temples from local donations, and spend years, decades even, in making these cultural focal points into objects of artistic pride and functional meaning.

The medium, oracle and shaman are three different functionaries within the Chinese system, with a different word for each role. The medium, whose body is occupied by a spirit while in trance, the shaman, who travels into the afterlife, whether the underworld or the heavens, and the oracle, who speaks in the words of a bystanding spirit, fulfil the roles of seer, healer and keeper of justice in villages where the spiritual power of the temple and the religious system provides more stability than the rapidly changing political and industrial forces of change. The medium and the shaman have tended to multiply in those areas where political stability is repressive or lacking (such as Taiwan, Korea, the Philippines and South-East Asia) and practically to disappear where economic growth or strictly enforced political discipline is dominant, as in Japan or mainland China [40].

Conclusion

The power of the folk religion in modern China, whether in the diaspora or mainland, has not been destroyed but rather simplified and strengthened by modernization and political change. Proto-scientific systems such as *feng-shui*, or the placing of buildings to utilize the wind and the sun, and *di-li* or the placing of graves so as to preserve natural watersheds, are quite visible throughout maritime China. The festivals and their paraphernalia such as incense, paper money and paper clothes are still seen in the countryside and outlying areas of mainland China. Religion dies hard in modern Asian society because it is a vehicle for self-expression and cultural identity, giving the ego a firm place in family, society and nation. Just as the Chinese who have emigrated to South-East Asia and America are finding new meaning in asserting the festivals of the past, so the peasants and masses of mainland China will restore the celebrations of life's cycle which give meaning to existence in a vital socialist society. Such a phenomenon is possible because religion is a cultural force in China, affirming and strengthening the smooth working of human relationships in the difficult struggle for survival in a hard-working peasant and industrial environment. Religion brings joy and meaning to the passage of life and death in a truly social context.

NOTES

1. 'Irenic' signifies an attitude of peace and acceptance towards other people and their ideas, stemming from the self. 'Ecumenic' connotes a positive effort to understand points held in common between two opposing religious systems. Thus, to the Chinese, Buddhism is a system for the afterlife, Taoism for the present (natural) life and Confucianism for moral virtue. The self is inwardly irenic, outwardly ecumenic with regard to the three religious teachings. There can never be an ecumenism of dogma, only of religious experience.
2. 'Eidetic visualization' means the constructing of an imaginative picture of the Taoist heavens, the arrival of Taoist spirits, or other imaginative contemplations rather in the style of the Ignatian Spiritual Exercises known in Western Christian terms. 'Eidetic' means that the outlines of the meditation are drawn by the classical text, while the meditator himself or herself fills in the outlines with a complete devotional experience of the text. Thus the *eidos* or substantial form of the meditation is fixed by custom, whereas the qualitative or devotional aspects are determined by the meditator.

BIBLIOGRAPHY

1. *Li-Chi* (*Lĭ Kĭ*) (Book of Rites) (tr. J. Legge), Oxford, Clarendon Press, 1885 (Sacred Books of the East, XXVII, XXVIII); Delhi, Motilal Banarsidass, 1966. The text of LIN PO-T'UNG, *Kuan-Hun-Sang-Chi*, Canton, 1845, is translated in SASO, M., *Blue Dragon, White Tiger* (see item 6 below), summarizing the modern adaptations of the *Li-chi* and the *Ta-T'ang K'ai-yüan Li*, Szu-ku Ch'uan-shu, Toyo Bunka, Tokyo, Iwanami Press, 1972.

2. *Complete Home Rituals* (Chia-li Ta-ch'eng), Hsinchu, Chu-lin Press, 1960. This and similar volumes are found throughout maritime China, as popular summaries of the works cited in item 1 above.

3. *Cheng-t'ung Tao-tsang* and *Wan-li Tao-tsang*, Ming dynasty versions of the Taoist Canon, are reprinted in Taiwan and readily available for library and private use; e.g. Taipei, I-wen Press, 1961.

4. SASO, M., *Chuang-lin Hsü Tao-tsang* (The Chuang and Lin Family collections of the Lung-hu Shan Taoist Canon), Taipei, Ch'eng-wen Press, 1975; also SASO, M., *Dōkyō Hiketsu Shusei* (A Collection of Taoist Esoterica), Tokyo, Ryukei Shosha, 1978

5. EBERHARD, W., *The Local Cultures of South and East China* (tr. A. Eberhard), Leiden, Brill, 1968; see also KARLGREN, B., 'Legends and cults in ancient China', *Bulletin of the Museum of Far Eastern Antiquities*, vol. 18, 1946

6. SASO, M., *Blue Dragon, White Tiger* (forthcoming) ch. 2
   BODDE, D., *Festivals in Classical China*, Princeton, NJ, Princeton University Press, 1975

7. KEIGHTLEY, D., *Sources of Shang History: The Oracle-Bone Inscriptions of Bronze Age China*, Berkeley, Calif., University of California Press, 1978

8. LEGGE, J., *The Chinese Classics*, 4 vols., Taipei, 1961; prev. publ., 5 vols., Hong Kong, Author/London, Trübner, 1861–72; 2nd edn, Oxford, Clarendon Press, 1893–5; London, Oxford University Press, 1935; also, Hong Kong University Press, 1960, repr. 1970; New York, Krishna, n.d.

9. FÊNG, YU-LAN, *A History of Chinese Philosophy* (tr. D. Bodde), 2 vols., Princeton, NJ, Princeton University Press, 1952–3

10. LAO, D.C. (tr.), *Lao Tzu: Tao te Ching*, Harmondsworth, Middlesex, Baltimore, Md, Penguin Books, 1963
    WATSON, B. (tr.), *Chuang Tzu: The Complete Works*, New York, Columbia University Press, 1968

11. WATSON, B. (tr.), *Mo Tzu: Basic Writings*, New York, Columbia University Press, 1963

12. KU, CHIEH-KANG, *Ch'in-Han de Fang-shih yü Juei-shih* (Proto-Taoists and Confucianists of the Ch'in-Han Period), Shanghai, Chun-lien Press, 1954

13. LIU, TS'UN-YEN, *Selected Papers*, Leiden, Brill, 1976, ch. 3, pp. 76–148

14. SASO, M., *The Teachings of Taoist Master Chuang*, New Haven, Conn., Yale University Press, 1978, ch. 1 (for a traditional Taoist view of its history, using Chinese and Japanese sources)

15. KUBO, NORITADA, *Chūgoku no Shūkyo Kaikaku*, Kyoto, Hōzōkan, 1966 (The Religious Reformation of China)

16. GROOT, J. J. M. DE, *Sectarianism and Religious Persecution in China*, 2 vols., Amsterdam, Müller, 1903–4; Taipei, Literature House, 1963; other edns: Shannon, Irish University Press, 1973, New York, Barnes & Noble, 1974

17. GROOT, J. J. M. DE, *The Religious System of China*, 6 vols., Leiden, Brill, 1892–1910; Taipei, Literature House, 1964, Ch'eng Wen, 1976
DORÉ, H., *Researches into Chinese Superstitions* (tr. M. Kennelly *et al.*), 13 vols., Shanghai, T'usewei, 1914–; repr. Taipei, Ch'eng Wen, 1966

18. WOLF, A. (ed.), *Religion and Ritual in Chinese Society*, Stanford, Calif., Stanford University Press, 1974. The views of Wolf and Freedman are expressed in the Introduction and Chapter 1, respectively.

19. THOMPSON, L. G., *Chinese Religion: An Introduction*, 3rd edn, Belmont, Calif., Wadsworth, 1979
THOMPSON, L. G., *Studies of Chinese Religion: A Comprehensive and Classified Bibliography* . . ., Encino, Calif., Dickenson, 1976

20. SCHIPPER, K. M., *Le Fen-teng, rituel taôiste*, Paris, École Française d'Extrême-Orient, 1975
AHERN, E., *The Cult of the Dead in a Chinese Village*, Stanford, Calif., Stanford University Press, 1973
JORDAN, D. K., *Gods, Ghosts and Ancestors*, Berkeley, Calif., University of California Press, 1972
LIU, CHIH-WAN, *Rites of Propitiation* (Sung-shan Ch'i-an Chien Chiao Chi-tien), Nankang, Academia Sinica, 1967

21. KUBO, NORITADA, *Dōkyō-shi* (A History of Taoism), Tokyo, Yomakawa Press, 1978

22. LIU, CHIH-WAN, *Chung-kuo Min-chien Hsinyang Lun-chi* (A Treatise on Chinese Popular Religion), Nankang, Academia Sinica, 1974

23. SASO, M., *Taoism and the Rite of Cosmic Renewal*, Pullman, Wash., Washington State University Press, 1972

24. SASO, M., and CHAPPELL, D. (eds.), *Buddhist and Taoist Notions of Transcendence*, Honolulu, University of Hawaii Press, 1977 (Buddhist and Taoist Studies 1)

25. *Rites of Origin: A Taoist Festival* (videotape production, ¾ in. KCA, ½ in. Betamax, 30 mins.), Honolulu, University of Hawaii, Department of Religion, 1980 (a visual study of the ritual)

26. 'Monthly Commands' chapter, *Book of Rites* (Li-chi, Yüeh-ling) reveals the Confucian origin of this Taoist rite. See SASO, M., 'On the Ling-pao Chen-wen', *Tōhō Shūkyō* (Tokyo), vol. 50, November 1977, pp. 22–40

27. 'The Tao-ch'ang ritual', *Rites of Origin*, item 25 above, last segment

28. *Lao Tzu: Tao te Ching* (see item 10 above), ch. 66
29. *Li-Chi* (see item 1 above), 1885, bk 1, pp. 62, 116, 257
30. FÊNG, YU-LAN, *A Short History of Chinese Philosophy* (tr. and ed. D. Bodde), New York, Macmillan, 1962, pp. 42–8; prev. publ. 1948
31. MORGAN, E., *Tao, The Great Luminant*, Shanghai, Kelly & Walsh, repr. Taipei, Ch'eng Wen, 1966 (Translations from the Huai-nan-tzu); London, Trübner, 1935; New York, Paragon, 1969
32. GROOT, J. J. M. DE, *Buddhist Masses for the Dead at Amoy: Acts of the Sixth International Conference of Orientalists*, Leiden, 1885
33. EBERHARD, W., *Guilt and Sin in Traditional China*, Berkeley, Calif., University of California Press, 1967, pp. 47–55
34. WOLF, A., 'Gods, ghosts and ancestors', in: A. Wolf (ed.), see item 18 above, pp. 179–82 (discusses the various uses of paper money)
35. SUZUKI, S., *Kan-kon-so-sai* (The Chinese Rites of Passage), Taipei, Nichi-nichi Press, 1934
36. IKEDA, T., *Taiwan no Katei Seikatsu* (Daily Life and Customs in Taiwan), Taipei, Toto Press, 1944
37. LIN, PO-T'UNG, *Kuan-Hun-Sang-Chi* (The Rites of Passage), 3 vols., Canton, 1845 (for the rites of marriage and burial) (wood-block prints)
38. BODDE, D. (ed. and tr.), TUN, LI-CH'ÊN, *Annual Customs and Festivals in Peking, as Recorded in the Yen-ching Sui-shih-chi*, 2nd edn, Hong Kong University Press, 1965; also EBERHARD, W., *Chinese Festivals*, Taipei, 1964, prev. publ. New York, H. Schuman, 1952, London, New York, A. Schuman, 1958, and SASO, M., *Blue Dragon, White Tiger* (see item 6 above)
39. SASO, M., *Taoism and the Rite of Cosmic Renewal* (see item 23 above)
40. WALEY, A., *The Nine Songs: A Study of Shamanism in Ancient China*, London, Allen & Unwin, 1955

D. REID

Introduction

Religion is frequently studied as a matter of personal belief. This is not always possible in Japan, where religious phenomena include many dimensions to which faith is irrelevant. Shinto festivals and Buddhist mortuary rites, for example, are not commonly thought of as part of personal religion. None the less, there are also dimensions where personal belief is essential, as in the majority of sects (Shinto, Buddhist, Christian and other). Yet again, a few sects (mainly Buddhist) place no emphasis whatever on faith, preferring a 'try-it-and-see' attitude. One thing that these disparate religious phenomena have in common is behaviour. In this discussion, behaviour will be recognized as 'religious' if it expresses a relationship with a divine being or beings, as in Shinto, popular Buddhism, Christianity and folk religion, or with a life-transforming ultimate/immanent principle, as in elite forms of Buddhism.

Living religion in Japan, as in other countries, includes an organizational dimension. Religious organizations have their own internal histories, to be sure, but for the student of Japanese religion and society more important is the question of the changing relationships between religious organizations and the state. Throughout most Japanese history, the state has set the terms within which such organizations could exist. It is important, therefore, to give a brief account of the continuing story of the interplay between religious organizations and state power.

RELIGIOUS STUDIES IN JAPAN

Broadly construed, the term 'religious studies' as used in Japan includes every academic discipline that takes religion as its object of study. Narrowly construed, the term excludes not only theological and philosophical studies but also historical and textual studies. It is limited to disciplines in which contemporary religious phenomena are studied empirically and, at least in principle, comparatively. Phenomenology of religion, anthropology of religion, psychology of religion, and sociology of religion constitute the principal disciplines.

THE 'LITTLE TRADITION' MATRIX

'Great' traditions are usually distinguished from 'little' traditions by the existence of highly developed systems of thought and doctrine in the former and the relatively weak development of such systems in the latter. On this basis, the term 'little tradition' will be applied to Shinto in its three principal forms: folk Shinto, Shrine Shinto and Sect Shinto. The term 'great traditions' will refer to Buddhism, Confucianism and Christianity.

Shinto has a highly complex history of its own. It resists systematic portrayal. One may identify, however, two general tendencies in Japanese ways of thinking that have their roots in Shinto. One deep-seated and far-reaching motif is the emphasis on Shinto as something that unifies. Ideally, its festivals unite people with the *kami*, the divine beings, more immanent than transcendent, who desire to see their people enjoying a life of communal harmony and abundance, filled with dynamic vitality and purity of heart. Socially, this unity is sought primarily at two levels: the local community and the national community. In both cases the expectation is that the oneness achieved, whether or not interpreted religiously, will lead to increasing productivity, creativity and prosperity. In all this, the role of the Emperor is central. For historical reasons to be touched on later, the Emperor is the chief priest of the Shinto world. In modern Japan (from 1868 onwards), he has also played a key role in the Japanese state. Together, these two roles helped shape the stubborn problem of the relationship between religion and state power. From 701 CE, when the law of the land was first codified, until 1945, when defeat in war led to the institutionalization of the hitherto alien value of government neutrality in respect of religion, the dominant assumption was that upright religion was properly at the service of the state [18: 162]. This centuries-old feature of the 'little tradition', issuing as a general tendency, strongly affected the way people perceived, evaluated and modified the imported 'great traditions'.

The other motif of Shinto thought to be considered here is the emphasis on different kinds of divinities or *kami*. Ichiro Hori distinguishes between two main types: clan *kami* and charismatic *kami* [16: 30–34]. Clan *kami*, associated with rites for the ancestors, were initially the ritual focus of territorially limited and mutually exclusive quasi-genealogical bodies. Generally beneficent, *kami* of this type had no clearly defined personalities or functions. Charismatic *kami*, associated with local shrines, were originally objects of faith who united people from different social groups. Such *kami* had sharply defined personalities and performed specific functions, such as healing. Over the years, these two types became intertwined. In modern Japan, Shrine Shinto can be viewed as a religion of clan *kami* in an enlarged, more comprehensive sense. The *kami* of local communities have their parishes, and the *kami* associated with the imperial household embrace the entire nation. In both cases they unite people in a sense that transcends the genealogical nexus. The charismatic *kami* come into view primarily in the new religious movements. These movements will receive consideration later, but here it should be emphasized that for centuries people with urgent personal problems have sought help from one charismatic *kami* or another, one shamanic leader or another. Such practices and expectations have given rise to the general tendency to assume that religion oriented to a 'living *kami*' should provide tangible, this-worldly benefits. This tendency has likewise guided people's perceptions, evaluations and modifications of the imported 'great traditions'.

Religious Traditions in Japanese History

The story of the interaction between religious traditions and the state is a continuing one. Borrowing the administrative classifications employed in the organization of statistical data (see Table 10.1), we shall divide this history into four periods representing cumulative layers of religious tradition.

SHINTO PERIOD (PRE-SIXTH CENTURY CE)

The key development in the first period was the regionally limited establishment, about the middle of the fourth century CE, of a hereditary priestly rule that, exceptions aside, continues to the present day in the imperial household. The religious practices later given the name 'Shinto' are closely tied to the priestly role of the Empresses and Emperors in this line. These practices, fundamentally concerned with food and the sun, involved priestly tasks not only for the chief ruler but also for the heads of the many clans. The beings whose favour they sought, the *kami*, were of many kinds: *kami* of nature, *kami* of ideas, *kami* in outstanding people, ancestral *kami* etc. [15:672]. Two major festivals were held, one in the spring to pray for a successful harvest, the other in the autumn to celebrate the harvest granted. Divination and purification were important features. The reigning Empress or Emperor, who had to observe many taboos, was regarded as possessing the mystical power to receive influences from the sun goddess, augment the food supply, and thereby control the well-being of the people.

SHINTO-BUDDHIST PERIOD (538-1549)

In 538 (or 552 according to some scholars) when Buddhism was introduced from Korea, the political situation in Japan was unsettled. Clan heads were in effect the heads of village states. Imperial court control, though growing,

Table 10.1. Numbers of adherents to major classes of religious tradition in Japan between 1953 and 1978

| Year | Annual numbers of adherents by tradition | | | | | Population of Japan |
	Shinto	Buddhist	Christian	Other	Total	
1953	77,780,324	47,714,876	485,399	3,419,471	129,400,070	86,981,463
1958	76,844,827	48,974,838	652,518	4,010,745	130,482,928	91,767,079
1963	80,284,643	69,843,367	711,636	5,350,790	156,190,436	96,155,847
1968	83,458,684	83,278,496	831,335	6,768,042	174,336,557	101,330,883
1973	87,414,779	84,573,828	879,477	10,002,986	182,871,070	109,103,610
1978	98,545,703	88,020,880	950,491	13,729,376	201,246,450	115,174,112

Sources: Figures on adherents are taken from the Ministry of Education *Shukyo Nenkan* (Religions Yearbook). They represent the numbers of people claimed by religious organizations as of 31 December in a given year. The population figures are estimates prepared by the Bureau of Statistics, Office of the Prime Minister. They represent the situation as of 1 October in a given year.

was by no means complete. Buddhism was seen, on the one hand, by the court as a way of promoting a spiritual outlook that would support its claims to 'universality' with magico-religious power, but, on the other hand, by village-state heads as a threat to autonomy and tradition. Confucian morality, entering Japan in the fifth century together with the Chinese system of writing, weakly complemented Buddhism as an ordering of human relation-ships that strengthened the hand of male power-holders. Efforts to centralize political power included the development of official compilations of Shinto myth and legend, so organized as to centre on the imperial house.

Between 538 and 1549, Buddhism took deeper root in successive waves of sectarian tradition (see Figure 10.1). The Nara, Tendai and Shingon sects were imported from China between the seventh and ninth centuries, when political power resided in the imperial court. The Pure Land, Zen and Nichiren sects, more interested in winning believers among the masses, began just before and during the Kamakura period (1185–1333) when leading men of the military or samurai class were seizing political power and the Emperor was sinking into obscurity. The changing relationships between Shinto and Buddhism reflect these political conditions. When power was held by the court, Buddhist thinkers, then in favour, accommodated Shinto to Buddhism. When power fell to the Kamakura military government, Shinto thinkers, in reaction, accommodated Buddhism to Shinto. In time, the two became interwoven both doctrinally and institutionally.

SHINTO–BUDDHIST–CHRISTIAN PERIOD (1549–1802)

Christianity entered the scene in 1549. The shogunate (government under the shogun or leading general) was then at a low ebb. Fief heads or daimyos, relatively autonomous, warred with one another to enlarge their domains. Tendai, Nichiren and Pure Land soldier-monks armed themselves, fortified their monasteries and took sides in the fray. Under Nobunaga Oda (1534–82) order was restored in central Japan, but in the process opposing monasteries were razed and thousands of monks killed. His successor, Hideyoshi Toyotomi (1536–98), established a military dictatorship over the entire country. Christianity was outlawed in a series of inconsistently enforced edicts that began with Hideyoshi's expulsion of Catholic missionaries in 1587 and his crucifixion of twenty-six Japanese and foreign Christians in 1596. It grew under Ieyasu Tokugawa (1542–1616) to include the exiling of Japanese Christians to Manila and Macao in 1612 and the further executing of Christians under his son Hidetada (1578–1632). The opposition to Christianity cul-minated in an absolute prohibition following the abortive Shimabara Revolt of 1637–8.

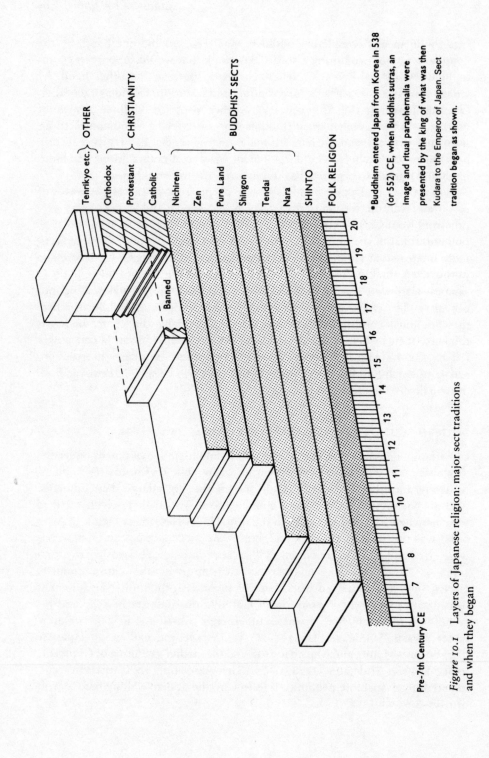

*Buddhism entered Japan from Korea in 538 (or 552) CE, when Buddhist sutras, an image and ritual paraphernalia were presented by the king of what was then Kudara to the Emperor of Japan. Sect tradition began as shown.

OTHER
CHRISTIANITY
BUDDHIST SECTS

Tenrikyo etc.
Orthodox
Protestant
Catholic
Nichiren
Zen
Pure Land
Shingon
Tendai
Nara
SHINTO
FOLK RELIGION

Banned

20 19 18 17 16 15 14 13 12 11 10 9 8 7

Pre-7th Century CE

Figure 10.1 Layers of Japanese religion: major sect traditions and when they began

Buddhism was put into government service with the establishment of the *danka seido* (1638), a system that required every Japanese household to affiliate with a local temple, and the *terauke seido* (1662), where every adult was required to obtain annually from this temple a certificate attesting that he or she was innocent of association with subversive religion. These developments led to the formation of underground Christian congregations – some of which persist today. Not surprisingly, mandatory ties to Buddhist temples, the only institutions then authorized to conduct mortuary rites, weakened voluntary interest in Buddhism. Temple ties became more a matter of obtaining ritual services for the household dead than a matter of seeking enlightenment.

One stream of religious tradition conspicuous in this period is *shugendo*, the way that leads to magico-religious power through ascetic practices in the mountains (see Figure 10.2). A blend of folk Shinto, esoteric Buddhism and *yin–yang* Taoist magic (see pages 349ff), this tradition traces its origin to the legend-surrounded shaman En-no-Gyoja of the Nara period (710–94). Several centuries later, under the hereditary Tokugawa shogunate, the formerly unregulated ascetics were brought under government control as part of an overall policy towards religious movements and organizations.

During the seventeenth century, Neo-Confucianism came to play an influential role. The Tokugawa shogunate encouraged Confucian studies both in its own schools and in fief schools throughout the nation in order to mould samurai ideas and behaviour. In the eighteenth century, through private schools for commoners, Confucian principles spread among craftsmen, merchants and farmers. In the Mito fief (part of what is now Ibaraki Prefecture, located just north-east of Tokyo) these studies led to the *Dai Nihon Shi*, a multi-volume history of Japan inculcating the idea of the *kami*-descended imperial line as the only legitimate basis of authority and enlarging the principles of loyalty and filial piety by identifying the Emperor as the supreme object of such virtues. These ideas, transmuted into Shinto restorationism, helped bring an end to seven centuries of samurai rule.

SHINTO–BUDDHIST–CHRISTIAN–OTHER PERIOD (1802–)

Since 1802, two major developments affecting the Japanese people and their institutions have taken place. One was the restoration of the Emperor (1868), the other defeat in war (1945). (Post-1945 developments are treated in the final section.)

During the turbulent closing years of the Tokugawa shogunate and the early years of the restoration government, a number of new religious organizations appeared (see Table 10.2). The harbinger of this development appeared in 1802, which thus marks the turn from the preceding to the present period.

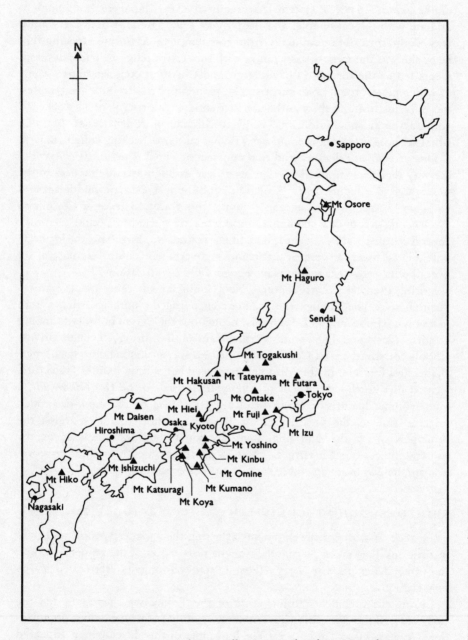

Figure 10.2   Japanese mountains historically associated with magico-religious power

Table 10.2. Some surviving new religious organizations in Japan: year of origin, classification and current membership

Period	Shinto Origin	Name	Members	Buddhist Origin	Name	Members	Other Origin	Name	Members
1801–1900	1814	Kurozumi-kyo	218,240	1802	Nyorai-kyo	34,030	1838	Tenrikyo	2,525,759
	1840	Misogikyo	124,960	1857	Honmon Butsuryushu	465,158			
	1843	Shinrikyo	266,120						
	1859	Konkokyo	480,072						
	1873	Maruyama-kyo	3,251						
	1873	Ontake-kyo	734,390						
	1873	Izumo Oyashirokyo	1,051,206						
	1892	Omoto	163,760						
1901–45	1913	Honmichi	480,072	1914	Kokuchukai	22,706	1919	Ennokyo	306,975
				1917	Nihonzan Myohoji	1,120	1924	PL (Perfect Liberty) Kyodan	2,658,872
				1923	Reiyukai	2,838,000	1930	Seicho no Ie	3,242,911
				1925	Nenpo Shinkyo	862,030	1934	Sekai Kyuseikyo	803,841
				1929	Gedatsukai	216,528			
				1930	Soka Gakkai	16,539,375			
				1935	Kodo Kyodan	417,636			
				1938	Rissho Koseikai	5,081,286			
Post-1945	1949	Ananaikyo	201,360	1948	Shinnyo-en	543,959	1945	Tensho Kotai Jingukyo	401,572
				1950	Myochikai Kyodan	686,205	1947	Zenrinkai	602,153
				1950	Bussho Gonenkai	1,354,662			
				1951	Saijo Inari-kyo	286,270			

Sources: Membership figures, voluntarily reported, are for 31 December 1978, as found in the 1979 edition of the Shukyo Nenkan (Religions Yearbook). The list of organizations follows Murakami [24: 170–71].

Nyorai-kyo, a body classified as Buddhist, began as a faith-healing sect based on the belief that its founder, a peasant woman named Kino (1756–1826), was a living *kami* and prophet of a better life in the next world. When the restoration government took control, it disestablished Buddhism and established Shinto in its place, identifying it not as a religion, which would have made it voluntary, but as an ethic, obligatory for all the Emperor's subjects. Institutionally intertwined for centuries, Shinto and Buddhism were forcibly separated. The *shugendo* organizations, an inseparable amalgam of traditions, were ordered to disband. Many *shugendo* ideas, however, were taken up into the new religious organizations – ideas such as spirit-possession, exorcism, faith-healing and leaders deemed living *kami* or living buddhas.[1]

The government classification for most of the new religious organizations of these years was (and is) Sect Shinto, a term coined to distinguish them from 'non-religious' State Shinto. The movements thus grouped together can be understood as belonging to four types:

Shinto revivalism: Shinrikyo, Izumo Oyashirokyo.
Purification: Misogikyo.
Mountain worship: Maruyama-kyo, Ontake-kyo.
Faith-healing: Kurozumi-kyo, Tenrikyo, Konkokyo, Omoto. (Tenrikyo, in order to emphasize its universality, was reclassified as 'Other' at its own request in 1970.)

Honmon Butsuryushu, founded in 1857 by the Nichiren Buddhist priest Nissen Nagamatsu (1817–90), is significant as the first of the lay Buddhist associations to emphasize conversion to faith in the *Lotus Sutra* as essential to the welfare of individuals and of the nation.

From 1859 on, Christian missionaries reintroduced Christianity. Churches, schools and medical care were the main forms through which Christians, Japanese and foreign, sought to plant the new faith. Christianity found a moderate welcome as Japan ended over two centuries of seclusion from the West, but met with disapproval as nationalistic feeling and war fever began to mount from about 1890. It remains a minority religion.

The anti-Buddhist iconoclasm that occurred in many areas with the turn to State Shinto lasted only a few years. When cooler heads prevailed, Buddhism was given government protection. Until 1945, however, the mythology of State Shinto became an increasingly rigid norm. New religious bodies were required to conform or be crushed by state power [24: 48–51, 95–109].

It can be seen that continental Buddhism entered Japan during the shift from clan government to imperial government when a difficult reorientation of values was in process. Buddhism as a popular religion took hold during the shift from imperial to military government, another reorientation. Christianity arrived during a temporary shift to domain government, was ousted soon after the restoration of centralized military rule when Neo-Confucian influence was strong, and returned during the swing to a new imperial government under the aegis of Shinto Restorationism. The new religious organizations came into being during the decades bracketing the restoration of imperial rule, during the economic depression and totalitarian controls following the First World War, and, to anticipate, during the period of economic and spiritual distress following the Second World War. In broad perspective, then, it appears that significant religious developments have tended to coincide with periods of political unrest and value-confusion. This finding is reinforced when one turns to the religious leaders of these times.

Religious Leaders and Their Teachings

One cultural thread evident throughout Japanese history is the tendency to honour only what has a clearly traceable lineage. Arguments supporting the legitimacy of the imperial house rarely fail to mention its 'direct and un-broken succession' – a cultural norm even if not a historical fact. In the same way, a person recognized as an outstanding religious leader is frequently revered not only for what he taught but also because he founded a sect that takes pride in tracing its origin back to 'the founder'.

Saicho (767–822), who founded the Japanese Tendai sect tradition in 805 after studying it in China, exemplifies a tendency now common among Japanese Buddhists: to seek the absolute not beyond but within the present world. He was the first to coin the phrase *sokushin jobutsu*, 'to become a living buddha'. This has come to mean that one need not await countless rebirths or undergo endless austerities in order to achieve buddhahood; one can become a living buddha in this lifetime. This teaching has had an immense influence on new Buddhist organizations in the modern period, particularly those that, with Tendai, attach special importance to the *Lotus Sutra* and its doctrine that all forms of existence, animate and inanimate, are filled with – and can realize – the Buddha nature.

Kukai (774–835), after studying Tantric Buddhism in China, founded the Japanese Shingon sect in 816. He taught that the entire universe is the body of the Supreme Buddha, Vairocana, and thus that absolute truth and this-worldly phenomena are essentially identical. Synthesizing Buddhist and non-Buddhist philosophies into ten stages of realization culminating in Tantrism, he further taught that meditation, ritual postures and mystical syllables are uniquely important as symbolic representations of, and channels for, the living substance of the cosmos. This teaching appears to underlie the wide-spread ritual practice of chanting the title of the *Lotus Sutra*.

Honen (1133–1212) and his disciple Shinran (1173–1262) lived at a time when the idea of the impending dissolution of the world was current. Like earlier itinerant holy men, they sought to make the way of enlightenment available to people of all classes and conditions. Both taught that the way of enlightenment most appropriate for 'this degenerate age' was not that of ascetic exercises but rather of simple reliance on the power and compassion of Amitabha (Japanese: Amida) Buddha, who had vowed to help people and was sure to welcome them into his Pure Land. Honen, urging people to call on Amida and gain enlightenment, founded the Pure Land Sect in 1175. Shinran, more radical, held that Amida had already fulfilled his vow and that people only needed to accept their enlightenment through faith. This made the celibate monastic life, till then deemed essential to salvation, logically unnecessary. Shinran therefore renounced it, married, and demonstrated that Amida's way applied unconditionally to lay people in the secular world. His organization, the True Pure Land sect, dates from 1224.

The two main forms of Zen Buddhism, Rinzai and Soto, were introduced from China by the Japanese priests Eisai (1141–1215) and Dogen (1200–53). Eisai, favoured by the Kamakura shogunate, taught a way of enlightenment through enigmatic questions that threw the seeker into a quandary but could lead to a flash of saving insight. His ties were mainly with the newly dominant samurai class. Dogen, less reliant on political patronage but more reliant on scriptural authority, taught that the way to enlightenment is through *shikan taza*, 'seated meditation alone'. His ties were mainly with the unlettered and often superstitious peasant class. The present influence of Zen is seen not only in chastely styled architecture and gardens that communicate a oneness with nature and ultimate reality, but also in cultural and martial-arts groups where mastery of techniques goes hand in hand with spiritual training (rarely thought of as religious).

Nichiren (1222–82) is by far the most confrontational of Japanese religious leaders, and the sect tradition that bears his name has been the most prone to schism. Like many before him, including Saicho and Dogen, Nichiren treated the *Lotus Sutra* as the highest scriptural authority, but unlike his predecessors, he taught that it was imperative for the welfare of Japan that the government rid the nation of false ways (primarily the Shingon, Zen and Pure Land sects) and establish as the state religion the true Buddhism he proclaimed. This teaching, in subsequent variations, looms large in the development of several new religious organizations.

In the Shinto world Kanetomo Yoshida (1435–1511), founder of Yoshida Shinto, took as his point of departure a thirteenth-century school of thought called Ise Shinto. In contrast with Buddhist thinkers who had interpreted the Shinto *kami* as demigods in need of enlightenment or, later, as avataras (see page 200) of specific buddhas and *bodhisattvas*, Ise Shinto had declared that the basic reality of the universe was a *kami* through whom the buddhas and *bodhisattvas* had their being. Yoshida, going a step further, sought to develop a Shinto free of Buddhist influences by emphasizing purity of heart as a mystical form of worship.

Japanese Neo-Confucianism began with Seika Fujiwara (1561–1619). Both he and his illustrious disciple Razan Hayashi (1583–1657), one of the most influential Confucian advisers to the first Tokugawa shogun, taught that the way of Confucius was virtuous in so far as it fitted into the way of the *kami*, the way of the Emperor. They regarded Buddhism as inferior for teaching a universal law that concealed differential obligations according to social rank. As often noted, the traditional Confucian doctrines of abdication and justifiable rebellion could not be accommodated in Japan. Under Mitsukuni Tokugawa (1628–1700), founder of the Mito school, Neo-Confucian teachings were recast in such a way as to uphold the superiority of the Emperor over daimyo and shogun, yet also in such a way as to soften the distinction between ruler and ruled by presenting the Emperor as a caring father.

Norinaga Motoori (1730–1801) was the founder of a movement to purify Shinto of all Buddhist and Confucian accretions. Atsutane Hirata (1776–1843) went even further, developing into an anti-foreign chauvinist as he promoted restoration of power to the imperial house. The influence of these and other leaders – Buddhist, Confucian and Shinto – who cannot all be dealt with here, lives on in modern Japan.

The Religious Population of Contemporary Japan

SOME STATISTICS

The estimated population of Japan on 1 October 1978 was 115 million. Of this number, how many people belonged to religious organizations and, more broadly, how many regarded themselves as religious?

To answer the first question, data from the *Shukyo Nenkan* (Religions Yearbook) are usually employed. But immediately one confronts an anomaly. In 1978 the total number of adherents to the major classes of religious tradition was 201 million, a figure almost 75 per cent larger than the population (see Figure 10.3 and Table 10.1). This 'discrepancy' is generally accounted for by two facts: dual or multiple affiliation; and inflated membership reports. Whatever the case, it is useless to compare these figures (population and adherents) in the expectation of determining what proportion of the population belongs to religious organizations and what proportion does not. One can, however, consider survey findings. One survey, published in 1979, asked

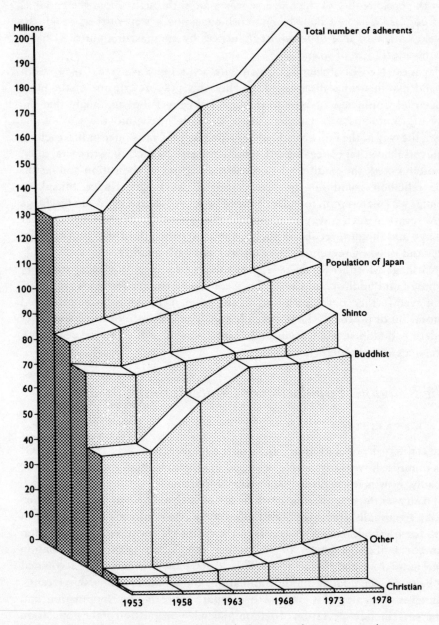

Figure 10.3 Adherents to major classes of religious tradition in Japan between 1953 and 1978 (see also Table 10.2)

people about their membership in organizations of various kinds. With regard to religious organizations, only 13·6 per cent said they were members [14: 133]. This percentage, applied to the 1978 population, suggests that only 15·6 million out of 115 million people counted themselves as adherents of religious organizations.

Living religion is by no means limited to members of religious organizations. Another survey, conducted in 1979, asked people if they professed any religious faith. Affirmative replies to this question amounted to 33·6 per cent [14: 133]. Most people replying in the affirmative went on to identify their faith as Buddhist (78·4 per cent). Only a handful (3·3 per cent) identified their faith as Shinto – almost certainly Sect Shinto rather than the district-organized Shrine Shinto in which the question of faith rarely occurs. But since most Japanese people of religious persuasion are both Shinto parishioners and Buddhist temple supporters, it is perhaps not unreasonable to suppose that about the same number of people can be found in both camps. If so, the religious population of present-day Japan can be reckoned at about one-third of the total population.

CONTEMPORARY RELIGIOUS PRACTICES

Before 1945 Japanese households traditionally had both a *kami* altar (*kami-dana*) and a buddha altar (*butsudan*). To a lesser extent, the same holds true today. Rural households, especially, often have several *kami* altars: one main altar and other minor altars. In a rough division of labour, the *kami* altar is generally associated with life and the avoidance of whatever impedes vitality and productivity, the buddha altar with death and the veneration of those who are becoming or who have become ancestors. On both, offerings of food and drink are reverently presented at the beginning of each day.

The Shinto and Buddhist practices of ordinary people may be grouped under two headings: the annual cycle and the life-cycle. (For a list of major festivals see Table 10.3; for a picture of the pattern they form see Figure 10.4.)

The New Year season involves a number of activities now largely associated with Shinto. Some of these activities are oriented to the household, some to the national community. At the end of a year, households throughout the land 'clean the slate' by giving the house, yard and adjacent road a thorough cleaning and by paying off all debts due. Entrances are decorated with ever-greens and shafts of cut bamboo. (According to the widely accepted theory of Kunio Yanagita, New Year was originally a festival to welcome the ancestral spirits, apparently conceived of as diminutive, like songbirds or fire-flies. He saw the bamboo shafts as their 'landing sites'.) For three days or so, people lay aside their daily work in order to be with their families, send

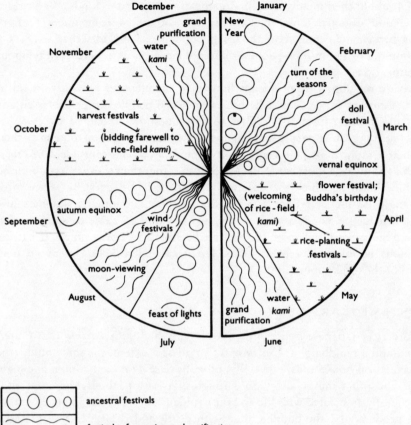

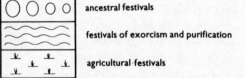

Figure 10.4 Annual pattern of major Japanese festivals (see also Table 10.3)

out New Year's greetings, call on and give gifts to elderly relatives, teachers and others. They wear their best clothes and eat special foods. Today, any awareness of the purported connection between New Year and the ancestors is dim, except that if a family loses one of its members, it will not celebrate the next New Year. Closer to the spirit of national community is the practice of visiting a big-name shrine or temple at New Year. According to police estimates, the number of people who went to such institutions rose from 25 million in 1965 to 60 million in 1976. In 1979 some 56 per cent of the total population made such visits.

Table 10.3. Annual major festivals (see also Figure 10.4)*

Date or period	Japanese name	English paraphrase
1–6 January	Shogatsu	New Year
3 February	Setsubun	Turn of the seasons
3 March	Hina Matsuri	Doll festival
21 March	Haru no Higan	Vernal equinox
8 April	Hana Matsuri	Flower festival; Buddha's birthday
April–May	Taue Matsuri	Rice-planting festivals†
15 June	Suijin Matsuri	Water *kami* festival
30 June	Oharai	Grand purification
‡13–16 July	Bon	Feast of lights
‡15 August	Tsukimi	Moon-viewing
‡August	Kaza Matsuri	Wind festivals†
23 September	Aki no Higan	Autumnal equinox
October–November	Shukaku Matsuri	Harvest festivals†
1 December	Suijin Matsuri	Water *kami* festival
31 December	Oharai	Grand purification

* For explanations of these and other festivals, see Hori [18: 126–32]; for a remarkable essay on one local festival, see Yanagawa [35].

† Where the word 'festivals' occurs, festival observance dates vary with the locality.

‡ These dates and periods are those of the lunar calendar, presently about one month ahead of the solar calendar.

The midsummer feast of lights or Bon festival is a community-wide activity in which, traditionally, individual households welcome their visiting ancestral spirits and entertain them communally. At this time the house is cleaned and decorated with fresh fruit and flowers. Meat foods are generally taboo. A small welcoming fire is built just outside the gate in order to guide the spirits. People dress up in light, summer-weight kimonos, and entire communities hold outdoor dances and displays of fireworks to celebrate the occasion. It closes with 'seeing-off' fires, in some areas prepared on hundreds of tiny floats set adrift on streams or lakes at nightfall – a spectacular sight. Most of today's urban residents or their recent forebears came from a rural area where the 'old homestead' is still located and where the ancestral tablets are kept. Millions of people, therefore, travel to the country for these family reunions and, a few days later, return to the cities. Officially, the Bon festival is not a national holiday. Some idea of its importance to ordinary people can be gained, however, from the realization that over half the industries in Japan give workers a few days off at this time.

The spring and autumn equinoxes are also times when the ancestors are honoured. Trips to the 'old homestead' are not necessary. Instead, a few relatives get together and visit the family grave in their area. They clean and sweep the site, pour water on the gravestone, present flowers, incense, food and drink, and offer silent prayer. If nobody has died recently and the pain of parting has passed, the occasion may well be a happy one, with the children playing games and all enjoying a picnic.

Community-wide festivals associated with Shinto shrines are usually held once a year. The timing varies with the community, but the major festivals follow much the same pattern: a formal service for purification of the parish representatives and for invocation of the *kami*; removal of the *kami*-symbol from the inner sanctuary and its ritual installation in a scaled-down portable shrine (often weighing several tons); a solemn or boisterous procession whereby the *kami* tours and infuses new life into the parish; a feast at the shrine where the priest and parish representatives enjoy food, drink and entertainment expressive of the new vigour bestowed by the *kami*; and the formal rite of ushering the *kami* back into the inner sanctuary. In small, rural communities, as young people leave for the towns and cities, it becomes increasingly difficult to hold festivals in the usual way. Not uncommonly, the scaled-down shrine now has to be borne not on the shoulders of stalwart young men chanting in rhythm but on a truck equipped with a loudspeaker. Conversely, in growing communities festivals find considerable support, usually for a combination of reasons, sometimes mainly religious, at others mainly secular.

The life-cycle has its focus in the individual, but its context is the family. *Birth* is associated with the local Shinto shrine. On or about the thirtieth day after birth, the child is taken to the shrine and presented to the *kami*. From that time on, the child is under the care of the divinity. This point receives ritual reinforcement a few years later when girls of three and seven years of age, and boys of five, are dressed up and taken to the shrine in mid-November. *Marriage* did not become a religious ceremony until the twentieth century. Since 1901, when the first Shinto wedding was performed, Shinto rites have gradually become the accepted way of uniting households through matrimony, though Christian rites (not necessarily requiring faith) are becoming increasingly popular. *Death* is by far the most complex rite of passage. Buddhism is the main religious tradition involved, but the legal abolition of the extended family and its replacement by the nuclear family is leading to a different way of identifying the ancestors. Until 1945 the ancestors in the paternal line were the principal objects of veneration. Women who married out of the family had their names struck out of the family record, and affines were treated, in death, more as guests than as family members. Since 1945, however, many people, especially those in their thirties and forties, are coming to venerate both the paternal and maternal lines. As before, the process of becoming an ancestor calls for thirty-three to fifty years of ritual observances, some at the Buddhist temple, others before the buddha altar in the home.

Post-1945 Developments

In 1945, as a direct result of defeat in war, religious freedom supported by government neutrality *vis-à-vis* religion became a reality for the first time in Japanese history. In this new situation hundreds of new religious organizations sprang up. Most proved ephemeral, some downright fraudulent. Most of the sizeable groups trace their origin to the years between the First and Second World Wars, but it was after 1945 that they grew by leaps and bounds (see Figures 10.5 and 10.6). This growth provided part of the stimulus for internal reform movements among several older bodies.

With regard to the surviving new religious organizations, some of which are listed in Table 10.2, those mentioned may be considered representative of many [18: 89–104]. The most conspicuous organizations, like Honmon Butsuryushu before them, are associations of lay Buddhists who give pride of place to the *Lotus Sutra* and seek to reform Japanese society. Two streams may be distinguished. The first is Soka Gakkai. Largest of all, it is theoretically under the Nichiren Shoshu, a monastic organization that claims exclusive legitimacy as heir to the teachings of Nichiren. One of the fundamental goals of the Nichiren Shoshu is to see the Emperor and the government converted to the form of Buddhism it proclaims as exclusively true. Religious freedom and government neutrality towards religion have no place in its world-view. But its independently formed lay association, Soka Gakkai, has come out in favour of religious freedom and separation of state and religion. The short history of the relationship between Soka Gakkai and the Nichiren Shoshu, not to mention the latter's other lay associations, has been one of tension and near-schism. Through its network of neighbourhood groups, however, Soka Gakkai has brought help to millions of people more concerned about personal problems than about abstract questions of principle and authority.

The second stream runs through the tradition connecting Reiyukai and one of its many offshoots, Rissho Koseikai. The importance of memorial rites for ancestors and faith in the *Lotus Sutra* are the two main tenets of Reiyukai. Particularly notable in this group is its practice of having members venerate ancestors in both the paternal and maternal lines. Some scholars derive this practice from the circumstance that in its early days Reiyukai drew its members from economically peripheral families in which both parents had to work for pay. At any rate it anticipated the bilateral memorial rites increasingly practised among Japanese families in general since legal entitlement of the nuclear family and the growth of the idea of male–female equality.

Rissho Koseikai also honours the *Lotus Sutra* and the ancestors, but its

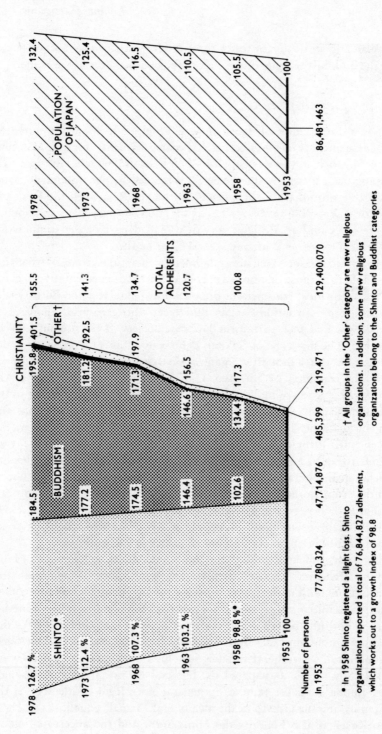

Figure 10.5 Growth indices for major classes of religious tradition in Japan between 1953 and 1978

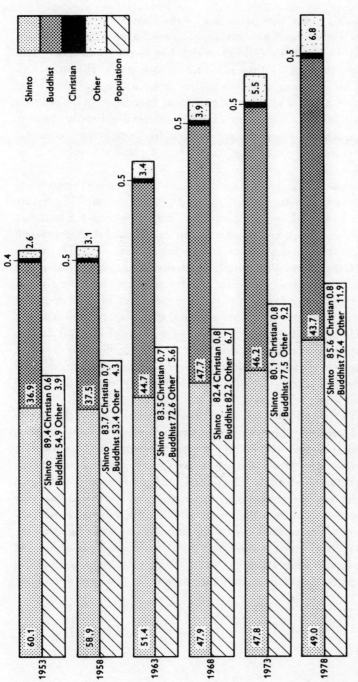

Legend:
- Shinto
- Buddhist
- Christian
- Other
- Population

1953
- 60.1
- 36.9
- 0.4
- 2.6
- Shinto 89.4 Christian 0.6
- Buddhist 54.9 Other 3.9

1958
- 58.9
- 37.5
- 0.5
- 3.1
- Shinto 83.7 Christian 0.7
- Buddhist 53.4 Other 4.3

1963
- 51.4
- 44.7
- 0.5
- 3.4
- Shinto 83.5 Christian 0.7
- Buddhist 72.6 Other 5.6

1968
- 47.9
- 47.7
- 0.5
- 3.9
- Shinto 82.4 Christian 0.8
- Buddhist 82.2 Other 6.7

1973
- 47.8
- 46.2
- 0.5
- 5.5
- Shinto 80.1 Christian 0.8
- Buddhist 77.5 Other 9.2

1978
- 49.0
- 43.7
- 0.5
- 6.8
- Shinto 85.6 Christian 0.8
- Buddhist 76.4 Other 11.9

For each year, the left-hand panel has four vertical bars each of which, at its upper limit, represents 100 per cent of the population. The different levels in the bars show the percentages of the population classified as belonging to the Shinto, Buddhist, Christian, or Other categories. These percentages, when added together, regularly total over 100 owing to both dual or multiple affiliation and inflated membership reports. The right-hand panel shows what the percentages are when the numbers of adherents in all four categories are added together and the total treated as 100 per cent.

Figure 10.6 Percentages of adherents of Japanese traditions between 1953 and 1978

distinctive emphasis has been on perfection of the individual through group counselling circles where leaders give guidance on personal problems in the light of *Sutra* teaching. Unlike Soka Gakkai, which has direct connections with the political world through its formally autonomous party (the Komeito), Rissho Koseikai, in company with other new religious organizations, has chosen not to form a political party but to form friendships with political figures and, as occasion demands, to exercise influence indirectly through dialogue and through the votes of its members. Its social-reform concerns are particularly evident in its interreligious agency, the World Conference on Religion and Peace.

The principal reason that people join the new religious organizations is to find help with health, marital, financial and other problems. The nature of the help offered varies. In general, however, one can perceive a tendency to affirm that health, wealth and happiness can be obtained if a person will only have implicit faith in the leader, and in the divinity or divine reality he or she represents, participate whole-heartedly in the activities of the organization, and win others by holding out the promise of the help available through this supportive fellowship. Because they often blended doctrinal interpretations with elements of folk religion and even magical practices, the new religious organizations were at first viewed with suspicion and disdain by educated people. In recent years, however, the new bodies have to some extent rid themselves of such features, rationalized their operations, and reached a stage where leaders are no longer likely to be regarded as near-divine wonder-workers.

Living religion in Japan involves more than annual and life-cycle rites of passage, internal reform in established organizations, and new religious organizations that promise help with personal problems. It also involves questions of law and state power. For over 1,000 years, government officials and religious leaders alike took it for granted that government could legitimately police religious organizations in the interests of the state. The year 1945 brought imposition of the value of government neutrality towards religious organizations. This value is only some thirty years old in Japanese institutional history. Its meaning is a subject of public debate, legal action and political manoeuvre. In what changing forms religious freedom will survive in a Japan that values both tradition and internationalism remains to be seen.

NOTE

1. Capital letters have been employed for *the* Buddha (and its derivatives, Buddhism, Buddhist etc.), lower-case for all others (a 'living buddha', 'buddha altar' (the altar for the household dead) etc.) who become buddhas, whether through enlightenment or through death (death-related attribution of buddhahood is unique to Japan).

BIBLIOGRAPHY

1. ABE, Y., 'Religious freedom under the Meiji constitution', *Contemporary Religions in Japan*, IX, iv, 1968, pp. 268–338 (and serially in the next five issues of this journal)
2. ANDREWS, A. A., *The Teachings Essential for Rebirth: A Study of Genshin's Ōjōyōshū*, Tokyo, Sophia University, 1973
3. ANESAKI, M., *History of Japanese Religion*, Rutland, Vt, Tuttle, 1963; first publ. London, Kegan Paul, 1930
4. BELLAH, R. N., *Tokugawa Religion: The Values of Pre-Industrial Japan*, Glencoe, Ill., Free Press, 1957
5. BERTHIER-CAILLET, L., *Fêtes et rites des quatre saisons au Japon*, Paris, Publications Orientalistes de France, 1981
6. BLACKER, C., *The Catalpa Bow: A Study of Shamanistic Practices in Japan*, London, Allen & Unwin/Totowa, NJ, Rowman, 1975
7. CALDAROLA, C., *Christianity: The Japanese Way*, Leiden, Brill, 1979
8. COLLCUTT, M., *Five Mountains: The Rinzai Zen Monastic Institution in Medieval Japan*, Cambridge, Mass., Council on East Asian Studies, Harvard University, 1981
9. CREEMERS, W. H. M., *Shrine Shinto after World War II*, Leiden, Brill, 1968
10. DAVIS, W. B., *Dojo: Magic and Exorcism in Modern Japan*, Stanford, Calif., Stanford University Press, 1980
11. DRUMMOND, R. H., *A History of Christianity in Japan*, Grand Rapids, Mich., Eerdmans, 1971
12. EARHART, H. B., *Japanese Religion: Unity and Diversity*, 3rd edn, Belmont, Calif., Wadsworth, 1982
13. ELIOT, SIR CHARLES, *Japanese Buddhism*, London, Routledge/New York, Barnes & Noble, 1959; first publ. London, Arnold, 1935
14. FUJII, M., 'Gendaijin no Shūkyō Kōdō' (The religious behaviour of contemporary Japanese people), *Jurisuto*, no. 21, 1981, pp. 132–8
15. HIRAI, N., 'Shinto', *Encyclopaedia Britannica*, 15th edn, *Macropaedia*, vol. 16, Chicago, EB, copyr. 1974, 1982

16. HORI, I., *Folk Religion in Japan: Continuity and Change*, Chicago, Ill., University of Chicago Press, 1968, 1974; University of Tokyo Press, 1968

17. HORI, I., 'Japanese religion', *Encyclopaedia Britannica*, 15th edn, *Macropaedia*, vol. 10, Chicago, Ill., EB, copyr. 1974, 1982

18. HORI, I., *et al.* (eds.), *Japanese Religion*, Tokyo, Palo Alto, Calif., Kodansha International, 1972

19. KITAGAWA, J. M., *Religion in Japanese History*, New York, Columbia University Press, 1966

20. LEBRA, T. S., *Japanese Patterns of Behavior*, Honolulu, University Press of Hawaii, 1976

21. MATSUMOTO, S., *Motoori Norinaga: 1730–1801*, Cambridge, Mass., Harvard University Press, 1970

22. MORIOKA, K., *Religion in Changing Japanese Society*, University of Tokyo Press, 1975

23. MORIOKA, K., and NEWELL, W. H. (eds.), *The Sociology of Japanese Religion*, Leiden, Brill, 1968 (repr. from *Journal of Asian and African Studies*, vol. 3, nos. 1–2, 1968)

24. MURAKAMI, S., *Japanese Religion in the Modern Century* (tr. H. B. Earhart), Tokyo, University of Tokyo Press, 1980

25. NAKAMURA, H., 'Japanese philosophy', *Encyclopaedia Britannica*, 15th edn, *Macropaedia*, vol. 10, Chicago, Ill., EB, copyr. 1974, 1982

26. NAKAMURA, H., *Ways of Thinking of Eastern Peoples: India, China, Tibet, Japan* (rev. English tr., ed. P. P. Wiener), Honolulu, East–West Center Press, 1964

27. NORBECK, E., *Religion and Society in Modern Japan: Continuity and Change*, Houston, Tex., Tourmaline Press, 1970

28. ROTERMUND, H. O., *Die Yamabushi: Aspekte ihres Glaubens, Lebens und ihrer sozialen Funktion im japanischen Mittelalter*, Hamburg, Cram & De Gruyter, 1968

29. SMITH, R. J., *Ancestor Worship in Contemporary Japan*, Stanford, Calif., Stanford University Press, 1974

30. SMITH, W. W., *Confucianism in Modern Japan: A Study of Conservatism in Japanese Intellectual History*, 2nd edn, Tokyo, Hokuseido Press, 1973

31. SPAE, J. J., *Itô Jinsai: A Philosopher, Educator and Sinologist of the Tokugawa Period*, New York, Paragon Book Reprint, 1967; first publ. Peiping, Catholic University of Peking, 1948

32. SUGIMOTO, M., and SWAIN, D. L., *Science and Culture in Traditional Japan: A.D. 600–1854*, Cambridge, Mass., MIT, 1978

33. SWYNGEDOUW, J., 'Japanese religiosity in an age of internationalization', *Japanese Journal of Religious Studies*, V, ii–iii, 1978, pp. 87–106

34. TAKAKUSU, J., *The Essentials of Buddhist Philosophy* (ed. W. T. Chan and C. A. Moore), 2nd edn, Honolulu, University of Hawaii, 1949

35. YANAGAWA, K., 'Theological and scientific thinking about festivals', *Japanese Journal of Religious Studies*, I, i, 1974, pp. 5–49

APPENDIX: SOURCES FOR STUDY

The brief list of primary sources that follows is limited to texts of Japanese provenance. Omitted, therefore, are the pre-Japanese *sutras* on which Japanese Buddhist schools rely. For the convenience of the reader, works available in English translation predominate, but it should be remembered that such works constitute only a fraction of the whole. For more complete bibliographical information on Western-language works, see: J. M. Kitagawa, 'The religions of Japan', in C. J. Adams (ed.), *A Reader's Guide to the Great Religions* (New York, Free Press/London, Collier-Macmillan, 1965), pp. 161–90; J. Swyngedouw, 'A brief guide to English-language materials on Japan's religions', *Contemporary Religions in Japan*, XI, i–ii, 1970, pp. 80–97; H. B. Earhart, *The New Religions of Japan: A Bibliography of Western-Language Materials*, 2nd edn, Boston, Mass., G. K. Hall (forthcoming).

EARLY PERIOD (PRIOR TO 1185)

To begin with materials generally associated with Shinto, the *Kojiki*, drawing on traditions that antedate its completion in 712, is the earliest cultural sourcebook. See the D. L. Philippi translation (University of Tokyo Press, 1968). A close second is the *Nihongi* (720), still available in the 1896 translation of W. G. Aston (London, Allen & Unwin, 1956). About one-fourth of an anthology of some 4,000 poems reflecting life in seventh- and eighth-century Japan may be found in *The Manyōshū* (New York, Columbia University Press, 1965). The *Izumo Fudoki*, translated by M. Y. Aoki (Tokyo, Sophia University, 1971), is an eighth-century compilation of factual and etymological information that includes a unique collection of myths. Of the fifty books specifying administrative regulations of the tenth century, the first ten, covering festivals, deities, rituals etc., are now accessible in the *Engi-Shiki*, 2 vols., translated by F. G. Bock (Tokyo, Sophia University, 1970, 1972).

Buddhist and Confucian influences converge in Prince Shōtoku's 'Seventeen-Article Constitution' of 604, translated in R. Tsunoda *et al.*, *Sources of the Japanese Tradition* (New York, Columbia University Press, 1958). Excerpts from the works of Saichō may be found in the same source. Some works of his contemporary Kūkai appear in Y. S. Hakeda's *Kūkai* (New York, Columbia University Press, 1972). Another important Buddhist work of this period, often compared to the *Divine Comedy*, is Genshin's *Ōjōyōshū*, a partial translation of which was published by A. K. Reischauer in the *Transactions of the Asiatic Society of Japan* (2nd ser., VII, 1930).

MEDIEVAL PERIOD (1185–1868)

Neither Hōnen's central work, the *Senjaku Hongan Nenbutsu Shū* (Collection of passages on the original vow of Amida), nor the main scriptures and commentaries of the Pure Land school are yet available in a commendable translation, but Shinran's *magnum opus*, the *Kyōgyōshinshō* (Teaching, practice, faith and attainment), appeared serially in annotated translation in the *Eastern Buddhist* (beginning with vol. VIII, no. iii, November 1957). The chief scriptures of the True Pure Land school exist in a difficult translation by K. Yamamoto entitled *The Shinshu Seiten* (Honolulu, Honpa Hongwanji Mission of Hawaii, 1955). Important in this connection is the *Tannishō* (Notes lamenting differences), a good translation of which is that by R. Fujiwara (Kyoto, Ryukoku Translation Center, Ryukoku University, 1962). For Zen Buddhism see Eisai's *Kōzen Gokoku Ron* (Propagation of Zen for the protection of the country), the preface to which is translated in *Sources of the Japanese Tradition*, and Dōgen's *Shōbō Genzō: The Eye and Treasury of the True Law*, 3 vols., translated by K. Nishiyama and J. Stevens (Tokyo, Nakayama Shobō, 1975, 1977, 1982). Nichiren's noted *Risshō Ankoku Ron* (Treatise on the establishment of the orthodox teaching and the peace of the nation), together with other primary materials, appears in L. R. Rodd, *Nichiren: Selected Writings* (Honolulu, University Press of Hawaii, 1980). Also to be noted is the remarkable thirteenth-century work *Gukanshō* (Some modest views), a rare Buddhist interpretation of Japanese history, now available in English as *The Future and the Past: A Translation and Study of the Gukanshō* by D. M. Brown and I. Ishida (Berkeley, Calif., University of California Press, 1979).

Shinto, overshadowed in religion by Buddhism and in philosophy by Confucianism, sought to redress the balance from about the fourteenth century. Here we find the purportedly archaic 'Five classics of Shinto' (*Shintō gobusho*) associated with Ise Shinto, but unfortunately still untranslated, as are: (1) K. Yoshida's *Yuiitsu Shintō Myōhō Yōshū* (Essentials of the eminent law of pure Shinto), an early argument for Shinto primacy; (2) the *Dai Nihon Shi* (History of Japan), a 397-volume work which, though not completed until 1906, was begun in 1657 and is said to have exercised great influence on Shinto 'restorationist' thought and action; (3) the highly regarded works of N. Motoori, a leading scholar of Japanese classical literature and thought; and (4) the works of his chauvinistic disciple A. Hirata.

The latter years of this period mark the beginning of several new religious organizations. The primary sources for the study of such groups, however, are treated below in connection with the modern period.

MODERN PERIOD (1868–)

A list of the scriptures of the new religious organizations (which is not easy to come by) is presented here. It covers only the better-known organizations and is adapted from N. Inoue *et al.*, *Shinshūkyō Kenkyū Chōsa Handobukku* (Handbook for the study of new religious organizations) (Tokyo, Yūzankaku Shuppan, 1981, pp. 220–43): (1) Ananaikyō: *Reikai de Mita Uchū* (The cosmos seen in the spirit world); (2) Iesu no Mitama Kyōkai Kyōdan: *Seisho* (The Bible); (3) Izumo Taishakyō: *Kyōshi Taiyō* (Essentials of the teaching), plus eleven other titles; (4) Ennōkyō: *Ennōkyō Kyōten* (Ennōkyō scriptures), plus three other titles; (5) Ōmoto: *Reikai Monogatari* (Tales of the spirit world), eighty-one vols., plus one other title; (6) Ontakekyō: *Ontakekyō Nagomi no Oshie* (The Ontakekyō 7–5–3 doctrine); (7) Kyūsei Shukyō: *Mioshie* (The eminent teaching); (8) Kurozumikyō: *Kyōso no Mikunsei* (Admonitions of the founder); (9) Gedatsukai: *Hannyashin-gyō* (Essence of wisdom *sutra*); (10) Kōdō Kyōdan: *Hoke Sanbukyō* (*Lotus Sutra* trilogy); (11) Konkōkyō: *Konkōkyō Kyōten* (Konkōkyō scriptures), plus two other titles; (12) GLA (God-Light Association) Sōgō Honbu: *Shinkō Kiganbun* (Prayerbook of spirit and action); (13) Shinshūkyō: *Uchū no Seishin* (Spirit of the universe), plus four other titles; (14) Shinnyoen: *Ichinyo no Michi* (The way of indivisible reality); (15) Shinrikyō: *Kyōso no Dōtō* (The lineage of the founder's path); (16) Shinreikyō: *Akeyuku Sekai* (The dawning world); (17) Seichō no Ie: *Seimei no Jissō* (The reality of life), forty vols., plus four other titles; (18) Sekai Kyūseikyō: *Tengoku no Ishizue* (The cornerstone of heaven), plus eight other titles; (19) Sekai Mahikari Bunmei Kyōdan: *Miseigenshū* (Sacred utterances), plus one other title; (20) Zenrinkai: *Seikyō* (Sacred scripture) plus one other title; (21) Sōka Gakkai: *Nichiren Daishōnin Gosho* (Writings of the great Nichiren), plus one other title; (22) Daijōkyō: *Hokekyō* (*Lotus Sutra*); (23) Tenshō Kōtai Jingūkyō: *Seisho* (Words of life); (24) Tenrikyō: *Ofudesaki* (Tip of the divine writing brush), plus three other titles; (25) Nakayama Shingo Shōshū: *Gozabun* (Writings from the dais); (26) Nyoraikyō: *Okyōsama* (Sacred scriptures); (27) Nenpō Shinkyō: *Nenpō Hōgoshū* (Nenpō teachings), plus one other title; (28) PL (Perfect Liberty) Kyōdan: *PL Kyōten* (PL scriptures), plus one other title; (29) Bussho Gonenkai Kyōdan; *Kunyaku Hokekyō Heikaishi* (*Lotus Sutra* in Japanese translation with commentary); (30) Bentenshū Myō'ōji: *Shūso Sonjo Okotoba Shūsei* (Collected sayings of the foundress); (31) Honmichi: *Ofudesaki* (Tip of the divine writing brush), plus three other titles; (32) Honmon Butsuryūshū: *Hokekyō* (*Lotus Sutra*); (33) Maruyamakyō: *Oshirabe* (The quest); (34) Misogikyō: *Yuiitsu Mondōsho* (The pure catechism); (35) Myōchikai Kyōdan: *Asayu no Otsutome* (Daily tasks), plus one other title; (36) Myōdōkai Kyōdan: *Myōhō Rengekyō* (The lotus of the wonderful law), plus one other title; (37) Risshō Kōseikai: *Hoke Sanbukyō* (*Lotus Sutra* trilogy), plus one other title; (38) Reiyūkai: *Namu Myōhō Rengekyō* (*Lotus Sutra*), plus one other title.

Some of these works are doubtless available in English. Those interested may consult the organizational headquarters of the relevant group, the addresses for nearly all of which are given in Hori [18: 170–232].

Religions in Primal Societies

A. North American Indian Religions

JOSEPH EPES BROWN

Introduction

THE STUDY OF NORTH AMERICAN INDIAN RELIGIONS

The first scholarly attention given to the rich complex of American Indian cultures coincides with the early formative periods of the anthropological sciences in the late 1800s. Fortunately for historians of religion, the works of such pioneers as Franz Boas, J. O. Dorsey, Alice C. Fletcher, A. L. Kroeber, R. J. Lowie and Clark Wissler [21] often reflected an enduring interest in recording the religious phenomena of indigenous North American cultures. A prime motivation underlying this quantity of materials on American Indians was undoubtedly the pervasive conviction of the time that most Indian cultures were disappearing. Immediate recording of the traditions was therefore considered imperative. It is fortunate that these scholars accomplished their urgent work, but also that time has proven their assumptions wrong, as is evidenced by accelerating population figures and contemporary movements for the revitalization of religious traditions (see section D below). Ironically, many of these early 'salvage' studies have recently been instrumental in providing Indian peoples with sacred lore which had been lost or neglected, thus supporting the revitalization process.

There have been shifts in methodology in the study of American Indian cultures in the past decade, specifically regarding the role of religion. Whereas the anthropological studies mentioned above were largely descriptive, such works have become more and more theoretical. Perhaps in response to this trend, historians of religion are increasingly giving attention to expressions of living primal religions – in this case, American Indian religious traditions. Such works, appearing with ever greater frequency, represent a more balanced approach, in which religious phenomena are examined in and for themselves. Leading this new development are such scholars as Mircea Eliade and, especially, Åke Hultkrantz, who has chosen to focus almost exclusively on the phenomena of American Indian religions using the methodologies of both anthropology and the history of religions [11]. It is also important to mention the rapidly growing number of American Indian authors who are presenting their experience and understanding of their own religions without outside recorders and interpreters, joining the many unknown Indian elders who have explained their sacred lore to earlier students.

Because there are hundreds of extant American tribal groups, each with its own distinctive culture and history, a single study could not do justice to this complex subject. Three attempts at comprehensive anthropological synthesis are Wissler, 1917 [21], Spencer and Jennings, 1965 [17], and Driver, 1961 [5]. Most recent and perhaps best are the occasionally appearing volumes of *The Handbook of North American Indians*, published by the Smithsonian Institution [18]. But none of these valuable texts gives sufficient attention to the meaning of religious phenomena within the multiple dimensions of Indian culture. The initial attempt to do so was Underhill, 1965, a selective and somewhat general but welcome volume [20]. The first adequate treatment of Indian religions – though it is presented in summary manner and attempts to include all the Americas – is Hultkrantz, 1979 [11]. The most recent is Gill, 1981 [7; 8].

The present discussion of elements of American Indian living religions must obviously be both cursory and selective. Even where emphasis is to be upon the present living reality and viability of religious elements, account must be taken of at least the following three major interrelated factors. First, American Indian religions represent examples of primal traditions which have existed for some 30,000 to 60,000 years. Fundamental elements not only survive in living communities, in many cases they are being reaffirmed with increasing vigour. Second, out of this heritage of primal qualities has developed a rich plurality of differentiated religious traditions, which makes it impossible to describe American Indian religions in generalizations. Third, ever-increasing contact from the late fifteenth century with representatives of diverse European cultures has led to vast changes across indigenous Indian cultures. Under this impact certain tribal groups became extinct, whereas others became acculturated into the dominant societies. Most surviving groups have shown a remarkable ability to cope with change by adapting to and borrowing from the non-Indian world selectively, making it possible both to survive and to retain at least core elements of traditional ways. The 'new' religious movements of revitalization should therefore be understood in terms of a continuity of traditional elements rather than as innovations completely unrelated to the peoples' history. The impact of Christianity and the special meaning of 'conversion' to the American Indian should also be understood in this larger context.

THE PRIMAL FOUNDATIONS

Those primal elements universal to virtually all North American Indian religious traditions must include at least the following:

1. That which we refer to in current usage as 'religion' cannot be conceived as separable from any aspects of American Indian culture. In no American Indian language is there a term which could translate as 'religion'. It is thus preferable to use a word like 'tradition' when referring to religion among Indians.

2. For American Indians, words have a special potency integral to their specific sounds. What is named is therefore understood as present in the name, not merely as a symbol of it. It is understood that words in their sounds are borne by the breath of the being from whom they proceed, and since breath is identified with the life principle, words are sacred and must be used with care and responsibility. Such a quality of the spoken word is enhanced by the understood proximity of the source of breath, the lungs, with the heart, which is associated with the being's spiritual centre.

Just as words bear power, a statement or a thought is understood to have a potency of its own, especially when it occurs in a ritual context. Thus recitation of a myth of creation, for example, is understood as an *actual*, not a symbolic re-enactment of that primordial creative process, which is not bound by time [19].

3. A similar mode of understanding, paralleling that of language, is expressed in the way American Indian peoples view their arts and crafts. The natural materials they use manifest sacred powers; and the completed form, the external representation, is understood to manifest its own sacred potency. Such quality of experience is essential to understanding Indian art forms [6].

4. Further basic American Indian concepts are found in experience of time and process, which are universally understood not in Western lineal manner, but in terms of the cyclical and reciprocal. The seasons of nature, the span of a life, human or non-human, are understood in such cyclical manner and are re-expressed formally in architecture and ritual.

5. As with diverse primal societies, American Indians have developed an accumulated pragmatic lore regarding the natural environment upon which they depend. This has always been interrelated with a sacred lore; together these can be said to constitute a metaphysic of nature. Subsistence activities

can be described as sacred modes of hunting and fishing, and detailed cosmological lore can be seen in agricultural pursuits. American Indian peoples are today giving new attention to the wisdom of these traditions, a re-evaluation which has had strong impact upon certain non-Indian groups that are concerned with environmental degradation in industrialized societies.

Generalizations regarding American Indians are impossible, owing to the enormous differences that they show, due to their migrations over successive time periods, in their diversity of physical types, the thousand or more tribal groups with several hundred mutually unintelligible languages in North America alone, and the contrasts of geography and climatic zones to which the peoples have adapted. Clark Wissler's synthesizing concept of Native American 'culture areas' also raises some problems, but it is a useful approach to follow here in order to organize descriptive materials and to employ certain circumscribed generalizations. The five culture areas selected for description here represent a cross-section of North American indigenous peoples and provide examples of religious traditions as related to contrasting subsistence patterns (see Figure 11.1 and Table 11.1). They can be said to constitute living religions in the sense that core elements of sacred tradition and native language are held today by certain segments of the populations, and it is through their leaders that movements for revitalization are appearing with increasing frequency.

The Arctic Eskimo

The Eskimo of the Arctic coast, representatives of a larger circumpolar region, are often excluded from descriptions of Indian groups to the south. This is arbitrary, as evidence suggests that many Arctic and sub-Arctic religious themes diffused southward, where they survive in modified form among the eastern woodland Algonquin hunting peoples, the Athabascans of the western sub-Arctic, and even the peoples of the Plains and Prairie cultural area.

The Eskimos experience their world of barren coast and expanse of sea and ice as peopled with hosts of spirits, whose qualities and powers are specific to each facet of the natural environment. There are also spirits from realms unrelated to the phenomenal world; they are graphically depicted in ancient traditional stone carvings or contemporary lithographs. Dependency upon sea or land animals is interrelated with beliefs in a soul (or souls) specific to all beings. In slaying animals the hunter bears responsibility for releasing the souls (*anua*) of living beings. Rites must therefore be observed in relation to all aspects of hunting.

The Eskimos hold that the greatest danger in their lives is not the cold or

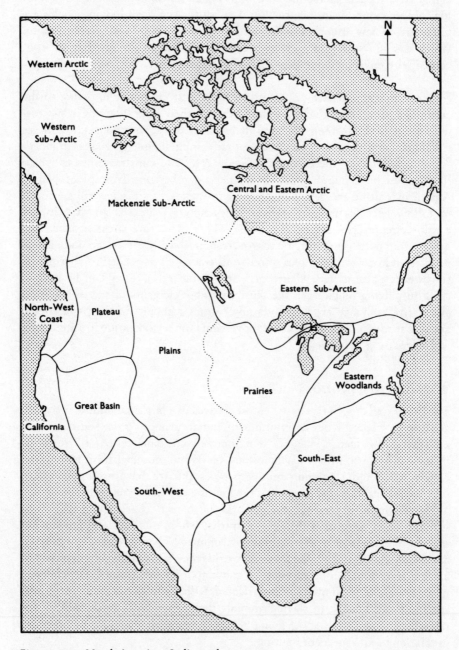

Figure 11.1   North American Indian culture areas

starvation, but the fact that their existence depends on taking the lives of other beings. In a world where such a precarious balance obtains between life and death, where a thin line divides physical appearances from the spirits, there must be mechanisms by which equilibrium can be maintained. This equilibrium depends upon observing a host of taboos. Where behavioural codes are broken, or where the hunter's attitudes are not respectful towards the game, it is believed that the animals will not present themselves willingly as a sacrificial offering to the hunter. Such traditions are supported by beliefs in an all-powerful goddess, half human and half fish, called Sedna or *Takānâluk*, who dwells in a great cave or pool under the sea where she keeps all the sea mammals, which she releases or withholds according to the degree to which the people observe the taboos.

Parallel to Sedna, there are Masters or Keepers of the various species of land animals who release or withhold their kind according to the behaviour and attitudes of the hunter and his people. Further, the multiplicity of spirits and souls of all sea life coalesce into a kind of unity in the single underwater Sea Power – as, similarly, the spirits of land animals are unified under the great Master or Keeper. Although the Eskimo may not conceive of a High God responsible for all life – as is found in most Indian tribes to the south – there are occasional references to a unity of all living beings, of sea and land, in the figure of the Great Meat Dish. If such an ultimate concept is not central to Eskimo experience, it is because human survival here means that attention must be given to the specific elements of a harsh and precarious environment.

In this uncertain Arctic world, the central religious practitioner is the *angakut*, or shaman. He/she helps the people maintain the necessary delicate balance between this world of pragmatic necessities and the more subtle world of spirits, acting as an intermediary between these worlds. The shaman's wisdom and special powers are critical to communal life and human survival. Through his familiarity with the spirit realms and his ability to send out in ecstatic trance one of his souls (often called the 'free soul') on a spiritual journey, he is able to discern who has broken the taboos causing the disappearance of game. He is also able to placate Sedna or discover the cause of illness perhaps associated with 'soul loss', or he may foretell future weather conditions and thus the appropriate time for travel. The methods of becoming a shaman are common to many American Indian groups. The apprentice must have a guide who has travelled and knows the way. Among many disciplines, he must learn how to divest himself in sacred manner of the outer layers of his own flesh, then to name all the bones of his skeleton. In such magical lore are clarified the deep meanings underlying widespread traditions of shamanic art forms found throughout the Arctic and Indian Americas, wherein the outer covering of beings is understood as transparent, like a kind of X-ray vision focusing on depicted inner realities understood spiritually [15]. To gain shamanic lore, apprentices must also engage in a retreat where, in solitude and suffering, through fasting and exposure to cold, the worthy will receive sacred powers through visions and the teachings of a helping spirit.

The novice shaman must observe special taboos and requirements when he returns to his people whom he can now lead through that delicate balance of life and death. Such powers must be demonstrated in periodic communal gatherings where, aided by drum and vocal rhythms and a rich array of props and techniques, the shaman enters into ecstatic trance, during which his soul travels to find and return with the needed knowledge. His success or failure as a shaman is established by the pragmatic or spiritual results thus obtained. [15]

The Eastern Sub-Arctic

Despite contact with Euro-American hunters, traders and Christian missionaries, the hunting practices and religious traditions of the northern Algonquin hunters are still imbued with beliefs and practices similar to those of the Arctic peoples. Here, however, there are rich mythologies of creation with an anthropomorphic Creator who moves upon the primordial waters, accompanied by aquatic birds and animals who bring to the surface the primal mud from which the earth is fashioned. This particular myth teaches that creation is not just an event of time past but an ever-continuing process. Here also are tales of ambivalent 'trickster' hero figures who bring desirable things to the people and who define through their acts the parameters of acceptable behaviour.

The conical-frame wigwam of these peoples is conceived as an image of the cosmos, or of man as a microcosm; this is also reflected in their dome-shaped 'sweat lodge'. In such lodges the regenerative forces of earth, air, fire and water are combined to restore that original purity of man which can be lost through the breaking of innumerable hunting taboos or through contact with the ritual impurity of women's menstrual cycles. Smoking-pipes and tobacco are used in this area with profound sacred meanings [1]. In the sub-Arctic the shaman does not send out in ecstatic trance one of his souls to accomplish a mission; rather, in dramatic ceremony within the lodge he conjures *in* to himself his spirit helpers, whom he has experienced in the course of a 'vision quest'. These spirits demonstrate their presence through mysterious sounds and by tapping and shaking the lodge. The spirits, who are usually the practitioner's 'guardian spirits', are then instructed to seek out and bring back what is desired of them.

Appropriately for a people whose lives are dependent upon the hunting and trapping of game, there is rich sacred lore relating to all the animals in their world of experience. Special qualities which can be communicated to people are specific to each species of animal. Animals are thus considered teachers and in this sense are superior to man. There are secret societies of animal lodges, often ranked in accordance with gradations of powers of the animal involved. The bear, for example, is considered most powerful, thus complex rites and ceremonies occur in the hunting, slaying and finally the sacred treatment of this animal's remains. The key Algonquin term for such sacred power is *manitu*, and *Kitchi Manitou* is the totality of such powers. [10]

Eastern Woodlands

As climate and habitat become more favourable in the eastern woodlands south of the sub-Arctic, religious rites become increasingly complex. This is well illustrated by the practices of the *Midéwiwin*, the Medicine Lodge society of the Ojibwa–Chippewa of the Great Lakes region [10], whose ceremonies usually occur annually, in late spring and early autumn. Candidates seek initiation into the sacred society for a variety of reasons, but most often they have had dream or vision experiences indicating that they should do so. Such persons are then instructed by the *midé* priests in the sacred lore.

The *Midéwiwin* rites are conducted within a long lodge conceived as an image of the universe. Within the lodge and guarding the doorways are forms identified with animal-spirit helpers. Purification in a sweat lodge is required prior to participation in the ceremonies, which may last from two to eight days, depending on the degrees which the candidates are entering. The first of these cumulative degrees is associated with aquatic animals referred to in myths of creation: the mink, otter, musk-rat or beaver. The second is associated with beings of the air, such as an owl or hawk; and the third with more powerful beings of the earth such as the serpent or wildcat. The fourth and ultimate degree, which may be achieved in old age and which demands much preparation, is represented by the most powerful land animal, the bear. In the lodge, myths of creation and sacred migration are recited by the priests or 'medicine men'. The climax of the ceremonies comes when the candidates are ritually 'shot' by the priests, using an otter-skin bag from which the sacred *mi'gis* (cowrie shell) is magically propelled into the candidate, who drops to the ground in spiritual death. In being brought back to life by the priest, the candidate is understood to be reborn into a new world of deeper spiritual understanding. Despite various external compromising influences (Christianity and the fur trade for example), the rites of the Algonquin (especially those of the *Midéwiwin*) are being increasingly practised. This may partly be explained by new pan-Indian movements which facilitate inter-tribal exchange.

The dominant Iroquoian-speaking peoples of a still more favourable eastern woodland environment represent even greater cultural complexity, with their dual subsistence patterns of seasonal hunting and horticulture. The basic structure of their six-nation socio-political league still endures beneath the obvious external evidence of change. This is also true of many traditional Iroquoian religious expressions.

Iroquoian religion gives ultimate attention to a supreme unitary principle which, although claimed by many to be of Christian origin, seems to have been integral from earliest times to the Iroquoian world-view. Their term *orenda* – an extension of spiritual power(s) – is a widespread concept across American Indian cultures. Such abstract concepts are basic to Iroquoian cosmological dualisms of heaven and earth, which are understood as necessary reciprocal forces of a unitary principle. The structure of Iroquoian long houses, in which complex dance–drama ceremonies, often of thanksgiving, are enacted, expresses these cosmological values. The Iroquoian carved masks of the 'false face' curing societies represent the spirit forces of the woodlands, their powers intensified in that the masks must be carved *in situ* out of a living tree. The Iroquois have rites of purification; and a youth is expected at puberty to engage in the 'vision quest', often to seek out his guardian spirit, which is usually associated with his new sacred name.

With the disruption of much of Iroquoian culture under intensified Euro-American pressure for change, there appeared in the 1800s the Seneca chief Handsome Lake, whom the people prefer to call the Life-Bringer, with his messianic teaching and its strict codes of conduct. As with the messianic movement of the 1890 Ghost Dance, or that of the peyote cult which became incorporated as the Native American Church in 1918, Life-Bringer's code integrated indigenous elements with selected Christian ideas [11]. It is in terms of such synthetic reformulations that many Iroquois live their religions today.

Plains and Prairie

The cultures of Native American peoples in Plains and Prairie regions have been influenced by the groups described above, by agricultural traditions of the South-East and by certain Uto-Aztecan peoples. But adaptation to the environment of this region has forged a unique commonality of religio-cultural traits which can be summarized generally.

The Plains peoples experience a multitude of differentiated spirits which are: (1) specific to each part of the natural world; (2) associated with an animating life principle; and (3) synonymous with certain subtle qualities which, it is believed, can be transferred to other beings or to inanimate forms. Because to these peoples all phenomena are animate in some manner, they make no hard distinction between the animate and inanimate. The sacred quality of powers is referred to in such terms as the Dakota *wakan* – not a noun implying limitation, but an adjective conveying a sense of the mysterious. The multiplicity of sacred mysteries coalesces into an ultimate unity expressed through such polysynthetic terms as the Lakota *Wakan-Tanka*, Great Mysterious. The oft-used translation Great Spirit employs a noun, changing the original meaning, and is undoubtedly the result of Christian influence. Almost all Plains tribal groups stress the obligation of individual participation in a ritualized 'vision quest' or, less frequently, a quest to receive one's personal guardian spirit. Both are accomplished in solitary retreat with fasting and sacrifice. Sacred powers appearing in such experiences are usually associated with animal beings or other natural phenomena. They may indicate the seeker's sacred name, or they may constitute the origin or validation of sacred songs, art forms or tribal rites. Robert Lowie has called this process democratized shamanism.

The Plains peoples' classical dwelling is the portable conical *tipi*, which expresses cosmological ideas and is still used for ceremonial occasions and summer pow-wows. The shelter is understood as a world or universe or, microcosmically, as man. The central open fire is the presence of the Great Mysterious, and the smoke hole above it is the place and path of liberation. Although today most Plains people live in permanent frame houses, they nevertheless often have their sweat lodges near by.

The Sun Dance, also called Medicine Dance or Thirst Lodge, is a complex annual springtime world- or self-renewal ceremony which today is instrumental in revitalizing many traditional religious elements. A large circular open-frame lodge is ritually constructed in imitation of the world's creation; the sacred cottonwood tree at the centre is the axis linking sky and earth. Those who have already made the vow participate in a sacrificial dance–fast in the lodge for three to four days, supported by large drums and heroic songs. They move from the circumference to the tree at the centre and back again, always facing and concentrating on the tree or on the sacred eagle or bison head attached to it. Certain groups, such as the Lakota, periodically shift positions within the lodge so that the dancers always gaze towards the sun, which is associated with the source of life. Some dancers vow to have their chest muscles pierced. Into the cuts thongs are attached which have been tied to a high point in the tree, so that the dancer is now virtually tied to the centre. He dances until the flesh breaks loose. Through the rigours and sacrificial elements of these rites the participants often receive, by means of visions, sacred powers which are communicated to those present.

The tobacco pipes used by Plains peoples express all that is most sacred to them [1]. Such pipes are used on all ritual and other important occasions, and any agreement or relationship sealed with the smoking of a pipe is held inviolate. The pipes have mythological origins, and it is still believed that if ever they are no longer used, or respected, the people will lose their centre and cease to be a people. These pipes, with their long wooden stems and stone bowls, are perceived as an axis defining the path between heaven and earth. Microcosmically, the pipe is identified with man: the stem is the breath passage leading to the bowl, the spiritual centre or heart. In prayer, as each grain of carefully prepared tobacco is placed in the pipe, some aspect of creation is mentioned, so that when the bowl is full it contains the totality of time, space and all of creation, including man. When the fire consumes this consecrated tobacco with the aid of man's breath, the identity of all creation with the fire – which is the presence of the Great Mysterious – is affirmed. Participants in the communal smoking often conclude by reciting, 'We are all related.' Some Christian priests now attempt to integrate these rites with the celebration of Holy Communion, but many younger traditional Indians have ambivalent feelings about such practice.

Religious practitioners in the Plains are often termed medicine men/women, for they know the lore of curative herbs, a knowledge transferred, validated and increased in the 'vision quest'. Others, too, receive especially sacred powers through visions – as is sometimes the case with the medicine men – and are thereby qualified to guide those seeking experience of the sacred. As in the sub-Arctic, the practitioner calls in his spirit helpers and then dispatches them to discover the cause of an illness, to find lost objects or to answer spiritual questions. The contemporary *Yuwipi* ceremonies, very popular among many Plains tribes, are a good example of such practices.

All these rites of purification – the pipe, 'vision quests', Sun Dances and other traditional ceremonies – are practised increasingly by Plains peoples today, often with younger tribal members as leaders. Traditional values are also being affirmed in such new contexts as the summer pow-wow circuit, which offers a type of nomadism with inter-tribal emphasis. Even the once militant American Indian Movement, which has used religious themes to support protest activities, is minimizing militancy in favour of sincerely reliving traditional religious ways, in which are found more enduring answers to problems of identity. Statistics are not available, but significant evidence from Plains areas suggests that the once rapidly expanding ceremonial use of peyote in the syncretistic Native American Church is being superseded by the more satisfying realities found in the traditional lore of the people – which, moreover, is transmitted through their own languages.

South-West: Pueblos and Navajo

The cultural and linguistic diversity of the peoples of the American South-West is considerable. It is possible to treat here only two dominant groups, the Pueblos and the Navajo, or *Diné* (the people), as they prefer to be called.

THE PUEBLOS

The roots of sedentary Pueblo cultures in the South-West trace back to both the Palaeo-Indian big-game hunters of approximately 10,000 BCE and the expansive 'desert culture' of *c.* 3000 BCE with its evidence of incipient agriculture. Since then, the peoples have developed complex cultures identified with specific regions and have migrated a number of times before settling in their present sites along the Rio Grande to the east and across to the Arizona mesas of the Hopi in the west. Despite Spanish incursions, Christian missions and the detraditionalizing policies of American government agencies, the Pueblos have resisted outside pressures. Through bitter experience these remarkably viable peoples have learned the wisdom of appearing to acquiesce while holding in secret to their own traditional beliefs and rites, which they continue to practise today.

Although each of the many Pueblo communities holds to its own ways, it is nevertheless possible to discern some general characteristics of these peoples if one views the differences as dialects of a commonly shared spiritual language. The Puebloian cosmos is portrayed in myths as incorporating a number of spheres pierced through by a hollow vertical axis. Among the Zuñi there are seven of these spheres. Commencing with the realm of *A'wonawil'ona*, a supreme life-giving bisexual power, the second and third spheres are identified with the Sun Father, giver of light and warmth, and the Moon Mother, who gives light at night, divides the year into months, and expresses the life-cycle of living beings. The central terrestrial fourth realm of the Earth Mother is the provider of all vegetation. The fifth subterrestrial realm is associated with the gods of war, the twin culture heroes and the Corn Mother. The gods of the sixth realm are represented by persons wearing masks (the *koko*), who appear in seasonal dance–dramas; and the seventh realm is identified with animal gods. Mythic accounts of humans and animals emerging into the terrestrial realm commence with descriptions of a dark underworld, an eminently sacred realm of undeveloped possibility. In the process of emergence, amorphous 'human' beings are led by solar heroes and aided by animal beings who explore in turn each sphere to the four horizontal cardinal directions. The process of vertical emergence is aided by four types of sacred trees upon which the beings climb upwards into this world of limit and hardness, but illuminated by the light of the sun. Through these myths, periodically retold in dramatic manner, everything of importance for the people of this world is defined in sacred terms: the heavenly elements of sun and moon; the four directions of horizontal space with their specific colours and identifying mountain ranges; the meanings associated with the categories of tree peoples; and the lore specific to each of the animals and birds which is central to the structure and values of the people's secret societies.

The Puebloian cosmos is also defined in terms of a duality: the sacred worlds below as distinct from the more profane world into which the people emerged. The Tewa describe this dualism in such terms as *ochu* (green, unripe, eminently sacred), distinguished from a *seht'a* (cooked, ripe, hardened); social categories, with their supernatural counterparts, are defined and supported by such formulations [13].

The most sacred place of the Pueblos is the *kiva*, an underground ceremonial chamber at the bottom of which is a hollow shaft, the *sipapu*, leading underground and understood to be the very place of emergence, the Centre of centres, and the underworld connection to the shrines located in the sacred mountains of the four directions. Access to the *kiva* is by ladder – so that descent leads back to the sacred realm and ascent recapitulates the mythic process of emergence. Within the *kivas*, present in varying numbers at each pueblo or settlement, preparations take place for rites and for the dance–dramas of masked deities, which are enacted according to a seasonal calendar marked by the dualities of summer and winter solstices. The strict observance of the ceremonial cycle is controlled by a priest of a specific clan, who observes the annual movements of the sun. The dance–dramas, prepared by the men in the *kivas*, are performed in open village plazas. This seasonal return of the sacred deities re-establishes contact with sacred realms. Without the rites it is believed that the recycling of life-sustaining powers would cease, whereupon the world and its people would die. The force of such ritually enacted beliefs inhibits acculturation into the non-Pueblo world of other values, both religious (e.g. Christian) and secular. [4; 14]

THE NAVAJO

Because the Navajo were intruders, who arrived from the north *c.* 1200–1400 CE into an area of enormous cultural complexity, many threads of their present culture represent a variety of elements borrowed from the Pueblos, the Spanish, the Spanish-Americans and the ever-changing presence of the American non-Indian world. But despite contacts with these peoples, the Navajo have not only remained independent, they have also increased. Their number was approximately 8,000 in 1868. It rose to 50,000 in 1950 and 85,000 in 1961, and is at least 175,000 at present. Christian missions, government 'civilizing' educational policies and new syncretistic religious movements (e.g. the Native American Church) have neither been fused into Navajo culture nor compartmentalized (unlike the Pueblo response to pressures for change), but rather have been incorporated around a central framework that remains to this day distinctly Navajo. The essence of this structure, outlined below, is identified with elements of a basic northern Athabascan heritage reinterpreted through creative adaptations of Puebloian cosmologies and ceremonial expressions.

Central to the Navajo view of reality is the understanding that the human personality is a whole, with every facet interrelated both within itself and with the totality of phenomena. In this totality everything exists in two parts, the good and bad, the positive and negative, the elements of male and female; they complement one another and belong together. Normally these elements are present in a manner that is balanced, harmonious, ordered and thus of beauty. This ideal equilibrium, however, is precarious and can be put out of balance in an indefinite number of ways, which must be avoided: doing anything to excess, violating taboos, contamination through contact with ghosts, harbouring evil thoughts, initiating or being the victim of acts of witchcraft, or showing disrespect or carelessness in one's relations with the forces of a natural world which normally is in a state of balance.

Symptoms of any illness indicate that the normal balance has been upset and must be restored. Such restoration of health for the Navajo necessitates participation in one of several hundred ceremonial 'chantways' of two to fourteen days' duration. The chantway specific to the illness is determined by a special quasi-shaman diagnostician or 'hand trembler'. A singer (*hatali*) who knows the selected chantway is then contacted, and elaborate preparations begin. Sacred ceremonies must always be enacted within a *hogan*, the traditional Navajo circular or octagonal dwelling with an opening in the domed roof. Such dwellings, as well as the Athabascan-type conical sweat lodge, are considered by the people to be the world or cosmos, with its place of release in the opening above.

Reminiscent of Pueblo practice is the use of plumed prayer wands, set to the four directions outside the ceremonial *hogan* to compel the *yei* (gods) to be present with their curative spiritual powers. Central to the complex ceremonies within the *hogan* is the singer's chanting of myths of creation, the stories of heroes who purified the earth in primal times, or other mythic episodes related to the cause of the illness. These chants must be recited without any error whatsoever. At appropriate times, multi-coloured dry-paintings are laid out with precision on the clean sand of the *hogan* floor; the patient is seated on the centre of these so that the powers of the depicted gods and other beings can work for the restoration of harmony, balance and thus health. Although the patient is the central beneficiary of these sacred rites, it is understood that powers thus generated spread from the centre to bless those who are present and eventually extend outwards without limit.

With the maintenance of balance and harmony as the presiding idea of their religion, it is understandable that the Navajo must be under considerable stress in their confrontations with a threatening and unpredictable surrounding world. Participation with this larger American world in foreign wars has intensified these pressures (although the Navajo are proud of their abilities in warfare), for slaying an enemy involves contact with his potentially dangerous ghost. One avenue of release from such tensions has been increased witchcraft practices. Because such practices are institutionalized, they provide controlled release and thus do not jeopardize the basic structures of Navajo life. Other types of responses are in a sense paradoxical, for they have resulted, on the one hand, in intensification of traditional ceremonial activities in order to 'decontaminate' those who have been exposed to dangerous forces associated with the dead or the unfamiliar. On the other hand, the Navajo now pragmatically seek any available additional means for curing their increasing and complex ailments. This partly explains the Navajo use of non-Indian health services and their increasing participation in the Native American Church, in which they use the hallucinogenic peyote as a curative agent.

Increased adherence to Christian denominations also involves identification of the Christian message with curative forces. Historically, however, Catholic missions have enjoyed less success among the Navajo than have Protestant or Mormon missions because there is an incompatibility between core Navajo religious structure and the central rites of the Catholic Church. Not only do the Navajo fear contamination with ghosts of the dead in relation to the crucifixion of Jesus, but also the central rites of communion involve what to them may be abhorrent acts of 'cannibalism'. [16]

Christian 'Conversion' among American Indians

Christian missions have influenced probably all American Indian peoples. Gradations of Indian affiliation to Christianity span two extremes: some have fully accepted the new faith and consciously rejected their own traditions. Others have been exposed to Christianity, and once even may have accepted it, but have since returned to an often intensified participation in their own sacred ways. But the incomplete evidence suggests that these two groups are in the minority in relation to those situated between the extremes. A key element in the evaluation of Indian affiliation with Christianity, to which sufficient attention has not been given in the scholarly literature or in Church documents, lies in the special meaning of conversion for most American Indians – as indeed for most representatives of the primal traditions who have had contact with Christianity.

The following perspective is fundamental to this inquiry: in virtually every indigenous American Indian tradition, a basic, pervasive theme has always been that all forces of the experienced natural environment can communicate to man the totality of what is to be known of the sacred mysteries of creation, and thus of the sacred essence of being and beings. Beliefs and practices which have evolved from cumulative personal and tribal experience assure the intensification and continuity of participation in the sacred. Such conditioned openness to experiences of the sacred makes it understandable that for American Indians religious matters – of whatever origin – are not open to debate. When, therefore, the Christian message came to the people through dedicated missionaries who led exemplary and sacrificial lives, the people easily understood the message and example because of the profundity of their own beliefs. They adapted the new expressions of values into the sacred fabric of their own religious culture. The historical phenomenon represented here is thus not one of conversion as understood exclusivistically by bearers of Christianity; it is simply a continuation of the people's ancient and traditional facility for what can be termed non-exclusive cumulative adhesion.

It is important to add that, if this process of synthesis can be accomplished with neither confusion nor dissonance it is ultimately due to the ability of American Indian peoples to penetrate and comprehend the central, most profound nature of all experience and reality. In a very practical sense, it must also be noted that if these groups had been unable to accommodate selectively the traits of alien cultures, they simply would not have survived as distinct peoples.

For Bibliography, see page 449 below.

Table 11.1. North American Indian culture areas showing language families and selected representative tribal groups

Culture areas	Language families		Representative tribal groups
1 Coastal Arctic (Western, Central and Eastern)	Eskimo-Aleut		Trans-Arctic Eskimo Eastern and Western Aleut
2.1 Sub-Arctic (Western and Mackenzie)	(a) Athabascan (Na-Déné)		Dogrib Slave Hare Beaver Kutchin Kaska Carrier Yellowknife
2.2 Sub-Arctic (Eastern)	(b) Algonquian		Cree Montagnais Naskapi
3 Eastern Woodland	(a) Algonquian		Micmac Malecite Abnaki Penobscot Mahican Pennacook Massachusett Delaware
	(b) Iroquoian		Iroquois Mohawk Oneida Onondaga Cayuga Seneca Huron Tuscarora
4 South-East	Muskogean		Natchez Creek Chickasaw Choctaw Biloxi Mobile

5	*Plains/Prairie*	
	(a) Siouan	Crow / Hidatsa, Asiniboine / Iowa, Omaha / Osaga, Dakota / Mandan
	(b) Algonquian	Prairie Cree / Blackfeet, Plains Ojibwa / Atsina, Cheyenne / Arapaho
	(c) Athabascan (Na-Déné)	Sarsi / Kiowa-Apache
	(d) Caddoan	Pawnee / Arikara, Wichita / Caddo
	(e) Uto-Aztecan	Shoshone / Comanche, Ute
6	*Basin*	
	Uto-Aztecan	Mono / Paiute, Mohave / Washo, Shoshone / Bannock, Ute / Gosiute
7	*South-West*	
	(a) Tanoan	
	Tiwa	Taos / Picuris, Isleta / Sandia
	Tewa	San Juan / Santa-Clara, San Ildefonso / Tesuque, Nanbe / Hano
	Towa	Jemez / Santo Domingo, San Felipe
	(b) Keresan	Acoma / Santa Ana, Cochiti / Laguna, Zia

Table 11.1 – contd

Culture areas	Language families	Representative tribal groups	
	(c) Uto-Aztecan	Hopi, Pima, Yaqui	Huichol, Papago, Mayo
	(d) Zuñian	Zuñi	
	(e) Athabascan	Navajo	Apaches (Eastern and Western)
	(f) Yuman	Walapai, Havasupai, Cocopa	Yavapai, Mohave, Maricopa
8 Plateau	(a) Sahaptin	Nez Percé	Sahaptin
	(b) Salish	Lillouet, Kutenai, Spokan, Yakima, Umatilla	Flathead, Kalispel, Cœur d'Alène, Shuswap, Klamath
9 California	(a) Algonquian	Yurok	Wiyot
	(b) Athabascan (Na-Déné)	Hupa	Tolowa
	(c) Hokan	Diegueño, Yuman, Shasta, Yana	Kamia, Pomo, Seri, Chumash
	(d) Uto-Aztecan	Luiseño, Gabrielino, Serrano	Cahuilla, Kawaiisu

10 *North-West Coast*

(e) Penutian — Yokuts, Costanoan, Wintun { Miwok, Maidu

(f) Yukian — Yuki { Wappo

(a) Athabascan (Na-Déné) — Tlingit, Haida { Chilkat

(b) Penutian — Chinook, Coos, Klamath { Tsimshian, Takelman, Sahaptin

(c) Wakashan — Kwakiutl, Heilsuk, Nootka { Haisla, Bella Bella, Makah

(d) Salishan — Bella Coola, Lummi, Twana, Klallam, Skagit, Chehalis { Quinault, Cowichan, Puyallup, Snuqualmie, Tillamook

Figure 11.2   Western islands of the Pacific Ocean

B. Pacific Religions

B. COLLESS AND P. DONOVAN

Introduction

FOREWORD

The Pacific Ocean covers nearly a third of the earth's surface. Geographically and historically its island inhabitants form four main groups: Indonesian, Australian, Melanesian and Polynesian (see Figures 11.2 and 11.3). Apart from Indonesia, which has been subject to Indian influences for nearly 2,000 years and Islamic contact for over 1,000, the remaining Pacific territories have enjoyed many centuries of isolation from the rest of the world. In their small, remote communities, the native peoples have developed cultures in which religious belief and practice play a vital and distinctive part. They provide some of the world's best examples of primal religions. Modern history of religion in the Pacific, however, is dominated by the increasing intrusion of Europeans since the sixteenth and seventeenth centuries, and the response of native societies to European culture, including its Christian religion. Writing about the Pacific has largely reflected European viewpoints and concerns. Only recently have indigenous writers and scholars begun to emerge, recording Pacific Islanders' own reactions to the foreign impact, and attempting to recover and appreciate afresh their ancient beliefs and ways.

SOURCES FOR STUDY

Primal religions of the Pacific have no written traditions. Reducing to writing their myths and teachings, and recording their practices, has been the work of a wide variety of foreigners (including explorers, missionaries and colonial officers) for many of whom scholarly objectivity was not a primary concern. Some descriptions by colonists and missionaries, however, provide invaluable records of native beliefs at a stage before the invading world seriously altered their character. Among these are the collection of Polynesian legends and myths by Sir George Grey [1], R. H. Codrington [2] on the beliefs and practices of Melanesians, and Carl Strehlow [3] on the myths of central Australia. Emerging modern anthropology, with its systematic and analytical field-work, had notable representatives, including Bronislaw Malinowski [4], F. E.

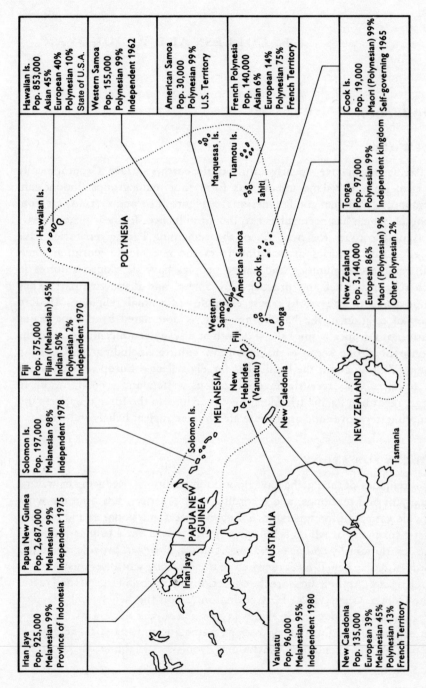

Figure 11.3 Eastern islands of the Pacific Ocean

Hawaiian Is.
Pop. 853,000
Asian 45%
European 40%
Polynesian 10%
State of U.S.A.

Western Samoa
Pop. 155,000
Polynesian 99%
Independent 1962

American Samoa
Pop. 30,000
Polynesian 99%
U.S. Territory

French Polynesia
Pop. 140,000
Asian 6%
European 14%
Polynesian 75%
French Territory

Cook Is.
Pop. 19,000
Maori (Polynesian) 99%
Self-governing 1965

Tonga
Pop. 97,000
Polynesian 99%
Independent kingdom

New Zealand
Pop. 3,140,000
European 86%
Maori (Polynesian) 9%
Other Polynesian 2%

Fiji
Pop. 575,000
Fijian (Melanesian) 45%
Indian 50%
Polynesian 2%
Independent 1970

Solomon Is.
Pop. 197,000
Melanesian 98%
Independent 1978

Papua New Guinea
Pop. 2,687,000
Melanesian 99%
Independent 1975

Irian Jaya
Pop. 925,000
Melanesian 99%
Province of Indonesia

Vanuatu
Pop. 96,000
Melanesian 95%
Independent 1980

New Caledonia
Pop. 135,000
European 39%
Melanesian 45%
Polynesian 13%
French Territory

POLYNESIA

MELANESIA

NEW ZEALAND

AUSTRALIA

Hawaiian Is.

Marquesas Is.

Tuamotu Is.

Tahiti

Western Samoa

American Samoa

Cook Is.

Tonga

Fiji

New Hebrides (Vanuatu)

New Caledonia

Solomon Is.

PAPUA NEW GUINEA

Irian Jaya

Tasmania

Williams [5], Sir Baldwin Spencer [6] and A. P. Elkin [7]. Classical descriptions of the culture of Polynesian peoples were produced by the Maori scholar Sir Peter Buck [8]; E. S. C. Handy [9] and R. W. Williamson [10] recorded in detail the religion and mythology of Central Polynesia; and Elsdon Best [11] compiled records of the traditions of the New Zealand Maori.

Greater justice has been done to local and regional diversity through the many ethnographic studies in Oceania in recent years, by scholars eager to record information about these rapidly changing societies. Archaeology is also making important contributions, especially to the study of patterns of migration. Recent works particularly concerned with religion include Ronald and Catherine Berndt [12] on Australian Aborigines, I. H. N. Evans [13] and Erik Jensen [14] on Borneo tribespeople, Clifford Geertz [15] and Niels Mulder [16] on the Javanese, and P. Lawrence and M. J. Meggitt [17] on Melanesia. Roslyn Poignant [18] has produced an illustrated account of the major mythologies of Pacific islanders.

The effects of contact with a dominant foreign culture, and reactions by way of prophetic cults and new religious movements, have especially attracted the attention of scholars. Some writers, such as Peter Worsley [19], see these phenomena as primarily of sociological and political interest; others find in them evidence of distinctively religious patterns, with native peoples reviving aspects of their traditional belief-systems, in an effort to regain power and initiative through spiritual means. Examples can be found in the studies by Kenelm Burridge [20], Philip van Akkeren [21], R. M. Berndt [22], with many more recorded in the bibliography of new religious movements prepared by Harold W. Turner [23]. Investigation of such movements reveals the many ways in which the primal heritage may remain a vital force within modern religious and political life.

Scholars in the field of history of religions bring to the study of primal religions the further refinements of their phenomenological and comparative method. They use classifications developed especially to permit the religious data to be viewed within the worlds of meaning and experience to which they belong. Mircea Eliade, for instance, has written on Australian primal religion [24]. Present-day scholars in Pacific universities, theological colleges and other centres for the study of religion and culture are producing valuable studies in this field [25–8]. Crucially important is the contribution by indigenous researchers and writers, who record oral traditions from the fast-disappearing older generation; and who reflect on their own generation's reactions to its experiences of colonialism and independence, conversion to foreign religions, and contact with the wider world. Though often unpublished, or appearing only in locally produced journals or books, writing of this nature provides the best evidence of the extent to which primal and traditional elements still assert themselves in the religious life of Pacific peoples.

The four main regions are now considered in turn. For each, the general features of the beliefs and practices of Pacific primal religions are discussed; foreign influences, which have produced major disruptions of traditional life, are considered; and an account is given of modern developments, showing the ways in which underlying primal elements remain alive.

Indonesia

BELIEFS

Throughout the Pacific region we encounter myths of a marriage between Earth (Mother) and Sky (Father), and their eventual separation (it is usually their children who break their creative embrace, as in Polynesia). Indonesia is no exception, but here we also find sacred marriage in the context of the production of the staple food. In Java it is Sri and Sadono (the Hindu Lakshmi and Vishnu, see pages 198–200) who unite to produce rice, the divine plant of life. For tribespeople and village farmers a mystical relationship between man and rice establishes the unity of society and its symbiosis with nature. The Indonesian world is inhabited by humans and spirits whose wishes sometimes clash, and propitiation is required. The word *adat* is widely used for the correct behaviour expected of people, as also of spirits and animals, to maintain cosmic order. Conceptions of an impersonal supernatural power (like Polynesian *mana*) are widespread. In Javanese mysticism (*kebatinan*), the idea of *rasa* or *roso*, intuitive inner feeling leading to higher knowledge, is cultivated. The belief in a soul is usually complex, involving a substance which can be increased, by certain techniques, alongside a personal spirit. An afterlife is everywhere acknowledged and is not an innovation from Islam or Christianity; nor have Hindu or Buddhist ideas of reincarnation had much influence here, save in Hindu Bali.

PRACTICES

In Indonesia the religious year revolves round the life-cycle of rice. In Borneo, for example, the cycle begins with divination to find the right place in the jungle for farming, followed by slashing and burning; rituals accompany planting, growth, ripening, harvesting and storing. In Java and Bali the ritual pattern is similar, but there the grain is cultivated in irrigated terraces. Great reverence is shown to the spirit or soul of the rice; it is treated as a person.

In many places the 'rice mother' (a bundle from the harvest) is set up to represent the whole field and be ritually cared for.

Spirits of many kinds have to be propitiated in every part of the village and landscape, and at every turn in life. In Java every significant occasion is marked with a *slametan*, a religious meal aimed at producing *slamet*, peace and well-being, in the community and in the spirit world; the spirits eat the essence of the food and are satisfied. There is a Muslim prayer in Arabic to solemnize the ceremony, but the purpose is propitiation of spirits. In funerary rites, burial is the normal method of disposal of the dead body, but in Hindu Bali it is cremation. Ritual specialists are on hand to ensure a good departure for the soul of the deceased.

FOREIGN INFLUENCES

The legacy of India to Indonesia is evident from the monuments and temples on the landscape of Sumatra, Java and Bali. Hindu–Buddhist images of metal and stone are always being discovered. There are traces of Muslim iconoclasm, which has made archaeologists' work more difficult, but there is general tolerance between religions. Whereas Sunni Islam of the Shafi'ite school (see pages 136f) is firmly established in the archipelago, Bali remains Hindu and Java is not prepared to jettison its old and proven tradition when it accepts new faiths. In Java's ricefields the God of the new religions must allow a place for the rice goddess, who goes under the Hindu name Dewi Sri. In Java and Bali those who espouse exclusive Islam or Christianity are not at home in the village and must live in the cities or establish new settlements.

MODERN DEVELOPMENTS

The ideas 'modernity' and 'development' are in great vogue in the Republic of Indonesia today, as the diverse religious and ethnic groups strive to build a modern developed nation. Its motto is 'Unity in Diversity' (a phrase of religious origin from the Hindu past) and the first of its five principles of nationhood (the *Panca Sila*) is 'belief in God'. In the 1970s the government actually fostered religion, declaring that the development of religion and belief in the Oneness of God was necessary to create harmony as the various communities sought to build the new society together. Christianity has its independent churches, notably the Batak churches of Sumatra and the indigenous church of East Java (see pages 444f); and the mosque is the centre of countless communities; but gurus are rising up in increasing numbers in Java to teach Javanese mysticism. Some of these gurus mix Muslim and Christian ideas into their Hindu–Javanese teachings, but go on to offer day-by-day revelations. Admittedly some of these intuitions relate to the national lottery, but more significantly these specialists of the sacred (who are usually also involved in the secular world as mechanics, teachers, soldiers, politicians and so on) offer their disciples individual and social harmony.

Australia

BELIEFS

Aboriginal myths usually recount the wanderings of supernatural beings in the creative period, conventionally known as 'the Dream Time' or 'the Eternal Dreaming'. In south-eastern Australia there are traces of a male supreme being who now lives in the sky but once walked upon the earth to establish it. In the north, however, instead of this All-Father we find Earth as Mother of all. The Rainbow Snake is widely represented in the mythology, sometimes as male, sometimes as female. It is associated with rain or water, and is often held to be the first creator, as the maker of all living creatures.

Australian religion is said to be totemic. Totemism involves a relationship between a person or group and some natural object, phenomenon or species. It is an affirmation of a kinship bond between mankind and nature: they share the same life essence and exist for the mutual imparting of life. Totemism is also a declaration of strong attachment to one's own land and people, and a symbolic expression of Aboriginal social values and relationships. An Aboriginal Australian is not a materialist. His possessiveness extends only to his totem and a few sacred objects; he fosters the life of the spirit religiously. The person's spirit exists before birth and survives after death, but there is no heaven or hell. The spirit simply remains on or in the land.

PRACTICES

The greater part of sacred lore and law is in the hands of males, especially older men and medicine men. Males also direct most of the religious rituals in Aboriginal religion, but women take part in some of them and have their own secret ceremonies. Myth and rite are complementary: rituals are either enactments of myths or validated by myths (for example, stories giving the origin of circumcision and subincision as performed on boys at initiation). Of vital importance are the increase rituals, for stimulating spirit beings to augment food supplies, or fertility, or love between a woman and a man. In the case of food or weather, each totemic group (kangaroo, honey-ant, sun, rain and so on) has its own special dance ritual for increasing the supply.

A potent ingredient to ritual practices is human blood (obtained not from sacrificial victims but from a man's own subincised urethra or arm veins) or its substitute, red ochre. For ceremonial occasions human bodies are decorated with feathers, fat, clay, colouring and blood. Thus arrayed the people dance and sing. Typical ritual objects are: secret and sacred carved boards (often used as bullroarers); thread crosses (wool and hairstring threaded on a frame of two or three sticks, worn on the hair or on the back in dances, but sometimes large and elaborate, with sacred boards and spears as the framework); and symbolic designs drawn on the ground or painted on walls.

FOREIGN INFLUENCES

Before the coming of the European to Australia in 1788, the Aborigines had lived in isolation. In the north there had been contacts with Melanesians and Indonesians (reflected in songs, rituals and paintings) but the surface was only ruffled at the edges by such encounters. The invasion of the British was more catastrophic. From the very start their diseases spread with ease; smallpox ravaged the black population for half a century. Disseminating their Christian religion was not so easy; Aborigines found no spiritual or political relevance in it to their own well-ordered world. Iconoclastic-minded missionaries found no heathen idols to smash, and they inclined to the opinion that they were dealing with subhuman savages who had no religion and were beyond redemption, a view still held by some frustrated evangelists today. Though the European missionary could not impose his morals on the Aboriginal, he nevertheless imparted demoralization. In recent years one of this apparently dying race said with grave humour to the anthropologist W. E. H. Stanner: 'When all the blackfellows are dead all the whitefellows will get lost in the bush, and there'll be no one to find them and bring them home.' Aboriginal religion contains, however, the sacred secret of survival on the dry southern continent.

MODERN DEVELOPMENTS

Christianity has made a few conquests. Part-Aborigines who have no clear relation to a tribe or locality can find a sense of belonging and unity in Christian conventions which bring them together to sing and pray. By contrast, 'the Jigalong mob' in Western Australia are a group of Aborigines of mixed origins who have resisted the missionaries by pooling their various cultural resources and holding on to them. The Bandjalang of northern New South Wales offer an example of a syncretistic movement, a synthesis of Pentecostal Christianity with their own myth and ritual (which had been branded as the work of devils by the missionaries who had taught them). The whites with their prosperity and power are linked with the Romans who crucified Jesus. When Christ returns it will be the blacks that he favours. While the whites are thus denigrated and demoted, Aboriginal women are promoted to sharing in knowledge of religious lore, since they too are 'baptized in the Spirit'. In general, though, Aboriginals are disturbed that so much of their secret heritage is being published in books and magazines, exposing women and uninitiates to danger or disaster from breaking taboos. Although radio valves and light bulbs are turning up among their sacred objects (as at Jigalong), this does not mean that the Aborigines are prone to instituting cargo cults. Aboriginal Australians are not acquisitive, and so far they have not shown themselves desirous of gaining the whole world at the cost of losing their own soul.

Melanesia

BELIEFS

Central to all Melanesian religion is belief in ancestor-spirits who through their access to supernatural powers can bring good or ill to their living descendants. Gods, demons, land-spirits (*masalai* in pidgin) and other forces of the unseen environment also intervene in human affairs. While there is little speculation about the origins of the wider world, creative gods and culture-heroes are credited with having given both the local culture and the means of livelihood. Animals, reptiles or fish may be regarded as totems, providing a bond between clan groups and their natural habitat.

Prosperity and order in the small communities depends on effective control of spiritual power (sometimes called *mana*) which shows itself in practical achievements such as successful warfare, trading, pig-rearing or crop-growing. Gods and spirits are believed to supervise communal morality, bringing illness or accident to those who misbehave or break taboos. Magic and sorcery are widely believed in and practised. Spirits of the recently dead are commonly sought by the living, through divination, in order to discover why their death occurred. Premature deaths and suicides raise the suspicion of sorcery, for which pay-back (appropriate recompense) must be sought, before the spirit will be free to journey to its final destination.

PRACTICES

Through individual and communal rituals, spirits of ancestors are honoured and their help is sought in the affairs of life. Male cult rites take place at the ceremonial house (*haus tambaran*), where the spirits make their presence known through sacred masks, musical instruments, dreams, prophecy and trance-mediums. In these rites, young men are introduced to the inner secrets of tribal lore. Birth, puberty, marriage, trade exchanges and funerals are all marked by communal ceremonies, commonly involving feasts and dances (*singsings*). Ceremonial distributions of wealth and food strengthen ties among the living and with the unseen powers.

Techniques of sympathetic magic, spells, incantations and herbal medicines, known to sorcerers and other religious specialists, are used in private rituals for healing, divination and success in hunting or courting, as well as for protection from dangerous animals, malicious ghosts and demons, and the effects of sorcery.

FOREIGN INFLUENCES

In the past century, Melanesia has been invaded by European trade, government and religions. The new sources of power which foreigners brought (wealth, weapons, medicines) deeply disrupted communities in which status rested on traditionally recognized achievements. Colonial governments brought an end to tribal warfare, depriving village societies of an important customary source of prestige, and of the need for much religious ritual.

However, since power is believed to be essentially a religious matter, native people assumed that by adopting European beliefs and practices they could share the higher levels of power and prosperity which Europeans appeared to enjoy. Christianity, then, was found by many to be a peaceful means of attaining the traditionally sought religious goal, a safer and more prosperous life in harmony with nature and society. In some cases, the impact of foreign culture was resisted by an established means of defence, namely religious revival and ritual. 'Nativistic' movements, often led by prophets (male or female), have been accompanied by mass enthusiasm and ecstatic behaviour, sometimes involving total rejection or selective reinterpretation of mission teachings. Of such movements, the widely discussed 'cargo cults' form only one of several distinct types (see Chapter 14 below).

MODERN DEVELOPMENTS

Melanesia has experienced vigorous missionary activity since the mid nineteenth century. Converts from other Pacific islands, brought by some of the missions, played an important part. Melanesian converts themselves actively spread Christianity. Under colonial administration, foreign missions helped establish communications, were responsible for health and education, and provided a spiritual rationale for the adoption of European ways. The Pacific

War of 1941–5 brought great changes: missions lost property and personnel; European prestige and control declined; and, of necessity, Melanesian initiative and experience in Church affairs increased. In the post-war period, foreign missions have increasingly given place to autonomous national churches, among which ecumenical cooperation is extensive. Many smaller evangelical missions have been introduced, and other groups, including Jehovah's Witnesses, Latter-Day Saints, and the Baha'i faith, are active. Indonesian rule of Irian Jaya (Western New Guinea) will mean increasing contact with the religion of Islam.

Despite major foreign influences, the cultural roots of primal religion remain vital, not only underlying cults and independent churches, but contributing generally to the identity and aspirations of Melanesia's newly independent peoples. The 'localization' of theology, as well as of liturgy and Church administration, is actively promoted by Christian leaders. They point to similarities between their own primal heritage and the biblical world; a pragmatic and communal experience of life; respect for forefathers; guidance from prophets, dreams and visions; and salvation through a fruitful relationship with higher powers. From this common basis Christian leaders seek to develop an indigenous Christianity, freed from associations with colonialism and white cultural dominance.

Polynesia

BELIEFS

For the Polynesians, life is lived within a world peopled by supernatural beings. The great creator god Tangaroa (or Io, in Maori religion) brought the cosmos into existence out of an original void. Earth and Sky begot lesser gods (*atua*) who in turn produced humans and continue to preside over important human concerns (Tane is god of forests and woodcutting; Tu, god of warfare; Hina, goddess of motherhood and weaving, etc.). Lesser spirits, ghosts and demons abound. Gods stand at the head of long lines of noble ancestors, transmitting through them the creative power (*mana*) which brings life and prosperity to their living descendants. Genealogies and migration stories trace family histories back to the mythical homeland Hawaiki, where spirits of the dead return to rest.

Although gods and ancestor-spirits are felt to be close at hand, mystery and awe lies at the heart of Polynesian religion. Direct access to the power and favour of the gods was traditionally reserved for chiefs (themselves once divinized) and for priests (*tohunga*), who possessed secret knowledge of lore and ritual.

PRACTICES

Gods and ancestor-spirits were invoked by the *tohunga* with sacred chants at a shrine or on a *marae* (gathering place for communal occasions). Honoured by rituals of offering, feast and dance, the gods in return granted *mana* to the chiefs, their people and their tribal lands. Food to nourish the gods and ensure their favour included the offering of human sacrifices. The first enemy killed was, for instance, offered to the god of war. First-fruits from freshly gathered foods or a catch of fish were likewise returned to the patron god. Human sacrifice was also commonly used in the consecration of buildings, war canoes and other types of sacred object.

Equally important were rites of purification from the effects of *tapu* (taboo). (*Tapu* formed a system of restraints and prohibitions to preserve the effectiveness of *mana*.) Water, the chief purifying agent, was sprinkled on new-born children, bloodstained warriors and those contaminated by sickness or death, in order to free them from *tapu* and make them safe for contact with other people. Priests used a variety of further rituals and chants for healing and divination, protection from sorcery or evil spirits, and for the burial of the dead to ensure their peaceful departure to the spirit-land.

FOREIGN INFLUENCES

The impact of European culture brought new diseases and weapons, reducing island populations and altering the balance of inter-tribal rivalry. Foreign trading undermined the native economies; dependence on foreign political and religious leadership destroyed the *mana* of chiefs; and the destruction of sacred objects and places by converts to Christianity challenged the authority of priests and the efficacy of traditional beliefs. Missionaries appropriated local languages for preaching and translating the Bible. Mission stations became centres for the spreading of foreign ways of life, while former villages and sacred places were abandoned. Sometimes, when chiefs were befriended by missionaries and embraced the new faith, conversions of whole tribes followed. Native converts, trained as teachers and preachers, became the chief agents of further expansion.

Disillusionment came for many when the expected benefits did not all follow conversion. Conflicts between different churches, the neglect of Christian moral teachings by other Europeans, and the involvement of missionaries in colonialist politics all contributed to a loss of confidence in the new religion's claims. However, after customary priestcraft, ritual and sacred places had been outlawed by mission decree or government law, it was not possible for the ways of the past to be completely reinstated. Resurgences of primal beliefs have from time to time occurred in the form of nativistic movements which either rejected foreign ways (as with the Mamaia cult in Tahiti in the 1820s) or, under prophet leaders, drew from biblical and traditional sources to produce indigenous versions of Christianity (as with the Ringatu and Ratana movements, which have become major churches among New Zealand Maori today).

MODERN DEVELOPMENTS

Although Christianizing helped bring peace and stability during two centuries of disruption, European missionary attitudes and policies inevitably resulted in the Polynesian peoples becoming ashamed of and abandoning many valuable features of their own heritage. Recovering those features (while protecting them from debasement by tourism) is a concern of leaders in Pacific culture today. A Pacific Conference of Churches actively promotes a local theology and a sense of continuity with the faith of non-Christian ancestors and their religion. The Pacific Theological College in Suva, Fiji, is a centre for such developments. Universities in Hawaii, Fiji, Australia and New Zealand have departments concerned with Pacific history and culture, including religion.

Mormonism (active in the Pacific since the 1840s), the Baha'i faith (introduced in the 1950s) and other new religions compete with post-Christian and secular ideologies for the support of the rising generation. But whether in scattered island villages or among migrant communities in city suburbs, the patterns set by the main missions – Congregationalist, Wesleyan, Roman Catholic, Anglican and Seventh-day Adventist – remain, for the foreseeable future, the familiar forms of religion for the great majority of Polynesians. In New Zealand, a current revival of Maoritanga (Maori culture) includes an emphasis by Maori Christian leaders on retaining traditional ways and concepts within Christian faith and practice. Among these are healing and exorcism rites, ceremonies of burial and mourning, respect for elders and ancestors, and other values embodied in the custom of the *marae*. To this extent, at least, primal religion remains alive.

For Bibliography, see page 451 below.

C. African Religions

AYLWARD SHORTER

Introduction

The term 'African religions' is used here to refer to the indigenous, ethnic religions of sub-Saharan Africa. The concept of tribe or ethnic group is a fluid one in Africa, for ethnic identities shade into one another and there have been continual migrations and amalgamations throughout African history. Basically the tribe is a category of interaction among heterogeneous peoples, but it has a cultural core which consists of a human tradition in a given physical environment. Such an environment offers a limited number of choices for solving the problems of daily living and each society has developed its social and cultural institutions in accordance with a chosen economy. Within the framework provided by physical environment and human tradition, African societies have interrogated human existence, have developed their own religious imagery and symbolic classifications and have evolved their own organic universe. Any attempt to classify the tribes of Africa is necessarily arbitrary. One such attempt has been that of G. P. Murdock, who lists 742 sub-Saharan tribes [1]. This conservative estimate conveys some idea of the size and complexity of the subject.

Nevertheless, indigenous religion in Africa is not strictly identifiable with the tribe, however it is defined, even though beliefs and values are articulated within tribal structures and traditions. Religious concepts and practices have been shared over wide areas in the history of Africa and certain religious institutions, such as ancestor veneration, have a near-universal currency. Particularist or holistic studies inevitably present a false picture although they are a necessary stage in our understanding of African religion and provide the primary sources of information. Such studies have been made by social anthropologists, early travellers and explorers and by scientifically minded missionaries. Participant observation, as a method, is required by the oral and ritual nature of the material. Subsequent comparative studies by scholars of religion have been based on this ethnographic material, particularly on recorded prayer-literature. The recent development of oral history has carried the study of African religions considerably further, providing, as it does, hard evidence for the interaction of peoples and the spread of ideas. Finally, modern

African poets, novelists, playwrights and political philosophers have added their interpretations to the growing literature on African religion.

Students of African religion were at first sceptical about the possibility of historical studies. Today there is no doubt that they are both possible and worth while. Religion permeated every aspect of life in traditional African societies and its history is inseparable from that of their social and political institutions. Over much of the continent, particularly eastern, central and southern Africa, populations have been small and scattered, and poverty of resources has imposed a subsistence economy in the shape of hunting-gathering, shifting cultivation and pastoralism. Such societies did not elaborate rich material cultures, but discovered parables for the spiritual realities of existence in the phenomena of an all-embracing nature. The theologies of such religions, though often subtle, were not elaborate. In the lake regions and forest fringes where soils are richer and rainfall more plentiful, settlement has been more dense and culture technologically more advanced. In such societies theology has been patterned more on the interplay of personalities, divinities and deified human beings, while religious practice has centred on holy places, graves, shrines, temples and mausoleums. All over the continent territorial and royal cults are found which have played an important role in politico-religious history.

In the colonial era (late nineteenth century to mid twentieth century) ritual leaders were mostly secularized, and immigrant religions, such as Islam and Christianity, acted as catalysts in an enlargement of social and theological scales. They also added to the doctrinal repertory of African traditional religion and stimulated reinterpretation, particularly with regard to belief in a supreme being or 'High God'. Certain indigenous belief-systems crossed the Atlantic as a result of the slave trade and survive in recognizable form in Cuba, Brazil and the Caribbean [2]. Such are the well-known *vodun* snake cult from Benin (see Figure 11.4) which has become the *voodoo* of Haiti and Jamaica, and the religious traditions from Nigeria, Zaire, Angola and Mozambique which survive as the Candomble brotherhoods in Brazil, the Umbanda and Macumba spirit cults and the syncretic Batuque traditions.

Within Africa itself ethnic religious values and traditions have lent a special colour to Islam and Christianity in their orthodox or mission-related forms. They have also taken new forms of their own in the so-called independent Church movements, some of which are not so much neo-Christian or neo-Judaic as neo-traditional, a good example being Elijah Masinde's Religion of the Ancestors (*Dini ya Misambwa*) in Kenya. Finally, contemporary Africa is witnessing the appearance of numerous communities of affliction, practising spirit mediumship therapy and also witch-eradication movements.

Racial and religious prejudice often bedevilled early accounts of African

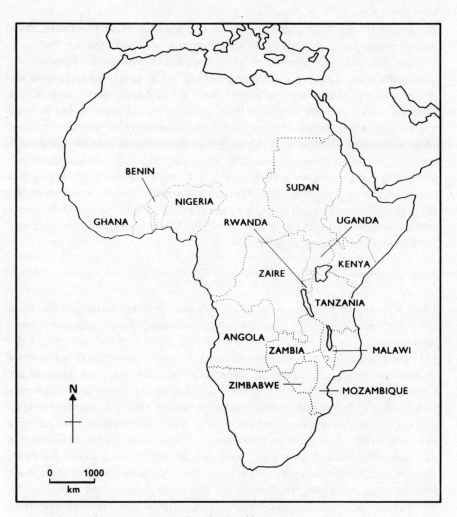

Figure 11.4 African countries referred to in the text

religions, and it was felt that peoples who were technologically inferior were incapable of 'higher' religious feelings and behaviour. Symbolism and mythology were held in contempt by Westerners, who considered scientific facts to be the only realities. Naïve evolutionism was replaced by misguided missionary progressionism and the effort to find vestiges of a 'primitive revelation'. It was social anthropology that began to appreciate African religions on their own terms, but even then Eurocentric criteria were responsible for concepts such as the 'withdrawn' or 'lazy' God (*deus otiosus*), the so-called 'High God' and for dualistic or polytheistic interpretations. With regard to comparative analysis, Evans-Pritchard advocated the 'limited comparative method' [3] (the study of dissimilarities among contiguous and historically related peoples) while Mary Douglas has proposed categorization on the basis of 'definable social experience' [4: IX]. Theologians, such as J. S. Mbiti [5] and E. B. Idowu [6], believe in the essential comparability of all ethnic religions, a 'super-religion' which purports to belong to all Africans, while historians, such as B. A. Ogot [7], I. N. Kimambo, T. O. Ranger [8] and R. Gray [9], advocate a more factual, but necessarily more restricted, analysis. Finally, African writers such as Chinua Achebe [10], Ngugi wa Thiongo [11] and Wole Soyinka [12] have chronicled the destruction of the old organic universe; used African religion as an allegory for modern sociopolitical processes; replaced it with an alien, Marxist ideology; or sought to secularize it in modern, tragic theatre.

The Teachings of African Religions

Africa's approach to the numinous is both personal and 'trans-personal'. In many instances 'spirit' is a category which includes inanimate medicines and fetishes as well as personal beings. Sometimes the concept is unified and the different levels of spirit are seen as 'refractions' of an ultimately powerful being, symbolically associated with the sky. This is the case for the northern Nilotes of Sudan, the Nuer [13] and Dinka [14]. In other instances a supreme being is more clearly and exclusively personalized as a Creator and/or Life-Giver, again employing sky-symbolism: sun, rainbow or lightning for example (see Figure 11.5). The supreme being has also been associated with mountains and high hills, Mounts Kenya and Kilimanjaro (the latter in Tanzania) being the most celebrated examples, and it is possible that hill-symbolism represents an older stratum of belief than sky-symbolism (see Figure 11.6).

Generally speaking, African experience of nature is classified as being either life-fulfilling or life-diminishing – and there is a third, enigmatic category of natural phenomena which seem to share human life or characteristics [15; 16: 9–26]. Thus classified, nature reveals the existence of spiritual realities, beings and powers, as well as means of human communication with the numinous. Very often nature spirits are thought to control the wild animals, as well as the trees and plants that grow in the wilderness, or they are associated with lakes, streams or rock-formations. A special place is reserved for the Earth and its (usually female) personalization in African cosmology. Occasionally, Sky–Earth opposition results in a clearly bisexual representation of the supreme being. The ultimate source of evil and disorder in the world is rarely personalized as a spirit, but more commonly traced to the witch,

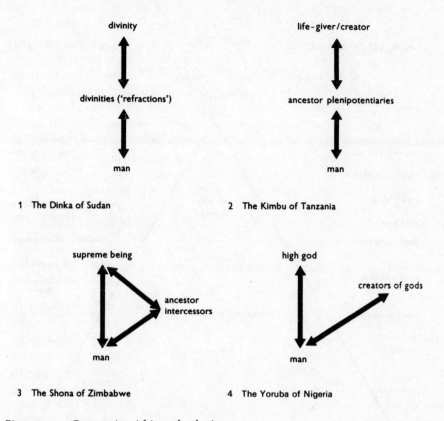

1   The Dinka of Sudan

2   The Kimbu of Tanzania

3   The Shona of Zimbabwe

4   The Yoruba of Nigeria

Figure 11.5   Contrasting African theologies

a human being who possesses preternatural powers to harm others secretly and malevolently.

Although there are well-documented instances of totemic spirits who are invoked as the guardians of clans and lineages, the patrons of society are usually the spirits of the dead, the ancestors. The spiritual world of the ancestors is patterned after life on earth. The recently dead and the un-remembered collectivity of the remotely deceased, are invoked by, and on behalf of, the family community. The territorial spirits who are the ancestors of chiefs or who are eminent personalities of the past are invoked on behalf of larger social groupings. Ancestors are thought to be mediators in one sense or another. They are perhaps seldom conceived of as intercessors, like the Christian saints. More often they are plenipotentiaries of the supreme being, mediating his providence and receiving worship in his name. Occasionally

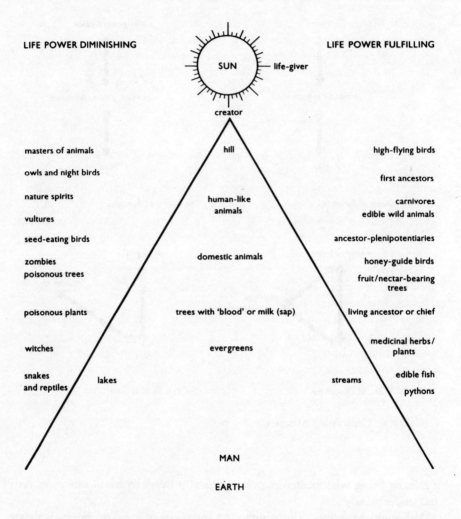

LIFE POWER DIMINISHING

LIFE POWER FULFILLING

SUN — life-giver

creator

masters of animals

owls and night birds

nature spirits

vultures

seed-eating birds

zombies
poisonous trees

poisonous plants

witches

snakes
and reptiles

lakes

hill

human-like
animals

domestic animals

trees with 'blood' or milk (sap)

evergreens

streams

high-flying birds

first ancestors

carnivores
edible wild animals

ancestor-plenipotentiaries

honey-guide birds

fruit/nectar-bearing
trees

living ancestor or chief

medicinal herbs/
plants

edible fish

pythons

MAN

EARTH

Figure 11.6   Cosmology of the Kimbu of Tanzania: pattern of symbols representing spiritual powers

they are seen as mankind's companions in the approach to the supreme being, guarantors of authentic worship [17 and 18 *passim*]. Much of traditional morality is concerned with pleasing the ancestors and living in harmony with them, since they are the most important members of the total community.

Leadership in traditional Africa was basically ritual leadership, whether of divine kings, or of prophet-arbitrators or spirit-mediums. In the shifting political situation of the pastoralists the leaders were members of prophet-clans which were credited with exceptional spiritual power. Among more settled peoples, the rulers were kings whose own life and well-being was linked cosmo-biologically with that of the universe. Royal cults like that of the 'High God' Mwari in Zimbabwe, or the divinity M'Bona in the Shire and Zambezi valleys (Malawi and Mozambique), were often manipulated by rulers [19]. In certain cases, the ruler was himself possessed by, or descended from, a divinity. This was the case of the king (or Reth) of the Shilluk in Sudan who was believed to be possessed by the deified spirit of the first king, Nyikang. It was also true of the Yoruba kings of Nigeria who were said to be descended from the god Odudua, the creator of the Earth, and of the King (Kabaka) of Buganda (Uganda) who was said to be descended from the deified first king, Kintu. Other kings like the King of Ashanti (Ghana) or the King of Ankole (Uganda) possessed the soul or spirit of their people in an important item of their regalia, the 'Golden Stool' or the royal drum (Figure 11.7).

It is particularly in the highly developed, monarchical societies that the greatest theological pluralism is encountered. When Christian missionaries appeared on the scene, it was sometimes difficult for them to select a supreme divinity with which they could identify the Christian god. In Buganda, for example, there were three candidates – the god of the sky, the creator god and the first god-king – while in the Yoruba religion the supreme being was king of the gods, but he was neither the creator of the earth nor of mankind. Such pluralism was basically unsystematic and the question of which divinity was supreme was often unimportant to those concerned. The experience of the numinous consisted in the dialectical interplay between the various spiritual beings. This was expressed mythologically and acted out in various ritual forms. Thus the tensions of human society were reproduced at the spiritual level.

In the precarious existence led by members of traditional African society, life and the transmission of life were important values. Death presented a paradox, since it was both a diminution of life and the gateway to a more powerful participation in life as an ancestor. Generally, one could only qualify for ancestorship by becoming oneself a life-giver, and the afterlife was bound up with a person's remembrance by the living. Humans could become ancestors, and in certain cases ancestors could become humans again. Peoples like the Ashanti of Ghana have a very clear concept of reincarnation. For them a person is reincarnated again and again until his life-work is complete and he is qualified to enter the world of the ancestors [20: 39–41]. Literal reincarnation is rarer than forms of nominal reincarnation whereby the living benefit by a special protection from their ancestor namesakes. Many people, like the Shona of Zimbabwe, believe that ancestral spirits can possess the living.

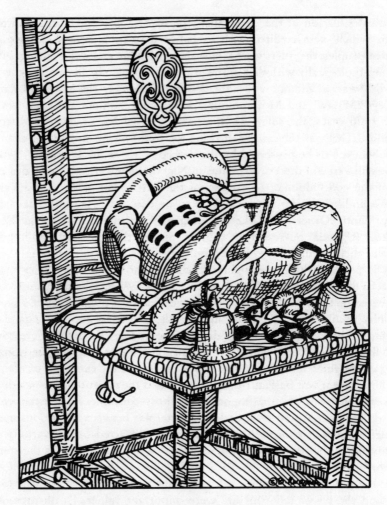

Figure 11.7   The Golden Stool of the Ashanti, Ghana

African Religious Practices

Foremost among the religious practices of traditional Africa is sacrifice. Among pastoralists it tends to have a markedly piacular (or expiatory) character and to be offered wholly or mainly to the supreme being. It is, typically, cow-sacrifice and is a feature of the cattle-culture complex. Sacrifice in other groups, however, is far from being reserved to the supreme being alone. It is modelled on human gift-exchange and on customs connected with the sharing of food and drink. First-fruits sacrifices are very common, from the first portions of meat set aside by the hunter when he butchers his quarry or the first portions of harvested grain, to the first mouthfuls of cooked food or the first mouthfuls of beer. Formal sacrifice at graves and shrines is usually a gift-oblation and is mostly a foodstuff or a libation. However, non-edible goods are also offered, and sometimes living animals, cows, goats or chickens are dedicated without immolation. When sacrifice is made to ancestors it is often likened to the feeding of, and caring for, old people, but it clearly goes beyond purely human ideas of eating and drinking. Ancestors are credited with exceptional knowledge and power, and sacrifice to them is an acknowledgement of their powerful role in human society. Misfortunes are very frequently attributed to a failure to offer sacrifice in due form or due time.

A very great proportion of African religious ritual is ancestral or funerary. This is especially true of territorial cults. The chief is often in some sense a 'living ancestor', ruling on behalf of his forebears and ensuring that a regular ancestral cult takes place. The rulers of chiefdom societies in western Tanzania were responsible for periodic offerings at their ancestors' graves. The rulers of the East African lake kingdoms also regulated the ritual that took place in the tomb-houses of their predecessors and at the shrines where their jawbones and umbilical cords were preserved. The Divine King (Oba) of Benin in Nigeria is still obliged to venerate the funerary altars of his ancestors, while in the kingdom of Ashanti the ritually blackened stools of deceased local chiefs are assembled before the king and his Golden Stool, in an important rite of national solidarity. In Ashanti also the embalmed bodies of former kings are preserved in a special mausoleum and continually repaired with gold-dust.

Mention has already been made of royal, ritual objects such as the Golden Stool of Ashanti, believed to have been conjured from heaven by the priest Anokye, and of royal drums like Byagendanwa of Ankole (Uganda). Such objects are often personified. The Golden Stool, for example, has its own stool, umbrella and attendants, and the Ankole drum has its own wives, servants and household. The ghost-horn blown during the territorial rituals of the Kimbu in western Tanzania is also symbolically identified with the country itself.

In traditional Africa practically every element of life had a religious aspect and this was the case especially with the rites of passage. Religious invocations and offerings played a part in birth-rites and naming ceremonies, in puberty rituals and other forms of initiation, as well as in marriage ceremonial and in funerals, mourning and inheritance ceremonies. There were numerous professional associations with their own religious rituals. In the more pluralistic societies, where ego-centred networks were as strong as, or stronger than, group loyalties, there were numerous particular cults of spirits or divinities with their own ceremonial repertory of song and dance, and their own traditions of ethical behaviour.

African notions of moral evil include the factual breaking of taboos and the ordinary laws of life, as well as the more grave anti-social actions. The first may be regarded fairly lightly, with only the culprit himself to blame. In the second case, it has to be remembered that traditional society in Africa included the dead as well as the living. An offence against society was, therefore, also an offence against the guardians of society. Redressive and reconciliatory rituals consequently often contained prayer for salvation from sin and its social effects. Although sickness, suffering and misfortune were thought to reveal such offences, a clear distinction was drawn between the state of sin and its effects. Redressive rituals were typically communal, since anti-social behaviour incurred collective guilt and punishment [21]. These rites often involved public confession of faults and symbolic purification. Sometimes, they included a communal gesture of renouncing the evil that had brought the misfortune.

Liminal rituals are very common in Africa. These celebrate – and, indeed, try to re-create – the liminal or marginal phase in rites of passage [22: 94–203]. It is an experience of temporary loss of status and social distinctions in which the deep springs of human interrelatedness are rediscovered. In the past, such rituals were performed by secret or semi-secret dance-societies or mask-societies. Often they acted out traditional cosmological myths or impersonated ancestors and historical personalities. Such were the Nyau societies of Central Malawi and the Egungun society of the Yoruba (Nigeria).

Whether it took a magical or a religious form, divination was always an important stage in the celebration of rituals in Africa. It was the divination process that decided which ritual was appropriate, and thus many religious ceremonies began with divination. If divination itself was a religious ritual it could take the form of spirit-mediumship. In some cases there was a god or divinity of divination who was thought to be the spokesman of the spirit world and who could identify which spirits or ancestors should be approached on a given occasion. Ifa, in the Yoruba pantheon, was such a god of divination.

Popular Manifestations of African Religion

At the popular level the African believer is often more engrossed in the identification of human sources of evil, and in counteracting them, than in the acknowledgement and worship of superior forces of good. The African, it has been said, is 'naked in front of evil' [23: 32]. Principally, this means that witch-finding is an important activity, and it involves recourse to the diviner and medicine man. The client approaches the diviner with certain presuppositions and suspicions, and these are rendered explicit in the divination process. The latter affords social approval for a retaliatory course of action against his enemies, and the medicine man provides protective rituals and medicines, as well as retaliatory ones.

The application of magic to areas of religious belief and practice is as rife in Africa as it is in the popular forms taken by religions elsewhere. There are societies, for example, in which it is believed that nature spirits and ancestors can be manipulated through magical processes. The Ganda (Uganda) believe that ancestral spirits can be conjured into medicine horns and then 'sent' to harm an enemy or rival. There is also the belief that a troublesome spirit can be disposed of by conjuring it into a pot which is then totally burnt and destroyed. There is also the possibility that prayer and sacrifice may take on the character of a magical technique with infallible results, if it is correctly performed.

Spirit-mediumship occurs sometimes as a popular form of prayer. It is obviously satisfactory for the worshipper to feel that he is in direct contact with the spirit he addresses and that he can obtain an immediate answer to prayer, even though the message may be somewhat enigmatic. Spirit-mediums may be possessed by nature spirits who are objects of propitiation or by ancestors and hero-divinities. In some cases the medium is mentally dissociated and speaks in trance; at other times, he or she simply speaks unfalteringly from the heart, believing that what is said in perfect truth and sincerity is the message of the spirit. This is the case with the Kubandwa mediumship of Rwanda and of the Lubaale spirit-mediumship (personally observed at Kampala, 31 July 1975) in Uganda. Worshippers seek information and guidance from the spirits in this way, and they also give gifts and offer praise to them.

Popular worship takes place in the family context, chiefly through ancestral or totemic rituals. Graves and ancestor shrines or figures play an important part in this worship (Figure 11.8). The wearing of protective charms and emblems is also often thought to be a means through which ancestors exercise their guardianship, and territorial rites of passage, the arrival and departure of travellers, house-moving or the opening up of new cultivation are also occasions for invoking the ancestors and possibly other spirits. Birth-rites, weddings and funerals are fundamentally family celebrations, and in many areas puberty initiation has become a family, rather than a community, affair as a result of the breakdown of traditional social structure. Reconciliation ceremonies take place at neighbourhood level when disputes have to be settled, and these may have a religious, even a sacrificial, character. Although on formal community occasions prayer takes on the form of a lengthy praise-poem, or of litanic song, in the ordinary household the typical prayer formula

Figure 11.8   Yoruba ancestor shrine, Nigeria

is a short and familiar petition, directly stating the needs of an individual or family. Religious values enter into much of the oral literature of African peoples. Not only in myth and aetiological folk-tales are there cosmological and moral themes, but religious ideas underlie proverbs and other didactic forms. Spontaneous oaths and blessings also take a religious form.

Modern Developments in African Religions

It has been estimated that between 30 and 40 per cent of the population of contemporary Africa still practise traditional African religion [24]. If Christians and Muslims who also resort occasionally to traditional practices are included, then the percentage might reach 70 per cent. It remains true, nevertheless, that African religion in its visible form, that is, as structured through pre-colonial tribal institutions, has been severely weakened. As far as ritual is concerned, the trend has been away from communitarian forms and towards individual and familial ones. With regard to concepts, beliefs and values, traditional religion is more tenacious than might be thought. Old ideas survive in new forms. Religion in Africa has always been highly absorbent and prone to syncretism, if not to reinterpretation. The playwright Wole Soyinka has described African religious symbolism as 'protean' [12: 122]. Certainly African religion has a remarkable resilience and a surprising capacity to survive in a submerged form.

Islam and Christianity have undoubtedly helped to bring about a monotheistic reinterpretation of traditional theology in some clear instances. Monica Wilson has shown how Kyala, the hero-divinity of the Nyakyusa (Tanzania) developed, under missionary influence, into the Christian God [25: 187ff], while Soyinka has argued that Idowu's concept of 'diffused monotheism', as applied to the Yoruba pantheon (Nigeria) is a Eurocentric reinterpretation [12: 108]. It is generally agreed that Christian eschatology has made a strong impact on traditional religious thought in Africa, and the idea of a bodily resurrection and future bodily existence is certainly attractive to people for whom bodily life and physical generation are important values. It may be that the conceptual formulations of Christian theology have unwittingly encouraged a literal and materialistic understanding of heaven and hell among Africans [26].

Accelerated organizational change has encouraged the growth of new forms for African traditional religion. One of these is the witch-eradication movement, which has been a recurring phenomenon in central Africa and southern Tanzania. This is, in a sense, a millenarian phenomenon in which a group of 'experts' who are possessed of a new and effective technique claim to be able to cleanse a whole community or countryside of witches and sorcerers. Travelling from place to place, they organize collective rites of purification and reconciliation in which people renounce their witchcraft and their evil powers are neutralized. A new golden age is proclaimed in which people will be free from the fear of witchcraft and sorcery. However, disillusionment usually follows, and there may eventually be further visits from the eradicators. Tomo Nyirenda's Mwana Lesa movement and Alice Lenshina's Lumpa Church (both in Zambia) are perhaps the most famous of modern, millenarist eradication movements, but there have been numerous others. [27: 45–75; and see pages 443f below)

Some so-called 'independent churches' are also traditionalist revivals rather than splinter groups from established mission churches. Other neo-traditional 'churches' are racially or ethnically conscious movements which attempt to purge foreign elements, while still other modern religious movements are frankly syncretist. Even an independent church like the Maria Legio Church of Kenya, which is ostensibly a schism from the Roman Catholic Church, inspired by the lay association known as the Legion of Mary, is in fact better understood in terms of the *juogi* spirit beliefs of the Luo tribe. But even those independent movements like the Religion of the Ancestors (*Dini ya Misambwa*, also in Kenya) or the ethnically conscious Kikuyu churches which nurtured the Mau Mau protest that precipitated Kenyan independence, were reinterpretations of traditional religion under the influence of Christianity.

Of equal interest is the way in which traditional values and institutions have shaped or affected religious movements which are demonstrably Christian and even orthodox Christianity itself [28 *passim*]. Many Christian independent churches have an organization which derives from traditional models of ritual or prophetical leadership. Dreams, mythology and spirit-mediumship may also play an important part in the life of these churches. In the mission-related churches, now under African leadership, the exercise of authority, as well as liturgical and musical adaptations, owes much to non-Christian traditions. Moreover, since Christian missionaries refused to accept African traditional religion as a coherent philosophy (albeit couched in symbolic and mythological language) neophytes have not been required to renounce their previous religion effectively. The result, as Robin Horton indicates, is a process of 'adhesion', rather than 'conversion', resulting in a crypto-traditionalism [29].

An interest which unites traditional religion, independent church movements, mission-related Christianity and the various forms of Islam is undoubtedly spirit-mediumship and spirit-healing. Among Christians the Pentecostal movement has exerted a strong influence, but the exorcism of evil spirits is also gaining popularity and even official approval. In the case of exorcism, the practice owes more to traditional ideas about morally neutral, but none the less malevolent, personifications of misfortune, than to Christian demonology. The Islamic jinn are also comparable to these traditional spirits. Many independent churches are basically pentecostal, and it has been conjectured that the pentecostalism which is now influencing Africa derives in part from spirit-possession cults which were carried to the New World by African slaves in the first place [30]. Certainly the neo-African and syncretic cults in Brazil and elsewhere tend to emphasize spirit-mediumship [2].

Finally, it cannot be denied that politicians and statesmen in independent African countries have exploited traditional beliefs as well as the politico-religious character of traditional leadership in order to consolidate their power. This opportunism has been denounced by – among others – Wole Soyinka as a trivialization of the essential, 'with catch-all diversionary slogans such as "authenticité"' [12: 109]. In spite of such false prophets of retrieval, traditional religious values continue to exert their influence both within and outside the religious organizations of contemporary Black Africa and to presage the transformation even of Islam and Christianity.

D. New Religious Movements
in Primal Societies

HAROLD W. TURNER

Introduction

In the last few centuries, and notably in the present century, the tribal peoples of the Americas, Asia, Africa and the Pacific have responded to their increasing interaction with the more sophisticated and powerful societies and religions by developing their own new religious movements. These usually differ at some important points both from the local tribal (here called primal) religion and the more universal religion concerned. Such movements have arisen in the interaction with Western culture and the Christian religion following the expansion of the European peoples across the world, but they also occur in relation to Hindu, Buddhist and, to a lesser extent, Islamic contacts.

Most of these religious movements possess no written sacred texts or other sources and have depended instead on a new oral tradition. This oral tradition enshrines the account of the origins of the movement, often the story of the founder's call and early struggles. These may also have been recorded in a diary or journal, or as a written testimony, and they can then assume the status of an authoritative canon or incipient scriptures. Sometimes this material is presented as having been given in written form from heaven, or otherwise divinely revealed. The oral tradition may also include new forms of old myths, and very often a body of sacred songs and prayers that may become the basis for a printed hymn-book or liturgy, as commonly in Africa and among New Zealand Maoris. In general, however, much earlier information comes not from such primary sources but from the rather hostile accounts of outsiders – colonial-government agents or soldiers, travellers and missionaries. Since the mid twentieth century there has been an increasing flow of scholarly information from more systematic and sympathetic academic studies.

There seem to have been few if any equivalent movements among the tribal peoples of North Africa and Europe during the earlier Christian expansion into these areas. The history of these movements may be said to start with European colonial and missionary expansion into Central and South America. Probably the earliest recorded movement occurred in Guatemala in 1530, followed by others in Colombia, Brazil, Paraguay, Bolivia, Peru etc., up to the present day. In the sixteenth century similar movements appeared in west central Africa after the conversion of the old Kingdom of the Kongo by Portuguese missionaries. Few of these movements lasted long, and it is in North America that the first of the movements still surviving appeared: the Narragansett Indian Church in Rhode Island in the 1740s, and the Handsome Lake Religion among the Seneca from 1800. These were followed by the Peyote cult or Native American Church, which has spread over much of North America in the last 100 years and is now the main Indian example (see page 400 above). Although the first Caribbean movement was George Liele's Native Baptist Church in Jamaica in the 1780s, most movements – Pocomania, Revival Zion, Bedwardism, Convince, Santería, Shango, Spiritual Baptists, Rastafarianism etc. – were later nineteenth- and twentieth-century developments. Modern movements in Black Africa trace back to Ntsikana and Makanna, Xhosa prophets at the beginning of the nineteenth century, but the great proliferation of independent churches (as most intend to be) began late in the century and has continued ever since. Similar developments occurred in the Philippines and in Oceania throughout the nineteenth century, especially among the New Zealand Maoris as in the Pai Marire and Ringatu religions. But it is in Melanesia, and since the 1930s, that most movements have appeared – usually small, short-lived and of the cargo-cult form [1]. In Asia the new religions of Japan are rather different phenomena, but the 200 that have appeared in Korea in the past century or more are somewhat closer to the new tribal movements. Elsewhere in Asia these have occurred in Siberia, in India among the scheduled tribes interacting with Hindu or Christian traditions since the eighteenth century, and in Burma and South-East Asia among the hill tribal peoples influenced by Buddhist culture or Christian missions in the same period. Indonesian movements have appeared in the later nineteenth and the twentieth century, either in relation to Christian contacts, or with an Islamic background, but the latter shade off into Islamic mystical movements that differ from new tribal religions.

The first major scholarly study in this field was James Mooney's on the Ghost Dance religion, in 1896 [2]; this also included substantial accounts of most other movements among Indians in the United States. Other anthropologists developed the study further both in the Americas and in other parts of the world, giving us the common terms 'nativistic' [3] and 'revitalization' [4] for these movements, seen as acculturation phenomena, together with various systems of classification. Other human sciences have produced major studies, each in terms of its own categories. Sociologists have seen the movements as products of social change and in relation to traditional social structures; economists have been concerned with material wants, with relative deprivation, and hence with cargo cults as a search for wealth in irrational ways; political scientists have studied the effects of colonialism and spoken of 'protest' movements, and indeed earlier movements often did come into violent clashes with governments and were suppressed; psychologists have used the categories of neurosis and crisis, and investigated the psyche of founders and leaders; and historians have sought to place these new movements in their wider context and trace their development over the years, as well as stress the place of the individual in the appearance and shaping of the movement. By contrast the first major study of African movements was that of the missionary-scholar, B. G. M. Sundkler, in 1948 [5]; while using many of the above categories he also gave attention to the religious features and the spiritual search apparent in the Zulu prophet movements he surveyed. Other scholars in the religious disciplines produced most of the major African studies until the more recent advent of the historians and social scientists [6; 7].

Since these movements are now better understood as religious developments, although necessarily conditioned by the various other factors identified above, a classification may be offered in terms of the degree of interaction between the two religious traditions concerned. Those seeking to remodel the existing primal religion with some borrowed elements may be called neo-primal; those deliberately rejecting the local and the invading traditions in favour of a new composite form drawn from both of the others may be called synthetist; in the case of those related to Christianity a third type of movement which resembles the religion of ancient Israel and stresses the Hebrew Scriptures or 'Old Testament' may be called Hebraist; those which go beyond this point in their biblical content and possess some form of Christology may be called independent churches (see Figure 11.9). Some movements, of course, overlap these analytic categories. Various names have been used – 'millennial' and 'messianic' movements, 'prophet', 'syncretist' or 'separatist' cults etc. The term 'adjustment movements', commonly used of Melanesia, is useful, but the best working name is probably 'new religious movements' (i.e. in primal societies interacting with more powerful societies and their universal religions).

Basic Beliefs

Common to most movements is the belief in a new revelation specially given from the spirit world to a local founder or leader. This often occurs through a dream or a mystical experience of dying, visiting heaven and being commissioned to return to earth with a new ritual and moral code, and with divine power, especially for healing. There is usually an emphasis upon a single supreme and personal God, either as a development from a possibly remote High God in the traditional primal religion, or in replacement of the former spirits and divinities. Some of the latter may be transposed into angels or saints, or else demoted as the devil. Reliance on this supreme and powerful

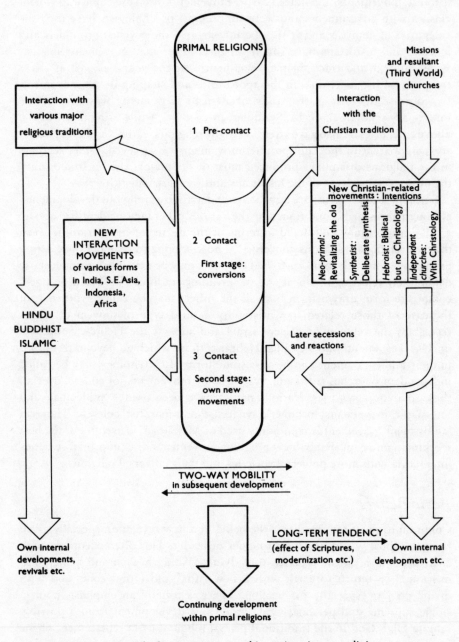

PRIMAL RELIGIONS

Interaction with
various major
religious traditions

Missions
and resultant
(Third World)
churches

Interaction
with the
Christian tradition

1 Pre-contact

New Christian-related
movements : Intentions

NEW
INTERACTION
MOVEMENTS
of various forms
in India, S.E.Asia,
Indonesia,
Africa

2 Contact

First stage:
conversions

Neo-primal:
Revitalizing the ola

Synthetist:
Deliberate synthesis

Hebraist: Biblical
but no Christology

Independent
churches:
With Christology

HINDU
BUDDHIST
ISLAMIC

3 Contact

Second stage:
own new
movements

Later secessions
and reactions

TWO-WAY MOBILITY
in subsequent development

Own internal
developments,
revivals etc.

LONG-TERM TENDENCY
(effect of Scriptures,
modernization etc.)

Own internal
development etc.

Continuing development
within primal religions

Figure 11.9 Varieties of religious content and intentions in new religious
movements in primal societies

God usually results in rejection of the use of magic, although belief in its effectiveness when used by others may continue.

The new religion usually offers definite practical blessings, here and now, in the form of mental or physical healing, further individual revelations for guidance from the spirit world, promises of success and prosperity, or of protection from evil forces. These blessings may be set within the wider promise of a new social or world order that is shortly to appear, perhaps through some cataclysmic event or messianic leader. This new order may introduce a paradisal era of peace, health and plenty; lost lands or a previous state of sinlessness may be recovered, oppression and humiliation at the hands of conquerors or colonial powers will cease, and the tables may even be turned with the tribal peoples in a dominant position. Such millennialism is common in some regions, as in Melanesian cargo cults, but is rarer in other regions, as in Africa where the emphasis is upon immediate practical benefits.

These promised blessings lead to a new hopeful and confident attitude to life, as well as to a new self-respect, a sense of dignity and of identity among peoples whose morale has been undermined by the traumatic effects of inter-action with the invading society. This confidence rests upon the belief in the new authoritative revelation given especially for themselves, and upon the conviction that supernatural help is to be given towards these various blessings. This help may come from God or Jesus or some other being in the spirit world, such as guardian angels, ancestors or culture-heroes, or the deceased founder returning from the dead once again. Receipt of the blessings also depends upon faithful observance of the new forms of worship, perhaps upon extensive performance of the new ritual dances (as in the 'Ghost', i.e. ancestor, dances of the North American Indians) or of prayers, fastings and other disciplines, and the observance of a strict moral code.

Whereas primal religions are characteristically confined to one tribal group, the new religious movements show various degrees of a more universal out-look. The revelation and the blessings are then regarded as given for other adjacent tribes, for all of their own race, or even for the whole world including the whites, who will then depend upon the tribal people for their full salvation. Thus while Godianism, a sophisticated neo-primal religion in eastern Nigeria, promotes a single God of Africa and rejects Christianity as for whites only, another Nigerian movement calls itself 'The Church of the Lord (Aladura) Throughout the World', and has had the occasional white member and branches in Britain.

Two of the basic drives at work in these new religious movements are the search for meaning and the quest for spiritual power. On the one hand confidence in the traditional primal world-view with its religious beliefs and practices has been eroded, for it cannot cope with the new intercultural situation or defend its adherents against the religious system and world-view of the invasive society. On the other hand there are many for whom the new religion, in the foreign form in which it arrives, also fails to provide the necessary meaning and spiritual power for daily living in a situation of great cultural change. (See Figure 11.10.) Peoples across the tribal world have therefore created new religious systems of their own, combining in various degrees something of their existing world-view and cultural forms with the new views and practices of the more powerful invasive religion. Sets of beliefs from the two systems may merely coexist somewhat incongruously; in other cases there is a creative synthesis into a new belief-system that brings meaning and power to its adherents. The new system of belief will be implied and expressed in concrete popular forms of prophecy, ritual, dance, song, story, healing, code of conduct etc.; it is less likely to articulate the analysis used here or to take the form of theology, doctrine or creed in a Western Christian manner.

Characteristic Practices

Many movements engage in a selective and dramatic rejection of some of the old ways, in preparation for the expected new order. Cargo cultists may kill the pigs, cease gardening and even destroy the food stores in view of the imminent supernatural abundance; Siberian shamans' drums have been burnt and North American Indian medicine-bags thrown away. These are more extreme examples but it is common to destroy ritual objects or shrines and especially magic paraphernalia, for the power formerly sought in this way is now derived from faith in the new God.

There are, however, substantial retentions of the old ways, especially in the continued reliance on dreams and visions as a means of revelation, and in the acceptance of trance and possession as signs of the presence of spirit power. Other traditional practices such as acceptance of a highly authoritative 'chiefly' leader, purification rites, ritual uncleanness of women, and polygamous marriage may continue. A minority of movements, however, insist on monogamy, and in many areas there have been notable examples of women as founders or leaders, as with Alice Lenshina in the Lumpa Church in Zambia from 1953, Angganitha the Biak area prophetess in Irian Jaya around 1940, and Mama Chi of the Guaymi people in Panama in the 1960s. Since these women have usually been young they represent a double revolution in societies dominated by male elders.

The new movements usually stress frequent or prolonged communal worship. The forms derive from both the old and the new religion, so that drums, dancing and reporting of dreams consort with band instruments, Bibles, hymns and preaching, imported vestments and church layouts. There

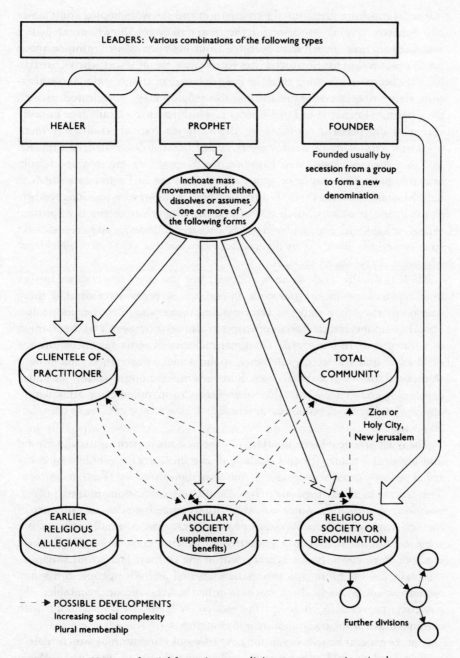

Figure 11.10 Variety of social forms in new religious movements in primal societies

is usually much congregational participation and the worshipping community is a cohesive central structure for the new movement. Newly created rites and festivals may incorporate features from both the contributing religious traditions; some of the borrowed rites receive new meanings, as when Christian baptism becomes a healing ritual or a mere badge of congregational membership. Other rites important in the invasive religion may be neglected, as with the Christian Eucharist or Lord's Supper, which tends to be rare even in fairly Christian independent churches in Africa. Major festivals commonly focus on a new Holy City, a headquarters village or area designated or regarded as Zion, the new Jerusalem, Paradise, the Happy City etc. Members from afar will gather here once or twice a year, perhaps at Easter, as with Zion City Moriah in the northern Transvaal where there may be 100,000 members of the Zion Christian Church. Otherwise the holy centre serves as a spiritual focus (perhaps with a mausoleum for the deceased founder), and administrative base sometimes involved in diverse activities such as economic enterprises, educational and health services.

There is usually a new code of conduct. In a few cases this goes no further than replacement of the old code by an era of permissiveness, but more commonly there is a rigorous reforming ethic stressing love, peaceableness, sexual discipline, humanitarian practices and industriousness, and the position of women is often improved. The great majority of movements ban the use of alcohol and tobacco, even where palm wine or cereal beer have been traditional and local missions have allowed smoking and drinking. In newly developing countries, where alcohol and tobacco manufacturing are most inappropriate forms of economic development, this ascetic ethic is of considerable value.

The chief practical blessing offered by the new movements is usually mental and physical healing, for this deals with the most urgent problem of many tribal peoples, often accentuated rather than diminished by Western contacts. The central methods used are religious, such as confession, prayer, fasting, anointment with holy water or other rituals, together with the support of the believing community. Western physical treatment is usually rejected but some traditional herbal and purgative treatments may be retained. These methods have considerable efficacy within the cultural and social situation, especially for the more psychosomatic ailments, and with people for whom modern scientific medical treatment is either inaccessible or unsuitable. The tendency, however, is to accept the modern scientific treatment along with continued use of the traditional religious methods.

A more general benefit lies in the new religious communities which replace or transcend the old tribal groups and, where these are disrupted, offer a new 'place to belong', with new roles, especially for women and for the young men. There are often many official positions with ranks, titles, uniforms and insignia. The social structure ranges from loosely associated decentralized groups such as the Native American Church or the Rastafarians to highly integrated and centralized bodies with hierarchical systems such as some of the larger African independent churches. Either social form may span many tribal peoples within the one movement, and especially in Africa may transcend international boundaries; some Nigerian independent churches have spread around West Africa and to Britain, and the Kimbanguist Church in Zaire has many members in a number of central African countries. This expansion as a more universal faith reveals a remarkable missionary zeal once a movement breaks from its original tribal context, something that was quite unknown in the original primal ethnocentric religion. Some movements, however, remain essentially tribal, such as the great Nazarite Church of Shembe among the Zulu, and gain part of their strength from revitalization of the local culture.

In their early stages many movements have clashed with governments, often violently, and have been repressed as subversive, rebellious or harmful to their adherents. In the case of the more exotic movements, or of founders who were charlatans, this has been unavoidable, but too often the authorities have failed to appreciate the genuine religious motivations embedded in the new forms. The age-old conflict between rulers and prophets is seen again in these movements, but once they are established many settle down to an apolitical existence, concentrating on worship, their pastoral functions, the spreading of the movement and any associated economic or developmental activities.

More Recent Developments

The considerable amount of study given to these movements since the 1950s has assisted governments (and others) to a better understanding, although clashes are still possible. In the New Hebrides of the 1970s there was tension between the Nagriamel movement of Jimmy Stevens and the authorities, culminating in an attempted secession from the new Vanuatu state in 1980. This had to be dealt with by military means; what is not as widely known is that there was a new syncretistic Christian dimension to this movement and that this continued in a more apolitical form.

In the Philippines the potential for conflict remains but the largest of the new movements, the Iglesia ni Cristo, has had an understanding with the Marcos government, to their mutual advantage, since the late 1960s. Similarly in South Africa some of the independent or Zionist churches have cooperated with the government in spite of the apartheid policy, and for some years in the 1970s the government even provided a theological training college for their ministers. The Kimbanguist Church in Zaire has been regarded favourably by the government, and even the much-persecuted Peyote cult or Native American Church in the U.S.A. is securing religious freedom as state banning and other opposition are being removed. In contrast, during the 1970s there were several African countries where governments proscribed a wide range of indigenous movements, even if not always very effectively, and in Melanesia new cargo cults or revival movements that conflict with public order or welfare will continue to be problems to the government.

The great majority of movements, especially in more recent times, have arisen by interaction with the Christian tradition, and since about 1960 there has been considerable change in the attitudes of churches and missions towards them. Hostility, suspicion and ignorance are giving way to a better appreciation and a desire to cooperate with the new movements where possible. These are seen as extensive forms of grass-roots indigenization of the Christian faith, showing considerable creativity in forms of worship and styles of life, with a valuable if sometimes unorthodox evangelistic achievement, and performing a pastoral function in local cultural terms. Some of the African independent churches have been admitted to the World Council of Churches and to national Christian councils, and in West Africa, Zimbabwe, Kenya etc., various mission bodies have entered into partnership with some of the independent churches for Bible study and leadership training. Elsewhere fraternal relations may be established, as with the Ratana and Ringatu faiths in New Zealand, the Daku community in Fiji, the Hallelujah religion in Guyana, and even with the Rastafarians in Jamaica and the peyote cult in the U.S.A.

One sign of the developing interest in these movements was the establishment in the University of Aberdeen in 1973 of a documentation centre for this subject. In 1981 this unique collection of resources, covering all continents, was transferred to the Selly Oak Colleges, Birmingham, England, as a Study Centre for New Religious Movements in Primal Societies, and microfilmed copies of its resources were made available across the Third World. Doctoral candidates in the latter, as well as in Western countries, commonly choose one of these new movements for their research, and academic interest in many disciplines has been increasing. It is realized that many of the processes and problems of social, cultural and religious change in the developing world or among tribal peoples can fruitfully be studied through these specific and spontaneous manifestations of such changes. Development agencies, however, have not shown interest in the modernization and development potential of these new movements; this is considerable, for all such movements represent local transitions, and the grass-roots level and in varying degrees, from the old order to the new. The movements themselves also show changes in their religious content. There is a tendency for those towards the left of the four-point spectrum outlined above (page 442) to move to the right, becoming more acculturated and identified with the religious forms and contents of the invasive religion, especially where this is the Christian tradition. Here the influence of the Scriptures and the association with Western modernization contribute to this result. Examples of the opposite movement are less common, as with the Hebraist movement, the Bayudaya of Uganda, which is now clearly an African Judaism whereas in the 1920s it began as a Christian movement. In general, and contrary to the interpretations of earlier observers before the 1960s, these movements function as bridges into the future rather than back to the past.

They also represent a massive response to the traumatic changes experienced by the tribal peoples in the twentieth century, although statistics are somewhat uncertain. The greatest proliferation has been in Africa, where there could be upwards of 10 million people in 8,000/10,000 movements, some 3,000 of them in South Africa alone, and over 500 in Ghana. Many are small and some are ephemeral but their places are taken by others and the larger ones dating from earlier in the century are well established. The largest is the Kimbanguist Church and the 3 million adherents claimed for it may not be too inaccurate. The Iglesia ni Cristo in the Philippines may have the 1 million members it claims, and there are probably well over 500 other movements there. The Ratana and Ringatu movements in New Zealand have some 40,000 census members, about one-seventh of the Maori population. It is probably safe to say that there are between 12 and 20 million people involved in this development across the continents, although any figure depends on how these movements are defined. What is clear is that they are extensive, still growing, and of considerable significance from religious as well as from other viewpoints. [10]

BIBLIOGRAPHY

A. NORTH AMERICAN INDIAN RELIGIONS (J. E. Brown)

1. BROWN, J. E., *The Sacred Pipe: Black Elk's Account of the Seven Rites of the Oglala Sioux*, Norman, Okla, University of Oklahoma Press, 1953; Harmondsworth, Middx, Baltimore, Md, Penguin Books, 1972

2. CAPPS, W. H. (ed.), *Seeing with a Native Eye: Essays on Native American Religion*, New York, Harper & Row, 1976

3. DENSMORE, F., *Teton Sioux Music*, New York, Da Capo, 1972, repr. of the 1918 edn, which was issued as Bulletin 61 of the Smithsonian Institution, Bureau of American Ethnology

4. DOZIER, E. P., *The Pueblo Indians of North America*, New York, Holt, Rinehart & Winston, 1970

5. DRIVER, H. E., *Indians of North America*, Chicago, Ill., University of Chicago Press, 1961

6. FEDER, N., *American Indian Art*, New York, Abrams, 1965, 1971

7. GILL, S., *Native American Traditions: Sources and Interpretations*, Belmont, Calif., Wadsworth, 1981

8. GILL, S., *Beyond 'the Primitive': Religions of Nonliterate Peoples*, Englewood Cliffs, NJ, Prentice-Hall, 1982

9. GRINNELL, G. B., *The Cheyenne Indians*, 2 vols., New York, Cooper Square Publishers, 1962

10. HOFFMAN, W. J., 'The Midewiwin or "Grand Medicine Society" of the Ojibwa', *Annual Reports of the Bureau of American Ethnology*, VII, 1891, pp. 143–300

11. HULTKRANTZ, Å., *The Religions of the American Indians* (tr. M. Setterwall), Berkeley, Calif., University of California Press, 1979 (original Swedish edn, 1967)

12. JOSEPHY, A. M., *The Indian Heritage of America*, New York, Bantam, 1969, copyr. 1968; first publ. New York, Knopf, 1968

13. ORTIZ, A., *The Tewa World: Space, Time, Being and Becoming in a Pueblo Society*, Chicago, Ill., London, Chicago University Press, 1969

14. ORTIZ, A. (ed.), *New Perspectives on the Pueblos*, Albuquerque, N. Mex., University of New Mexico Press, 1972

15. RASMUSSEN, K., *Intellectual Culture of the Iglulik Eskimos*, Copenhagen, Gyldendalske Boghandel, 1929 (Report of the Fifth Thule Expedition, 1921–4, vol. VII, i–iii)

16. REICHARD, G. A., *Navaho Religion: A Study in Symbolism*, 2 vols., New York, Pantheon, 1950; 2nd edn, Princeton, NJ, Princeton University Press, 1963

17. SPENCER, R. F., and JENNINGS, J. D., *The Native Americans: Prehistory and Ethnology of the North American Indians*, New York, London, Harper & Row, 1965

18. TEDLOCK, D., 'Verbal art', ch. 50 of *Handbook of North American Indians*, vol. I, *Introduction* (ed. W. C. Sturtevant), Washington DC, Smithsonian Institution, forthcoming

19. TEDLOCK, D. and TEDLOCK, B. (eds.), *Teachings from the American Earth: Indian Religion and Philosophy*, New York, Liveright, 1975

20. UNDERHILL, R. M., *Red Man's Religion: Beliefs and Practices of the Indians North of Mexico*, Chicago, Ill., London, University of Chicago Press, 1965

21. WISSLER, C., *The American Indian: An Introduction to the Anthropology of the New World*, New York, McMurtrie, 1917; 3rd edn, New York, Oxford University Press, 1938, repr. New York, Peter Smith, 1950

B. PACIFIC RELIGIONS (B. Colless and P. Donovan)

1. GREY, SIR GEORGE, *Polynesian Mythology*, London, John Murray, 1855, repr. Christchurch, Whitcombe & Tombs, 1956; repr. of 1906 edn, New York, AMS, 1976
2. CODRINGTON, R. H., *The Melanesians*, Oxford, Clarendon Press, 1891, repr. New York, Dover, 1972
3. STREHLOW, C., *Die Aranda- und Loritja-Stämme in Zentral-Australien*, Städtisches Völker-Museum, Frankfurt, Baer, 1907–20
4. MALINOWSKI, B., *Argonauts of the Western Pacific*, London, Routledge, 1922, 1978; New York, Dutton, 1922, 1961
5. WILLIAMS, F. E., *Drama of Orokolo*, Oxford, Clarendon Press, 1940
6. SPENCER, SIR BALDWIN and GILLEN, F. J., *The Arunta: A Study of a Stone Age People*, London, Macmillan, 1927
7. ELKIN, A. P., *The Australian Aborigines: How to Understand Them*, Sydney, London, Angus & Robertson, 1938; 5th edn, 1974
8. BUCK, SIR PETER (Te Rangi Hiroa), *The Coming of the Maori*, Wellington, Maori Purposes Fund Board/Whitcombe & Tombs, 1949; 2nd edn, 1950
9. HANDY, E. S. C., *Polynesian Religion*, Honolulu, 1927 (Bernice P. Bishop Museum Bulletin 34); repr. New York, Kraus, 1971
10. WILLIAMSON, R. W., *Religious and Cosmic Beliefs of Central Polynesia*, vols. I and II, Cambridge, Cambridge University Press, 1933, repr. New York, AMS, 1977
11. BEST, E., *Maori Religion and Mythology*, Wellington, 1924 (Dominion Museum Bulletin, 10); repr. Wellington, Government Printer, 1976; New York, AMS, 1976
12. BERNDT, R. M. and C. H., *The World of the First Australians*, London, Angus & Robertson, 1964; 2nd edn, Sydney, Ure Smith, 1977
13. EVANS, I. H. N., *The Religion of the Tempasuk Dusuns of North Borneo*, Cambridge, Cambridge University Press, 1953
14. JENSEN, E., *The Iban and Their Religion*, Oxford, Clarendon Press, 1974
15. GEERTZ, C., *The Religion of Java*, Glencoe, Ill., Free Press, 1960; Chicago, Ill., University of Chicago Press, 1976
16. MULDER, N., *Mysticism and Everyday Life in Contemporary Java*, Singapore, Singapore University Press, 1978
17. *Gods, Ghosts and Men in Melanesia* (ed. P. Lawrence and M. J. Meggitt), Melbourne, London, New York, Oxford University Press, 1965
18. POIGNANT, R., *Oceanic Mythology: The Myths of Polynesia, Micronesia, Melanesia, Australia*, London, Hamlyn, 1967; Melbourne, Sun Books, 1970
19. WORSLEY, P., *The Trumpet Shall Sound: A Study of 'Cargo' Cults in Melanesia*, 2nd edn, London, MacGibbon & Kee, 1968

20. BURRIDGE, K., *New Heaven, New Earth: A Study of Millenarian Activities*, Oxford, Blackwell, 1969
21. AKKEREN, P. VAN, *Sri and Christ: A Study of the Indigenous Church in East Java* (tr. A. Mackie), London, Lutterworth, 1970
22. BERNDT, R. M., *An Adjustment Movement in Arnhem Land, Northern Territory of Australia*, The Hague, Paris, Mouton, 1962
23. TURNER, H. W., *Bibliography of New Religious Movements in Primal Societies*, vol. 3, *Oceania*, Boston, Mass., G. K. Hall (forthcoming)
24. ELIADE, M., *Australian Religions: An Introduction*, Ithaca, NY, Cornell University Press, 1973
25. *Te Ao Hurihuri: The World Moves On: Aspects of Maoritanga* (ed. M. King), Wellington, Hicks Smith, 1975
26. SALMOND, A., *Hui: A Study of Maori Ceremonial Gatherings*, Wellington, London, Reed, 1975
27. *Prophets of Melanesia* (ed. Gary Trompf), Port Moresby, Institute of Papua New Guinea Studies, 1977
28. *Powers, Plumes and Piglets* (ed. Norman C. Habel), Bedford Park, South Australia, Australian Association for the Study of Religions, 1979

C. AFRICAN RELIGIONS (A. Shorter)

1. MURDOCK, G. P., *Africa: Its Peoples and Their Culture History*, New York, McGraw-Hill, 1959
2. BASTIDE, R., *The African Religions of Brazil* (tr. H. Sebba), Baltimore, Md, London, Johns Hopkins University Press, 1978; *Les Religions africaines au Brésil*, Paris, Presses Universitaires de France, 1960
3. EVANS-PRITCHARD, SIR EDWARD E., *The Comparative Method in Social Anthropology*, London, Athlone Press, 1963 (L. T. Hobhouse Memorial Lecture, 33)
4. DOUGLAS, M., *Natural Symbols: Explorations in Cosmology*, London, Barrie & Rockliff/New York, Pantheon, 1970; 2nd edn, London, Barrie & Jenkins/New York, Vintage, 1973
5. MBITI, J. S., *African Religions and Philosophy*, London, Ibadan, Heinemann/New York, Praeger, 1969
6. IDOWU, E. B., *African Traditional Religion – A Definition*, London, SCM/Maryknoll, NY, Orbis, 1973
7. OGOT, B. A., *History of the Southern Luo*, vol. 1, *Migration and Settlement, 1500–1900*, Nairobi, East African Publishing House, 1967
8. RANGER, T. O., and KIMAMBO, I. N., *The Historical Study of African Religion*, London, Heinemann, 1972; Berkeley, Calif., University of California Press, 1972, repr. 1976
9. GRAY, R., 'Christianity and religious change in Africa', *The Church in a Changing Society, CIHEC Conference, Uppsala, 1977*, Stockholm, Almqvist & Wiksell (distr.), 1978, pp. 345–52

10. ACHEBE, C., *Things Fall Apart*, London, Heinemann, 1958; New York, McDowell, Obolensky, 1959

11. NGUGI WA THIONGO, *Petals of Blood*, London, Heinemann, 1977

12. SOYINKA, W., *Myth, Literature and the African World*, Cambridge, Cambridge University Press, 1978; first edn, 1976

13. EVANS-PRITCHARD, SIR EDWARD E., *Nuer Religion*, Oxford, Clarendon Press, 1962, first publ. 1956; new edn, London, Oxford University Press, 1970

14. LIENHARDT, G., *Divinity and Experience: The Religion of the Dinka*, Oxford, Clarendon Press, 1961

15. DOUGLAS, M., *Purity and Danger: An Analysis of Concepts of Pollution and Taboo*, London, Routledge/New York, Praeger, 1966

16. DOUGLAS, M., *Implicit Meanings: Essays in Anthropology*, London, Boston, Mass., Routledge, 1975

17. BERNARDI, B., *The Mugwe, A Failing Prophet: A Study of a Religious and Public Dignitary of the Meru of Kenya*, London, New York, Oxford University Press/International African Institute, 1959

18. KENYATTA, J., *Facing Mount Kenya: The Tribal Life of the Gikuyu*, London, Secker & Warburg, 1938, repr. 1953; school edn, Nairobi, Heinemann, 1971

19. SCHOFFELEERS, M., 'The interaction of the M'Bona cult and Christianity, 1859–1963', in T. O. Ranger and J. Weller (eds.), *Themes in the Christian History of Central Africa*, London, Heinemann/Berkeley, Calif., University of California Press, 1975, pp. 14–29

20. SARPONG, P. K., *Ghana in Retrospect: Some Aspects of Ghanaian Culture*, Tema, Ghana Publishing Corporation, 1974

21. TURNER, V. W., *Schism and Continuity in an African Society: A Study of Ndembu Village Life*, Manchester, Manchester University Press, 1957

22. TURNER, V. W., *The Ritual Process: Structure and Anti-Structure*, London, Routledge/Chicago, Ill., Aldine, 1969

23. ILIFFE, J., *A Modern History of Tanganyika*, Cambridge, New York, Cambridge University Press, 1979

24. ARINZE, F., and TSHIBANGU, T., 'Rapport du groupe des religions traditionnelles africaines', *Bulletin: Secretariatus pro non-Christianis* (Vatican City), XIV, ii–iii, 1979, pp. 187–190

25. WILSON, M., *Communal Rituals of the Nyakyusa*, London, New York, Oxford University Press/International African Institute, 1959

26. MBITI, J. S., *New Testament Eschatology in an African Background*, London, Oxford University Press, 1971

27. RANGER, T. O., 'The Mwana Lesa movement of 1925', in Ranger and Weller, op. cit., see item 19 above, pp. 45–75

28. FASHOLÉ-LUKE, E. W., *et al.* (eds.), *Christianity in Independent Africa*, London, R. Collings/Bloomington, Ind., Indiana University Press, 1978

29. HORTON, R., 'On the reality of conversion in Africa', *Africa*, VII, ii, 1975, pp. 132–64

30. BECKMANN, D. M., *Eden Revival: Spiritual Churches in Ghana*, St Louis Miss., Concordia, 1975

D. NEW RELIGIOUS MOVEMENTS

IN PRIMAL SOCIETIES (H. W. Turner)

1. STEINBAUER, F., *Melanesian Cargo Cults: New Salvation Movements in the South Pacific* (tr. M. Wohlwill), London, George Prior/St Lucia, University of Queensland Press, 1979

2. MOONEY, J., *The Ghost Dance Religion and the Sioux Outbreak of 1890*, Washington DC, Government Printing Office, 1896; abr., Chicago, Ill., Chicago University Press, 1965; orig. formed pt 2 of the *Fourteenth Annual Report of the Bureau of Ethnology, 1892–3*

3. LINTON, R., 'Nativistic movements', *American Anthropologist*, XLV, ii, 1943, pp. 230–40

4. WALLACE, A. F. C., 'Revitalization movements', *American Anthropologist*, LVIII, ii, 1956, pp. 264–81

5. SUNDKLER, B. G. M., *Bantu Prophets in South Africa*, London, Lutterworth, 1948; 2nd edn, London, New York, Oxford University Press/International African Institute, 1961

6. TURNER, H. W., *Bibliography of New Religious Movements in Primal Societies*, Boston, Mass., G. K. Hall, vol. 1, *Black Africa*, 1977; vol. 2, *North America*, 1979; vol. 3, *Oceania* (forthcoming)

7. TURNER, H. W., *Religious Innovation in Africa*, Boston, G. K. Hall, 1980

8. BASTIDE, R., *The African Religions of Brazil* (tr. H. Sebba), Baltimore, Md, London, Johns Hopkins University Press, 1978; *Les Religions africaines au Brésil*, Paris, Presses Universitaires de France, 1960

9. BINNEY, J., CHAPLIN, G., and WALLACE, C., *Mihaia: The Prophet Rua Kenana and His Community at Maungapohatu*, Wellington, NZ, Oxford University Press, 1979

10. HESSELGRAVE, D. J. (ed.), *Dynamic Religious Movements: Case Studies of Rapidly Growing Religious Movements Around the World*, Grand Rapids, Mich., Baker Book House, 1978

12   *Modern Alternative Religions in the West*

J. GORDON MELTON

Introduction

During the twentieth century, the West has experienced a phenomenon it has not encountered since the reign of Constantine: the growth of and significant visible presence of a variety of non-Christian and non-orthodox Christian bodies competing for the religious allegiance of the public. This growth of so many alternatives religiously is forcing a new situation on the West in which the still dominant Christian religion must share its centuries-old hegemony in a new pluralistic religious environment.

The recognition of what was happening was slow in coming. Early in the twentieth century, conservative religious leaders, primarily fundamentalist Christians, felt the presence of some alternative religions such as Spiritualism and Christian Science and new religious perspectives such as Humanism and modernism. Seeing a threat to orthodoxy, they attacked the alternatives as heresies, apostasy and the influence of Satan, and developed the 'cult' model for understanding these groups. Each author assailed those groups that offered the greatest threat to their particular orthodox perspective. Social scientists also lumped these different religions together as 'the cults', rather than calling them churches or sects, but did little research on them. More recently, in response to the rapid growth of the alternative religions in the 1970s, a new group of scholars has arisen who see the alternatives as 'new' religions and who have viewed their growth in the 1970s as the emergence of a new religious consciousness in the West during the last two decades. Although this is a more positive point of view, the concept of 'a new religious consciousness' ignores the more mundane forces leading to the rise of alternative religions in the West and mistakenly views the presence of 'alternatives' as a peculiarly recent phenomenon.

Beginnings

As both political and intellectual forces in the eighteenth century freed the religious environment from state Church controls and fostered first religious tolerance and then genuine religious liberties, alternative religions began to appear. First came the Quakers, then the perfectionists (i.e. the Wesleyans), the Deists, the Swedenborgians and the Millennialists. By the beginning of the nineteenth century, a cycle of religious growth had been established. Periodically, every twenty-five to thirty years, the West convulsed with a religious revival as the Churches, no longer always supported by state taxes, were forced to find ways to gain the voluntary support of the populace. Each wave of religious fervour, beginning with the well-known 'Second Great Awakening' at the start of the nineteenth century, saw the birth of new alternative Churches and religions. Older, minuscule groups would seize the opportunity of the revivals to jump into prominence. Thus the 'Second Awakening' launched the Methodists, Baptists, Disciples of Christ and Cumberland Presbyterians into the prominent position they established firmly during the rest of the century and initiated an era of prosperity for the Shakers. Later revivals saw the rise of Spiritualism, Latter-Day Saints, the Holiness Churches, New Thought, Christian Science and Pentecostalism. From their American beginnings, each soon travelled abroad, some gaining their greatest acceptance in a European (Spiritualism) or South American (Pentecostalism) home.

Until the end of the nineteenth century, the alternatives were basically indigenous to the West. England (with Ann Lee 1736–84, Joanna Southcott 1730–1814), the Continent (Swedenborg, the French Prophets), and the New World (Joseph Smith 1805–44, Mary Baker Eddy 1821–1910) each contributed new leadership. However, in 1893 a new set of 'alternatives' arrived in the West. In that year, the League of Liberal Clergymen of Chicago, Illinois, sponsored the World Parliament of Religions, when for the first time representatives of all the major world faiths assembled in a large Western city for a religious show-case without precedent. Buddhists, Hindus, Sikhs, Muslims, Confucians and Jews joined Spiritualists, Taoists, Parsis and Christians of every perspective for this giant conclave. Some saw the gathering as merely a big religious show, with little future significance. Yet the Parliament initiated some profound changes, especially among the religions of the East. The enthusiastic welcome given to Eastern thinkers such as Vivekananda, A. R. M. Webb and Shaku Soyen led directly to the founding of centres of Hinduism, Islam and Buddhism in the United States and to their spread in the West. Spurred by the warm experience, Eastern religious leaders began to see the West as a fertile mission field and set as their goal the returning of the favour accorded them by the nineteenth-century Christian missionary movement into Asia.

The mere fact of the Parliament being held underscored a new attitude of respect among Western scholars and religious leaders for the non-Christian religions of the world. Although many years were to pass before a majority of Christians would move beyond the view that other religions were at best pagan and heathen (and those of Asia a major source of degradation), the Parliament gave many the opportunity to see at first hand the depth and sophistication of non-Christian religious thought. After the Parliament, the various Eastern religions began to appear in the urban landscape, despite strong anti-Asian prejudice in many parts of the West. The growth of Eastern religions suffered a severe blow in 1917 when the United States passed an immigration law which stopped all immigration from Asia except by a small number of Japanese.

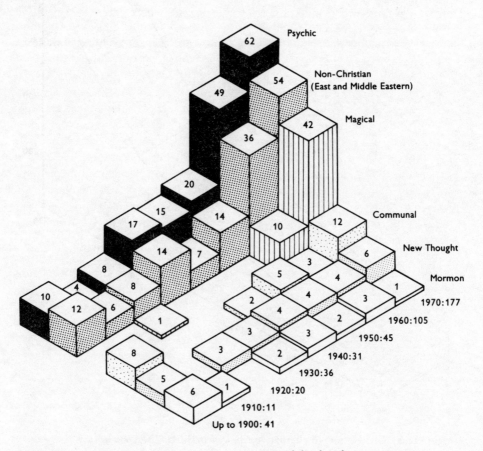

Figure 12.1 Alternative religions in the U.S.A.: growth by decades, 1900 to 1970 (after Melton, 1977 |8|)

While Asian religions grew slowly in the West, metaphysical and occult religions expanded rapidly following the founding of the Church of Christ, Scientist (1875), the National Spiritualist Association of Churches (1893) and the International New Thought Alliance (1914). The earliest metaphysical and occult groups tended to be Christian in orientation and follow Christian

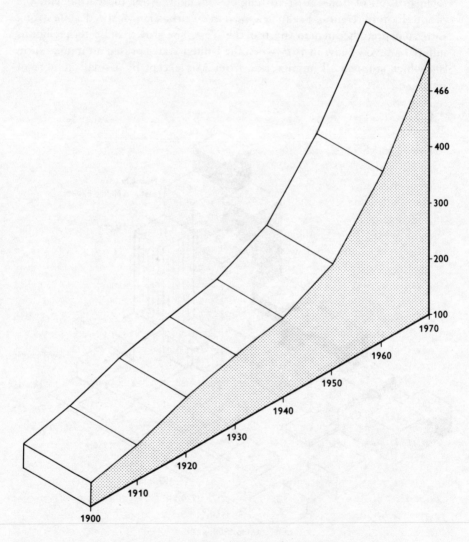

Figure 12.2 Growth rate of alternative religions in the U.S.A., 1900 to 1970 (after Melton, 1977 |8|)

patterns as much as possible, but as the century progressed, newer branches tended to drop any Christian veneer, with the exception of occasional references to Jesus as a great teacher.

The growth of the metaphysical and occult religions, and the presence, especially in the Asian communities in the West, of Hindu and Buddhist groups, set the stage for 1965. In that year, without fanfare, President Lyndon Johnson opened the United States once again to Asian immigrants, an act performed partly to allow refugees from Maoist China to come into the United States from Hong Kong. The results were quite unexpected, however, as large numbers of Japanese and Indians took advantage of the new situation and filled the quotas. Among all the Asians, the gurus, swamis and Zen masters travelled to the new homes ready not only to meet the spiritual needs of the immigrants, but also to spread the Eastern message to the West in general.

Having founded numerous movements in the 1960s, the Eastern religions were ready to reap the harvest when the latest phase of religious enthusiasm swept the West in the early and mid-1970s (see Figures 12.1 and 12.2). Small local movements grew to national proportions and quickly spread to Europe, while movements previously established in Great Britain soon set up branches in the United States and Canada. Eastern religions were joined by Jewish and Islamic groups. These Middle Eastern groups had been swollen by post-Second World War immigration into England and the United States. Islam took root and flowered within the black community from a thin shoot originally planted in the 1930s. The religious revival of the 1970s gave impetus and growth to every family of 'alternative religion' and the emergence of the pluralistic situation allowed all kinds of deviation from the old norm of mainline Christianity. Once a new form of faith appeared it soon found cause to splinter, thus enlarging the number of available religious options from which a new believer could choose. By 1980, in the United States alone, over 900 Christian sects and 600 alternative religious bodies competed for members. A similar situation, if on a lesser scale, could be found in most Western countries.

The Families of Alternative Religions

While over 600 alternative religions appeared in the United States, they and the other religions that now have communities of faith in other Western countries can, as a whole, be grouped into eight 'families' of alternative religions. Member groups of each family share a common thought world, life-style and heritage. These families represent the major directions that alternative religious groups have taken.

THE LATTER-DAY SAINT FAMILY

The Latter-Day Saints are held together by a shared belief in the revelations of Joseph Smith, which they collected into a set of books that now serve as authoritative literature alongside the Bible. The most famous piece of Latter-Day Saint scripture, the *Book of Mormon* (from which they take their more popular designation as Mormons) stands beside other volumes, the *Doctrines and Covenants* and the *Pearl of Great Price*. Smith also produced an inspired version of the Bible which some Mormon groups use.

Central to Latter-Day Saint belief is the idea of the Restoration. According to Smith, true Christianity died with the death of the last of the original apostles, but was restored through Joseph Smith's ordination and ministry. The Restoration was to find an earthly visible manifestation in Zion and a new Temple. Also, in the first generations, the Saints adopted the United Order, a communal self-help structure (which was, however, abandoned by most Mormons soon after the move to Utah in 1847). Over the years no less than twenty-five distinct Latter-Day Saint bodies have appeared and disappeared while that many more survive to the present day. They usually began with a prophet providing new revelations to supplement those left by Smith. Polygamy, practised and then abandoned by the main body of Mormons, has arisen anew as young Fundamentalists, i.e. those who practise polygamy, have become more vocal and visible during the 1970s.

THE COMMUNAL FAMILY

The communal impulse constantly reappears in all religious traditions, but, even in its more accepted monastic form, it implies a life-style that separates its practitioners from the mainstream of culture and religion. In the 1960s and 1970s a host of communes were established in every country of the Western world, and most that survived were overtly religious.

The major groups formed in the twentieth century were either Christians who took a very literal approach to scripture and particularly the injunction to hold all things in common (*Acts* 2), or groups with a distinctly Eastern mystical perspective (though they seem very eclectic theologically). In either case, they agree that the main fact of their life and thought is the challenge of communal existence. Most communal groups have a very low profile and are not well known, though a few like The Farm and the Church of Armegeddon have become visible because of their activism and their brushes with the legal authorities.

THE NEW THOUGHT METAPHYSICAL FAMILY

New Thought, a very eclectic movement, draws inspiration from mesmerism, New England transcendentalism, *laissez-faire* economics and a basic intuition that religion must be practical and applied to the major problems of everyday life. New Thought grew out of the life and work of Phineas Parkhurst Quimby, a clock-maker and amateur mesmerist from Maine (1802–66). Reflection upon his work as a magnetic healer led him to develop a practical philosophy of life which became the metaphysical basis for his healing work. The metaphysical movement teaches its members to move towards a state of health, wealth and happiness by a process of adjusting their mental perspectives. If the patient could gain a healthy positive outlook on life, a healing could occur. Quimby taught that the good, God's abundance, was ultimately the only reality. Thus if one could attune to God, all could flow to one. A major thrust of the practical activity of the members of New Thought churches consists in 'demonstrating' their attunement as they manifest God's filling of the lacks in their life.

Soon after Quimby's death, his students disagreed among themselves and parted company. The most famous and successful, Mary Baker Eddy (1821–1910), developed her own perspectives and founded the Church of Christ, Scientist. That body is most reluctant to admit any reliance upon Quimby or to associate with any other metaphysical churches. Other Quimby students, as well as some of Eddy's students who left her Church, formed the loose federation known as the International New Thought Alliance. Among the most noteworthy of the New Thought churches are the Unity School of Christianity, the Church of Religious Science (now split into several branches) and the Church of Divine Science. The New Thought movement has splintered into no less than thirty-five independent bodies. One Japanese-based group, the Seicho-No-Ie, has become an international body with centres throughout the Western world.

THE PSYCHIC/NEW AGE FAMILY

Possibly the largest of the alternative families contains the groups built around the experience of various forms of psychic phenomena. They have a continuous history in the West, at least since the time of Emanuel Swedenborg (1688–1772). These groups are the most ahistorical in their perspective, and few contemporary leaders of psychic groups know about, or are willing to acknowledge their debt to, the thought and practices of their predecessors. The psychic groups share a common relationship to science, in that they believe that psychic phenomena demonstrate 'scientifically' the truth of their religious perspective. They look to parapsychology for a verification of their religion, and have grown as the recognition of psychical research has grown. They might be said, however, to have an attitude better labelled 'scientism', that is, they have a love of things scientific but little knowledge, or appreciation, of science and scientific methodology.

Historically, the psychic community dates from two eighteenth-century figures: Swedenborg, the Swedish seer, and Franz Anton Mesmer (1734–1815), whose ideas about animal magnetism fostered a movement that, while not being directly religious itself, gave content and an early rationale to the psychic groups. From the thin thread of mesmerism and Swedenborg's New Church, Spiritualism emerged in New York. Andrew Jackson Davis (1826–1910), Spiritualism's great prophet, counted Swedenborg among his main spirit contacts. From New York Spiritualism spread across North America and to Europe, where it enjoyed a much greater acceptance in England and France than it did in the land of its origin. Once Spiritualism had spread and provided the base, other psychic groups could emerge. Among the earliest to come out of Spiritualism was Theosophy, founded in New York City in 1875 by Mme Helena Petrovna Blavatsky. She began to integrate the occult teachings of former centuries and the immediate phenomena of Spiritualism into a new 'gnostic' synthesis. Blavatsky soon replaced Davis as the major teacher of twentieth-century occultists.

During the twentieth century, the psychic–occult movement has grown and diversified widely. Each generation has fathered a host of psychics with variant revelations and a wide range of attitudes towards the dominant Christian perspective in society. More recently, groups founded upon psychedelic-drug experiences and 'flying saucer' sightings have created even more variations. The splintering of psychic groups can be seen as due to the complete lack of any central authority system or support from the dominant culture, coupled with a drive among members for an immediate experience of some form of psychic phenomenon, an impulse not unlike the Pentecostal drive to experience the gifts of the Spirit. Leaders rest their claim to authority on their ability to produce psychic phenomena or on their relation to someone who can.

Over 300 of the alternative religions are psychic–occult groups.

THE MAGICAL FAMILY

The magical family consists of those groups which include as a significant element in their life the practice of magic, which can be defined as the art of employing cosmic, paranormal forces (believed to underpin the universe) in order to produce desired effects at will. Magic has two major forms. In working high magic, the major focus of change is the magician's own consciousness. Low magic refers to the production of alterations in the mundane world such as healing the body, locating a better job, improving one's love life or cursing an enemy. While the practice of magic in itself is not necessarily religious, in the modern West its practice is most commonly found as an integral aspect of magical groups which provide all the traditional religious functions for their members.

Almost eliminated from the West in the eighteenth century, magic began a remarkable comeback in the nineteenth century, a comeback culminating in the formation of the Hermetic Order of the Golden Dawn (OGD) in the 1880s. From that group, and in particular from one of its members, Aleister Crowley (1875–1947), the magical revival began [9]. Crowley, and his secretary-student Israel Regardie, first published the majority of the OGD material, thus making it available to the wider occult community. Then, through his voluminous writings, Crowley provided occultists with perhaps their single most coherent digest of magical practice and most widely accepted presentation of magical thought. All three major groupings of modern magical 'religions' draw heavily upon the work of Crowley (even in those cases where groups and individuals openly separate themselves from Crowley and his more controversial and objectionable aspect, the emphasis upon sex magic).

Magic returned in the form of ceremonial magic, centred upon the disciplined practice of ritual invocation and evocation for the working of high magic. The OGD assembled the work of prior magical teachers such as Eliphas Levi (1810–75), added the writings of their own scholar-teacher S. L. MacGregor Mathers (1854–1918), and formed the first magic group to spread throughout the British Isles, on to the Continent and across the ocean to America. While several groups, such as the California-based Builders of the Adytum and the Fraternity of the Inner Light and the Servants of the Light, both British-based, carry on the Golden Dawn tradition, most ceremonial-magic groups can be traced to Aleister Crowley. After leaving the OGD, Crowley joined the German-based Ordo Templi Orientis and eventually became its Outer Head. He imposed his unique brand of magic, 'thelema' (from the Greek word for 'will'), upon the Order (which led to a split in the German section). Through his travels and writings he expanded the Order into a world-wide organization. In the early 1980s, the OTO branch headed by Grady McMurty of Berkeley, California, was the single largest magical group in the West, with centres in North America, New Zealand, Australia, Europe and even behind the Iron Curtain. Several other OTO branches, such as that led by British thelemite Kenneth Grant, have an international membership also. More recently, new offshoots of thelemic magic based upon Maat, the Egyptian goddess of truth and justice, have appeared, such as the London/Chicago-based Ordo Adeptorum Invisiblum. Together the various OTO and

Maatian organizations include the overwhelming majority of ritual magicians in the West.

Witchcraft, the second major grouping of magical religion, presents a confusing picture to the average observer. The word 'witchcraft' is popularly used to describe at least four distinct phenomena, frequently if mistakenly equated with each other. Anthropologists use the word to refer to the art of the tribal shaman in pre-technological (or primal) societies. Biblical scholars use it to describe the *ob*, such as the famous *ob* of Endor (1 *Samuel* 28), whose accomplishments included knowledge of herbs and poisons and the art of mediumship. The Western historian usually means the worship of the Devil, i.e. Satanism, with all of its associated practice of malevolent sorcery, the black mass and witchhunters.

However, modern witchcraft, as practised in Western technological society, is neither of these three. Rather it is a form of polytheistic nature religion based upon the worship of the Mother Goddess. This new witchcraft, more properly called Neo-Paganism, was created during the 1940s and 1950s by Gerald Gardner (1884–1964), a retired British civil servant who had spent most of his life in southern Asia. Gardner attempted to develop a popular magical religion. He combined elements of both Western and Asian magic, Masonic rituals, nudity and Goddess worship with liberal doses of Aleister Crowley. First made public in the 1950s, Gardnerian witchcraft spread quickly in England and came to America in the 1960s. Numerous variations of Goddess worship, which (in spite of claims to the contrary) can be traced almost entirely to Gardner, appeared, and by 1980 included literally hundreds of covens and groves (the small groups which meet together to practise their nature-oriented faith) in Europe, North America, Australia and South Africa. The Neo-Pagan witches view their task as reviving the old religion(s) of pre-Christian Europe. With the movement's growth into its second generation, it has experienced constant change as different covens have put various ethnic façades (Scandinavian, Welsh, Greek) on to their practice and have experimented with newly written rituals and new alternative magical techniques. Low magic predominates in witchcraft's rituals and practice, an emphasis that generally differentiates Neo-Pagans from ceremonial magicians.

The third group of magical religionists flashed into prominence momentarily in the late 1960s, and was heard from with less and less frequency during the 70s. The Satanists, those who actually worship the Devil and whose magic consists of the invocation of him or one of his demonic legion, have gradually faded from the occult world. Generally occultists, including ceremonial magicians and witches, dislike and fear the worshippers of Satan as much as Christians do. Contemporary Neo-Pagans consistently try to separate themselves from the taint of Satanic images constantly being thrown at them. Neo-Pagans assert that they practise a positive religion with their own Pagan deities, rather than a negative religion based upon the Devil of Christianity. Satanism is a magical religion which has as its central dynamic the rejection of and an attack upon Christianity. Modern Satanists have drawn their image of his Infernal Majesty from the snake in the Garden of Eden, the bringer of knowledge, and Lucifer, the light-bearer. This modern Satan is the giver of wisdom and builder of the individual ego. His worshippers, though few in number, can be found throughout the Christian world in small disconnected groups.

THE EASTERN FAMILY

Since 1965 the high level of visibility of Buddhism, Hinduism, Sikhism and Jainism indicates a significant proliferation of Eastern religion in the West. Several hundred different Eastern groups now operate in the West and, most significantly, they have broken out of the ethnic communities, serving Caucasian and black members as well as Japanese, Chinese and Indians. In actual practice, groups serving ethnic communities find it difficult to include non-ethnic members in the life of their own group.

Typically, the Eastern groups have a single teacher, a guru, though the title varies from group to group. The guru teaches the techniques by which the members can gain enlightenment or mystic vision, and members view the guru as an accomplished master of the system he/she teaches. Within Eastern groups, systems and practices vary as widely as they do within the whole of Western Christianity. Some are ascetic (Hare Krishna), some philosophical (Vedanta), some indulgent (Tantra) and some rigorous (certain types of *yoga*). While nominally led by the guru, the groups also present a wide variety of organizational strength, and ask for differing degrees of commitment from their members. Among the Hare Krishna, an ascetic monastic model of life has been adopted; some *siddha yoga* groups are based on the absolute obedience given to the guru; other groups merely respect the guru as a learned teacher, but have formed a rather loose organization. Some groups seek the total commitment of the members' time, money and energy; others seek only a few hours a week and a modest donation of financial resources and labour.

The media have given large amounts of space to the Eastern groups, whose beliefs and practices seem strange to the average Westerner. The success of these groups, however, is much more limited than the media coverage would tend to suggest. The largest guru-oriented group still numbers fewer than 10,000 and most have only a few hundred members. Their major accomplishment in the 1970s was to attract members from all segments of Western society in such numbers as to establish a permanent base for future expansion.

THE MIDDLE EASTERN FAMILY

Judaism has been in the West longer than Christianity, but, for a variety of historical and theological reasons, has remained a minority religion. The events of the Second World War dramatically reshaped the total Jewish community and scattered most of what was not destroyed of Eastern European Jewry. That war brought many Jews to the United States and Canada, and they brought with them varieties of Judaism never before seen in North America – the many Chasidic groups. (Chasidism is a mystical Orthodox form of Judaism – see pages 28–9 above.)

The post-war era has also seen many Muslims coming to the West, where large Islamic communities are appearing for the first time. The proliferation of both Judaism and Islam has been remarkable, with over thirty mystical Jewish groups and almost as many Islamic groups establishing communities. There have been important differences in their patterns of growth. Jewish groups have tended to grow primarily within the Jewish community. The Chasids have promoted large families and advocated the conversion of more liberal Jews and of non-practising Jews. Muslims have bolstered their immigrant communities by spreading Islam among blacks and by the penetration of mystical Islam (Sufism) among young adult middle-class whites, the group most attracted to Eastern faiths in general. (Figure 12.3)

Opposition to Alternative Religions

The growth of alternative religions in the twentieth century generated a counter-movement headed by those who saw the establishment of alternative religious communities as a threat. In the early part of the century, opposition started within conservative Christian bodies which saw members being seduced by exotic forms of faith. For many years these bodies produced books, pamphlets and tracts warning of the dangerous beliefs of such groups – primarily Mormonism, Christian Science, Spiritualism, Theosophy and Seventh-day Adventism. Several organizations, such as the Christian Research Institute founded by Baptist minister Walter Martin and the Religious Analysis Service in Minneapolis, Minnesota, were established to coordinate anti-cult activity and channel literature to Christians engaged in a ministry to cults. [13]

In labelling the alternative religions as 'cults', anti-cultists assumed that in some measure the alternative religions were essentially all alike, an assumption that has proved completely false. The only characteristic they share is a negative evaluation; they each present an alternative to traditional Chris-

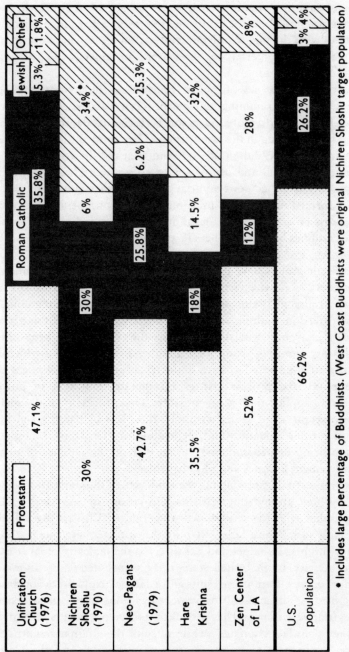

	Protestant	Roman Catholic	Jewish	Other
Unification Church (1976)	47.1%	35.8%	5.3%	11.8%
Nichiren Shoshu (1970)	30%	30%	6%	34%*
Neo-Pagans (1979)	42.7%	25.8%	6.2%	25.3%
Hare Krishna	35.5%	18%	14.5%	32%
Zen Center of LA	52%	12%	28%	8%
U.S. population	66.2%	26.2%	3%	4%

* Includes large percentage of Buddhists. (West Coast Buddhists were original Nichiren Shoshu target population)

Figure 12.3 Religious backgrounds of members of alternative religions in the U.S.A. (based on Judah, 1974 [5], McCloy Layman, 1976 [6] and Melton, 1970 [7]

tianity. The assumption of similarity has also been used to attack the 'cults': by attributing to all of them the faults and excesses of any one of them. This practice, along with the highly polemic motivation underlying most anti-cult literature, makes such materials the least useful in understanding the nature of life in alternative religions.

In the early 1970s a new form of opposition to alternative religions developed: the de-programming movement. Ted Patrick, whose son had associated with the Children of God in southern California, soon found other parents who had offspring in the same group. They formed FREECOG (Free Our Children from the Children of God) and attacked the group for its communal living, odd beliefs and use of sex in recruiting. They were, in turn, joined by parents who had sons and daughters in other alternative religions and together formed the Citizens' Freedom Foundation, the first of a number of groups across North America, and more recently in Great Britain, mainly composed of families having members in an 'unapproved' alternative religious group.

These anti-cult groups have developed a working rationale in which they see cult members as passive victims of recruitment processes through which the alternative religions brainwash and hypnotize members to the point that they lose their freedom to think and make decisions. To alleviate this problem, it is argued, it may be necessary to kidnap the 'victim' and keep him (or her) locked away from his group for a number of days, during which he is subjected to a high-powered counter-indoctrination process. While seen as freeing the mind, the process centres on the manipulation of powerful emotional forces applied with great pressure. This process typically includes fatigue, the desecration of sacred symbols, the pleas of parents and family members, intense interrogation and, depending on the degree of resistance of the person being de-programmed, it can include the absence of privacy, physical confinement in ropes and physical abuse.

The major target of the anti-cult movement has been the Unification Church, a small group built around the charisma and visions of Sun Myung Moon, a Korean prophet who has expounded a version of Christianity called the Divine Principle (see Figure 12.4). In 1965 the anti-cult movement took the Unification Church as its target and has directed the majority of its efforts to inhibiting its activity. In the United States this has included de-programmings, attempted anti-cult legislation, civil suits and a campaign of vilification directed through the media. The anti-cult movement has been largely unsuccessful in obtaining legislative action, and has provoked its own opponents. In particular several of the 'main-line churches', while wary of the alternative faiths, have joined forces with them to oppose anti-cult legislation; and the National Council of Churches in the U.S.A. has denounced the practice of de-programming as an offence to religious liberty. [16]

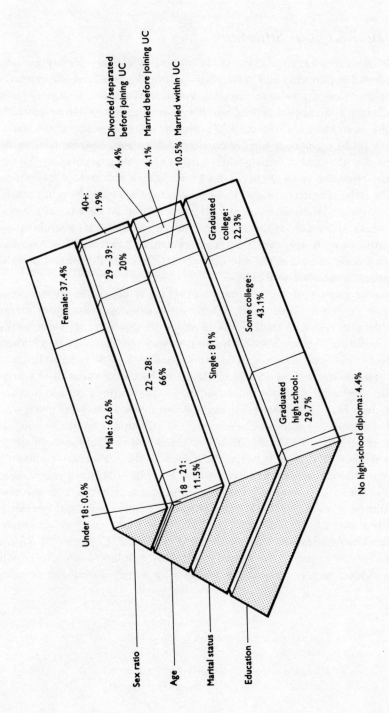

Divorced/separated
before joining UC
4.4%

Married before joining UC
4.1%

10.5% Married within UC

40+:
1.9%

29 – 39:
20%

Graduated
college:
22.3%

Female: 37.4%

Some college:
43.1%

22 – 28:
66%

Single: 81%

Male: 62.6%

Graduated
high school:
29.7%

18 – 21:
11.5%

No high-school diploma: 4.4%

Under 18: 0.6%

Sex ratio

Age

Marital status

Education

Figure 12.4   Unification Church membership profile, U.S.A., 1976

The New Religious Situation

Religious observers have for many years spoken of Western society moving into a post-Christian era, and certainly Christian leaders have experienced a marked erosion of power in directing culture. Most commentators have seen secularism and unbelief as the Church's major competitor. However much truth there is to the post-Christian hypothesis, the emergence of the many alternative faiths signifies a further erosion of Christian hegemony. During the 1970s the alternative faiths, while growing not nearly so much as the anti-cultists would have us believe, did grow enough to create a qualitative shift in the religious environment. They penetrated society to the point where they can no longer be dismissed as an odd phenomenon on the edge of society. The members, drawn from the educated, middle-to-upper-middle class, including professionals and career business executives, can no longer be dismissed as merely the alienated and oppressed. They see themselves as full, active participants in Western culture.

The visible impact of the alternative religions is highest in urban areas (see Figure 12.5 and Table 12.1), where their worship centres dot street corners, their stores open their doors in shopping districts and their books rest on bookstore shelves beside Christian devotional texts. Their children now attend public schools in which Buddhists, Scientologists, Hindus, Unificationists, Jews, Sikhs and an occasional Pagan sit beside all varieties of Christians. The alternative religions moved quickly to institutionalize and prepare future leaders. Hastily prepared training sessions in the 1960s have given way to the Unification Theological Seminary, the Religious Science School of Ministry, the Dharma Realm Buddhist University and the California Institute of Asian Studies. Dialogues between the leaders of these alternative religions and of main-line churches, the obvious next step, have begun, though these occurred in the 1970s primarily at the instigation of several of the more successful alternative religions. In Berkeley, California, a very successful Interfaith Council has offered a model for local dialogue and action on common problems. The Unification Church initiated a Global Congress of World Religion that has attracted the attention of many scholars. Such efforts will in all likelihood largely replace the anti-cult approach during the decades ahead.

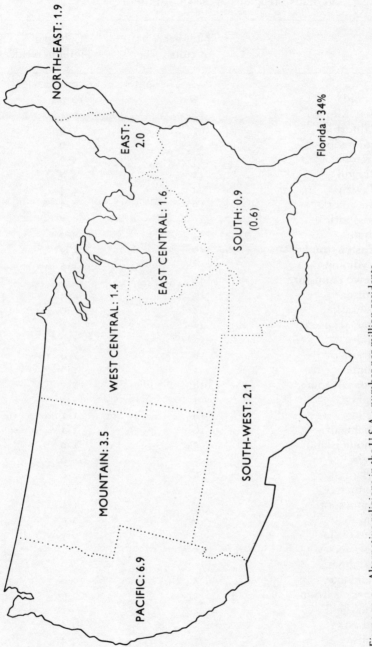

Figure 12.5   Alternative religions in the U.S.A.: number per million residents
by region

Table 12.1. Alternative religions in the U.S.A. (mid-1970s)

State	Number of cults	Cults per million residents
1. Nevada	6	10·0
2. New Mexico	10	9·1
3. California	167	7·9
4. Colorado	15	6·0
5. Arizona	13	5·9
6. Oregon	11	4·8
7. Hawaii	4	4·4
8. New York	59	3·3
9. Missouri	15	3·1
10. Illinois	34	3·0
11. Washington	10	2·9
12. Wyoming	1	2·5
13. New Hampshire	2	2·5
14. Florida	20	2·4
15. Nebraska	3	2·0
16. Massachusetts	11	1·9
17. Utah	2*	1·7
18. Virginia	8	1·6
19. Connecticut	5	1·6
20. Pennsylvania	18	1·5
21. Idaho	1	1·3
22. Texas	14	1·2
23. Michigan	10	1·1
24. Rhode Island	1	1·0
25. Iowa	3	1·0
26. Arkansas	2	1·0
27. Tennessee	4	1·0
28. Minnesota	4	1·0
29. Ohio	9	0·8
30. Wisconsin	3	0·7
31. New Jersey	5	0·7
32. Oklahoma	2	0·7
33. Alabama	2	0·6
34. North Carolina	3	0·6
35. Maryland	2	0·5
36. Indiana	5	0·5
37. Kansas	1	0·4
38. Georgia	2	0·4

State	Number of cults	Cults per million residents
39. South Carolina	1	0.4
40. Kentucky	1	0.3
41. Louisiana	1	0.3

Alaska, Delaware, Maine, Mississippi, Montana, North Dakota, South Dakota, Vermont and West Virginia had none.

Washington DC	11	15.7

* Utah Mormon groups omitted.
Source: Melton, 1978 [9]; Stark, Bainbridge and Doyle, 1979 [14].

BIBLIOGRAPHY

1. BROMLEY, D. G., and SHUPE, A. D., *Strange Gods*, Boston, Mass., Beacon 1981
2. ELLWOOD, R. S., *Alternative Altars: Unconventional and Eastern Spirituality in America*, Chicago, Ill., University of Chicago Press, 1979
3. ELLWOOD, R. S., *Religious and Spiritual Groups in Modern America*, Englewood Cliffs, NJ, Prentice-Hall, 1973
4. GLOCK, C. Y., and BELLAH, R. N. (eds.), *The New Religious Consciousness*, Berkeley, Calif., University of California Press, 1976
5. JUDAH, J. S., *Hare Krishna and the Counter Culture*, New York, Wiley, 1974
6. LAYMAN, E. M., *Buddhism in America*, Chicago, Ill., Nelson Hall, 1976
7. MELTON, J. G., 'The Neo Pagans of America: An Alternative Religion' (paper presented to the American Academy of Religion, 1970)
8. MELTON, J. G., *A Directory of Religious Bodies in the United States*, New York, Garland, 1977
9. MELTON, J. G., *The Encyclopedia of American Religions*, Wilmington, NC, McGrath, 1979, copyr. 1978
10. MELTON, J. G., *Paganism, Magick and Witchcraft*, New York, Garland, 1981

11. NEEDLEMAN, J., and BAKER, G. (eds.), *Understanding the New Religions*, New York, Seabury, 1978
12. NELSON, G. K., *Spiritualism and Society*, New York, Schocken/London, Routledge, 1969
13. SHUPE, A. D., and BROMLEY, D. G., *The New Vigilantes: Deprogrammers, Anti-cultists, and the New Religions*, Beverly Hills, Calif., Sage, 1980
14. STARK, R., BAINBRIDGE, W. S., and DOYLE, D. P., 'Cults of America: a reconnaissance in space and time', *Sociological Analysis*, 40, 4, 1979, pp. 347–59
15. WUTHNOW, R., *The Consciousness Reformation*, Berkeley, Calif., University of California Press, 1976
16. WUTHNOW, R., *Experimentation in American Religion: The New Mysticisms and Their Implications for the Churches*, Berkeley, Calif., University of California Press, 1978
17. ZARETSKY, I. I., and LEONE, M. P. (eds.), *Religious Movements in Contemporary America*, Princeton, N J, Princeton University Press, 1974

Baha'ism

DENIS MacEOIN

Introduction

Among the new religious movements clamouring for attention in the modern
West, Baha'ism (the Baha'i faith) stands out as something of an anomaly.
The movement originated in the 1860s as a faction within Babism (founder:
the Bab, 1819–50), a messianic sect of Shi'a Islam (see page 154 above) that
began in Iraq and Iran in 1844. The founder of Baha'ism, Baha' Allah (1817–
92), claimed to be a new prophet and expounded his religion as the latest
in a long line of divine revelations. Confined to the Middle East, it is likely
that Baha'ism would have joined the ranks of the numerous heterodox Islamic
sects there, with most of which it shares common features. But in 1894 the
movement became one of the first missionizing Eastern religions to reach the
West, arriving in the United States while still in a state of flux after its
emergence from Shi'a Islam. Unlike the Ahmadiyya and some recent Sufi
groups that have sought converts in Europe and America, the Baha'is had
consciously broken their connection with Islam and were in search of a means
of defining their identity as a community based on a separate revelation,
something which had proved difficult in Islamic countries, but which they
found possible in more pluralist societies. The original move to North America
had been unintentional and the work of one individual, but the moment was
perfect, and early successes among fringe-group adherents encouraged the
Baha'i leadership to divert considerable energies to the promulgation of
Baha'ism in the West as a 'new world faith' destined to supersede all established religions. This development was given considerable impetus by the
Western preaching journeys of 'Abd al-Baha' (1844–1921), Baha' Allah's
son and successor. The head of the movement from 1921, Shoghi Effendi
(1897–1957), accelerated this process of Westernization, and by the time of
his death in 1957 the religion had changed its character enormously.

Although the Baha'i conversion rate in North America and Europe has
been severely limited and is likely to remain so, since the 1950s the movement has had remarkable success in establishing itself as a vigorous contender
in the mission fields of Africa, India, parts of South America and East Asia,
thus outstripping other new religions in the extent of diffusion, if not in

numbers. The most important Baha'i community is still that of Iran, where adherents constitute the largest religious minority. The history of Baha'ism in Iran has been chequered, however, with periodic bouts of persecution and a continuing pattern of discrimination. The community has never succeeded in winning official recognition. Since 1979, Iranian Baha'is have been under threat from the Islamic regime: over one hundred have been killed, many have been imprisoned and property has been confiscated [1].

The outsider is faced with a genuine ambiguity in seeking a relatively un-biased approach to Baha'ism. In terms of numbers, influence, social position, voluntariness of membership, and so on, it is most usefully treated as a sect or denomination (with major regional fluctuations), rather than as a wholly independent tradition. But Baha'is themselves emphasize other criteria, such as the lives of the movement's founders and saints, the richness of its scriptural literature, the breadth and rapidity of its geographical expansion, and the ontological assumption of a divine revelation subsequent to and abrogatory of Islam. The scholar must try to shift between these and other approaches as far as possible. Perhaps the central focus of interest lies in the conscious promulgation of an alternative religion, not primarily as an outgrowth of an existing major tradition, but as a potential new tradition. In its earliest phases, Baha'ism experienced the normal processes of small-scale religious development and, in terms of internal routinization, high participation, zeal to convert and to confirm new adherents, it has continued to do so. But the use of aggressive, centrally planned missionary tactics since the late 1930s has made it possible to transform theological assumptions about status more and more into empirical realities or (which may be as significant) into assump-tions in the minds of the public, moulded by careful presentation of data. What we are witnessing, in other words, is the planned construction of a 'world religion' according to objectives derived from external theories about what actually constitutes such a phenomenon.

SOURCES

The question of sources for Baha'i history and doctrine is a vexed and compli-cated one, in spite of the comparative modernity of the movement. In the case of historical materials, in particular, there has been sharp controversy since the late nineteenth century, and, if anything, this seems to be increasing. There are several reasons for this. The first is that, almost from the inception of the religion, Baha'is themselves have been deeply concerned with historical issues, and numerous general 'official' histories have been written, including some either penned or vetted by leaders of the movement [e.g. 2–5]. Valuable as they are, these and other works by adherents are highly tendentious. Independent scholars since E. G. Browne (d. 1926), have criticized this central tradition of Baha'i historiography, but until recently limited access to primary source materials and lack of scholarly interest have restricted the production of alternative versions.

A second problem is that Baha'i history is characterized from the very beginning by severe factionalism. With the virtual exception of the Azali Babis in Iran, however, alternative or sectarian groupings have tended to fade out. At the same time, idealizing tendencies in what is now the mainstream of the movement have played down or concealed the historical significance of earlier disputes and the personalities associated with them. Useful fractional literature is scarce, while many crucial documents remain in private hands or are kept in official archives to which the researcher has little or no access.

Nevertheless, ample primary materials do exist and, in recent years, many of these have been used as the basis for radical reinterpretations of Baha'i and, in particular, Babi history. Many important manuscripts were obtained by European scholars in the late nineteenth century, the main collections being in Cambridge, London and Paris. Unfortunately, the largest manuscript collections are those of the National Baha'i Archives in Iran and the International Baha'i Archives at the Baha'i World Centre in Haifa, Israel, neither of which is accessible to the public. In general, more primary materials are available for the earlier than for the later period. The introduction of a rationalized administrative system from the 1920s onwards has meant that crucial materials have gone straight into official archives, while printed materials have tended to become blander and less inclined to reveal the full range of developments or events behind the scenes. This is noticeably true of recent volumes of the official yearbook, *The Baha'i World* [6].

In the case of scriptural writings, the problems are fewer and less critical. Strictly speaking, Baha'i scripture consists of the Arabic and Persian writings of the Bab, Baha' Allah and 'Abd al-Baha', the first two representing 'revealed' scripture (in the Qur'anic sense of direct verbal inspiration), the third infallible commentary on and extension of the former. The writings of the Bab fall into an ambiguous position, in that they are technically regarded as abrogated by those of Baha' Allah. Although not regarded as scripture, the writings in Persian and English of Shoghi Effendi are deemed infallible interpretations of the sacred text and occupy a high position in the religion (especially in Iran, where prayers written by him are used in devotions). Taken together, these materials constitute a formidable canon, the full extent of which is difficult to gauge because so much still remains in manuscript. The main collection of original manuscripts is at Haifa, but reliable copies may be found elsewhere.

The works of the Bab were composed over only six years, but they fall, nevertheless, into at least two distinct periods, with major shifts in his thought between the two. These works are couched in highly ungrammatical Arabic and idiosyncratic Persian, and are at times almost unreadable, leading to serious problems of interpretation. Modern Baha'is, even Iranians, are almost wholly ignorant of these works, except in the form of selective quotations in later books. [On works of the early period, see 7: 157–67.] There are French translations by Nicolas of works from the later period [8–10]. A recent Baha'i publication [11] provides interpretative translations of carefully selected and not very representative passages from major works.

The writings of Baha' Allah also fall into two main periods: works between about 1852 and 1867 (up to his break with Babism), and those to 1892. Works from the first period [e.g. 12–14] are largely concerned with ethical issues, mysticism and scriptural interpretation, those from the second [e.g. 15; 16] increasingly with apologetics for his new religion, and with the formulation of laws, rituals and so on. Compilation volumes including early and late writings have been published [e.g. 17].

'Abd al-Baha's works consist principally of collected letters and lectures, many of which have been translated into English [e.g. 18–20]. Shoghi Effendi wrote in both Persian and English, but his best-known works are in the latter language [e.g. 5; 21; 22]. His rhetorical and exaggerated English style has become a model for later Baha'i writing, particularly that produced by official bodies. Two collections of English letters from the Universal House of Justice have been published [23; 24].

Two problems concerning scriptural materials deserve mention. The first is that no critical editions of any original-language texts have been published. The second relates to translations. Baha'i sources state that translations exist in about 700 languages, but this is misleading in that these often consist of no more that a tiny prayer-book or less. Significantly, however, all current translations are made, not from original Arabic or Persian texts, but from the English translations of Shoghi Effendi. These latter are written in fluent if somewhat archaic English, are highly interpretative and are wholly lacking in critical apparatuses. For the majority of Baha'is, therefore, access to scriptural authority is possible only in mediated form. Recent translations made at Haifa adopt both the style and technique of Shoghi Effendi. Apologetic and polemical literature is extensive and easily obtained. A straightforward example of contemporary Baha'i apologetics, which presents historical and doctrinal material uncritically and often unreliably, is [25]. There is a large body of anti-Baha'i polemic in Persian, most of which is of limited value. A smaller corpus of anti-Baha'i writing exists in English, the most recent example of which is [26]. For an example of sectarian writing within the movement, see [27].

HISTORY

Baha'is have inherited from Islam a view of history as a linear process directed by the divine will and marked by the periodic appearance of major and minor prophets, some of whom bring books and laws and found religious communities. Whereas Muslims see Muhammad as the 'Seal of the Prophets' and Islam as the final religion, for Baha'is this is only true in the sense that Islam completes a series of revelations that together comprise a 6,000-year 'prophetic cycle', the first part of a much longer 'universal cycle' (see Figure 13.1). According to modern Baha'i theory, the second part of the 'universal cycle', the 'cycle of fulfilment' (i.e. of prophecy) or 'Baha'i cycle', was initiated on 22 May 1844 by the 'declaration' of a young Iranian, the Bab (1819–50), to be the 'promised one' of Islam. Although regarded as an independent prophet by Baha'is, the Bab's central function is that of a herald for the advent of Mirza Husayn 'Ali Baha' Allah (1817–92), who announced his mission in Baghdad in 1863. Baha' Allah is regarded as the promised saviour of all ages and religions, the 'universal manifestation' of the divinity, who presides over the present universal cycle. His dispensation will last at least 1,000 years, and the Baha'i cycle about 500,000. It is anticipated that, before the end of this dispensation, the Baha'i religion will become the dominant faith of the planet, uniting the nations in a single theocratic system based on the religious and political teaching of Baha' Allah and his successors. In retrospect, the lives of the Bab, Baha' Allah, and his son 'Abbas ('Abd al-Baha') (1844–1921) are deemed by Baha'is to be the 'sacred time' *par excellence*, within which divine activity can be seen at work in temporal affairs. The historicity of events connected with this period is, therefore, crucial to Baha'is in much the same way that the life of the Prophet is crucial to Muslims. In reality, however, empirical historical processes have inevitably been much overlaid by preconceived schematic representations of events and personalities [see in particular 5]. The following account attempts to present a relatively neutral picture of the main phases of Babi and Baha'i history.

In the 1840s, Iranian Shi'ism was undergoing important changes, particularly with respect to the question of religious authority. During the 1820s and 1830s, an important heterodox but religiously conservative movement known as Shaykhism emerged in Iraq and Iran, emphasizing the need for continuing inspiration from the Prophet and his successors, the Imams. Later developments in Shaykhism by the early 1840s were concerned with the theme of an age of inner truth succeeding that of external law in Islam. At the beginning of 1844, the leader of the Shaykhi sect died in Iraq, and the movement rapidly split over the question of succession. The most radical faction was that formed by a group of mostly Iranian clerics (*ulama*), initially in Shiraz, Iran, then

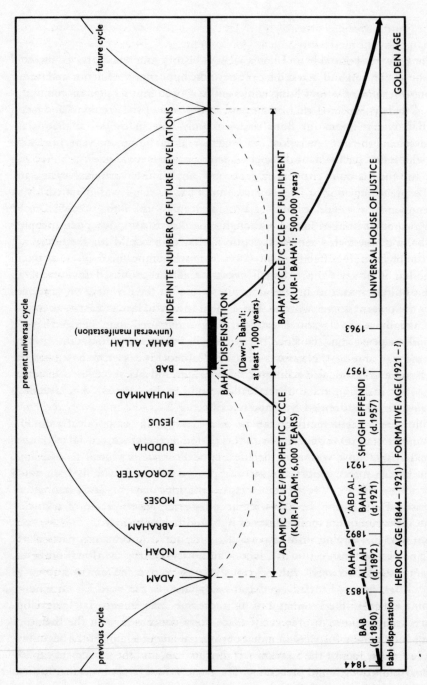

Figure 13.1   The Baha'i view of history

at the Shi'ite shrine centres of Iraq. This group focused on the claims of an Iranian Shaykhi merchant, Sayyid 'Ali Muhammad Shirazi [3; 28], to be the *bab* or gate between men and the hidden twelfth Imam [on early claims, see 7: 168–75]. The Bab directed his earliest followers to proclaim the imminent advent of the Imam, for which he himself had been sent to prepare the way. It was widely expected that this event would occur in Iraq in 1845, when the Bab would appear to lead the final holy war. This he failed to do, however, and the movement lost much of its original momentum, particularly after the Bab's seclusion and repeated recantation of his claims in Shiraz in 1845 and the fission of the central group in Iraq. Renewed impetus was given by the preaching work of several members of the original Babi hierarchy, pre-eminently a female scholar called Qurrat al-'Ayn, who radicalized the Iraqi group. The Bab resumed his activities in secret from 1846, was arrested in 1847, and transferred to prison in Adharbayjan province, where he continued to write prolifically. Effective control of the movement was, however, by then in the hands of several provincial leaders. In late 1847, the Bab claimed to be the hidden Imam in his persona as the Mahdi, and in 1848 a conclave of his followers met in Mazandaran to abrogate the outward laws of Islam and inaugurate the age of inner truth. These activities were soon followed by outbreaks of mass violence between militant Babis and state troops in Mazandaran (1848–9), Nayriz (1850) and Zanjan (1850–51), in the course of which some 3,000 to 4,000 Babis were killed (Baha'i sources increase this figure to 20,000), including most of the leadership. The Bab himself was executed by firing squad in Tabriz on 8 or 9 July 1850.

Following a Babi attempt on the life of the King of Iran, Nasir al-Din Shah, in August 1852 and the execution of several remaining leaders, a largely non-clerical group chose voluntary exile in Baghdad from early 1853. Leadership of this group initially fell to the son of an Iranian state official, Mirza Yahya Nuri Subh-i Azal (*c.* 1830–1912), regarded by many as the Bab's appointed successor. Even during the Bab's lifetime, however, there had been problems in the movement concerning authority, and later theories of theophany had encouraged a veritable rash of conflicting claims to some form of divinity. The question of authority was concentrated by the early 1860s in a growing power struggle between Yahya and his half-brother, Mirza Husayn 'Ali Baha' Allah [29], who had by then become the *de facto* leader of a large section of the Baghdad community. Whereas the Azali faction was essentially conservative, seeking to preserve the late doctrines and laws of the Bab, the Baha'i sect sought for radical modifications in doctrine and practice. In his early writings, Baha' Allah effectively restructured the Bab's highly complex system, simplifying it and preaching tolerance and love in place of the legalism and severity of the later Babi books. In this, he seems to have been much influenced by close contact with Sufi circles. Perhaps the most crucial change, however, was the explicit repudiation of Babi militancy in favour of political quietism and obedience to the state. In 1863, most of the Baghdad community was exiled via Istanbul to Edirne in European Turkey. Whether or not he had actually made his claims semi-public before leaving Baghdad, Baha' Allah now proclaimed himself a divine manifestation and set about the task of dismantling the Babi system and remaking it as the Baha'i faith.

The last twenty-four years of Baha' Allah's life were spent in exile in Palestine, first in Acre, then in its vicinity, where he died at Bahji on 29 May 1892. Curiously and significantly, remarkably little is known of his life there, in spite of the considerable freedom he possessed after leaving Acre. He continued to write extensively, drawing up laws and ordinances for his community, and incorporating European ideas into his teachings. Though not a recluse, he was in little contact with the outside world, living a somewhat distant existence surrounded by numerous Iranian followers, by whom he was regarded with extreme deference. Before his death, he followed the Shi'ite system of directly appointing his eldest son 'Abbas [30] as the head of the community and inspired interpreter of the sacred text. A split nevertheless occurred between the followers of 'Abbas and those of his younger half-brother, Mirza Muhammad 'Ali, the effects of which lasted for some time. The largely progressive faction of 'Abbas succeeded in gaining control, partly through the superior charismatic appeal of 'Abd al-Baha' himself, partly by his readiness to excommunicate his opponents.

The first Western converts came into the movement in 1894, and during the early years of the present century small groups were established in the United States, Britain, France and Germany. These were, for the most part, drawn from the cultic milieu of the period, often combining membership with continued affiliation to churches or cult movements such as Theosophy. But following 'Abd al-Baha's Western travels (1911, 1912–13) and the dispatch of orthodox teachers to America, Western Baha'ism became increasingly exclusive, while methods of routinized administration began to take precedence over earlier metaphysical and occult concerns. Several factional disputes, including a serious one in 1917–18, which involved the setting up of a 'Committee of Investigation' to determine doctrinal purity, led to the eventual predominance within the movement of those concerned mainly with social and moral issues and committed to organizational restructuring.

The appointment of Shoghi Effendi Rabbani (1897–1957) [31] as first Guardian of the Cause of God (wali-ye amr Allah, originally a Shi'i term for the Imam) proved singularly important for the later development of the movement. In his first years as Guardian, Shoghi made strenuous efforts to demystify and organize the communities under his centralized leadership.

Between 1921 and 1937, he concentrated on the establishment of local and national administrative bodies throughout the Baha'i world, had by-laws drawn up for their operation, instituted the regularization of publications, and began to create an image of Baha'ism as a dynamic new world religion. Having consolidated his own authority and firmly established the principles of Baha'i organization, he turned his attention to missionary enterprise, which he directed through a series of 'plans' designed to introduce Baha'ism into all parts of the globe.

Shoghi Effendi's death in 1957 provoked a serious crisis in the movement, the details of which remain unclear. He had been appointed first of a line of Guardians intended to lead the Baha'i community in tandem with the then unestablished legislative body, the Universal House of Justice, but had died without issue and without leaving any instructions as to the future leadership of the religion. He had, moreover, by then excommunicated all his living male relatives, so that there did not seem to be any way of perpetuating the Guardianship through a collateral line. 'Abd al-Baha' had been explicit about future Guardians in his will and testament, and Shoghi himself had stressed that, without the Guardianship, the Baha'i system would be 'mutilated and permanently deprived of (the) hereditary principle' [21: 148]. The effective termination of a hereditary Guardianship thus called into question certain basic assumptions about the workings of the system and left open the possibility of future factionalism, an eventuality which the present Baha'i leadership has come to regard as particularly threatening. It is, however, a measure of Shoghi Effendi's success in creating a functional religious bureaucracy that, in 1963, the National Assemblies elected the first Universal House of Justice without undue opposition. The centralizing authority of this institution, combined with others since created at the Baha'i World Centre in Israel, has so far proved an effective means of preserving the unity of the Baha'i community in the face of occasional factionalism (see Figure 13.2).

DEVELOPMENTS IN SCHOLARSHIP

Popular and academic interest in Babism was sparked off by the extensive account given of the sect by Gobineau in 1865 [32], but the first serious research on the subject was carried out after 1889 by the Cambridge orientalist, E. G. Browne, who met Baha' Allah, Subh-i Azal and 'Abd al-Baha', corresponded with numerous Baha'is and Azalis, and built up an impressive collection of manuscripts. Although now dated, Browne's work [e.g. 2; 4; 33 and see 34: 29–36] is still immensely useful for its detailed examination of the basic historical and scriptural materials. It was Browne and his French contemporary A. L. M. Nicolas [see 34: 36–40] who first drew attention to the

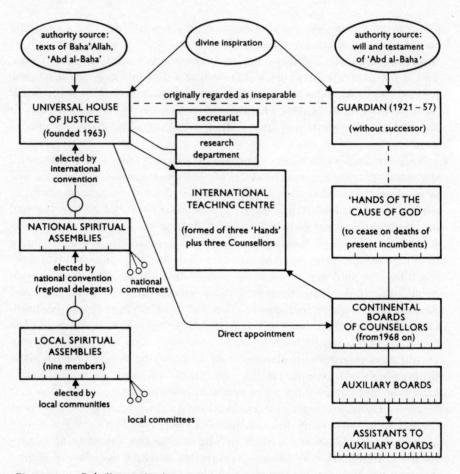

Figure 13.2   Baha'i organization

controversial character of much Baha'i historical writing, a point which continues to be a focus of scholarly interest. Inevitably, such early studies approached the subject from an 'orientalist' perspective, seeing it purely in its Iranian and Islamic contexts, but, with significant changes in the nature and distribution of Baha'ism, such an approach became increasingly less satisfactory. At the same time, there was little scholarly interest in the contemporary cultic milieu, and techniques for the study of small-scale movements were still undeveloped, so it is not altogether surprising that after Browne's death in 1926 there was a significant hiatus in academic work on the subject. Orientalists lost interest in a movement that had in most ways passed out of their field, and the apologetic nature of contemporary Baha'i writing did little to inspire fresh interest elsewhere.

Beginning with Peter Berger's doctoral dissertation on Baha'ism in 1954 [35], a number of basically sociological studies of the movement as a whole have been produced in the West [36–8]. At the same time, several recent studies have revived serious research on Babism and Shaykhism [7; 39], incorporating a wide body of previously unused primary sources and analysing the material within the context of modern scholarship on Islam, Shi'ism and Iranian history. For the most part, such studies present an interpretation of the origins of Baha'ism radically different from that provided within the movement itself, and it seems likely that future research will continue to emphasize this disparity. Whereas official Baha'i doctrine conflates the two movements (and makes Shaykhism a prophetic movement preparing for the Bab), academics are stressing increasingly the significance of Babism as an extremist movement within nineteenth-century Shi'ism, with only tenuous links to what developed outside Iran as Baha'ism. It seems, therefore, that, although studies of the overall Babi to Baha'i development are both possible and desirable, the main thrust of future research is likely to be in two directions, one towards Babism and its Shi'i roots, the other towards Baha'ism and its move away from Islam, particularly in the West.

A tradition of Baha'i scholarship was built up in Iran throughout this century, notably by Gulpaygani, Mazandarani and Ishraq-Khavari. This adopted the standard methodology of contemporary Islamic scholarship, with little or no room for radical historical or textual criticism, and it continues to dominate Baha'i writing, not only in Iran, but in the West as well, where a knowledge of sources rather than an ability to analyse them is the main scholarly criterion. This problem has been exacerbated by the priority given in the movement to works of propagation, so that writing is either openly apologetic or produced with apologetic criteria in mind, and by the mandatory vetting by special committees of all materials to be published by Baha'is. Recent years, however, have seen the beginnings of what may prove to be a crisis for the movement as several younger scholars in the West have tried to question some basic assumptions of existing historiography and hermeneutics. How successful this group will be depends on how much real freedom the official bodies are willing to extend to them, particularly in the matter of publication.

Teachings

The characteristic doctrines of Baha'ism have been succinctly described by Shoghi Effendi as follows:

> The Baha'i Faith upholds the unity of God, recognizes the unity of His Prophets, and inculcates the principle of the oneness and wholeness of the entire human race. It proclaims the necessity and inevitability of the unification of mankind ... enjoins upon its followers the primary duty of an unfettered search after truth, condemns all manner of prejudice and superstition, declares the purpose of religion to be the promotion of amity and concord, proclaims its essential harmony with science, and recognizes it as the foremost agency for the pacification and the orderly progress of human society. It unequivocally maintains the principle of equal rights, opportunities, and privileges for men and women, insists on compulsory education, eliminates extremes of poverty and wealth, abolishes the institution of priesthood, prohibits slavery, asceticism, mendicancy, and monasticism, prescribes monogamy, discourages divorce, emphasizes the necessity of strict obedience to one's government, exalts any work performed in the spirit of service to the level of worship, urges either the creation or the selection of an auxiliary international language, and delineates the outlines of those institutions that must establish and perpetuate the general peace of mankind [40: 3–4].

It is vital to the faith of Baha'is that these and other doctrines contained in their Scriptures be regarded as wholly original, not merely in the sense of being largely 'new', but as emanating directly from God himself. This view owes much to the Islamic theory of divine revelation as a unidirectional process whereby the uncreated word is conveyed to men unaltered through the inert medium of the prophet. The Bab and Baha' Allah are regarded as 'manifestations of God', a term borrowed from Shi'ism and theosophical Sufism. They are, in other words, incarnations of the eternal Logos, which has appeared in all previous major prophets, and as such possess the dual conditions of humanity and divinity. In the later writings of Baha' Allah, however, this comes close to a doctrine of incarnationism in statements such as 'the essence of the pre-existent has appeared'. The knowledge of God can only be obtained through recognition of his manifestations, a recognition which in turn entails absolute obedience to their laws [17: 49–50, 329–30]. Divine revelation is progressive (though sporadic rather than continuous), in accordance with the exigencies of changing human circumstances. At the same time, all developments in the human sphere are ultimately generated by the creative power of the divine word in each age [17: 141–2]. This doctrine entails the more problematic corollary that the teachings of a prophet must be chronologically prior to expressions of the same ideas in the world at large (in itself evidence that the prophet has not been influenced by the thoughts of others). Such a view, while clearly important as a means of establishing the credentials of Baha'ism for its followers, is clearly difficult to sustain empirically and has the disadvantage of obscuring the actual process through which the Baha'i teachings developed. The following remarks may help to clarify that process.

The majority of Baha'is today are converts from non-Islamic backgrounds and, as a result, there is widespread ignorance within the community of the extent to which the basic doctrines of the religion are Islamic (and, in particular, Shi'ite) in origin. Leaving aside for the moment the question of individual doctrines, it is incontrovertible that the context within which these operate differs in no radical sense from the central presuppositions of Islam. History is a process directed by periodic divine intervention, the purpose of which is to reveal the will of God in the form of a *shari'a*, a comprehensive ethical, legal and social system designed to fashion and regulate the affairs of society at all levels. Western distinctions between Church and state, religion and politics, do not strictly apply here, for the sacred law embraces all areas of human experience. The Baha'i *shari'a* is derived from two primary sources: the sacred text and the legislation of the Universal House of Justice. In practice, only a small portion of Baha'i law is either known or acted on outside Islamic countries.

Yet another central theme developed from Shi'ism is the notion of the 'covenant', through which the authority of 'Abd al-Baha', Shoghi Effendi, and the present leadership is guaranteed and the unity of the religion in theory assured. Thus Baha' Allah appointed 'Abd al-Baha', who in turn appointed Shoghi Effendi; the Universal House of Justice is similarly elected on the authority of a statement by Baha' Allah to the effect that such a body would be divinely guided. As in Shi'ism, this concept involves the corollary of the expulsion from the community and the subsequent shunning of those who have rebelled against the authority of the appointed head of the faith.

Even several apparently modernist teachings, such as the harmony of religion and science, the oneness of mankind, or the unity of revealed religion are, in essence, typically Islamic. This primary Islamic stratum in Baha'ism was modified in two ways: first, in Baha' Allah's reaction against Babism; and second, in his response to external influences, particularly modernist and Western ideas. Although Baha' Allah retained and simplified most of the religious and metaphysical teachings of the Bab, he reacted strongly against many of his laws and ordinances, especially those which underpinned the fanaticism and exclusivism that characterized the Babi movement. Many of Baha' Allah's earliest writings speak of the reforms he had instituted among the Babis, notably in the abrogation of laws directed against non-believers, above all the waging of holy war. 'Abd al-Baha' was later to characterize Baha'ism as, in a sense, the diametrical opposite of Babism. Whereas the latter emphasized 'the striking of necks, the burning of books and papers, the destruction of shrines, and the universal slaughter of all save those who believed and were faithful', the former stressed compassion, mercy, association with all peoples, trustworthiness towards men, and the unification of mankind [40a]. Later, however, Shoghi Effendi's wholesale conflation of Babism and Baha'ism served to obscure this important distinction, and modern Baha'i writing often describes as 'the teachings of the Bab and Baha'u'kkah' what are, in fact, mainly doctrines of the latter [e.g. 34: XXIII–XXV].

Baha' Allah was clearly influenced in this direction by Sufi and, it appears, Christian doctrines, both quite obvious in his early writings, where he quotes extensively from Sufi writers and the New Testament. In his later exiles to Turkey and Palestine, he came into contact with Europeans and Islamic modernists, as did 'Abd al-Baha', and seems to have been extremely receptive to the Western ideas then widespread in the Ottoman Empire. As a result, his writings in Acre incorporated notions such as collective security, world government, the use of an international auxiliary language and script, universal compulsory education and so on. 'Abd al-Baha' seems to have been particularly interested in these and related matters, as is obvious from an early work [41], and in his later talks and letters he addressed himself increasingly to topics of interest to Western converts. He spoke at length concerning the equality of the sexes, the need for an independent search after truth, the harmony of science and religion, and the solution of economic problems, and frequently referred to issues such as evolution, social and scientific progress, labour relations, socialism and education.

Having been an essentially progressivist movement in the early years of this century, Baha'ism is still portrayed as such in contemporary literature, and Baha'is continue to identify themselves with what are seen as 'progressive' causes, such as world government or religious and racial harmony. In practice, however, there are problems with this assessment, and in some respects Baha'ism has begun to take on a somewhat conservative appearance. Thus, for example, Baha'is refuse to involve themselves in human rights, disarmament or anti-apartheid movements because doing so would mean 'involvement in politics'. In principle, society takes its shape from revelation, not vice versa, and there is, therefore, little desire to adapt to changing attitudes in the outside world. Without scriptural authority, there can be no rethinking of established positions, and it is likely that Baha'is will become increasingly out of step with wider developments.

Another source of potential confusion is the sometimes uneasy coexistence of contradictory elements within the doctrinal spectrum. Thus, for example, modern Baha'i teaching on sexual equality is little supported by the legislation of the *Aqdas*, which permits a man two wives and assigns to women a decidedly inferior position in matters such as inheritance. More fundamentally, perhaps, the important principle of non-involvement in politics stands in stark conflict with the overtly political character of many basic teachings and, above all, with the concept that religion must be concerned with all areas of human life, not least that of government. As Baha'is continue to work towards the establishment of Baha'i states, they are certain to find this anomaly particularly difficult. How easily problems of this kind can be resolved remains to be seen. There are already signs that some of the more Islamic-style regulations are being gradually introduced to the West and, as this process accelerates, something of a crisis may develop as liberal Western adherents find themselves increasingly ill at ease with the more authoritarian side of their religion. Conversely, this may result in a fresh appeal of the movement to different sections of society.

Practices

The question of contemporary religious practice in Baha'ism is complicated by the existence of a gap between prescriptive regulations (which are extensive) and actual practices (which are limited), particularly outside Iran, although as time goes on more and more ritual and other prescribed practices are being introduced. The basic pattern is again Islamic, the main religious obligations being those of ritual prayer (*salat*), annual fasting (*sawm*) and pilgrimage (*hajj* and *ziyara*) (see pages 136–49). Many customary rites in Islam (such as the rites of passage) tend to be prescriptive in Baha'ism, always according to Islamic norms.

Salat is private, with three alternative versions to be performed (once in twenty-four hours, once at noon, or thrice daily), with ritual ablutions. The prayer-direction (*qibla*) is the tomb of Baha' Allah near Acre. Fasting takes place during the last month of the solar Baha'i year (2–20 March) on the Islamic pattern. As in Islam, there are exemptions for certain categories, such as the sick or pregnant women. Pilgrimage is less well defined. Strictly speaking, the Islamic *hajj* to Mecca has been replaced by two pilgrimages, both of which are restricted to men. These are to the house of the Bab in Shiraz and that of Baha' Allah in Baghdad, and both involve elaborate ritual ceremonies. In practice, it has never been possible for Baha'is to perform these *hajj* rites, and the destruction of the house of the Bab in 1979 following the Iranian revolution has introduced a fresh complication. 'Abd al-Baha' made obligatory what may be termed 'lesser pilgrimage' (*ziyara*) to the tombs of

Baha' Allah and the Bab (now in Haifa), this being the form of visitation made by Shi'is to the tombs of Imams and their relatives or by Sunnis to the shrines of saints. Visitation to the shrines in Israel has become the standard Baha'i pilgrimage, and most non-Iranian Baha'is are unaware that other forms exist and even imagine the *ziyara* to be the ritual equivalent of the Islamic *hajj*, which it is not. *Ziyaras* can also be made to numerous other Baha'i holy sites, particularly in Iran, and special prayers exist for recitation at these. The grave of Shoghi Effendi in London has become an important pilgrimage site in recent years.

Devotional and ceremonial practices are generally informal. At the local level, communal activities are organized by local assemblies, which are elected annually. As in Islam, there is no priesthood, but recent years have seen the emergence of a semi-professional appointed hierarchy responsible for propagation and protection from external attacks and internal dissent. In Arabic, these individuals (who include women) are known as *'ulama*, although their functions are not currently comparable to those of the Islamic clergy. They perform no ceremonial or intercessory functions. The principal communal gatherings are those held for the Nineteen-Day Feast on the first day of each Baha'i month (of which there are nineteen, each of nineteen days) and for the nine principal holy days during the year (on which work has to be suspended) (see Appendix). Feasts, which are preferably held in the homes of individuals, consist of three portions: the reading of prayers and sacred texts; administrative consultation; and the sharing of food and drink. Holy-day meetings generally consist of prayers and devotional texts designated for the occasion, sometimes with sermons or historical readings relevant to commemorative festivals.

Most Baha'i communities meet in private homes or halls rented or purchased for the purpose. There are in existence only five Houses of Worship, which are show-pieces built on a continental basis and at present used largely for public gatherings. They follow a common pattern of circular design incorporating nine entrances and a dome, but are otherwise architecturally diverse and, in several cases, represent fine examples of modern religious architecture.

Rites of passage are limited to naming ceremonies for babies (circumcision is not mandatory), marriage and funeral rites. Marriage is conditional on the consent of both parties and all living parents; arranged marriages are permitted and are common in Iran and elsewhere. The ceremony is flexible, the minimum requirement being the recitation by the bride and groom in the presence of witnesses of two verses adapted from the Persian *Bayan*. Simplicity is preferred, but ceremonies are usually expanded with music and readings from sacred texts and tend to follow cultural norms. The preparation and burial of the dead are carried out according to complex regulations. Cremation is not prohibited but is regarded as undesirable. The place of burial is to be no more than one hour's journey from the place of death and the plot is to be arranged so that the feet of the dead face the Baha'i *qibla*. The ritual *salat* for the dead (used only for adults) is the only occasion on which communal recitation of prayer is permitted.

Babism followed popular Shi'ism in being particularly rich in thaumaturgical and magical practices, such as the use of talismans, engraved stones and incantatory prayers. There are fewer such practices in Baha'ism, but they have not been wholly eradicated. There are numerous thaumaturgical, protective and supererogatory prayers, most of them as yet little known outside Iran. A calligraphic representation of the 'greatest name of God' in Arabic is found in most Baha'i homes:

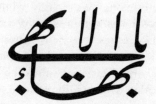

Ya baha' al-abha – O splendour of the most splendid

Equally common is the much stylized representation of the name Baha' designed to be engraved on ringstones, which owes much of its form to magical symbols found in popular Islam:

Strictly speaking, the symbol of the Baha'i religion is a five-pointed star, but it is much more common to find a nine-pointed star on jewellery and publications, as well as on gravestones.

Distribution

The key element in the growth of Baha'ism during the past fifty years has been its carefully planned character, a theme developed by Hampson [37] in the only full-length study of the subject. Since 1937, a series of national, regional and global missionary 'plans' have been conceived to coordinate the expansion and consolidation of the religion. Growth is assessed in terms of adherents, territories and localities represented, administrative bodies founded, assemblies legally incorporated, property purchased or constructed, literature translated or published, and so on. The result has been an impressive overall increase in all these areas, laying the base for future expansion. Significant gains have been made since the 1950s in several Third World countries, notably India, South Vietnam, Uganda and Bolivia, to the extent that 'the Baha'i Faith ... has started to become a predominantly third world religion' [38: 370]. The densest community remains that of Iran, while Iranians, Americans and Europeans are still the most active in missionary and administrative work.

How widespread Baha'ism has become is extremely difficult to assess, and the figures in Table 13.1 must be regarded as highly approximate for several reasons. Although the organizational statistics provided by the Baha'i authorities may be regarded as generally reliable, they are open to criticism

Table 13.1. Statistics on Baha'ism

Year	Total countries 'opened'	Total national assemblies	Total local assemblies	Total localities (with or without assemblies)
1921	35			
1953	128(i.e. 35 + 93)	12	611	2,425
1964	240	56	4,566	15,186
1973	335	113	17,037	69,541
1979	343	125	(over) 25,000	(over) 102,000

*Estimated number of adherents (1973)**		
Africa	236,987	
North America	74,635	*Estimated number of indigenous tribes, races and ethnic groups (1973)*
South America	128,693	
Asia (except Iran)†	399,002	1,607
Australia and Pacific	22,827	
Europe	29,601	
Total	891,745	

* *Source*: Hampson, 1980 [37: 457].

† Estimates for Iran vary between 150,000 and 300,000.

on a number of counts; official figures often conceal as much as they show, since impressive growth figures are regarded as important evidence of the status of Baha'ism as a 'world religion'. The principal difficulty lies in interpreting figures for institutions (national and local assemblies) or geographical areas ('countries opened', 'localities in which Baha'is reside') in terms of individuals. Individual Bha'is are encouraged to travel as 'pioneers' to unopened towns or districts, so that 'localities' frequently have only one or two adherents. As soon as local assemblies are established with nine members, great encouragement is given to surplus members to move elsewhere, so that 'assemblies' often amount to around nine individuals. The problems that can emerge from misinterpretation of such figures are evident in the detailed numbers given for Baha'is around the world in the *World Christian Encyclopedia*. For example, this work gives a figure of 14,600 Baha'is in the U.K. in 1975, when the community probably numbered around 5,000, a large percentage of whom were Iranian pioneers. It may be assumed, therefore, that the *Encyclopedia*'s overall figure of 3,822,630 Baha'is world-wide in 1980 is similarly exaggerated.

Other distortions are caused by the lack of accurate figures for disaffiliated and inactive believers. The Baha'i administration sets low requirements for membership but insists on formal withdrawal. Understandably, this latter is seldom forthcoming and, as a result, large numbers of individuals and even localities continue to be officially registered long after informal disaffiliation. That figures for disaffection may be high is suggested by Hampson's statistic indicating that, in 1976, mail was returned unopened from the addresses of 31 per cent of U.S. adherents [37:230]. It is also difficult to estimate how successful post-registration consolidation has been in mass-conversion areas in the Third World. In some places, there appear to be problems of multiple affiliation. Perhaps more seriously, little fresh information has been made available about the conditions of large Baha'i populations in areas of political disturbance, such as Uganda or Vietnam.

A significant shift in policy occurred in early 1983, when the Universal House of Justice decreed that all newly born children be automatically registered as Baha'is, which suggests the beginnings of a move away from earlier emphases on voluntary membership.

Conclusion

The development of Baha'ism may prove to be an important paradigm for future trends in the religious sphere. In the past, religious traditions have developed self-consciousness as distinct, reified systems only after lengthy periods of growth. With the partial exception of Islam, no major tradition has been founded or initially developed as a self-defined entity separate from others. The notion of 'world religions' is itself relatively recent. [On these and related points, see 42.]

In the modern period, however, it does not seem possible for unselfconscious development of this kind to take place. New movements emerge into a universe of already reified and competing systems. In order to compete, they are obliged to define themselves within terms of the prevailing norms. Baha'ism would seem to be the first of the new religious movements that shows signs of developing as an independent tradition. In origin, it belongs wholly to the pre-modern world of nineteenth-century Iran, but the significant phases of its development are marked by various responses to Western ideas and methods. Since the 1920s, its leaders have planned, systematized and organized in order to make it conceptually and actually a 'new world faith'. It has, in Hampson's words, 'managed its own development' [37:2]. The future progress of Baha'ism must remain speculative, but without doubt a firm basis has been laid for continued expansion in some regions. It would be surprising if the movement succeeded in resisting tendencies towards fission, heterodoxy and popularization if it moves much beyond its present sectarian dimensions. But there is already much to learn from its progress so far. Conscious planning, rational organization and long-term strategies have, it seems, become keys to religious growth in the modern age.

APPENDIX: THE BAHA'I CALENDAR

The Baha'i calendar is known as the Badi' Calendar and was devised by the Bab. It is based on a solar year of nineteen months, each of nineteen days plus four intercalary days (five in leap years). There are also cycles (*vahids*) of nineteen years, nineteen of which constitute a *Kullu shay'*. Baha'is date the commencement of the Badi' era from the New Year's Day (21 March) preceding the announcement of the Bab's mission in May 1844.

DAYS OF THE WEEK

Days	Arabic name	English name	Translation
1st	Jalāl	Saturday	Glory
2nd	Jamāl	Sunday	Beauty
3rd	Kamāl	Monday	Perfection
4th	Fiḍāl	Tuesday	Grace
5th	'Idāl	Wednesday	Justice
6th	Istijlāl	Thursday	Majesty
7th	Istiqlāl	Friday	Independence

NAMES OF THE MONTHS

Month	Arabic name	Translation	First days
1st	Bahā	Splendour	21 March
2nd	Jalāl	Glory	9 April
3rd	Jamāl	Beauty	28 April
4th	'Aẓamat	Grandeur	17 May
5th	Nūr	Light	5 June
6th	Raḥmat	Mercy	24 June
7th	Kalimāt	Words	13 July
8th	Kamāl	Perfection	1 August
9th	Asmā'	Names	20 August
10th	'Izzat	Might	8 September
11th	Mashīyyat	Will	27 September
12th	'Ilm	Knowledge	16 October
13th	Qudrat	Power	4 November
14th	Qawl	Speech	23 November
15th	Masā'il	Questions	12 December
16th	Sharaf	Honour	31 December
17th	Sulṭān	Sovereignty	19 January
18th	Mulk	Dominion	7 February
19th	'Alā'	Loftiness	2 March

Ayyám-i-Há (intercalary days): 26 February to 1 March inclusive

FEASTS, ANNIVERSARIES
AND DAYS OF FASTING

Feast of Riḍvān (Declaration of Bahā' Allāh), 21 April to 2 May 1863
Feast of Naw-Rūz (New Year), 21 March
Declaration of the Bāb, 23 May 1844
The Day of the Covenant, 26 November
Birth of Bahā' Allāh, 12 November 1817
Birth of the Bāb, 20 October 1819
Birth of 'Abd al-Bahā, 23 May 1844
Ascension of Bahā' Allāh, 29 May 1892
Martyrdom of the Bāb, 9 July 1850
Ascension of 'Abd al-Bahā, 28 November 1921
Fasting season lasts nineteen days beginning with the first day of the month
of 'Alā', 2 March – the Feast of Naw-Rūz follows immediately after.

HOLY DAYS ON WHICH WORK
SHOULD BE SUSPENDED

The first day of Riḍvān
The ninth day of Riḍvān
The twelfth day of Riḍvān
The anniversary of the declaration of the Bāb
The anniversary of the birth of Bahā' Allāh
The anniversary of the birth of the Bāb
The anniversary of the ascension of Bahā' Allāh
The anniversary of the martyrdom of the Bāb
The feast of Naw-Rūz

BIBLIOGRAPHY

1. COOPER, R., *The Baha'is of Iran*, London, Benjamin Franklin House, 1982 (Minority Rights Group Report no. 51)
2. 'ABD AL-BAHĀ, *A Traveller's Narrative Written to Illustrate the Episode of the Bāb* (ed. and tr. E. G. Browne), 2 vols., London, Cambridge University Press, 1891; repr. Amsterdam, Philo Press, 1975; new edn Wilmette, Ill., Baha'i Publishing Trust, 1980
3. NABĪL-I-A'ZAM (Mullā Muḥammad Zarandī), *The Dawn-Breakers: Nabīl's Narrative of the Early Days of the Baha'i Revelation* (tr. and ed. Shoghi Effendi), New York, Baha'i Publishing Committee, 1932; British edn (abr.), London, Baha'i Publishing Trust, 1953
4. ḤUSAIN HAMADĀNĪ, M., *The New History (Tārīkh-i-Jadīd) of Mīrzā 'Alī Muḥammed the Bāb by Mīrzā Ḥuseyn of Hamadān* (tr. and ed. E. G. Browne), Cambridge, Cambridge University Press, 1893; repr. Amsterdam, Philo Press, 1975
5. SHOGHI EFFENDI, *God Passes By*, Wilmette, Ill., Baha'i Publishing Committee, 1944; rev. edn, 1974
6. *The Bahā'ī Yearbook, 1925–1926*, New York, Baha'i Publishing Committee, 1926; subsequently publ. as *The Bahā'ī World*, vols. 2–7, New York, 1928–39; vol. 8, Wilmette, Ill., 1942; vol. 9, New York, 1945; vols. 10–12, Wilmette, Ill., 1949–56; vols. 13–18, Haifa, 1971–82
7. MACEOIN, D. M., *From Shaykhism to Babism: A Study in Charismatic Renewal in Shī'ī Islam*, Cambridge, University of Cambridge, 1979 (Ph.D. dissertation) (University Microfilms 81–70,043)
8. NICOLAS, A. L. M. (tr.), *Le Livre des sept preuves de la mission du Bāb* (by 'Ali Muḥammad Shīrāzī, called the Bāb), Paris, Maisonneuve, 1902

9. NICOLAS, A. L. M. (tr.), *Le Béyân arabe* (by 'Ali Muḥammad Shīrāzī, called the Bāb), Paris, Leroux, 1905

10. NICOLAS, A. L. M. (tr.), *Le Béyân persan* (by 'Ali Muḥammad Shīrāzī, called the Bāb), 4 vols., Paris, 1911–14

11. TAHERZADEH, M. (tr.), *Selections from the Writings of the Bāb* (by 'Ali Muḥammad Shīrāzī, called the Bāb), Haifa, Baha'i World Centre, 1976

12. SHOGHI EFFENDI (tr.), BAHĀ'U'LLĀH: *The Kitāb-i-Īqān. The Book of Certitude*, 1931, New York, Baha'i Publishing Committee, (1937); 2nd edn, London, Baha'i Publishing Trust, 1961; rev. edn, Wilmette, Ill., Baha'i Publishing Trust, 1974

13. SHOGHI EFFENDI (tr.), BAHĀ'U'LLĀH: *The Hidden Words*, London, Baha'i Publishing Trust, 1932, 1944; Wilmette, Ill., Baha'i Publishing Trust, 1939, rev. edn, 1954

14. ALĪ-KULI KHĀN (tr.), BAHĀ'U'LLĀH: *The Seven Valleys and the Four Valleys*, Wilmette, Ill., Baha'i Publishing Committee, 1945 (New York, 1936); 3rd rev. edn, Baha'i Publishing Trust, 1978

15. ELDER, E. E., and MILLER, W. MCE. (trs.), BAHĀ'U'LLĀH: *Al-Kitāb al-Aqdas, or, The Most Holy Book*, London, Royal Asiatic Society, 1961 (i.e. 1962)

16. SHOGHI EFFENDI (tr.), BAHĀ'U'LLĀH: *Epistle to the Son of the Wolf*, Wilmette, Ill., Baha'i Publishing Committee, 1941, rev. edn, Baha'i Publishing Trust, 1976

17. SHOGHI EFFENDI (tr.), BAHĀ'U'LLĀH: *Gleanings from the Writings of Bahā'u'llāh*, Wilmette, Ill., Baha'i Publishing Committee, (1948), New York, 1935; London, 1949; 2nd rev. edn, Wilmette, Ill., Baha'i Publishing Trust, 1976

18. GAIL, M. (tr.), 'ABD AL-BAHĀ: *Selections from the Writings of 'Abdu'l-Bahā* ... (tr. by a committee at the Baha'i World Centre and by Marzieh Gail), Haifa, Baha'i World Centre; Wilmette, Ill., Baha'i Publishing Trust, 1978

19. BARNEY, L. C. (tr.), 'ABD AL-BAHĀ: *Some Answered Questions*, London, Trübner/Philadelphia, Pa, Lippincott, 1908; London, Baha'i Publishing Trust, 1961; Wilmette, Ill., Baha'i Publishing Trust, 1981

20. 'ABD AL-BAHĀ, *Talks by Abdul Baha Given in Paris*, London, Baha'i Publishing Society/East Sheen, Unity Press, 1912; 4th edn, London, G. Bell, 1920; Amer. edn with title, *The Wisdom of Abdu'l-Baha*, New York, Baha'i Publishing Committee, 1924; Brit. edn: *Paris Talks*, London, Baha'i Publishing Trust, 1961

21. SHOGHI EFFENDI, *The World Order of Bahā'u'llāh*, New York, Baha'i Publishing Committee, 1938, rev. edn, Wilmette, Ill., Baha'i Publishing Trust, 1965, copyr. 1955

22. SHOGHI EFFENDI, *The Promised Day is Come*, Wilmette, Ill., Baha'i Publishing Committee, 1941, rev. edn, Baha'i Publishing Trust, 1980; Bombay, Baha'i Assembly of Bombay, 1942

23. UNIVERSAL HOUSE OF JUSTICE, *Wellspring of Guidance: Messages, 1963–1968*, Wilmette, Ill., Baha'i Publishing Trust, 1969, rev. edn, 1976

24. UNIVERSAL HOUSE OF JUSTICE, *Messages, 1968–1973*, Wilmette, Ill., Baha'i Publishing Trust, 1976

25. PERKINS, M., and HAINSWORTH, P., *The Bahā'ī Faith*, London, Ward Lock Educational, 1980

26. MILLER, W. MCE., *The Bahā'ī Faith: Its History and Teachings*, South Pasadena, Calif., William Carey Library, 1974

27. SOHRAB, MIRZA AHMAD, *The Broken Silence: The Story of Today's Struggle for Religious Freedom*, New York, Universal Publishing Co./New History Foundation, 1942

28. BALYUZI, H. M., *The Bāb*, Oxford, George Ronald, 1973

29. BALYUZI, H. M., *Bahā'u'llāh*, Oxford, George Ronald, 1980

30. BALYUZI, H. M., *'Abdu'l-Bahā*, London, George Ronald, 1971, Wilmette, Ill., Baha'i Publishing Trust in the U.S.A.

31. RUHIYYIH RABBANI, *The Priceless Pearl*, London, Wilmette, Ill., Baha'i Publishing Trust, 1969

32. GOBINEAU, J. A. DE, *Les Religions et philosophies dans l'Asie centrale*, Paris, Didier, 1865; 10th edn, Paris, Gallimard, 1957

33. BROWNE, E. G. (ed.), *Materials for the Study of the Bābī Religion*, Cambridge, Cambridge University Press, 1918

34. MOMEN, M. (ed.), *The Bābī and Bahā'ī Religions, 1844–1944: Some Contemporary Western Accounts*, Oxford, George Ronald, 1981

35. BERGER, P., *From Sect to Church: A Sociological Interpretation of the Baha'i Movement*, New York, New School for Social Research, 1954 (Ph.D. dissertation)

36. JOHNSON, V., *An Historical Analysis of Critical Transformations in the Evolution of the Baha'i World Faith*, Waco, Tex., Baylor University, 1974 (Ph.D. dissertation) (University Microfilms 75–20,564)

37. HAMPSON, A., *The Growth and Spread of the Baha'i Faith*, Honolulu, University of Hawaii, 1980 (Ph.D. dissertation) (University Microfilms 80–22,655)

38. SMITH, P., *A Sociological Study of the Babi and Baha'i Religions*, Lancaster, University of Lancaster, 1982 (Ph.D. dissertation)

39. AMANAT, ABBAS, *The Early Years of the Babi Movement*, Oxford, University of Oxford, 1981 (Ph.D. dissertation)

40. SHOGHI EFFENDI, *Guidance for Today and Tomorrow*, London, Wilmette, Ill., Baha'i Publishing Trust, 1953

40a. *Makatib-i 'Abd al-Baha'*, vol. 2, Cairo, 1912, p. 266

41. GAIL, M. (tr.), 'ABD AL-BAHĀ: *The Secret of Divine Civilization*, Wilmette, Ill., Baha'i Publishing Trust, 1957, 2nd edn, 1970

42. SMITH, W. CANTWELL, *The Meaning and End of Religion*, New York, Macmillan, 1962 (1963); London, New English Library, 1965, SPCK, 1978

General Bibliography

1. ELIADE, M., *The Sacred and the Profane: The Nature of Religion* (tr. W. R. Trask), New York, Harper, 1961; prev. publ. New York, Harcourt, Brace, 1959, repr. 1968
2. EVANS-PRITCHARD, SIR EDWARD E., *Theories of Primitive Religion*, Oxford, Clarendon Press, 1965, London, Oxford University Press, 1967
3. GENNEP, A. VAN, *The Rites of Passage* (tr. M. B. Vizedom and G. L. Caffee), London, Routledge, 1960, new edn 1977; Chicago, Ill., Chicago University Press, 1960, 1961
4. LEEUW, G. VAN DER, *Religion in Essence and Manifestation: A Study in Phenomenology* (tr. J. E. Turner), London, Allen & Unwin, 1938; German original *Phänomenologie der Religion*, publ. 1933
5. ROBERTSON, R., *Sociology of Religion: Selected Readings*, Harmondsworth, Baltimore, Md, Penguin Books, 1969
6. SHARPE, E. J., *Comparative Religion: A History*, London, Duckworth, 1975, new edn 1976; New York, Scribner, 1976
7. SKORUPSKI, J., *Symbol and Theory: A Philosophical Study of Theories of Religion in Social Anthropology*, Cambridge, New York, Cambridge University Press, 1976
8. SMART, N., *The Phenomenon of Religion*, London, Macmillan/New York, Herder, 1973; 2nd rev. edn, Oxford, Mowbray, 1978
9. SMITH, W. CANTWELL, *Belief and History*, Charlottesville, Va, University Press of Virginia, 1977
10. SMITH, W. CANTWELL, *The Meaning and End of Religion: A New Approach to the Religious Traditions of Mankind*, New York, New American Library (Mentor), 1964; London, New York, SPCK, 1978; New York, Harper & Row, 1978; first publ. New York, Macmillan, 1963
11. WAARDENBURG, J. J., *Classical Approaches to the Study of Religion: Aims, Methods and Theories of Research*, 2 vols., The Hague, Paris, Hawthorne, NY, Mouton, 1973-4
12. WERBLOWSKY, R. J. Z., *Beyond Tradition and Modernity: Changing Religions in a Changing World*, London, Athlone, 1976; in U.S.A. and Canada (distributors): Atlantic Highlands, NJ, Humanities

Acknowledgements

The Editor gratefully acknowledges permission to reproduce copyright material in this book. Every effort has been made to trace copyright holders and the publishers would be interested to hear from any copyright holders not here acknowledged.

Christianity: Figure 2.1: From the late J. M. Harness, by permission. Figure 2.4: From a drawing by June Reed, for *The Work of William Perkins* (ed. I Breward), Sutton Courtenay Press, 1969. Figures 2.7, 2.8 and 2.9: Based on D. B. Barrett, *World Christian Encyclopedia*, Oxford University Press, 1982. *Islam:* Figures 3.2 and 3.5 After Kenneth Cragg, *Islam and the Muslim* (figs. 5 and 10), Milton Keynes, The Open University Press, 1978 (Man's Religious Quest, Units 20–21). *Zoroastrianism:* Figure 4.4: From an architect's plan kindly provided by Faribourz Nariman. *Hinduism:* Figure 5.8: The British Museum. *Religions in Primal Societies:* Figures 5.10 and 5.11 are based, by permission, on S. M. Bhardwaj, *Hindu Places of Pilgrimage in India*, University of California Press, 1973, pp. 81 and 89. Figures 11.7 and 11.8: Drawings by Ben Rwegoshora. *Modern Alternative Religions in the West:* Figures 12.1 and 12.2: Drawn from J. Gordon Melton, *A Directory of Religious Bodies in the United States*, New York, Garland, 1977.

Index

The broad aim of this Index has been to achieve consistency with the General Index in *The Penguin Dictionary of Religions*. However, different scholars do hold differing (and strongly held) views on the correct spelling of technical terms, particularly where these involve transliteration from a non-Roman script or concern the use of diacriticals on words which have been anglicized (e.g. with the suffix 'ism'), and such professional differences have been respected. Full diacritical apparatus has been included for readers who require such information.

Reluctantly, it was decided not to index references to individual scholars. So many are mentioned that this would have increased the size of the Index dramatically unless arbitrary selections were made. Normally, contributions by Western scholars will be found through the entry 'Western scholarship' in the Index.

All references (including figure and table references) are to page numbers. Numbers in bold type indicate principal entries.